International Encyclopedia of Organization Studies

International Encyclopedia of Organization Studies

2

Editors

Stewart R. Clegg
University of Technology, Sydney, Australia, and University of Aston, Birmingham, UK

James R. Bailey
George Washington University

A SAGE Reference Publication

Los Angeles • London • New Delhi • Singapore

Copyright © 2008 by SAGE Publications, Inc.

All rights reserved. No part of this book may be reproduced or utilized in any form or by any means, electronic or mechanical, including photocopying, recording, or by any information storage and retrieval system, without permission in writing from the publisher.

For information:

SAGE Publications, Inc.
2455 Teller Road
Thousand Oaks, California 91320
E-mail: order@sagepub.com

SAGE Publications Ltd.
1 Oliver's Yard
55 City Road
London EC1Y 1SP
United Kingdom

SAGE Publications India Pvt. Ltd.
B 1/I 1 Mohan Cooperative Industrial Area
Mathura Road, New Delhi 110 044
India

SAGE Publications Asia-Pacific Pte. Ltd.
33 Pekin Street #02–01
Far East Square
Singapore 048763

Printed in the United States of America

Library of Congress Cataloging-in-Publication Data

International encyclopedia of organization studies/general editors, Stewart R. Clegg, James R. Bailey.
   p. cm.
Includes bibliographical references and index.
ISBN 978-1-4129-1515-1 (cloth)
  1. Organization—Encyclopedias. 2. Management—Encyclopedias.
3. Organizational sociology—Encyclopedias. I. Clegg, Stewart. II. Bailey, James Russell, 1963-

HD31.I564 2008
302.3′503—dc22   2007015688

This book is printed on acid-free paper.

07 08 09 10 11   10 9 8 7 6 5 4 3 2 1

Publisher:	Rolf A. Janke
Acquisitions Editor:	Al Bruckner
Developmental Editor:	Yvette Pollastrini
Reference Systems Manager:	Leticia Gutierrez
Project Editor:	Libby Larson
Copy Editors:	Bonnie Freeman, Geof Garvey
	Teresa Herlinger, Cate Huisman
	Trey Thoelcke, Glenn Wright
Typesetter/Designer:	C&M Digitals (P) Ltd.
Proofreaders:	Theresa Kay, Dennis Webb
Indexer:	Kathy Paparchontis
Cover Designer:	Michelle Kenny
Marketing Manager:	Carmel Withers

Contents

List of Entries, *vii*

Reader's Guide, *xv*

Entries

Volume 1: A–D

1–412

Volume 2: E–L

413–836

Volume 3: M–O

837–1214

Volume 4: P–Z

1215–1640

Index, *I-1–I-60*

List of Entries

Absorptive Capacity
Accountability
Accounting, Impact on Organizations and Society
Action
Actionable Knowledge
Action Learning
Action Research
Activism
Actor-Network Theory
Adaptive Learning
Adhocracies
Adult Learning
Aesthetics of Organization
Affect
Agency
Agency-Structure Debate
Agency Theory
Alliances
Alterity (Otherness)
Analytical Empiricism
Anthropology
Antirationalism
Antirealism
Archetypes
Architecture and Organizations
Arts and Organizations
Asset Specificity
Attitudes
Attribution Theory
Authenticity
Authoritarianism
Authority
Autopoiesis

Balanced Scorecard
Behavior. *See* Organizational Behavior
Behavioral Theory of the Firm
Behaviorism
Boundaryless Career
Bounded Emotionality
Bounded Rationality
Bureaucracy
Bureaucratization
Business Ethics
Business History
Business Journalism
Business Networks
Business Process Redesign. *See* Reengineering
Business Process Reengineering.
　See Reengineering
Buyer-Supplier Relationships

Call Centers
Capitalism, Models of
Capital Markets
Capital Movement, Migration, and Maquiladoras
Chaos Theory
Civil Society
Class
Classical Management
Clinical Perspective
Closed System Approach
Clusters
Coaching
Coalitions
Coase Theorem
Coercion

Cognitive Approach
Cognitive Dissonance
Cognitive Mapping
Cohesion
Collaboration and Cooperation
Collective Social Phenomena
Collectivism
Communication
Communicative Action
Communities of Practice
Community and Organizations
Competition
Competitive Advantage
Complex Adaptive Systems
Complexity of Decision Making
Complexity Theory
Complex Organizations
Compliance
Computer-Based Learning
Computer-Based Simulation Research
Computer-Mediated Communication
Configuration Theory
Conflict
Conservatism
Constructivism
Consumer Culture
Contingent Employment
Contingent Workers
Control
Convergence Model
Conversation
Coordination
Corporate Branding
Corporate Citizenship
Corporate Crime and Corruption
Corporate Culture
Corporate Governance
Corporate Social Responsibility
Corporate Values
Creativity
Crime and Corruption. *See* Corporate Crime and Corruption
Critical Analysis
Critical Management Education
Critical Management Studies

Critical Modernists
Critical Realism
Critical Theory
Cross-Cultural Management
Cross-Level Analysis
Cultural Capital
Cultural Intelligence
Culture. *See* Organizational Culture
Cybernetics
Cynicism

Data
Decentralization
Decision-Making Theory
Deconstruction
Dehumanization
Deinstitutionalization
Delphi Technique
Democracy. *See* Organizational Democracy
Demographic Process
Design Space Management
Dialogue
Diffusion
Digital Divide
Discipline
Discourse. *See* Organizational Discourse
Discourse Analysis
Discrimination
Disorganization
Diversity
Domination
Downsizing
Dramaturgy
Dynamic Capabilities

Ecological Change
Ecology. *See* Organizational Ecology
E-Commerce
Economic Rationalism
Economic Sociology
Effectiveness
Emergent Theory
Emic
Emotion
Emotional Intelligence

Emotional Patterns in Organizations
Employment Relations
Empowerment
Engineering-Managerial Discourse
Enterprise Culture
Entrepreneurship
Environment. *See* Organizational Environments
Environmental Determinism
Environmentalism and Organizations
Epistemic Communities
Epistemology
Equity Theory
Ergonomics
Ethnicity
Ethnography
Ethnomethodology
Etic
Evolutionary Theory
Expectancy Theory
Experiential Learning
Explicit Knowledge
Exploitation

Family Business
Fashion
Feminism. *See* Radical Feminism
Fit
Five Forces
Followership
Foresight
Formal Organizations
Foucauldian Turn
Frankfurt School
Free-Rider Problem
Functionalism

Game Theory
Garbage Can Model
Gender Division
Gendered Organization
Gender Stereotypes
Genealogical Analysis
General Systems Theory
Glass Ceiling
Globalization

Global Village
Goal-Setting Theory
Governmentality
Grand Narratives
Grounded Theory Building
Guanxi

Hawthorne Studies
Hegemony
Hermeneutics
Hierarchy
High Involvement Management
High-Risk Technologies and Organizations
Historical Analysis of Organization Theory
Human-Computer Interaction
Human Engineering
Humanism
Human Relations School
Human Resource Management
Human Rights
Humor
Hypocrisy

Identification
Identity
Ideology
Impression Management
Improvisation
Incommensurability
Individualism
Industrial Democracy
Industrial Relations
Industrial Revolution
Influence
Informal Economy
Information
Information and Communication Technology
Information Processing
Innovation
Institutional Entrepreneurship
Institutional Isomorphism
Institutional Legitimacy
Institutional Theory
Integrity
Intellectual Property

Intelligence. *See* Cultural Intelligence
Interaction Analysis
Interactionism
Intergroup Conflict
International Business
International Human Resource Management
Internationalization School
International Management
Interorganizational Relations and Collaborations
Interpretive Theory
Iron Law of Oligarchy
Irrationality

Japanese Management
Job Evaluation
Job Satisfaction
Joint Stock Companies
Justice. *See* Organizational Justice
Just-in-Time Management

Karoshi
Keiretsu
Knowledge
Knowledge Creation
Knowledge-Intensive Firms
Knowledge Management

Labor and Offshoring
Labor Relations
Lacanian Psychoanalysis
Language and Organizations
Law and Economics
Leadership, Charisma
Leadership, Dispersed
Leadership, Servant
Leadership, Styles
Leadership, Transactional
Leadership, Transformational
Leadership Theory
Lean Production
Learning
Learning, Double-Loop
Learning Organization
Liberalism
Liberal Technologies of Regulation

Life Cycle
Liminality
Literary Theory
Locus of Control
Logical Positivism
Long-Wave Theory
Loose Coupling

Machine Bureaucracy
Magic in Organizing
Management and Organization of Local Governments
Management and Public Policy
Management Consultants
Management Fashions and Fads
Management Learning
Managerial and Organizational Cognition
Managerial Capitalism
Managerial Cultural Capital
Managerialism
Managerial Rationality
Managerial Revolution
Maquiladoras. *See* Capital Movement, Migration, and Maquiladoras
Marginalization
Market-Based Theory
Masculinities and Management
Matrix Organization
McDonaldization
Measurement
Mechanistic Organizations
Meta-Analysis
Metaphor and Organization
Middle-Range Theory
Migration. *See* Capital Movement, Migration, and Maquiladoras
Military Organization
Minimal Network
Minimal Structure
Modernism
Modernity
Morale
Moral Hazard
Motivation
Multiculturalism

Multidivisional Form
Multinational Enterprises
Multisubsidiary Form
Music and Work

Narcissism
Narratives
National Culture
Negotiation
Neoclassical Economics
Neocontingency Model
Neoinstitutional Theory
Neoliberalism and Organization
Network Coevolution
Networks
Network Society and Organizations
New Institutionalism
New Public Management
Nongovernmental Organizations
Nonprofit Organizations
Normal Accidents

Objectivity
Ontology
Open Systems
Operant Conditioning
Opportunistic Behavior
Oppression
Organic Organizations
Organizational Adaptation
Organizational Anthropology
Organizational Art. *See* Arts and Organizations
Organizational Behavior
Organizational Capabilities
Organizational Change
Organizational Citizenship Behaviors
Organizational Climate
Organizational Communication
Organizational Culture
Organizational Democracy
Organizational Demography
Organizational Design
Organizational Development
Organizational Discourse
Organizational Ecology

Organizational Economics
Organizational Environments
Organizational Ethnography
Organizational Evolution
Organizational Existentialism
Organizational Field
Organizational Identity
Organizational Image
Organizational Justice
Organizational Knowledge
Organizational Language. *See* Language and Organizations
Organizational Learning
Organizational Literature, African
Organizational Literature, Anglo-Saxon
Organizational Literature, Arabic
Organizational Literature, Asian
Organizational Literature, Brazilian
Organizational Literature, Eastern European
Organizational Literature, Francophone
Organizational Literature, Germanic
Organizational Literature, Latin American
Organizational Literature, Scandinavian
Organizational Man
Organizational Memory
Organizational Misbehavior
Organizational Mortality
Organizational Paradox
Organizational Paranoia
Organizational Performance
Organizational Philosophy
Organizational Politics
Organizational Resilience
Organizational Rhetoric
Organizational Rituals
Organizational Routines
Organizational Rules
Organizational Spirituality
Organizational Stigma
Organizational Strategy
Organizational Structure
Organizational Subcultures
Organizational Symbolism
Organizational Taboos
Organizational Theory

Organizational Therapy
Organizational Toxicity
Organization Theory, Historical Analysis
Otherness. *See* Alterity (Otherness)
Outsourcing
Ownership and Control

Panopticism
Paradigm Incommensurability
Paradigms
Paradox
Participation
Perceived Organizational Support
Performance Appraisal
Performance-Driven Evaluation
Personality, Five-Factor Model
Phenomenology
Philosophy. *See* Organizational Philosophy
Philosophy of Science
Play
Political Economy of Organizations
Politics
Politics of Organizational Culture
Popular Culture
Positive Organizational Scholarship
Positive Psychology
Positivism
Post-Bureaucratic Organizations
Postcolonial Theory
Post-Fordist Economy
Postmodernism
Postmodernity
Poststructuralism
Power
Practice
Pragmatism
Prescriptive Theory
Prisoner's Dilemma
Procedural Justice
Procrastination
Product Innovation
Professional Service Firms
Professions
Project Management

Protestant Ethic
Psychoanalytic Approach
Psychological Contract
Psychological Safety
Public Choice Theory
Punishment and Violence in Organizations

Qualitative Approaches
Qualitative Interview
Quantitative Models and Methods

Radical Feminism
Radical Humanism
Rational Choice Theory
Realism
Recruiting
Reengineering
Reflective Practice
Reflexivity
Regionalization and Capital Movement
Relativism
Replication Strategy
Resistance to Change
Resource-Based View of the Firm
Resource Dependence
Reverse Culture Shock
Risk Management
Rituals. *See* Organizational Rituals

Scenario Planning
Scientific Management
Self-Efficacy
Self-Employment Identities
Sensemaking
Serendipity
Servant Leadership. *See* Leadership, Servant
Sexuality
Shareholders
Skill
Slavery
Small and Medium-Sized Enterprises
Social Capital
Social Constructionism
Social Identity Theory
Socialization

Social Movements
Social System
Social Theory
Sociological Approach
Sociology of Work and Employment
Sociotechnical Systems
Spatial Organization
Stakeholders
Storytelling
Strategic Alliances
Strategic Choice
Strategic Discourse
Strategic Human Resource Management
Strategic Management
Structural Contingency Theory
Structural Determinism
Structural Functionalism
Structuration
Structure. *See* Organizational Structure
Subcultures. *See* Organizational Subcultures
Subjectivity
Subordination
Surveillance
Sustainable Development
Sweatshops
Symbolic Interactionism
Symbolism, *See* Organizational Symbolism

Taboos. *See* Organizational Taboos
Tacit Knowledge
Team Development
Team Diversity
Team Leadership
Team Learning
Team Performance
Team Process
Teams, Cross-Cultural
Teams, Virtual

Technological Determinism
Technology
Theory Building
Theory X
Theory Y
Theory Z
Time-Space Relations
Total Quality Management
TQM. *See* Total Quality Management
Training
Transaction Cost Theory
Transnational Corporations
Transnational/Postcolonial Feminist Theorizing
Triangulation
Trust
Truth

Uncertainty
Unemployment
Unionism
Utilitarianism
Utopia

Value Chains
Value-Free Conception of Science
Values
Vertical Integration
Viable System Model
Violence
Virtual Organization
Virtual Reality
Virtue Ethics

Wage Inequities
Worker Rights
Work-Family Balance
Working Time
Workplace Incivility

Reader's Guide

The Reader's Guide is provided to assist readers in locating articles on related topics. It classifies articles into 20 general topical categories:

- Approaches to Management Theory
- Approaches to Organization Theory
- Culture and Symbolism
- Human Resource Management
- Innovation and Creativity
- International Approaches
- Issues in Organizational Structure
- Issues in Organization Practices
- Knowledge and Learning
- Leadership Theory
- Organizational Behavior
- Organizational Cognition, Change, and Communication
- Organizational Economics
- Organizational Power, Politics, and Conflict
- Organizational Relations
- Philosophy of Organizations
- Research Practice and Methodology
- Social Issues
- Teams
- Technologies

Entries may be listed under more than one topic.

Approaches to Management Theory

Classical Management
Critical Management Education
Critical Management Studies
Cross-Cultural Management
Engineering-Managerial Discourse
Entrepreneurship
Hawthorne Studies
High Involvement Management
Human Relations School
International Management
Management and Organization of Local Governments
Management and Public Policy
Management Consultants
Management Fashions and Fads
Management Learning
Managerial and Organizational Cognition
Managerial Capitalism
Managerialism
Managerial Rationality
Managerial Revolution
Masculinities and Management
New Public Management
Scientific Management
Strategic Management
Theory X
Theory Y
Theory Z
Total Quality Management

Approaches to Organization Theory

Actor-Network Theory
Autopoiesis
Behavioral Theory of the Firm
Chaos Theory
Classical Management
Closed System Approach
Collective Social Phenomena
Complexity Theory
Complex Organizations
Configuration Theory
Convergence Model
Critical Management Studies
Critical Modernists
Cybernetics
Deinstitutionalization
Economic Sociology
Engineering-Managerial Discourse
Environmental Determinism
Equity Theory
Ergonomics
Evolutionary Theory
Expectancy Theory
Formal Organizations
Functionalism
Gendered Organization
General Systems Theory
Hawthorne Studies
Hermeneutics
Historical Analysis of Organization Theory
Human Relations School
Institutional Isomorphism
Institutional Legitimacy
Institutional Theory
Interaction Analysis
Interactionism
Interpretive Theory
Life Cycle
Literary Theory
Long-Wave Theory
Management Fashions and Fads
Managerialism
McDonaldization
Metaphor and Organization
Middle-Range Theory
Narratives
Neocontingency Model
Neoinstitutional Theory
New Institutionalism
New Public Management
Open Systems
Organizational Adaptation
Organizational Demography
Organizational Ecology
Organizational Economics
Organizational Environments
Organizational Field

Organizational Rhetoric
Organizational Theory
Organization Theory, Historical Analysis
Positive Organizational Scholarship
Postcolonial Theory
Public Choice Theory
Radical Feminism
Radical Humanism
Rational Choice Theory
Resource-Based View of the Firm
Resource Dependence
Social Constructionism
Social Identity Theory
Social System
Social Theory
Sociological Approach
Sociology of Work and Employment
Strategic Choice
Structural Contingency Theory
Structural Functionalism
Structuration
Symbolic Interactionism
Theory X
Theory Y
Theory Z
Time–Space Relations
Transnational/Postcolonial Feminist Theorizing
Viable System Model

Culture and Symbolism

Aesthetics of Organization
Alterity (Otherness)
Anthropology
Archetypes
Authenticity
Consumer Culture
Corporate Citizenship
Corporate Culture
Corporate Values
Cross-Cultural Management
Cultural Capital
Cultural Intelligence
Dramaturgy
Enterprise Culture

Ethnicity
Fashion
Humor
Hypocrisy
Identity
Integrity
Language and Organizations
Liminality
Magic in Organizing
Management and Public Policy
Managerial Cultural Capital
Masculinities and Management
Multiculturalism
Music and Work
Narcissism
National Culture
Organizational Culture
Organizational Rituals
Organizational Subcultures
Organizational Symbolism
Organizational Taboos
Popular Culture
Reverse Culture Shock
Self-Employment Identities
Sexuality
Socialization
Utopia

Human Resource Management

Balanced Scorecard
Boundaryless Career
Coaching
Contingent Employment
Contingent Workers
Downsizing
Employment Relations
Glass Ceiling
Human Resource Management
Industrial Relations
International Human Resources Management
Job Evaluation
Job Satisfaction
Labor and Offshoring
Labor Relations

Outsourcing
Performance Appraisal
Performance-Driven Evaluation
Professions
Recruiting
Reengineering
Strategic Human Resource Management
Training
Unemployment
Unionism
Wage Inequities
Worker Rights
Work-Family Balance
Working Time
Workplace Incivility

Innovation and Creativity

Creativity
Foresight
Innovation
Intellectual Property
Knowledge Creation
Learning Organization
Product Innovation
Reflective Practice
Serendipity
Uncertainty

International Approaches

International Business
International Human Resources Management
Internationalization School
International Management
Japanese Management
Organizational Literature, African
Organizational Literature, Anglo-Saxon
Organizational Literature, Arabic
Organizational Literature, Asian
Organizational Literature, Brazilian
Organizational Literature, Eastern European
Organizational Literature, Francophone
Organizational Literature, Germanic
Organizational Literature, Latin American
Organizational Literature, Scandinavian
Transnational Corporations

Issues in Organizational Structure

Absorptive Capacity
Adhocracies
Architecture and Organizations
Bureaucracy
Bureaucratization
Decentralization
Demographic Process
Design Space Management
Downsizing
Ecological Change
Fit
Five Forces
Hierarchy
Locus of Control
Loose Coupling
Machine Bureaucracy
Management and Organization of Local Governments
Matrix Organization
Mechanistic Organizations
Military Organization
Minimal Network
Minimal Structure
Multidivisional Form
Multisubsidiary Form
Nongovernmental Organizations
Nonprofit Organizations
Organic Organizations
Organizational Design
Organizational Evolution
Organizational Rules
Organizational Structure
Post-Bureaucratic Organizations
Small and Medium-Sized Enterprises
Spatial Organization
Structural Determinism

Virtual Organization
Virtual Reality

Issues in Organization Practices

Balanced Scorecard
Boundaryless Career
Complexity of Decision Making
Contingent Employment
Contingent Workers
Control
Conversation
Coordination
Corporate Branding
Dehumanization
Diversity
Dynamic Capabilities
Effectiveness
Emotional Patterns in Organizations
Gender Division
Gender Stereotypes
Human Resource Management
Information
Irrationality
Job Evaluation
Just-in-Time Management
Karoshi
Lean Production
Managerial Revolution
Normal Accidents
Organizational Capabilities
Organizational Citizenship Behaviors
Organizational Discourse
Organizational Identity
Organizational Image
Organizational Man
Organizational Misbehavior
Organizational Mortality
Organizational Paradox
Organizational Paranoia
Ownership and Control
Panopticism
Participation
Perceived Organizational Support

Performance Appraisal
Performance-Driven Evaluation
Play
Practice
Procedural Justice
Procrastination
Project Management
Recruiting
Reengineering
Risk Management
Scenario Planning
Scientific Management
Strategic Human Resource Management
Strategic Management
Total Quality Management
Vertical Integration

Knowledge and Learning

Actionable Knowledge
Action Learning
Adaptative Learning
Adult Learning
Business Journalism
Coaching
Communities of Practice
Cultural Intelligence
Dialogue
Diffusion
Emotional Intelligence
Entrepreneurship
Experiential Learning
Explicit Knowledge
Exploitation
Information
Information Processing
Knowledge
Knowledge Creation
Knowledge-Intensive Firms
Knowledge Management
Learning
Learning, Double-Loop
Learning Organization
Management Learning

Managerial and Organizational Cognition
Organizational Knowledge
Organizational Learning
Professional Service Firms
Professions
Skill
Storytelling
Tacit Knowledge
Training

Leadership Theory

Authenticity
Authority
Coercion
Followership
Influence
Leadership, Charisma
Leadership, Dispersed
Leadership, Servant
Leadership, Styles
Leadership, Transactional
Leadership, Transformational
Leadership Theory
Subordination
Team Leadership

Organizational Behavior

Action
Affect
Asset Specificity
Attitudes
Attribution Theory
Bounded Emotionality
Clinical Perspective
Cohesion
Emotion
Followership
Goal-Setting Theory
High Involvement Management
Identification
Impression Management
Individualism
Influence
Intergroup Conflict
Job Satisfaction
Leadership, Charisma
Leadership, Dispersed
Leadership, Servant
Leadership, Styles
Leadership, Transactional
Leadership, Transformational
Leadership Theory
Morale
Motivation
Negotiation
Operant Conditioning
Opportunistic Behavior
Organizational Behavior
Organizational Climate
Organizational Memory
Organizational Performance
Organizational Resilience
Organizational Routines
Organizational Spirituality
Organizational Stigma
Organizational Therapy
Organizational Toxicity
Personality, Five-Factor Model
Self-Efficacy
Subjectivity
Trust
Values

Organizational Cognition, Change, and Communication

Bounded Rationality
Cognitive Approach
Cognitive Dissonance
Cognitive Mapping
Communication
Communicative Action
Decision-Making Theory
Garbage Can Model
Institutional Entrepreneurship
Managerial Rationality
Organizational Change
Organizational Communication

Organizational Development
Positive Psychology
Prisoner's Dilemma
Psychological Contract
Psychological Safety
Resistance to Change
Sensemaking

Organizational Economics

Agency
Agency Theory
Business History
Capital Markets
Coase Theorem
Competition
Competitive Advantage
Corporate Governance
Economic Rationalism
Free-Rider Problem
Game Theory
Joint-Stock Companies
Law and Economics
Market-Based Theory
Moral Hazard
Multinational Enterprises
Neoclassical Economics
Shareholders
Transaction Cost Theory
Utilitarianism
Value Chains

Organizational Power, Politics, and Conflict

Alterity (Otherness)
Authoritarianism
Authority
Coercion
Compliance
Conflict
Cynicism
Discipline
Discrimination
Domination
Empowerment
Glass Ceiling
Governmentality
Hegemony
Human Rights
Ideology
Iron Law of Oligarchy
Labor and Offshoring
Labor Relations
Oppression
Organizational Democracy
Organizational Justice
Organizational Politics
Political Economy of Organizations
Politics
Politics of Organizational Culture
Power
Punishment and Violence in Organizations
Slavery
Strategic Discourse
Subordination
Surveillance
Sweatshops
Violence
Wage Inequities
Worker Rights
Workplace Incivility

Organizational Relations

Alliances
Business Networks
Buyer-Supplier Relationships
Coalitions
Collaboration and Cooperation
Collectivism
Communities of Practice
Complex Adaptive Systems
Employment Relations
Guanxi
Industrial Relations
Interorganizational Relations and Collaboration
Keiretsu
Network Coevolution
Networks

Network Society and Organizations
Organizational Strategy
Outsourcing
Stakeholders
Strategic Alliances

Philosophy of Organizations

Agency-Structure Debate
Analytical Empiricism
Antirationalism
Antirealism
Constructivism
Critical Realism
Critical Theory
Deconstruction
Disorganization
Epistemic Communities
Epistemology
Foucauldian Turn
Frankfurt School
Grand Narratives
Humanism
Improvisation
Incommensurability
Lacanian Psychoanalysis
Logical Positivism
Modernism
Objectivity
Ontology
Organizational Existentialism
Organizational Philosophy
Paradigm Incommensurability
Paradigms
Phenomenology
Philosophy of Science
Positivism
Postmodernism
Poststructuralism
Pragmatism
Realism
Relativism
Theory Building
Truth

Research Practice and Methodology

Action Research
Arts and Organizations
Behaviorism
Critical Analysis
Cross-Level Analysis
Data
Delphi Technique
Discourse Analysis
Emergent Theory
Emic
Ethnography
Ethnomethodology
Etic
Genealogical Analysis
Grounded Theory Building
Measurement
Meta-Analysis
Organizational Anthropology
Organizational Ethnography
Paradox
Prescriptive Theory
Psychoanalytic Approach
Qualitative Approaches
Qualitative Interview
Quantitative Models and Methods
Reflexivity
Replication Strategy
Triangulation
Value-Free Conception of Science

Social Issues

Accountability
Accounting, Impact on Organizations
   and Society
Activism
Business Ethics
Capitalism, Models of
Capital Movement, Migration, and Maquiladoras
Civil Society
Class
Clusters
Community and Organizations

Conservatism
Corporate Crime and Corruption
Corporate Social Responsibility
Critical Management Education
Environmentalism and Organizations
Family Business
Globalization
Global Village
Industrial Democracy
Industrial Revolution
Informal Economy
Liberalism
Liberal Technologies of Regulation
Managerial Capitalism
Marginalization
Modernity
Neoliberalism and Organization
Post-Fordist Economy
Postmodernity
Protestant Ethic
Regionalization and
 Capital Movement
Social Capital
Social Movements
Sustainable Development
Unemployment
Unionism
Virtue Ethics
Work-Family Balance
Working Time

Teams

Cohesion
Diffusion
Free-Rider Problem
Psychological Safety
Team Development
Team Diversity
Team Leadership
Team Learning
Team Performance
Team Process
Teams, Cross-Cultural
Teams, Virtual

Technologies

Call Centers
Computer-Based Learning
Computer-Based Simulation Research
Computer-Mediated Communication
Digital Divide
E-Commerce
High-Risk Technologies and Organizations
Human-Computer Interaction
Human Engineering
Information and
 Communication Technology
Sociotechnical Systems
Technological Determinism
Technology

Ecological Change

Organizational ecology refers to the study of how populations adapt, through competitive and cooperative dynamics, to various niches, terrains, and resource spaces. These dynamics and niche interactions occur within the broader context of the community in which the organizational populations are embedded. *Ecological change* refers to the changes in the character of the community or its constituent populations as they adapt—that is, to any organizational group's evolutionary path. Research in evolutionary biology, economics, political science, and sociology has demonstrated that adaptation is nonfunctional, historic, holistic, and based on contestation within and between community populations. Recent research in the sciences has also underscored the importance of rapid, and often punctuated, change in populations and ecosystems, challenging the long-standing assertions that inertia and gradual change are pervasive.

Conceptual Overview

Two sets of concepts are essential for understanding ecological change: first, the mechanisms of adaptation, and second, different types of adaptive outcomes. The progenitors of organizational ecology, Howard Aldrich, Michael Hannan, John Freeman, Glenn Carroll, Bill McKelvey, and others, all argue that adaptation occurs through variation, selection, and retention by constituent populations within a community. These classic mechanisms are now known not to operate in purely Darwinian terms, but to involve some degree of Lamarckian (learning-based) evolution. *Variation*, the creation of new methods or forms within a population, may occur intentionally, not just via random chance or experimentation. Institutional entrepreneuring through innovation, creative destruction, and the leveraging of intangible resources can create new models of organizing. *Selection* of various alternatives involves not just competition, but also cooperation and networked interdependence among population members. Innovations are often selected by networks of common interest or supportive social movements. *Retention*, the encoded preservation of new alternatives, can occur not only for highly individualistic, rational reasons, but also for less individualistic and rational ones. Hannan, Freeman, Carroll, and colleagues have convincingly shown that both competition and legitimacy pressure are at work in shaping this path and the survival of different population members.

The end point of evolution for a community is not knowable in advance. Nevertheless, evolution is path dependent, and there may be stable evolutionary points of ecological change based on a specific population or community's path. Stability may occur within a population once diffusion of an innovation has been taken up as a solution yet has not reached saturation point, e.g., when density dependence has reached a temporary equilibrium based on the joint effects of legitimacy and competition. Stability across populations may occur when there is some ordering principle by domain or level that serves the majority of subpopulations. For instance, resource partitioning may lead to a dual market structure where large generalists compete in the core and small specialists become located in the periphery. Stability of the whole may occur not only under different diffusion periods and new orderings of domains, but also when the community has reorganized to better utilize existing resources. For example, the existing workforce within an industry may have re-sorted into new employment models. Indeed, as Aldrich, Rickard Sandell, and others have argued, growth itself may not characterize community or population change along all evolutionary paths, a point echoed today by environmental ecologists.

Critical Commentary and Future Directions

The most fundamental critique of the population ecology paradigm, and by extension organizational ecology, is Ruth Young's from 1988. The basic argument is that Hannan and Freeman and colleagues have done a poor job of transferring the central ecological constructs of species, niche, competition, fitness, and survival from biology to organization studies. Going further, Young maintains that trying to use the metaphor (or analogy) of evolution as found in biology in organizational ecology is a fundamentally flawed intellectual move, for firms are much more plastic than members of animal species: Firms can change templates (genetic code), they can fill more than one niche, and they can avoid death.

Challenges like Young's have actually stimulated work in the last 15 years on these issues, leading to a broader empirical foci (e.g., the use of interpopulation and community levels of analysis as opposed to the previously dominant population-level approach), a better specification of niches (e.g., as types and with partitions), a deeper examination of competition (e.g., as variants and partial cooperation), and an elaboration of survival (e.g., as variation in change rates, forms, and identities). In particular, ecologists have returned to consider community contexts more carefully to the point that there are few ecology articles that do not draw upon other contextual frames, such as institutional theory, learning, social movements, and state theory. In addition, ecologists have updated their biological notions of evolution by including coevolutionary processes and transformation (of identity or ecosystem).

In the future, each of these topic areas will see continued work. Another area that will likely see increased attention, mirroring similar efforts in biology, environmental studies and evolutionary law, and economics, is *global ecological change*. Are there global populations of firms? If so, what are their dynamics and how do they affect the global community in which these populations are embedded? Indeed, in spite of 30 years of study, the variety of organizational forms still needs further attention. Ecologists may find, as environmental ecologists like Jared Diamond claim, that the chief global ecological change is not the expansion in form variety, but the collapse.

—*P. Devereaux Jennings and Michael Lounsbury*

See also Adaptative Learning; Community and Organizations; Evolutionary Theory; Global Village; Organizational Change; Organizational Ecology

Further Readings

Aldrich, H. E. (1999). *Organizations evolving.* London: Sage.

Baum, J. A. C. (1996). Organizational ecology. In S. R. Clegg, C. Hardy, & W. R. Nord (Eds.), *The handbook of organization studies* (pp. 77–114). London: Sage.

Carroll, G. R., & Hannan, M. T. (2000). *The demography of corporations and industries.* Princeton, NJ: Princeton University Press.

Hannan, M. T., & Carroll, G. R. (1992). *Dynamics of organizational populations: Density, competition, and legitimation.* New York: Oxford University Press.

Hannan, M. T., & Freeman, J. H. (1977). The population ecology of organizations. *American Journal of Sociology, 83,* 929–984.

Hawley, A. H. (1950). *Human ecology: A theory of community structure.* New York: Ronald Press.

Young, R. C. (1988). Is population ecology a useful paradigm for the study of organizations? *American Journal of Sociology, 94,* 1–24.

Ecology

See Organizational Ecology

E-Commerce

E-commerce is the exchange of digitized information within and across organizations relating to communications, electronic ordering, and management of product and service activities. Distinctively in e-commerce, technology operates simultaneously as the tool that automates business transactions and workflows and as an organization's additional touch point or primary/sole interface with its customers. E-commerce signifies business activity and financial and commercial transactions carried out over the Internet and an ever increasing array of other technology devices.

Conceptual Overview

E-commerce business models are based on business being conducted 24 hours a day, 7 days a week. At the core of e-commerce is the technology required to operate it. In all business organizations, technology provides a functional supporting role. By contrast, e-commerce is not just the application of technology to an organization or a marketing issue but a strategic business model with a complex embedded information system. It is a system that integrates the internal management of an organization's activities in tandem with establishing the required interactive access with customers, business partners, and suppliers to facilitate real-time gathering and organizationwide generation and application of customer intelligence. Information gathered on clients can then be used to foster long-term customer management and value, adding to an organization's offerings.

In e-commerce, customer focus changes to the demand side rather than supply. Clients have a potential role in the development of enhancements to products and services through provision of feedback. This is seen as an opportunity to strengthen customer and business relations.

Capability for ongoing assessment of organizational performance is also enhanced through integrated information exchange, enabling better analysis of competitors and relevant market forces so that adjustments to strategy, efficiencies in processes, streamlining of the value chain, reconciling off-line and online channels, and cost reductions can be applied. For example, reusable online product information and advice can be provided very cost effectively so that self-service options replace skilled retailers.

True market orientation is dependent on organizational learning, and learning is advanced through versatile information and business exchanges across departments, business units, product groups, or geographically dispersed company divisions. This is vital as low market entry barriers mean that competitive advantage is sustainable only if it can counter competitor duplication by a strategic focus imbued throughout the organization to capitalize on an organization's strengths. For instance, Web sites are easily duplicated, and it is the value added to client offerings that will counter customers clicking to a competitor site.

Critical Commentary and Future Directions

For the future of e-commerce, security of payment transactions, privacy of personal information, and access to redress when transactions go wrong will continue to be a focus. Trust is the underlying element that will determine whether more consumers will evolve from gathering information online to actually ordering products or services and becoming long-term loyal customers.

E-commerce has changed the focus of marketing from a separate but necessary component to a fundamental driver of strategy. The level of sophistication required for market communications will continue to increase in order to match consumer insight. With every business competing for consumer attention, the volume of market communications will be invasive. Permission marketing will become more important, with customers exchanging personal information with organizations because they can trust that marketing messages will be delivered only if they are pertinent.

For e-commerce businesses to prosper, the notion of organizationwide sharing of information needs to be pervasive. Equally important, every customer contact with the business needs to be handled expertly and knowledge gained from each interaction used to develop organizational learning.

Changes in organizational culture are necessary for the success of e-commerce and a top-down focus is required. Management needs to embrace change at the same pace that e-business technology and its applications are evolving. Organizational structures such as internal administration need to support flexibility and counter internal rivalries. Performance rewards based on customer satisfaction can be linked to management roles. High-level customer relationship management at senior levels allows the organization's holistic cultural focus to be the driver of strategic decision making rather than just reactionary modifications to existing approaches.

Research has examined the interplay of e-commerce with organizational structure, IT structures, and brand management, each in isolation. The findings have concluded that when pursuing e-commerce activities, all three need to be factored into formative planning as e-commerce will alter the structure of each of these. For instance, consideration must not only be given to individual brands but also to the companies' total brand architecture.

The development of intuitive-to-use portable devices and the degree to which customers will be able to personalize content of technology mediated environments to suit their unique individual needs are key elements of the e-commerce future.

Contemporary e-commerce technology essentially limits one's virtual encounters with products to use of one's vision and hearing senses. The potential to extend one's sensory experience of the virtual environment leaves much to be developed for the future. However, current research indicates that technology enhancement must link directly to key product characteristics and not just the application of technology for the sake of it.

Increasingly, advances in technology reflect a country's economic progress, and determinations of that success can provide comparative data for cross-country analysis. What remains to be established are effective benchmark definitions that encompass transactional elements of e-commerce and the concomitant economic facets needed to gauge the ability of governments, organizations, market segments, and consumers to use the available technology infrastructures. A country's capacity for e-commerce has been linked to numbers of technology devices per person, the skill with which they are used by the general public, transparency in business and legal systems, and overall governmental support and procurement of technologies. Fundamental operational elements can be tracked for comparisons and these are important in the context of societal impacts. Data on levels of city-based usage of technologies can be compared with rural use; comparisons may be made between information-only transactions versus purchases; and sociological characteristics can be studied.

The ultimate future of e-commerce will be reflected in the ingenuity of the technologies invented and the skills applied to drive them.

—*Daphne Freeder*

See also Balanced Scorecard; Digital Divide; Enterprise Culture; Human–Computer Interaction; Organizational Learning

Further Readings

Rayport, J. F., & Jaworski, B. J. (2004). *Introduction to e-commerce.* Boston: McGraw-Hill.

Strebinger, A., & Treiblmaier, H. (2006, January). The impact of business to consumer e-commerce on organizational structure, brand architecture, IT structure and their interrelations. *Schmalenbach Business Review, 58*(1), 81–113.

Suh, K., & Lee, Y. (2005, December). The effects of virtual reality on consumer learning: An empirical investigation. *MIS Quarterly, 4,* 673–697.

Van Bentum, R., & Stone, M. (2005). Customer relationship management and the impact of corporate culture: A European study. *Database Marketing and Customer Strategy Management, 13*(1), 28–54.

Economic Rationalism

Economic rationalism is a typically Australian term that refers to government decision making based on neoclassical, neoliberalist economic ideas. It encompasses a range of economic propositions about the liberalization of markets. These economic ideas act as the strategic guide for government policy making including how the public sector organizations are managed and structured.

Conceptual Overview

Classical economics and liberalism, from which economic rationalist ideas are derived, originally developed in the 17th to 19th centuries through the work of economists and liberalists such as John Locke, Adam Smith, and John Stuart Mill. Neoclassical economics, or economic rationalism, involved a repromotion of these classical ideas from the 1960s by contemporary economists, including Milton Friedman and Friedrich Hayek. Influential think tanks, academic schools, and supranational organizations, such as the World Bank and the International Monetary Fund, were significant actors in seeding the ideas within political arenas.

This was at a time when governments were confronting global oil crises, stagflation, and high government debt—problems that were not addressed adequately within the postwar, Keynesian decision-making paradigm. It was not until the late 1970s, though, that Keynesianism notions of a mixed economy, welfarism, and collectivism were finally rejected by governments in favor of economic rationalism. Notably, Prime Minister Margaret Thatcher of the United Kingdom and President Ronald Reagan of the United States were early adopters, followed quickly by Canada, Australia, and New Zealand. In its modern interpretation, economic rationalism is based on a number of theoretical and conceptual ideas about the role and size of governments, as well as the role of actors within organizations.

Conceptually, economic rationalist ideas question the traditional role of government and suggest that governments should facilitate free market activity rather than directly regulate or control markets. This will achieve economic growth that might be facilitated through deregulation of financial markets, the establishment of strong financial management architecture and new institutional building, the reduction in corporate tax, and the removal of barriers to international trade. Incentives are offered to businesses to attract foreign direct investment and to support the competitive development of home industries.

Economic rationalism also suggests that governments need to give businesses the power to manage their organizations. This might involve governments legislating for industrial relations reform with changes to bargaining approaches requiring a shift away from collective bargaining to employer/employee–negotiated, enterprise-by-enterprise agreements. These are meant to reduce the power of trade unions in political and business arenas.

In governments' direct role, as a provider of public goods and services, economic rationalism moves governments' strategic decision making from a demand- to a supply-side determination. This usually means a reduction in spending on welfare policies and the implementation of fiscal and monetarist policies that reduce government debt. Conceptually, economic rationalism is a resource-based paradigm with limited attention given to collectivist, social concerns.

Such moves toward efficiency and competition involve the downsizing and reorganization of the public sector to make it more businesslike, with organizations adopting private sector managerial techniques. Thus, monopolistic and nationalized government organizations, pertaining to sectors such as banking, energy, health, education, and airlines, are likely to be restructured. This usually occurs in a number of different and combined ways.

A corporatization approach keeps a specific organization in government ownership but in a way that requires efficient business operations. Privatization and contracting out involve the selling off of the public sector organization or the contracting of specific organizational services, to the private or not-for-profit sectors. A public–private partnership, for the development of infrastructure or service provision, may involve long-term contractual arrangements between government and private sector organizations. Governments might create a contrived marketplace, whereby large monopolistic government organizations may be disaggregated into competing businesses.

Important theories are those relating to public choice, transaction costs, and agency. For example, public choice suggests that the delivery of public goods and services needs to involve a much greater choice of product and delivery mode, similar to the way markets operate. Transaction costs analysis addresses issues of efficiency and economy in government. This is done because many government programs are subsidized, so it is important to identify the precise costs of service delivery through transaction costs analysis. Agency theory examines the relationship between a principal (for example, government) and its agent (for example, a senior public sector chief executive officer) and proposes contractual arrangements designed to ensure that the agent acts in the interests of the principal. This can occur through systems such as senior executive services where the assumed tendency toward self-interested budget-maximizing behavior can be ameliorated through performance contracts and incentives.

Critical Commentary and Future Directions

While economic rationalism started as a New Right ideology of conservative governments, adoption has been economically pragmatic, as well as ideological. Effectively, the ideas of economic rationalism have become a global grand narrative and a preferred strategy of economic reform for many governments. The acceptance of economic rationalism, as a dominant paradigm, has occurred through the use of strong rhetoric and promotion by early adopters, within significant international networks. This has led to global acceptance of the broad ideas.

The knowledge assumptions of economic rationalism, however, while promoted by neoclassical economists, are largely ideological, philosophical, and theoretical, rather than empirical and rational. When the ideological aspects are considered, it is apparent that economic rationalism favors elite capitalists and businesses. Economic gains for many countries are undeniable, but adoption has created social, technological, and economic divisions, especially within developing polities.

Democratic processes, where they exist, allow voters to determine the extent to which they will support economic rationalist governments. As an elitist-directed strategic thrust, economic rationalism certainly challenges some democratic principles, particularly pluralist, citizen participation in representative government.

Critics of economic rationalism suggest that, in practice, adopting governments have ceded considerable power to markets and have become subservient to big-business interests. They argue that the political context of many organizations in the public sector is different from that of markets, which demonstrate no particular social conscience. While critical objectives of public sector organizations may be focused on efficiency, there is an absence of profit motive, especially where the provision of public goods with a social interest is concerned. Therefore, the adoption of economic rationalism is inappropriate. Proponents of economic rationalism assert that organizations, whether in the public or private sectors, can be managed on the basis of efficiency and economy, regardless of context.

While there are degrees of economic rationalism in practice, few governments have attempted a pure model of implementation. Thus, hybrid models of economic rationalism have emerged, some of which attempt to combine good economic management of a polity with a stronger sense of social responsibility and concern. Governments' future approach to economic rationalism may be dependent upon their level of ideological commitment to the paradigm and the social conscience that, collectively, they possess.

—*Judy Johnston*

See also Management and Public Policy; Neoclassical Economics; Neoliberalism and Organization; New Public Management

Further Readings

Emy, H. V., & Hughes, O. E. (1991). *Australian politics: Realities in conflict.* Sydney, Australia: Macmillan.

James, C., Jones, C., & Norton, A. (Eds). (1993). *A defence of economic rationalism.* St. Leonards, NSW, Australia: Allen & Unwin.

King, S., & Lloyd, P. (Eds). (1993). *Economic rationalism: Dead end or way forward?* St. Leonards, NSW, Australia: Allen & Unwin.

Pusey, M. (1991). *Economic rationalism in Canberra: A nation-building state changes its mind.* Sydney/New York: Cambridge University Press.

ECONOMIC SOCIOLOGY

There are authors who claim economic sociology for economics, those who claim it for sociology, and those who argue that it is situated somewhere in the gray area between these two disciplines. Usually, however, economic sociology is understood to be a subfield of sociology, and it is then defined as the sociological approach applied to economic phenomena. A fuller definition would be that economic sociology analyzes the production, distribution, and consumption of goods and services with the help of sociological concepts and methods. Following the argument of Max Weber in 1954, one may want to add that economic sociology should not only look at economic phenomena, but also at so-called economically relevant phenomena and economically conditioned phenomena. By the former is meant noneconomic phenomena that influence the economy (e.g., religion), and by the latter economic phenomena that influence noneconomic phenomena (e.g., politics).

Conceptual Overview

As opposed to mainstream economics, which is based on microeconomics, economic sociology lacks a closely interrelated set of basic concepts. Instead it draws on a series of concepts and ideas that come from different traditions in sociology, such as Marxism, Weberian sociology, organizational sociology, and the sociology of work. A central role is played by the work of Karl Polanyi, whose concepts are used by a large number of people who are currently active in economic sociology.

If one were to single out three central figures in economic sociology, whose works have deeply influenced the field and are still being drawn upon, it would be Karl Marx, Max Weber, and Karl Polanyi. Marx introduced, first of all, the idea of capitalism as a social system with its own internal motor in the form of a search for ever more profit. He also invented the notion of class struggle, caused by the organization of labor and factors of production, and more generally the idea that social structures are deeply influenced by economic factors. Firms as such play little role in Marx's work, however, and the reader of *Capital* will only find references to factories and the impersonal figure of the capitalist.

Weber laid a conceptual foundation for economic sociology in *Economy and Society* (1978), especially in the chapter entitled "Sociological Categories of Economic Action." Weber suggests that the basic analytical unit of economic sociology is economic social action or economic action that is oriented to other actors. This unit is then used to construct other and more complex categories in Weber's economic sociology. When two actors orient their actions to one another, for example a buyer and a seller, a social and economic relationship is formed. Social and economic relationships can be open or closed, with a local fruit and vegetable market illustrating the former and a modern profession the latter. Closed economic relationships turn into firms when they are oriented to a set of economic goals to be realized, and when there is a staff to see to it this gets done. Economic systems that are centered on the idea of a household (such as feudalism or socialism) tend to be static, while those that are centered on profit making (where capitalism is the prime example) tend to be dynamic.

The firm plays a central role in the modern type of capitalism, which Weber calls rational capitalism and which has its origin exclusively in the West. The modern shareholding firm has evolved very slowly from the household and the economic partnership, and is today characterized by a methodical search for profit and its use of bureaucracy. Weber portrays bureaucracy as an efficient administrative machine that tends to stifle the search for profit unless it is counteracted by the entrepreneur. Weber's famous description of what characterizes a bureaucracy can be found in Chapter 11 in *Economy and Society*.

Polanyi argues that while the view of the economy that can be found among mainstream economists is abstract and can be described as formal, the one that is used by sociologists and anthropologists is centered on the livelihood or materiality of life and can be characterized as substantive. While mainstream economists also tend to focus exclusively on the economy at the expense of its social structure and origin, sociologists and anthropologists see it as an instituted process or as embedded in social, political, and religious institutions. Polanyi also finally argues that all economies can be organized in one of three ways: as reciprocity, redistribution, or exchange. A concrete economy typically draws on each of these, while one is usually predominant. In the economy of a modern European society, for example, one can find reciprocity in the household, redistribution in the state, and exchange in the corporate sector.

Finally, modern economic sociology has added its own set of concepts to the tradition of economic sociology. The most famous of these are embeddedness and the social construction of the economy. The former is taken from the work of Polanyi but is given a significantly different meaning. While Polanyi had argued that capitalist economies are disembedded in the sense that they are no longer embedded in religious and political institutions, the argument of Mark Granovetter (1985) and others is that *all* economies are embedded in social structures, including capitalist economies. While Granovetter argues that economic actions are always embedded in networks of social relations (relational or structural embeddedness), other economic sociologists refer also to cultural embeddedness, political embeddedness, and so on.

The notion that the economy and anything economic can be seen as an economic construction has its origin in a famous work by Peter Befger and Thomas Luckmann from 1967. The key idea is that nothing in the economy should be taken for granted or somehow seen as "natural" by the sociologist. Everything is a social construction, with its own distinct history, from *homo economicus* to the modern shopping mall. A related idea in modern economic sociology is the notion that the economy is not a thing, but something that always has to be acted out according to a script. These scripts come naturally to people but can also be invented by economists (performativity).

Critical Commentary and Future Directions

Modern economic sociology, as illustrated by the 2005 edition of *The Handbook of Economic Sociology*, covers a huge number of topics, from the center of the economy to its intersections with law, culture, religion, and more. Much of this literature is directly relevant for those interested in a critical management perspective, while some parts are of more peripheral interest. When Viviana Zelizer, for example, in her study from 2005, argues that intimate personal values and economic values are typically interwoven, rather than antagonistic to one another, this is an insight that is more relevant to the individual in his or her capacity as a family member, partner, and so on than as a manager or worker.

Firms and organizations appear in many parts of modern economic sociology, not least in its attempts to analyze markets. According to a well-known article from 1981 by Harrison White, for example, production markets are seen as the social structures that come into being when a small number of firms closely watch each other for clues about prices and levels of production. Markets, in brief, are viewed as social structures, created by firms in their interactions and ways of orienting themselves to one another. White's theory is sometimes complemented with the idea that firms enter into status and power hierarchies in their respective markets. Production firms may similarly be conceptualized in terms of networks, either inside a single market or as networks connecting markets that exist upstream and downstream.

The tool of network theory is also often used to explore the connections between firms and organizations more generally. There exists today, for example, a fairly extensive literature on the way that organizations are connected by the fact that some board member of a firm is also a member of the board of another firm. The existence of these so-called interlocks can usually be established with the help of publicly available information, and then analyzed with the help of various mathematical tools. Drawing on the assumption that one tie equals one, many important diffusion studies, for example, have been produced.

The early optimism that one could capture the social structure that exists between organizations with the help of quantitative network analysis has, however, turned out to be premature. Exactly what the existence of interlocks between firms signifies, it has gradually been realized, depends crucially on what it is that is being transmitted through the ties. This is something that can only be established by getting more information than what is available in the public accounts of who the board members are. While this type of extra information can clearly be produced, for example, through interviews, the idea of a common metric becomes, if not lost, suddenly more problematic.

Economic sociologists have recently turned to entrepreneurship, and here also the idea of network has come in handy. In a 2005 article by Ronald Burt, for example, one can find an elaboration of the idea that corporations as well as individuals can exploit opportunities and be entrepreneurial by spanning so-called structural holes or nonredundant social contacts. Burt also casts this phenomenon in terms of Georg Simmels's notion of *tertius gaudens,* or one actor who plays off two actors against one another.

Economic sociologists have for a long time tried to break with the idea of the entrepreneur as a kind of economic hero who singlehandedly drives the economic system forward, along the lines of Joseph Schumpeter. Through a combination of qualitative and quantitative studies, Rosabeth Moss Kanter showed in 1983 that entrepreneurship in the modern firm is not individual but typically takes place in teams. She also outlined the various roles in this type of "intrapreneurship" that are played by different people. While someone may be in charge of getting the necessary resources together, someone else has as a task to protect the team from interference while it is doing its work, and so on. To this may be added a growing sociological literature on start-ups, including rates of start-ups in a number of Organisation for Economic Co-operation and Development (OECD) countries.

Kanter is also a pioneer in analyzing the role of women in the corporation and her study on this topic from 1977 is considered a classic. Female lower staff members, for example, may not seize the few opportunities that they have to advance because of the solidarity they feel with their coworkers. Moreover, the women who do get ahead, for example in management, may have to face the situation that they are the only woman in this type of position. When this is the case, the person in question is seen not as an individual but as a representative of a category (tokenism).

One may want to contrast Kanter's famous picture of the difficulties that women face in the average corporation with the situation in a women-run industry with a very different type of corporate culture. This is done in a study by Nicole Biggart (1989), which focuses on direct-selling organizations such as Tupperware and Mary Kay Cosmetics. In this type of organization, women often work on their own and use their personal networks to locate potential clients; they may also create new networks for this purpose.

Finally, economic sociologists have tried to diagnose the situation of firms in today's neoliberal economy. The argument is currently being made in Neil Fligstein's *The Architecture of Markets* and other works that the overriding goal of major corporations in the United States is to exclusively try to satisfy the shareholders, by bringing in as much profit as possible. This emphasis on shareholder value means that the parts of the corporation that deal with production and distribution are seen as subordinate to finance, something which is a historically new development. As is shown by Dirk Zorn (2003), the 1990s saw, for example, the rise and institutionalization of the chief financial officer in the modern U.S. firm.

—*Richard Swedberg*

See also Organizational Theory

Further Readings

Berger, P., & Luckmann, T. (1967). *The social construction of reality: A treatise in the sociology of knowledge.* New York: Doubleday.

Burt, R. (2005). *Brokerage and closure: An introduction to social capital.* New York: Oxford University Press.

Fligstein, N. (2001). *The architecture of markets.* Princeton, NJ: Princeton University Press.

Granovetter, M. (1985). Economic action and social structure: The problem of embeddedness. *American Journal of Sociology, 91,* 81–510.

Kanter, R. M. (1977). *Men and women of the corporation.* New York: Basic Books.

Kanter, R. M. (1983). *The change masters: Innovation and entrepreneurship in America.* New York: Simon & Schuster.

Marx, K. (1990). *Capital.* London: Penguin.

Polanyi, K. (1977). *The livelihood of man.* New York: Academic Press.

Smelser, N., & Swedberg, R. (Eds.). (2005). *The handbook of economic sociology* (2nd ed.). Princeton, NJ/New York: Princeton University Press/Russell Sage Foundation.

Weber, M. (1954). *Methodology of the social sciences.* New York: Free Press.

Weber, M. (1978). *Economy and society: An outline of interpretive sociology.* Berkeley: University of California Press.

White, H. (1981). Where do markets come from? *American Journal of Sociology, 87,* 517–547.

Zelizer, V. (2005). *The purchase of intimacy.* Princeton, NJ: Princeton University Press.

Zorn, D. (2003). Here a chief, there a chief: The rise of the CFO in the American firm. *American Sociological Review, 69,* 345–63.

Effectiveness

Effectiveness is the capability to produce or bring about a desired outcome or result. It is contingent upon goals and the agent, method, process, or "way" the goal is achieved, as well as the context and circumstances in which achievement is reached. Its usefulness as a concept is situationally specific. Virtually all fields use it as a performance measure. However, because of the innumerable ways in which effectiveness can be defined, a widely agreed-upon definition does not exist. Nonetheless, how effectiveness is defined has important implications for how organizations measure success and for the development of useful models of organizational theory.

Conceptual Overview

A universally adopted definition of effectiveness continues to elude both academicians and practitioners. Adam Smith proposed that effectiveness, or rather efficiency, was derived through specialization of production and subsequent exchange of goods and services. Fredrick Taylor's principles of scientific management argued for the division of labor and for understanding an organization's processes to find the one best way of efficiently executing those processes. Unfortunately, after more than 200 years, researchers still lack a single conceptual definition of effectiveness.

The concept of effectiveness in the organizational research literature has dozens, if not hundreds, of criteria permutations. Researchers often derive these definitions as a matter of convenience. Also, the definitions can reflect the values or bias held by the researcher rather than that of the organization being studied. Furthermore, criteria are varied, often including both objective measures such as profit and revenue growth, and subjective measures such as employee and customer satisfaction.

A major source of variation in defining effectiveness is that the term is often used interchangeably with concepts such as productivity and efficiency. The implied meaning of these terms is similar, though many authors suggest subtle, yet important, differences. One common view among scholars contends that efficiency is a subset of the broader concept of effectiveness. Organizational efficiency is typically considered a short-run measure that focuses on process inputs and outputs and the minimization of waste, expense, or effort. Organizational effectiveness, then, is the efficient attainment of organizational goals or outcomes. From this perspective, anything that is effective must be efficient.

Alternatively, some hold that efficiency and effectiveness are distinct but related constructs. From this perspective, effectiveness is solely concerned with goal attainment. It does not necessarily imply a concern with the amount of resources used to achieve the desired result. Further, efficiency refers only to the ratio of inputs and outputs without consideration of whether or not those outputs achieve the desired results or outcome. In this conceptualization, an organization can be effective, efficient, or any combination of the two. Consideration is given to understanding the existence of trade-offs between efficiency and effectiveness, as well as the antecedents and outcomes of the identified dimensional combinations.

Measures of Effectiveness

The familiar saying of *what gets measured gets done* is especially relevant to effectiveness. The measures that an organization uses to assess its effectiveness are reflective of goals and priorities, whether explicit or not. These goals define the organization's purpose and reason for existence. Therefore, determining the underlying goals of an organization is critical to understanding that organization and enabling its development. However, the diversity of organizational structures, situations, and environments necessitates a contingency approach to studying effectiveness.

Given the variety of definitions of effectiveness, it follows that there are as many, if not more, measurement methods. For example, organizational effectiveness may be characterized by financial results such as revenues, profits, or return on equity. It may have a market or customer orientation such as market share, product diversification, or customer satisfaction. Effectiveness might also be considered from an operational or production perspective with measures of unit production, quality, or resource utilization. More recently, organizations have considered a more balanced and comprehensive view of the organization with measures such as the balanced scorecard. The Malcolm Baldrige National Quality Award is a reflection of this perspective. This annual self-evaluation covers organizational elements such as leadership, planning, market focus, information management, human resources, process management, and various aspects of business results. With pressures resulting from globalization and efforts toward improving environmental stewardship, companies are also including measures of social responsibility such as pollution rates and charitable projects.

Models of Organizational Effectiveness

A number of approaches or perspectives are used to analyze organizational effectiveness. One perspective holds that effectiveness criteria can be reduced to three basic models—the resource model, the process model, and the goal model. The resource model focuses on the acquisition and management of organizational inputs, the process approach centers on efficient utilization of resources, and the goal model emphasizes the outputs and effects of the organization's activities. While each of these models produces useful insights, the narrowness of their respective scopes limits their overall utility.

In an attempt to address this issue, Robert Quinn and John Rohrbaugh offer a spatial model of organizational effectiveness that integrates several previous models. Their competing values model is built on the premise that different organizations need different measures of effectiveness. The value of this type of model is that it provides a multidimensional view of organizations that allows for different organizational priorities. Organizational life cycle, industry, competitive position, or strategic planning might dictate priorities.

Other more recent paradigms have also been considered. The stakeholder model considers effectiveness measures associated with an organization's key constituents such as employees, customers, suppliers, investors, and creditors. Other views of effectiveness have shifted from an emphasis on efficiency to one on flexibility and ability to adapt to changes in the organization's environment. This view is often associated with the adoption of a biological view of an organization versus the mechanistic paradigm that has been historically predominant.

Levels of Analysis

While an accurate model of organizations is important to those studying organizational effectiveness, it is also useful to consider other levels of analysis. Different levels of analysis can dictate different measures of effectiveness. The three main levels of analysis are individual, group, and organization. At the most granular level is the individual men and women who are the building blocks of an organization. Investigations at this level look at factors such as employee motivation and job satisfaction. The group level might represent project-specific work teams or even entire departments. Finally, the organizational level might consider specific business processes or interdepartmental cooperation as areas of interest in understanding effectiveness. A more recent addition is the environmental or interorganizational level of analysis. This meso level looks at collections of organizations according to market, location, size, or other classification method.

Critical Commentary and Future Directions

Because no single definition of organizational effectiveness exists, the field lacks a well-supported theory grounded by a significant body of sound empirical research. As previously mentioned, related to the lack of a consensus definition is the multitude of ways that effectiveness is measured. Past research in organization studies has focused on single- as well as multi-component criteria. For example, one study may utilize profitability, another may use shareholder value, while yet another may use a combination of measures that reflects multiple aspects of the organization's activities. These divergent combinations of criteria lead to conflicting conclusions and fragmentation in organizational research. Moreover, there appears to be a general belief among organizational scholars that a single definition of effectiveness is impossible, giving scholars little incentive to strive for such a goal.

Another issue in effectiveness research is whether the variables being considered are predictors of organizational effectiveness or simply indicators of effectiveness. For instance, an alcoholic beverage manufacturer may be deemed operationally effective, but the social impacts of that effectiveness may not be deemed successful from certain perspectives. Furthermore, it is likely that variables in each of these classifications may change from predictor to indicator, depending on the nature of the organization or the context of the analysis. This raises the question of whether research should focus on measurable outcomes of organizational effectiveness or the effects of the outcomes.

Recognizing these issues, future organization studies must utilize careful judgment in developing and conducting effectiveness research. Given the level of disagreement and the diversity of perspectives, it is likely that scholars will be afforded a fair amount of latitude in defining effectiveness, as long as such criteria are specific and justifiable for the given context. The key will be in identifying, explaining, and assessing the unique contradictions and paradoxes inherent in organizations that define effectiveness for each.

The Nature of Change and Effectiveness

The conceptualization of effectiveness has experienced several transitions over the years. At the turn of the previous century, automation was a revolutionary step in business practice, launching us from single-unit production via guilds and craftspeople to high-volume, mass-produced items at considerably lower prices. From the early days of scientific management, the belief solidified that specialization and division of labor were the key antecedents of effectiveness. The next evolution was mass customization, in which consumers have nearly unlimited choices, enjoy the price benefits of mass production, and expect the delivery speeds of highly efficient supply chains. A focus on quality and the adoption of programs like Total Quality Management and Six Sigma drove another sea change in the expectations of industry. Largely due to the competitive pressures of a developing global marketplace, poor quality was no longer tolerated by consumers who had grown increasingly savvy.

Today, the concept of organizational effectiveness is changing yet again. Elements of corporate social responsibility are rapidly being incorporated into the mission statements and strategic plans of companies large and small. Operational and financial performance is no longer enough. Stakeholders have begun to expand their expectations of organizations to include consistently ethical behavior as well as environmental and social responsibility.

In all of these trends one theme is evident: The nature of organizational effectiveness is intrinsically linked to an organization's ability to successfully adapt to changes in its environment. Furthermore, as our definitions of effectiveness change, our measures of organizational effectiveness must continue to change as well. This realization has challenged the work of both scholars and practitioners alike. On one hand, the implication is that in order for organizations to be effective, they must adapt to changing business needs. On the other hand, application of the theory requires that regardless of change, someone or something has to measure how well the organization is meeting stakeholder needs at any specific point in time to assess current effectiveness. Consequently, a widely held theory or concept of effectiveness (other than a contingency model) is practically impossible.

—*George Hrivnak, Jr. and Terry Halfhill*

See also Bureaucracy; Cohesion; Decentralization; Hierarchy; Lean Production; Technology

Further Readings

Cameron, K. S., & Whetten, D. A. (Eds.). (1983). *Organizational effectiveness: A comparison of multiple models.* New York: Academic Press.

Huber, G. P. (1984). The nature and design of post-industrial organizations. *Management Science, 30,* 928–951.

Peters, T. J., & Waterman, R. H. (1983). *In search of excellence: Lessons from America's best run companies.* New York: Harper & Row.

Quinn, R. E., & Rohrbaugh, J. (1983). A spatial model of effectiveness criteria: Toward a competing values approach to organizational analysis. *Management Science 29,* 363–377.

EMERGENT THEORY

Emergent theory (ET) is an outcome of organization research in which theory is allowed to come to light through a systematic data collection and analysis process called grounded theory, a research approach committed to discovery, direct contact with the social phenomenon of interest, and a rejection of explicit a priori theorizing.

Conceptual Overview

ET is a product of grounded theory (GT), a widely recognized and adopted research approach associated with sociologists Barney Glaser and Anselm Strauss. The two successfully collaborated on this qualitative research style in which theories, concepts, and hypotheses emerge from the data rather than from investigation of the literature.

The methods and analysis for GT are drawn from inductive quantitative analysis developed in the Department of Sociology and the Bureau of Applied Social Research at Columbia University in the 1950s and 1960s. In 1967, Glaser and Strauss published what has become the seminal work on ET in organization studies, in which the authors describe the importance of systematically and theoretically modeling social processes and propose that the researcher asks two formal questions that allow theory to emerge from data. The researcher asks, what is the chief concern or problem in the social phenomenon and what accounts for most of the variation in processing the problem? The researcher also asks, what category or what property of category does the incident under study indicate? Guided by these two questions, the researcher then includes the following perspectives and methods to ensure theoretical emergence.

First, the researcher does not explicitly introduce specific theoretical knowledge from the literature a priori. Next, the researcher adopts a perspective that allows abstract significant *categories* to be discovered from the data, an approach Glaser and Strauss termed *theoretical sensitivity.* The researcher also adopts a *constant comparison method* where *incidents,* rather than individuals or organizations, are observed, compared, analyzed and *coded* in order to identify, revisit, and redefine important concepts, categories of concepts, and interrelationships among concepts and categories. Next, as significant categories emerge from the data, the researcher may then turn to relevant literature to help inform on the emerging theory. Thus, the literature is treated as another set of data informing the researcher on the ET.

In the early 1990s, after nearly three decades as collaborators and advocates for the importance of ET to organization studies, Glaser and Strauss went down different paths. In 1990, Strauss and Corbin developed a newer framework of GT, which allowed the researcher to examine relevant literature before a study began. In 1992, Glaser responded critically to this approach, expressing concern for the loss of true ET if literature could be introduced a priori, and reinforcing the original precepts of GT. Both the original and the newer GT approaches continue to have their strong advocates among new and senior researchers and ET, whether informed with little or no explicit a priori theorizing, continues to be a highly regarded product of qualitative research, evidenced by the number of recent organizational scholars publishing on the subject or adopting one or both of the GT approaches.

Critical Commentary and Future Directions

While ET is widely recognized, it is not without its controversies, most notably made public when Glaser responded to the Strauss and Corbin framework by describing it as a destructive misconception of the original GT that would "force" categories on the data rather than allow concepts and categories to emerge. Glaser demanded that the authors withdraw their book from publication, and while this did not occur, a 1998 second edition by Strauss and Corbin added commentary that addressed several of Glaser's major concerns.

Another area of concern about ET relates to vulnerability regarding the researcher's capacity for putting aside preconceptions, being open to the data, and allowing theories to emerge from the data. It is argued that the researcher cannot have a complete tabula rasa, dropping personal experiences sufficiently to allow theories to emerge, without some effect from the researcher's own theoretical lenses. Related to this is a second area of concern specific to GT, but affecting ET, that methodologies necessary to achieve true ET require extensive training in sociological theory and are thus of limited use to novices in empirical research. On the one hand, Glaser and Strauss's original work is criticized for not providing enough detail on *how* the researcher is to accomplish theoretical sensitivity, for example, so that novices in this research can move toward proficiency. On the other hand, Strauss and Corbin's work, which aimed to overcome this concern, has been described as formulaic in its approach to this problem.

With these concerns come opportunities for the future of ET, which has now been a validated product of organization studies for over four decades. There is still a need to help the novice researcher who wants to effectively combine an open mind on new data with the theoretical sensitivity espoused by some ET proponents. The complexity and potential for tediousness of the GT research process lend itself to newer approaches using technologies that can help overcome this tediousness. In addition, proponents of action research—an approach in which the researcher alternates between action in and reflection on the social phenomenon of interest—suggest that it can be a method for collecting data from which ET can be derived. While scholars of both domains make clear distinctions between action research and ET, there are opportunities for scholars interested in the complementarity of the two. Finally, ET will persist as a highly regarded product of organization research in general, and qualitative research in particular, regardless of whether the sources of hypotheses for ET are drawn from literature or drawn from data. The researcher's choices will affect ET processes and outcomes in either event, but these choices affect research outcomes in any research approach.

—*Sherrie E. Human*

See also Action Research; Grounded Theory Building; Qualitative Approaches

Further Readings

Eisenhardt, K. (1989). Building theories from case study research. *Academy of Management Review, 14*(4), 532–550.

Glaser, B. (1992). *Emergence vs. forcing: Basics of grounded theory analysis.* Mill Valley, CA: Sociology Press.

Glaser, B., & Strauss, A. (1967). *Discovery of grounded theory.* Chicago: Aldine.

Human, S., & Provan, K. (1997). An emergent theory of structure and outcomes in small-firm strategic manufacturing networks. *Academy of Management Journal, 40*(2), 368–403.

Locke, K. (2001). *Grounded theory in management research.* London: Sage.

Strauss, A., & Corbin, J. (1990). *Basics of qualitative research.* Thousand Oaks, CA: Sage.

Strauss, A., & Corbin, J. (1998). *Basics of qualitative research* (2nd ed.). Thousand Oaks, CA: Sage.

Emic

The linguist Kenneth L. Pike used *emic unit* (see also *etic*) to refer to all aspects of behavior that are meaningful in a particular social situation (e.g., family meal, work situation, religious ceremony) for a particular society. Emic units contrast with behavior that the society does not notice or disregards. Pike uses *emic system* to refer to a society's complete set of interrelated behaviors and meanings. *Emic standpoint, viewpoint,* or *analysis* refers to methods of learning about a society that identify its emic units and systems. Scholars often use "emic" in ways that differ from Pike's. Some use it to refer to phenomena that are unique to a particular society. Some restrict emic methods to induction from direct observation without reference to comparative theory and data.

Conceptual Overview

Pike derived *emic* unit from the concept of phon*eme*, a meaningful element of sound in a particular language. For example, tones convey phonemic differences in word meanings in the indigenous American tonal languages that Pike studied. Generalizing from phoneme, Pike coined the word "tagmeme" to refer to the meaning of a grammatical construction, and "behavioreme" to refer to the meaning of a behavior. He later dropped the term "behavioreme" in favor of "emic unit." In Pike's view, explicit statements about meaningful behaviors implicitly refer to other aspects of behavior and meaning.

Emic analysis focuses on one culture at a time, but theoretical systems developed in other societies (see the entry for "etic") are what Pike calls an essential initial approach to an alien system. Central to Pike's methodology is that a newcomer must systematically combine prior theory with the general human capacity to intuit when learning an emic system. Emic analysis discovers emic units; it does not create them. Since an emic unit is embedded within a set of meanings that abstractions only partially re-create, an emic unit is not created by being defined. Explicit knowledge rests on a tacit or nonconscious base. The conclusions of an emic analysis are adequate to the extent that they correspond to the intuition of someone living within the emic system, hence the link of "emic standpoint" to "insider perspective." An emic unit is successfully identified when an insider responds to it as being different from other emic units.

Pike used the distinction between insiders' and outsiders' experience as a heuristic base to formalize the application of phoneme to behavior. He does so by referring to the insider (linked to emic) compared to the outsider (linked to etic) perspective in language analysis.

A newcomer inevitably begins from theoretical rather than emic understanding and presents theoretical conclusions to other outsider analysts. However, the newcomer increasingly develops an emic stance in personal interactions with a system. The transition to emic understanding is analogous to language learning. The language learner begins by translating unfamiliar words into his or her first language. The learner progresses to the point where words include meaning in relation to other words in the second language and to the experiences of native speakers. Pike developed a procedure for learning unwritten languages that relied heavily on induction and largely bypassed translation. This procedure encouraged cultural anthropologists to use inductive methods and has influenced other fields as well.

Critical Commentary and Future Directions

The meaning of emic in other fields has drifted substantially from Pike's original use. The drift is due in part to the multifaceted quality of the term and applied linguistics purpose of the original description. It is also due to differences in the phenomena and perspectives taken in linguistics as compared to other fields.

Anthropologists use the term emic (see also *etic*) for at least two purposes. Cultural anthropologists studying living cultural groups can follow Pike's assumption that an analyst can develop personal experience with a group's emic system. Cultural anthropologists who study prehistoric societies adapted the concept to suit the need to infer uses of archaeological objects by drawing analogies with similar objects in other societies.

The idea of emic (and etic) was brought into cross-cultural psychology through its application to the design of questionnaire surveys. Berry advocated identifying emic units by oscillating among designing questionnaires using prior theory, trying them in a new setting, statistically checking which parts reflected emic units that were actually meaningful in the new setting, and revising the survey based on an intuitive analysis of the new setting. The process he prescribes reflects the complementary roles Pike envisioned for combining prior theory with local induction.

Other scholars depart from Pike's use, believing that using prior theory tends to harm more than help understand emic units. Some evoke the term "emic" to argue that analysts should rely solely on intuition and direct interactions with a society's members, not prior theory. Others in the same spirit take the view that texts written or stories told by a society's members provide the appropriate materials for emic analysis. Still further from Pike's usage, scholars sometimes refer to "emic theory" as that which applies to a particular society as distinct from "etic theory" as that which applies to many societies.

Scholars often invoke emic meanings to highlight things that analysts miss by importing theories developed in one society to analyze a new society. Blame for the omission is placed on foreign biases in the theoretical structure or intuition of outsider analysts. The critic then suggests using a less traditionally scientific, more intuitive method to access the less theoretically structured and more comprehensively intuitive understandings of the society's insiders. In contrast, Pike's view was that analysts should combine prior theory with structured application of intuition to analyze the emic system of a new society.

For future use, its conceptual drift and variability in current use makes "emic" difficult to use without creating misunderstanding. Nevertheless, Pike's original point remains that cultural analysis that ends by relying on generalized categories is insufficient to allow a newcomer to understand or function adequately in an unfamiliar society.

—*Mark F. Peterson*

See also Etic

Further Readings

Headland, T. N., Pike, K. L., & Harris, M. (Eds.). *Emics and etics: The insider/outsider debate.* Newbury Park, CA: Sage.

Peterson, M. F., & Pike, K. L. (2002). Emics and etics for organizational studies: A lesson in contrast from linguistics. *International Journal of Cross Cultural Management, 2,* 5–19.

Pike, K. L. (1967). *Language in relation to a unified theory of the structure of human behavior* (2nd ed.). The Hague, the Netherlands: Mouton.

Pike, K.L. (1993). *Talk, thought, and thing: The emic road toward conscious knowledge.* Dallas, TX: Summer Institute of Linguistics.

Pike, K. L., & Pike, E. G. (1983). *Text and tagmeme.* Norwood, NJ: Ablex.

EMOTION

The term *emotion* has it roots in the Latin *emovere*, which means to stir up or move. In that crucial sense, emotions such as fear, love, anxiety, jealousy, joy, and anger play a key role in signaling to ourselves and others how well or safely we are performing. Emotions will shape the meaning we attribute to experiences as well as impelling or inhibiting particular behaviors. Emotions thus implicate a number of different processes, especially subjective feelings and their outward expressions and the social contexts in which they are learned or exchanged.

The study of emotion in organizations has become particularly significant in the past decade. It focuses on the way that organizational life is energized and formed through feelings. So emotions are more than just side issues or interferences in the business of organization; they lie at the very heart of organizational experiences, politics, and order. Moreover, organizations are not simply empty receptacles for their employees' emotions; organizations shape and control emotions, sometimes specifically toward productive ends.

Conceptual Overview

To grasp the detail of what emotion *is* requires an appreciation of the different perspectives that inform our understanding of emotion. These can be broadly classified as biological, cognitive, psychodynamic, and social constructionist.

A biological viewpoint holds that emotional responses are rooted fundamentally in the way our neurological and chemical system is "wired," a product of many millennia of human evolutionary development. Indeed, there is persuasive evidence that specific areas of the brain, especially a small region called the amygdala, signal when anger, fear, or aggression is required. Following the insights of Charles Darwin's *The Expression of Emotions in Man and Animals,* emotions such as fear, anger, and rage are seen to have been biologically crucial for our primitive ancestors in dealing with threats to their very survival. Such impulses are still present in our emotional makeup, even though threats to life and limb are now far less likely than threats to one's esteem or competence, such as from feeling insulted, unfairly treated, or demeaned. The biological perspective typically seeks universal trends, and researchers such as Paul Ekman have revealed that some facial expressions of emotions such as fear, sadness, disgust, and enjoyment are recognizable across very different national cultures. The shadows of our Stone Age past are, according to evolutionary organizational psychologists, still detectable in particular present-day organizational behaviors, such as in patterns of hierarchy, male dominance, alliances, and aggression. They suggest that this is a "given" that inevitably limits attempts to democratize the workplace.

Cognitive approaches take a rather different starting point: It is the *appraisal* of what we see or hear that determines the kind of feeling we experience and the emotion we express. Appraisal refers to the way we make sense or meaning of what is before us; an emotional response then follows. A snake may be appraised as dangerous, triggering fear and flight; a look of disapproval from a boss elicits anxiety and wariness. Richard Lazarus and his colleagues have been predominant advocates of appraisal theory. They refer to *primary appraisal* and *secondary appraisal.* The former determines the extent to which a particular situation is felt to impinge on the person: "What's this got to do with me?" And if it does, secondary appraisal addresses "What can I do about it?" Appraisal theory has been influential in our understanding of stress responses in the workplace and, more recently, a broader range of emotions.

Through a psychoanalyst's eyes, the workplace is a cauldron of mixed emotions, especially from fantasies, threats, and desires. Following the teachings of Sigmund Freud, individuals are seen to suppress or repress such impulses because of the anxiety they provoke and their social unacceptability. Different psychological defense mechanisms—such as *projecting* one's own feeling onto others, and *regressing* to childlike behaviors—offer ways of coping and self-protection, but they also undermine organizational rationality. For example, nurses may become very bureaucratic, even unfeeling, toward patients as a way of coping with the anxiety of dealing with the overwhelming demands of sickness and dying. The psychoanalytic perspective asserts that, to an extent, we are all prisoners of our past, and we carry our early vulnerabilities and pains into organizational settings, often in ways in which we are not consciously aware; our aspirations are not always what they seem. So, personal agendas, politicking, and plotting stem, in large measure, from the way organizational members act out their past, in the present. These effects are evident in a wide range of organizational processes, such as tensions in work groups and teams, as well as what Manfred Kets de Vries has termed "neurotic" leadership—inconsistent, impulsive, authoritarian. A key goal of organizational psychoanalysts is to help organizational members acknowledge and address the roots of their anxieties, and so free them to act more rationally, in line with the manifest goals and objectives of the organization.

The social construction of emotion emphasizes the different ways in which emotion is influenced by interpersonal, social, and cultural settings. In other words, we learn what emotional expressions we ought to display in certain settings (e.g., grief at a funeral, enjoyment at a party, humility before a superior), but these can vary according to the norms or conventions of a society or particular social group. For example, beating an opponent in a competition should result in expressions of pride in many Western settings, but humility in some Asian cultures. Some writers, such as Arlie

Hochschild, suggest that social learning also extends to what we privately feel; there are societal "feeling rules" that we internalize, such as "achievement makes you happy" and "we always love our children." The subtleties of emotion are evident in the everyday "emotion work" that goes into managing appearances, appearances that may or may not correspond to private feelings. Emotion work cuts across, or overwrites, any primal urges, or the legacies of early childhood, as emphasized by the other emotion perspectives. Social constructionists, therefore, see emotion as the vibrant product of a wide range of social influences, but emotion scripts, narratives, and the conventions of language frame the way emotion is felt and expressed. These scripts are often gendered—there are "right" emotions for men and for women—as well as peculiar to one's occupation or status, such as what a judge, doctor, receptionist, or flight attendant can emotionally reveal. Some scripts are fairly flexible, such as when teenagers test the boundaries of acceptable emotional behaviors with their parents and peers, or when professional negotiators present different emotional postures (frowns, grimaces, smiles) to influence each other. In contrast, "macro" social constructionist writers have been interested in the way major social emotions, or "master passions," shape much broader societal trends. They point, particularly, to the role of shame, embarrassment, and envy in triggering national and international disputes, as well as driving major corporate takeovers and leadership battles.

A significant strand in social constructionist thinking is about emotional labor. Emotional labor refers to circumstances where everyday emotion work is more than incidental to the performance of a job; it is an essential and often explicit part. Emotional labor has most often been associated with front-line service jobs, where being "nice" and smiling is required by the employer of the supermarket clerk, flight attendant, theme park worker, or hamburger salesperson. In these circumstances, a positive demeanor is often sought when the employee is recruited, reinforced through training, and monitored directly by managers. Call centers reflect a similar form, where "smiling down the phone" is often a core requirement of the operator. Emotional laborers may be found in other "face work" settings where maintaining an appropriate emotional front—such as "warm," "compassionate," "sincere," "firm," or "serious"—is crucial to effective performance, but is not necessarily formally prescribed or monitored. Paralegals, judges, nurses, social workers, teachers, doctors, politicians, police officers, and security staff fit this bill. The emotion laborer's lot can be an onerous one, especially when having to maintain the required demeanor for hours on end and under pressure to perform a high volume of work. Arlie Hochschild has referred to the different kinds of acting required of emotional laborers. For some it is "deep acting," where the worker is strongly encouraged to take the emotional expectations of the job to heart, to "really feel what they are supposed to feel"; others get by with "surface acting," putting on a smile but easily dropping it. While sustained emotional labor is undoubtedly stressful for some, particularly for deep actors who cannot readily "switch off," recent research has shown a more mixed picture. Some emotional laborers very much enjoy the "act," and treat it as a game or, as Sharon Bolton notes, something that they willing give as a gift (philanthropic emotional labor), while others seek relief in different sections or zones at work, where different emotion rules apply—areas such as the galley of an aircraft, a coffee room, or the corner of a corridor.

Critical Commentary and Future Directions

Our understanding of emotion in organizations has developed considerably through the different conceptual lenses outlined. While organization studies has borrowed freely from them, each has its strengths and weaknesses, and strict allegiance to one will obscure insights from the others. Evolution has provided humans with remarkable emotional capacities—signaling systems. They give us an instant readout on how we are relating to the world and what we should do, as well as lend general shape to our societal arrangements. All is not fixed, however, and in different ways, psychoanalytic and social constructionist approaches reveal how important learning is—be it from early emotional experiences or surrounding cultural and organizational mores. There are, however, continuing debates about the extent to which the different perspectives can be fused. Challenges include the over-determinism of biological and evolutionary approaches—the question of whether we are really as "hard-wired" as is claimed; psychoanalysts' preoccupation with negative/anxiety emotions and irrationality; and some social constructionists' neglect of "personal agency"—we are not simply swept along by established social/emotional forces.

Emotion theory has raised serious questions about the notion of rationality in organizations. Traditionally, emotions have been seen to be the enemy of rationality, interfering with deliberations when seeking an optimal decision. Emotions, accordingly, are viewed as sand in the machinery of organization. This view has now been countered by sociological, psychological, and neuroscience researchers. In their different ways, they argue that separating thinking from feeling is a false dichotomy, sustained by an outmoded conception of cognitive and affective process. Thinking and feeling interpenetrate. Decision makers often rely on "gut feelings" and intuitions to create a sense of coherence or break a deadlock. Moods matter and, broadly, it would be impossible to even approximate the "rational" without feelings to steer the way, and emotions themselves can be rational in their directions and ends. From this viewpoint, emotions lubricate rather than clog the machinery of organization. This does not mean that the discourse of rationality is dead; it is still powerfully institutionalized in much organizational and management thought. A social constructionist perspective alerts us to the way that organizational decisions, particularly in Western settings, still have to be presented as if they were rationally derived—a viewpoint still imbued with a male notion of being "unemotional."

The "emotional turn" in organization studies has led organizational researchers to high-profile emotion in their studies. Issues tackled include the emotions of organizational change, the nature of compassion in organizations, toxic emotions at work, positive emotions at work, the emotions of justice and injustice in the workplace, decision making and emotions, virtuality and emotions, emotions and management learning, and emotional intelligence. These studies vary in their approach, ranging from positivist and quantitative, to social constructionist and qualitative. There have been lively debates as to which of the approaches is "best." For example, can emotion be adequately represented through traditional social research protocols such as questionnaires and psychometric devices, or do we need different approaches? One view is that measurement tends to grind down and atomize emotional experience, divorcing it from its political and social context. In contrast, qualitative approaches, such as ethnographies and storytelling, can reveal the mix and flow of organizational processes in which emotion is embedded—in the participant's rather than the researcher's language. They chime with social constructionist's vision of emotions interactively produced and reproduced in the mundane chat, gossip, and stories of organizational life. In sum, the study of emotion challenges the limits and possibilities of the social scientific method, to the extent that some researchers believe that new methods are required, such as ways of experience-sampling, and different uses of video, pictorial, and poetic imagery.

Emotion Politics and Power

A critical appreciation of emotion in organizations draws our attention to the less visible, sometimes oppressive features of organization—such as toxic emotions.

Peter Frost has coined the phrase "toxin handler" for the individual who takes on the role of absorbing the pain generated by a boss who has little concern or understanding of the harm engendered by his or her abrasive style of leadership. The toxin handler takes the flak, so to speak, sheltering others from the worst effects. Toxin handlers can provide a valuable screen, but in so doing eventually endanger their own health, while also propping up a dysfunctional organizational leadership.

A close examination of contexts of emotional labor where the corporate smile is a "must"—such as the fast-food industry—suggests it is not always as benign as it appears to the customer. Corporate regimes of emotion management, coupled with close surveillance of their workers, can be unforgiving for employees who fail to toe the "happy" line—when the working conditions and the worker's personal circumstances may be far from conducive to maintaining a cheery disposition. In other words, the prescribed emotion management becomes a device that exploits a relatively powerless sector of employees: If they want the job, they have to act the part, regardless. In commercial hospitality settings, a similar dynamic has been observed. For example, hotel staff are required to present an upbeat, seductive image to attract customers, but can then be susceptible to harassment from clients who exploit the "invitation" of the smile.

Some professional groups, similarly, have to practice emotional labor in conditions that test their coping capacities. In the United Kingdom, for example, groups such as nurses and social workers operate in a "new managerialist" climate of strict targets of patient/client throughput, as well as low personal remuneration. In these circumstances, maintaining an empathetic composure while also meeting imposed targets can be an unequal struggle, and it is caring that, ultimately, becomes the casualty. A common organizational response is to "blame the worker" and require him or her to undergo further training, such as to improve his or her "stress fitness." An alternative approach, of course, is to look to the conditions of work that produce the tensions in the first place.

The politics of positiveness at work has come under the gaze of critical scholars. For example, prescribed "fun-at-work" has become, paradoxically, a serious Human Resource Management tool. Organized fun, such as play areas for workers, theme dressing, and games, offers employees an opportunity to let go of their frustrations and share positive, fun feelings through a contagious ripple of amusement. For management, it is seen as a way of keeping employees motivated in jobs that can be intrinsically demotivating, such as call-center work. A critical viewpoint regards such activities as reinforcing management control, but wrapped in a "positive" package. It can exert pressure on some employees to participate in events that they would prefer not to, and which are not experienced as fun. It can also displace opportunities for natural, or spontaneous, humor at work. Finally, it can be used to deflect attention from unsavory working conditions that management should be addressing.

The pursuit of positive feelings at work has been a central aim of "positive organizational scholars." Positive organizational scholarship celebrates qualities and outcomes such as well-being, happiness, optimism, flow, satisfaction, joy, pleasure, hope, faith, and love. It also embraces a moral agenda to create a just, honest, and humane workplace where negative emotions do not prevail. Positive organizational scholarship presents a refreshing contrast to a traditional focus on organizational pathologies and individual anxieties. It represents a swing away from studying what is wrong to what is good and positive. Yet in doing so, critical theorists have sounded a note of caution. For a start, by focusing exclusively on positive emotions, there is neglect of the symbiotic nature of the positive and negative feelings: They can be seen as coproduced and often mixed in their valuation (love can be joyful and painful; fear can be exciting and scary). Second, positiveness promotes a particular Westernized set of values based on optimism, individualism, and expressed self-confidence. There are national cultures, such as in parts of Asia and Europe, where emotion norms favor self-effacement, humility, and blending with the crowd. Positiveness has yet to account for such variations, or the different emotional nuances of gender and ethnicity. A similar criticism has also been leveled at popular renditions of emotional intelligence, such as that advocated by Daniel Goleman. Goleman describes emotionally intelligent managers as those who display "positive mental attitude"—enthusiasm, optimism, hope, and initiative—a syndrome very much rooted in American individualism.

Emotion holds the promise of bridging disciplinary boundaries, especially between social psychology, organizational psychology, sociology, and the brain sciences. Yet at present, save a few notable exceptions, each discipline tends to keep emotion to itself, and speaks more or less exclusively to its own members. This accentuates paradigmatic differences as well as approaches to the understanding of emotion. We can, hopefully, look forward to a rapprochement here where, for instance, critical organizational ethnographies play as large a part as measurement and statistical studies. We still have some way to go in understanding what work feels like at its most basic and mundane; the everyday is as important as the exceptional and crisis-laden. Other challenges for emotion researchers include mapping the shifts in the emotionology of a culture that define changes in emotion expectations at an organizational level. We also have more to learn how the embodied, corporeal sense of emotion is mediated by organizational power structures. Recent work on "aesthetic labor" shows promise here, where employees are expected to literally represent the product or service they are offering through their physical appearance. Finally, there are theoretical and empirical challenges for emotion in the proliferation of virtual organizations. How do we construct and communicate emotion when face-to-face contact hardly ever occurs? What happens to bonding and trust?

—Stephen Fineman

See also Emotional Intelligence; Positive Organizational Scholarship; Positive Psychology; Psychoanalytic Approach; Social Constructionism

Further Readings

Albrow, M. (1992). Sine ira studio—or do organizations have feelings? *Organization Studies, 13*(3), 313–329.
Bolton, S. (2004). *Emotion management in the workplace.* London: Routledge.
Ekman, P. (1973). Cross-cultural studies of facial expression. In P. Ekman (Ed.), *Darwin and facial expression: A century of research in review.* New York: Academic Press.
Fineman, S. (2000). *Emotion in organizations* (2nd ed.). London: Sage.
Fineman, S. (2003). *Understanding emotion at work.* London: Sage.
Fineman, S. (2004). Getting the measure of emotion—and the cautionary tale of emotional intelligence. *Human Relations, 57*(6), 719–740.
Fineman, S. (2006). On being positive: Concerns and counterpoints. *Academy of Management Review, 31*(2), 270–291.
Gabriel, Y. (1999). *Organizations in depth.* London: Sage.
Hochschild, A. (1983). *The managed heart.* Berkeley: University of California Press.
Kets de Vries, M. F. R. (Ed.). (1991). *Organizations on the couch.* San Francisco: Jossey-Bass.
Lazarus, R. S., & Cohen-Charash, Y. (2001). Discrete emotions in organizational life. In R. L. Payne & C. Cooper (Eds.), *Emotions at work.* Chichester, UK: Wiley.
Witz, A., Warhurst, C., & Nickson, D. (2003). The labour of aesthetics and the aesthetics of labour. *Organization, 10*(1), 33–54.

Emotional Intelligence

Emotional intelligence (EI) is a relatively new construct that emerged from the body of research concerning social and multiple intelligences. Generally, EI may be defined as the ability to recognize and manage one's emotions and the emotions of others. As a result, individuals, groups, and organizations high in EI might prove more capable of utilizing emotion to better adapt to and capitalize on environmental demands. Today, many organizations recognize EI as a set of emotional competencies that allow people to use emotions to facilitate desired outcomes.

Emotion is generally defined as a learned mood or feeling in response to stimuli that guides our reactions and decision making in relationship to others. Emotion is the precursor for action, setting the schema by which we interact with our environment. Intelligence is generally defined as the ability to learn facts and skills, and to apply those facts and skills to novel situations. Although emotion is a reaction to external simulation, intelligence, in more general terms, is the use of reason to better understand and adapt to those reactions. Therefore, EI becomes the overlap between emotion and intelligence, or more simply, the intelligent use of emotions.

Conceptual Overview

EI has particular value to organizations. Current research validates that individuals who improve their EI and emotional competencies in ways that parallel job demands demonstrate higher levels of performance. The list of behaviors potentially influenced by EI includes such diverse outcomes as job performance, positive work attitudes, leadership potential, self-efficacy, and change management. How well one can recognize and manage the emotions of oneself and others may constitute a differentiating characteristic between success and failure for individuals, teams, and organizations. Although the evidence is mixed regarding the extent of the influence of EI on performance, there are clear indications that EI does determine a significant variance in the overall effectiveness of employees and their organization.

To understand EI, a review of the primary architects is required. EI finds its construction within a body of research concerning *social intelligence*. The historical authors and constructs are Thorndike's *practical intelligence*, Gardner's *intra-* and *interpersonal intelligence*, and Bar-On's *emotional quotient* (EQ). The modern construction credits Salovey and Mayer with originating the EI concept and Goleman with popularizing EI.

Thorndike believed in three distinct types of intelligence: (1) abstract or scholastic intelligence, defined as the ability to understand and manage ideas; (2) mechanical or visual-spatial intelligence, defined as the ability to understand and manipulate concrete objects; and (3) social or practical intelligence, defined as the ability to understand others, manage people, and act wisely in social contexts. While social or practical intelligence resonated intuitively, psychologists focused on the first aspect, abstract or scholastic intelligence, as attempts to refine, measure, and understand social intelligence proved unsuccessful.

Gardner continued the inquiry into multiple intelligences in an effort to answer the question of what additional capacities are attributed to our potentials for productivity. Gardner illuminated a distinction between intellectual and emotional capacities, classifying these additional intelligences as inter- and intrapersonal. *Inter*personal intelligence is the capacity to understand other people and, consequently, to work effectively with others. *Intra*personal intelligence is the capacity to understand oneself and to use such information effectively in regulating one's own life. These two definitions provide the theoretical basis for EI and are the common denominators for most contemporary conceptions of EI.

Bar-On was the first author to coin the term EQ (which in today's literature is largely synonymous with EI), focusing on the impact of emotional and social functioning. He was also the first author to develop a measure of EQ, viewing the construct along five interdependent dimensions: (1) intrapersonal, (2) interpersonal, (3) stress management, (4) adaptability, and (5) general mood. The greater the number of effective EQ competencies, the more positive the prediction for effective functioning in meeting environmental demands and pressures. Bar-On continues as one of the lead authors in the field of EI.

There are literally hundreds of articles on EI, with dozens of competing models and measures that utilize the EI term. However, two main streams of research in the literature helped to develop and popularize the concept of EI and form the basis for the majority of current conceptions of EI. The two streams may be characterized as competing paradigms of EI, based on their contending underlying assumptions and different methods for measurement. The two paradigms are (1) "emotional ability," developed by Salovey and Mayer; and (2) "emotional competency," proposed by Goleman. Most contemporary models of EI tend toward one or the other of these paradigms.

Salovey and Mayer are frequently cited as the originators of the modern EI construct, defining EI as a form of intelligence that involves the ability to monitor one's own and others' feelings and emotions, to discriminate among them, and to use this information to guide one's thinking and actions. The authors maintain that EI is best understood as ability, distinct from other types of intelligence, but as contributing to one's overall cognitive capacity to process and capitalize on information. According to Mayer and Salovey, EI reflects not just a single ability, but rather a composite of the distinct emotional reasoning abilities of perceiving, understanding, and regulating emotions.

Although the previous authors set the stage, it was Goleman's best-selling book, *Emotional Intelligence: Why It Can Matter More Than IQ*, that popularized the concept, placing EI squarely within Western culture's concept of superior performance. Goleman teamed with Boyatzis to develop the emotional competency model of EI, which categorized and benchmarked behavior along the four broad clusters of (1) self-awareness, (2) self-management, (3) social awareness, and (4) relationship management. According to Boyatzis and Goleman, EI is observed when a person demonstrates emotional competencies at appropriate times and with sufficient frequency to be effective in a given situation. EI is now a contemporary construct with its principles incorporated into business, consulting, counseling, and education, highlighting the importance of emotions in our daily lives.

Critical Commentary and Future Directions

Although EI has achieved acclaim during the past 15 years, the construct is still in its infancy. There is still a core question regarding the parameters of EI, specifically relating to the content domain and scope of EI, the measurement of EI, the relationship of EI to other related constructs, and the impact of EI on performance. The current state of EI can be characterized as demonstrating significant potential but poor actual performance.

EI derives out of a Western business philosophy, specifically the aspect of management and its implied functions of planning; organizing; leading; and most important, control. That is, the implied assumption of EI is to recognize and reward those employees who supplant their own needs and the needs of others toward the attainment of organizational goals.

Further, EI, and the benefits posited to organizations that select and place those who accept high EI as critical to their own success, may limit potential creative talents that are outside the bounds of the construct. The research supporting EI assumes that all employees, their motivations, and job demands are equal. The link between one's role in the organization and the degree of EI required must be clarified before EI can be attributed as a determinant of global high performance.

In addition, there is concern with the application of EI to more diverse populations. The assumptions and propositions put forth by prior researchers suggest that EI has universal dimensions across ethnic, cultural, and gender borders. However, little research has substantiated these claims, making the assumptions tenable at best.

Confounding the issue is the theory of EI itself, which recognizes the impact of experiential learning upon EI development, meaning that our awareness and response to emotional signals are likely to vary with our life experiences. In other words, distinctions in our ethnic, cultural, or national backgrounds can and should lead to changes in our demonstrated EI competencies.

Furthermore, even though EI may, in fact, contribute to Western business acumen, organizations from other countries may not experience the same contributions. EI clearly incorporates a Western cultural value distinction. Therefore, different cultures, with their own distinct values (for example, differentiating levels of control and cooperation), may find the construct limiting and perhaps even disadvantageous to their operation and understanding of effective performance. Future research should include critical demographic information as well as explore the multicultural dimension of EI to better understand these distinctions.

Another area for concern is the multitude of definitions, models, and measures of EI currently available. Each set of authors advocates its own version of the construct. As such, what one researcher views as an emotionally intelligent person may be contrary to the views of a competing researcher. In effect, the scope of the domain of EI has yet to be determined, hindering the development of an integrative theory of EI and our understanding of the core emotional determinants to effective performance.

Even if the domain issue can be resolved, there are still questions as to the elusive nature of the theory in question. Researchers have been attempting to refine the various conceptions of social intelligence for a number of years with limited success. There is concern as to whether EI even qualifies as an actual scientific theory, falling instead into categories of data, typologies, or metaphors, rather than being a true organizational theory.

In order to secure its position within the field of organizational studies, EI will require the continued conceptual and empirical contributions to establish an agreed content of domain, a more definitive theory, and clearer boundaries between what EI is and, perhaps more important, what it is not. In the end, although the concept of EI may be a major factor in successful outcomes, our science may be inadequate to justify a construct of EI.

—*Craig R. Seal and Rayshad Holmes*

See also Attitudes; Bounded Emotionality; Competitive Advantage; Cultural Intelligence; Emotion; Management Fashions and Fads

Further Readings

Bar-On, R. (1985). *The development of an operational concept of psychological well-being.* Unpublished doctoral dissertation, Rhodes University, Grahamstown, South Africa.

Gardner, H. (1983). *Frames of mind: The theory of multiple intelligences.* New York: Basic Books.

Goleman, D. (1995). *Emotional intelligence: Why it can matter more than IQ.* New York: Bantam.

Salovey, P., & Mayer, J. D. (1990). Emotional intelligence. *Imagination, Cognition and Personality, 9*(3), 185–211.

Thorndike, E. L. (1920). Intelligence and its uses. *Harper's Magazine, 140,* 227–235.

Tomer, J. F. (2003). Personal capital and emotional intelligence: An increasingly important tangible source of economic growth. *Eastern Economic Journal, 29*(3), 453.

Emotional Patterns in Organizations

The suggestion that organizations have emotions may be considered as excessive anthropomorphizing. Emotional *patterns,* however, can exist in organizations. These patterns refer to groups of organization members who can feel or display similar emotional states.

Conceptual Overview

Emotional patterns—felt or displayed—can arise in organizations, thanks to various social-psychological mechanisms.

Felt Emotional Patterns

A number of mechanisms can create patterns of felt (experienced) emotional states. Faced with an important organizational event, a large number of employees across various work roles can feel shared emotions if they have similar beliefs, which lead to similar appraisals and ways of feeling. Culture represents a subtle yet powerful form of control that acts to inform, guide, and control the emotions of organization members.

Moreover, members who strongly identify themselves with their organization are likely to experience similar emotions when faced with events that enhance or threaten the identity of their organization. Perceived threats (e.g., a hostile takeover or competitive price wars) can particularly increase the need for solidarity among people who believe they are confronting the same situation.

However, in large organizations inhabited by different groups with different roles, values, and interests, dramatic organizational events may not trigger such a coming together. An organization's members may not experience the same emotions when faced with the same organizational event. For example, Quy Huy has documented how different groups of middle managers with different goals and political agendas felt very different kinds of emotions when faced with the same organizational event, in this case radical change. Certain groups felt enthusiastic because they actively played the role of change agents. Other groups felt angry and fearful because they felt they were the targets of their change-agent colleagues.

Members belonging to the same group can feel the same emotions when they identify strongly with one another. Moreover, a group's emotional charge, when amplified through mutual interaction, can promote further group cohesion. Because emotions can spread through various processes, unconscious and conscious, emotional contagion can also convert individual emotions into group ones.

Unconscious emotional contagion occurs through a very fast process of automatic and synchronous nonverbal mimicry and feedback, posited to come from an innate human tendency toward mimicking the behavior of others. By contrast, conscious processes involve cognitive social comparison in which people compare their feelings with those of relevant others in their social environment and then respond according to what seems appropriate for the situation. The recipient uses emotion as a type of social information to understand how he or she should be feeling. Once a group experiences shared emotions toward certain organizational events, these emotions influence the group's cognitive processes and motivate collective action. Emotions that are shared by many members of a group can influence their cognition and behavior even more than emotions felt by single members.

Displayed Emotional Patterns

These patterns arise in organizations to the extent that an organization's members feel they must display some emotions and suppress others. The former are those perceived to be needed to sustain the image of the organization or those deemed necessary for effective collective action. Thus, emotion can be used as a tool of social influence in a variety of organizational roles, especially in front-line service functions. For instance, bankers have to display calm to inspire trust and confidence. Different emotional displays are required for Disneyland entertainers or for funeral parlor workers. Organizations select and retain their members based on certain specific emotional habits they want displayed. These organizational emotions relate to the performance of particular roles and should not be confused with individual private emotions.

Thus, members do not necessarily experience privately the same emotion they display. They may be required to display or act out a "legitimate" emotion in response to various organizational events, such as the death of the company's founder. Moreover, being part of a group—rather than an individual acting alone—makes it easier to display such an emotion because group membership boosts people's feelings of power by making them bolder through anonymity. Displaying or acting out emotions—in other words, emotion-related behaviors—can in the long run become organizational routines that govern what emotions members *should* display or feel in their interactions with other stakeholders.

Critical Commentary and Future Directions

In a large organization, many members belonging to a group may feel similar emotions, although different groups may feel different emotions. Thus, different patterns of emotions can be present at the same time. Future research can explore how these patterns influence various organizational processes such as resistance to change, organizational learning, collective mobilization, and organizational creativity. In addition, although Huy has suggested that those organizations that can develop their emotional capability through emotion-related routines that acknowledge, recognize, monitor, discriminate, and attend to their members' emotions are likely to be able to realize major strategic change, if and when needed, more quickly and with less cost, very little empirical research has been conducted in this area. Valid measurement scales remain to be developed to enable testing of the theory. Finally, developing emotional capability and embedding it in organizational routines holds the promise of not requiring a large number of emotionally intelligent individuals in influential positions, who risk using their emotional intelligence to maximize their personal interests instead of collective interests. Future research can explore the interdependence and interaction between individual-level emotional intelligence and organizational-level emotional capability.

—*Quy Nguyen Huy*

See also Cross-Cultural Management; Identity; Organizational Change; Organizational Culture

Further Readings

Barsade, S. G. (2002). The ripple effect: Emotional contagion and its influence on group behavior. *Administrative Science Quarterly, 47,* 644–675.

Bartel, C. A., & Saavedra, R. (2000). The collective construction of work group moods. *Administrative Science Quarterly, 45,* 197–231.

Huy, Q. (1999). Emotional capability, emotional intelligence, and radical change. *Academy of Management Review, 14*(2), 325–345.

Huy, Q. (2002). Emotional balancing of organizational continuity and radical change: The contribution of middle managers. *Administrative Science Quarterly, 47,* 31–69.

Employment Relations

A broad definition of employment relations (ER) includes all aspects of the employment relationship, including industrial relations (IR) and human resource management (HRM). IR may be regarded as dealing more with the macro and institutional aspects of the employment relationship, while HRM can be seen as focusing rather on the micro- and enterprise-level aspects; each is complementary to the other. The term ER is sometimes used in the literature to reflect the interconnectedness of labor–management relations, IR, and HRM.

Conceptual Overview

Although the study of ER focuses on the regulation of work, it must also take account of the wider economic and social influences on the relative power of capital and labor, and the interactions among employers, workers, their collective organizations, and the state. A full understanding of ER requires an interdisciplinary approach that uses analytical tools drawn from several academic fields, including accounting, economics, history, law, politics, psychology, sociology, and other elements of management studies.

One can focus on ER at various levels, including the workplace; enterprise; industry; locality, state, or province; the nation; or at an international level. There is much to be gained from adopting an internationally comparative approach to ER. However, this requires not only insights from several disciplines, but also knowledge of different national contexts. Some scholars distinguish between comparative and international studies in this field. Comparative ER may involve describing and systematically analyzing two or more countries. By contrast, international ER involves exploring institutions and phenomena that cross national boundaries, such as the labor market roles and the behavior of intergovernmental organizations (e.g., International Labor Organization), multinational enterprises (MNEs), and unions. This is a useful distinction, but this entry inclines toward a broader perspective whereby internationally comparative ER includes a range of studies that traverse boundaries between countries.

There are several reasons why it is beneficial to study internationally comparative ER. Such a focus provides a contribution to one's knowledge about ER in different countries and a source of models for policy development. Increased economic interconnectedness associated with globalization has produced a greater need for information about ER practices in other countries and has led to a resurgence of interest in internationally comparative ER. Such comparative analysis offers possibilities for theoretical development and an understanding of the impact of globalization on national patterns of ER.

Critical Commentary and Future Directions

Keith Sisson argues that the fields of study contributing to ER could be criticized for being overly descriptive, and that academics in these fields have generally not developed straightforward causal explanations of relevant phenomena. The descriptive nature of and relative lack of theory in the study of IR and HRM reflect the practitioner and policy orientation of these subjects.

Thomas Kochan has proposed an analytical framework guiding research in ER in terms of four important enterprise-level employment practices:

1. Changes in work organization due to the introduction of new technologies and the adoption of new competitive strategies (such as decentralization or team systems); linked to these changes are new work rules and patterns of employee participation within enterprises;

2. Changing patterns of skill acquisition and training to match the needs of enterprises; this takes account of the shifting balance between the public and private provision of education and training;

3. New pay systems, which affect many categories of employees; and

4. Staffing, employment security, and recruitment, which affect the way in which enterprises adjust their workforce when faced with cyclical or long-term structural changes in demand for their output.

The framework used to explain variations in these employment practices includes two competing hypotheses for the degree of transformation in ER. One hypothesis stresses the importance of the persistence of institutional structures (at the national, industry, and enterprise levels), which limit the discretion of enterprises and other actors in ER. This can be referred to as the *institutionalist* ER perspective, and is discussed below. An alternative hypothesis emphasizes the range of strategic choices available to enterprises and the pressures associated with international competition and technological changes.

There are at least four important trends in ER. Harry Katz and Owen Darbishire find, first, the enterprise is increasingly seen as an important locus for strategy and decision making in ER. At least from a U.S. perspective, management is generally the driving force for change, albeit sometimes in collaboration with governments, unions, or works councils. Second, decentralization of ER structures is accompanied by the search for greater flexibility in work organization and the deployment of labor. Third, many firms, and governments in most countries, appear to be increasing their rhetoric about the importance of investment in training and skill development, which is often associated with a trend toward skill-related pay systems. (However, the rhetoric in practice is not always consistent with the realities.) Fourth, unions are experiencing major challenges in most countries as the pace of restructuring intensifies, the workplace becomes more diverse, and there is a decrease in the average size of enterprises.

At least three types of tension can be observed from these emerging trends and their likely influence on the future direction of ER. First, low-road (cost-cutting) and high-road (value-added) competitive strategies coexist uneasily. Value adding may result from a firm's long-term investment in research and development, training and development of the workforce, and quality assurance, whereas low-cost competitive strategies may militate against such initiatives. Second, the drive for increased flexibility in work organization and related employment practices has the potential for polarization between workers with access to good jobs and secure employment and those without. Third, while unions in many countries are experiencing declining influence and membership, arguably there is a growing need for a stronger employee voice in corporate decision making as well as in industry-level interactions and national policy making. Yet, there is little evidence that ER issues are consistently attracting much greater attention in corporate decision making. A simple reconstruction of union membership and power along traditional lines appears unlikely in the foreseeable future, although new forms and approaches to employee voice and representation might emerge.

Critical political economy is another tradition in ER scholarship, which can potentially overcome some of the limitations of other approaches and provide the basis for greater insight into the factors that mediate the relationship between international economic change and national patterns of ER. This includes defining ER as the study of the social relations in production, adopting a view of ER as structured antagonism and regarding mechanisms such as collective bargaining as essential and enduring. Political economy sees ER as an institutionalized compromise between workers and employers, which may be affected by changes in the balance of power between them. This intellectual tradition also argues that a key difference between the liberal-pluralist tradition and critical political economy is the way in which issues like globalization are conceptualized. Whereas the mainstream sees such changes as having an impact on ER, Anthony Giles and Gregor Murray note that political economy sees changing workplace relations as central.

From a political economy perspective, changes in the international economy, associated with globalization, should be considered along with the analysis of national or sectoral patterns of ER. However, while a critical political economy perspective offers a range of conceptual tools, which would potentially provide insights into the relationship between globalization and national patterns of ER, in many ways it is yet to live up to its promise. Such authors as Richard Hyman suggest that this reflects the difficulty of integrating the different levels of analysis required of such an approach into a single framework.

Murray et al. provide one example of how a critical political economy approach can be operationalized to provide insight into the relationship between globalization and ER. These authors argue that, rather than deregulation, there is a reregulation of employment relationship taking place in the context of an increasingly globalized economy. To understand the nature of the reregulation of ER taking place, it is important to focus on how globalization either alters or accentuates such key relationships as the indeterminacy of the employment relationship; the uncertainty and contingency faced by enterprises; the power, scope for agency, and level of interdependence of actors; and the interconnectedness between different sources of regulation.

By working with critical political economy concepts, it is possible to go beyond establishing whether the dominant trend in national patterns of ER is convergence or divergence. Rather, a critical political economy perspective makes it possible to specify a range of factors, including international economic change and historical and institutional traditions, which are likely to shape national patterns of ER.

Some comparative studies also emphasize the importance of differences in national-level institutions for explaining differences in patterns of ER. Anthony Ferner and Hyman point to the reemergence of societal corporatism in some European economies during the 1990s as evidence that states possess a key role in the reconfiguration of the relations between social regulation and markets (including labor markets). They also develop the notion that some forms of labor market institutions can adapt to international economic changes better than others. In explaining the persistence of systems of labor market regulation, education and training, and corporate governance at the national level across a range of countries, Peter Hall and David Soskice differentiate between liberal market economies (LME) and coordinated market economies (CMEs). In coordinated economies, these authors identify extensive nonmarket relationships, and forms of coordination that rely on collaboration rather than the interaction of formal, competitive market arrangements that characterize LMEs.

An institutionalist approach represents a useful corrective to the simple globalization thesis of convergence to a common pattern of ER. The focus on the mediating role of institutions helps to explain patterns of persistent national differences and demonstrates that the relationship between globalization and national ER is neither simple nor deterministic. It also points to key variables that play a decisive role in determining distinctive national patterns of ER, many of which may be national in character.

ER, then, involves the interrelation of two fields of study, IR and HRM. For many, these fields of study cannot be considered separate and distinct because of trends and developments in the world of work that include the impact of globalization, the decline in collective bargaining coverage, the decentralization of bargaining to the level of the enterprise, and the decline of union density. While arguably IR and HRM will remain important fields in their own right, ER is likely to grow in relevance as academics and practitioners seek to understand and explain phenomena that cross the boundaries of these two areas. Giles has argued for the use of the broader notion of *work relations* to take into account also such issues as self-employment, subcontracting, and voluntary work.

—*Greg J. Bamber and Michael Barry*

See also Human Resource Management; Industrial Relations; Labor Relations; Political Economy of Organizations

Further Readings

Bamber, G. J., Lansbury, R. D., & Wailes, N. (Eds). (2004). *International and comparative employment relations: Globalisation and the developed market economies* (4th ed., p. 486). London: Sage.

Bamber, G. J., & Sheldon, P. (2004). Collective bargaining: Towards decentralization? In R. Blanpain (Ed.), *Comparative Labour Law and Industrial Relations in Industrialized Market Economies* (8th ed., pp. 509–548). The Hague, the Netherlands: Kluwer Law.

Ferner, A., & Hyman, R. (1998). Introduction: Towards European industrial relations? In A. Ferner & R. Hyman (Eds.), *Changing industrial relations in Europe* (2nd ed.). London: Blackwell.

Giles, A. (2000). Industrial relations at the millennium: Beyond employment? *Labour/Le Travail, 46*, 37–67.

Giles, A., & Murray, G. (1997). Industrial relations theory and critical political economy. In J. Barbash & N. Meltz (Eds.), *Theorising in industrial relations: Approaches and applications.* Sydney: Australian Centre for Industrial Relations Research and Training.

Hall, P., & Soskice, D. (2001). *Varieties of capitalism: The institutional foundations of comparative advantage.* Oxford, UK: Oxford University Press.

Hyman, R. (1980). Theory in industrial relations: Towards a materialist analysis. In P. Boreham & G. Dow (Ed.), *Work and inequality, Volume 2: Ideology and control in the labour process.* Melbourne, Australia: Macmillan.

Katz, H., & Darbishire, O. (2000). *Converging divergence: Worldwide changes in employment systems.* Ithaca, NY: Cornell University Press.

Kochan, T., Katz, H., & McKersie, B. (1984). *The transformation of American industrial relations.* New York: Basic Books.

Martin, R., & Bamber, G. J. (2004). International comparative employment relations theory: Developing the political economy perspective. In B. E. Kaufman (Ed.), *Theoretical perspectives on work and the employment relationship,* pp. 293–320 (Annual Research Volume). Champaign, IL: Industrial Relations Research Association.

Murray, G., Levesque, C., & Vallee, G. (2000). The re-regulation of labour in a global context: Conceptual vignettes from Canada. *Journal of Industrial Relations 42*(2), 234–257.

EMPOWERMENT

Empowerment is a term used widely but loosely in the management field. The term *empowerment* is normally used to refer to initiatives designed to allow employees to make decisions relating to work. It is largely focused on task-based involvement and attitudinal change. Unlike notions of industrial democracy, there is no notion of workers having a "right" to a say; it is for employers to decide whether and how to empower employees. Thus, "empowerment" takes place within the context of a strict management agenda: Workers are authorized to carry out specific activities or responsibilities. Empowerment schemes tend to be direct and based on individuals or small groups (usually the work group).

Conceptual Overview

Empowerment is normally associated with a distribution of power to those in subordinate positions. A number of perspectives on empowerment are evident in the literature and range from psychological empowerment, which emphasizes feelings of self-determination and competence, to more structural forms, which focus on the autonomy or influence afforded by the environment within which people work.

While empowerment may be a new label, the underlying ideas are long-standing. One can identify two sets of arguments being used to justify the utilization of empowerment. The first is democratic humanism, which is usually seen as a response to the excesses of scientific management. The sociotechnical systems school stressed the need to design technical and social components alongside each other to optimize the two. Their influential study of coal mining in Britain showed how work could be redesigned within the existing technical basis so as to retain traditional features such as skill variety and a degree of autonomy. In the 1970s, the Quality of Working Life (QWL) movement developed these ideas and put them into practice, most famously in the Swedish car plants such as Volvo at Kalmar, Sweden. More recently, it has been argued that developments in the broader political and social environment, including more educated workers, have led to a higher level of expectation concerning quality of working life, and the notion of citizenship is important here. There is also an economic case for empowerment. It is assumed that workers have the opportunity to contribute to organizational success, and as they are closer to the work situation they may be able to suggest improvements that management would be unable to by virtue of their position in the hierarchy.

There are a number of ways in which empowerment could be seen as contributing to effectiveness. First, empowerment could enable workers to work harder. Second, where empowerment involves direct staff taking on additional responsibilities that others would otherwise have to perform (e.g., record keeping, inspection, task allocation), costs for indirect staff are reduced. Finally, the most important potential benefit of empowerment results from its ability to improve employees' competence, thus making them more effective workers.

Critical Commentary and Future Directions

There has been little detailed discussion of the issues likely to arise when implementing empowerment or the conditions that are necessary for such an approach to be successful. It is assumed that employees will simply welcome empowerment and regard it as beneficial to them. The literature also takes a universalistic approach, regarding empowerment as appropriate to all organizations in all circumstances. However, key contingencies include production uncertainty, product market competition, and labor–management relations. In addition, the literature underplays the conflict that exists within organizations and ignores the context within which empowerment takes place.

While there is evidence that empowerment has a positive impact on performance, there are a number of reasons to be cautious. It is difficult to isolate the impact of just one aspect of management practice from other factors that can influence behavior at work. For example, labor turnover is likely to be influenced by relative pay levels and the availability of other jobs as much as the presence or absence of empowerment. Even if it were possible to find a significant association between empowerment and performance, it is very difficult to determine the direction of causality. It is just as likely that superior organizational performance leads to more positive employee attitudes as it is that the process of empowerment causes employees to work harder and more effectively. In short, the view that empowerment is connected with high levels of commitment and organizational performance is predicated upon a series of assumptions, none of which can be taken for granted. Finally, there is the issue of evaluation and on whose terms it should be done. Should assessments be made in terms of merely having a form of empowerment (i.e., the process) or in terms of how things may be changed due to empowerment (i.e., the outcomes)?

While there is evidence that workers welcome the removal of irritants (e.g., close supervision) and welcome the opportunity to address problems at their source as well as the ability to decide work allocation, there is also evidence that employees are not sufficiently trained for empowerment, especially where empowerment is a result of downsizing. For employers, empowerment is not free but carries costs in terms of establishing a new approach to management. From a business perspective, a concern is the implication in terms of a loss of management control. Thus, it is likely there will always be tension between empowerment and control in modern organizations, and future study is needed to map out these tensions. Research is gradually coming to see empowerment less in universal terms and more in relation to the context of work in particular circumstances.

—Adrian Wilkinson

See also High Involvement Management; Industrial Democracy; Participation

Further Readings

Conger, J., & Kanungo, R. (1988). The empowerment process: Integrating theory and practice. *Academy of Management Review, 13*(3), 471–482.

Denham Lincoln, N., Travers, C., Ackers, P., & Wilkinson, A. (2002). The meaning of empowerment: The interdisciplinary etymology of a new management concept. *International Journal of Management Reviews, 4*(3), 271–290.

Foy, N. (1994). *Empowering people at work*. London: Gower.

Marchington, M., & Wilkinson, A. (2005). Direct participation and involvement. In S. Bach (Ed.), *Personnel management* (4th ed.). Oxford, UK: Blackwell.

Wall, T., Wood, S., & Leach, D. (2004). Empowerment and performance. *International Review of Industrial and Organizational Psychology, 19*, 1–46.

Wilkinson, A. (1998). Empowerment: A review and a critique. *Personnel Review, 27*(1), 40–56.

Wilkinson, A. (2002). Empowerment. In M. Warner (Ed.), *International encyclopaedia of business and management* (2nd ed., 1720–1730). London: International Thomson Learning.

ENGINEERING-MANAGERIAL DISCOURSE

Managerial discourse first emerged in the late 19th century within engineering circles. The icons of "systems" and "efficiency," so central in engineering, were translated to include managerial and organizational domains. A loose band of mechanical and industrial engineers has disseminated this newly emerging vision through practice, magazines, and professional associations. The influence of this group, against the backdrop of the cultural and political forces existing at the time, constitutes the backbone of managerial discourse and practice in the United States today. In other industrial countries for which researchers have information, the nexus between engineering and management has been weaker.

Conceptual Overview

In the 1850s, the first practicing managers in the United States were civil engineers, but it was mechanical engineering that spawned and nurtured the management movement until it reformed and reorganized American industry. At first, mechanical engineers were professionally concerned with the formulation of uniform codes and standards, and with achieving predictability and regularity in production. With the rapid growth of the large corporate firm, mechanical engineers expanded their professional engagement to include administrative and organizational systems. They brought in professional road maps, tools, and the (predominant) metaphor that the organization is analogous to a machine composed of interchangeable parts. John Dunlap, editor of *Engineering Magazine,* has argued that the cold logic of the machine may be more effective in industrial reform than in any humanitarian reform. Dexter Kimball, Dean of Engineering at Cornell University and later a president of the American Society of Mechanical Engineers (ASME), suggested extending the principles of standardization to the human element in production, assuming that human and nonhuman entities are interchangeable and can equally be subjected to engineering manipulation, as noted by Yehouda Shenhav in 1999. Individuals such as Alexander Church and Dunlap, among others—who were labeled by historians as "systematizers"—applied mechanical engineering methods to the administrative restructuring of firms, to design systems of accountancy, determine wages, and determine selection criteria in employment.

The extension of engineering practices and systems ideology to human organizations was an act of translation, affirming an underlying unity between elements distinct from one another and creating convergences and homologies by relating things that were previously unrelated. Despite objections to the systems ideology, the so-called Progressive Era (circa 1900–1917) in the United States was instrumental to the diffusion of this discourse. It provided legitimacy to the roles of professionals, including engineers, as experts. The (Theodore) Roosevelt administration, for example, maintained close relationships with all engineering societies, and these societies supported Roosevelt's attempts to bring efficiency and rational management into industry and government. At the end of the Progressive period, business philosophy was solidified around secular engineering ideals rather than around religious, philanthropic, or social Darwinist ones. With the engineering discourse, resorting to politics could be redefined in technical terms. Engineering expertise seemed most appropriate for the management of large systems and for the resolution of labor unrest. The efforts to view organizations as systems received public visibility with the work of Frederick Taylor and his followers. Taylor's conceptualization of industrial bureaucracy—the extension and codification of mechanical engineering—involved an explicit attempt to systematize the firm. His suggestions were made under the banner of social physics, a science of production that was supposed to be objective, systematic, and rational.

In 1912, the study of management and organizations was defined in the engineering literature as a separate scientific field, a little sister of sociology as a science of human nature. In 1915, Dunlap, the editor of *Engineering Magazine* and the most active journalistic sponsor of the management movement, documented what he labeled as the historic events in the development of a new science. The discourse on organization systems, which first entered engineering literature in the 1880s, rose to an average of 26% of the literature on management during the Progressive period. During the first half of the 20th century, this rhetoric and practice traveled from engineering circles to additional fields and became widely known in American industry and academia. In 1916, Dunlap inaugurated *Industrial Management,* which was devoted to issues of organizational systematization and became a professional outlet for managerial thought. *Industrial Management* established a regular section on personality and employment issues, and more specific magazines such as *System: The Magazine of Business and Personnel* were established. The embryonic engineering/management ideas that were published in these magazines were later collected and collated in books, written by individuals such as Harringtom Emerson, Henry Gantt, Alexander Hamilton Church, Charles Bedaux, Chester Barnard, Luther Gulick and Lyndall Urwick, James Mooney and Alan Reiley, Fritz Roethlisberger and William Dickson, or George Terry. These books were read by sociologists, psychologists, engineers, and political scientists, and became the seedbed from which discourse on management developed.

Critical Commentary and Future Directions

While the managerial-engineering discourse emerged in the United States, one should not necessarily assume that this was the case for other industrialized countries. Both Frank Dobbin and Mauro Guillen argue in critical comparative perspectives that cultural and political factors yield different results in countries such as Germany, Britain, France, Sweden, Japan, or Spain. Throughout the 19th century, German engineers neglected management and organization ideas. Historical documents attest to a strong hostility that German managers and entrepreneurs felt for the general orientation of German engineering. Compared with the American magazines *American Machinist* and *Engineering Magazine*, the German counterparts such as *Zeitschrift* were heavily tilted toward theoretical discussions, as noted by Kees Gispen in 1989. It was only at the turn of the century that German engineers shifted attention to the United States, and only in the late 1910s and throughout the 1920s were American engineering-management techniques imported to Germany.

At the level of the profession, British engineers and their American compatriots had similar trajectories. They were well entrenched in technical work and respected apprenticeship at the floor level. They differed, however, at the cultural and ideological levels. British engineers rejected the association with management and rejected Taylorism. Of the 201 factories that introduced Taylorism worldwide in the beginning of the century, only four were in England. Likewise, French engineers refrained from applying Taylorism in industry, except for a few large firms in the automobile industry. It was only after the Second World War with the Marshall Plan that Taylorism was imported to France. Slow importation of Taylorism was also the case in Sweden and Japan. It should be noted, however, that the introduction of these techniques in other societies (other than the United States) was not a simple imitation, but rather a hybridization of Taylorism with elements of the receiving culture.

Thus, in Japan and Jewish Palestine, for example, these programs were blends of industrial relations, industrial democracy, and Taylorism. Furthermore, in Palestine, as well as in other national societies such as Spain, scientific management was adapted as an instrument of national development, as noted by Guillen. This is to say that the rise of engineering-based managerial discourse is not the inevitable outcome of economic imperatives, but rather a combination of culturally specific factors.

—Yehouda Shenhav

See also Managerial Rationality; Managerial Revolution; Scientific Management

Further Readings

Bendix, R. (1974). *Work and authority in industry*. Berkeley: University of California Press. (Original work published 1956)

Boltanski, L. (1987). *The making of a class: Cadres in French society*. Cambridge, UK: Cambridge University Press.

Boltanski, L. (1990). Visions of American management in post-war France. In S. Zukin & P. DiMaggio (Eds.), *Structures of capital: The social organization of the economy* (pp. 343–372). Cambridge, UK: Cambridge University Press.

Dobbin, F. (1994). *Forging industrial policy: The United States, Britain and France in the railway age*. Cambridge, UK: Cambridge University Press.

Frenkel, M., Shenhav, Y., & Herzog, H. (1997). The political embeddedness of managerial ideologies in pre-state Israel: The case of PPL 1920–1948. *Journal of Management History, 3,* 120–144.

Gispen, K. (1989). *New profession, old order: Engineers and German society, 1815–1914*. Cambridge, UK: Cambridge University Press.

Guillen, M. F. (1994). *Models of management: Work, authority, and organization in a comparative perspective*. Chicago: University of Chicago Press.

Hounshell, D. A. (1984). *From the American system to mass production, 1800–1932: The development of manufacturing technology in the United States*. Baltimore: Johns Hopkins University Press.

Kalev, A., Shenhav, Y., & De-Vries, D. (in press). The State and the labor process: Regulatory means and normative framing in the diffusion of managerial models. *Administrative Science Quarterly*.

Lash, S., & Urry, J. (1987). *The end of organized capitalism*. New York: Polity.

Layton, E. T. (1971). *The revolt of the engineers: Social responsibility and the American engineering profession.* Cleveland, OH: The Press of Case Western Reserve University.

Locke, R. R. (1984). *The end of the practical man: Entrepreneurship and higher education in Germany, France, and Great Britain, 1880–1940.* London: JAI.

Maier, C. (1987). *In search of stability: Explorations in historical political economy.* Cambridge, MA: Harvard University Press.

Noble, D. F. (1977). *America by design: Science, technology, and the rise of corporate capitalism.* New York: Oxford University Press.

Shenhav, Y. (1995). From chaos to systems: The engineering foundations of organization theory, 1877–1932. *Administrative Science Quarterly, 40,* 557–585.

Shenhav, Y. (1999). *Manufacturing rationality: The foundations of the managerial revolution.* Oxford, UK: Oxford University Press.

ENTERPRISE CULTURE

Enterprise culture enshrines the values of liberal economics, emphasizing three key principles: the efficiency of markets, the liberty of individuals, and the noninterventionism of the state. The term is particularly associated with the United Kingdom and, initially, was connected to Thatcherism. The opposite of enterprise culture is the "culture of dependency," which implies that both organizations and individuals are dependent on the "nanny state" for handouts, grants, bailouts, or subsidies.

Conceptual Overview

Formed in Britain while the Conservatives were in opposition in the 1970s, the notion of enterprise culture flowered with the election of Margaret Thatcher as prime minister in 1979. Concerned about economic decline, she took steps to increase the competitiveness of the private sector and to decrease a perceived drain on the public purse. Along with shrinking the state, Thatcher promoted enterprise culture at every level of society. These actions were intended to increase prosperity.

Enterprise culture was to be nurtured by organizations and professed by individuals. Enterprising individuals are creative, risk taking, and responsible, understanding that no one owes them a living. Therefore, to become enterprising, welfare recipients were expected to give up the culture of dependency and get a job; the middle class were to stop passively relying on their employers for a paycheck and were instead to work actively to increase productivity, thereby adding value. At the top of the social hierarchy, elites were encouraged to give up the aristocratic values of the gentry, replacing anticommercialism with entrepreneurialism. For their part, organizations were to become enterprising by empowering employees to take the initiative rather than to wait for instructions. Firms and small businesses were to embrace enterprise culture to boost productivity, increase UK competitiveness, and foster the creation of wealth. Public and voluntary organizations were to adopt enterprise culture in order to cater more effectively to their clientele. Enterprise culture reflected core beliefs of Thatcherism, and continued to thrive under Tony Blair's New Labor.

On a more specific level, enterprise culture has at least two distinct applications. First, it is associated with administrative reform and privatization in the public sector. Thatcher literally privatized many national industries and, in a different sense, also "privatized" other areas such as health, culture, and education. In these sectors, government was no longer to be seen as the sole provider of funds. Organizations such as museums, universities, and the National Health Service were pressed to run themselves in the manner of private businesses, to use marketing tools to serve "customers" (rather than students or patients), and to seek supplemental funding from private sources. Along these lines, Thatcher reformed the civil service, introducing market forces. Russell Keats argues that the formation of enterprise culture represents a "de-differentiation" of previously distinct modes of organization, as public and nongovernmental organizations come more closely to resemble business firms. Government put into place a number of incentives to encourage, or force, these organizations to adopt business principles. This created serious debate, both within and outside these organizations, as to whether market forces should be introduced into sectors not traditionally measured by economic yardsticks.

Second, enterprise culture is associated with a championing of entrepreneurial values in business organizations. One might think that this logic was already firmly embedded within that sector; however, large businesses (along with the state apparatus) were seen as potentially or actually bureaucratized, and therefore, inflexible and uncompetitive. The United Kingdom was seen to be behind other nations in the creation of small, innovative firms. Thatcher feared the effects of an antibusiness, and specifically, anti-entrepreneurial spirit, which was thought to permeate the nation. Enterprise culture called out to established business firms to become more entrepreneurial and more competitive, in order to meet international challenges. Likewise, it encouraged small business and self-employment, highlighting their crucial role in wealth creation. Changes in public policy, tax reform, and the like were introduced to combat the decline of British industrial might, with the key ingredients of the prescription being freedom from state control and the adoption of enterprise values: unencumbered, competitive markets and the will to win. Although the term arose in the British context, it has been used to describe movements elsewhere that put a premium on open markets, the initiative of individuals, and a laissez-faire state.

Critical Commentary and Future Directions

Enterprise culture is an ambiguous and multifaceted term. In one sense, it is a catchphrase for the positive values of self-reliance and entrepreneurship. In another, it is a reviled slogan representing the mindless imposition of managerialism into the public sector. Yet it is important in that it embodies crucial, if contested, aspects of British cultural values.

The effectiveness of enterprise culture, with respect to its more concrete applications, is unclear. It represents beliefs about the proper antidote to welfare dependency, anticommercial values, and concerns about global competitiveness, but it is not a coherent policy per se. The actions of successive British governments—deprofessionalization, privatization, a "rolling back" of the state, and a shift in favor of business-friendly policies—might have been made in the name of enterprise culture, but are indicative of general trends in modern capitalist economies. Nevertheless, enterprise culture, as David Marquand argues, represents an "aspiration" that has been achieved in part, even if it can never be achieved fully. The British economy has strengthened since the 1970s, a pro-business stance is no longer a matter for embarrassment, and significant market forces have been introduced into sectors previously shielded from them.

Enterprise culture embodies a number of unresolved, or even contradictory, propositions: It celebrates competition and winners, but ignores the inevitable losers. Theorists such as Mary Douglas question whether it is possible to change culture through government policy, or through any external action. David Marquand suggests that as the state takes action to create a more favorable business environment, it strengthens itself, ironically contradicting its own calls for its diminution. In addition, as many writers have pointed out, the inculcation of enterprise culture is not just a business proposition. It is an ideological, indeed, a moral project, which is based on Western, conservative, and specifically Christian beliefs. Enterprise culture also raises wider debates about the highly individualistic form of capitalism that underpins it, including such issues as increasing social inequality, work–life balance, and the decline of community.

—*Victoria D. Alexander*

See also Entrepreneurship; Management and Public Policy; Nongovernmental Organizations; Organizational Culture; Small and Medium-Sized Enterprises

Further Readings

Gray, C. (1998). *Enterprise and culture.* London: Routledge.

Heap, S. H., & Ross, A. (Eds.). (1992). *Understanding the enterprise culture: Themes in the work of Mary Douglas.* Edinburgh, Scotland: Edinburgh University Press.

Heelas, P., & Morris, P. (Eds.). (1992). *The values of the enterprise culture.* London: Routledge.

Keat, R., & Abercrombie, N. (Eds.). (1991). *Enterprise culture.* London: Routledge.

Thompson, F. M. L. (2003). *Gentrification and the enterprise culture.* Oxford, UK: Oxford University Press.

Entrepreneurship

Entrepreneurship is the process whereby newness is created in the market and society at large through creating new organizations or through transforming existing organizations, which in turn is called *intrapreneurship* or *corporate entrepreneurship*. Entrepreneurship allows organization studies to focus on organizational emergence and organizational innovation and to understand the "event" of organization, which is how organizational processes are created and changed or are continuously in the making. Entrepreneurship is also important for organization studies as it allows assessment of the impact of organizations on people's everyday lives in both a critical and generative sense as illustrated by the phenomena of "enterprising selves" and "entrepreneurial history making."

Conceptual Overview

Entrepreneurship is of primary interest for organization studies because it does not take the existence of organizations for granted but allows for the study and explanation of how organizations come into existence, either as individual new firms or as new industries, and to emphasize that organizations always need to develop new products and services and to innovate in order to perpetuate their existence. To describe the significance of the concept of entrepreneurship for organization studies, it is important to indicate that entrepreneurship has developed into an academic field in and of itself, as Scott Shane and Sankaran Venkataraman suggest, implying that entrepreneurship studies and organization studies share an interface with organizational emergence at its core. Entrepreneurship is thus both related to both small and medium-sized firms, since new venture creation focuses on how young and (for that reason) smaller firms are started up, develop, and grow, as well as to organizational change and innovation processes of larger and more established organizations. Entrepreneurship thus brings creativity and newness under the attention of organization studies. The focus on newness and innovation for the most part goes back to Joseph Schumpeter who defined entrepreneurship as the creation of new combinations in the form of new goods and services, new methods of production, new markets, new sources of supply, and new organization of the industry. For Schumpeter, creative destruction is central, since entrepreneurship both overwrites current products, services, and markets and develops new ones. For instance, the mobile phone replaced the practice of wired phoning and reorganized the sector of telecommunication.

Within the field of entrepreneurship studies, it is debated whether the creation of new combinations requires the creation of a new organization or if it is also made possible through innovation in existing organization. William Gartner sees entrepreneurship as the study of the creation of organizations or so-called new venture creation. He conceives entrepreneurship as organizational emergence and hence shifts the focus from the individual entrepreneur to the more complex process of how organizations are created through the interplay of four perspectives: characteristics of the individuals who start the venture, the organization that they create, the environment surrounding the new venture, and the process by which the new venture is started. Historically, entrepreneurship has been reduced to characteristics of the entrepreneurs, trying to identify personality features and cognitive abilities to distinguish entrepreneurs from other people, such as managers. However, there is no empirical support that can identify such discriminating personality characteristics or cognitive styles. Gartner therefore suggests studying the behaviors and activities that lead to the creation of a new organization.

Shane and Venkataraman refocus entrepreneurship beyond the creation of new organizations as they emphasize opportunity recognition and exploitation and as they leave it open whether opportunities are exploited through creating a new venture or through changing an existing organization. Entrepreneurship is seen as an activity that involves the discovery, evaluation, and exploitation of opportunities to introduce new goods, services, and ways of organizing, as well as new markets, processes, and raw materials through organizing efforts that previously had not existed. Simultaneously, the focus on individuals and their actions is reintroduced as entrepreneurship becomes explained through the nexus of enterprising individuals and valuable opportunities.

However, the meeting between entrepreneurial behavior and organizational behavior has not always been self-evident. Historically, scholars from organization studies have shown little interest in the process of entrepreneurship and new venture creation, as they focused mostly on mature organizations and cross-sectional designs. This prompted entrepreneurship scholars to claim that most theories of organization are not valid for the context of start-ups and that entrepreneurship needed its own theory of organization. More and more, it has become clear that understanding the entrepreneurial process is a quintessence for developing organizational concepts and for theorizing organizational processes.

Entrepreneurship has contributed considerably to the understanding of organizations with regard to how such central organizational notions as culture, structure, and strategy have been conceptualized. Both Andrew Pettigrew and Edgar Schein have studied entrepreneurial organizations to understand the creation of organizational cultures. Schein documented how the values and practices of entrepreneurs and their close collaborators became constitutive for the values and practices of the overall organizational culture, while Pettigrew developed a longitudinal-processual analysis of culture through studying the birth and development of a private boarding school. With regard to the concept of structure, Henry Mintzberg has for his structural theory of configurations used the context of smaller and innovative organizations to understand how the so-called *simple structure* and *adhocracy* emerge. Simple structure was held to represent the traditional hierarchical structure of a small firm with one boss, a few line managers, and a broad group of employees, while new structural forms—such as adhocracies—represent more fluid and less hierarchical networks of collaboration through ad hoc project groups. Furthermore, Mintzberg studied entrepreneurial and innovative organizations to look at strategy formation and to transform the idea of strategy as something planned into the concept of strategy as emerging.

Besides the development of central organizational concepts, the focus on entrepreneurship has contributed especially to the understanding of organizational processes. First, the models that address the so-called growing pains of young organizations as they become bigger have been captured in *stage models*—life-cycle models and models of organizational development. For instance, Greiner describes different cycles of growth that young companies have to cope with during different crises and moments of evolution and revolution. Second, *evolutionary* approaches to process do not focus on the stages of development of a single organization but study how organizations are founded and disbanded by following the movements of populations of organizations and how certain organizations—through processes of selection—survive while others disappear from the organizational landscape. Third, *interpretive and social constructionist* approaches to process have rephrased the entrepreneurial process as "entrepreneuring" and contributed to what Karl Weick has called organizing by focusing on how variation is enacted and comes into play. New venture creation is seen here as a process of sensemaking whereby new ideas and possibilities become enacted, selected, and legitimated until they become accepted by potential users. Entrepreneurship is hence about seeing a crack or a flaw in the prevailing social construction of reality and interpreting it as an opportunity to actualize new ideas of what the world could and should look like.

The concept of entrepreneuring focuses on the ongoing construction of reality, which is negotiated through connecting the discourses of several participants into a common process of sensemaking. Rene Bouwen and Chris Steyaert use the concept of texture to explain that entrepreneuring consists of interweaving evolving tasks and organizational roles that become tried out, practiced, made sense of, and negotiated within the entrepreneurial team and the expanding group of actors. *Texture* refers to a quasi-stable and provisional collective frame of discourses and practices that guide and enact the interaction processes. These interaction processes often consist of improvisation and bricolage, as Ted Baker has pointed out. Entrepreneurs work with improvised practices and designs and create something from nothing by constructing their own resources from what is at hand. A fourth and related approach focuses on the *narrative* processes that construct reality and the role of stories used for self-presentation, legitimation, and sensemaking. Narrative is seen as ontological, as life itself is storied. As an ontological condition of social life, a narrative perspective of entrepreneurship claims that new organizations become constructed through myriad stories that perpetually repeat, contradict, and extend each other. Entrepreneurship is a process of storytelling through which people become implied in an ongoing employment where actors and networks become connected and disconnected. Stories are not individual expressions of entrepreneurs but are shot through with public narratives of what entrepreneurs do and don't do, and with cultural narratives of what it means to take risks or what it means to fail a business. In that sense, a narrative perspective conceives the entrepreneurial process in relationship to the construction of time, legitimacy, morality, and everyday survival. The question of which cultural or public narratives or discourses are drawn on is related to the issue of power, as focused on in critical (discursive) perspectives, which the next section addresses.

Critical Commentary and Future Directions

As the critical perspective gathered momentum within organization studies, an interest was taken in entrepreneurship examining critically how entrepreneurial discourse has taken center stage in all aspects of working life. An enterprise culture is pervading all organizations in which people are expected to perform their jobs as entrepreneurial selves, turning every employee into a potential entrepreneur and into someone who has no choice but to be creative, responsible, and flexible. The critical study of enterprising selves and of what Nikolas Rose has called "the governing of the soul" looks at the interrelation of power and subjectivity as rooted in the work of Michel Foucault. Rather than seeing people (or entrepreneurs) as the masters of their own creation, this critical perspective indicates how entrepreneurial identities are formed in the webs of actualized discourses and their inherent power struggles that prioritize certain realities above others. For Foucault, subjectivity is not an existing thing per se, but is created by systems of social organization that give shape to and control how people are expected to act, for instance, as healthy people; as factory workers; and indeed, as entrepreneurial people. People's subjectivity is then more their concept of how they are expected to think of themselves as they are exposed to these values and images in education, in family life, or in the media. Discourses create truth effects and power effects, implying that all forms of truth and knowledge entail disciplinary power, since people's actions and identities become shaped in an expected way. For instance, in an analogy to Foucault's notion of governmentality, Attila Bruni, Silvia Gherardi, and Barbara Poggio speak of "entrepreneur mentality" to seize how entrepreneurial discourse proclaims a system of acting and thinking that normalizes certain forms of being an entrepreneur and excludes other forms. Though female entrepreneurship is rendered invisible by mass media and scholarly articles, the available studies of the female entrepreneur tend to implicitly reproduce the male experience as a preferred norm.

Discursive studies of entrepreneurs thus take a critical stance on entrepreneurship studies itself and take issue with the assumption that it seems to act as a value-free endeavor (such as gender-free or culture-free). Entrepreneurship studies are hence construed as supporting a hegemonic ideology of enterprising that fits certain (economically dominant) parts of the world, and that forms the latest version of governmentality through which people become subject to certain scripts of behaving actively, responsibly, and full of initiative. As entrepreneurship is continuously exported to all domains of society, including education, government, health, or art, which are all said to "need" entrepreneurship (as in for instance the entrepreneurial university or the *culturepreneur*), critical studies of entrepreneurship become primordial. This can be documented by the phenomenon of social entrepreneurship that, more recently, has taken center stage in the discourse of politics, media, and academics, where it is seen as the cure-all balm for achieving social change and for bettering the world. As a consequence, the image of social entrepreneurs as heroes who can single-handedly change the world for the better is reinstalled. In this hype, it is neither acknowledged that entrepreneurship studies have already abandoned this individual perspective, nor is the political and ideological impact of reconstructing societal problems through this individualized lens critically examined and historically contextualized. Instead, many social problems become an issue of economist thinking and of managerial solutions.

As entrepreneurship is not solely seen as connected to economic progress but is more and more related to society, other studies have examined how entrepreneurship affects practices of living and everyday life. New organizations—through the new entrepreneurial products and services and the new combinations they produce—have a strong impact on how people's lives take form and how major aspects of society become transformed. From the automobile to the mobile phone, from the pencil to the personal computer, each of these new devices has had enormous implications for how transport, communication, writing, and work have been produced and practiced. In the example of the mobile phone, it is clear that the mobile phone is not just a new form of phoning or that it has merely reshaped the telecommunication sector, but it has fundamentally changed people's practices of communicating; the experience of time, distance, and reachability; and how people experience the relationship between their body and objects. While people used to "go" to the phone, they now always carry a phone with them, allowing them to send at any time a text message or to check email, and possibly interrupting (their participation in) a local meeting to give priority to a virtual interaction. In this vein, Charles Spinosa, Fernando Flores, and Hubert L. Dreyfus consider entrepreneurship to be a form of history making, as entrepreneurs are sensitive to how the problem they sense has its roots in people's pervasive way of living and in people's lifestyle. The changes brought about in the entrepreneurial process are changes of historical magnitude because they change the way people see and understand things in the relevant domain.

The entrepreneurial process is started by sensing that certain practices form an anomaly and can thus be done differently. Crucial is how one can hold onto this anomaly and reveal how the commonsense way of acting somehow fails and is doomed to perish as a new practice is slowly developed and becomes visible. For instance, digital technology has quickly rendered the taping of sound and images on music and video cassettes obsolete. This anomaly that drives the entrepreneurial process forms a historical possibility that, once recognized through a new shared practice, will be practiced by most people in roughly the same way. In the example of the cell phone, the idea of wireless phoning was at first unbelievable but very quickly, people saw the advantages of this artifact and even further developed it by practicing, for instance, a text-messaging culture. Now some people no longer have a fixed ("landline") phone connection at home, or in the city of Nokia there is no longer the possibility to install a fixed connection.

As entrepreneurship is more and more connected to everyday life and practices, it is clear that entrepreneurship and entrepreneurs become less exclusive and can be observed in less obvious contexts than one normally expects. This pervasiveness, however, differs from the increasing homogeneity pinpointed by the critique of entrepreneurial selves, since it is assumed that entrepreneurship—as it changes significantly people's forms and styles of living—is continuously questioning and bringing variations to how life is organized. Ultimately, when entrepreneurs give form to the future face of society and when it is the task of entrepreneurship to create *from* the society people have to live in, the society people *want* to live in, as Saras Sarasvathy has noted, entrepreneurship brings multiplicity and creativity to the organizing of society.

However, how exactly the dreams and dangers of entrepreneurship can be understood remains a future challenge. Entrepreneurship is a contested and hybrid phenomenon that is simultaneously bestowed with the hope for regional development, for battling poverty or for ecological sustainability, and the fear that it will reduce society and all people into a bunch of egoistic self-maximizers. There is thus a need to develop an approach that integrates a critical and affirmative perspective into one processual understanding of entrepreneurship, which is especially pressing as the critical perspective on entrepreneurship being imported from organization studies and social sciences still stays at the margins of the field. As the world becomes more and more globalized, networked, and virtualized, the idea of entrepreneurship as a process of cocreation whereby the new products, services, and combinations (that Schumpeter pointed at) will themselves become more ephemeral and constantly in the making as users in particular take part in the shaping of the form and the use of the new artifact. This tendency holds, once again, an enormous potential to support the theorizing of organizing that has been radicalized by an ontology of "becoming" into a process of flux, and to emphasize that notions of creativity and invention are primary concepts to understand the unfolding of newness. This process of creation—which considers creation not as subject to the individual creator but as forming a collective assemblage—implies uncertainty, open-endedness, and risk, and it is that which creates the double-sidedness of entrepreneurship, its promise and its danger, and which urges more than ever a critical, yet affirmative understanding of entrepreneurship.

—*Chris Steyaert*

See also Adhocracies; Creativity; Enterprise Culture; Improvisation; Individualism; Innovation; Opportunistic Behavior; Serendipity; Small and Medium-Sized Enterprises; Uncertainty

Further Readings

Aldrich, H. (1999). *Organizations evolving.* London: Sage.
Baker, T., Aldrich, H. E., & Liou, N. (1997). Invisible entrepeneurs: The neglect of women business owners by mass media and scholarly journal in the USA. *Entrepreneurship and Regional Development, 9,* 221–238.
Baker, T., & Nelson, R. E. (2005). Creating something from nothing: Construction through entrepreneurial bricolage. *Administrative Science Quarterly, 50,* 329–366.
Bouwen, R., & Steyaert, C. (1990). Construing organizational texture in young entrepreneurial firms. *Journal of Management Studies, 27*(6), 637–649.
Bruni, A., Gherardi, S., & Poggio, B. (2004). Entrepreneur-mentality, gender and the study of women entrepreneurs. *Journal of Organizational Change Management, 17*(3), 256–268.
du Gay, P. (2004). Against "Enterprise" (but not against "enterprise," for that would make no sense). *Organization, 11*(1), 37–57.
Gartner, W. B. (1985). A framework for describing the phenomenon of new venture creation. *Academy of Management Review, 10*(4), 696–706.
Hjorth, D., & Steyaert, C. (2004). *Narrative and discursive approaches in entrepreneurship.* Cheltenham, UK: Edward Elgar.
Ogbor, J. O. (2000). Mythicizing and reification in entrepreneurial discourse: Ideology-critique of entrepreneurship studies. *Journal of Management Studies, 37*(5), 605–635.
Rose, N. (1989). *Governing the soul: The shaping of the private self.* London: Routledge.
Sarasvathy, S. D. (2001). Entrepreneurship as economics with imagination [Special issue: The Ruffin Series 3]. *Business Ethics Quarterly,* 95–112.
Shane, S., & Venkataraman, S. (2002). The promise of entrepreneurship as a field of research. *Academy of Management Review, 25*(1), 217–226.
Spinosa, C., Flores, F., & Dreyfus, H. L. (1997). *Disclosing new worlds.* Cambridge, MA: MIT Press.
Steyaert, C., & Katz, J. (2004). Reclaiming the space of entrepreneurship in society: Geographical, discursive and social dimensions. *Entrepreneurship and Regional Development, 16*(3), 179–196.

Environment

See Organizational Environments

Environmental Determinism

Environmental determinism is the doctrine or viewpoint that asserts organizational features are causally determined by aspects of the environment. In this view, the environment is treated as a concrete thing or natural fact that exists independently of its human, social, and economic constituents. This view assumes a one-directional flow of resources and influence from the environment to the organization. Human agency and free will are thus assumed to be irrelevant to organizational actions and outcomes.

Conceptual Overview

Environmental determinism assumes the environment is a concrete, self-sufficient phenomenon external to the organization. The environment causes or determines all internal features of organizations including how members think and act, how organizational structures are shaped, which organizational technologies are adopted, criteria of organizational effectiveness, and whether organizations stand or fall. The strong form of environmental determinism assumes there is little or no agency or free will in the choices made by organizational members. In essence, organizational choices, actions, and meanings are seen as the causally determined outcomes of environmental features. The organization thus reflects and is directly determined by the features of the environment.

Environmental determinism is consistent with the social system view of organizations that Conrad and Haynes discuss in 2001. The doctrine of the social system focuses on external constraints on organizations that determine their structural configuration. This view uses a language of objectivity and externality to depict actors' choices as severely constrained or determined by features of the situation. Constraints are strong but imperfect influences that are not equivalent to determinism. There is a tendency for theories that examine constraints or influence as key processes to employ deterministic arguments.

The social system view contrasts with a social action perspective that assumes behavior is voluntary and based in human agency. Thus, a key challenge facing organizational theories that seek to avoid being overly deterministic is to describe organizational action in ways that show how it is guided by actual pressures while avoiding the view that the situation fully determines organizational actions.

Early organizational theory was characterized by a closed system perspective that addressed internal organizational features and neglected how the environment influences organizations. However, later organizational theories adopted an open systems perspective to examine how organizational components are imported into the organization and how the organization is influenced by the environment. John Child, writing in 1997, notes that key organization perspectives including ecological, institutional, and contingency theories assume organizational characteristics are determined by environmental conditions.

Three forms of determinism are evident in these theories. One form is natural determinism, which assumes natural selection determines organizational features. This is evidenced in population ecology theory, developed by Michael Hannan and John Freeman, that examines the population of organizations to understand why certain types of organizations survive. Survival is based on the fit between the environment and the organization. This theory is highly deterministic because it assumes that environments select or determine which organizations will survive by providing or failing to provide essential resources. Management has little influence on organizational outcomes. Hannan and Freeman modified their approach into a less deterministic view in 1989 that they referred to as organizational ecology. Organizational ecology emphasizes adaptability rather than selection: where a particular variant or form does not fit its environment, managerial skills can help an organization to adapt.

A second form of determinism is social determinism, which assumes that norms and social processes external to the organization determine organizational characteristics. For example, the institutional theory of organizations uses social determinism because it asserts that social and cultural pressures to conform to conventional beliefs and myths in the environment influence the organization to adopt socially desirable organizational characteristics. Organizational structures and other internal features of organizations are thus conceived to be outcomes of environmental processes that make organizations similar in appearance to their environments. Social determinism operates here through the assumption that organizational survival is based in successful adoption of environmental elements that allow the organization to maintain its legitimacy and social fitness.

A third form of determinism is rational determinism, which assumes that reason and rationality determine the best fit between environmental characteristics and organizational features and processes. For example, the structural contingency theory of organizations uses rational determinism by assuming that (1) organizational performance is an outcome of the fit or match between environmental features and organizational characteristics, and (2) managers rationally assess and recognize this match and take conscious action to shape the organization to fit the limited range of environmental contingencies or features that allow it to continue to exist.

Critical Commentary and Future Directions

A significant implication of environmental determinism is that organizational features are caused by the environment, hence human agency or free will in organizations is (relatively) ineffectual for changing organizations or influencing performance outcomes. However, the assumption that human agency and choice do not influence organizational features and outcomes differs from the everyday life assumption that managers and employees can influence organizations, an assumption that is also consistent with the social action perspective. Many organizational theories, including organizational ecology, institutional theory, and contingency theory, have thus been elaborated to address the possibility of human free will (agency) and strategic choice making in organizations.

There are other limitations to the doctrine of environmental determinism that limit its usefulness from a critical perspective. First, the environment is at least partly a human construction. The human and social processes through which environments determine, constrain, or influence organizations need to be better understood. Otherwise, the environment will continue to be treated as a concrete phenomenon, external to humans, that is difficult for humans to comprehend and manage. Second, conceptions of the environment are based on human values, not natural facts. Future research thus needs to address how values and ideologies influence people's conceptions of the environment. Third, the different processes that constitute environmental impacts on organizations, including determinism, influence, and constraints, are not well conceptualized by environmentally deterministic organizational theories. These processes need to be better conceptualized and understood. Finally, highly determinist views tend to reflect and encourage the value-based assumption that the competitive success of individuals and organizations reflects their superior characteristics and social value. Environmental determinism needs to be questioned and challenged in future research, particularly where it supports rationalized myths that legitimate inequality.

Environmental determinism results in misleading and incomplete research frameworks. Future research needs to examine a wide range of ways that environments influence organizations and to use perspectives that assume people can influence organizations and environments. Further, research on environmental determinism should define the boundary conditions for each kind of influence or determination and the human meanings and explanations given by members when they seek to make sense of environmental influences on organizations.

—*Robert P. Gephart, Jr. and Cagri Topal*

See also Institutional Theory; Social Theory; Structural Contingency Theory

Furthur Readings

Child, J. (1997). Strategic choice in the analysis of action, structure, organizations and environment: Retrospect and prospect. *Organization Studies, 18*(1), 43–76.

Conra, C., & Haynes, J. (2001). Development of key constructs. In F. Jablin & L. Putnam (Eds.), *The new handbook of organizational communication: Advances in theory, research, and methods*. Thousand Oaks, CA: Sage.

Hannan, J., & Freeman, J. (1989). *Organizational ecology*. Cambridge, MA: Harvard University Press.

Scott, W. R. (1992). *Organizations: Rational, natural, and open systems*. Englewood Cliffs, NJ: Prentice Hall.

Environmentalism and Organizations

Environmentalism is the set of human beliefs and behaviors that are oriented toward preserving, conserving, or otherwise protecting one or more aspects of the natural environment. Environmentalism is a multi-level concept in which these values and actions that seek to establish more positive human relationships with nature are evident in individuals, organizations, and societies. While human organizations from their beginnings have existed in and have been affected by their respective natural environments, only recently have a number of these organizations perceived themselves, and been perceived by others, both as affecting and as being part of those natural environments. As Mark Starik and Gordon Rands have suggested, typical human organizations, often grouped into business, government, and nonprofit organization sectors, as well as the more informal types of organization, including households, affinity groups, neighborhoods, communities, and societies, all use natural environment inputs (such as air, water, land, and biomass), employ natural environment processes (such as photosynthesis, combustion, heat transfer, and material alteration), and create natural environment outputs (such as products, services, pollution, and depleted resources). Ecologists generally conceptualize natural environments as the various sets of biophysical spheres (atmosphere, hydrosphere, lithosphere, and biosphere) and the locations, forces, and cycles within which they exist and interact. In the early part of the 21st century, Lester Brown identified that numerous global, regional, and local natural environments were being stressed—some extremely so—by rising temperatures, falling water tables, reduced fish stocks, advancing deserts, shrinking forests, dwindling species, and increasing toxicity, not insignificantly due to human organization actions and inactions.

Conceptual Overview

Beginning in the early 1990s, organization researchers such as Rogene Buchholz, Alfred Marcus, and James Post described numerous cases that highlighted that natural environment inputs, processes, and outputs associated with human organization vary significantly by organizational type, size, location, values, strategy, and behavior. Larger organizations and those in resource-intensive industries (such as mining, manufacturing, forestry, fishing, transportation, and agriculture) are often perceived as affecting and being affected by their natural environments more than others. In addition, those organizations associated with locations that are especially eco-sensitive, such as those conducting business in or near tropical rainforests, coastlines, and shallow underground water tables, are seen to potentially impact and be impacted by their natural environments more than other organizations. Finally, organizations vary significantly in their values, strategies, and behaviors regarding their use of or reaction to natural environment phenomena. While some well-known organizations have been identified as either very bad or very good actors due to their environmental policies, plans, practices, or performance, most organizations likely fall between these extremes and are slowly advancing from the former to the latter.

Organizations have approached their relationships with their natural environments using widely varying orientations. Based on a number of factors mentioned earlier, as well as on the environmental values, strategies, and behaviors adopted by these organizations, they typically have been perceived as occupying one or more positions on a proactiveness continuum. Paul Shrivastava, Carolyn Egri, and Susan Herman identified that leaders in organization and environment issues often are led by very visible top executives who help develop attitudes of serious environmental appreciation within their organizations and among their external stakeholders. These CEOs, executive directors, and board members have been known to set environmentally friendly examples by using nonautomobile transportation, by donating to pro-wildlife causes, and by encouraging recycling practices, among other environmental culture–instilling behaviors. They and other environmentally inclined organization members have also formed environmental committees and task forces; set overall and departmental environmental objectives; and established general and specific strategies for reducing pollution, using nontoxic materials and processes, and otherwise more positively interacting with their multiple natural environments. Starik and Alfred Marcus have indicated that leading organizations in environmental issues have designed and implemented systems (including human resources, research and development, production, distribution, and information systems) to follow through on their environmental objectives and strategies. These have included Design for the Environment life cycle analysis (a program of the U.S. Environmental Protection Agency), environmental management information, pollution and depletion reduction, energy management, and environmental management systems (EMS).

Regarding the latter, recent research led by Nicole Darnall suggests that these EMS approaches may be key among these organizational programs or behaviors, since environmental management systems can adopt comprehensive and integrated views of an organization's interactions with its natural environments, and since these systems can be certified under ISO 14001, an emerging international voluntary standard for environmental management systems. This standard requires an organization to establish an environmental policy and plan, identify its environmental impacts and aspects, document how it is implementing its plan to address these impacts and aspects, and establish continuous improvement and management review processes. Attaining this certification does not necessarily mean that an organization is an environmentally excellent one, only that it has a documented system in place to move in that direction.

Critical Commentary and Future Directions

While leading organizations have often attained ISO 14001 certification and implemented one or more of the other systems above, and though some have done much more, many organizations, whether formal businesses, governments, or nonprofit organizations, or more informal organizations of households, communities, or societies, have not developed their environmental orientations to such an extent. These organizations often, but not always, are smaller in size and operating in less resource-intensive industries or less sensitive natural environments, and in countries with less effective environmental regulation than those that have attained ISO 14001 certification. These organizations are often constrained by top executives who have not been able or willing to focus on their organization's interaction with its natural environments. As Ruth Hilary has indicated, often these mostly noncertified organizations also have not experienced external pressures to develop environmental management systems, nor do they perceive themselves as having the resources, such as time, money, and personnel, necessary to develop and implement them. However, some organizations with large advertising or public relations budgets, whether ISO 14001 certified or not, have the capability, and some the reputation, for preaching rather than practicing environmentalism, often referred to as *greenwashing*.

Future directions of the development of the relationships between human organizations and their natural environments are difficult to ascertain, since both organizations and environments are coevolving, affecting one another's substance and processes. What is apparent is that human organizations, as they grow in size, number, and technological capacity, will negatively affect their natural environments to a greater (and perhaps more frequent) extent than in the past. Human populations continue to urbanize, to congregate near coastlines, and to otherwise move toward potentially greater macro concentration and micro dispersion (such as evidenced by urban sprawl). What appears necessary for a continuation or improvement in the environmental quality of life of most humans around the world is a far more prudent relationship with their natural environments than has been exhibited in the past. David Suzuki has suggested that these more effective interactions will likely involve a concerted strategic effort on the part of many human organizations and individuals to assess their current impacts on their multiple natural environments; to identify more sustainable approaches to interacting with them; and, finally, to change human behavior so that their relationships with these environments are far more benign, perhaps even restorative.

Numerous suggestions have been forwarded to implement these three strategies. Regarding assessment of impacts, a wide range of techniques have been developed, both those with a strong qualitative element (such as the development of the human sensory appreciation of the beauty and power of natural phenomena) and those with a strong quantitative element (such as geographic information systems, or GIS, which allow mapping of both natural and demographic phenomena). Approaches that combine both qualitative and quantitative elements include environmental education, in general, and environmental footprint and environmental impact audits and life cycle analysis, specifically. Regarding the identification of more sustainable approaches to human organization–natural environment interactions, many models have been proposed, including Design for the Environment, Strategic Environmental Management, and the Natural Step, each of which takes into account multiple human values, including those related to natural environments. For example, Starik and Archie Carroll suggest that Strategic Environmental Management can encourage organizations to identify "greening" opportunities both within and outside these organizations, to hone them to levels of excellence, and to integrate them with one another so that, for instance, an organization's environmental strategy matches its environmental stakeholders, including its staff. Finally, regarding changing human behavior that fosters more nurturing natural environmental outcomes, again, multiple suggestions have been made by organization and environment researchers, from altering environmental policies to provide incentives for humans, including their organizations, to more positively interact with their natural environments (such as pollution charges and renewable energy investments), to political and social marketing campaigns designed to make both macro and micro changes in how human individuals and organizations can more prudently produce and consume only what they need, ensuring that the natural environments that support them are enhanced rather than depleted.

The prospects for a smooth transition from an industrial approach to human organization production and consumption that involves significant pollution and depletion to one that has been described by Paul Hawkin, Amory Lovins, and Hunter Lovins as "biomimicry" (or the emulation of natural systems behavior by humans and their organizations that is seen to be far more benign and restorative than the industrial model) are unclear at best. Nearly a quarter of one hundred trillion dollars of human world annual economic activity will apparently need to change its inputs, processes, and outputs to significantly affect the daunting challenges human organizations face as they more prudently align themselves with those of nature. Entire human organization sectors, not simply industries, will apparently need to reinvent themselves, using far different (less- or nontoxic) materials; more energy-efficient, renewable, and less polluting energy sources; find radically different suppliers and customers who share their environmental values and strategies; and collaborate with partner organizations in other sectors around the world (as well as locally and regionally) who can provide the political and other support and resources these sectors will need to transform themselves into integrated sets of ecologically sustainable organizations.

Happily, a number of organizations have identified possible pathways toward sustainability (or the ability of an entity to both survive and thrive over a long period of time). As Monika Winn, Sanjay Sharma, and others have found, numerous human organizations are now actively involved in establishing environmental visions, missions, objectives, and strategies leading toward the creation of a more sustainable human organization future. In all three sectors and in most countries, businesses, governments, and nonprofit organizations, as well as informal human organizations, are working separately and together to alter human behavior toward this ideal.

Projections that Earth's climate is changing and its species are becoming extinct at alarming rates, as well as the general decline in multiple world ecosystems, due in part to human population and organization behaviors, have prompted many concerned observers to urge human organizations to begin to address their multiple natural environment impacts. Organizations as diverse as tourism operators, mining companies, local governments, insurance companies, civic groups, dry cleaners, and the United Nations have begun to assess these impacts, develop appropriate responses, and put these into action. For all human organizations, as well as for human individuals and those of the other species with whom humans share the planet, an era of both environmental crises and hope appears to be the organization and natural environment reality in the early 21st century.

—*Mark Starik*

See also Community and Organizations; Corporate Social Responsibility; Interorganizational Relations and Collaboration; Stakeholders; Sustainable Development

Further Readings

Brown, L. (2003). *Plan B*. New York: Norton.

Buchholz, R. A., Marcus, A. A., & Post, J. E. (1992). *Managing environmental issues: A casebook*. Englewood Cliffs, NJ: Prentice Hall.

Darnall, N., Gallagher, D., Andrews, R. N. L., & Amaral, D. (2000). Environmental Management Systems: Opportunities for improved environmental and business strategy? *Environmental Quality Management, 9*(3), 1–9.

Egri, C. P., & Herman, S. (2000). Leadership in the North American environmental sector: Values, leadership styles, and contexts of environmental leaders and their organizations. *Academy of Management Journal, 43,* 571–604.

Hawken, P., Lovins, A., & Lovins, H. (1999). *Natural capitalism*. Snowmass, CO: Rocky Mountain Institute.

Hilary, R. (Ed.). (2000). *Small and medium-sized enterprises and the environment: Business imperatives*. Sheffield, UK: Greenleaf.

Sharma, S. (2000). Managerial interpretations and organizational context as predictors of corporate choice of environmental strategy. *Academy of Management Journal, 43,* 936–960.

Shrivastava, P. (1996). *Greening business*. Cincinnati, OH: Thomson Executive Press.

Starik, M., & Carroll, A. B. (1992). Strategic environmental management: Business as if the Earth really mattered. In D. Ludwig & K. Paul (Eds.), *Contemporary issues in the business environment* (pp. 143–169). Lewiston, PA: Edwin Mellen Press.

Starik, M., & Marcus, A. A. (2000). Introduction to the Special Research Forum on the Management of Organizations in the Natural Environment: A field emerging from multiple paths, with many challenges ahead. *Academy of Management Journal, 43*(4), 539–546.

Starik, M., & Rands, G. P. (1995). Weaving an integrated web: Multi-level and multi-systems perspectives of ecologically sustainable organizations. *Academy of Management Review, 20,* 908–935.

Suzuki, D. (1994). *Time to change*. Toronto, ON., Canada: Stoddart.

Winn, M. (1995). Corporate leadership and policies for the environment. In D. Collins & M. Starik (Eds.), *Research in corporate social policy and performance—Sustaining the natural environment: Empirical studies on the interface between nature and organizations* (pp. 127–162). Greenwich, CT: JAI.

EPISTEMIC COMMUNITIES

Generally, the notion of an epistemic community (EC) refers to socialities, such as disciplines, professions, or other kinds of expert groups, favoring a particular mode of production and use of knowledge. Such knowledgeable communities, which enjoy a substantial degree of autonomy, are highly significant in a society characterized by an increasing division of (knowledge) labor, the emergence of increasingly specialized occupations, and so forth. Societies and organizations may benefit from communicating with such knowledge-based expertise. However, reliance on ECs also entails a risk that efficiency or democracy may suffer.

Conceptual Overview

Basically, the *epistemic community* notion refers to the way in which expert groups deal with and operate on knowledge. As discussed by Burkart Holzner and John Marx in 1979, this notion signals a prime interest in the kinds of epistemic criteria that different communities apply and how these interpenetrate with the embedding social and cultural context. The discussion by Peter Haas in 1992 shows how the general EC idea may be further elaborated. For him, an EC is a network of professionals with recognized expertise and competence in a particular domain. Those who belong to such an EC may come from a variety of disciplines, but they should have (1) a shared set of normative and principled beliefs, (2) shared causal beliefs, (3) shared notions of validity, and (4) a common policy enterprise. Haas notices that such a characterization of ECs somewhat resembles Thomas Kuhn's sociological definition of a paradigm. Using the above criteria, it follows that interest groups that lack shared causal beliefs do not belong to the EC category, nor do disciplines or professions that lack those principled values, ethical standards, and common enterprise associated with ECs. To illustrate, he claims that while economists as a whole constitute a discipline or profession, Keynesians may constitute an EC, systematically contributing to a set of projects informed by their views, beliefs, and ideas.

A second highly influential source of inspiration for those who theorize about knowledge work within sciences, disciplines, professions, occupations, or the like, are the writings of Karin Knorr-Cetina. In her 1981 book, she portrays the manufacture of knowledge in scientific laboratories as a highly contextual and socially situated activity, where a multitude of diverse contingencies and interests interplay. Scientific laboratories should therefore be conceived as *transscientific fields,* mirroring how laboratories are constantly traversed and sustained by social relationships that transcend the site of research. Later, in her 1999 book, Knorr-Cetina introduces the notion of *epistemic culture* to signify, not the knowledge production per se, but the entire amalgams of arrangements and mechanisms deployed in its production. This brings the great diversity of specific epistemic cultures to the fore and suggests the power of this machinery to reconfigure both objects and scientists into fitting derivative devices.

Within organizational analysis, explicit references to the epistemic community notion appear predominantly in connection with attempts to extend or complement the discourse about the communities of practice. References to the works of Knorr-Cetina are a recurrent feature here. The 2001 article by John Seely Brown and Paul Duguid is particularly informative in making a clear distinction between *communities of practice,* referring to tightly knit groups working in close proximity, and loosely connected epistemic *networks of practice,* which refers to large occupational or professional groups extending beyond the firm, where members may neither know nor have met each other. By participating in a similar practice, they acquire communal know-how and tacit knowledge, which paves the way for communication and knowledge transfer.

Critical Commentary and Future Directions

The notion of EC and its cognates constitutes a field of inquiry that is attracting a growing interest in the literature. However, elaborated conceptual discussions are currently in short supply and the somewhat diverse strands presented above are among the few that are informative. While all focus on similar empirical settings, i.e., larger expert systems such as professions, occupations, and so forth, they use a slightly variegated terminology and add nuances by introducing a network and culture terminology. In doing that, they downplay somewhat the notion of community, which is understandable considering the idealist connotations associated with that notion (see Lars Lindkvist). However, such a shift may bring little relief as both the network and the culture notion appear notoriously difficult to define.

There is also a shortage of empirical studies investigating the benefits and the negative effects of relying on these kinds of expert systems. The study by Jacky Swan, Harry Scarbrough, and Maxine Robertson showing how networks of practice may restrain knowledge transfer, and Gernot Grabher's analysis of how project organizations tend to be embedded in a variety of professional and personal network systems, represent a few recent examples of the kind of studies that could be undertaken.

Finally, the dominating perspective in the literature strongly favors contextual, social, or sociocultural conceptions of knowledge work, and pays less attention to explanations in terms of individuality or to rational and generic aspects of knowledge production. As a result, there appears to be a need for alternative conceptions, where individuals and decontextualized knowledge processes matter more.

—*Lars Lindkvist*

See also Communities of Practice; Epistemology; Networks; Professions

Further Readings

Brown, J. S., & Duguid, P. (2001). Knowledge and organization: A social-practice perspective. *Organization Science, 12,* 198–213.

Grabher, G. (2004). Temporary architectures of learning: Knowledge governance in project ecologies. *Organization Studies, 25,* 1491–1514.

Haas, P. M. (1992). Introduction: Epistemic communities and international policy coordination. *International Organization, 46,* 1–35.

Holzner, B., & Marx, J. H. (1979). *Knowledge application: The knowledge system in society.* Boston: Allyn & Bacon.

Knorr-Cetina, K. D. (1981). *The manufacture of knowledge: An essay on the constructivist and contextual nature of science.* Oxford, UK: Pergamon Press.

Knorr-Cetina, K. D. (1999). *Epistemic cultures: How the sciences make knowledge.* Cambridge, MA: Harvard University Press.

Kuhn, T. S. (1970). *The structure of scientific revolutions.* Chicago: The University of Chicago Press.

Lindkvist, L. (2005). Knowledge communities and knowledge collectivities: A typology of knowledge work in groups. *Journal of Management Studies, 42,* 1189–1210.

Swan, J., Scarbrough, H., & Robertson, M. (2002). The construction of "communities of practice" in the management of innovation. *Management Learning, 33,* 477–496.

Epistemology

Conceptual Overview

Epistemology concerns the philosophy underpinning any given science. It is not the study of scientific methods (methodology), but the study of postulates, hypotheses, and the way that knowledge is produced in a given scientific field, designed to identify the origin of that knowledge, the logic of its articulation, and how its findings fit within the framework of an a posteriori evaluation. Epistemology denotes the idea of a theory of knowledge, including the connections constituted between the "human being," or knowing subject, and the "object" of his or her knowledge. Hence, it addresses issues that have to do with the extent to which a representation is appropriate. Two meanings of epistemology will be applied to organization: the organization as a tangible object (such as a given company) and the organization as a concept. The organization as an object raises the question of the independence (or not) of the object organization from the human being who observes it and who dwells within its spaces and shadows. We find here the duality between "positivism" and "constructivism."

The opposition between positivism and constructivism in organization science (OS) is a common one. Positivism argues that there is, in principle, one best way of apprehending the world of phenomena; constructivism sees that world as always existing in a relationship constituted by all the relevancies and interests of the knower. From the latter perspective, any best way will always be considered as such because some broader historical or social project has been able to establish it as such. Knowledge is contingent on its social and historical construction and the phenomena of social life have no necessary story attached to them. Such concerns raise the question of what constitutes an adequate representation of the world and of the relations between phenomena and the place of the human being who apprehends that world in which he or she is immersed. In a universe of "organizations" these are questions with significant consequences because if the organization has a necessary and sufficient one best way of being apprehended, then this stands as a revision of any other attempts to make sense of it; if, on the other hand, the organization is rather more of an effect of the varied ways in which differing people constitute, understand, and relate to it, then how are appropriate theoretical models built, with the aim of giving an understanding as well as a satisfactory application of actions within organizations? We can more dissociate than oppose, item by item, the positivist posture from the constructivist one:

Positivism

1. Ontological principle of reality of the principle of representation of the real (the reality is considered as existing and immediately accessible)
2. Principle of a determined universe: the "real" is given
3. Principle of objectivity (independent human being—object)
4. Principle of evidence (I see so I know)
5. Principle of the unique optimum

Constructivism

1. Principle of representation of the real (experience of the reality)
2. Principle of a constructed universe: the real is perceived
3. Principle of interaction of human being—object
4. Principle of argumentation of the logic (considered as rhetoric; we see what we want to see)
5. Principle of the intelligent action

Positivism embraces a set of propositions originally formulated by Auguste Comte as a doctrine based on a rationalist vision of nature as a general principle for the understanding of all phenomena pertaining to the social, in which research has to look for laws related to experienced causalities. It is premised on knowledge of facts rather than on theoretical intuition or introspection. It regards the type of certainty supplied by experimental sciences to be privileged and sees this as being based on empirical exposure to "facts" through structured and replicable experience. The understandings held by the subjects whose work underlies the materialization of the phenomena in question is inaccessible; positivism condemns any form of idealism in favor of realism. Thus, reflection should concentrate on the causal relations between phenomena and understand these in terms of law-like explanations.

By contrast, constructivism is a deconstruction of positivist postulates: Organizations have no given substance and cannot be represented as such. Organizations are places where people may be observed identifying relevant phenomena, which in turn constitutes their understanding of those phenomena. Thus, in this perspective, the knowledge that science must work with results from a prior organization of perceptions, such that constructivism sees the organization as a consequence of the autonomy of the perceptions that its many participants and observers make. The elements of systematicity and complexity of the phenomena will thus be an effect of the social constructions that are made. Consequently, a teleological hypothesis replaces a determinist hypothesis (positivism); the necessary ambiguity of the end—organization as a result of organizing—is given priority instead of an analysis of the efficient causes that might have produced the concrete organization.

We distinguish a radical constructivism, which denies the existence of any reality independent of the observer and ends on a total relativism of interpretation (subjectivism) from a moderated constructivism. Without definitely ruling on the construction of facts, moderated constructivism recognizes an interaction "observer"—"facts" as a foundation of the interpretation. In this perspective, there is, at first, a refusal of a natural evidence of a given sense for the "object" (i.e., for the organization here). These objects result from historic constructions. "Reality" is not outside the observer (unlike the "realistic" perspective, the simple one, where reality would offer itself in direct perception, as well as the "elaborated" one, where reality would offer itself through the mediation of a representation), but is a truly personal and collective invention.

The organization as "concept" raises the question of the status of the representation, in so far as, with organizations, as for any social object, we always catch it through a representation. The question of representation is one of the oldest questions of philosophy. It is related to the question of truth, i.e., the correspondence between ideas and objects. The notion of representation contains constants: It is a reproduction of a reality regarded from a certain point of view, as we find in the use of the term for theater and painting (Gareth Morgan discusses such approaches in OS).

The art of representation is seen to be truthful, to have achieved verisimilitude, when it is considered a fair or approximate imitation. The question that arises is that of the truth (or not) that exists beyond the representation, a truth which is in the object itself and not in the duplication. Representation is an ideal that offers only a limited account of reality. Representation also raises the problem of proofs. Representation eclipses foundations, in terms of what is real, actual, necessary, and determinate: Instead it offers valuation of what is preferable, achieved through discourse. Representation is more a project of coherence than a fact of equivalence with a reality. Representation raises the question of passive and active justification (it is the case of "selling" a model with a set of arguments of coherence, and internal relevance regarding the represented object).

Representation also refers to conviction about what is more important and relevant, as for instance when one searches for an effective power as a will to drive control within organizations (act for profit!). Representation has then the power to be a project for the "others" so that they mobilize their power to act in the sense proposed by the representation. Conventionally, the project of many organizational representations is seen to be to govern indecision in order to produce wealth, as in much of the discourse of strategy, for instance. Yet if, analytically, representation is a replica, where does the original come from? Is it previous to or outside the representation? What is it that lends credence and coherence to the representational impulses of one way of representing the phenomena rather than another, where one cannot assume that there is a reality independent of the means of representation that can act as a referee or umpire?

Representation establishes the represented object. It is the case when an organization is postulated as ever changing. Representation makes it exist to the point, ultimately, of being able to replace it. Think of the way that performance management indicators often end up being managed for their own sake, to make a good impression, while in doing so one actually neglects the underlying phenomena that these are meant to represent.

Representing is a reflexive expression, which consists in appropriating objects to incorporate within a conceptual scheme. Individuals, with their specific mentalities and shared discourses, create representations as a conscious tableaux or display (i.e., they are built upon a theatrical device). This display of "objects" means imagining them in a process in which others create them through a project articulating thought and action. It is a subjective activity of access to the world, but a world outside and inside the self at the same moment.

Representation also raises the question of conviction, i.e., that of the connections between human beings and their thoughts. Living experience and the representation are built at the same time. Representation coupled with conviction is a mode of destruction of doubts and uncertainty. The conviction accompanying representations is not a representation in itself. It is an act, at the same time passive (we submit ourselves because we are "overcome" by the force of a representation) and active (we shall then overcome those who are sent a representation). It is again the case when an organization is considered as being organized according to given standards.

Critical Commentary and Future Directions

The restricted definition of epistemology has been fruitful for contemporary European philosophic schools. It is particularly the case with Michel Foucault, who made a distinction between successive historic periods within which thought gets organized around those concepts it produces. Following Foucault, we can say that the notion of organization is not so much the result of an epistemology as much as an object of an epistemological production. It is then possible to emphasize that today we attend to an institutionalization of the idea of organization, i.e., the development of a belief in a situation where any sociality should be reasoned in terms of organizational categories (Henry Mintzberg). In its ideological version, this perspective is translated into managerialism, which considers organizational categories capable of being applied to all kind of social objects.

An epistemology of organizations raises the questions of the specification of organization as an observable empirical object and asks that we be clear about how we claim to know how to distinguish, among social objects, those that are specifically an organization.

OS is based on the specification of organizational elements. OS illustrates the argumentation proposed by Bruno Latour that its discourse refers to the organization and its categories as a "normal" questioning, as far as its statements are taken as facts and as far as all important agents are now produced and persuaded by the validity of the object. The eclipse of the social construction and the history of this construction are now legitimate in the positivist perspective just as in managerialism. Is organization a normal object? The utopia of the true representation in OS is the sign of a dream to make of this domain a social science, a dream at the same time darkening its profoundly political dimension, because, of course, what the science makes out organizations to be is a political choice. If they are chosen to be seen as sustainable enterprises or profit maximizers or exploiters of labor or as havens of rationality, then these decisions in favor of particular representations have political consequences.

The epistemology of organizations also raises the question of the status of an organizations' theory (OT) as being capable of founding OS. OS is based on the implicit postulate of the continuity "individual—group—community—company—organization—institutions—state—society" reduced to a fragment, the company, as the archetype of the organization. The theories of organizations drive then to a reification of the company in an ahistoric dimension, reducing their formal variety into the double dimension of the organization (as an entity) and organizing (as a process).

The way we use the term *organization* today is a recent and peculiar notion that, in OT, has been developing as a conceptual autonomy since the beginning of the 20th century. It results from conceptual efforts displayed by engineers and company leaders, to generate general principles of organization and management. It gathers knowledge acquired on organizational functioning, on the behavior of their various members (their motivations, the modalities that govern their processes of communication and those that govern the way they make decisions) and on the way they manage organizations. OT builds a rationalist project of the study of the most rational possible conditions of organizational functioning, which serve to further the development of organizational techniques. It is from this perspective that references to principles of organization are developed.

OTs present several advantages (Maria Bonnafous-Boucher): They traverse different disciplines of management; they offer a speculative dimension by contrast to the operational perspective, and by being theoretical, they appear to hold a premier role in the managerial fields of knowledge. In OT, the search for repetitions in the interdependence of "organization—environment" has led to the elaboration of the contingency program. In the name of contingency, the same causes produce the same effects according to the influence of determinants. And allomorphic organizational practices (i.e., observation of same practices), which are thus contingent, can then be considered as isomorphic (noncontingent), ending up with the idea that all organizations should operate in the same way. Should OTs be taken as an epistemology of organizations?

Let us also recall a parallelism established between institution and organization. Both terms operate according to their focus. "Institution" (i.e., established institutions) is also understood as "institutionalization" (i.e., the instituting modalities) just as "organization" is also convenient for "organizing." In both cases (institution and organization), it is also a question of considering these two objects as places of authority, observation, evaluation, and judgment and places of evidence for their instruments (particularly their instruments of direction). According to managerialism, the company (and its categories) would be the reference organization, and OS then should offer a scientific understanding of the institutions. In a way, by adopting organizational patterns, the institution is losing its legal and political characteristics. That is why it is then possible to speak about a "de-institutionalization of the institutions" and an "institutionalization of the organization." It is then a question of speaking about a world where societies would be dissolved into their constituting organizations, which are finally then considered as institutionalized organizations, which would allow one to think of the whole society as an organization.

—Yvon Pesqueux

See also Constructivism; Hermeneutics; Ideology; Logical Positivism; Metaphor and Organization; Ontology; Organizational Behavior; Organizational Rhetoric; Organizational Theory; Paradigms; Positivism; Realism; Relativism; Theory Building

Further Readings

Berger, G. (1941). *Recherche sur les conditions de la connaissance.* Paris: PUF.
Bonnafous-Boucher, M. (2005). *Anthropologie et gestion.* Paris: Economica.
Foucault, M. (1966). *Les mots et les choses.* Paris: Gallimard.
Foucault, M. (1969). *Archéologie du savoir.* Paris: Gallimard.
Latour, B. (1987). *Science in action: How to follow scientists and engineers.* Cambridge, MA: Harvard University Press.
Latour, B., & Woolgar, S. (1993). *La vie de laboratoire: La production des faits scientifiques.* Paris: La Découverte.
Mintzberg, H. (1989). *Mintzberg on management: Inside our strange world of organization.* New York: Free Press.
Morgan, G. (1996). *Images of organization.* London: Sage.

Equity Theory

Equity (E) is the state, ideal, or quality of being just, impartial, and fair. Aristotle defined E as synonymous with justice: the rectification of the law when it is insufficient given its universal character. In other words, the law considers human beings as equals in all their characteristics. Given that actual people are very different across fields, the general character of the law is often inadequate to understand the specific nature of each individual. As a result, the law can produce unfair outcomes at individual levels. Equity theory (ET) is therefore the attempt to face this dilemma.

Conceptual Overview

One of the most important difficulties that ET faces, given the fact that human beings are different, is its attachment to distributive justice. These interpersonal differences are so crucial to the individual that it is impossible to measure with a certain degree of precision the real impact on each individual of an equity-aimed intervention. Equality of resources, for example, has been defended as one simple way to achieve equity; however, the degree of happiness or welfare achieved by each individual, even assuming they began with the same level of resources, might be very different. Moreover, personality and luck are not the only variables to consider; desires and merit, effort and capacity must also be taken into account. Then one must ask how to achieve equity if human beings are so different, if one human being with the same resources achieves different results, both objectively (i.e., wealth) and subjectively (i.e., felicity).

Three big blocks of literature in ET might be useful to deal with the problem of equity, what can be called the libertarian, the liberal, and the communitarian approaches. For the libertarian, to achieve equity implies to take seriously the Kantian maxim that individuals should be taken always as ends and never as means. The state involvement is minimized, only assuring that human beings can enjoy their basic rights to property and life. Therefore, to be forced to contribute to another's welfare violates the rights of an individual because it violates the self-ownership principle: The first and most important possession of an individual is him- or herself. The problem, then, with the attempt to equalize is that it tends to intervene arbitrarily over the self-ownership of persons. Trying to cope with inequity creating artificial rules or norms can only produce worse effects on liberty because nobody can assure that a distributional system is not used under the effects of envy rather than justice.

The liberal position, with Rawls as its main personality, argues for freedom as a main value, but considers unacceptable that injustice be allowed in the name of liberty. Entitlements are often arbitrary (i.e., gene provisions of an individual), so nobody strictly "deserves" his or her talents or capacities. It is true, the liberals say, that envy exists and therefore it is important that any mechanism for equity and justice address this. Rawls argues that we are different but that we have an equal moral status that forces us to create impartial institutions. Impartial institutions can achieve equity, since they take the differences among human beings into consideration and assure that the arbitrary advantages of some ultimately work to produce better results for the less advantaged people (principle of difference). Under conditions of equality, under a "veil of ignorance," Rawls argues that rational persons, without knowing their advantaged or disadvantaged position in life and society, would argue for a principle of difference. Perfect equality would not be possible, but equity would be, since the natural and logical differences among humans would produce the best results available even for the less advantaged (under the principle of *maximin*).

The communitarian position criticizes the libertarian and the liberal ones. Against libertarians the argument is that they are defending entitlements, not freedom. Cohen shows that property seems to be the most important variable for Nozick because the appropriation is what defines a human being. Against the liberals, Sandel argues for the extremely abstract conception of the individual, where their defense fails to understand that persons are part of communities, defending moral values stemming from different sources rather than abstract ones stemming from individual possessions, capacities, or universal moral principles. To talk about equity, we must talk about the social networks that people have built to understand the world and relate with others.

Critical Commentary and Future Directions

Beyond the philosophical discussion within ET, the general mechanisms to achieve equity are also under discussion. There are different types of equity: subjective, relative, equal resources, rank order, and equal opportunity. Each of them takes into considerations different characteristics of the recipients, in order to calculate the level of equity: need, fitness, deserts, status, and position.

This typology (similar to that of Rae) allows one to classify the equity mechanisms into two broad categories: those that depend upon the characteristics of the recipients and those that do not. Moreover, it implies that there are at least three broad conceptions of equity at this level: parity (all treated equally), proportionality (divides according to the differences among participants), and priority (where the persons with the greatest claim to the good get it). At the end, equity can be achieved depending on the principal categories used: trying to create one form of equity can affect negatively other types of equity.

ET faces the necessity of evolving toward a more specific definition of the different types of possible *equities* and the interaction (both positive and negative) between different specific instruments to achieve equity in complex organizational and social settings. This discussion will yield more instruments to deal with the challenge of developing more E, but it is also clear that the values and ideological elements involved in the process of instrumentation of ET guarantee a constant debate with important difficulties to produce substantial practical instruments to achieve E in concrete situations.

—*David Arellano-Gault*

Further Readings

Cohen, G. A. (1995). *Self-ownership, freedom and equality*. Cambridge, MA: Cambridge University Press

Elster, J. (1993). *Local justice*. London: Sage.

Karen, S., & Hegtvedt, K. (1983). Distributive justice, equity, and equality. *Annual Review of Sociology, 9,* 217–241.

Nozick, R. (1974). *Anarchy, state, and utopia*. New York: Basic Books.

Rae, D. (1981). *Equalities*. Cambridge, MA. Harvard University Press.

Rawls, J. (1971). *A theory of justice*. Cambridge, MA: Harvard University Press.

Sandel, M. (1982). *Liberalism and the limits of justice*. Cambridge, MA: Cambridge University Press.

Young, P. (1994). *Equity: In theory and practice*. Princeton, NJ: Princeton University Press.

Ergonomics

Ergonomics is the study of human beings and their interactions with objects and systems in the environment. Its aim is to use knowledge about human abilities and limitations to design and build objects and systems that match human capabilities and limitations, thereby optimizing human well-being and overall system performance.

Conceptual Overview

Ergonomics is generally thought of as a relatively new discipline, with Hywel Murrell having played a central role in defining it in 1949. The term *ergonomics*, meaning the science of work, was first used in 1857 by Wojciech Jastrzebowski. It stems from the Greek *ergon*, meaning work, and *nomos*, meaning natural laws. Ergonomics draws heavily on the disciplines of psychology (cognitive, social, and organizational), anatomy, physiology, and engineering. The effectiveness of the interaction between humans and machines is affected by the degree of fit between the human operator and the machine he or she is operating. In practice, this means that the interface between the human and the machine or system, and the way the human and machine are intended to interact, should be designed to fit the human needs, rather than as a technological or aesthetic solution to an engineering problem. For example, a car designed for an average man may be virtually undrivable by a small woman. Fitting that car with seats that can vary the driving position, and a steering column that is similarly adjustable, results in a machine that is equally usable by both drivers. Within the car, the positioning, shape and feel of the controls, the design of the speedometer, and the layout of the dashboard also form part of an ergonomist's work. Infrequently used controls should be placed where they are unlikely to interfere with regular driving activities, important displays such as speed should occupy a more central position, and both controls and displays should behave as the driver would expect. These control and display issues are often seen as the core business of ergonomics; however, with the increasing range and complexity both of technology and of the systems of which they form a part, the scope of the discipline has widened. It now encompasses issues from crew resource management, teamwork, and communication to protective work wear and safety provision.

The user of the tool, equipment, or system is therefore at the heart of good ergonomic design. Furthermore, the user will be using the equipment in certain environmental conditions that may place a range of other demands on him or her. For example, there might be excessive noise or other task-related distractions. Some users may be very experienced and have a high level of expertise in using a system, others may be novice users with limited understanding of what is required, and there may also be a wide range of intermittent or occasional users. For example, it is reasonable to expect that a great deal of training is needed before it is possible to use the controls in the cockpit of a plane, whereas it must be possible to know immediately how to use a machine that dispenses parking tickets with no training or prior knowledge. These different users have different needs of the system, the interface, and the technology generally. The ergonomist therefore needs to consider the range of the human capabilities and expectations and also the features of the environment in which the system is operating in order to develop usable tools, machines, and jobs. Typically ergonomists consider the human-machine *system*, each element of which has its own strengths and limitations.

While the origins of ergonomics stem from wartime concerns over human performance (efficiency and effectiveness) under stressful conditions, ergonomic concerns clearly encompass both work and nonwork activities. Researchers, notably Donald Norman, have discussed how many of the frustrations of modern life stem from poor design. While most people are familiar with the complications of figuring out how to get the best out of a cell phone or video recorder, poor design can affect one's use of objects as basic as a door. People may pull when they should push, or try to open a door at the hinge side. Typically, people blame themselves for such mistakes; however, ergonomists would argue that the blame should be placed on the designer for not considering the humans that will use the technology.

Domain of Ergonomics

The driving principle of ergonomics is that the user should be placed at the center of the human-machine system, whether the system is a door, a job, or a mobile phone. This is the essence of user-centered design: The focus is on making the environment *usable* for the humans operating within it. This means that things should do what one expects them to do. They should provide the functionality one requires and should be easy to learn with appropriate training or instruction, and easy to use as far as is possible. If a person does make a mistake, he or she should have the chance to rectify that mistake before the result is catastrophic, and the consequences of what the person does should be apparent at the point at which he or she interacts with the system. In order to accommodate these requirements, system designers need to know who the users will be and what they want, need, and expect from any system in use.

Broadly speaking, ergonomics can be divided into three domains.

Physical ergonomics concentrates on the human body and how it responds to physical and physiological load. Designing a workplace that physically accommodates the people who will work within it requires consideration of size, space and accessibility, reach and visual clarity, noise and temperature, environmental risks and danger, and physical demands of the job. The knowledge base for this branch of ergonomics tends to be anatomy, anthropometry (the measurement of the dimensions of people), and physiology. Employers are legally required to ensure their establishments are safe and healthy places to work, and that they do not pose a risk of injury, either through accidents or mistakes, or through prolonged loading resulting in musculoskeletal disorder—for example, repetitive strain injury. This branch of ergonomics goes a long way toward ensuring that employers meet these requirements. It is perhaps most closely aligned to the classic description of "fitting the task to the man."

While the ideal situation would be to design a work environment from scratch to take account of these concerns, frequently the ergonomic contribution is a remedial one. Problems in the work environment are identified and solutions sought. These may include redesigning the equipment, tools, or technology to make it more user friendly. Provision of adjustable furniture and instruction on how to use it effectively can overcome many musculoskeletal problems associated with office work. Redesigning the structure of the task, perhaps incorporating rest breaks or task variety to limit static loading, may similarly overcome problems of fatigue and stress. Improving the physical environment by introducing air-conditioning to manage extremes of temperature or controlling noise levels by installing double glazing may further improve an environment that otherwise makes its users feel uncomfortable or ill.

Cognitive ergonomics focuses on understanding people's mental models of systems and of the world, and appreciating human psychological limitations on information processing. While the physical environment clearly presents specific hazards and challenges to people at work, much contemporary ergonomic activity is focused on mental workload and making systems usable. Mental models are continuously evolving internal representations of objects and actions and the relationships between them. They are typically incomplete and unstable, but tend to develop in both detail and accuracy through repeated interaction with the system. At a basic level, turning a knob clockwise to increase the value of whatever the knob affects is an illustration of a good mapping of the physical environment to people's mental model of how things work. At a more complex level, the desktop metaphor originally developed for the Apple Macintosh computer captures an existing model and overlays it onto a new technology. People know what a "desk" is and what it is for—they "put things on" it, things like "documents" or "folders" or "tools" (applications). Using the metaphor (model) that people are familiar with, Apple constructed a user interface that tallies with that existing mental model. While this is now taken for granted, when it was first developed it was a major breakthrough in user interface design and now is a standard system image across most operating systems. This concept is used in aviation where the term *situation awareness* is used by Mica Endsley (among many other researchers) to describe how aircrew build a picture of what is going on around them, what it means, and how things will develop in the future. The study of mental models as used in situation awareness has become a major focus of a large body of research in aviation and related areas.

Mental models are very useful to system designers; however, the question is raised as to whose mental model a system should represent. With repeated use of a system, people develop more sophisticated mental models of it, so the model an expert user may have could be quite different from the model of a novice user. Moreover, a system designer is likely to have yet another mental model of the system under design. Thus, again the concern is for the end users of a system, and ideally they should be involved in the design and testing of any new system.

Another dimension of cognitive ergonomics is consideration of how people use information to make decisions, and also how mistakes can arise. The basic elements of performance are sensing, information storage, information processing and retrieval, and action. Both humans and machines can do most of these most of the time, but they are not equally good at all of them in all circumstances. Understanding what people attend to, what they remember, and how they use available information to make decisions further contributes to ergonomists' understanding of how to design for users. People are good at organizing information, drawing inferences, and making decisions based on often incomplete information. However, people are not as good as computers at retrieving (recalling) information that has been stored for a long time, or performing complex calculations quickly and accurately. Therefore, the allocation of tasks to different elements of a human-machine system should reflect these differing abilities. Cell phone designers therefore group together related functions in a hierarchical fashion and offer structured menus that limit the available options at any point. This directs the users to groups of relevant functions rather than overloading them with too many choices, some of which are extremely unlikely to be needed at that stage in an interaction. Inbuilt storage of phone numbers and other personal details saves the user from the effort of having to recall all contacts. The system designer needs to consider which aspects of a task are best done by machine and which are best left to the human decision maker.

Organizational ergonomics considers the macro environment in which systems interact. It incorporates concerns over how activity is organized and the ways in which performance is controlled in the social environment. This may include organizational policies and procedures, issues of motivation, and the culture and values—particularly attitudes to safety and risk—that shape the work environment. Such considerations expand the issue of usability to incorporate issues of acceptability—does a new system not only do what is needed, but does it also do so in a way that is acceptable to those who are required to use it?

Some of these organizational developments stem from changes in technology, others from changes in economics or work values. The rise of location-free working, for example, while facilitated by the Internet and broadband communications technology, presents the ergonomist with issues such as how to manage information and people working at a distance and how to ensure that health and safety is maintained, but also how to ensure that the individual social needs are met and that the organization's culture and values are upheld both for the individual and by the individual. In this context, interventions may include activities that are not directly performance related but affect the way the job is done or how the individual is managed. Issues of motivation, job satisfaction, work scheduling, and organizational policies may all need reconsidering as the nature of work changes and the difference between work and home is reduced.

Critical Commentary and Future Directions

Much of the original "knobs and dials" focus that was seen to be the early bones of ergonomics is now ubiquitous. Good practice in design and basic heuristics of mapping, grouping, and chunking are so ingrained in contemporary design as to be virtually invisible (until you find an object that you habitually misuse!). The development of more sophisticated Internet and communication technology (ICT) has presented ergonomists with a new range of challenges and opportunities. Indeed, an entirely new field of study, human computer interaction (HCI), has come into being to address these issues. Still, there remains a tendency among designers to focus on what is technically achievable rather than what is required by the end user; to put it another way, there is expanding functionality at the expense of usability. As a result, most of the functionality of everyday technology is never used by most users. Moreover, the provision of such complexity serves to confuse novice users and can prevent them from engaging with the technology at all.

As a counterpoint to this, and coupled with changes to production technology and product markets, and better identification and profiling of specific user groups, greater differentiation of products tailored to particular user needs becomes possible. This may range from a phone with only basic functionality, through phones designed as a fashion statement, to highly integrated mobile technologies and personal digital assistants (PDAs). Each product meets the needs of the particular group for which it is designed. While these groups may not present any unique problems for the ergonomics community, they do combine issues in novel ways that result in design trade-offs being required. Couple this with the increased rate of product development, and limited opportunity for user testing, and the ergonomist's role becomes increasingly challenging. Early involvement in systems design is usually seen as the solution to this issue; designing for usability rather than seeing usability as an add-on in later stages of system development has long been recognized as the most effective way of operating.

Advances in technology also give rise increasingly to new forms of work and new forms of interaction between colleagues, within teams and across boundaries. Much of this work is now electronically mediated; physical collocation is no longer a requirement of team membership. Designing systems to support such virtual teamworking is perhaps one of the biggest challenges of the ergonomist generally and of HCI specialists in particular. Computer-supported cooperative work (CSCW) is different from cooperative work within a collocated team: It can be both more democratic and more emotive. Shy team members may feel more able to voice opinions over an email than they would in a meeting, but the generally more casual style of conversing via email coupled with the lack of physical cues (body language, voice tone, and inflection) to the meaning of messages may result in small perceived slights becoming major arguments and flame wars ensue. Developing an appropriate protocol for such interactions—rules of engagement—remains a challenge.

As systems become increasingly complex, whether through technological development or advances in social understanding, the possibilities for error and mistake potentially grow also. While it may be feasible to "design out" the chance of making certain mistakes, there are circumstances in which that may be undesirable. In safety-critical systems, for example, there is a natural desire to design out the possibility of accidental mistakes. However, if this reduces a skilled role to one of automation or artificial intelligence, there may be social consequences for the organization as a whole. Risk homeostasis, for example, suggests that each person assumes that a certain level of risk is tolerable. Forcing one to be less risky in some situations only creates "spare risk" that may induce more risky behavior elsewhere. Plus, on the rare occasions when skilled performance is required (in the case of system failure), the operators may be so far removed from their technical knowledge that they cannot solve the problem they are presented with. Removing all human agency in a system is unlikely to be positive for the humans concerned, therefore the designer has difficult choices to make in the allocation of function and responsibility to human or machine. Rather than designing a system such that the individual cannot engage in an action that could lead to an accident, it may be preferable to rely on perceptions of risk to induce vigilance, coupled with the provision of warning signals within a culture that emphasizes safety and safe behavior.

New forms of interaction continue to develop. Effective speech recognition, high-quality graphics, and increasing variety in control devices allow for new combinations of experiences with technology. Given the rate of change of technology, it is becoming increasingly possible for the challenges of multiple users and contrasting user needs to be accommodated by adaptive systems that respond to the user's level of expertise. Understanding the development of expertise and translating that into adaptive or learning systems is a rapidly developing area with huge promise for humane and informed working. However, as with most developments in this domain, the locus of control in system operation still needs to reside with the user for social as well as psychological reasons.

Fundamentally, the integration of ergonomics into all aspects of design at an early stage has been and remains the key challenge to the profession. The tendency to accept human flexibility as the preferred solution to bad design should not be acceptable.

—*Ann Davis and Patrick Tissington*

See also Cognitive Mapping; Human–Computer Interaction; Information Processing; Sociotechnical Systems

Further Readings

Edholm, O. G., & Murell, K. F. H. (1974). *The Ergonomics Society: A history, 1949–1970.* London: Taylor & Francis. (Published as a supplement to *Ergonomics*)

Endsley, M. R., & Garland, D. L. (Eds.). (2000). *Situation awareness analysis and measurement.* Mahwah, NJ: LEA.

Karwowski, W. (2005). Ergonomics and human factors: The paradigms for science, engineering, design, technology and management of human-compatible systems. *Ergonomics, 48,* 436–463.

McCormick, E. J., & Sanders, M. S. (1992). *Human factors in engineering and design* (7th ed.). New York: McGraw-Hill.

Norman, D. A. (1988). *The psychology of everyday things.* New York: Basic Books.

Wickens, C. D., & Hollands, J. G. (2000). *Engineering psychology and human performance.* Englewood Cliffs, NJ: Prentice Hall.

ETHNICITY

Ethnicity is about the ways that groups of people define themselves or are defined by others as a group with a shared common background with regard to history and culture. In the current era of globalization, contacts between groups with various cultural and historical backgrounds, both inside and between nation states, are increasing. This has resulted in a growing interest in the concept of ethnicity, inside as well as outside of organizations.

Conceptual Overview

Ethnicity has been the subject of numerous debates and definitions in the past decades. The two extreme poles in defining the concept have been the essentialist and nonessentialist, or constructionist, positions. The essentialists emphasize the primordial aspect of ethnicity, in which the source of communality is to be found in the common cultural content and the shared history of the members of an ethnic group. The second group opts for a contextual and situational approach to ethnicity, in which the focus is on the construction of an imagined sameness and history in order to emphasize the markers of otherness situated in time and space.

The groundbreaking book of the anthropologist Fredrik Barth, *Ethnic Groups and Boundaries: The Social Organization of Cultural Difference,* resulted in a shift toward a more nonessentialist approach to ethnicity within the social sciences. His emphasis on ethnic boundary instead of the "cultural stuff" that it encloses had a great impact on the perception of ethnicity as a dynamic construction of otherness rather than a focus on *being* the other. In Barth's analysis, individuals are not captured within their social and cultural settings, but are people who consciously pursue goals.

In this way, Barth offers an approach of ethnic and other social identities as somewhat fluid, situationally contingent, and contextual. Barth's focus on boundaries as a means of understanding group formation and dynamics could be compared with an influential theory in social psychology: social identity theory (SIT). Compared with Barth's emphasis on boundaries, SIT holds that individuals tend to classify themselves and others into social categories that have a significant effect on social interaction. The formation of social categories is a result of the comparisons made both inside and outside the group. In this sense, individuals' identity formation is approached from the group level and considered in opposition to the other (or rather "others"). The difference between Barth's approach and SIT is that whereas Barth emphasizes the relational and contextual aspect of ethnic formation, SIT focuses mainly on the self-definition of the group. However, Stella Nkomo and Taylor Cox observe a shift that took place at the beginning of the 1990s, when some SIT scholars started to choose the social construction approach in relation to the topic of diversity in organizations.

Coming back to the social sciences, the most recent approach with respect to ethnicity is to distance from the two mentioned extremes (essentialist and nonessentialist) and try to find a way in between: the third way. This means at the same time to accept that ethnicity has to do with certain shared patterns of culture or history, and yet to avoid considering these patterns as unchangeable and fixed essences. In this view, these shared patterns from the past are subject to change in time and in relation to a variety of locations and situations. As Stuart Hall puts it, as soon as an ethnic group lays claims to a shared past, the past undergoes transformation since the claim is situated in the present time and locality. In this way, ethnicity is both about being and becoming: *being* through the existence of certain cultural or historical markers of otherness, and *becoming* since these markers are constructed, and for that matter situated, in the present context.

Three Approaches to Ethnicity in Organizations

The issue of ethnicity within organizations has been part of the broader focus on diversity in organizations. The great impact of the functionalist approach of power within organizations has made us believe for a long time that the natural processes within modern organizations would result in selecting the most qualified person for a job. This selection of a perfect match for the organization was assumed to be neutral with regard to gender, race, or ethnicity. Influenced by this line of approach, many studies have pointed to a lack of qualifications among ethnic minorities as the reason for their exclusion from the workforce. Following the meritocratic principle, these scholars of the so-called deficit approach believe that when migrants improve their skills, they will be able to participate in the labor market on an equal basis. In this way, the notion of a "norm employee" has often been related to quality and availability: The norm employee is an assumingly disembodied worker, a worker without gender or ethnicity.

This point of view has met with much criticism from the side of gender and race studies. Joan Acker, for example, shows that this seemingly neutral notion of the disembodied worker is anything but neutral; it is gendered. Various other scholars have shown that the norm employee has a certain ethnicity, the dominant ethnicity. They argue that the construction of the norm is influenced by culturally and somatically desired images existing within organizations. These images contribute to certain processes of inclusion or exclusion within organizations in which some have better access to higher (power) positions than others. Thus, it is not accidental that mostly men of dominant ethnicities occupy the top positions, while women and ethnic minorities are facing the so-called glass ceiling in their careers within modern organizations. While the deficit approach ignores the issue of power difference as a factor for exclusion, the gender/race studies bring power, in the sense of domination, back to the core of organizations. In these studies, the focus is mainly on the ways that ethnic minorities have been denied entrance and proper participation because they are discriminated against by the dominant parties within organizations.

The third approach to ethnicity within organizations, known as the culturalist approach, is the one in which ethnic diversity is not seen as the base of a problem (be it deficit or discrimination) but rather as something that could be approached in a positive way. The idea is that knowledge of different cultural contents enables the members and especially the managers of organizations to develop the competence to deal with the issues raised by cultural/ethnic differences within organizations. The assumption is that an increased level of cultural consciousness will provide room for productive interaction within organizations. This implies the belief that knowledge of different cultures will contribute to a smoother interaction between the members of those cultures. Within the culturalist approach, attention mainly focuses on the cultural contents of ethnic groups as exclusively different.

Critical Commentary and Future Directions

In spite of the influential contributions of some of the above-mentioned approaches, they do not seem to reach far enough. The main problem of these perspectives on organizations is their rather essentialist approach of ethnic groups as closed entities with fixed cultural contents. The members of the ethnic groups are considered either as incompetent to fit the organization or are discriminated against because they are different. Even in the case of the culturalist approach in which the possible value of ethnic diversity is underscored, the viewpoint remains essentialist. This approach does not consider the contextual and situational ways in which individual members of groups shape and reshape their ethnicity through interaction with other individuals. Also, these approaches neglect the possibility of a hybrid positioning within organizations in which individual members could combine elements from various available cultural and ethnic resources.

In order to work toward more inclusive organizations in which diversity is not considered as something incidental but as the point of departure of the organization, it is important to distance oneself from categorical thinking, which attempts to explain all human actions and motivation through the fixed and closed categories of which they are supposed to form a part. People are not prisoners of their culture or their ethnicity; they have a certain agency and subjectivity toward their background, although this is a limited form of agency. This means that organizational members are in some ways subjected to their backgrounds and to the various settings of which they are a part, yet they are not blind reproducers. It is in relation to others that individuals make a selection from the various discourses of which they are a part, and through these selections they shape and reshape their (ethnic) boundaries within a given context and situation. Departing from ethnic or cultural categories to understand the actions of organizational members does not allow one to put these actions into a broader perspective and to include all the factors needed to understand connections and conflicts within organizations. For this, one must create more space for organizational processes of inclusion and exclusion from which the choices of organizational members are to be understood. In order to do that, one needs to depart from the situational logic of practice, whereby one can situate the choices of members and their strategies. By doing this, one is able to broaden the context of analysis and include other factors such as power relations, the history of the organization or the unit, and the societal context, to name but a few, in order to understand ethnic interactions and possible exclusions based on ethnicity.

To do this, one needs to distance oneself from an instrumental and limited approach to ethnicity within organizations, in which the core attention is on integrating difference into the organization, be it through compensating for the deficit or by eliminating discrimination. One needs to adopt an integral approach to diversity within organizations in which ethnicity is approached not as a given, and taken-for-granted, category but as a category in motion, shaped and reshaped in relation to others and influenced by various processes and discourses within organizations. In this sense, one needs to make room for a new approach to ethnicity within organizations in which there is space to understand individual choices and practices through the ways they are positioned within the intersection of various contextual and organizational discourses. The work of Roosevelt Thomas emphasizes individual differences with respect to managing diversity within organizations. But one could also think about the conditions that enable experimenting with ethnic boundaries within organizations, allowing new mixtures and hybrid positioning instead of stimulating ethnic groups to protect their boundaries and to use their ethnicity strategically within various power struggles. Therefore, more ethnographic studies on ethnicity within organizations that pay attention to spoken and nonspoken patterns of inclusion and exclusion are needed, studies that depart from daily practices and processes within organizations and dare to use unorthodox ways of approaching ethnicity in organizations.

—*Halleh Ghorashi*

See also Anthropology; Cross-Cultural Management; Cultural Intelligence; Globalization; Identity; Power; Social Identity Theory; Socialization

Further Readings

Acker, J. (1992). Gendering organizational theory. In A. J. Mills & P. Tancred (Eds.), *Gendering organizational analysis* (pp. 248–260). Newbury Park, CA: Sage.

Barth, F. (1969). *Ethnic groups and boundaries: The social organization of cultural difference.* Boston: Little Brown.

Cox, T., Jr. (1994). *Cultural diversity in organizations.* San Francisco: Berret-Koehler.

Hall, S. (1990). Cultural identity and diaspora. In J. Rutherford (Ed.), *Identity: community, culture, difference* (pp. 222–237). London: Lawrence & Wishart.

Hardy, C., & Clegg, S. R. (1996). Some dare call it power. In S.R. Clegg & C. Hardy (Eds.), *Studying organization: Theory & method* (pp. 368–387). London: Sage.

Nkomo, S. M., & Cox, T., Jr. (1997). Diverse identities in organizations. In S. Clegg, C. Hardy, & W.R. Nord (Eds.), *The Sage handbook of organization studies* (pp. 338–356). London: Sage.

Thomas, R., Jr. (1999). *Building a house for diversity: How a fable about a giraffe and an elephant offers new strategies for today's workforce.* New York: Amacom.

ETHNOGRAPHY

Like many if not most social science terms, *ethnography* is a word with a history and multiple meanings. In its most general sense, ethnography refers to the study and representation of culture. It is a research practice that many claim to be the most scientific of the humanities and the most humanistic of the sciences and has become something of a storytelling institution possessing a good deal of scholarly legitimacy. Ethnography claims a sort of documentary status by the fact that a researcher, for a time, lives with and, to a degree, lives *like* those who are studied. A logic of discovery rather than a logic of verification governs the practice in both its research and representational phases.

These are matters that are more or less given. They are not up for debate. One becomes an ethnographer by going out and doing it (and writing it up). Fieldwork of the immersive sort is by and large expected of those in the trade. Yet fieldwork practices are also biographically and situationally varied—spectaculary so. Studies differ in terms of working style, place, pace, time, and evidentiary approaches. They also vary by textual styles and, like fieldwork approaches, they change over time as new ways of doing old things and old ways to do new things emerge and establish a hold on at least some ethnographers. Contemporary students of culture emphasize representational forms and thus look to define ethnography in terms of its topical, stylistic, and rhetorical features. Earlier and more traditional or conventional uses of the term highlight the methods and evidence an ethnographer relies on when fashioning a cultural description.

Conceptual Overview

The origins of ethnography are sometimes traced to the unknown sources of the Greek historian Herodotus, but modern versions of ethnography did not begin to emerge until the 19th century. A problem faced by the early ethnographers was just how to set off their own cultural depictions as different in kind from the writings of others such as travelers, missionaries, adventurers, and governmental and military officials. Anticipating the eventual emergence of scientific cultural study, a member of the pioneering *Societes des Observateurs de l'Homme,* Joseph-Maria Dégerando, suggested in 1800 that the problem "with observations of explorers on savages is their incompleteness [which was] only to be expected given the shortness of their stay, the division of their attention, and the absense of any regular tabulation of their findings." While the beginnings of a professional ethnography appear during the early 19th century, another 100 or so years would pass before a more or less intensive form of fieldwork would become the recognized method of ethnography.

The turn to firsthand experience in ethnography is credited in Britain to Bronislaw Malinowski, a Polish anthropologist, who, under house arrest by the British and conveniently confined to the South Pacific for the duration of World War I, found himself living alongside the natives of the Trobriand Islands for several years. In America, Franz Boas is credited with pushing the ethnographer from the university and museums into the lifeworlds of those about whom they wrote. The crucial contribution of both men was to urge students to stop relying on secondhand reports (correspondent or native) and to go to the field themselves to collect their own data.

By the late 1920s, fieldwork and the image of a trained fieldworker engaged in participant observation by living with and (with some reservations) living like the natives under study had become the cornerstone of ethnography. In the clever phrasing of Clifford Geertz in his 1974 work, the goal of contemporary ethnographic fieldwork is "to figure out from what the native says and does, what the devil he thinks he's up to, the result being an interpretation of the way a people live that is neither imprisoned within their mental horizons, an ethnography of witchcraft written by a witch, nor systematically deaf to the distinct tonalities of their existence, the ethnography of witchcraft written by a geometer." While Geertz's interpretive practices are not always acceptable to all ethnographers, his means are certainly taken for granted—to learn of culture "from what the native says and does." Such learning typically begins with fieldwork, but fieldwork itself is now viewed as only a part of ethnographic work, necessary but not sufficient to understand ethnography as both a process and a product.

Critical Commentary and Future Directions

Viewed as a process, there are three discernible activity phases—moments—associated with ethnography. The first moment concerns the collection of information or data on a specified culture. The second refers to the construction of an ethnographic report—in particular, the compositional practices used by an ethnographer to fashion a cultural portrait. The third moment of ethnography deals with the reading and reception an ethnography receives across relevant audience segments both narrow and broad. Each phase raises distinctive problems.

The most attention in the social sciences has been directed to the first moment of ethnography—fieldwork. This form of social research is both a consequence of and a reaction to the cultural studies of the mid- to late 19th and early 20th centuries. There is, however, a good deal of variation in terms of just what activities are involved in fieldwork and, more critically, just how such activities result in a written depiction of culture. Current practices include intensive interviewing, participant observation, count-and-classify survey work, taking part in everyday routines or occasioned ceremonies engaged in by those studied, the collecting of samples of native talk and behavior across a range of social situations, and so on. There is now a rather large literature designed to help novice or veteran fieldworkers carry out ethnographic research.

Yet much of the advice offered in fieldwork manuals defies codification and lacks the consensual approval of those who produce ethnographies. Field notes, for example, are more or less de rigueur in terms of documenting what is learned in the field, but there is little agreement as to what a standard field note—much less a collection of field notes—might be. Moreover, how one moves from a period of lengthy in situ study to a written account presumably based on such study is by no means clear. Despite 70 or so years of practice, fieldwork remains a sprawling and quite diverse activity and is quite likely to remain that way.

The second moment of ethnography—writing it up—has by and large been organized by a genre termed *ethnographic realism*. It is a genre that has itself shifted over time from a relatively unreflective, closed, and general ("holistic") description of native sayings and doings to a more tentative, open, and partial interpretation of native sayings and doings. Yet realism remains a governing style for a good deal of ethnography, descriptive or interpretive. It is marked by a number of compositional conventions that include, for example, the suppression of the individual cultural member's perspective in favor of a typified or common denominator native's point of view, the placement of a culture within a timeless ethnographic present, and a claim for descriptive or interpretive validity based on the author's "being there" (fieldwork) experience.

Some ethnographers, though by no means all, express a degree of dissatisfaction with ethnographic realism. Partly in response to critics located outside ethnographic circles who wonder just how personal experience serves as the basis for a scientific study of culture, some ethnographers make visible—or, more accurately, textualize—their discovery practices and procedures. *Confessional ethnography* results when the fieldwork process itself becomes the focus in an ethnographic text. Its highly reflexive composition rests on moving the fieldworker to center stage and displaying how the writer comes to know a given culture. While often carefully segregated from an author's realist writings, confessional ethnography frequently manages to convey a good deal of the same sort of cultural knowledge put forth in conventional realist works but in a more personalized fashion. Other recognized genres utilized for ethnographic reporting are available as well.

A good deal of the narrative variety of ethnographic writing is a consequence of the post-1970s spread of the specialized and relatively insular disciplinary aims of anthropology and, to a lesser degree, sociology. Growing interest in the contemporary idea of culture—as something held by all identifiable groups, organizations, and societies—has put ethnography in play virtually everywhere. No longer is ethnography organized simply by geographic region, society, or community. Adjectival ethnographies have become common, and sizable literatures can be found in such areas as medical ethnography, organizational ethnography, conversation ethnography, school ethnography, occupational ethnography, family ethnography, and many more. The results of the intellectual and territorial moves of both away and at-home ethnography include a proliferation of styles across domains and an increase in the number of experimental or provisional forms in which ethnography is cast.

This expansion of ethnographic interests, methods, and styles is a product of the third moment of ethnography—the reading of ethnographic texts by particular audiences and the kinds of responses these texts appear to generate. Of particular interest are the categories of readers an ethnographer recognizes and courts through the topical choices, analytic techniques, and composition practices displayed in a text. Three audience categories stand out. Collegial readers are those who follow particular ethnographic domains most avidly. They are usually the most careful and critical readers of one another's work and the most familiar with the past and present of ethnography. General social science readers, a second category, operate outside of ethnographic circles. These are readers attracted to a particular ethnography because the presumed facts (and perhaps the arguments) conveyed in the work help further their own research agendas. Finally, there are some who read ethnography for pleasure more so than professional enlightenment. Certain ethnographic works attract a large, unspecialized, lay audience for whom the storytelling and allegorical nature of an ethnography is salient. Such readers look for familiar formats—the traveler's tale; the adventure story; the investigative report; and, perhaps most frequently, the popular ethnographic classics of the past—when appraising the writing. Ironically, the ethnographer charged with being a novelist manqué by colleagues and other social scientists is quite likely to be the ethnographer with the largest number of readers.

For each reader segment, particular ethnographic styles are more or less attractive. Collegial readers may take in stride what those outside the field find inelegant, pinched, and abstruse. Moreover, the growing segmentation across collegial readers suggests that many may be puzzled as to what nominal ethnographic colleagues are up to with their increasingly focused research techniques and refined, seemingly indecipherable prose styles. This creates something of a dilemma for ethnographers for it suggests the distance between the general reader and the ethnographic specialist as well as the distance between differing segments of ethnographic specialists themselves is growing. While ethnography itself is in little or no danger of vanishing, those who read broadly across ethnographic fields may be fewer in number than in generations past. This is a shame for, strictly speaking, an unread ethnography is no ethnography at all.

—*John Van Maanen*

See also Anthropology; Consumer Culture; Corporate Culture; Cross-Cultural Management; Emic; Enterprise Culture; Grounded Theory; Interactionism; Literary Theory; National Culture; Narratives; Organizational Anthropology; Organizational Culture; Organizational Ethnography; Organizational Rituals; Organizational Subcultures; Politics of Organizational Culture; Popular Culture; Qualitative Approaches; Reflexivity; Symbolic Interactionism

Further Readings

Agar, M. (1980). *The professional stranger.* New York: Academic Press.

Behar, R. (1996). *The vulnerable observer.* Boston: Beacon Press.

Bernard, H. R. (2001). *Research methods in anthropology.* Walnut Creek, CA: Alta Mira Press.

Burawoy, M., Burton, A., Ferguson, A., & Fox, K. J. (1991). *Ethnography unbound: Power and resistance in the modern metropolis.* Berkeley: University of California Press.

Clifford, J. (1983). On ethnographic authority. *Representations, 1,* 118–146.

Clifford, J., & Marcus, G. E. (Eds.). (1986). *Writing culture.* Berkeley: University of California Press.

Dégerando, J-M. (1969). *The observation of savage peoples* (F. C. T. Moore, Trans.). Berkeley: University of California Press. (Original work published 1800)

Emerson, R. B., Fretz, R. I., & Shaw, L. (1995). *Writing ethnographic fieldnotes.* Chicago: University of Chicago Press.

Geertz, C. (1973). *The interpretation of cultures.* New York: Basic Books.

Geertz, C. (1974). From the natives' point of view. *Bulletin of the American Academy of Arts and Sciences, 28,* 27–45.

Hammersley, M. (1995). *Ethnography: Principles in practice* (2nd ed.). London: Routledge.

Kuper, A. (1977). *Anthropology and anthropologists.* London: Routledge.

Kuper, A. (1999). *Culture: The anthropologists' account.* Cambridge, MA: Harvard University Press.

Lowie, R. (1937). *The history of ethnological theory.* New York: Holt, Rinehart and Winston.

Marcus, G. E. (1998). *Ethnography through thick and thin.* Princeton, NJ: Princeton University Press.

Marcus, G. E., & Fisher, M. (1986). *Anthropology as cultural critique.* Chicago: University of Chicago Press.

Orner, S. (1999). *The fate of culture: Geertz and beyond.* Berkeley: University of California Press.

Rabinow, P. (1977). *Reflections on fieldwork in Morocco.* Berkeley: University of California Press.

Sanjek, R. (Ed.). (1990). *Fieldnotes.* Ithaca, NY: Cornell University Press.

Shore, B. (1982). *Sala'ilua: A Samoan mystery.* New York: Columbia University Press.

Spradley, J. P. (1979). *The ethnographic interview.* New York: Holt, Rinehart & Winston.

Stocking, G. W. (Ed.). (1974). *A Franz Boas reader.* Chicago: University of Chicago Press.

Stocking, G. W. (Ed.). (1983). *Observers observed.* Madison: University of Wisconsin Press.

Stocking, G. W. (1987). *Victorian anthropology.* New York: The Free Press.

Stocking, G. W. (1992). *The ethnographer's magic.* Madison: The University of Wisconsin Press.

Van Maanen, J. (1988). *Tales of the field.* Chicago: University of Chicago Press.

Van Maanen, J. (Ed.). (1995). *Representation in ethnography.* Newbury Park, CA: Sage.

Wax, M. (1972). Tenting with Malinowski. *American Sociological Review, 37*, 1–13.
Willis, P. (1977). *Learning to labour.* London: Routledge.
Wolfe, M. (1992). *A thrice-told tale: Feminism, postmodernism and ethnographic responsibility.* Palo Alto, CA: Stanford University Press.

ETHNOMETHODOLOGY

Ethnomethodology (EM) is the study of the ways in which an organization's staff, its members, organize and produce work in their interactions together. EM focuses on the courses of practical action and practical reasoning, or the work practices, that inhabit work and that provide for its organized achievement. EM studies of work are particularly concerned to uncover the work practices involved in the production of formal structures of practical action, such as policies, plans, procedures, processes, workflows, and the other structures of action that populate organizational life. Uncovering or explicating (rather than explaining) work practice enables EM to identify how the organization itself is reflexively produced as an objective feature of everyday life by the members who inhabit it. EM uncovers work practice by attending to the local, situated, and particular details of works' collaboratively produced interactional achievement. The lived details of work make the art and craft of its achievement visible and display the real-world, real-time character of organization in a wide variety of occupational domains across industry, institutional life, science, medicine, and the arts.

Conceptual Overview

EM initially emerged in the field of sociology and was pioneered by Harold Garfinkel. Garfinkel substituted the prevalent concern in sociology to account for work and organization through generic representational theorizing—modeling, developing coding or classification schemes, specifying ideal types, administering compliance documents such as questionnaires, and so forth. EM suspends the use of social science accounting practices and replaces them with a concern to unpack the accounting practices that are endogenous, or internal to work and organization, and which are, as such, a natural feature of it. Garfinkel's seminal insight is that work and organization possess their own natural accountability and that the use of extraneous accounting practices obscures this.

The core notion of "accountability" extends in EM beyond its ordinary meaning to draw attention to the ways in which members make sense of work. Extending the philosophical insights of the later Wittgenstein, EM suggests that sensemaking is embodied (in conversation and gesture), material (tied to equipment, artifacts, and technologies), situated (in time, place, and physical environments), and achieved in concert (interactionally and collaboratively). EM takes it that the ways in which members make sense of work in the course of its production, make it accountable and intelligible to one another as it unfolds and are identical to the work practices they devise and exploit to accomplish and organize work. Thus, in accomplishing work practice, members "reflexively," at the same time, construct the organization of work.

This view of work and organization suspends the logic of exteriority that populates organizational theories. The logic of exteriority essentially construes of organization as a container that in diverse ways specified by the social sciences, and detailed in this encyclopedia and a veritable host of academic texts as well, shapes, constrains, and coordinates the actions of individuals within. EM offers the alternate view that organization might instead be understood as a practical ordering of and arrangement to interaction. EM holds that just what the practical order and arrangement of interaction consists of in any organizational setting, and just how that order and arrangement are interactionally produced, is to be found concretely in the natural and reflexive accountability of members' work practices.

The "reflexivity of accounts" is a ubiquitous social phenomenon that permeates work and organizations as members everywhere are constantly engaged in making their work accountable and available to one another. EM seeks to unpack the phenomenon by describing how distinct arrangements of work are "formulated" or constructed in interaction. Initial examination of formulations in EM was directed toward unpacking the ways in which conversation is organized by members, who then as now conduct work activities in large part through talk. This line of inquiry led to the development of a specialized field of EM study, *conversation analysis,* which was championed by the late Harvey Sacks and has over the course of its development identified a sophisticated turn-taking machinery organizing the production of accounts.

EM studies extend beyond a concern with the machinery organizing talk, however, to examine other ways in which work is formulated, focusing particularly on the work that talk achieves in interaction (what talk does as it unfolds or its practical effect) with the equipment (documents, tools, and other artifacts) that are involved in the accomplishment of work, and the local constellations of collaboration and assistance that are involved in the production of distinct arrangements of work. This latter and more comprehensive field of study represents EM's "radical studies of work" program, which is occupied with the "shop floor problem."

The shop floor problem recognizes that formal structures of practical action are key ingredients in the organization of work. The shop floor problem asks of formal structures of practical action, how are they produced as naturally accountable achievements of members' work? When social science accounts are consulted, the embodied, material, situated, collaborative, and interactional just what and just how—or the "haecceities"—of this achievement cannot be found. The practicalities of the achievement have been substituted for abstract accounts generated through practices of generic representational theorizing, which inevitably remove the actual details of work's achievement. There is, then, a significant gap in the social science literature on work and organization, which consists of what Harvey Sacks referred to as the missing interactional what of organizational studies.

EM's program is directed toward explicating the missing interactional what of organizational studies. The program is radical in that it inverts the accounting relationship, suspending generic representational theorizing under the policy of "ethnomethodological indifference." This policy, adopted from Edmund Husserl's phenomenological investigations of the origins of natural science, sets social science accounting practices aside on the basis that the natural accountability of work and organization is necessarily replaced by them. Alternately, EM accounts for work and organization by describing the haecceities that inhabit work and that make it visible on any occasion as the work that it uniquely is. These detailed portraits of work replace abstract, decontextualized, and generic accounts with corrigible sketch accounts that exhibit the lived production of formal structures of practical action on the shop floor and wherever else it is that work is carried out.

EM studies of work are done through ethnographic practices of data collection (e.g., participant observation and the gathering of data through the production of field notes; photography, audio, and video recording; and the collection of artifacts from the setting, such as documents, process descriptions, and job descriptions). EM's use of ethnographic methods differs from anthropological uses in one crucial respect, however: EM replaces the contemporary ethnographic concern with analytic reflexivity, or the act of ethnography and ethnographic reportage, with a concern to satisfy the unique adequacy requirement of methods. This demands that the analyst suspend concerns with his or her relation to members, and the ways in which he or she may influence our understanding of work and organization, and instead *develop competence in the work under study.* The unique adequacy requirement of methods is a requirement for the analyst to be able to recognize work in its detail as members recognize it and recognize the work practices that organize it. It is not a requirement for the analyst to "go native," but rather to understand just what the "missing interactional what" consists of and just how work is thereby organized and produced by members on the shop floor.

Critical Commentary and Future Directions

The critical emphasis of EM is on descriptive adequacy and the ways in which generic representational theorizing is used as a means of representing work and organization. This method of representation, which inevitably transforms naturally accountable features of work and organization into abstract signs indicative of a general and even universal phenomenon, is insufficient for understanding the interactional production of work and organization, and so EM dispenses with it. EM is not concerned then with the integration of its findings with organizational theory, managerial or otherwise, or with the further development of theory, for EM has *no work* for theory to do. EM instead places critical emphasis on the explication of working practice and working competence through careful description of the naturally accountable ways in which an organization's staff orient to work from within their local and situated circumstances and display the practical relevancies of its production to one another over the unfolding course of "getting the work done." Thus, EM suspends the use of generic representational theorizing to describe work and organization and instead describes and represents work in terms of the phenomenal field properties of ordinary human jobs.

EM's unique focus on work has contributed to a critical understanding of work and organization in three main ways. First, EM has unpacked the lived production of work and organization in a wide variety of different settings: industrial, entrepreneurial, financial, government, law and order, transportation, medicine, and science, to name but a few. Second, these studies have permitted the explication of recurrent activities and themes such as rationality, planning, coordination, rule use, calculation, measurement, knowledge management, representation, decision making, competence, skill, and so on. Third, with its interactional focus on the embodied, material, and situated character of work, EM has made a strong contribution to understanding the social character of technology in work and organization. EM studies of work place emphasis on technology as a sociotechnical system and address the practical incorporation of technology into the everyday working world. This strand of research has been of particular utility to the development of information technology (IT) for the workplace. EM studies have been and continue to be a stable feature of dedicated fields of IT research, particularly Computer-Supported Cooperative Work (CSCW) and Human–Computer Interaction (HCI), and they are exploited today in academic and industrial contexts alike. The purchase of EM studies in this context lies in the attention paid to actual technology use, which largely goes unnoticed in other sociological studies of technology, and to the working knowledge, practices, and competences that the effective incorporation of IT into work and organization relies upon. In short, EM studies make the organizationally embedded nature of technology use visible and support the design of IT systems that resonate with the real-world, real-time nature of work.

While incommensurable with conventional social science studies, EM need not be seen and treated as antithetical to or in competition with them as it often is by opponents and proponents alike. An alternate position might be adopted instead where, in addressing the missing interactional what of organizational studies, EM is seen and treated as asymmetrical but complementary insofar as it addresses the gap in the literature that inevitably emerges from practices of generic representational theorizing. The future of EM does not turn upon its reconciliation with conventional studies, however, even when the two are treated as complementary literatures on work and organization with one articulating formal structures of practical action and the other displaying the art and craft of their interactional production. Rather, the future of EM turns upon the "hybridization" of the studies of work programs. The status of EM studies in IT research provides a concrete example of what is meant by hybridization: the incorporation of EM studies into the *practice* of technology research and development. Hybridization sees EM move out of its sociological home and become part and parcel of new professions such that, for example, studies of technology use become part and parcel of the practice of technology design in the workplace. The principal challenge for EM is to continue its diversification, moving away from its sociological home into organizational practice to support effective sociological intervention in the business of everyday life.

—*Andy Crabtree and Mark Rouncefield*

See also Accountability; Ethnography; Phenomenology; Reflexivity; Symbolic Interactionism

Further Readings

Boden, D. (1994). *The business of talk: Organizations in action.* Cambridge, UK: Polity Press.

Button, G. (Ed.). (1991). *Ethnomethodology and the human sciences.* Cambridge, UK: Cambridge University Press.

Garfinkel, H. (1967). *Studies in ethnomethodology.* Englewood Cliffs, NJ: Prentice Hall.

Garfinkel, H. (1986). *Ethnomethodological studies of work.* London: Routledge/Kegan Paul.

Garfinkel, H. (2002). *Ethnomethodology's program: Working out Durkheim's aphorism.* Lanham, MD: Rowman & Littlefield.

Lynch, M. (1994). *Scientific practice and ordinary action: Ethnomethodological and social studies of science.* Cambridge, UK: Cambridge University Press.

Lynch, M., & Sharrock, W. (Eds.). (2003). *Harold Garfinkel.* London: Sage.

Sacks, H. (1992). *Lectures on conversation.* Oxford, UK: Blackwell.

Etic

The linguist Kenneth L. Pike coined the term etic (see also *emic*) to refer to the theoretical taxonomic categories that analysts use to construct an explicit, scientific system. Etic units are analogous to the units used in phon*etics,* the linguistic analysis of sounds. An *etic standpoint, viewpoint,* or *analysis* is one that compares societies. Pike refers to *etic system* as the theory, methods, and observations in a field of science. An adequate etic system meets ordinary norms of science and provides a basis for a newcomer unfamiliar with a given society to begin an analysis. Current uses of the term *etic* have drifted from Pike's original meaning. Scholars often use "etic" to refer to aspects of societies, measures, or theories that are identical everywhere, or treat "etic" research as imposing foreign concepts that impede understanding a new society.

Conceptual Overview

The frequent link of etic viewpoints to outsider viewpoint follows from Pike's work as a field linguist. Field linguists enter societies that have languages with no written form. As outsiders, they have prior theory, scientific methods and observations, and a capacity to induce from direct experience. They begin by applying the prior tools to see what linguistic sounds members of the unfamiliar society find meaningful. Anything from the prior etic base found meaningful is then said to have an emic (see *emic*) meaning in the unfamiliar society. Misunderstandings or communication failures indicate that the society's members are responding to something that the outsider analyst does not notice. Misunderstanding suggests an area where inductive work is needed that relies on human abilities to intuit.

Pike viewed an etic starting point as essential for beginners to approach an unfamiliar situation or society, but viewed etic knowledge as inadequate to fully function in a society. Newcomers use prior etic theory as a basis for contrast with direct observation of the unfamiliar situation. Contrasts raise questions and stimulate inductive analysis that depends on the human capacity to use intuition to explicate experience (see *emic*). Pike describes how to use etic systems to start analyzing new situations and use lessons from new situations to improve etic systems.

Berry applied Pike's view of etic analysis to questionnaire research in a way that stays faithful to Pike's intent. When scholars apply an existing survey to a new society, they take an *imposed etic* approach. The contrasts with prior research that appear when the questionnaire data are statistically analyzed provide the basis to develop a *derived etic.* Some scholars extend this logic to suggest how inductive methods can be used to redesign a questionnaire before using it in a new setting. Others depart from Pike's use to argue that an imposed etic approach is inappropriate or that etic research is limited to that which identifies commonalities among societies.

The nuances of Pikes meaning of etic are affected by his work to develop a comprehensive taxonomy of linguistic sounds. His phonetic taxonomy included both qualities of sounds that are common to most languages and those unique to particular linguistic groups. He was particularly interested in tonality among the indigenous languages of southwestern North America. Representing them required that Pike augment prior linguistic research by developing methods that take advantage of the perceptual and psychological processes that scientists use to create abstractions from observation. Pike observed that applying prior theory to tonal languages identified contrasts, points of inadequacy in the prior theory that encouraged him to induce from observation.

Pike's original idea and applications of etic systems reflect debates about science during the mid-20th century. He deliberately drew from Einstein's addition of observer position to the then standard Newtonian view of particle, wave, and field to develop etic theories of grammar and behavior. Pike's view of emic and etic is similar to his contemporary Michael Polanyi's distinction between tacit and explicit knowledge and the way scientists move between the two.

Critical Commentary and Future Directions

Pike's experience in developing a phonetic system lent his view of etic analysis and science two qualities that scholars frequently miss. One is that universally found characteristics of a phenomenon, frequently found characteristics, and rarely found characteristics are all part of any etic system. Departing from Pike, scholars frequently restrict etic systems to measures, concepts, and empirical relationships that are equivalent in many societies. Similarly, scholars frequently restrict "emic" (see also) to research findings that apply to a particular society but are rarely found elsewhere. The second is that Pike proposed a reciprocal process between prior research and intuition that contributes both to scientific progress and the ability to function in a society. Once a phenomenon has been documented explicitly, and systematically following scientific norms, that documentation becomes an addition or revision to the etic system.

The conceptual drift and complexity in the meaning and implications of the term etic makes it difficult to use the term without creating confusion. In future work, scholars would be best advised to identify the particular aspects of the concept of etic that they wish to use rather than the more multifaceted term itself. For scholars who wish to draw further inspiration from Pike's ideas, the most significant themes in Pike's view are precisely those that are most often missed. That is, explicit analysis following norms of science and implicit analysis using intuition and direct observation complement one another both in learning to live in unfamiliar societies and in improving scientific explication.

—*Mark F. Peterson*

See also Emic; Explicit Knowledge; Knowledge Creation; Philosophy of Science; Tacit Knowledge

Further Readings

Berry, J. W. (1969). On cross-cultural comparability. *International Journal of Psychology, 4,* 119–128.

Morris, M. W., Leung, K., Ames, D., & Lickel, B. (1999). Views from inside and outside: Integrating emic and etic insights about culture and justice judgment. *Academy of Management Review, 24,* 781–796.

Peterson, M. F., & Ruiz-Quintanilla, S. A. (2003). Emics and etics in cross-cultural organizational studies: Universal and local, tacit and explicit. In D. Tjosvold & K. Leung (Eds.), *Cross-cultural management: Foundations and future* (pp. 73–101). Hampshire, UK: Ashgate.

Pike, K. L. (1967). *Language in relation to a unified theory of the structure of human behavior* (2nd ed.). The Hague, the Netherlands: Mouton.

Pike, K. L. (1993). *Talk, thought, and thing: The emic road toward conscious knowledge.* Dallas, TX: Summer Institute of Linguistics.

Polanyi, M. (1962). *Personal knowledge: Towards a post-critical philosophy.* Chicago: University of Chicago Press. (Original work published 1958)

Evolutionary Theory

The term *evolution* (and its variants) is widely used in common parlance to denote any gradual or incremental variation, often connoting progress. It is also used analogically or metaphorically by students of history, technology, and development. Population ecologists, among others, have used it to mean any change arising from processes of selection operating on variation occurring in phenomena. Although these uses persist, the stricter Darwinian sense of evolution is "descent with modification." Descent requires replication, which is now known to occur via the medium of the gene, a process that only occurs in biological reproduction.

The "replication" of ideas, technologies, or organizational forms is a metaphor when writers on these subjects invoke evolutionary concepts.

The logic of biological evolution is unique and compelling. In order to understand this logic, it is important to distinguish between genotype and phenotype. The *genotype* of an organism is the class to which an organism belongs, which is determined by the physical material made up of DNA that was inherited by the organism from its parents. The *phenotype* of an organism is the class to which an organism belongs as determined by the physical and behavioral characteristics of the organism—e.g., size and shape, metabolic activity, and so forth. This logic of evolution says that selection mostly does not occur at the level of the genotype, but rather the phenotype. It is individuals and groups that have to survive the pressures of hazardous environments, invasive pathogens, and other predators long enough to be able to reproduce, thereby transmitting their genes to their offspring. Any causal connection between genotype and phenotype is therefore subject to the logic of evolution—those that confer reproductive fitness will be more likely to be replicated; those that impede or that are irrelevant to fitness will become extinct.

This is natural selection—Darwin's great and "dangerous" idea, so-called by the philosopher Daniel Dennett because its inexorable logic is a "universal acid" that burns through to the evolutionary origins of any feature of organic design. To this Darwin added a corollary insight: the concept of sexual selection. It is not enough to have a phenotype that will survive environmental predations. One also needs to have reproductive opportunities of the best quality possible to enhance the probability of one's genes passing through to multiple future generations. The phenotypic expression is the search for mates who bear signs of "good genes" themselves, i.e., they represent the best chances for one's future offspring to survive and prosper. The consequence is a competitive market for mating opportunities in most species, where the most attractive, nurturing, fierce, or well resourced survive. Any quality can be the target of this selection and this depends on the environmental context, its demands and constraints.

This opens the path for coevolution to occur—for reciprocal change to occur in both context and the target. Frequency-dependent selection is one such process—as one type becomes dominant through natural and sexual selection in a population (e.g., tough and dominant individuals) its value decreases and the value of other types (e.g., nurturing and pacific individuals) increases. Population variation can occur around any number of characteristics that attain equilibrium by this comparative advantage, as is visible in our society's profiles of many fitness-relevant characteristics, such as handedness, personality, and body type.

A third key element to the Darwinian insight that was added in the 20th century is the idea of kin selection or inclusive fitness. This recognizes that phenotypic behavior that raises the reproductive fitness of kin, i.e., other individuals and groups bearing the same genes, will also be advantageous—hence the willingness in many species of individuals to sacrifice their lives for their close relatives.

Conceptual Overview

Applying these concepts to humans has major and radical implications for the social sciences. It raises the question of how much of human thought, emotion, social behavior, institutional preferences, and cultural preferences might be subject to the logic of selection, and systemically linked with the human genotype. In other words, might human psychology and social behavior have heritable aspects?

Traditional models of human nature have regarded the brain as a blank slate and free of social constructions. This traditional view, referred to as the *standard social science model* by evolutionists John Tooby and Leda Cosmides, has been challenged by evolutionary psychology (EP) as logically and empirically untenable. Although humans are prodigious learners, like all other species, not least our primate cousins, they could not function without innate biases, capabilities, and drives, suffusing out affective, cognitive, and conative systems. Any characteristic that repeatedly proves to be fitness enhancing gets incorporated into the evolved design. It is labor saving to have a blueprint rather than learning de novo for each succeeding generation. The human design evolved over the 4 million years of human ancestral line to the first hominids, and became stabilized around 200,000 years ago with the appearance of *Homo sapiens*. Humans continue to evolve in various particulars (e.g., food tolerances) but the basic architecture of mind and body remains unchanged in its ancestral form—adapted to and for the existence of clan-dwelling hunter-gatherers. For example, humans have genes for speech and grammar, but none for reading and writing, so recent has been their advent as fitness-enhancing characteristics.

The evolutionary perspective is the project that arises from this reasoning—to identify the legacy of human evolution, understand its effects on human behavior, and find new and better ways of accommodating the human design in how we choose to arrange our social institutions, including the design of jobs, organizations, and institutions. This entry shall provide an overview of a couple of areas in which these ideas are being most closely examined.

Readers will discern that the evolutionary perspective applies potentially to every area of human activity, including human culture and institutions, since they are the embodiment of human goals, fears, and intentions. The evolutionary perspective shuns dualism—the separation of mind vs. body, or human nature vs. culture. It does, of course, allow phenomena and features to be untouched by natural selection. Many aspects of human life and behavior are not the direct outcome of evolutionary processes, but the result of random or accidental elements. However, even these are not exempt from the forces of evolutionary selection if they have any bearing on reproductive fitness, however indirect.

Because of the great potential breadth of application, such a short review as this must be highly selective. Therefore, this entry will focus on aspects of human cognition (a) because the application of Darwinian logic to human rationality is a test case for its viability against the implicit dualism of much discourse about reason, and (b) because it has far-reaching practical implications for management science.

Applying the Theory to Cognition

Much of the literature on decision making makes the assumption that the mind functions as a general purpose algorithm. The evolutionary perspective on cognition takes the view that natural selection shaped human reasoning by creating domain-specific, specialized mechanisms that are designed to solve specific adaptive problems that the human species encountered. The assumption of a domain-independent architecture has led in this line of research to the use of decision tasks devoid of content. For example, within this paradigm, the decision to choose which car to buy and whom to date are considered as being the same as long as the logical structure underlying these two decisions is similar. However, there has been a series of studies that demonstrate the domain-specific nature of human reasoning, which demonstrate the robustness of an evolutionary explanation for these findings. Notably, Cosmides used the Wason selection method, a logical reasoning task in which people have to infer if a set of conditional rules have been violated. For example, people are shown a set of four cards placed on a table, each of which has a number on one side and a colored patch on the other side. The visible faces of the cards show 3, 8, red, and brown. Which cards should one turn over in order to test the truth of the proposition that if a card shows an even number, then its opposite face shows a primary color? People's ability to solve this puzzle varies according to how the elements in the problem are framed. Success is much higher when the framing is around detecting cheating behavior, triggering what Tooby and Cosmides call the *social contract algorithm*. Invoking an evolutionary explanation, Cosmides argues that detecting cheating behavior is a cognitive adaptation that evolved to enable humans as a species to punish free-riding behavior in hunter-gatherer groups.

A large proportion of applied cognitive research focuses on the area of cognitive biases, inspired by the pioneering work of Daniel Kahneman and Amos Tversky generically known as behavioral decision research. This work has generally not theorized about prime causes, so much as critiqued the assumptions of the rational decision-maker model that have prevailed in economics and allied areas. One exception has been Gerd Gigerenzer, who has led a stream of research into heuristics arguing that inferences people make about the social world are guided by a cognitive toolbox, including many heuristics that evolved as adaptive solutions to the ecological problems faced by human beings over millennia.

The primary argument that Gigerenzer and colleagues make is that human beings are endowed with an ability to make fast and frugal decisions under uncertainty. One example is the *recognition heuristic*, a cognitive tool whose utility lies in its ability to help solve the adaptive problem of with whom to form alliances, that is, who has more resources and other valued attributes. The alternative is trial and error—which would be unnecessarily risky if applied to our choice of human associates and potentially fatal if applied to food getting or some equally fundamental utility. In demonstrating the adaptive nature of this heuristic, Gigerenzer and colleagues found that in the highly competitive stock market, the recognition heuristic on average matched or outperformed major mutual funds, the market, randomly picked stocks, and the less recognized stocks.

A third area of cognition that has attracted much interest is altruism; there has been much debate about the evolution of prosocial behaviors among humans, and our close primate relatives. In evolutionary terms, altruism is defined as the voluntary action of an organism that increases the inclusive fitness of another organism. The paradox altruism presents is that it appears to contradict the principle of natural selection, for by definition an altruistic act reduces the reproductive fitness of an organism. A number of explanations have been proposed and remain contested by evolutionary scholars.

Debate has centered on the concept of group selection. It has been defended by Elliot Sober and David Sloan Wilson, who theorize that as the proportion of altruists in a population increase, the groups they constitute will have enhanced fitness. The principle of natural selection operates at the level of the group, setting in motion a virtuous cycle in which successive generations of altruists get selected. However, this argument has been fraught with controversy as there is no explanation of how altruists originate in the first place. Some have argued that since genetic evolution operates at the level of the gene and its carrier—the individual organism—there is no mechanism to support the transmission of the gene between generations.

In response, it can be argued that coevolutionary processes can produce attributes at the group level, without abandoning the idea that selection operates at the level of the individual "replicator"—the agent of selection is the group, whose cultural norms have become adapted to environmental contingencies. Thus altruism could have evolved as a consequence of sexual selection under the contingency of social norms.

Sociologists have argued that a generalized norm of reciprocity exists in every human society, and among the explanations at the level are kin selection—individual organisms sacrificing themselves to increase the reproductive fitness of their close relatives—and reciprocal altruism. The latter idea, developed by Robert Trivers, is that altruistic acts are performed in expectation of the return of unspecified favors at a future date. An important corollary for reciprocal altruism to emerge is the capacity for observers to detect thwarted or unreciprocated altruistic acts, and for them then to be punished by social approbation or sanctions (a cheating-detection mechanism at work). A recent extension of this thinking, advocated by Herbert Gintis, Samuel Bowles, Robert Boyd, and Ernest Fehr, is the idea that human beings exhibit a trait called *strong reciprocity*, which is a predisposition to cooperate with others and to punish those who violate the norms of cooperation even at a cost that may never be paid back.

Scholars such as Robert Frank and Nigel Nicholson have argued that the best way to secure the reciprocal benefits of altruism is to act consistently. It is more economical to have a hardwired drive to be altruistic, even when there is no possibility of detection (e.g., making anonymous donations to strangers), than to have to calculate in every instance whether altruism will lead to a payback.

A further set of relevant arguments has been advanced around the idea of self-handicapping. The *handicap principle* in evolutionary biology, developed by Amotz Zahavi and Avishag Zahavi, suggests that costly behaviors or physical features are inherently reliable signals of reproductive fitness because they are difficult to fake. For example, according to this principle, long and heavy tails help peacocks find and attract mates, who are impressed by the possessor's ability to bear a needless and hazardous burden. According to Eric Smith and Rebecca Bliege Bird, two important conditions for a signal to be effective are that they must be a reliably diagnostic of an organism's ability, and the cost of bearing the burden of possessing the signal must be in proportion to the quality of the ability that is demonstrated by the signal. It has recently been suggested by Sabrina Deutsch Salamon and Yuval Deutsch that altruism in organizations— studied under the rubric of organizational citizenship behavior—can be seen as the demonstration of a person's fitness as a citizen. They are demonstrating their ability to bear the costs associated with organizational citizenship behavior and that it credibly signals their underlying qualities to others.

Critical Commentary and Future Directions

We have only covered a fraction of the current and potential applications of evolutionary theory to organizations. One of the most important and distinguishing features of evolutionary theory is its commitment to traversing levels of analysis and unifying cross-disciplinary approaches, as noted by Tooby and Cosmides and by E. O. Wilson. According to Nicholson, evolutionary theory is widely misrepresented as being reductionist, deterministic, and normative. It is also attributed to crudely support gender stereotypes and supremacist ideas about leadership, whereas the reality is a much more differentiated and context-dependent set of ideas.

Interactionism and coevolution are critically important ideas here, and are likely to be at the forefront of future advances in the theory and its applications.

Interactionism connotes the interplay between inborn propensities, impulses and susceptibilities, and the environments that evoke them. People's altruistic impulses can be suppressed as well as encouraged. Some of the most interesting advances on these interactions are going to come from behavior genetics and neuroscience. Behavior geneticists Remus Ilies, Richard Arvey, and Thomas Bouchard note the heritability of organizational concepts such as job satisfaction, personality, and leadership. Attention seems likely to focus increasingly on the factors that mediate these associations, such as management interventions, in developing employee potential and shaping employee attitudes.

The study of biological influences on human behavior is thriving, with research focusing on the role of neurotransmitters and hormones in stimulating or guiding behavior. Testosterone—underlying a suite of male behaviors, including dominance striving—has been the focus of attention, including in one recent study by Rod White, Stewart Thornhill, and Elizabeth Hampson, on the propensity to found ventures. This effect was mediated by individuals' willingness to take risks (higher risk propensity strengthens the link with entrepreneurial behavior).

Neuroscience is a growing contributor to many disciplines. Functional magnetic resonance imaging (fMRI) and methods of imaging that rely on objective measurement of neuronal activity in the brain are being borrowed from medical science to investigate the neural correlates of behaviors, thoughts, and emotions. These applications have proved so successful as to spawn new synthetic fields, such as neuroeconomics and social neuroscience.

It seems likely that there will be increasing convergence between the behavioral, neuroscience, and genetic approaches to overt behavior and mental events at various levels—e.g., individual differences in risk behavior, susceptibility to influence, and interpersonal reactions. Second, one can expect broader and more ambitious theorizing around coevolutionary hypotheses, drawing together evolutionary approaches emanating from psychology, anthropology, and economics. Currently, cross-cultural theorizing is weak and descriptive, with one or two notable exceptions. The Darwinian framework provides a fresh opportunity to achieve a deeper understanding of how organizations are able to sustain viable cultures that attract and retain people, and to design communitarian systems and incentives that help to reinforce the values of the culture. There is one case, documented by Mandy Johnson, of an Australian-based travel business that claims its remarkable growth and success are attributable to its explicitly Darwinian "family-village-tribe" model of organizing.

One may anticipate bolder theorists venturing to discuss variations in national cultures. These are the product of the unique compromises that emerge from coevolutionary processes to determine what kinds of social norms, systems, and mores are accepted as "normal," and how self-selection, migration, socialization, and other adaptive processes shape the evolution of cultural identity.

At the start of this entry it was noted that in common speech the concept of evolution carries connotations of progress. In the stricter Darwinian sense of evolution, progress is illusory. Species adapt, migrate to new habitats, or become extinct in response to environmental pressure and change. No species today—human included—is any better or more refined than any forerunner, or indeed than any successor. Cultural "evolution" is different, if only because progress is a distinctly human concept that we are highly motivated to believe in. It can be a reality, to the extent that by virtue of our reflexivity—our unique capacity to conceive of ourselves and our possible futures—the insights of evolutionary theory can be turned to our advantage and help us steer cultural development toward forms that are congruent with our evolved human nature.

—*Nigel Nicholson and Jayanth Narayanan*

See also Bounded Rationality; Complexity of Decision Making; Decision-Making Theory; Free-Rider Problem; Game Theory; Irrationality; Organic Organizations; Organizational Anthropology; Organizational Culture; Paradigms; Risk Management; Trust

Further Readings

Cosmides, L. (1989). The logic of social exchange: Has natural selection shaped how humans reason? Studies with the Wason selection task. *Cognition, 31,* 187–276.

Dennett, D. C. (1995). *Darwin's dangerous idea: Evolution and the meanings of life.* New York: Simon & Schuster.

Frank, R. (1988). *Passions within reason.* New York: Norton.

Gigerenzer, G. (2000). *Adaptive thinking: Rationality in the real world.* New York: Oxford University Press.

Gintis, H., Bowles, S., Boyd, R., & Fehr, E. (2003). Explaining altruistic behavior in humans. *Evolution and Human Behavior,* 24,153–172.

Ilies, R., Arvey, R. D., & Bouchard, T. J. (2006). Darwinism, behavioral genetics, and organizational behavior: A review and agenda for future research. *Journal of Organizational Behavior,* 27,121–142.

Johnson, M. (2005). *Family, village, tribe: The story of the Flight Centre Ltd.* Sydney, Australia: Random House.

Nicholson, N. (2000). *Managing the human animal.* London: Texere.

Nicholson, N. (2005). Objections to evolutionary psychology: Reflections, implications and the leadership exemplar. *Human Relations, 26,* 137–154.

Salamon, S. D., & Deutsch, Y. (2006). OCB as a handicap: An evolutionary psychological perspective. *Journal of Organizational Behavior,* 27, 185–200.

Smith, E. A., & Bliege Bird, R. (2000). Turtle hunting and tombstone opening: Public generosity as costly signaling. *Evolution and Human Behavior, 21,* 245–261.

Sober, E., & Wilson, D. S. (1998). *Unto others: The evolution and psychology of unselfish behaviors.* Cambridge, MA: Harvard University Press.

Tooby, J., & Cosmides, L. (1992). The psychological foundations of culture. In J. H. Barkow, L. Cosmides, & J. Tooby (Eds.), *The adapted mind: Evolutionary psychology and the generation of culture.* Oxford, UK: Oxford University Press.

Trivers, R. L. (1971). The evolution of reciprocal altruism. *Quarterly Review of Biology, 46,* 35–57.

Tversky, A., & Kahneman, D. (1974). Judgment under uncertainty: Heuristics and biases. *Science, 185,* 1124–1131.

White, R. E., Thornhill, S., & Hampson, E. (in press). Entrepreneurs and evolutionary biology: The relationship between testosterone and new venture creation. *Organizational Behavior and Human Decision Processes.*

Wilson, E. O. (1998). *Consilience: The unity of knowledge.* New York: Vintage Books.

Zahavi, A., & Zahavi, A. (1997). *The handicap principle: A missing piece in Darwin's puzzle.* New York: Oxford University Press.

Expectancy Theory

Expectancy theory provides an understanding of the motivation to engage in work-related tasks or to make decisions about one's own behavior concerning choices in organizational environments. According to this theory, personal motivation is influenced by the expectation that a certain level of effort will lead to a specific level of performance and the outcomes associated with it. Thus, the more a person expects to obtain the desired outcomes by means of a determined behavior, the stronger will be his or her motivational force—the higher the level of importance given to the results, the stronger the motivational force.

Conceptual Overview

Expectancy theory is based on cognitive theories of motivation proposed by W. Edwards, K. Lewin, and others. Victor H. Vroom's expectancy model is the best known and most utilized for explaining human behavior in industrial and organizational psychology. Expansions and modifications from Lyman Porter and Edward Lawler in 1965 and from John Campbell and Robert Pritchard in 1976 generated a large field for research related to the prediction of work performance and occupational choice.

Vroom developed the expectancy-valence theory of work motivation, but other authors explain this theory as a function of three specific variables: valence (V), expectancy (E), and instrumentality (I). This model strives to predict choices between jobs, tasks, and levels of effort necessary to produce the highest benefits for each individual concerned. In this vision, that which motivates a person to make a decision (motivational force—MF) is the product of the degree to which a person desires a reward (valence), the person's estimate of the probability that his or her effort will result in a successful performance (expectancy), and the person's belief that his or her performance is the way to reach the reward (instrumentality). These relationships were presented in a mathematical equation:

$$MF = E_* \Sigma\, (V_* I)$$

Valence

Valence is the force of one's preference for a certain type of reward or result. It expresses the strength of one's desire to attain a personal goal that could be a raise in salary, a promotion, a recognition, a better quality job, and so forth. The valence of a reward is unique for each individual, being conditioned to his or her experiences, and could vary substantially over a period of time. Once anterior necessities are satisfied, newer ones always emerge to take their place.

Valences may be expressed by either positive or negative values, according to whether a person pursues positive or negative preferences for a specific outcome. Within a job situation, one could expect that a salary raise would be evaluated as a positive valence while a reprimand from a supervisor would provide a negative valence. However, if a person is indifferent to a given reward, the valence can be considered as zero. When an individual fulfills a task, the individual gives him- or herself a reward from the simple fact that the task was finished. This is called an *intrinsic* reward or outcome. On the other hand, rewards that are provided by organizations or supervisors are called *extrinsic* rewards or outcomes.

Valence has its focus on the relationship between personal goals and rewards. This means it is related to the degree to which rewards come to satisfy personal objectives or individual necessities and the attractiveness of these potential rewards for each person.

Instrumentality

Instrumentality represents an individual's belief that a reward will be received as a function of his or her performance. A person makes a subjective judgment with regard to the probability that the organization will value his or her performance and furnish a reward based on its success. It is also necessary that the individual perceives the system as being just. For example, the employee perceives that rewards are obtained by satisfactory performance, and not based on the fact that he or she is a friend of the boss.

Instrumentality has its focus on the relationship between performance and reward. It measures a person's perception as to what level of performance is necessary to obtain a reward from the organization. If an employee perceives that a reward such as a salary raise, a promotion, and so forth are related to evaluation data on performance, instrumentality will tend to be evaluated positively (merit system). On the other hand, if this relationship is not clear, a low estimation will tend to be made.

Expectancy

Expectancy is the belief that a certain level of effort related to the job will result in a corresponding level of performance. Performance, in this case, may simply mean the conclusion of a task. Expectancy is expressed in terms of probability: a person estimates to what point his or her performance will be determined by the effort given. By expressing the probability as a connection between effort and performance, its value may vary from zero to 1 or from zero to 100%. If the individual does not perceive there is a chance that a given effort may lead to a desired performance, his or her expectancy level is zero. On the other hand, if the person is highly confident that his or her effort will lead to a desired performance, the person's expectancy level has the value of 1 (100%).

Expectancy, therefore, has its focus on the relationship between effort and performance. This means that a given degree of effort will lead to satisfactory performance.

Critical Commentary and Future Directions

As Nadler and Lawler note, various studies have been performed with the intention of testing the validity of the expectancy theory with regard to the predictions that it proposes concerning human behavior in diverse job areas. Terence Mitchell, however, advised that the use of the expectancy theory to predict behavior should only be attempted when the options of choice can be clearly identified and are mutually exclusive. According to this author, Vroom clearly sees the expectancy theory as an individual choice. Regardless of this, the majority of researchers have tested the model on expectancy theory more from a group aspect than from an individual approach.

Another contradiction pointed out by Mitchell is that the usual procedure applied has been to compute a simple motivational force value for each individual tested (only one alternative) and to compare it with the standard expected. For example, take the motivational force "to be a volunteer." A correct theoretical approach would be to compute an alternative motivational force for each individual, usually in the opposite direction, modifying the original tendency and then subtracting it from the other. The more the resulting force is either positive or negative, the more probable it is that the original or the alternative motivational force would be more influential in individual decision.

For example, in 1997 Robert Allen, Margaret Lucero, and Kathleen Van Norman made use of Mitchell's approach, emphasizing the necessity for comparisons of the individual forces that attract someone to the two behavioral patterns under study. Personal involvement in organizational programs was analyzed with the subject being either a volunteer (motivated to get involved or to avoid the status quo) or a nonvolunteer (motivated to maintain the status quo or to avoid involvement). This way, it was possible to assume that people react rationally to alternative choices and that they have access to adequate information concerning all relevant variables for decision making. This means, in the perspective of Vroom's model, that they are capable of distinguishing valences, instrumentalities, and expectancies for all choice options.

Lawler emphasizes the fact that content theories, such as Maslow's needs hierarchy theory, assume that results are attractive to a person because he or she possesses some impulse, motive, or need. On the other hand, Vroom approaches motivation from a different angle: The expectancy model simply says that outcomes have value if they lead to rewards valued by an individual. Nothing is mentioned on the reason why people give value to rewards or why certain rewards are more valued then others. Although this may facilitate comprehension of the attractiveness of individual rewards, it sacrifices its predictive power. The theory of needs hierarchy, on the other hand, establishes, a priori, what rewards will probably be appreciated and what affects their values.

Marisa Salanova, Pedro Hontangas, and José Peiró understand that other aspects are also influential in determining the level of effort that a person will apply to accomplish a task: past experience, personality traits, emotions, skills, opportunities, and the strategies required to fulfill that task. Although not interfering with the applicability of the expectancy model, it is important for research to approach these aspects.

Nadler and Lawler perceived the necessity of comprehending the behavioral types that the expectancy model explains and the situations that influence its predictions. They believe the model is based on the assumption that people make decisions in a rational manner after exploring and pondering the possible rewards of all available alternatives. Nonetheless, it can be observed that personal decisions are not always made on the basis of so complete an analysis. Human beings have limits to the amount of information they can use for decision making.

Another source of criticism in relation to expectancy theory emerges from the multiplication aspect of the formula for motivational force, supposing that two negative values for any of the three components—valences, instrumentalities, and expectancy—would provide a positive motivational force. After testing the validity of this model, however, Hugh J. Arnold, in 1981, found evidence that supports the proposed interactions among the variables for determining motivational force.

In terms of future directions, the expectancy theory of Vroom will probably continue to provide a good tool for managers to perform diagnoses of motivation, especially when combined with goal setting or other motivation cognitive theories. The approach is specifically useful when facing changes in organizational procedures or in order to understand the behavior process utilized to satisfy personal needs for career development. However, situational moderators must be observed in order to make the expectancy theory functional. These can include differences such as opportunity and externally oriented predictors (e.g., wife/family index), or individual differences, such as hesitance or risk-taking propensity.

Expectancy theory should continue to be as useful as it is practical. As the base for the development of motivational programs, it provides the consequent rise in productivity among employees. One of the best roads to obtain this outcome is to promote the importance of task performance. The employees may feel motivated when they perceive their contributions to the organization and the rewards associated with them.

—*Helder Pontes Regis, James Anthony Falk, and Sonia Calado Dias*

See also Equity Theory; Goal-Setting Theory; Job Satisfaction

Further Readings

Allen, R. E., Lucero, M. A., & Van Norman, K. L. (1997, March). An examination of the individual's decision to participate in an employee involvement program. *Group and Organization Management, 22*(1), 117–143.

Campbell, J. P., & Pritchard, R. D. (1976). Motivation theory in industrial and organizational psychology. In M. D. Dunnette (Ed.), *Handbook of industrial and organizational psychology* (pp. 63–130). Chicago: Rand McNally.

Kanfer, R. (1990). Motivation theory and industrial/organizational psychology. In M. D. Dunnette & L. M. Hough (Eds.), *Handbook of industrial and organization psychology* (2nd ed., vol. 1). Palo Alto, CA: Consulting Psychologists Press.

Latham, G. P. (2006). *Work motivation: History, theory, research, and practice.* Thousand Oaks, CA: Sage.

Lawler, E. E., III. (1991). Drives, needs, and outcomes. In B. M. Staw (Ed.), *Psychological dimensions of organizational behavior* (2nd ed). Upper Saddle River, NJ: Prentice Hall.

Mitchell, T. R. (1974). Expectancy model of job satisfaction, occupational preference and effort: A theoretical, methodological, and empirical appraisal. *Psychological Bulletin, 81,* 1053–1077.

Mitchell, T. R. (1982, January). Motivation: New directions for theory, research, and practice. *Academy of Management Review,* 80–88.

Nadler, D. A., & Lawler, E. E., III. (1991). Motivation: A diagnostic approach. In B. M. Staw (Ed.), *Psychological dimensions of organizational behavior* (2nd ed). Upper Saddle River, NJ: Prentice Hall.

Parker, D. F., & Dyer, L. (1976). Expectancy theory as a within-person behavioral choice model: An empirical test of some conceptual and methodological refinements. *Organization Behavior and Human Performance, 17*(4), 97–117.

Porter, L. W., & Lawler, E. E., III. (1965). Properties of organisation structure in relation to job attributes and job behaviour. *Psychological Bulletin, 64,* 23–51.

Salanova, M., Hontangas, P. M., & Peiró, J. M. (1996). Motivación laboral. In J. M. Peiró & F. Prieto (Eds.), *Tratado de Psicología del Trabajo. Vol. I: La actividad laboral en su contexto.* Madrid, Spain: Editorial Síntesis.

Vroom, V. H. (1964). *Work and motivation.* New York. Wiley.

Experiential Learning

Experiential learning theory or ELT, which was developed and published by David A. Kolb in 1984, is a learning process involving the combination of grasping and transforming knowledge through experience. In 1998, Russ Vince stated that ELT is the most influential theory, particularly in the area of managerial and leadership learning and development. Its popularity and international acclaim make this important especially because of its use at individual and team levels.

Conceptual Overview

Grasping Knowledge

Apprehension and comprehension are two key aspects central to the theory of experiential learning representing the dialectically related ways in which we grasp knowledge. The apprehension-comprehension dialectic is derived from dual knowledge theory, which states that there are two distinct (yet inseparable) ways of knowing: concrete and abstract. Apprehension is defined as "concrete knowing," and refers to that which is experienced as both immediate and feeling oriented. It is a subjective process largely based in older regions of the human brain that serve as gatekeepers, monitoring the physiological and emotional dimensions of learning. Comprehension is defined as "abstract knowing," which is experienced as the linguistic, conceptual, interpretive process based in the newer left cerebral cortex of the brain. In short, this dialectic can be stated as the emotional-conceptual dialectic.

We grasp experience by either being involved through apprehension using the concrete experience (CE) learning mode or through comprehension using the abstract conceptualization (AC) learning mode. The CE mode is one where we interact with our environment through immersion, experiencing it with our senses, feelings, and emotions; we are involved with the tangible aspects of our surroundings. On the other hand, one can also grasp knowledge through the AC mode by thinking, analyzing, and theorizing to gain knowledge without being immersed in the environment.

Transforming Knowledge

Apart from how knowledge is grasped, Kolb articulates that the transforming of knowledge is also central to the theory of experiential learning. Simple perception of experience alone is not sufficient for learning; something must be done with what we have taken in, or grasped. Intension is the act of reflecting on or observing some state or experience, whereas extension is the actual action—deliberate or experimental—that will generate new states and experiences. This dialectic involves the praxis of action and reflection.

We transform knowledge by either being involved through the reflective observation (RO) learning mode or the active experimentation (AE) learning mode. The RO mode is one where we incorporate diverse perspectives from the knowledge we gained through reflection or observation. The dialectical related mode of active experimentation is one where the focus is to do something about the knowledge we gained.

The Experiential Learning Cycle

Kolb asserts that most effective learning happens as one goes through a cycle using all four modes. Constant use of these modes would also cause individuals to develop learning flexibility. One could enter the cycle at any modal point; however, entering the cycle in a particular mode indicates an individual's tendency or preference for how to grasp or transform information.

Consider a person (let's call her Jane) who is promoted to the position of manager based on her superior performance as an engineer. As a manager, Jane is immersed in a completely new work environment and in the first few months, experiences the stress related to the requirements, demands, and expectations of this role. Starting her learning cycle from concrete experience, Jane would then reflect on the job and even begin to observe other managers to learn how they function successfully. She may also engage in conversations with other managers to obtain as many perspectives as possible to inform her own experience. In doing so, Jane has moved through two modes: CE and RO. Jane may then need to gain more knowledge and reads more about how to succeed as a new manager. As she gathers this information, she comes up with her own ideas and concepts of how to succeed. At this stage, Jane is engaging in the AC mode and develops her own working theories of successful behaviors for her new role. Finally, Jane decides to act by incorporating these new behaviors in her job by engaging in the AE mode. As she now interacts with her environment and employs these new behaviors, she engages in concrete experience and the cycle continues.

The original diagram showing this learning cycle can be found in Kolb (1984: 42, Figure 3.1).

Learning Styles

Going through all four modes of the learning cycle provides the ideal well-rounded learning process. However, at times one might realize a preference for particular modes and tend to skip others. Further, when we interact with others we may notice that they also have such learning tendencies. As we progress into adulthood, we develop certain predispositions or preferences for how we grasp and transform knowledge. This tendency to choose certain learning modes is indicative of a learning style.

Diverging

An individual with a diverging learning style tends to choose concrete experience in grasping information and reflective observation in transforming knowledge. Such individuals tend to be personally involved in any situation or event and are sensitive to feelings and people. Individuals with a diverging learning style also tend to view issues from many or different perspectives, to look for the meaning of things, and also to carefully observe a situation before making any judgments. Their interest in knowledge and idea generation is the reason for such a style to be labeled as "diverging." As such, they tend to do well and even thrive in situations that involve the bringing together of diverse perspectives such as brainstorming. Their passion for gathering information is ideal for tasks or work involving creativity or the arts, entertainment, and service. Such people also tend to be imaginative, have the ability to listen with an open mind, and to function as excellent team players. In a classroom setting, discussion forums work well for individuals having diverging learning styles.

Assimilating

Individuals with an assimilating learning style tend to use abstract conceptualization to grasp knowledge and reflective observation for transforming knowledge. The diverging and assimilating styles share the same preference for transforming knowledge in that they tend to look at diverse perspectives but with a specific intention to understand. Individuals with this preference tend to distill information to seek clarity and precision. They tend to logically analyze ideas, and to plan systematically. People with this learning style have a tendency to remove themselves emotionally and instead seek to understand situations intellectually. Their focus on achieving clarity makes them thrive in tasks or work areas involving theories, and ideas that promote precision such as the sciences, research and development, and most academic environments. They tend to work well on their own and have very high standards in their work. In a classroom setting, assigned readings, listening to lectures, and developing conceptual models work well for individuals with assimilating learning styles.

Converging

Sharing the preference for abstract conceptualization in grasping knowledge with the assimilating learning style, people with a converging learning style tend to prefer active experimentation in transforming information. Individuals with this learning style have an interest in not just understanding a situation or event but they also want to be able to take action using this knowledge. Unlike the individual that focuses on the soundness of a theory (those with assimilating learning styles), an individual with a converging learning style focuses on the practicality of theoretical models. These individuals' propensity to use ideas to solve problems makes them ideal for careers in technology, engineering, and design. As such, they prefer to work with technical tasks than to deal with social problems or interpersonal issues. Individuals with converging learning styles thrive when they are given tasks with clear parameters or boundaries. In a classroom setting, using case studies, simulations, and laboratory assignments works well for people with converging learning styles. Educational environments that focus on examinations and tests align with the converging learning style.

Accommodating

Individuals with an accommodating learning style tend to prefer immersing themselves in concrete experience to grasp information and active experimentation to transform information. Similar to individuals with diverging learning styles, those with an accommodating learning style tend to be sensitive to feelings and people and are concerned about relating to others. However, people with this learning style are also very focused on being able to get things done, take risks, and influence people through action. They tend to accommodate (or adapt) to the environment they are immersed in. Such individuals focus on having "hands-on" experience as their primary mode of interacting with their environment, tending to act on their "gut" rather than using logical analysis. They also do well in tasks or jobs related to sales, marketing, and management due to the emphasis on action or getting things done. As with the diverging learning style, those with an accommodating learning style also like to work in teams but with the focus on getting things done, completing a project, or doing field work. In a classroom setting, completing assignments, fulfilling tangible tasks, and doing presentations work well for individuals with accommodating learning styles. Although individuals have preferred learning styles, it is important to know that each individual does have four scores for each learning mode—suggesting that ELT is not a typological model but a dynamic one where individuals can learn to become more flexible by continuously using all four modes as they go through the learning cycle. It is the constant use of the four modes that is the focus of the experiential learning theory of development.

Experiential Learning Theory of Development

The experiential learning theory of development is a fundamental part of Kolb's experiential learning theory (ELT). Although ELT deals with learning along the four modes (CE, RO, AC, and AE), it is a process whereby development occurs—particularly from the interaction between personal and social knowledge. In this theory, Kolb also states that the human developmental process is divided into three broad developmental stages: acquisition, specialization, and integration. In the *acquisition* stage, an individual embarks on acquiring the basic learning abilities and cognitive structures that lead toward a sense of self. Hence in this stage, one is registering, differentiating, and expanding one's sense of self. Formal higher education and career training influence the *specialization* stage. As this is an adaptive stage dealing with self-characteristics and environmental demands, one's learning style is the processing structure. In this stage, the self is content based and self-worth is measured against rewards and recognition. One is constantly interpreting, evaluating, and selecting information to suit one's talents and social needs. The third stage, *integration,* is marked by existential conflicts between specialization (imposed from society) and integration of oneself as a whole being. Kolb states that with this awareness, one would experience a shift in the frame of reference used to experience life, evaluate activities, and make choices to shape one's experience rather than observing and accepting experiences as they happen. Clearly during this stage, one is constantly integrating and carrying forward the flow of one's experience, centering one's purpose and focusing one's attention toward holistic development. Hence this stage focuses on the unique capabilities of the whole person—creativity, wisdom, and integrity.

As one constantly engages with the environment using the four modes, Kolb argues that integrating the diverse learning styles would result in achieving a higher level of skill in learning. Particularly when one combines learning styles that incorporate dialectically related modes (e.g., diverging and assimilating incorporating CE and AC), one will achieve a specific related higher level of learning complexity. Kolb describes four learning complexities (sometimes referred to as developmental dimensions) that could be achieved. As one begins this process, a lower level of learning complexity is possible (through interaction during the specialization stage). As one develops a better sense of self-awareness across diverse interactions, one would achieve a higher level of this learning complexity (through selection during the integration stage).

Affective Complexity

When one includes both accommodating and diverging learning styles constantly (i.e., combining the dialectically related modes of AE and RO), that person would achieve *affective complexity.* A simple example would be a visual artist being able to absorb a multitude of information from a scene (through the diverging learning style) and then beginning to paint the scene (through the accommodating learning style) on a canvas. At a lower level of affective complexity, an individual would be able to have a relativistic appreciation of values systems as one interacts across different environments, whereas at a higher level, one would engage in active value commitment in the context of that relativism.

Perceptual Complexity

When one includes both diverging and assimilating learning styles (i.e., combining the dialectically related modes of CE and AC), that person would achieve *perceptual complexity*. A simple example would be a detective absorbing a multitude of information from a crime scene (through the diverging learning style) and beginning to deduce clear ideas or theories as to how the crime could have occurred (through the assimilating learning style). At a lower level of perceptual complexity, an individual would be able to have a relativistic appreciation of observed schemes and perspectives as one interacts across different environments, whereas at a higher level, one would obtain a strong intuitive sense to choose meaningful perspectives and frameworks for interpreting experiences.

Symbolic Complexity

When one includes both assimilating and converging learning styles (i.e., combining the dialectically related modes of RO and AE), that person would achieve *symbolic complexity*. A simple example would be a scientist developing clear, logical theories (through the assimilating learning style) and beginning to test out these theories or ideas (through the converging learning style). At a lower level of symbolic complexity, an individual would be able to match creatively symbolic systems and concrete objects when interacting across different environments, whereas at a higher level, one would be able to have the capacity for finding and solving meaningful problems.

Behavioral Complexity

When one includes both converging and accommodating learning styles (i.e., combining the dialectically related modes of AC and CE), that person would achieve *behavioral complexity*. A simple example would be an expert snooker/pool player who understands the principles of angles of approach and reflection (from physics) and his or her bodily mechanical functions to obtain optimal positioning of the various parts of the body (through the converging learning style) and to finally hit the striker ball to achieve the desired end result (through the accommodating learning style). At a lower level of behavioral complexity, an individual would be able to develop an experimental, hypothesis-testing approach to action that introduces flexibility to goal-oriented behavior when interacting across different environments, whereas at a higher level, one would engage in active commitment to responsible action in an environment that is constantly changing or being created.

Critical Commentary and Future Directions

Extensive research has been conducted using the two axes of ELT: grasping and transforming knowledge. As of the year 1999, a total of 1,004 studies had been conducted including two doctoral dissertations that provided comprehensive reviews of ELT. In these studies, one main critique has been that the learning style inventory (LSI)—the major instrument for measuring individual approaches to learning—uses a forced choice method instead of a scale. Some researchers converted the LSI into a scale and found different combinations of the four modes. The majority of these studies show evidence of this two-factor structure with concrete experience (apprehension) and abstract conceptualization (comprehension) as one factor and active experimentation (extension) and reflective observation (intention) as another. In a UK review of learning styles conducted in 2004, some studies were cited that showed different combinations of the modes of learning (e.g., where apprehension and intension combined as one factor with extension and comprehension as another or where apprehension and extension combined as one factor while comprehension and intension combined as another). Although most of these studies offer methodological arguments (e.g., the ipsative design of the LSI), the theory of experiential learning continues to be the most influential theory used in research and practice in organizations and educational institutions across the globe.

Over the past 4 years, Kolb and some of his colleagues (who use ELT in their teaching and research) began exploring how ELT can be used at the group level. In 2003, David and Alice Kolb, with Christopher and Anna Kayes, developed the Kolb Team Learning Experience (KTLE) to help teams consider how to incorporate the different learning styles of its individual members so as to designate roles and functions to help the team perform better. In 2002, David Kolb, Patricia Jensen, and Ann Baker started exploring learning at the group level and developed the theory of conversational learning. Grounded in the theory and practice of experiential learning, conversational learning is a process whereby individuals construct meaning and transform experiences into knowledge conversations. As a construct, the authors define conversational learning as learning that occurs in a space bounded by five dialectics: grasping knowledge, transforming knowledge, connectedness, power, and time perception. Kolb, Baker, and Jensen mention that such a space would serve to emphasize the interpersonal experience among group members and to weave multiple voices into an interconnected whole, and they also offer this theory as a way to understand group and organizational interaction.

Although the anatomy of the space itself has been theoretically derived from experiential learning theory and tested qualitatively in four major studies, in 2004, Tony Lingham offered the first quantitative empirical research in this field by developing an instrument (based on the five dialectics proposed in conversational learning theory) that both measures and maps out a team's conversational space. His research to date has helped inform and refine the theory through rigorous empirical methodologies and to show that a team's conversational space is a group-level construct. Lingham's final 30-item Team Learning and Development Inventory (TLI) charts conversational spaces in teams along four major spaces—diverging, converging, shared leadership, and openness spaces—based on team members' responses on their actual and ideal conversational spaces and where the results facilitate teams to engage in team-directed learning and development. The TLI has been used internationally (United States, Europe, Africa, and Asia) in organizations and educational institutions.

—*Tony Lingham*

See also Action Learning; Adult Learning; Learning; Management Learning; Team Learning

Further Readings

Baker, A. C., Jensen, P. J., & Kolb, D. A. (Eds). (2002). *Conversational learning: An experiential approach to knowledge creation.* Westport, CT: Quorum Books.

Coffield, F., Moseley, D., Hall, E., & Ecclestone, K. (2004). *Learning styles and pedagogy in post-16 learning: A systematic and critical review.* London: Learning and Skills Research Centre. Available online at http://www.LSRC.ac.uk

Kayes, A. B., Kayes, D. C., & Kolb, D. A. (2005). Experiential learning in teams. *Simulation & Gaming, 36*(3), 330–354.

Kolb, A. Y., & Kolb, D.A. (2005). Learning styles and learning spaces: Enhancing experiential learning in higher education. *Academy of Management Learning and Education Journal, 4*(2), 193–212.

Kolb, A. Y., & Kolb, D. A. (2006). Experience Based Learning Systems, Inc. [Program for educators]. Available online at http://www.learningfromexperience.com

Kolb, A. Y., & Kolb, D. A. (2006). *Experiential learning theory bibliography: 1971–2005.* Cleveland, OH: Department of Organizational Behavior, Weatherhead School of Management, Case Western Reserve University.

Kolb, D. A. (1984). *Experiential learning: Experience as a source of learning and development.* Englewood Cliffs, NJ: Prentice Hall.

Lingham, T. (2004). *Developing a measure for conversational learning spaces in teams.* Unpublished doctoral dissertation, Case Western Reserve University, Cleveland, OH.

Lingham T. (2006). The Complexity and Uniqueness of Team Experience: A JIT measurement and mapping system to facilitate team-directed learning and development. *ESADE Business School Working Paper Series No. 202,* Barcelona, Spain.

Vince, R. (1998). Behind and beyond Kolb's learning cycle. *Journal of Management Education, 22*(3), 304–319.

Explicit Knowledge

Knowledge refers to personal beliefs of what is true, derived from accumulated information. Knowledge may be held by individuals or organizations; it becomes organizational as individuals share and create knowledge through social interactions. Individuals and organizations engage in action based on their existing knowledge. Whereas traditional epistemology emphasizes the static and absolute character of knowledge, knowledge creation theorists recognize its context-specific and relational nature by focusing on its development and evolution over time. Michael Polanyi distinguished between two forms of knowledge: explicit and tacit. Explicit knowledge is readily accessible to individuals in a format that enables them to understand, use, and communicate it.

Social science researchers have identified several distinguishing characteristics of explicit knowledge. First, it is expressed in a formal, systematic language of words or numbers. It may be represented in linguistic form or statistical measurements. Second, interested individuals may readily access it through records, such as databases, archives, and publications. Third, the premises on which explicit knowledge is based are transparent and readily tested by individuals who encounter it. Fourth, it generates from past events and experiences and is sequentially created as novel information becomes available. Finally, it can be reused for multiple purposes by different individuals or groups. Explicit knowledge resides outside and within the cognitive structures of those who create it. It is inherently mobile and may be purchased, sold, or protected through security mechanisms. Examples of explicit knowledge include published research findings, patents, documented procedures, and statistical reports.

Conceptual Overview

Ikujiro Nonaka has suggested that effective knowledge creation involves conversion between explicit and tacit forms of knowledge. This research identified three methods of knowledge creation that involve explicit knowledge. First, externalization translates tacit knowledge into explicit knowledge. In this process, implicitly held assumptions become explicit as they are expressed through written or verbal communication. Externalization may facilitate double-loop learning as it creates new understanding of experiences and new strategic options. Second, internalization converts explicit knowledge into tacit knowledge as individuals learn through their own actions. Finally, combination processes employ extant explicit knowledge to generate new explicit knowledge. These conversion processes apply to both individual and organizational knowledge creation; taken together, they represent a knowledge spiral that creates organizational knowledge by amplifying individual knowledge to higher ontological levels.

Empirical researchers commonly engage in explicit knowledge creation as they extend or integrate prior research findings. Organizations employ technology-enabled knowledge management systems to foster sharing of explicit knowledge among organizational members. Individuals who make decisions based on explicit knowledge can readily explain their thought process and actions to others. As new information becomes available, this knowledge can be updated to reflect changing conditions. Archival records enable researchers to create new knowledge from historical experiences in the absence of tacit knowledge that disappeared long ago.

Individuals' explicit and tacit knowledge has been the subject of scholarly interest in other fields, including cognitive science, neuroscience, and linguistics, stimulated by the work of Reber. These fields have contributed complementary and distinct findings to those of organizational researchers. These findings suggest that explicit knowledge and tacit knowledge reside in neurologically distinct parts of people's brains. In addition, explicit knowledge likely evolves later than tacit knowledge. While explicit knowledge is conscious, it may not be expressible in ways that others can recognize. Expression of explicit knowledge is sometimes imprecise and inaccurate but may improve with training and over time.

It is likely that most individual learning involves some combination of tacit and explicit knowledge. Bottom-up approaches to learning involve tacit learning first, followed by development of explicit knowledge about what it learned. Top-down approaches to learning involve explicit learning first, followed by the translation of this learning into practice. For tasks that are first learned tacitly, premature attempts to verbalize knowledge to make it explicit likely interfere with ongoing learning.

Critical Commentary and Future Directions

Despite the importance of explicit knowledge in the knowledge creation process, certain obstacles impede its understanding and creation. Organizational scholars' exploration of explicit knowledge sometimes lags behind that of researchers in other fields, who have developed more sophisticated indices of what such knowledge comprises and how it may be expressed. Even within organization studies, scholars and practitioners rarely engage each other in their efforts to create new explicit knowledge and explore its appropriateness for learning. Paradigmatic diversity among scholars regularly raises questions about how knowledge is created and what constitutes knowledge. Finally, academics and practitioners often engage in defensive practices that prevent their tacit knowledge from being made explicit.

Contemporary organizational research has increasingly shifted in focus away from explicit knowledge and toward tacit knowledge. Practitioners increasingly identify tacit knowledge and the intangible assets it carries as a more important means of differentiation and source of competitive advantage than explicit knowledge. Despite this de-emphasis on explicit knowledge, both forms of knowledge are necessary inputs to knowledge creation processes.

Technological advancements have greatly expanded the sharing of explicit knowledge within and across organizations. Knowledge management systems, online publications, and advanced search techniques provide individuals access to vast amounts of explicit knowledge. Future research on explicit knowledge could explain how individuals filter and evaluate these resources to discern knowledge that informs their decisions and behavior. Empirical testing of how externalization, internalization, and combination processes contribute to knowledge creation in organizations and their interactions would provide a clearer understanding of the unique contributions of these methods to effective performance and potential obstacles that individuals face as they engage them.

—*Ian J. Walsh and Jean M. Bartunek*

See also Knowledge Creation; Learning; Tacit Knowledge

Further Readings

Argyris, C. (2004). *Reasons and rationalizations: The limits to organizational knowledge.* Oxford, UK: Oxford University Press.

Nonaka, I. (1994). A dynamic theory of organizational knowledge creation. *Organization Science, 5,* 14–37.

Polanyi, M. (1966). *The tacit dimension.* London: Routledge & Kegan Paul.

Reber, A. S. (1967). Implicit learning of artificial grammars. *Journal of Verbal Learning and Verbal Behaviour 6,* 855–863.

Rynes, S. L., Bartunek, J. M., & Daft, R. L. (2001). Across the great divide: Knowledge creation and transfer between practitioners and academics. *Academy of Management Journal, 44,* 340–353.

Stewart, T. (2003). *The wealth of knowledge: Intellectual capital and the twenty-first century organization.* New York: Currency.

EXPLOITATION

Exploitation is defined here as one group of people appropriating another group's labor power for what Karl Marx in 1867 called *surplus value* (net profits), benefiting by paying them less than the necessity value (actual cost of wages) produced in a day. For example, assume in an 8-hour day, in the first 3 hours, a worker produces what it costs a capitalist to pay the wage and cover overhead, equipment, and other operating costs. That means that during the next 5 hours, the capitalist appropriates labor power (skill, experience, and activity of the worker) to expand surplus value. If a worker produces $50 worth of goods or services each hour (paying for wages and overhead in the first 3 hours), then that last 5 hours worked adds $250 in surplus value (net profit). Marx's formula for surplus value exploitation is well-known:

$$S = s/v * V; S = P * a'/a * n.$$

The individual terms are defined as follows:

- S is mass of surplus value supplied by individual workers in an average day.
- s is the variable capital advanced to purchase one worker's labor power.
- v is the sum total of variable capital (V).
- P is the value of an average worker's power.
- The degree of exploitation is defined as a'/a (surplus labor/necessary labor).
- n is the number of workers employed.

The greed for surplus labor value is such that many firms are motivated to stretch the working day, and ensure entire segments of society, classes, races, ethnicities, or nations are available not just for exploitation but also for superexploitation.

Conceptual Overview

Superexploitation

Workers paid above a living wage are exploited to the extent that surplus value exceeds the time workers need to work to cover necessities, but workers paid less than a living wage is what post-Marxists call *superexploitation*. Superexploitation is an elevation of exploitation to what Marx said was vampire-like. Capital sucks the living blood out of labor, and the vampire lives the more it sucks labor dry. Every last drop of blood and every nerve and muscle is exploited. That is how labor power purchased from labor is consumed.

Critical Commentary and Future Directions

Ethics

The ethics of superexploitation can be researched. Superexploitation includes slavery, colonialism, and contemporary global systems of sweatshop supply chains. Superexploitation violates Immanuel Kant's categorical imperative because humanity is treated as a means to an end: maximizing surplus value through superexploitation, rather than treating humanity as an end unto itself. Greed that harms one segment of humanity while ceding surplus value to another is legitimated by *practical reasoning ethics;* overworking a class of workers is the means to benefit another segment or class (lower prices at the retail store for consumers; higher dividends to shareholders; humungous salaries for executives).

Superexploitation of one class, race, or gender over another means that there is a racism, sexism, or ethnocentrism ideology in force legitimating inequitable pay for equal work. For example, Pakamani Basebanz reports that in 1986, average monthly earnings of an African worker were 28% of those of a white worker; people of color and Indian workers earned 35% and 52%, respectively, of monthly earnings received by whites.

Performativity

Performativity, defined by Marx as working labor unto death, can also be researched. Calculating systems are set up to use up the life of a worker within a set number of years. Performativity is embedded in the calculating system multinational corporations contract with subcontractors, in terms of production quotas, time-to-complete tasks, and so forth. Do these calculating systems perpetuate the performativity of superexploitation? Farm and garment-sweatshop workers often work at piece rates set by a contracting food or retail corporation. The piece rates and daily quotas are preset so workers can supposedly earn a subsistence wage in 8 or 10 hours, but often it can take 12 to 16 hours, and there is no pay for overtime. Jim Rosenbaum reports tomato workers picking in the field and processing in canneries get 4%, the farm owners get 9%, while the canneries get 83%. It's all about the calculations. In the United States, the EPA estimates that each year, 300,000 farm workers fall ill from toxic pesticides and herbicides used in the fields. Besides cancer, there are chronic skin rashes and kidney, liver, and chest cavity problems. Rosenbaum says women workers on these farms are seven times more likely to have miscarriages compared to women not working on farms. The small firms who hire immigrant works are often contracted by large global monopolies to avoid paying union workers.

Globalization and Superexploitation

Globalization, or what Marx called the "whirlpool of an international labor market dominated by the capitalist mode of production," seeks to extend the working day to 24 hours, snatching minutes or hours from workers by pilfering rest, meal, and leisure time. The vampire's hunger for surplus labor results in the slow sacrifice of humanity in global sweatshops that degenerate population of mostly young women, sacrificing their health in long hours of misery in some overcrowded, poorly ventilated House of Terror. Vampirism turns the natural day into night, "as a palliative." The vampire quenches its thirst for living blood of labor by usurping workers' time for body maintenance, growth, and development. The vampire steals time required for fresh air and sunlight while haggling over work breaks and meal times. The vampire steals workers' time to sleep and recuperate. Workers' bodily power is drained in the sweatshops until they are dead labor.

Contemporary vampirism includes ways that predominantly young women are exploited in garment and food production supplying commodities to major Western retail companies. Globalization of production feeds on mostly young women, located in Africa, Asia, and Latin America. These women make garments and grow food for firms subcontracting to major Western corporations without time to revitalize. According to Barry Mason, 75% of women in Chile's agricultural sector are hired to pick fruit on temporary work contracts. They put in more than 60 hours a week during the season. They earn below minimum wage. Mason reports that less than half of the women working in Bangladesh's textile and garment export firms have a work contract. The majority have no maternity or health coverage. In China's Guangdong province garment factories, young women work 150 hours of overtime each month. Again, most have no written contract and 90% have no access to social welfare.

Supply chain subcontractors compete with one another to offer the cheapest rates of labor to buyers from Western retail companies. Developing countries have created some 3,000 export processing zones (EPZs) in industrial parks that offer tax breaks and exempt subcontractors from heeding worker rights, as ways to attract subcontractors supplying to the large Western retail companies. The supply chains of sweatshop and agricultural sweat labor are exploitations of local workers (mostly women) by global business.

There are several methods of superexploitation besides paying nonliving wages and unequal pay that can be studied. For example, superexploiters can derive higher levels of surplus value: illegal systemic deductions from wages for overcrowded dorms or worm-ridden food, forcing workers to sign in early and work after punching out, sacking high-paid workers while replacing them with low-paid workers, understaffing production and retail or farms while keeping the quotas the same, underspending on training and equipment safety, nonexistent or overly expensive health benefits, and stealing meal and break time are common methods of superexploitation.

Micro Versus Structural Superexploitation

Micro-level superexploitation is what organizations do to workers in terms of differential working conditions, overwork, and pay inequity for one group, race, or gender of workers over another. Structural (macro-level) superexploitation is when organizations collaborate with the state to create segments of the populace with no option but to accept superexploitative work. For example, in Mexico, the Korean ambassador bargained to exempt 600 Korean maquiladora firms from labor laws, and lowering legal wages and age requirements. This sets up structural inequities, stacking the deck against the workers, denying them the right to join a union, and escalating physical, sexual, and verbal abuse in unsafe working conditions. The Kukdong factory, for example, often locked factory doors to prevent the workers from leaving—a common characteristic of a sweatshop, the hazard of being burned alive. And after the young women workers endured the brutality of a host of club-swinging thugs and militia and persevered to win their right to organize, what was the result? The conglomerates canceled their contracts. Kukdong reenacts a very old story. In Marx's view, "factory inspectors" allowed the mill owners to cheat the worker out of wages by making them start 15 minutes early and keep working 5 minutes into breaks, and this way they could steal as much as 5 hours and 40 minutes each week in uncompensated work time. Monitoring reports of this behavior were meaningless, as they were issued by corporate-contracted agents.

Research into superexploitation is not limited to developing nations. A 2004 study by Job Watch, a Victorian (Australia) employment rights legal service, reports that young people working in fast-food outlets are prone to injury and superexploitation. Tim Cobon and Susan Price, reporting on the study, provide several insights:

- 46% of fast-food workers suffered injury or illness at work, but 24% did not report it.
- 33% were not supervised adequately to ensure health and safety instructions were followed.
- 35% experienced bullying and violent assault, including sexual harassment at work.
- 10% were not paid the legal minimum wage.
- 23% were paid nothing for attending staff meetings.
- 32% worked 11 hours or more per day.
- 53% worked shifts longer than 8 hours.

Besides factory, farm, and retail worker superexploitation, there are such types as sex labor, animal, and natural resource superexploitation.

Sex Labor Superexploitation

When structural inequity occurs, leaving starvation as the only option for poor families, these families may sell their children to the sex industry. The International Labor Organization reports that 10 million children work in the globalized sex industry; 1 million enter each year. According to the Human Rights and Equal Opportunity Commission, well-to-do people, often Westerners, become sex tourists; 250,000 sex tourists visit Asia each year, with 25% coming from the United States, 16% from Germany, and 13% from both Australia and the United Kingdom. To exact higher prices from "johns," vaginal operations are performed to "renew" virginity. Debates rage on whether to consider voluntary prostitutes as exploited by sexism or only those forced into the trade, physically abused, or paid less than a living wage.

Animal Superexploitation

Animals are exploited to extract surplus value from their work and their meat. When animals are slaughtered while living, abused by overcrowding in cages, or their bodies mutilated or genetically altered to increase production, the threshold is crossed into superexploitation. People for the Ethical Treatment of Animals (PETA), for example, negotiates with several corporations for humane animal growing and killing processes that cut into surplus value extraction.

National Resource Superexploitation

When corporations cut the old growth forests so severely that there is no renewal and desertification occurs, when species diversity continues to decrease, and corporations patent seeds to deprive indigenous farmers of their livelihood, this too can be considered superexploitation.

Story Apologetics

Marx argues that superexploitation requires a story or ideology and a capitalistic anthropology to justify and excuse its material practices. One of the most persistent fantasies is free market capitalism. Free market capitalism is practical reasoning that overwork, underpay, and unsafe conditions are prices developing nations pay to join the global economy; that every nation began in slavery and pulled itself up by its boot straps; and that without government or activist interference, markets will be efficient, giving incentive for firms to be more humanitarian, when other firms become too superexploitative.

Organizations superexploiting workers is storied as a market failure, such as with monopoly. Many organization theories (transaction costs, principal agency theory) reverse the premise, focusing on how exploited capitalists are by their transaction agents (managers or executives who embezzle), as well as by (lazy) labor, and by the state that taxes corporations to pay for public goods, thereby making the market less efficient.

Another contemporary form of superexploitation is detailed in Donna Haraway's *Cyborg Manifesto.* In *informatics of domination,* new social forms of exploitation accompany a utopia-for-capital cover story. Marc Bousquet suggests that mostly young women become an integrated circuit of production, consumption, and exchange in new-media technologies, while being paid superexploited wages, accompanied by systematic destruction of health, education, welfare, and worker's rights, especially for women of color.

Corporate storytellers argue that sweatshop or sex work is an option to the drudgery farm or agricultural labor or to people starving if no such employment existed. It is argued that the subcontractors to multinational corporations must provide better conditions and pay than indigenous firms, thereby raising everyone's boat.

The minor improvements that have been realized in the conditions of the farm, sweatshop, and sex workers in recent years have been due mostly to the militant action of the workers themselves and supportive collaboration from activists. Without activism, there is retrogress, as Marx said, and old brutalities soon blossom out again.

—*David M. Boje*

See also Critical Theory; Labor and Offshoring; Storytelling; Sweatshops

Further Readings

Basabenz, P. (2005). *The African National Congress on the working class in the struggle for national liberation.* Accessed January 4, 2005, from http://www.anc.org.za/ancdocs/history/basabenz.html

Boje, D. M., Rosile, G. A., & Dámaso Miguel Alcantara Carrillo, J. (2001). *The Kukdong story: When the fox guards the henhouse.* Available online at http://cbae.nmsu.edu/~dboje/AA/kuk_dong_story.htm

Bousquet, M. (2005). *Politics of information, part II.* Accessed January 4, 2005, from http://www.electronicbookreview.com/thread/technocapitalism/introductory

Cobon, T., & Price, S. (2005). Young workers face "super sized" exploitation. *Green Left Weekly.* Accessed January 4, 2005, from http://www.greenleft.org.au/back/2005/ 641/641p7.htm

Haraway, D. (1991). *Simians, cyborgs, and women: The reinvention of nature.* New York: Routledge.

Human Rights and Equal Opportunity Commission. (2004, September 14). *Children and sexual exploitation.* Accessed January 5, 2006, from http://www.hreoc.gov.au/info_for_students

International Labor Organization. (2004, September 14). *Helping hands or shackled lives?* Accessed January 4, 2005, from http://www.ilo.org/public/english/ standards/ipec/publ/download/cdl_2004_helpinghands_en.pdf

Kant, I. (1993). *Grounding for the metaphysics of morals: On a supposed right to lie because of philanthropic concerns* (3rd ed.; J. W. Ellington, Trans.). Indianapolis, IN: Hackett. (Original work published 1785)

Marx, K. (1867). *Capital: A critique of political economy. Vol. 1: The process of capitalist production* (F. Engels, Ed.; S. Moore & E. Averling, Trans.). New York: International Publishers.

Mason, B. (2004, February). *Oxfam report: Trading away our rights: Women working in global supply chain.* Accessed January 4, 2005, from http://www.wsws.org/articles/2004/feb2004/wome-f25.shtml

Rosenbaum, J. (1989, December 15–31). The brutal exploitation of Mexican immigrant workers in the U.S. *Labor's Champion.* Accessed January 4, 2005, from http://www.geocities.com/acero.rm/US/meximm1.htm?20064

Family Business

A family business is a commercial organization in which decision making is influenced by multiple generations of a family—related by blood or marriage—who are closely identified with the firm through leadership or ownership. Owner-manager entrepreneurial firms are not considered to be family businesses because they lack the multigenerational dimension and family influence that create the unique dynamics and relationships of family businesses.

Conceptual Overview

Family business is the oldest and most common model of economic organization. The vast majority of businesses throughout the world—from corner shops to multinational, publicly listed organizations with hundreds of thousands of employees—can be considered family businesses.

The economic prevalence and importance of this kind of business are often underestimated. Throughout most of the 20th century, academics and economists were intrigued by a newer, "improved" model: large, publicly traded companies run in an apparently rational, bureaucratic manner by well-trained "organization men." Entrepreneurial and family firms, with their specific management models and complicated psychological processes, often fell short by comparison.

Privately owned or family-controlled enterprises are not always easy to study. In many cases, they are not subject to financial reporting requirements, and little information is made public about financial performance. Ownership may be distributed through trusts or holding companies, and family members themselves may not be fully informed about the ownership structure of their enterprise. However, as the 21st-century global economic model replaces the old industrial model, government policymakers, economists, and academics turn to entrepreneurial and family enterprises as a prime source of wealth creation and employment.

Family Business on the Couch

The academic field of family business—with university courses first offered in the late 1980s as a part of the multidisciplinary study of free enterprise and entrepreneurship—has been enriched by its strong historical and philosophical connections to psychology and psychoanalytic thinking. Family business is a derived discipline supported by constructs and theory from anthropology, economics, sociology, and psychology. While each of these social sciences offers important perspectives and understandings of the phenomenon, psychology provides the organizing concepts for the study of the interaction and interdependence of the family and business systems, and the emotional and social relationships they create.

Many of the early thinkers in the field were psychotherapists who, when working clinically with entrepreneurs and their families, recognized that their clients' symptoms and conflicts were based in their career and business relationships. Destructive individual or family behavior sometimes overwhelmed the family's attempts to deal with critical business issues. Therapists realized that family businesses are unique social organizations, requiring specialized interventions, techniques, and frameworks that take into account not only organizational behavioral issues and business values, but also the multiple roles and complex interpersonal relationships within the families who own these firms.

Two mutually informative perspectives have proved to be extremely helpful in addressing family business issues that fall outside the boundaries of traditional management theory: the psychodynamic perspective and the family systems approach.

The Psychodynamic Perspective

The psychodynamic perspective focuses on how individual thinking and behavior are shaped by previous developmental history. We are products of our life experiences and our family origin; therefore, the psychotherapist/psychoanalyst seeks to discover how our early experiences influence the way we interact with others as adults. Early interpersonal relationships set the stage for the kinds of interaction patterns adopted by the individual later in life. These clinical insights are helpful when deciphering the rational explanation for seemingly irrational behavior.

The Family Systems Approach

The family systems approach (which partially evolved from the psychodynamic model) looks at how the family currently interacts, and emphasizes the process of changing behavior to create more effective relationships. The family systems model recognizes the importance of past experiences but focuses its intervention on the "here and now." This is particularly useful in a business family in which people must interact on emotional *and* rational levels, in both family and business systems.

The advantage of using these two psychological perspectives when analyzing family business is that together they address the behavioral problems and enduring belief systems that underpin behavior at both the individual and family system levels. The psychodynamic model is like an income statement, showing trends and patterns over time: *Here's the overview of the last 10 years; it shows where we're coming from.* The family systems model is more like a balance sheet: *This is where we are today, and this is how we will deal with what we have.*

Sigmund Freud argued that the critical determinants of human satisfaction are love and work; this concept helps to explain why family businesses are unique. All family businesses experience to some degree a conflict between love (family) and work (the business), because families and businesses operate on different sets of values, assumptions, and agendas. In many family firms, the business system is not adequately separated from the family. The business becomes an extension of the family system, and its rules and behavior patterns. If the family pattern of functioning encourages clear boundaries and effective decision making, it will foster sound business processes. Conversely, when the family–business boundaries are blurred and the family functioning is ineffective or conflicted, management processes may be adversely affected.

Life cycle analysis yields another piece of the puzzle. Each of us plays a different role at different times in our lives, and as we age, our goals and our roles change. Business organizations and markets also have life cycles. In business-owning families, human development takes place in a matrix of business needs and family motivations, with individuals and families negotiating their roles and relationships over a lifetime. It is the interactions of the individual, the family, the business, and the marketplace life cycles that create many of the challenging situations faced by business-owning families.

The overriding challenge for a family business is how to address the structural conflicts that exist between the operating principles of the family and the business. Many constructs exist to help members of business families and their advisors identify and resolve weaknesses, build on strengths, and make emotional sense of the family's situation.

Concepts and Constructs

The Three Circles Model

The challenge for business families is that family, ownership, and business roles involve different and sometimes conflicting values, goals, and actions. For example, family members put a high priority on emotional capital—the family success that unites them through consecutive generations. Executives in the business are concerned about strategy and social capital—the reputation of their firm in the marketplace. Owners are interested in financial capital—performance in terms of wealth creation.

A three circles model is often used to show the three principal roles in a family-owned or -controlled organization: Family, Ownership, and Management. This model shows how the roles may overlap.

Everyone in the family (in all generations) obviously belongs to the Family circle, but some family members will never own shares in the family business, or ever work there. A family member is concerned with social capital (reputation within the community), dividends, and family unity.

The Ownership circle may include family members, investors, or employee-owners. An owner is concerned with financial capital (business performance and dividends).

The Management circle typically includes non–family members who are employed by the family business. Family members may also be employees. An employee is concerned with social capital (reputation) and emotional capital (career opportunities, bonuses, and fair performance measures).

A few people—for example, the founder or a senior family member—may hold all three roles: family member, owner, and employee. These individuals are intensely connected to the family business, and concerned with any or all of the above sources of value creation.

The Genogram

A genogram is an organization chart for the family. It is an enhanced family tree that not only shows family events like births and deaths, but also indicates the relationships (close, conflicted, cut off, etc.) among individuals in the family. It is a useful tool for spotting relationship patterns across generations and decrypting seemingly irrational behavior.

Family Myths

These myths—sets of beliefs that are shared by the family members—can play important defensive and protective roles in families. Myths help people cope with stress and anxiety and, by prescribing ritualistic behavior patterns, will enable them to establish a common front against the outside world. They provide a rationale for the way people behave, but because much of what makes up a family myth takes place deep beneath the surface, they also conceal the true issues, problems, and conflicts. Although these family myths can turn into a blueprint for family action, they can also turn into straitjackets, reducing a family's flexibility and capacity to respond to new situations.

Parallel Planning Processes

All businesses require planning, but business families face the additional planning task of balancing family and business demands. There are five critical issues where the needs of the family and the demands of the business overlap—and these require parallel planning action to ensure that business success does not create a family or business disaster.

1. Capital: How are the firm's financial resources allocated between different demands, including family demands?

2. Control: Who has decision-making power in the family and firm?

3. Careers: How are individuals selected for senior leadership and governance positions in the firm or family?

4. Conflict: How is this natural element of human relationships kept from becoming the default pattern of interaction?
5. Culture: How are the family and business values sustained and transmitted to owners, employees, and younger family members?

Fair Process

Fairness is a fundamental issue in family business decision making. Solutions that are perceived as fair by the family and business stakeholders are more likely to be accepted and supported. Fair process helps create organizational justice by engaging family members, whether as owners or employees, in a series of practical steps to address and resolve critical issues. Fair process lays a foundation for continued family participation over generations.

Critical Commentary and Future Directions

Current family business theory building seeks to identify the extent to which family control of social, emotional, and financial capital affects business performance. Quantitative research on the financial performance of family-influenced or -owned firms seeks to clarify whether family-controlled businesses perform better over time than publicly held organizations, and if so, why.

Research on conflict and decision making in family firms explores governance and control, and the intersections among family, management, and ownership roles. Governance is one area in which much work remains to be done; there are undoubtedly family and business governance models that more completely address both the social and technical (business) issues in organizations.

Family business strategy—specifically, long-term perspective, focus on core business, and innovation—is another area requiring additional exploration. Family firms are created by entrepreneurs, and the transition in culture created by professional management processes has implications for all organizations.

The final broad area of exploration is the unique psychological issues faced by family firms, and how family concerns affect management decisions related to leadership transitions and performance. All firms are strongly influenced by the human dimension (life cycle, personality, leadership style) of management and employees, but this has largely been ignored by organizational researchers. The impact of family dynamics on management is an area of research that should be more fully explored in the traditional business school curriculum.

Researchers of family business topics should continue to be informed by mainstream management theories, and conversely, academics whose primary interest lies in publicly held organizations should integrate the family business model into their own theoretical frameworks.

—*Manfred F. R. Kets de Vries, Randel Carlock, and Elizabeth Florent-Treacy*

See also Organizational Therapy

Further Readings

Carlock, R. S., & Ward, J. L. (2001). *Strategic planning for the family business: Parallel planning to unify the family and business.* London: Palgrave Macmillan.

Carter, B., & McGoldrick, M. (1999). *The expanded family life cycle* (3rd ed.). Boston: Allyn & Bacon.

Duvall, E. (1957). *Family development.* Philadelphia: Lippincott.

Freud, S. (1955). *Civilization and its discontents.* London: Hogard Press.

Gersick, K. E., Davis, J. A., Hampton, M. M., & Lansberg, I. (1997). *Generation to generation: Life cycles of the family business.* Boston: Harvard University Press.

Kets de Vries, M. F. R. (1996). *Family business: Human dilemmas in the family firm.* London: International Thompson Business Press.

McGoldrick, M., Gerson, R., & Shellenberger, S. (1999). *Genograms assessment and intervention* (2nd ed.). New York: Norton.

Van der Heyden, L., Blondel, C., & Carlock, R. S. (2005). Fair process: Striving for justice in the family firm. *Family Business Review, 18*(1), 1–21.

FASHION

The interest of social sciences in the phenomenon of *fashion*—the imitation of certain modes of appearance or certain ways of doing things during certain periods—is usually traced back to Herbert Spencer's *Ceremonial Institutions*, published in 1880. According to Spencer, fashion was intrinsically imitative, but the imitation could stem from two widely divergent motives. One was *reverential* imitation, such as the modification of a monarch's costume, no matter how absurd, being imitated by the courtiers. From Spencer onward, fashion was seen as the opposite of progress, connoting erratic changes in clothing, with no relation to utility or symbolic value.

The second type of imitation discerned by Spencer was motivated by *competition* or a desire to assert equality with the person imitated. The author who made the greatest contribution to this view of fashion, not the least in management and organization theory, was the economist Thorstein Veblen, author of the 1899 classic, *The Theory of the Leisure Class*. According to Veblen, fashion was the means of promoting *conspicuous consumption*, as contrasted with valuable productivity, and it was a pastime of the leisure classes.

Conceptual Overview

Thus, fashion was originally portrayed as an irrational deviation from rational behavior. Because of the stubbornness of the phenomenon, however, its simple denigration to the status of deviant behavior did not make it less conspicuous. This fact was noticed by the economist Paul Nystrom as early as 1928, when he set out to find a rational explanation of fashions. He adopted Veblen's insights, but applied business logic to them. As there is high demand for articles about what is and isn't fashionable, they must have utility, he reasoned, although this utility is, in fact, the advertisement of a capacity for conspicuous leisure or conspicuous consumption.

Quite early in the debate there also existed other ways of conceptualizing fashion. One early theoretician of fashion as a cultural phenomenon was Gabriel Tarde, who claimed in 1890 that fashion was already a strong force in antiquity, although he admitted, in agreement with the later scholars of fashion from Fernand Braudel to Elizabeth Wilson, that it was the 18th century that inaugurated the rule of fashion on a large scale. He was also first to point out fashion's paradoxical character: people follow fashion for the pleasure of change and to be different from others, but once the way dictated by fashion becomes truly popular, it becomes the common way of doing things and is no longer fashionable.

Writing in 1904, Georg Simmel seemed to agree with Spencer and Veblen, but he also continued along Tarde's train of thought. He saw in fashion a democratic and democratizing phenomenon, intensifying with the progress of civilization. This was because fashion connected two opposing tendencies: equalization and individualization.

The original focus on the trickle-down direction of reverential imitation diverted attention from the "trickle-up" and especially "trickle-across" effects. Yet, the trickle-up effect is not new. Simmel claimed that fashion for both genders is usually invented at the margins, and only legitimized when it has been adopted by higher classes, from which it then "trickles down" to the middle classes.

Unlike the many followers of trickle-down theory who tend to equate women's interest in fashionable clothes with capitalist exploitation and creation of consumable illusions, cultural scholars like Angela Partington have demonstrated how consumers are able to produce unexpected and subversive meanings around fashion goods. Another paradoxical observation is that fashion stands for change, but, as it is also repetitive, from a long-range perspective fashion stands for tradition as well. Indeed, as pointed out by Agnes Brook Young in 1937, fashion need not be seen as the opposite of progress, but rather as unrelated to progress, although it stands for modernity. Fashion, she claimed, is evolution without destination. Fashion is continuous change, unhampered by the restrictions of either aesthetics or practicality.

Young's notion of evolution without destination is also indebted to Simmel, who pointed out that although fashion operates through dramatized revolutions, it is evolutionary in character. The anthropologist Edward Sapir, who wrote the entry on fashion in the *Encyclopedia of the Social Sciences* in 1931, put it well when he said that fashion is "custom in the guise of departure from custom." Tarde would agree: In his view, fashion first opposes custom, and then, if successful, becomes a custom itself, only to be opposed by the next fashion.

Simmel's theory was not taken up until the late 1960s, by sociologist Herbert Blumer, who postulated that fashion is a *collective selection mechanism* that influences the market and distorts the demand and supply curves, both using and serving the economic competition. Its important element is a collective choice among competing tastes, things, and ideas; it is oriented toward finding but also toward creating what is typical of a given time. It can be added that fashion operates at the institutional fringes. On the one hand, its variety is limited by the "iron cage" of existing institutions, which fashion actually reproduces; on the other hand, fashion is engaged in a constant subversion of the existing institutional order, gnawing at its bars. This is yet another paradox connected to fashion: its simultaneous unimportance and saliency.

Fashion (together with other processes, like control or negotiation) introduces order and uniformity into what might seem an overwhelming variety of possibilities. In this sense, fashion helps people to come to grips with the present. At the same time, says Blumer, it helps them to detach from the grip of the past, to liberate their way of acting from past habits. As Simmel pointed out, fashion seems to occupy the dividing line between the past and the future, and, as a result, produces an enhanced feeling of the present. Fashion, in its gradual emergence, attenuates the surprises of the next fashion, and tunes into the collective by making it known to itself, as reflected in the present fashion and in the rejection of past fashions.

All scholars interested in fashion describe it as a highly paradoxical process. Its constitutive paradoxes are invention *and* imitation, variation *and* uniformity, distance *and* interest, novelty *and* conservatism, unity *and* segregation, conformity *and* deviation. It is therefore important to preserve this paradox in management studies of fashion, which translates into an imperative to study the *process* of fashion and not, as is more common, merely its results.

Fashion plays its tricks on fashion research, as well. Focusing on its products, scholars reach the conclusion that fashion is fickle and ephemeral. However, in reaching this conclusion, they miss the stable character of the production process itself. Similarly, there is a need to acknowledge the simultaneous homogenization and heterogenization that accompanies fashion. Fashion means that many people do the same thing at the same time across space, but fashion also means that they will be doing something else soon. Given a longer time horizon, however, it is likely that they will be doing the same thing, but in another place. As Kjell-Arne Røvik pointed out in his study of organizational fashions, fashion is a stable social mechanism that continually produces change.

There is no doubt that "fashion leaders" and "trend setters" exist; the point is, they are known only in retrospect. Therefore, the convenient focus on the "trickle-down" path must be complemented by tracing various kinds of "trickle ups," and, especially in the world of organizations, of "trickle acrosses."

Critical Commentary and Future Directions

Students of management are learning from students of culture in this endeavor, allowing that the world of management can learn from the world of fashion by way of analogy, not only by way of metaphor. Management is as fashion prone as clothing, interior design, and science. Moreover, as Elizabeth Wilson noted, the pointlessness of fashion that was so harshly criticized by Veblen might be that which makes it valuable in the first place. It is in the margins, where the decorative and the futile thrive, that not only a new aesthetic but a new cultural order may begin. It could be that even managers, while cultivating façades and futile practices, might be opening cracks in the solid rationality of formal prescriptions. It could also be, as postulated by Simmel, that they seek to save their freedom of action by sacrificing appearances to the dictates of the general public. This was the idea suggested by John W. Meyer and Brian Rowan when they said that organizational structures are ceremonial façades adopted in order to earn legitimacy. The managerial freedom of action might express itself in frauds and political games, but fashion deserves respect and curiosity.

In order to satisfy such curiosity, it is important to continue processual studies of fashion aimed at capturing how a fashion develops; this is where fashion research has been recently directed. As early as 1904, Simmel criticized the history of fashion for concentrating only on the development of its contents. It is important to report what is in fashion, but also to inquire, why this, and why now? Fashion is a historical concept; any specific fashion will be unintelligible if lifted out of its place in a sequence of fashions, as Sapir emphasized. Therefore, studies of fashion need to be firmly *situated*. That is, the following questions must always be asked: What was the previous fashion? What is the accessible repertoire at the time? What is happening elsewhere at the same time? This research direction promises to further redefine the role of fashion in management: from a deviant irrationality on the part of erring managers to the key to pattern recognition, permitting a better understanding of the dynamics of management across time and space.

—Barbara Czarniawska

See also Aesthetics of Organization; Arts and Organizations; Diffusion; Globalization; Management Fashions and Fads; New Institutionalism

Further Readings

Barthes, R. (1983). *The fashion system.* New York: Hill and Wang. (Original work published 1967)

Blumer, H. G. (1973). Fashion: From class differentiation to collective selection. In G. Wills & D. Midgley (Eds.), *Fashion marketing* (pp. 327–340). London: Allen & Unwin. (Original work published 1969)

Czarniawska, B. (2004). Gabriel Tarde and city management. *Distinktion,* 9, 81–95.

Czarniawska, B. (2005). Fashion in organizing. In B. Czarniawska & G. Sevón (Eds.), *Global ideas: How ideas, objects and practices travel in the global economy* (pp. 129–146). Malmö, Sweden: Liber/CBS.

Forty, A. (1986). *Objects of desire: Design and society, 1750–1980.* London: Cameron.

Leopold, E. (1992). The manufacture of the fashion system. In J. Ash & E. Wilson (Eds.), *Chic thrills: A fashion reader* (pp. 101–118). Berkeley: University of California Press.

Meyer, J., & Rowan, B. (1991). Institutionalized organizations: Formal structure as myth and ceremony. In W. W. Powell & P. J. DiMaggio (Eds.), *The new institutionalism in organizational analysis* (pp. 41–62). Chicago: University of Chicago Press. (Original work published 1977)

Nystrom, P. (1973). Character and direction of fashion movements. In G. Wills & D. Midgley (Eds.), *Fashion marketing* (pp. 193–205). London: Allen & Unwin. (Original work published 1928)

Partington, A. (1992). Popular fashion and working-class affluence. In J. Ash & E. Wilson (Eds.), *Chic thrills: A fashion reader* (pp.145–161). Berkeley: University of California Press.

Røvik, K-A. (1996) Deinstitutionalization and the logic of fashion. In B. Czarniawska & G. Sevón (Eds.), *Translating organizational change* (pp. 139–172). Berlin: de Gruyter.

Sapir, E. (1931). Fashion. *Encyclopedia of the social sciences* (pp.139–144). New York: McMillan.

Simmel, G. (1971). Fashion. In D. N. Levine (Ed.), *Georg Simmel on individuality and social forms* (pp. 294–323). Chicago, IL: University of Chicago Press. (Original work published 1904)

Spencer, H. (1880). *Ceremonial institutions: Being part IV of the principles of sociology.* New York: D. Appleton.

Tarde, G. (1903). *The laws of imitation.* New York: Henry Holt. (Original work published 1890)

Veblen, T. (1994). *The theory of the leisure class.* New York: Dover. (Original work published 1899)

Wilson, E. (1985). *Adorned in dreams: Fashion and modernity.* Berkeley: University of California Press.

Young, A. B. (1973). Recurring cycles of fashion. In G. Wills & D. Midgley (Eds.), *Fashion marketing* (pp.107–124). London: Allen & Unwin. (Original work published 1937)

FEMINISM

See RADICAL FEMINISM

FIT

Fit is the consistency either among a set of choices made by an organization, or between an organization's set of choices and its current environmental conditions.

Conceptual Overview

The concept of fit has a long tradition in the field of organization studies. As a result, it has been employed in many uses. While it is generally employed to describe a state of consistency among various elements, the nature of these elements can differ. Consequently, it is helpful to distinguish between two broad classes of fit: internal fit—the fit among various elements under the control of an organization—and external fit—the appropriateness of an organization's chosen elements given the organization's environment. Both types of fit will be discussed in turn.

Internal fit has been discussed at various levels of aggregation. At a high level, organizations need to seek, for instance, fit between their strategy and structure. At a lower level, organizations need to seek fit between their strategy and the various activities they put in place. At an even lower level, organizations need to seek fit among their various policies or organizational design elements. At each level, one can identify various combinations of elements that are internally consistent, or that form *configurations*.

At the heart of fit is the concept of *interaction*. Two elements interact when the value of one element is influenced by another element. For instance, the value of flexible manufacturing equipment is influenced by the breadth of products that are offered by a firm: The broader the product range, the more valuable the flexibility afforded by the equipment (and the more valuable is an increase in flexibility). As a result, the combinations of high flexibility and broad product range, and low flexibility and narrow product range, are both consistent—each pair of choices concerning equipment and product range displays internal fit.

A number of studies have conceptualized fit as such pairwise consistency, or complementarity. However, the concept of configuration usually goes one step further by identifying a whole set of elements that all fit with each other. Such a systemic viewpoint is particularly important if interactions exist across more than two elements and if interactions themselves are affected by other choices that an organization has taken.

A helpful visualization tool for the notion of fit is a performance landscape consisting of "horizontal" dimensions representing the various choice elements of an organization and a "vertical" dimension representing the resulting performance associated with each combination of choices. Interactions create multiple peaks on these landscapes, with each peak representing an internally consistent set of choices—a configuration that displays high internal fit. This visualization also suggests one precise definition of internal fit: A set of choices has internal fit if no incremental change can be found that would be performance enhancing.

The notion of external fit has played a prominent role in the work on contingency theory. For instance, various mappings between different organizational structures and different environmental conditions (e.g., volatility, complexity) have been proposed. Here, fit denotes a consistency between an organization's choice—for instance, with respect to its structure—and its environment. Again, the landscape visualization is helpful in this context. Given that the performance values of the landscape take into account all performance-relevant attributes (e.g., customer tastes, competitors' positions, available technology), the height of the landscape at a particular configuration represents the appropriateness of this configuration—that is, its external fit.

Critical Commentary and Future Directions

The distinction between internal and external fit is helpful as they do not have to go hand in hand. An organization may have a consistent set of activities (i.e., high internal fit) that is not very appropriate given the current environmental conditions (i.e., low external fit). For instance, the traditional mass manufacturing system, as developed by Ford, is still an internally consistent set of activities, yet its value has been eclipsed by a different internally consistent set of activities, the lean manufacturing system developed by Toyota.

One should note that it is the presence of multiple peaks (multiple consistent sets of choices) caused by the interactions among choices that drives a wedge between internal and external fit. If all choices an organization engaged in were independent from each other, the performance landscape would have a single peak. In that landscape, high internal fit and high external fit would go hand in hand, as an organization that maximized its internal fit would automatically also maximize its external fit (by sitting on the single peak of the landscape). With multiple peaks, internal fit can be associated with different levels of performance. This observation also implies that multiple peaks do not necessarily imply equifinality. Different internally consistent sets of choices might be available, but not all of them may lead to the same performance outcome.

The notions of internal and external fit raise a number of research challenges. With respect to internal fit, dynamic aspects have generally found little attention. How do organizations arrive at sets of internally consistent choices? What different developmental paths do organizations follow? What leads to different paths? What are the consequences of having developed along different paths, for instance, regarding an organization's ability to respond to environmental changes? With respect to external fit, a still unresolved question is what types of choices an organization should make if it faces multiple external conditions that require opposing actions. How can an organization find the right balance if contradictory requirements have to be met? Should an organization try to find a static balance, or perhaps change its structure over time so as to achieve a dynamic balance?

—*Nicolaj Siggelkow*

See also Complex Adaptive Systems; Complex Organizations; Structural Contingency Theory

Further Readings

Milgrom, P. R., & Roberts, J. (1995). Complementarities and fit: Strategy, structure, and organizational change in manufacturing. *Journal of Accounting and Economics, 19,* 179–208.

Miller, D., & Friesen, P. H. (1984). *Organizations: A quantum view.* Englewood Cliffs, NJ: Prentice Hall.

Siggelkow, N. (2002). Evolution toward fit. *Administrative Science Quarterly, 47,* 125–159.

Van de Ven, A. H., & Drazin, R. (1985). The concept of fit in contingency theory. *Research in Organizational Behavior, 7,* 333–365.

Venkatraman, N. (1989). The concept of fit in strategy research: Toward verbal and statistical correspondence. *Academy of Management Review, 14,* 423–444.

FIVE FORCES

The model of five forces is an industry structural model to understand the workings of competitive forces and to formulate a company's active and reactive competitive strategies against its rivals. An industry is a group of firms producing products and services that are close substitutes of each other's.

Conceptual Overview

These structural forces have a strong influence in determining the competitive strategies that are effectively and potentially available to the firm. In addition, since structural forces affect all firms equally, the key is to find the differing competencies of firms to deal with them.

The intensity of competition in an industry depends on five basic competitive forces; the profit potential of the industry, measured in terms of long-run return on invested profit depends on the five forces taken together. These five forces include the following: (1) threats from new entrants; (2) substitution of new products or services; (3) bargaining power of suppliers; (4) bargaining power of buyers; and finally, (5) the existing competitors.

The threat of new entry depends mainly on what sort of barriers there are to entry, whereas substitution depends on the rate of innovation in the industry. The bargaining power of suppliers and buyers has to do with the strategic configuration of the firm's value chain and its capacity to defend itself from the threat of forward and backward integration of its partners and customers.

The *threat of entry* into an industry depends on the barriers to entry that are present, together with the reaction from the existing rivals that the entrant can expect. If barriers are high or the newcomer can expect sharp retaliation from existing rivals, the threat of entry is low. If the opposite is true, entry is easy and profits are easily eroded. There are six major sources of barriers to entry: economies of scale, product differentiation, capital requirements, switching costs, access to distributing channels, and cost disadvantages independent of scale such as property rights and government policies.

Intensity of rivalry among existing competitors takes the form of fighting for position using price competition, and differentiation of product(s) and service(s) through advertising. Rivalry occurs because rivals feel the pressure or see the opportunity to improve competitive position in the market. Rivalry does not necessarily leave the industry better off in terms of profitability. If actions and reactions escalate, all firms in the industry may suffer and be worse off than before, especially following a price war. Price cuts are quickly and easily followed by rivals, and once matched, they lower revenues for all firms unless industry price elasticity is high enough. Conversely, advertising may expand demand or increase the level of product differentiation in the industry to the benefit for all firms.

Pressure for *substitute products* limits the potential returns of an industry by placing a limit on the prices firms can profitably charge. Two types of substitute products and services deserve more attention: those that show a price performance that is superior to those offered by the industry in question; and product(s)/service(s) that show average profit earnings above the industry average, and which can sustain a lowering of price without impairing their quality.

Bargaining power of buyers and suppliers may force price down, due to bargaining for higher quality in products and services, and driving competition against rivals to the detriment of the industry's profitability. The power of each buyer or seller segment depends on several characteristics, namely the credible threat of backward or forward integration and switching costs.

Competition in an industry continually works to drive the rate of return on invested capital down toward the competitive floor rate of return. The strength of competition forces in an industry determines the ability of firms to sustain above-average returns. The five forces reflect the fact that competition in an industry goes well beyond the established players. Customers, suppliers, substitutes, and potential entrants are considered "extended rivalry."

All five competitive forces jointly determine the intensity of an industry's competition and profitability, and the strongest force(s) is/are crucial to strategy formulation.

The underlying structure of an industry, reflected in the strength of the forces, should be distinguished from the many short-term factors that can affect competition and profitability in a transitory period. The focus of the structural analysis is on identifying industry rooted in its economics and technology, which shape the arena in which competitive strategy takes place. Firms will each have unique core competencies in dealing with industry structure, and these will change over time. Although the industry structure is historically built, an understanding of its basic forces is the starting point for analyzing the dynamics of firms' competitive strategies.

Critical Commentary and Future Directions

Methodologically, there is some controversy over the appropriate definition of an industry, which is centered on how close substitutes need to be in terms of products and processes. Also, the geographical boundaries of the industry are not clearly limited to a specific area, region, or nation, nor are they open to the world. Therefore, Porter's concept of a "national diamond" is an extension of the five forces model where "related industries" and national competitive advantage are treated in a dynamic context. The value chain of the enterprise is open to the world, and rivalry is questioned in terms of how firms can acquire competitive advantage in a specific national environment. Government and chance (natural resources, climate, size of the market) are incorporated into the model to explain comparative advantage of some firms within sectors. The role of government policies is explicitly recognized as a force impacting the industry structure and existing rivalry.

Although most of the structural analysis is performed in the short run, industry change is strategically important because it is a source of structural change. The trends holding the greatest importance from the strategic viewpoint are the most relevant for the competitive analysis. Therefore, structural analysis can be important in predicting the eventual profitability of an industry and the performance of innovative firms. In the long run, the important methodological task is to examine each competitive force, forecast the magnitude of each underlying cause, and then construct a landscape of the probable profit potential of the industry.

—*Sonia Dahab*

See also Competition; Market-Based Theory; Organizational Development; Organizational Structure; Structuration

Further Readings

Chandler, A. D., Jr., Solvell, O., & Hagstrom, P. (Eds.). (1998). *The dynamic firm: The role of technology, strategy, organization, and regions.* London: Oxford University Press.

Porter, M. E. (1979, March/April). How competitive forces shape strategy. *Harvard Business Review,* 66–75.

Porter, M. E. (1980a). *The competitive advantage of nations.* New York: Free Press.

Porter, M. E. (1980b). *Competitive strategy: Techniques for analyzing industries and competitors.* New York: Free Press.

FOLLOWERSHIP

In organization studies, followership is categorized as a field of study in the area of leadership and generally refers to what the followers of leaders do. More specifically, followership refers to the behavior exhibited by followers as a result of influence or guidance from a leader. Kelley is credited with providing the seminal piece of work on followership, which is recognized as a neglected field of study. Despite the fact that followership is of central importance to leadership, research into this area remains underexplored.

Conceptual Overview

Kelley's original contribution highlights the importance of the follower to leadership and challenges the pervading assumption that organizational success can be attributed solely to the actions of leaders. He also challenges the assumed passivity of followers and argues that, in actual fact, leaders contribute no more than 20% to the success of an organization and that the actions of followers are central to the remaining 80%. To support his claims, he developed a two-dimensional taxonomy of followership. The first dimension provides a measure for how followers think, ranging from uncritical dependent thinking to critical independent thinking. The second dimension provides a measure for the degree of follower engagement in work and ranges from active to passive involvement; the active style represents full participation, while the passive style represents limited participation and constant supervision by the leader. He argues that a greater understanding of the thinking and engagement styles of followers provides a rich source of information about who is contributing to organizational success. Based on this empirical classification of follower behavior, Kelley also developed a conceptual typology that identifies five roles that are central to followership, namely those of the *alienated follower, conformist follower, passive follower, effective follower,* and *pragmatic survivor.* In doing so, he provides insight into followership that moves its definition beyond the usual terms of conformity, weakness, and passivity, and signifies the broader contribution that followers make to the success of their organizations.

In more recent times, writers have defined leadership and followership in terms of a relationship based on mutual influence between leaders and followers who act with respect to shared purposes. Such a definition highlights the reciprocal nature of the relationship between leaders and followers and resonates with social exchange theory, leader–member exchange theory, and transactional leadership theory—the latter being recognized as a theory of leadership in which the follower is of central importance.

Critical Commentary and Future Directions

As already acknowledged, research in the field of leadership focuses primarily on the leaders of organizations; followers are relegated to a subservient position and relative obscurity. However, leadership is a necessary social phenomenon, and it cannot exist without followers. More to the point, the success of leadership is dependent on the constraints and opportunities presented and enabled by followers. Those writers interested in followership have focused on what followers do, in order to better understand the leadership/follower relationship. For example, charisma has been defined in terms of followers' reactions to the leader's personality traits as well his or her strategic vision and operational expertise; the heightened emotional states of followers in given situations; and, in more recent times, feelings of empowerment for followers. Conger points out, however, that while these studies have resulted in a greater understanding of the relationships between leadership behavior and follower compliance, knowledge concerning follower dispositions and the dynamics of dependency is limited.

In regard to compliance, in many cases writers treat followership and compliance as interchangeable concepts, yet one could argue that compliance offers little if any room for choice, and the term followership *implies* choice—one chooses the leader he or she wishes to follow.

The literature is also pervaded by theories and models aimed at promulgating what types of follower behavior will make followership successful. In this sense, the literature is somewhat normative. Following on from this point, the vast majority of writers neglect the complex nature of power relation between leaders and followers. Traditionally, the leader–follower relationship is one in which the leader is clearly differentiated from the follower on the basis of his or her superior power. To assume, as many approaches to followership do, that followers will question and engage in conflict with their leaders is sociologically vacuous and politically naïve. From a practical perspective, such a suggestion neglects the fact that when someone is in a leadership position, he or she is in a position of power; followers are well aware of this power and act accordingly, and in most cases this act is one of deference to the leader. Reflecting on the practical consequences of this point, some would argue that the practice of followership may result in the opposite of what its theory espouses; that is, those who practice followership may quite unwittingly reinforce the dominant position of the leader, resulting in an unobtrusive form of compliance, which, as mentioned previously, renders choice in followership problematic. In short, the literature suggests that "true" followership cannot be achieved without follower autonomy, which is somewhat paradoxical when one considers the nature of power relations between leaders and followers. There is no direct acknowledgment, let alone empirical verification, that provides insight into the practical consequences of such a paradox, and this area would be a particularly fruitful one for future research endeavors. The key focus of such research would be how, in both a sociological and cognitive sense, a follower can achieve autonomy while following a leader at the same time.

—*Raymond Daniel Gordon*

See also Empowerment; Influence; Leadership, Charisma; Leadership, Transactional; Power

Further Readings

Alcorn, D. S. (1992). Dynamic followership: Empowerment at work. *Management Quarterly, 33,* 9–13.

Conger, J. A. (1999). Charismatic and transformational leadership in organizations: An insider's perspective on these developing streams of research. *Leadership Quarterly, 10*(2), 145–179.

Kelley, R. E. (1988). In praise of followership. *Harvard Business Review, 66,* 142–148.

Kelley, R. E. (1992). *The power of followership.* New York: Doubleday.

FORESIGHT

Foresight is a word that emerged in the English language in the 14th century. In its simplest meaning, it is the ability to predict the future. This meaning is linked to foresight as the front sight of a gun—a piece of technology that helps one hit the target.

Most "futurists" have abandoned the earlier meaning, as the uncertainties that beset the future are now recognized as so complex and dynamic that their systemic behavior is quite unpredictable and thus unknowable. The general public, however, still tends to believe that the role of the futurist is to predict, and futurists do well to appreciate this anomaly. Within the "foresighting" community, the term foresight relates to the application of a perspective of care and attention as to possible future needs, as well as potential events and outcomes. It demands competencies in foreseeing and exploring multiple futures, and a motivation of "being prepared" in such a manner that both enables an organization to be adaptive to alternative futures and, wherever possible, to be generative by using foresight to change the way the future unfolds.

Conceptual Overview

Foresight in Practice

A foresight framework is increasingly used by businesses and organizations worldwide, and it is not uncommon to find people with job titles that include "foresight" and foresight-related descriptions. In recent years, for instance, the government of Singapore has established a scenario planning office, the brewing company Fosters Australia has an internal foresight group, and the University of Strathclyde in Scotland has in its business school the Centre for Scenario Planning and Future Studies.

Strategic planners and decision makers apply foresight in many ways and use diverse methodologies for delivering the benefits. The major broad methodologies are scenario planning and scenario thinking, with their accepted lineage from Shell in the seventies and eighties; integral futures as developed by Ken Wilber in the nineties and other devotees of holistic approaches; trend analysis; and frameworks like "three horizons." Scenarios, or coherent stories or narrative visions that describe plausible future states of the world as environments in which organizations will possibly have to operate, are common to most strategic approaches to the future.

Strategic Contexts

All foresight activities deal with change and are directed at improving our understanding of the future as a context for the development of better quality strategic decisions and evaluations about change being made today. As Pierre Wack described in a landmark article in the *Harvard Business Review* in 1984, the journey to alternative futures is designed to transform the way one sees the present: to "re-perceive" reality by learning from the future and applying these insights to decision making today.

Foresightful strategists would also do well to recognize that there are three key approaches to strategic development currently within organizations. The first approach follows the logic of "it'll be OK," whatever happens, in which organizations passively await the future with a sense of optimism. In current debates, the supporters of this approach argue, for example, that the future will not throw up anything that cannot be dealt with using current thinking or current technologies. Technology, it is argued, will save us from the exigencies of climate change, aging, health pandemics, water shortages, and so on. In scenario terms, these are the "brave old world" or "business as usual" scenarios.

The next approach to the future is preoccupied with predicting it while accepting the phenomenon of change. We call these the "getting it right" futures and they rely on spotting trends, extrapolation from past experiences, hopeful speculation, and what we call "preferred" or "normative" futures. The latter are those futures that express our vision of a world in which we would like to live, where we use our willpower to think a future into being and exert our deterministic powers to make it happen.

The third approach is the "not getting it wrong" futures. The essence is the idea of the learning self as a subsystem operating within the organizational system, which in turn is embedded within the environment in which it must operate. So the scenarios revealed are about alternative future environments to which the system must adapt and not, as is usually the case with the "getting it right" group, about alternative preferred futures of the system, or the single future suggested by the "it'll be OK" optimists. Scenarios produced are value free. They may be valued differently, but the processes by which they are created are not. The scenarios are actively anticipated, involve reflexive participation, and are cogenerated by the scenario builders.

Scenario Planning

Scenario planning can be conceptualized and applied as a social, reflexive, and transformative process of experiential learning that combines theoretical and philosophical rigor with practical application. Three cycles of such learning can be recognized, which are reflected in the mnemonic QUEST.

"QU" is for *questions*. It is the first step in the process—the first learning cycle—in which decisions are made about the strategic issues or questions for which we need the scenario process to provide contextual guidance. These could be a combination of "meta," "macro," or "micro" issues, depending on the task at hand. Whatever the focus, scenarios are usually employed to help us make strategic decisions, and without such an "issues" focus they will be too blunt to be of help. The outcome of this first learning cycle is a framing question or questions (the "focal" question in the Shell approach, sometimes called the strategic or scenario agenda).

"E" is for the future *environments* in which our questions will play out; this is the focus of the second learning cycle. Because we don't know which systemic combinations of the influences on those environments will emerge, the quest is for a range of different but plausible futures that result from the interplay and confluence of different "influences." The idea of influences is preferred over the more commonly adopted term "driving forces" because the constructs we create are quite neutral as to their intentionality. No one is doing the driving, and there is no inherent motive in the concepts. Influences are revealed through our [I]NSPECT process, which is a version of STEEP. Leaving the "I" to one side for a moment, the domains covered by the other letters of the mnemonic are influences from the Natural world, Society, Politics, Economics, Culture, and Technology. We use team brainstorming, Delphi interviewing, desk research, conversations with "remarkable" people, expert panels, and Socratic dialogue. The "I" stands for the self and emphasizes the significance of the worldviews of all of the participants in the process, on its outcomes. We talk sometimes of the "official" future of an organization, and in so doing we are suggesting how the theory of reality will converge for people who share organizational culture and views of the world.

The "S" in QUEST is for *scenarios*. We cluster, winnow, and focus the influences to create a list of "impaxes." In the Shell school, these are called "critical uncertainties," but our new word conveys the dynamics of the influences in a more dramatic way. An impax is an influence that is both important *and* uncertain, but also can be represented as an axis of different states. For example, oil prices, birth rates, and the acceptance of technology are all influences on future environments, each of which can be scaled along an axis of likely impact from low to high.

Some practitioners reduce the impaxes to the top two and then pitch them against each other in a matrix. This deductive method requires the two impaxes to be orthogonal and has the advantage of producing four mutually exclusive worlds. Its weaknesses are that we do not live in a two-dimensional world and that, at its heart, it is deterministic.

We favor the inductive approach, creating a scenario table of the top 10 or so influences in which we choose the state of any one impax, then the next, and so on until we have a set that creates an emergent scenario. Of course, we must test each scenario created for its plausibility, logic, and robustness, and then ensure that each scenario within our set of scenarios is suitably differentiated from the others.

Finally, "T" is for *transformation*. Foresight practitioners worldwide are involved with change. Change management is usually opposition management unless we understand that you cannot change organizations, you can only change people. So the first emphasis is on how people involved in the process of foresighting, whether using scenarios or not, are transformed by the process so that their perspectives on the world (the "I" in INSPECT) are now different. This transformation may be of two kinds. The first involves *changing your mind* about your worldview. Imagine you are a road builder. Your view may have been that your core business is building roads. After engaging in a foresighting process, you may now believe the business you are in is not building roads but creating databases about transport behavior, or leisure, or rainfall and storm water collection—and so on. The transformation is about content: "What I now see is different."

The second transformation has to do with *process*. Scenario building, for example, informs a person that the world contains multiple world views, and he or she may acquire learning that suggests that the person needs to embrace processes that inform him or her about them and help the individual to adapt his or her practice accordingly. When the individuals involved are transformed, it is now possible for them to transform their organization.

Most foresight practitioners are well aware that the big payoff from their work with people is to change the way they think about problems. Deterministic thinking stresses moving from problems to solutions. Leadership is often described as the ability to do that, and fast. However, scenario thinking requires us to contextualize problems and rehearse alternative actions before we move to a solution. And because all intervention is systemic by nature, we learn to be both cautious and reflexive in relation to our strategy.

The third transformation involves the exploration of current strategies and strategic plans with respect to their strengths and weaknesses in addressing the challenges of the imagined futures that are the outcomes of the previous transformation concerned with the building of the scenarios. In recent years, attention has been paid to the idea of strategic or critical conversations. Once a foresight process has been embarked upon and the "deliverables" delivered—such as, for example, a scenario book with mapped strategic implications for the organization—we need to embed a continuing and discursive conversation among the people at work that will keep the new awareness at a heightened state to the point of practical application.

Techniques to do this have one common feature: the need for discourse, which can be supported in many ways. Scenario practitioners use environmental monitoring and scanning, blogging, and "wind tunneling" as suitable means to achieve this end.

Critical Commentary and Future Directions

Foresight and scenario planning are increasing in popularity, although the potency and compelling nature of the "deliverables" are not yet secure. There is a shared understanding that the arrival of new futures is accelerating, and we should expect to see more changes in the next 25 years than we have seen in the last 100. The costs of not being prepared for the "discontinuities" or surprises that the future brings are accelerating as well.

If foresight practitioners are essentially involved with the business and organizational literacy of their clients, and these clients are essentially involved with the transactional success of their operations, the big question is, how do we connect the two in a way that makes the foresight deliverables an essential part of day-to-day activity for the organization? There are perhaps three ways this might happen:

1. *The impact of a crisis.* This occurs when something goes wrong in the operational environment from which people learn the need for foresight. Climate change has this capacity, as do "novel but critical" applications, using new technology.

2. *The need for risk management.* Reinsurers and their actuaries have been practicing foresight for many years. Climate change, terrorism, and health pandemics are among the many items with transactional risk potential that have been factored in so as to calculate insurance premiums. Organizations increasingly see the need to "be prepared," which foresight can deliver as an essential way of protecting the interests of shareholders and stakeholders.

3. *The need for innovation.* Few topics have become as important in business and organizational development innovation in the last 10 years. Innovation can be an adaptive response, but in most contexts it is generative. To the extent that generative innovation implies a discontinuity, a leap forward, it feeds off the contextualizing force of foresight. In the commercial world, competitive advantage is seen as a precious commodity that is under increasing pressure as innovation flies in from all directions.

—*Oliver Freeman*

See also Adaptive Learning; Delphi Technique; Organizational Learning; Risk Management; Scenario Planning; Strategic Choice; Technology; Uncertainty

Further Readings

Schwartz, P. (1991). *The art of the long views.* New York: Doubleday.

Van der Heijden, K. (2005). *Scenarios: The art of strategic conversation.* Chichester, UK: Wiley.

Van der Heijden, K., Bradfield, R., Burt, G., Cairns, G., & Wright, G. (2002). *The sixth sense: Accelerating organizational learning with scenarios.* Chichester, UK: Wiley.

Wack, P. (1984, September/October). Scenarios: The gentle art of reperceiving. *Harvard Business Review*, 73–89.

Formal Organizations

Formal organizations differ from generic forms of social organizations—e.g., groups, communities, societies—in that they are consciously designed social systems. Formal organizations are collectivities with highly formalized social structures. Formalization refers to the extent to which roles and relations are prescribed independently of the personal attributes and relations of specific participants. Formalization renders behavior more predictable by standardizing and regulating it. It allows for the design of social structure, treating it as an object to be manipulated—designed and redesigned. In contrast to informal organizations, such as neighborhood or friendship groups, formal organizations stress positions over persons and roles over personalities. Formal organizations also exhibit relatively high goal specificity. More so than most collectivities, they attempt to orient the design of their structures and the activities of their participants around a set of explicit, specialized objectives.

To focus on formal organizations is to emphasize the emergence, during the Enlightenment period, of social forms designed to achieve limited goals. Unlike kinship or diffuse patrimonial systems, these organizations were consciously established to achieve specified objectives. Gradually, over long periods of time, collective actors (organizations) were differentiated from individual actors (persons). Whereas earlier social forms, such as manors and guilds, wholly contained their members and possessed full authority over them, the new forms, such as city-states (and, subsequently, nation-states) and private companies distinguished between the rights of individuals and those of collective actors. The processes involved in bringing about these distinctive forms were not only technological progress and increasing economic interdependence, but also institutional work, including the construction of new categories of actors, rules, and social relationships. These developments were codified into political constitutions and legal statues: recognition during the late 17th and early 18th century of the rights of citizens separate from those of nation-states and, during the mid-1900s, creation of the limited liability corporation, in which the corporation was treated as a legal person and the liabilities of individual members were limited to their individual investments.

For many centuries, organizations were scarce, reserved primarily for military operations and major construction projects. Today, organizations are ubiquitous, employed in multiple private and public sectors, coordinating the production and supply of an astonishing array of specialized goods and services. One of the primary hallmarks of a "developed" or "modern" society is the size and variety of its organizational infrastructure.

Conceptual Overview

The importance of both public and private organizations was becoming apparent to scholars during the 19th century, as evidenced by the attention paid to public administrative forms ("bureaucracies") by scholars such as Max Weber and Robert Michels, and to industrial forms by Karl Marx, among others. In addition to these historical-descriptive accounts, early empirical work was pioneered principally by industrial engineers, such as Frederick W. Taylor.

Rational and Natural System Models

During the first half of the 20th century, two contrasting views of organizations emerged, which are still discernable in contemporary scholarship. Stemming primarily from studies by engineers and early administrative theorists, a *rational system* perspective developed that treated organizations as instrumental tools for accomplishing goals. Organizations were regarded as distinctive types of social structures that (1) pursue relatively specific goals; and (2) are characterized by relatively formalized structures. Goal specificity is important because the more specific the goal, the more clear are the criteria available for deciding how to organize, addressing issues such as who to recruit, how to allocate tasks among participants, how to design control and incentive systems, and how to coordinate activities to achieve objectives. As noted, formalization serves to objectify the structure, rendering it more independent of individual differences and more readily altered to fit changing circumstances. The presumption is that formal organizations are better suited to ensure both effectiveness and efficiency.

By contrast, a *natural system* perspective, which emerged with the work of social psychologists and sociologists during the 1930s and 1940s, insisted that organizations were not as distinctive as claimed. Goals were observed to be complex and multifaceted, not specific, and, while a formal skeleton might be erected, actual behavior was better predicted from informal structure—interpersonal networks and norms. Rather than being oriented to performance values, organizational behavior was seen to be more responsive to concerns for system survival and for protecting vested interests of participants. A conflict version of these arguments went further: Rational system models were accused of ignoring the importance of goal conflicts among members. Organizational structures were more reflective of power differences among members, enabling some participants to legitimately impose their will on others.

Attempts to reconcile these perspectives are manifold and ongoing up to the present. However, most organization theory and research can be seen to privilege one perspective over the other, the conflict forming a fault line along which dispute and debate continue.

Closed and Open System Models

By contrast, open system perspectives, emphasizing the importance of the wider context within which organizations operate, have largely supplanted earlier closed system models. *Closed system* views were widespread during the first half of the 20th century. During this time, most theorists and researchers treated organizations as relatively autonomous, self-contained systems. Indeed, great attention was accorded to the setting and policing of their boundaries. Scholars focused on participant behavior and relations, and on informal and formal structural characteristics. Topics such as centralization and decentralization, span of control, specialization and the division of labor, departmentalization and coordination, and leadership and morale dominated the agenda.

However, concepts and arguments from a broad, interdisciplinary perspective, termed "general systems theory," that arose during the late 1950s, quickly penetrated organization studies, transforming theoretical models and broadening research designs to include recognition of the role of the wider environment in organization structure and behavior. Since the 1950s, most of the influential theoretical perspectives guiding organization studies have embraced the insights of open system theory. These quickly were embraced and pursued by both rational and natural system scholars.

Combined Models
Rational Open System Approaches

Several theoretical approaches retained rational system assumptions but combined them with open system conceptions. Primary among these are the following:

- Bounded rationality—the view that organization structures are designed to help individual participants make the best decisions possible given the limited cognitive capacity of human actors faced with complex and uncertain environments
- Contingency theory—proposing that, in the interests of improving performance, organizations adapt their structures to the requirements of their environments
- Transaction cost analysis—an approach that argues that organizational structures exist and vary in design in order to reduce the costs of negotiating and monitoring economic exchanges
- Agency theory—viewing organization structures as systems designed by "principals" (owners or primary beneficiaries) to motivate and control "agents" (those hired to assist in the pursuit of principal's goals)
- Knowledge-based theories—arguing that organizations are usefully viewed as possessing distinctive bundles of dynamic capabilities encoded in their work routines and knowledge systems, allowing some to compete more effectively than others

All of these and related approaches stress the intentionally rational nature of organizations faced with varying environmental challenges.

Natural Open System Approaches

Confronting these views, a number of models combining open system with natural system assumptions have arisen during recent decades, including the following:

- Resource dependence—recognizing that although organizations are engaged in economic exchanges, these often give rise to power-dependence issues, which in turn may be managed by political processes, such as cooptation and lobbying
- Organizational ecology—a perspective embracing an evolutionary model viewing organizations as competing with similar forms to survive in a world of scarce resources
- Institutional theory—a collection of arguments emphasizing the importance of symbolic aspects of the environment—rules, norms, beliefs—that constrain and empower, constitute and penetrate organizational structures and processes.

Changes in Levels of Analysis

As theoretical models employed to examine organizations have shifted over time from closed to open system models, the level of analysis at which organizations are studied has moved ever upward. These changes affect the ways in which formal organizations are treated by scholars. Early accounts regarded organizations primarily as *contexts*—as a collection of structural and cultural features shaping the behavior of their participants. Somewhat later, analysts began to recognize organizations themselves as *corporate actors*—as systems containing distinctive structural features and capacities for action. More recently, organizations are increasingly viewed as *components* operating within larger systems of action. Thus, contingency theory posits the importance of an "organization set," identifying a focal organization in relation to a diverse collection of exchange partners; organizational ecology emphasizes the importance of the "organizational population," an aggregate of organizations exhibiting the same form or operating within the same environmental niche; and institutional theory stresses the value of the "organization field," a system of similar and diverse organizations operating within the same market or sector. In short, more organizational analysts view organizations not as isolated actors but as interdependent participants in wider sectoral, societal, and global systems.

Common and Divergent Features

Common Features

All organizations exhibit certain features in common. All organizations are social structures created by individuals to support the collaborative pursuit of goals. As such, all organizations confront a set of similar problems. All must define and redefine their objectives, select and recruit participants, produce incentives to motivate contributions, allocate tasks among participants, control and coordinate contributions, acquire necessary inputs from suppliers and locate markets or outlets for goods and services, cultivate legitimacy and support from oversight units and neighbors, and find ways of coping with the comings and goings of participants and changing environmental conditions.

The historic strength of organizations as a social forms has long been associated with three attributes: (1) their *durability*, in particular, their ability to replace participants and repair and renew structures in ways allowing them to persist over time; (2) their *reliability*, that is, their capacity to routinely perform a range of activities in a sustained manner; and (3) their *accountability*, stemming from their formal structures containing rules and authority systems that provide both guidelines and justifications for decisions and activities.

In addition to these and related common capacities, organizations are confronted by a number of common ills. In addition to the resources required for pursuing goals, substantial amounts must also be expended in the maintenance and restoration of the organization itself: All organizations must attend to support necessities as well as to the pursuit of avowed objectives. In situations where survival and goal attainment conflict, survival is likely to win out. Organization features intended as means can become ends in themselves. Discipline and attention to rules can merge into rigidity and ritualistic conformity. The very features that lead to reliability and predictability of performance are the source of inertia and can become competency traps, inhibiting improvement and learning. Contributions from similarly situated participants are never equal, and there will always be conflicts of interest among different categories of participants or "stakeholders."

Divergent Factors

Organizations pursue an enormous variety of objectives, incorporate individuals of varying characteristics and abilities, and operate in highly diverse contexts. They vary greatly in size, shape, scope of activities, and technologies employed. The largest contemporary organizations are military units and public administrative structures. The long-dominant manufacturing sector has been continuously shrinking in its share of employment throughout the 20th century to the point where today in the United States, only about 10% of the workforce is employed in manufacturing. Firms within service industries, such as Wal-Mart and McDonald's, are currently among the largest private companies. As a further indicator of the changing conditions of the labor market, in 2004, three of the largest five private employers were temporary employment agencies. At the beginning of the 21st century, America's most valuable foreign export was intellectual capital: the selling of licensing fees and royalties.

In addition to size, organizations vary greatly in organizational form. Early functionally differentiated, unitary forms, dominant during the latter half of the 19th century, gradually gave way to more diversified, multidivisional forms composed of a central office responsible for financial management and strategic planning, overseeing multiple divisions engaged in related and often unrelated businesses. However, toward the end of the 20th century, these forms, through processes ranging from unbundling to hostile takeovers followed by "bust-ups," have given way to more focused, lean enterprises. The latest forms to appear are network organizations, ranging from temporary alliances and joint ventures among independent companies, to "core ring" systems of geographically concentrated smaller firms clustered around a central assembly facility, to industrial districts composed of multiple cooperating and competing small firms, such as Silicon Valley in California.

Public agencies have also undergone related modifications, shifting from a reliance on large collections of insulated civil servants in centralized bureaucracies to increasing substitution of private providers and the contracting out of functions to both nonprofit and for-profit providers. Like private organizations, public agencies have undergone significant downsizing via privatization and outsourcing. Many public organizations are hybrid forms, operating as enterprises, dependent on the sale of their services, while others participate in elaborate systems of public–private partnerships.

In addition to employing organizations, large number of voluntary associations exist, including churches, professional societies, trade associations, fraternities and sororities, civic/service organizations, and reform and activist organizations, all constituting a vital societal infrastructure. In the United States at least, the structure of voluntary associations has shifted from primary dependence on the efforts of voluntary rank-and-file members to reliance on a professional staff structure in which volunteers play a greatly reduced role.

Many organizations are capital-intensive, relying primarily on machinery and automated equipment. Others are labor-intensive, depending on the knowledge and skills of a highly trained and experienced workforce. The gender composition of organizations has changed dramatically over the past century, from a token number of women employees to a point today where there are roughly equal numbers of men and women in the workforce. Still, to a surprising extent, the distribution of women varies greatly across sectors and by occupation and job category, and they remain severely underrepresented in top management positions.

Critical Commentary and Future Directions

There is no doubt that organizations and organization theory have undergone substantial change throughout their existence and particularly during the last half century. While changes are both evident and consequential, organizations exhibit some enduring features that are important to recognize.

Enduring Features

It is striking the extent to which rational and natural system conceptions continue to be applicable into the present era. For large numbers of observers, organizations continue to be viewed as rationally constructed structures for pursuing specific goals. Many stress the centrality of the interests of owners (shareholders), celebrating the discipline exercised by markets, as reflected in quarterly reports of financial gains and losses.

But such views continue to be challenged by the natural system perspective that organizations are more than tools. Organizations are not neutral instruments for achieving preset ends; rather, their structures and processes influence both means and ends, helping to determine what is possible as well as shaping ideas about what is desirable. The media (organization) influences, and often overrides, the message (goals).

The more balanced view of organizations recognizes their dual nature: melding technical and social features, economic and political processes, rational and nonrational elements. Rational and natural elements persist and operate in dynamic tension.

By contrast, as noted, open system models have largely supplanted closed system views of organizations. Indeed, in the most recent decades, the trajectory of changes in organization forms as well as of scholarly models of organizations largely reflects changes effected by environmental influences. As has been true for over 150 years, it remains the case that formal organizations are the workhorses of modern societies: They remain the fundamental vehicle by which complex work is carried out in every arena of social life.

Changing Features

In discussing sources of organizational divergence, we have alluded to some of the changes occurring in modes of organizing. Four types of change are particularly significant.

Organizational Boundaries

From the seminal discussion by Max Weber and continuing well into the 20th century, much attention has been devoted to organizational boundaries. Boundaries are marked and measured in all manner of ways: by physical barriers, inflections of activity, denseness of networks, temporal markings, or alterations in normative frameworks. A wide array of mechanisms and processes have been employed to "buffer" critical work units from environmental turbulence, including presorting and coding inputs, stockpiling essential inputs, and forecasting variations in supply and demand. Core employees are particularly well protected from market forces, being incorporated into internal labor markets bolstered by benefits, pensions, and other job protections.

There is no doubt, however, that the boundaries of today's modal organization have become more permeable and transitory. If asylums and prisons or other similar "total institutions" were a hallmark of 18th-century organizing, the "virtual" organization—in which participants, information flows, and production processes transcend and transgress any specific location—is the signature organization of the early part of the 21st century. Internal labor markets have been replaced by market-mediated employment contracts in which job security is reduced and work histories increasingly cross organizational boundaries. In many organizations, a smaller proportion of the rank-and-file workers and managerial participants are full-time employees. Workers and managers can be more readily dismissed or acquired as demand fluctuates.

Organizational Strategies

Related changes have occurred in the master strategies employed by organizations in relating to their environments. Throughout most of the 20th century, organizations pursued a strategy of internalization— increasingly incorporating workers, both earlier and later stages of production, marketing and distribution processes, and legal and financial expertise within the formal boundaries of the organization. Today, managers and designers are busily reversing these processes, attempting to decide which of all the diverse participants and activities are sufficiently crucial to be retained within the walls of the organizations and which can be outsourced. Employees are increasingly composed of temporary or contract workers; one function after another, including formerly core activities such as production, are contracted out to independent producers or alliance partners, and even management services are available off-the-shelf for hire. Contemporary forms are not nearly as concerned with durability as were their predecessors.

Some theorists suggest that the changing nature of organizational boundaries and strategies indicate that organizations are increasingly "absorbing society"—that more and more functions formerly conducted within the environment have been internalized by organizations. Others argue the reverse, that organizations are increasingly being absorbed by society. As more and more functional arenas are rationalized, and structures for managing them become more similar, it becomes ever easier to create partnerships or devise contracts to assemble disparate, appropriate units. The creation of these arrangements has been greatly facilitated by the increased speed and reduced cost of information flows associated with the revolution in information and communication technologies. The resulting network forms allow for rapid response to changing market demands.

Organizational Components

Important changes are also underway in subunits comprising organizational structures. For years, the central building block has been the job: formally defined, designed, and stable. Jobs were grouped into units and units collected into departments. Hierarchies are not just power and status structures but are also mechanisms of clustering units and departments. Stable jobs, rigid departmentalization, and centralization, however, are not well suited to confronting uncertainty and rapid change.

To increase the flexibility of organizations, stable, specialized jobs are being replaced by transitory teams composed of workers possessing more diffuse and varied skills. The division of work within teams can be altered as conditions require, and teams themselves can be readily reconfigured to deal with new and changing demands. Hierarchies are being delayered, and more discretion is moving to the edges of organizations and from managers to self-managing teams.

Organizational Power

Power relations in and around organizations have also undergone change. During the 19th century, as organizing processes became more complex and specialized, power migrated from the owners to accumulate in the hands of professional managers. As organizations grew in size and competition appeared to be threatened by increasing concentration, early in the 20th century, progressive political reformers succeeded in strengthening and extending public regulatory controls. Labor also improved their bargaining position, aided by the passage of legislation that was supportive of unions and collective bargaining. More recently, guided by neoliberal economic policies, governments increasingly have pursued deregulation policies and, as markets become globalized, financial agents exercise increased power. Stockholders—particularly big investment institutions—have demanded and secured a variety of changes in corporate governance that increase their power vis-à-vis managers and employees. Union membership and power, especially in the United States, are at an all-time low. At the same time, corporate power and influence in the political arena have never been stronger.

While current accounts stress the amount and rapidity of change in every aspect of organizational life, it is important not to overstate these trends. First, these developments apply primarily to newer industries and organizational forms while the universe of organizations is composed of many older, more traditional types that continue to operate. Second, observers attend more to change than to stability. Third, managerial and business press rhetoric is often mistaken for reality. Nevertheless, change is underway, not only in the empirical nature of organizations, but also in theoretical conceptions of organizations.

Changing Conceptions

Distinctions proposed by Musifer Emirbayer in discussing social organization in general seem particularly apt for describing general changes in the conceptual models guiding formal organization theorists. *Substantialist* definitions, as applied to organizations, view organizations as things or entities, possessing specific features or characteristics. These definitions encompass two subtypes. First, *substantialist self-action* definitions emphasize the discreteness and independence of organizations, and emphasize those features that distinguish organizations from other types of social collectivities. Such definitions were crafted by many scholars, including Max Weber, Herbert A. Simon, and Peter M. Blau. A second subtype, *substantialist interaction* definitions, began to emerge with the coming of the open system models. Although organizations continued to be conceptualized as discrete units, they were now seen to possess attributes that varied in response to external environments, whether technical, political, or institutional. The conceptions of Paul R. Lawrence, Philip Selznick, Jeffrey Pfeffer, and Michael Hannan are representative of this subtype.

During recent decades, more theorists are beginning to embrace a *relational* conception of organization. Such views recognize that organizations are constituted by and inseparable from the transactional contexts in which they are embedded. Their meaning and identity are the product of an ongoing set of social processes in which they participate and which they influence but do not determine. A wide range of recent scholars have embraced some version of a relational definition. Some, such as Karl E. Weick, argue that organizations are those processes by which participants create, maintain, and dissolve social collectivities. Barbara Czarniawska views organizations as continually produced and transformed by participants' stories or narratives—accounts of work and the arrangements that support it. Michael C. Jenson and William H. Meckling view organizations as a nexus of contracts, while Neil Fligstein and other theorists discuss organizations as a portfolio of financial assets or a bundle of dynamic capabilities. Network theorists are likely to view organizations as shifting collections of relational ties. Institutionalists, such as John W. Meyer, stress the ways in which organizational forms are constructed and reconstructed by symbolic processes.

In sum, most recent conceptions of formal organizations privilege process over structure. What is being processed varies from one theorist to another—for some it is symbols or words; for others, relations or contracts; for still others, assets or capabilities. However, in a relational conception, structures exist because they are being enacted and reproduced, and the identities and capabilities of actors—including organizations—are being continuously created and reconfigured.

—*W. Richard Scott*

See also Bureaucracy; Historical Analysis of Organization Theory; Organizational Design; Organizational Structure

Further Readings

Aldrich, H. E., & Ruef, M. (2006). *Organizations evolving* (2nd ed.). Thousand Oaks, CA: Sage.

Chandler, A. D., Jr. (1977). *The visible hand: The managerial revolution in American business.* Cambridge, MA: Belknap Press.

Child, J. (2005). *Organization: Contemporary principles and practice.* Oxford, UK: Blackwell.

Coleman, J. D. (1974). *Power and the structure of society.* New York: Norton.

DiMaggio, P. (Ed.). (2001). *The twenty-first-century firm: Changing economic organization in international perspective.* Princeton, NJ: Princeton University Press.

Emibayer, M. (1997). Manifesto for a relational sociology. *American Journal of Sociology, 103,* 282–317.

Hannan, M. T., & Freeman, J. (1989). *Organizational ecology.* Cambridge, MA: Harvard University Press.

Lawrence, P. R., & Lorsch, J. W. (1967). *Organization and environment: Managing differentiation and integration.* Boston: Graduate School of Business Administration, Harvard University.

March, J. G., & Simon, H. A. (1958). *Organizations.* New York: Wiley.

Micklethwait, J., & Wooldridge, A. (2003). *The company: A short history of a revolutionary idea.* New York: Modern Library.

Mintzberg, H. (1979). *The structure of organizations.* Upper Saddle River, NJ: Prentice Hall.

Perrow, C. (1986). *Complex organizations: A critical essay* (3rd ed.). New York: Random House.

Pfeffer, J., & Salancik, G. R. (1978). *The external control of organizations.* New York: Harper & Row.

Powell, W. W., & DiMaggio, P. J. (Eds.). (1991). *The new institutionalism in organizational analysis.* Chicago: University of Chicago Press.

Scott, W. R., & Davis, G. F. (2007). *Organizations and organizing: Rational, natural, and open system perspectives.* Upper Saddle River, NJ: Prentice Hall.

Weber, M. (1968). *Economy and society: An interpretive sociology* (G. Roth & C. Wittich, Trans.). New York: Bedminster Press. (Original work published 1924)

Williamson, O. E. (1985). *The economic institutions of capitalism.* New York: Free Press.

FOUCAULDIAN TURN

Michel Foucault's work straddles history and philosophy and has profoundly influenced every branch of the social sciences and humanities. His theory owes as much to phenomenology as it does to structuralism. The reasons for Foucault's appeal are manifold: in particular, the collapse of Marxism as a coherent philosophical and political project, and the elusive and open-ended nature of Foucault's work. Not the least of Foucault's attractions is the sheer beauty and drive of his historical writing—not qualities generally associated with his followers. The stark, cool tone he uses to describe an extraordinary 17th-century execution contrasts with the lush, poetic language he deploys to recount the mundane bureaucratic schedules that dominated institutional life from the mid-19th century.

Conceptual Overview

Foucault's books are typically structured around real or imaginary events, paintings, myths, and architectural drawings—visual imagery that disrupts as well as organizes the text. This is not an authorial conceit but is central to his historical method. First, the use of striking historical images captures not so much worlds that we have lost, but worlds that modern sensibilities find impossible to contemplate. Second, they act as a reminder that our modern world will seem no less strange to future commentators. Third, these images, particularly those that he knows are fictions, convey his disdain for teleological historical narratives that trace the emergence of the present from the absurdities or the failings of the past. Finally, Foucault uses the genealogical method to raise questions about the present. His histories, in other words, are not bounded by period but constantly seek to introduce concepts that can be used to interrogate contemporary assumptions, practices, and institutions. These are also the reasons for Foucault's controversial reputation as a historian. His aim was not to produce definitive accounts of the rise of the asylum or the prison but to throw doubt upon existing versions, to challenge the very notion of a single authoritative history, and to generate multiple alternative readings.

For Foucault, the Enlightenment marked the beginning of the human sciences, a departure in which the individual and society became the subject and object of our own knowledge. Foucault's genealogical studies of the hospital, the asylum, and the prison asked the same fundamental questions: Why did specific institutions emerge to deal with particular populations during the 18th century; why did the new sciences of the Enlightenment—medicine, psychiatry, penology—share a moral, humanist purpose; and why, despite this humanist imperative, did these new sciences and institutions produce regimes of isolation, repression, and exclusion? His answer is beguilingly simple. The Enlightenment project unleashed liberalism that both freed the individual from the necessity of monarchic and religious rule *and* created institutional regimes to regulate these newly liberated citizenries. While the experience of the patient and the prisoner, far less the doctor or warder, is all but absent from Foucault's accounts, there is a deep empathy that leaves little doubt where his sympathies lie. In this sense, Foucault's method relies on a hermeneutics that stresses the historicity of human subjectivity. Foucault's point is not that power uses or abuses knowledge for its own ends, nor that power corrupts knowledge. Rather, he insists that power and knowledge are necessarily intertwined. Power and knowledge are mutually constitutive. "Power/knowledge," as he styles it, acknowledges the ways in which specific abstract and applied knowledges provide the categories necessary for the operation of power. So, criminology and penology provides the categories of deviance and the policies and institutions designed to confirm and elaborate these categories. For Foucault, the practices that confirm and extend these categories are inherent in the organizational form, sometimes the very architecture, of institutions. Surveillance is essential to the development of power/knowledge. Populations have to be enclosed, tabulated, categorized, observed, and compared over time. From this, the impact of practical interventions can be compared, evaluated, and adjusted. Every human science shares the aim of controlling populations in order that individuals can be reformed, the better to manage themselves. The search is always for more effective, more efficient systems of governance in which individuals can be more securely relied upon to govern themselves. There is a danger that we misunderstand Foucault as the fatalistic prophet of a gray, wholly disciplined social world. Nothing could be further from the truth: Surveillant systems are always incomplete, always incapable of delivering the compliant prisoners, workers, or citizens that they promise.

Foucault was aware that his genealogical studies, particularly *Discipline and Punish*, which focused on power/knowledge, had been widely interpreted as determinist and neglectful of subjectivity. Subjectivity and identity were the main concerns of research in the decade before his death. In *The History of Sexuality*, Foucault set out to challenge any fixed conceptions of normality, identity, or morality. He was not a nihilist. Rather, his aim was to unsettle our conceptions of ourselves as having the almost limitless personal freedom promised by liberalism and to challenge the dystopian image of the wholly subjected modern individual ground down by bureaucratic routines that he had raised in *Discipline and Punish*. There is a clear echo between the later "ethical" Foucault and the earlier genealogist. That is, just as the political purpose of genealogy was to force us to think differently about the past *and* the present, so the purpose of Foucault's ethics is to call into question our contemporary moral categories, the better to think of alternatives. Through his discussion of Greek philosophy and sexual practices, Foucault invites us to live our lives as if every day were the first day of a new republic, a day of almost infinite personal and democratic possibilities. To become a citizen of this new republic entails the rejection of conventional mores and a constant skepticism about all forms of governance. He asks why we accept that everyday objects such as tables and chairs are considered works of art yet are startled by his demand that we think similarly of ourselves, that we treat our lives as aesthetic projects. Again, in this call to treat ourselves as works of art, Foucault returns to his lifelong dialogue with Kant. Far from lapsing into solipsism or narcissism, however, Foucault's pursuit of a care of the self is a call for a political engagement that refuses any boundary between the self and society.

Critical Commentary and Future Directions

Organization researchers have been remarkably narrow in their uptake of Foucault's work. Unfortunately, the reception of Foucault's work has been such that only one or two of his better-known formulations have been used, with researchers failing to pay attention to his overall project, as McKinlay and Starkey noted in 1998. Some researchers—such as Hoskin and Macve in 1988, Rose in 1989, and van Krieken in 1990—have begun to use Foucault's power/knowledge matrix to reinterpret the role of accounting techniques and psychological disciplines. Other contributors—for example, Burrell in 1988, Calás and Smircich in 1999, Clegg in 1989, and Knights and Vurdubakis in 1994—sought to redefine disciplinary analysis in the organizations field. Most popular has been a focus on surveillance and disciplinary mechanisms in organizations, notably in the work of Sewell in 1989. In part this may be because, as Hannah noted in 1997, Foucault focused on confining organizations, such as prisons and asylums, rather than organizations in general. One study that develops a systematic perspective on organizations that is influenced by Foucault's studies of power is Clegg, Courpasson, and Phillips' *Power and Organizations*.

Wider organizational issues have been explicitly addressed from a Foucauldian perspective by Jackson and Carter in 1998, du Gay in 2000, and van Krieken in 1996, looking at the use of forms of institutionalized regulation rather than prohibitory mechanisms to secure compliance. Studies in this vein, as organizations develop more sophisticated forms for shaping individual motivations, can be expected to increase in popularity, using Foucault to look at the fusion of organizational governance and the constitution of individual mentalities fashioned in the image of that governance—what Foucault referred to as "governmentality."

—*Alan McKinlay*

See also Actor-Network Theory; Critical Management Studies; Genealogical Analysis; Governmentality; Postmodernism; Power; Sexuality

Further Readings

Burrell, G. (1988). Modernism, post modernism and organizational analysis 2: The contribution of Michel Foucault. *Organization Studies, 9,* 221–235.

Calás, M., & Smircich, L. (1999). Past postmodernism? Reflections and tentative directions. *Academy of Management Review, 24*(4), 649–671.

Clegg, S. R. (1989). *Frameworks of power.* London: Sage.

Clegg, S. R., Courpasson, D., & Phillips, N. (2006). *Power and organizations.* London: Sage.

Foucault, M. (1965). *Madness and civilization: A history of insanity in the age of reason.* New York: Vintage.

Foucault, M. (1972). *The archaeology of knowledge.* London: Tavistock.

Foucault, M. (1977). *Discipline and punish: The birth of the prison* (A. Sheridan, Trans). London: Allen & Lane.

Foucault, M. (1979). Governmentality. *Ideology and Consciousness, 6,* 5–21.

Foucault, M. (1980). *Power/knowledge* (C. Gordon, Ed.). New York: Pantheon.

Foucault, M. (1988a). *Politics, philosophy, culture: Interviews and other writings, 1977–1984* (L. D. Kritzman, Ed.; A. Sheridan, Trans.). London: Routledge.

Foucault, M. (1988b). The care of the self as a practice of freedom. In J. Berbauer & D. Rasmussen (Eds.), *The final Foucault* (pp. 1–20). Cambridge, MA: MIT Press.

Foucault, M. (1990). *The history of sexuality.* London: Penguin.

Foucault, M. (2003). *Society must be defended* (D. Macey, Trans.). Harmondsworth, UK: Penguin.

Gay, P. du (2000). *In praise of bureaucracy: Weber, organization, ethics.* London: Sage.

Hannah, M. (1997). Imperfect panopticism: Envisioning the construction of perfect lives. In G. Benko & U. Stohmayer (Eds.), *Space and social theory: Interpreting modernity and postmodernity* (pp. 344–359). Oxford, UK: Blackwell.

Hoskin, K., & Macve, R. (1988). The genesis of accountability: The West Point connections. *Accounting, Organizations and Society, 13*(1), 37–73.

Jackson, N., & Carter, P. (1998). Labour as dressage. In A. McKinlay & K. Starkey (Eds.), *Foucault, management, and organization theory: From panopticon to technologies of self* (pp. 49–64). London: Sage.

Knights, D., & Vurdubakis, T. (1994). Power, resistance and all that. In J. M. Jermier, D. Knights, & W. R. Nord (Eds.), *Resistance and power in organizations* (pp. 167–198). London: Routledge.

Krieken, R. van. (1990). The organisation of the soul: Elias and Foucault on discipline and the self. *Archives Europeénes de Sociologie, 31*(2), 353–371.

Krieken, R. van. (1996). Proto-governmentalization and the historical formation of organizational subjectivity. *Economy and Society, 25*(2), 195–221.

McKinlay, A., & Starkey, K. (1997). *Foucault, management and organization theory: From panopticon to technologies of self.* London: Sage.

Rose, N. (1989). *Governing the soul.* London: Routledge.

Frankfurt School

The Frankfurt School was a group of predominantly German scholars including Max Horkheimer, Erich Fromm, Theodore Adorno, Herbert Marcuse, and Jürgen Habermas that developed a distinctive stream of post-Marxist thought beginning in the 1920s and ending in the 1970s. Their work, referred to as "critical theory," is a form of self-conscious critique aimed at change and emancipation through enlightenment while consciously working to avoid the tendency to cling dogmatically to its own doctrinal assumptions. Critical theory aims to produce a particular form of knowledge useful in realizing an emancipatory interest, specifically through a critique of consciousness and ideology.

Conceptual Overview

The Frankfurt School was established in February 1923. Its formal name was the Institute for Social Research and it was administratively associated with the University of Frankfurt. However, an endowment from the son of a wealthy grain merchant provided a significant amount of autonomy. The first director of the new institute was Carl Grünberg, who was unique in being the first professed Marxist to hold a chair at a German university. He was also unique among chaired professors of his time in his concern for what he saw as a tendency for German universities to focus on teaching at the expense of research and to produce academics that were only capable of supporting the status quo upon which their privilege and power depended. He also believed that Marxism provided the theoretical infrastructure to challenge this situation.

From the beginning, the institute's program focused on using Marxism as a frame for the empirical investigation of the social world. But Grünberg's view of Marxism was very different from the monistic materialism of many Marxists of the time who believed in transhistorical laws that explained the relation of the social and the economic and in simple, universal truths. Instead, he believed in a version of Marxism that was much more situational and limited in focus than was commonly believed by Marxists at the time.

While setting the stage for critical theory, Grünberg's view, however progressive, was largely rejected by the central figures of the Frankfurt School. In particular, his belief that the social was simply a product of the economic was rejected, along with his optimism about the general improvement of social institutions over time. What was retained, however, was a commitment to empirical research and a belief in the importance of history. The critical moment of Marxism combined with these latter beliefs in methodology provided an initial foothold for the development of critical theory as it became known.

The turning point for the Frankfurt School occurred when Grünberg retired in 1929 and Horkheimer took over as the director of the institute. Horkheimer quickly gathered together a diverse group including Fromm, Adorno, and Marcuse. Horkheimer continued Grünberg's concern for theoretical analysis and empirical investigation but moved the focus of the institute toward a much more radically historical and theoretical mode. He also believed strongly in the need for a reintegration of the disparate disciplines of the social sciences, as the state of fragmentation he saw was so advanced that no discipline could say it had any real ability to explore the historical reality at a place and time.

The institute was closed in 1933, under the Nazi regime, for "tendencies hostile to the state." Many members of the institute were Jewish, which was of course problematic at that time; in addition, their obvious interest in Marxism and their rather suspect international connections marked them out as enemies of the fascist state. Fortunately, Horkheimer had arranged to transfer much of the institute's financial endowment out of Germany. The institute first moved to Geneva and then, in 1935, to Columbia University in New York City. This forced emigration resulted in changes in both the tone and focus of the work of the institute and it also provided exposure for this work to the English-speaking academic world (particularly through the institute's English language journal, *Studies in Philosophy and Social Science*). Arguably, this period was at least partially responsible for later popularity of this work among British and American scholars.

The body of work produced by the Frankfurt School is interesting as much for its societal effects as for its influence on sociology and related disciplines. The work of those in the Frankfurt School caught the imagination of students and intellectuals in the 1960s and early 1970s and became an important influence in the development of various radical protest movements in those decades. The alternative interpretation of Marxist theory provided by the Frankfurt School, and the focus on issues and problems of common concern such as mass culture, the family, and sexuality, resonated with the concerns of many of the people involved in radical protest movements that characterized this period around the world.

Critical Commentary and Future Directions

The work of the Frankfurt School covers a wide range of topics and touches on many issues of interest to organization studies. Perhaps the most direct influence, however, is in critical management studies where much of the early work draws directly on the work of the Frankfurt School to develop a counterpoint to traditional functionalist organization theory.

Without the insights of the Frankfurt School, it is inconceivable that the more critical wing of organization studies could have created the well-developed frameworks that are now commonly used.

At the same time, the work of the Frankfurt School has proven to be very difficult to translate into mainstream organization studies. The writing style is often opaque and the theorizing complex and full of terms and concepts that find little traction in mainstream theorizing. It has therefore been uncommon for work drawing on the ideas of the Frankfurt School to appear in major journals, and the work done in critical management studies has had correspondingly little effect on the mainstream of organization theory. Much work remains to be done in translating the powerful ideas and deep insights of the Frankfurt School into the mainstream study of organizations.

—*Nelson Phillips*

See also Critical Management Studies; Empowerment; Exploitation; Ideology; Power; Radical Humanism; Reflexivity

Further Readings

Held, D. (1980). *Introduction to critical theory: Horkheimer to Habermas.* Cambridge, UK: Polity.

Jay, M. (1996). *The dialectical imagination: A history of the Frankfurt School and the Institute of Social Research, 1923–1950.* Berkeley: University of California Press.

McCarthy, T. (1989). *The critical theory of Jürgen Habermas.* Cambridge, MA: MIT Press.

FREE-RIDER PROBLEM

The free-rider problem (FRP) arises when, given a collectivity trying to produce a common good, a member rationally calculates that, assuming a collective good will be produced anyway, it is better for him or her not to contribute to the cooperative effort. In this fashion, the individual is taking advantage of the hard work of others.

Let's assume a large union carrying out a strike with the purpose of improving the benefits of its members. In order to accomplish this goal, the union asks all of its members to participate. Given that any improvement in salaries achieved by the union will go to all members regardless of individual level of participation, some members might calculate that their participation will not be missed. Here we have a perverse incentive to participation: On the one hand, it is likely that nobody will notice the absence of a member; yet, the nonparticipant will enjoy the benefits generated by these actions without assuming the costs implied by participating.

Conceptual Overview

The analysis of the FRP is rooted in the analysis of collectivities and the dilemmas they face when attempting to generate enough commitment and participation from their members. Throughout history, authors have complained of the costly effort needed to keep collectivities together and encourage equal participation among members. Personalities such as Aristotle, Hume, Adam Smith, John Stuart Mill, Pareto, and even Marx have made relevant contributions to the topic

For some, the main explanation is that the self-interest is the point of departure of politics, at any level. Machiavelli and Hobbes clearly made this assertion, creating a very influential definition of human nature: It is rational to be self-interested, since self-interest is the base for individual calculation. For Hobbes, individuals are self-determinate, selfish, and looking for satisfaction. This is the basis for the existence of a monarch or a leviathan state that limits the passions of its subjects through a legal frame or regulation.

The main problem is the discovery that, under certain circumstances, individuals selfishly looking for their own objectives will produce suboptimal results when working collectively. The market, given its size and multiple exchanges, produces a structure that, in theory at least, is able to produce collective Pareto optimum levels through the actions of ostensibly selfish individuals. However, when the exchange implies collective cooperation, the same selfishness might produce a counterintuitive effect: individuals facing collective incentives that, contradictorily, push them to act against the collective objective. The FRP is an enormous dilemma for those theories that depend upon individuals rationally calculating steps to achieve objectives based upon a selfish, individual-based, analysis. The FRP implies that, under certain circumstances, a rational person can produce irrational results, at least in collective situations.

Mancur Olson's *Logic of the Collective Action* is the best known seminal document on the FRP. Olson's argument starts by implying that an organization basically produces collective goods that cannot be denied to its members. When this happens, individuals have pervasive incentives not to participate. The larger the organization is, the bigger the possibility that individuals will defect due to an unfavorable calculation of the cost and benefits of participation. In other words, the bigger the organization, the harder it is to supervise equal participation among individuals. According to Olson, small groups are better prepared to monitor its members by generating easy and positive incentives for cooperation. For example, the benefit of a free ride is diminished by the increased cost associated with the high possibility that one will be observed cheating and then punished. For big groups to exist, they must decrease the possibility of employees cheating or free riding through the creation of specific incentives for cooperation. For Olson, these solutions are called the *n-group* and *selective incentives.*

N-group implies the reduction of the group or collectivity to an observable and monitored size (n-size) with the purpose of assuring reciprocity and cooperation. Selective incentives imply the definition of rewards, credible threats, and specific punishments in order to give both positive and negative incentives to encourage cooperation.

The behavioral complexity of the free rider can be seen as having two different sides. On one side, it is possible that a free rider agrees to participate in a collectivity knowing that he or she will be able to get away with not participating. On the other side, it is possible that a free rider initially wants to cooperate, but defects because he or she calculates the incentives associated with participation and finds it to not be worthwhile, making defection a rational act.

The FRP is therefore a complex phenomenon. Authors like Jon Elster mention that FRP may not necessarily be at the root of the problem.

Marwell and Oliver analyze the case of a free rider who decides to defect after a certain calculation regarding the final benefit obtained by cooperation. During the action, the employee's position can change as he or she decides to cooperate or not based on his or her expectation about the benefit or public good associated with the action. According to Marwell and Oliver, there are two different effects on a free rider. The first of these can be called the *order effect,* where the free rider evaluates his or her level of interest in the collective action. If an employee is not highly interested, then he or she decides rationally to participate only after the more interested employees have absorbed some of the costs. The second effect can be called *surplus,* which implies that the free rider calculates whether or not to cooperate by evaluating whether the personal benefits are higher that the costs. If the costs outweigh the benefits, then the free rider quits participation, assuming that the members more interested in cooperating will continue until they reach their optimum net benefit. If the free rider eventually finds cooperation to be profitable, he or she might decide to participate again. In contrast to the free rider, the participants in the collective action do think that such cooperative effort can succeed and their participation will be important for it. Noncooperation occurs, in this case, because free riders calculate at a certain point that the collectivity will fail to pursue its objectives to the end. In this way, both ideology and culture are important in order to balance the incentives defined by the collectivity.

Critical Commentary and Future Directions

The FRP synthesizes one of the most important debates in organization studies: why and when rational decisions not to cooperate arise in organizations. The simple answer for the supporters of FRP is that it all depends on the rational (therefore, selfish) calculus of individuals. Collective action is always a burdensome undertaking for an individual, given the capacity of others to defect. Cooperation is necessary, but uncertainty is always present regarding the intentions of others to keep cooperation running. This is why, at the extreme, the FRP assumes that the problem is not a moral one, but a practical one. In other words, defecting or free riding is not a moral issue because often to free ride is a rational action, a response against uncertainty or protection against the possibility of others defecting in a cooperative effort. The problem is that acting rationally, as an individual, probably produces negative effects at the collective level. If everybody can free ride, who would pay taxes, take care of the elderly, work for the public good, or achieve any other collective effort?

A particular example of this dilemma is the well-known *tragedy of the commons*. The idea, developed in 1968 by Garret Hardin, argues that wherever a group of individuals use and share a limited natural resource, the ultimate consequence will be its degradation, or even its disappearance. The classic example of the tragedy of the commons is about a group of cattle dealers who obtain income by selling cattle. It was understood by these dealers that the increase of cattle production by one or more dealers would decrease the price of the cattle and, therefore, their income. Nevertheless, there are no incentives for anyone to reduce the breeding, causing them to act in a spiral of increasing cattle production and, consequently, diminishing returns. In this situation, the temptation to be a free rider (and, in doing so, to avoid being the *victim* of a free rider) produces the tragic end results: increasing the cattle production at a level where the prairies will be destroyed. Each producer is locked into a system that compels him or her to increase the herd without limit. Communal property, under the tragedy of the commons, becomes nobody's property because of the possibility of becoming a free rider or the victim of one.

The FRP has been criticized for assuming a limited definition of human nature: selfish, egoistic, and calculative. However, it is also clear that there are important examples in which a free rider attitude is a rational behavior.

Another important practical problem that the FRP must face involves reflexivity: Is it not socially dangerous for this theory to teach people that to free ride is not immoral and is even rational/intelligent? Is it not important to explain to people that there are several benefits associated with cooperation that are beyond the egoistic calculus of individual rationality? Certainly, the FRP is a reflexive theory, with important lessons to teach regarding the positive and normative reaction of people under collective pressure.

The FRP will most certainly face these dilemmas as it strives to develop more intricate and specific models for different kinds of behavior: from the more acute model linked to classic economic behavior to the creation of formal models of calculative behavior that might lead to free-rider problems surfacing in politics, social organizations, and even families.

—David Arellano-Gault

See also New Institutionalism; Public Choice Theory; Rational Choice Theory; Transaction Cost Theory

Further Readings

Aristotle. (1998). *Politics* (C. D. C. Reeve, Trans.). Indianapolis, IN: Hackett.

Elster, J. (1985, October). Rationality, morality, and collective action. *Ethics, 96*(1), 136–155.

Hardin, G. (1968). The tragedy of the commons. *Science, 162,* 1243–1248.

Hardin, R. (1982). *Collective action.* Baltimore: Johns Hopkins University Press.

Heckathorn, D. D. (1996, April). The dynamics and dilemmas of collective action. *American Sociological Review, 61*(2), 250–277.

Hobbes, T. (1980). *Leviatan o la materia, forma y poder de una República eclesiástica y civil.* México: Fondo de Cultura Económica.

Hume, D. (1978). *A treatise of human nature* (L. A. Selby-Bigge & P. H. Nidditch, Eds.; 2nd ed.). Oxford, UK: Oxford University Press.

Marwell, G., & Ames, R. (1981). Economists free ride, does anyone else? *Journal of Public Economics, 15,* 295–310.

Marwell, G., & Oliver, P. (1983). *The critical mass in collective action: A micro social theory.* Cambridge, UK: Cambridge University Press.

Mill, J. S. (1965). Principles of political economy. In J. M. Robson (Ed.), *Collected works of John Stuart Mill* (7th ed., Vols. 2 and 3). Toronto: University of Toronto Press. (Original work published 1848)

Olson, M., Jr. (1965). *The logic of collective action.* Cambridge, MA: Harvard University Press.

Samuelson, P. A. (1954). The pure theory of public expenditure. *Review of Economics and Statistics, 36,* 387–389.

Smith, A. (1976). *An inquiry into the nature and causes of the wealth of nations.* Oxford, UK: Oxford University Press. (Original work published 1776)

Functionalism

While employed differently across disciplines such as sociology, linguistics, and psychology, at its core functionalism refers to an approach to the study of social and organizational systems that focuses on relating one aspect of such a system to another part, or indeed to the totality of the whole, in such a manner as to stress their mutual interdependence. Hence, any particular element of an organization—such as management—should be understood in terms of how it contributes to the functional stability or well-being of the organization as a whole. This also involves, however, recognizing that any such functional characteristics might not be immediately apparent to those involved, but might have a latent function that is either unrecognized or unintended, or indeed may be dysfunctional in that they operate to the detriment of the system as a whole.

Conceptual Overview

While functionalism has its origins in the work of the pioneering 19th-century French sociologist Emile Durkheim and his study of the division of labor in modernizing industrial societies, it is most widely associated today with American sociology and, in particular, the work of Robert Merton and his critique of the dysfunctions of bureaucracy, and Talcott Parsons who, in a series of general books and more specific organizationally focused articles such as those published in the first volume of *Administrative Science Quarterly* in 1956, developed a more general functionalist theory designed to explain both individual and macro-social behavior. From the functionalist perspective, in order to prosper, an organization must concern itself with the satisfaction of a number of what can be termed functional imperatives. Drawing on Parsons's general schema, these can be narrowed down to the identification of a set of goals toward which the activities of the organization as a whole can be oriented; a strategy of integration that ensures the common recognition and pursuit of these goals; the ability to recognize and adapt to environmental changes; and finally, a means by which internal patterns of belief and traditional action might be maintained and reproduced.

By the late 1950s, sociological functionalism within organization studies had started to combine with what is commonly referred to as *general systems theory*, itself generally attributed to the Viennese theoretical biologist Ludwig von Bertalanffy and popularized in organization studies by Kenneth Boulding. Indeed, during this period, systems theory, with its emphasis on integration, and functionalism with its attention to the role particular elements play within a system related to its continued stability, emerged as the largely accepted theoretical basis for mainstream organization studies, providing a growing sense of institutional legitimacy and practitioner recognition for the field.

The emergence of structural contingency theory during the 1960s cemented this dominance. Early pioneers such as Burns and Stalker and Lawrence and Lorsch, while accepting the basic functionalist tenets of systems theory, argued that greater attention needed to be paid to how functional requirements differed depending on a range of contingencies—both internal and external—that made differing demands on the organization at any point in time. Such an approach posited, therefore, an emphasis not merely on functional stability, but equally on the necessity of functional adaptability.

Despite something of a falling from favor over the last 10 to 20 years or so, functionalism continues to occupy an important theoretical space within organization studies. In part, this is due to its continued relevance to those strands of organizational research that are explicitly committed to the pursuit of managerial effectiveness and efficiency. Today, perhaps one of the most notable figures associated with this tradition is Lex Donaldson, professor of organizational design at the Australian Graduate School of Management, Sydney. In a number of contemporary articles and papers, he has been at pains to stress the continuing relevance of functionalism in an environment where complex organizations are required for the achievement of tasks that otherwise would be impossible to undertake and, as such, managers require meaningful evidence as to which structural arrangements within their organizations contribute to either their success or failure.

Critical Commentary and Future Directions

Functionalism, both within organization studies and the social sciences more generally, came under a high level of critical scrutiny during the latter decades of the 20th century. Central to this was the accusation that functionalism is not only unable to cope theoretically with revolutionary social and organizational change, but that it also displays an inherent conservatism that leads it to overlook the ways in which asymmetrical relations of power within organizations are structurally legitimated through an appeal to functionality. Burrell and Morgan's highly influential work, *Sociological Paradigms and Organisational Analysis*, did much within the field to cement this image of functionalism as a largely reactionary tradition, concerned primarily with the maintenance of managerial expertise and authority.

Today, functionalism continues to face opposition from a wide range of sources, both for its conservatism and its tendency toward something of a reductionist determinism. Approaches such as critical management studies, which draws upon a range of radical traditions within the social sciences such as critical theory, poststructuralism, and labor process theory, have been particularly dismissive—often more by implication than direct attack—while approaches such as strategic choice theory continue to be presented as a viable alternative to what is considered to be the lack of attention within functionalism to human agency and the complexities this engenders.

Despite this, functionalism, in for instance the form of structural contingency theory on the one hand, and the popular management press on the other, continues to thrive as both a theoretical disposition to organizational research as well as a political attitude toward the value of organization studies. In particular, it has even found its way into the study of somewhat esoteric fields of research such as the affective and the aesthetic in such a manner as to suggest that its future trajectory may lie not in the realm of traditional concerns with structural phenomena, but more significantly, in the very depths of those subjective relations from which emerges the organizational life-world.

—*Phillip Graham Hancock*

See also Paradigms; Sociological Approach; Structural Contingency Theory; Structural Functionalism

Further Readings

Burrell, G., & Morgan, G. (1979). *Sociological paradigms and organisational analysis.* London: Heinemann.

Donaldson, L. (2005). Vita contemplativa: Following the scientific method: How I became a committed functionalist and positivist. *Organization Studies, 26*(7), 1071–1088.

Parsons, T. (1956a). Suggestions for a sociological approach to the theory of organizations—I. *Administrative Science Quarterly, 1*(1), 63–85.

Parsons, T. (1956b). Suggestions for a sociological approach to the theory of organizations—II. *Administrative Science Quarterly, 1*(2), 225–239.

Game Theory

Although game theory was originally developed for use in applied mathematics, in 1944 John von Neumann and Oskar Morgenstern extended the reach of game theory by introducing *Theory of Games and Economic Behavior,* a classic look at the application of game theory to nonmathematical contexts.

Game theory by definition includes any situation in which there is strategic interaction that is framed by (and specifies) the behavior/decisions that players may display, but does not necessarily delineate the behavior/decisions that players *will* display, as noted by Martin Osborne and Ariel Rubinstein in 1994. The individuals involved (players) have an understanding that their outcomes are dependent on both their individual expected utilities and interests as well as the outcomes that result from the combination of their behavior and the other player or players' behavior, as noted by R. Duncan Luce and Howard Raiffa in 1957. Players work within a situation in which their interests can either conflict with or coincide with other players' interests. In a typical game theory scenario, there are a variety of outcomes that can result from the unique combination of all players' decisions, such that typically there is a conflict of interest between each individual's immediate self-interest, and the long-range interest in locating the most mutually beneficial set of outcomes.

Game theory is approached by many as a branch of the social sciences, a branch whose goal is to explore the behavior of decision makers who are interacting with one another. The mathematical axioms are valued to a certain extent in terms of their link to human intuition, as noted by Osborne and Rubinstein in 1994.

Conceptual Overview

Strategic Games

Typically a strategic game is one that is played only once, and in which each player assumes that the other players are behaving rationally. Even though the outcomes are a function of both the individual's choice and the other player's choice, players make their decisions independently and simultaneously—the only reference point being a matrix of the players' possible behaviors (decisions) and corresponding payoffs, as noted by Osborne and Rubinstein in 1994. In this case, the immediate payoff is highly salient to each player, since it involves only one trial.

Intertemporal, Repeated-Trial Games

These games are played over repeated trials, and involve a situation in which the player's behavior both has instantaneous consequences on personal payoffs, and can affect the other player's future behavior, as evidenced by the resulting joint payoffs. In this case the long-run, coordinated payoff is highly salient to each player, since it involves not only his or her individual decision on a single trial, but also the combined effects of his or her decision and the other player's decision.

Players

Any person, group, entity, organization, or country (geographic area) that has a single interest driving its decisions can be thought of as a player within a game theory paradigm, as noted by Luce and Raiffa in 1957. Although games are typically described in relation to two players, many are described as n-person games.

Utility

Assuming that utility is an economic measure of desired outcomes, it is expected that individuals and groups are inherently motivated to maximize their utility whenever possible, à la Jacob Marschak in 1950; however, it is also true that in some situations there is a conflict between immediate self-interest and long-run group interest.

Rational Behavior

It is assumed that individuals are rational and will behave in ways that are consistent with the goal of maximizing utility. For the purposes of game theory, it is necessary that one adopts a broad view of rational behavior. That is, a behavior may on its surface appear to be irrational, e.g., pilots volunteering to take immediate pay cuts; yet there is often an underlying, less obvious rationale behind the decision, e.g., pilots' self-imposed pay cuts help to maintain the long-run solvency of a commercial airline in a highly competitive market.

Zero-Sum Games

Games in which there are clear winners and losers are known as *zero-sum games*, and are noted as such because, by definition, the more outcomes one player receives, the fewer outcomes the other player receives, e.g., a tennis match between two people. Zero-sum games are by definition situations in which the sum of the utility functions associated with the game decisions is zero, as noted by Luce and Raiffa in 1957.

Non-Zero-Sum Games

Games in which there is not a fixed pie of outcomes—rather, there is an expanding-pie of outcomes—are often known as *non-zero-sum games*. In non-zero-sum games, there is an opportunity for all players to maximize their outcomes simultaneously, such that in the worst-case scenario, the outcomes of one player do not remove outcomes from any other player, and in the best-case scenario, the outcomes of one player may be interdependently linked to the maximization of the other player or players' outcomes, e.g., a merger between two organizations.

Nash Equilibrium

Nash equilibrium is a situation in which each player has an accurate understanding of the other player's behavior, and behaves rationally in response to this knowledge, as noted by Osborne and Rubinstein in 1994. In this way, there is a Nash equilibrium for each matrix-based scenario.

Games

As noted by Osborne and Rubinstein in 1994, there are several classic examples of games that effectively model a range of real-world situations, and these include, but are not limited to, the following:

Prisoner's Dilemma

The prisoner's dilemma, as noted by A. W. Tucker in 1955, occurs when two crime suspects are placed in separate rooms. The suspects are informed that if both of them confess (separately and simultaneously) to the crime, they will each receive three years in prison; however, if one of them confesses while the other does not confess, the confessing suspect receives no prison sentence, and the other suspect receives a four-year sentence; if neither suspect confesses, they will both receive only a one-year sentence. The best combination occurs via complete coordination wherein neither player confesses, and both suspects receive the lightest possible sentences.

Coordination

Coordination models any scenario within which players work to coordinate their responses (decisions), and further, they want to agree on the most desirable outcome. Like the "battle of the sexes" model below, these scenarios involve two people who want to share an experience together. For example, if two people are choosing between watching Olympic gymnastics and watching exhibition gymnastics—and assuming that Olympic gymnastics is the more desirable outcome for both—then Nash equilibrium occurs when there is an Olympics–Olympics match between players.

Battle of the Sexes

Suppose that two people are working toward making a decision about which music performance to attend: Bach or Stravinsky. Battle of the sexes models any scenario within which players work to coordinate their responses (decisions) but have competing goals. If the two people want to have a joint music experience, coordination is in order, and Nash equilibrium occurs when there is either a Bach–Bach or Stravinsky–Stravinsky combination.

Hawk and Dove

This is a game wherein two animals are fighting over prey, and each of the animals can behave like either a dove or a hawk. The worst outcome for each animal occurs when both animals act like hawks, and the best outcome for each animal occurs when one animal acts like a hawk in response to the other animal acting like a dove.

Fear Versus Greed

When comparing interactions between individuals with those between groups, intergroup interactions tend to be more competitive than interindividual interactions, a phenomenon that has been called the *discontinuity effect,* as noted by John Schopler and colleagues in 1993. In addition, the discontinuity between interindividual (e.g., two managers with conflicting goals) and intergroup (e.g., two work teams with conflicting goals) interactions is driven by both a *fear* of being taken advantage of by the other group, and *greed* for maximizing immediate self-interest, as noted by Schopler and colleagues.

In addition to the discontinuity effect, people tend to be more competitive in single-trial (one-time) interactions than in multitrial (repeated-time) interactions.

Critical Commentary and Future Directions

Bounded Rationality

Current game theory does not adequately address the issue of bounded rationality—specifically, the fact that individuals differ from each other in terms of how effectively they can assess a situation, analyze it, and ultimately produce the optimal strategy. Game theory models often assume a perfect *understanding* of the rules and parameters of the game, as well as an *ability* to effectively analyze the situation to reach optimal decisions, as noted by Osborne and Rubinstein in 1994. In reality, many individuals do not have a perfect understanding of the game, nor do they have the ability to locate optimal strategies at all times, so in this way game theory models do not account for bounded rationality. This would be an important topic for future work to more elaborately address.

Future Directions

Game theory has a wide array of applications, within domains such as marketing, economics, pricing, political science, negotiation, sports, bidding, and others, as noted by Arnold Reisman, Ashok Kumar, and Jaideep Motwani in 2001. Perhaps, researchers can look toward fully exploring the many applications of game theory, looking at not only the static, matrix-based models of behavior with perfect information, but also exploring some of the imperfections in behavioral decision making that make an individual human.

Implications

Whether there are two people, organizations, or nations engaging and interacting, each pair may soon realize that they are faced with a dilemma in which both sides will behave instinctively in their immediate self-interest, and will therefore be worse off in terms of their final outcomes, as noted by David P. Barash in 2003. There is an ever-present and inherent desire not only to maximize one's immediate self-interest, but to also minimize the interest of the other parties involved. It is in fact in this very situation that a temporary suspension of self-interest may ironically bring maximal outcomes to the cooperative individual.

—Nils Olsen

See also Collaboration and Cooperation; Competition; Complexity of Decision Making

Further Readings

Barash, D. P. (2003). *The survival game.* New York: Henry Holt.

Legut, J. (1986). Market games with a continuum of indivisible commodities. *Journal of Game Theory, 15,* 1–7.

Luce, R. D., & Raiffa, H. (1957). *Games and decisions: Introduction and critical survey.* New York: Dover.

Marschak, J. (1950). Rational behavior, uncertain prospects, and measurable utility. *Econometrica, 18,* 111–141.

Nasrallah, W. F. (2006). When does management matter in a dog-eat-dog world: An "interaction value analysis" model of organizational climate. *Compuational and Mathematical Organization Theory, 12,* 339.

Neumann, J. von, & Morgenstern, O. (1947). *Theory of games and economic behavior* (2nd ed.). Princeton, NJ: Princeton University Press.

Nowak, A. S. (1985). Universally measurable strategies in zero-sum stochastic games. *Annals of Probability, 13,* 269–287.

Osborne, M. J., & Rubinstein, A. (1994). *A course in game theory.* Cambridge, MA: MIT Press.

Radzik, T. (1991). Pure strategy epsilon-Nash equilibrium in two-person non-zero-sum games. *Games and Economic Behaviour, 3,* 356–367.

Reisman, A., Kumar, A., & Motwani, J. G. (2001). A meta review of game theory publications in the flagship US-based OR/MS journals. *Management Decision, 39,* 147.

Schopler, J., Insko, C. A., Graetz, K. A., Drigotas, S., Smith, V. A., & Dahl, K. (1993). Individual-group discontinuity: Further evidence for mediation by fear and greed. *Personality and Social Psychology Bulletin, 19,* 419–431.

Shubik, M. (1970). Game theory, behavior, and the paradox of the prisoner's dilemma: Three solutions. *Conflict Resolution, 14*(2), 181–193.

Tucker, A. W. (1955). *Game theory and programming.* Stillwater: The Oklahoma Agriculture and Mechanical College, Department of Mathematics.

Garbage Can Model

The phrase *garbage can* is frequently used to characterize organizational decision processes, usually as an attribution of nonstandard, chaotic, surprising, or disrupted patterns of attention. The source of the phrase is the 1972 article in which Michael D. Cohen, James G. March, and Johan P. Olsen suggested that decisions to a large extent are produced by temporal linkages: the arrival and departure times of independent, exogenous streams of problems, solutions, decision makers, and choice opportunities. While much attention has been given to its treatment of decision making in open structures, the central element of a garbage can process is that there is a substitution of a temporal order for a consequential order, not that there is completely open access. There is order, but it arises differently from the more common means–end order.

Conceptual Overview

The 1972 article noted above tried to make sense of some recurring empirical observations by supplementing conventional ideas about choice in organizations. The article introduced both a conceptual characterization of garbage can processes and a computational model that was used to deduce implications of the nonstandard assumptions proposed. Not all organizations were seen as unstructured. Hierarchical and specialized structures were specified along with the open access to choices, and the various structures were expected to influence outcomes differently by affecting the time patterns of connection among problems, solutions, participants, and choice opportunities, thus determining the allocation of attention and energy and thereby the outcomes.

The conceptual argument is built on three properties that are frequently observed in organizations, but contravene standard notions of how organizations work, or ought to work. Those properties of an *organized anarchy* are as follows:

1. Problematic preferences—the goals are either vague, inconsistent, or unstable

2. Unclear technology—the connection of means to ends is not well understood

3. Fluid participation—the attention to substantive decision domains by decision makers is unstable or indeterminate

To the extent these conditions are jointly present, organizational decision making, as commonly understood, becomes disconnected from its conventional grounds. Intentionally rational action rests on the projection and evaluation of consequences by stably participating actors. With unclear technology, projection of consequences becomes unreliable. With problematic preferences, evaluation of projected consequences breaks down. With fluid participation, the question of who shall decide becomes unresolved.

Since these conditions are frequently experienced in organizations, the article explored the consequences of a forthright reversal: What does one find if one assumes that the properties of organized anarchy hold?

This conceptual strategy is at once playful and serious. The former spirit is evident in the choice of terms such as *organized anarchy* and in the metaphorical suggestion that one can view a choice opportunity as a garbage can into which various kinds of problems, solutions, and participants are dumped, portraying an organization as a collection of choices looking for problems, issues and feelings looking for decision situations in which they might be aired, solutions looking for issues to which they might be the answer, and decision makers looking for work. The perspective allows readers to imagine severing connections between problems and choices that are usually taken for granted.

The conceptual strategy is serious in that it attempts to develop a coherent understanding of organizational processes that are not founded on the assumptions of forward-looking consequentialism shared by conventional theories. The garbage can perspective suggests that the meaning of organizational actions can develop out of a process of temporal sorting.

The computational model translated this conceptual perspective into a system of well-defined variables embodied in a Fortran program. The program was exercised under various assumptions to deduce some of the joint consequences of the properties of organized anarchy. Decision makers and problems were represented as moving through organizations, recombining under the influence of structural features that inhibit or promote their access to choice opportunities. In the model, decisions are made by *resolution* when decision makers having access to a choice contribute enough energy to meet the requirements of the problems attached to that choice. Arrivals of decision makers at a choice with few problems can produce decision by *oversight*. Departures of problems that become attached to other choices can leave behind actors whose energy produces decisions by *flight*.

Decision outcomes are sensitive to the precise mix of problems and solutions present in a choice opportunity (garbage can) at the moment of decision. This mix, in turn, depends on the number of decision arenas, the structure of access to them, the overall organizational load of problems and solutions, and the allocation of energy and attention across arenas. Flight and oversight, not the resolution of problems, are the most common styles of choice when the model is exercised. Important decisions are less likely to resolve problems than are unimportant ones. Processes within differing structures produce different problem-solving performances and different organizational climates (problem latency). In situations in which the load is heavy and the structure relatively open, intention is lost in the context-dependent flows.

There were a considerable number of nonlinear interactions in the processes that generated behaviors in the model. Standard mathematical models were not able to deal with the resulting complexity. The statistics collected were interpreted to reveal general relationship patterns (e.g., the patterns of movement among choices by decision makers and by problems are highly correlated, so that decision makers may have a feeling that they are always working on the same problems in different contexts, mostly without results). The patterns of the model's behaviors were also applied to make predictions about U.S. higher education. This was accomplished via additional assumptions about the way decreasing organizational slack would affect structural parameters of the model for different types of educational organizations, each with a different profile of resources. A number of the predicted patterns did indeed materialize over the subsequent decades.

Critical Commentary and Future Directions

The model has captured considerable professional attention. It is one of the most widely cited models in the social sciences and is included in standard textbooks and curricula. Jonathan Bendor, Terry Moe, and Kenneth Shotts questioned the value of the garbage can and claimed that only a radical remodeling could save what is of value in the original article. Olsen responded that their suggested model assumed away, rather than incorporated, key observations from behavioral studies of organizational decision making. Assumptions about stable participation and stable authority (principal–agent) relations were reintroduced together with standard assumptions from conventional theories of rational actors, instrumental organizations, and structural choice.

Ideas from the original article have flowed in many different directions. Some have seen the garbage can as a correct description yet argued that garbage elements should be eliminated from organizations as irrational and pathological. Others have viewed garbage can processes as unavoidable but susceptible to exploitation, or even as normatively desirable.

A result is that there exists a family of garbage can models, not just a single one. One line of development has centered on the computational model, and has involved replications, refinements, critiques, and extensions. Owing to its simplicity and early date, the model appears to be the most widely replicated computational model in organizational research. This literature has shown that the original formal model was moderately, but not perfectly, robust. Variations in some assumptions could occasionally produce changes in results, although most broad features of the results tend to be maintained.

Several other lines of less formalized theoretical work have deepened the development of the original insights by extending the organizational settings to which the model has been applied, including the organization of the World Wide Web, e-government, military units, policy making, and political institutions. Occasionally, the phrase *garbage can* has been used just to indicate that organizational processes appeared messy or apparently random; more detailed applications have generated theories of attention and decision making in organizational and political settings that serve as alternatives to rational consequentialism.

For example, Cohen and March suggested that it is possible to act intelligently in and manage garbage can worlds. John Kingdon developed a model that allowed control of the connections and separation of the four streams and the arrival and disposition of public policy "windows of opportunity." Following Kingdon, a number of policy areas have been explored, often with the aim of better understanding major policy shifts. March and Olsen have developed a "new institutionalism" that investigates the origins and dynamics of the structures that are treated as given in the garbage can model. Key questions are where structures come from; how they are maintained and transformed; and the relative importance of human intention, reflection, and choice.

The garbage can has also been portrayed as a design principle rather than an undesirable condition. Cohen showed how garbage can processes may sometimes increase the ability to maintain flexibility and repeatedly modify existing capabilities and routines in order to deal with rapidly emerging and often poorly understood new tasks. Christopher Hood found that garbage can processes can be useful (but also problematic) in dealing with corruption and opportunism.

Despite a wide variation among the many approaches influenced by the garbage can model, they have in common a perspective in which the meaning of choices is, to a substantial extent, determined endogenously by temporally unfolding processes of participation and attention. The meaning of a decision is not defined simply by reference to goals and action possibilities that are prior to and external to the choice opportunity. Rather, that meaning results from the path-dependent flows of decision makers, problems, and solutions. The garbage can perspective has been carried forward into later work in order to highlight the important roles of historical sequence and organizational structure in regulating participation and in directing attention to some organizational problems and solutions, and away from others.

The developments since the original article was published suggest three things: (1) The fundamental idea of temporal sorting has proven to be a useful frame for examining decision processes in many different kinds of situations. Scholars of quite different methodological and theoretical persuasions have adopted aspects of the ideas, not always in ways that are totally consistent either with each other or with the original article. (2) The garbage can perspective has not replaced other perspectives, such as ideas of rational choice, learning, evolution, or conflict, but has supplemented and helped to clarify them. Real decisions seem to involve a mélange of processes and rarely can be captured by a single perspective. (3) The specific computer model originally proposed has not itself become a major part of the canon, but it has stimulated a variety of elaborations that have clarified and extended the ideas and encouraged the development of simulation as a theoretical tool.

—*Michael D. Cohen,
James G. March, and Johan P. Olsen*

See also Bounded Rationality; Decision-Making Theory; Deinstitutionalization; Loose Coupling; New Institutionalism

Further Readings

Ansell, C. K. (2001). Garbage can model behavior. In N. J. Smelser & P. B. Baltes (Eds.), *International encyclopedia of the social and behavioral sciences* (vol. 9, pp. 5883–5886). Oxford, UK: Elsevier Science.

Bendor, J., Moe, T. M., & Shotts, K. W. (2001). Recycling the garbage can: An assessment of the research program. *American Political Science Review, 95,* 169–190.

Cohen, M. D. (1986). Artificial intelligence and the dynamic performance of organizational designs. In J. G. March & R. Weissinger-Baylon (Eds.), *Ambiguity and command* (pp. 53–71). Marshfield, MA: Pitman.

Cohen, M. D., & March, J.G. (1986). *Leadership and ambiguity* (2nd ed.). Boston: Harvard Business School Press.

Cohen, M. D., March, J. G., & Olsen, J. P. (1972). A garbage can model of organizational choice. *Administrative Science Quarterly, 17,* 1–25.

Hood, C. (1999). The garbage can model of organization: Describing a condition or a prescriptive design principle? In M. Egeberg & P. Lægreid (Eds.), *Organizing political institutions* (pp. 59–78). Oslo, Norway: Scandinavian University Press.

Jin, Y., & Levitt, R. E. (1996). The virtual design team: A computational model of project organizations. *Computational & Mathematical Organization Theory, 2,* 171–196.

Kingdon, J. W. (1995). *Agendas, alternatives, and public policies* (2nd ed.). New York: HarperCollins.

March, J. G., & Olsen, J. P. (1976). *Ambiguity and choice in organizations.* Bergen, Norway: Universitetsforlaget.

March, J. G., & Olsen, J. P. (1989). *Rediscovering institutions: The organizational basis of politics.* New York: Free Press.

March, J. G., & Weissinger-Baylon, R. (Eds.). (1986). *Ambiguity and command: Organizational perspectives on military decision making* Cambridge, MA: Ballinger.

Ocasio, W. (1997, Summer). Towards an attention-based view of the firm. *Strategic Management Journal, 18,* 187–206.

Olsen, J. P. (2001). Garbage cans, New Institutionalism, and the study of politics. *American Political Science Review, 95,* 191–198.

Padgett, J. F. (1980). Managing garbage can hierarchies. *Administrative Science Quarterly, 25,* 583–604.

GENDER DIVISION

Gender division is defined as the difference between female and male, feminine and masculine. These concepts are constructed as oppositional, dichotomous, and hierarchical in situations in which the masculine is privileged. Ideas, languages, and practices that depart from assumptions about gender differences contribute to gender division. Most cultures seem to include meanings and norms that prescribe gender differences and different activities for women and men. The present gender division is historically rooted in cultural systems of meaning and ideas about what is feminine or masculine and suitable/appropriate for women and men.

In organizations, gender division is reflected in the differences between the labor performed by males and that done by females. Today's labor market in the Western world is highly segregated both horizontally, where women and men work in different job areas, and vertically, where men occupy the large majority of the top positions. This results in inequalities where women are concentrated within lower-paid areas with lower-prestige jobs, fewer promotion prospects, and insecure work situations. It is also mirrored in the domestic sphere, where women are primarily responsible for domestic tasks and caring for children.

Conceptual Overview

Different explanations are offered to understand gender division. At the micro level, role theory, socialization theory, and psychoanalytic theory are salient. Socialization theory and role theory draw attention to expectations and norms, and how both influence the individual. By accepting culturally agreed-upon rules and norms, people are "forced" to internalize them and live up to their expectations. Stereotypes about women and men even make it seem natural that they perform different jobs. Furthermore, gendered socialization of girls and boys is believed to subsequently influence choices made in education and work. A result of this socialization is that women and men apply for different jobs, thus acknowledging an acceptance of different gender roles and positions. Many jobs are characterized by roles that are associated with either females or males, and there are strong norms prescribing the "proper" place for women and men. According to Nancy Chodorow, the gender division of labor found in parenting is also an important influencer in the development of the child's self-perception and helps us understand women's greater interest in social relations and social/humanistic jobs while men's interests tend to lie in technical and managerial jobs.

Meso-level theories include structural explanations, organizational policy, and organization culture theory. A seminal work within the structural approach is from Rosabeth Moss Kanter who emphasizes that gender per se does not matter as much for individual career aspirations as it does for individual structural situations, i.e., opportunity structures, structures of power, and proportional representations. Other studies, for example, Christine Williams's 1993 study, have raised some doubts about Kanter's claim that the number of people in a certain category is significant in order to understand what advances people's careers. It is argued that the person's gender may be more important, for employers may (re)produce the gender segregation of labor through organizational policies in which employers act as gatekeepers, recruiting people and deciding who does which job. Gender or job-based stereotypes underpin this explanation. The male-dominated power structures and a tendency toward homosocial reproduction contribute to the gendered division of labor. The third explanation within this meso level relates to organizational culture. Here, it is the meanings, ideas, values, and beliefs that are shared by a collective of people that underpin the explanation for gender segregation. Actions and other externalized phenomena such as formal structures and positions are seen as manifestations of these socially shared beliefs, ideas, and definitions.

The third level of explanations, the macro level, includes Marxist feminist analyses, patriarchy theories, and the dual systems theory. All of these tend to explain the gender division of labor as connected to capitalism, with the family as the foundation for women's subordination because the family serves as a necessary and functional means for the reproduction of labor. Hence, it is in the interest of capitalism to maintain the gender division of labor. For Marxist feminism, reproduction is central to understanding the gender division of labor in which women's domestic duties are seen as contributing to their unfavorable situation. Other explanations, for example that of radical feminists, put forth that men as a group dominate, and control, women as a group. The concept of patriarchy is used to explain women's universal and transhistorical oppression. It is argued that patriarchy has played a historic role in keeping women out of well-paid work and gendering this well-paid work as male. In the early capitalist industries, jobs were even designed according to one or the other gender, making it possible to employ women more cheaply because of the lower social value of their work. Finally, the dual systems theory, proposed by Heidi Hartmann in 1979, was an attempt to synthesize Marxist feminism with radical feminism. Here, patriarchy and capitalism are seen as two analytically distinct systems of power relations that work together, encouraging gender antagonisms. The present gender division of labor is then regarded as established in capitalist production relations, the result of a long process of interaction between patriarchy and capitalism that is fundamental for the reproduction of patriarchy. Capitalism has had a crucial role in maintaining, consolidating, and reconstructing precapitalist patterns of sex-typing and segregation, as noted by Harriet Bradley.

More recently, a social constructionist approach has become popular in gender division research. The constructionist approach avoids focusing too strongly on a particular analytical level, which makes it possible to generate connections between macro- and micro-level theory. In this approach, focusing on the ways in which organizations are gendered usually means paying attention to how organizational structures and processes are dominated by culturally defined masculine meanings. The concepts of masculinity and femininity can be used to describe cultural beliefs without connecting these very closely to men and women. Masculine meanings may be traced also in language, acts, and artifacts that are loosely coupled to sex/human bodies. What is "normal" for men and women guides, constrains, and traps people's occupational choices, leading them to acceptance/rejection of tasks. Although people may be more or less independent in relation to these guidelines and constraints, there exist profound ideas that certain types of education, career choices, work, and positions are connected with a particular gender. Most jobs are defined as masculine or feminine and thus are seen as natural for men or women, respectively. Jobs have a certain gender symbolism; they are seen as carrying a broader meaning stemming from a cultural logic behind the sex-typing. Constructing jobs as masculine makes them antithetical to women. Management and leadership are often viewed as socially constructed in masculine terms, making it difficult for women managers to strike a balance between being seen as a competent manager and as sufficiently feminine enough to avoid breaking with gender expectations. The social construction of education and jobs in terms of masculinity and femininity results in oppositional gender categories that play a crucial role in how men and women become located in the labor market and in organizations. According to Robin Leidner, most any job may be constructed as either male or female through emphasizing some dimensions and labeling it in a particular way. How jobs are constructed varies across cultures and groups. For example, when one gender comprises most of the jobholders, there tends to be a belief that this gender is particularly well suited to this job. However, many jobs have, over the years, been redefined in terms of gender—for example, when the association between a particular job and the biological sex is eroded.

Critical Commentary and Future Directions

The sex and gender role theory finds it difficult to explain what cannot be categorized in one-dimensional categories. If people were totally fused with their roles, there would be no need to discuss gender divisions; they would be given by nature. However, gender roles are normative and historically changeable, as they are culturally and socially constructed. For example, dealing with only the micro level means that individuals must disregard the other levels of explanation, i.e., the organizational, societal, and cultural contexts and structural factors that might help or hinder women or men. Therefore, a micro approach does not offer a strong basis for understanding collective patterns, for a variety of different forces and processes may well contribute to gender division of labor and to its de-differentiation.

Macro and meso theories tend to objectify women and men as passive reproducers of existing structures, which makes it difficult to conceive of women and men as actors on the historical scene. In this way, it becomes difficult to understand variations in women's and men's situations, such as the increase of women in positions of power, and men's inroads into female jobs. The idea that structures are reproduced by people and only exist in actions is not considered with these levels of explanations. These explanations' neglect of the importance of socialization and education preferences is also problematic. In the context of organization studies, more specific patterns, variations, and ambiguities are of interest to scholars.

The social construction approach must consider the risk of reproducing stereotypes and of arbitrarily imposing masculinity/femininity. What is masculine for one group or person may not be for another. The complex interplay between external pressures and internalized subjective orientations must be considered in order to truly understand gender division. The dichotomous way of thinking about genders leads to feminine/masculine reproduction of gender divisions that hide the internal differentiation within each concept. Furthermore, this dichotomy even obscures how males and females interact with other categories, i.e., ethnicity, age, and socioeconomic strata.

It is vital to appreciate the significance of identity to understand the role of cultural masculinity/femininity. People who break with established gender patterns can face significant difficulties. Males in typically female jobs are often stereotyped as feminine and are sometimes either accused of being too masculine for this kind of work or labeled homosexuals, as noted by Jim Allan. Power operates through normalization—through defining what is normal, natural, and acceptable, and through invoking fear and uncertainty about deviating from this ideal. Most people conform to social norms and feel natural when choosing an education, job, and career that are in line with cultural conventions or that at least do not break radically with these.

The gendered division of labor today is the result of a long historical process, with women and men sometimes in reversed roles The general cultural conceptions and expectations of the sexes are influenced by factors left over from a time when the roles of women and men were more fixed. These preconceptions still influence how we view, judge, and treat the two sexes. Poststructuralism's way of trying to go beyond dichotomy is to deconstruct language use. Two ways poststructuralism can advance the removal of gender divisions is through developing discourses whereby gender is created and re-created, or putting more weight on the subject's possible influence of the structures. Poststructuralism's contribution can be summed up as showing the instability in the concepts/categories of feminine/masculine and women/men. To be conscious about what Candace West and Don Zimmerman named the "doing of gender" and likewise about the doing of gender division is important if both the gender division and the consequences of this construction are to be removed.

—*Yvonne Due Billing*

See also Deconstruction; Discrimination; Equity Theory; Gender Stereotypes; Glass Ceiling; Identification; Identity; Masculinities and Management; Radical Feminism; Socialization

Further Readings

Allan, J. (1993). Male elementary teachers: Experiences and perspectives. In C. Williams (Ed.), *Doing "women's work": Men in non-traditional occupations.* Newbury Park, CA: Sage.

Bradley, H. (1994). Gendered jobs and social inequality. *The Polity reader in gender studies.* Cambridge, UK: Polity.

Chodorow, N. (1978). *The reproduction of mothering: Psychoanalysis and the sociology of gender.* Berkeley: University of California Press.

Hartmann, H. (1979, Summer). The unhappy marriage of Marxism and feminism: Towards a more progressive union. *Capital and Class, 8,* 1–22.

Kanter, R. M. (1977). *Men and women of the corporation.* New York: Basic Books.

Leidner, R. (1991). Serving hamburgers and selling insurance: Gender, work, and identity in interactive service jobs. *Gender & Society, 5*(2), 154–177.

West, C., & Zimmerman, D. (1987). Doing gender. *Gender & Society, 1,* 125–151.

Williams, C. (Ed.). (1993). *Doing "women's work": Men in nontraditional occupations.* Newbury Park, CA: Sage.

GENDERED ORGANIZATION

Organizations are gendered whether one experiences it or not. Despite this, the convention in organization studies has long been to consider organizations as gender neutral. This neglects any analysis of the gendered nature, gender differences, and gendered practices of organizations. More recently, however, commentators have argued that organizations and those who research them have actually blinded themselves to gender in that they ignore the fact that organizations are already gendered because they are dominated by masculine practices and values. To consider organizations as gendered is to understand them in terms of how their existence and behavior rely on power relations between the masculine and the feminine, relations that privilege the masculine and render the feminine marginal.

Conceptual Overview

Gender in Organizational Theory

Gender is socially constructed and it is performed—we "do" gender rather than "have" a gender. Joan Acker defines gender as patterns of meaning that are socially produced so as to enable people to distinguish between male and female, and masculine and feminine. Moreover, such meanings influence the ways that organizations are structured, cultures are produced and maintained, and behaviors are enacted. As Acker surmises, distinctions between the masculine or male and the feminine or female pattern the relations between advantage and disadvantage, exploitation and control, action and emotion, and so forth.

Fiona Wilson argues that because gender has not been a significant variable in organization and management theory, organizations have come to be understood as gender neutral. Critiquing this position, Stephen Linstead has suggested that organizations are better considered as being gender blind because they are dominantly conceived of in relation to the masculine. By this account, organizational meaning is dominated by a masculine norm where the feminine is excluded, marginalized, and rendered abject. Despite claims of gender neutrality in the majority of theories in organization studies, the foundational studies of, for example, Frederick Taylor and Abraham Maslow did actually account for gender, although it has been erased in subsequent uses of these theories. Taylor argued that organizing is about identifying the clearly observable principles on which work is founded, and against which they could be measured. Difference, like gender and ethnicity, does not affect these principles and people should manage according to the one best way. However, Taylor also argued that gender difference does affect the way people manage and work, and thus needs to be corrected for administratively. For example, he advocated allowing women two days' leave from work per month to enable them to cope with the menstrual cycle, therefore highlighting women's biological difference from men. Either way, Taylor's theories were gendered in that he believed scientific management would be beneficial for women by suppressing their difference from men. Maslow's famous hierarchy of needs is infused with an understanding of gender difference. In this model, the "self" in self-actualization is actually a male self, characterized by qualities such as the denial of relatedness and the pursuit of its own individual goals. This contrasts with a female model, which defines its self in relation to others. For Maslow, if women self-actualize, they do it in different ways from men—for example, through motherhood, rather than through organization or as expressed by the hierarchy of needs.

Gender in Organizations

As the above examples suggest, gender has long been considered a central aspect of organizations, albeit in problematic ways, and in ways that subsequent use of these theories has been blind to. What this does illustrate, however, is that a gendered analysis of organizations considers how gender influences organizational behavior and also how organizations create and re-create gendered practices and ways of knowing. Organizations are considered as being patriarchal or being characterized by hegemonic masculinity—that is, that in economic, cultural, and social spheres men are dominant, and privilege, power, and authority are invested in masculinity. Organizational masculinity informs the structural and cultural practices, and norms and behavior of organizational members in many possible different ways. Amanda Sinclair provides eight types of organizational masculinity found in organizations and that promote dominant types of behavior and cultures:

1. Traditional authoritarianism (which promotes bullying and a culture of fear)
2. Gentleman's club (where organizations are dominated by protectionism and paternalism, and which is based on the assumption that men are born to rule)
3. Entrepreneurialism (which has a task-oriented and a workaholic culture)
4. Informalism (where schoolboyish, larky behavior is common and is often attached to sporting and sexual rituals)
5. Careerism (where the organization values expertise and bureaucratic career progression)

6. Gender blind (where everyone, regardless of gender, is "one of the boys")

7. Feminist pretenders (where the organization is supportive of equality but the onus is on women to take the responsibility for developing equality)

8. Smart macho (which promotes and fosters a highly competitive environment and which is driven by performance. As such, the organization discriminates against those who cannot work at the desired pace or who question the competitive ethos)

As illustrated above, organizations have traditionally privileged masculinity; however, in recent times it has been suggested that management is becoming more feminized. The feminization of management thesis proposes that femininity is a necessary managerial capability. As Nanette Fondas argues, women are better positioned to fulfill contemporary expectations of organizations as their different skills render them closer to nature, passion, intuition, and emotion. This is said to offer new possibilities for women as their "special" skills are what is lacking in the higher echelons of management. Conversely, however, Judy Wajcman suggests that regardless of sex, masculinist career patterns and management practices prevail, with both men and women expected to behave in traditionally and stereotypically masculine ways.

Gender, Culture, and Identity

The study of gendered organizations is also related to issues of culture and identity in organizations. At issue here is that gendered organizational cultures (values, beliefs, assumptions, shared symbols, language use, etc.) produce and reproduce particular gendered relations, identities, practices, and power relations in organizations. Acker states that organizations are gendered at four levels: the level of the division of labor between males and females; the level of gendered symbols that may represent organizational culture, such as office space and corporate dress; the level of gendered social relations between individuals in organizations; and the level of gendered identities, which is how individuals construct their self-identities by drawing on masculine and feminine discourses.

Considerations of gendered organizational culture are also related to the way that gender in organizations can be theorized as a social practice. As espoused by Sylvia Gherardi, gender as social practice defines relations between men and women, and between male and female, in terms of how individuals enact their own gender in relation to the positionings of other people as reflected in situated discourses. Moreover, these discourses are located in specific locations and specific times. For example, as Gherardi shows, female position is often placed in relation to dominant masculine cultural practices of organizations in terms of whether women accept it, contest it, or impose themselves on it. Gherardi identifies six positions that assist in understanding female behavior in masculinist cultures. When the male positioning is friendly, females either *accept* this as "the guest" who is a cooperative relationship between men and women; *contest* it in the mismatched position of "the holiday maker"; or *impose* themselves on it as "the newcomer," which is an open-ended position of ambiguity and uncertainty. However, when the host male environment is hostile, female positioning changes, albeit with the same three positions of acceptance, contestation, or self-imposition. If females accept this hostile position, they are in the stigmatized position of "the marginal," if they contest it they are positioned as "the snake in the grass," and if they impose themselves on the culture they are "the intruder." In each case, it is the male position that remains primary, and the female position is a reaction.

In a lucid example of gender relations at work, Heather Höpfl examines the popular 1997 feature film *GI Jane*. In particular, she considers the position that Lieutenant Jordan O'Neill (played by Demi Moore) experiences when she enters the U.S. Navy SEALs (Sea, Air, and Land) training program as an experiment to integrate female combat fighters. Membership becomes central within a male-dominant and masculine culture. The viewer witnesses male regression as a response to the threat of feminine power, and GI Jane has two options open to her when faced with extreme hostility and marginalization—exclusion or incorporation. As a token female entering a male's world, her only choice if she wants to "make it" is to act like one of the guys, and this involves redefining herself as a man. What Höpfl shows is that complete incorporation into masculine naval culture—that is, being one of the men and becoming androgynous in her attempts to achieve equality—preserves the culture. As such, following Höpfl, women are incorporated into the military body both culturally and through inscription on their physical bodies. They become incorporated into the masculinist culture via a cancellation of the feminine; the only nonthreatening role for women is to become a man because subverting womanhood is challenging to men. We see GI Jane become successful and accepted by adopting a masculine role so as to overcome male prejudice about her sex.

While this film was heralded as a success story of a woman overcoming marginalization, Höpfl's critique argues that in becoming defeminized, GI Jane has to cancel her feminine power and therefore is not a valuable model for women in organizations. The example of GI Jane mirrors organizational events in which organizations try to induct, incorporate, or seduce their members into the masculine organizational culture.

Höpfl's poststructuralist reading of GI Jane demonstrates how gender is relational—that is, it concentrates on gender as being a product of social relations between men and women rather than indicative of the properties of their fixed identity positions. Alison Pullen's research on how middle managers construct their gendered identities shows how self and gender are embedded in and emerge from discursive structures and therefore appreciates the relationality and multiplicity of lived gendered experiences. As such, following Pullen, a relational approach to gender and organization provides increased discursive heterogeneity by demonstrating the wider variety of discourses through which people establish their gendered narratives of self; it also introduces the possibility of relational resistance and reveals the ways in which men and women relationally resist the discursive subject positions institutionally prescribed for them.

Critical Commentary and Future Directions

Studies of gender and organization have largely focused on the processes of "doing" gender as an organized performance, often a project of achievement and completeness—whether in producing or reproducing gendered identities and discourses or resisting and subverting them. However, such performance of gender involves considerable ambiguity, incompleteness, fragmentation, and fluidity—and it is often tied up with processes of undoing at levels of identity, self, text, and practice as David Knights and Pullen argue. In *Undoing Gender,* Judith Butler connects the performance of gender with both its organization and its disorganization with the experiences of becoming undone. She focuses on how gender gets done and undone in organizations and through organizing, and with what consequences, and how gender projects are caught up in a multiplicity of often conflicting desires, doubts, and discourses within shifting spaces and times that can indeed threaten the very concept of gender itself.

Reading gender as a linguistic or dramaturgical performance, Butler notes that language makes things happen, often in complex, indirect, and oblique ways. This performativity of language is critical to understanding gender and sexuality in terms of how they combine to make certain types of gender positioning possible. But Butler also considers that we weave streams of this general performativity into specific gender performances, and as such, organizational practice mediates the gendered performance of self. One way of challenging hegemonic masculinity in organizations is to rethink the ontology of gender as fragile and fragmented and to explore the multiplicity and fluidity of gender performance. Gender is seen as a multiplicity—any individual may have a number of different gender positions between which he or she shifts, and which are realized and changed in performance, as Linstead and Pullen contest. Accordingly, the focus of attention shifts to gendered cultural processes at work in the behavior of real men and women, rather than through abstract definitions. This means that males and females are not confined to their particular sex—that is, individuals are never purely masculine or purely feminine but are combinations of features that are multiple and shift constantly across dichotomous boundaries.

Poststructuralist developments in gender theory remind us that gender is relational and multiplex. Although gendered analyses of organizations have become more mainstream in recent years, future research needs to focus on the multiplicity and fluidity of doing and undoing gender to appreciate the complexity, ambiguity, and multiplicity of gendered organizational experiences. There is much need for investigation of underresearched organizational settings; the gendered experiences of underrepresented individuals in organizations; and neglected issues such as transgendering, degendering, or ungendering. But challenging gender inequality involves changing gendered organizational norms and practices, and this must involve disrupting taken-for-granted assumptions, and knowing and thinking differently—a politics for change.

—*Alison Pullen*

See also Identity; Masculinities and Management; Organizational Culture; Radical Feminism

Further Readings

Acker, J. (1990). Hierarchies, jobs, bodies: A theory of gendered organizations. *Gender and Society, 4*(2), 139–158.

Butler, J. (1990). *Gender trouble: Feminism and the subversion of identity.* New York: Routledge.

Butler, J. (2004). *Undoing gender.* London: Routledge.

Fondas, N. (1997). Feminization unveiled: Management qualities in contemporary writings. *Academy of Management Review, 22*(1), 257–282.

Gherardi, S. (1995). *Gender, symbolism and organizational culture.* London: Sage.

Höpfl, H. (2003). Becoming a (virile) member: Women and the military body. *Body and Society, 9*(4), 13–30.

Knights, D., & Pullen, A. (2006). Un-doing gender: Organizing and dis-organizing performance [Special Issue]. *Gender, Work and Organization.*

Linstead, S. A. (2000). Gender blindness or gender suppression? A comment on Fiona Wilson's research note. *Organization Studies, 21*(1), 297–303.

Linstead, S., & Pullen, A. (2006). Gender as multiplicity: Desire, difference and dispersion. *Human Relations, 59*(9), 1287–1310.

Pullen, A. (2006). *Managing identity.* London: Palgrave.

Sinclair, A. (1998). *Doing leadership differently: Gender, power and sexuality in a changing business culture.* Melbourne, Australia: Melbourne University Press.

Wajcman, J. (1998). *Managing like a man: Women and men in corporate management.* Cambridge, UK: Polity.

Wilson, F. (1996). Organizational theory: Blind and deaf to gender? *Organization Studies, 17*(5), 825–842.

Gender Stereotypes

The term *gender* refers to socially constructed sex, i.e., social practices and representations associated with femininity or masculinity. A stereotype is a typical and commonly shared picture that comes to mind when thinking about a particular social group or a category of people. Gender stereotypes are thus typical and socially shared representations of masculine or feminine traits and conducts.

Conceptual Overview

The American journalist Walter Lippmann introduced the concept of stereotype in 1922. It has since then been widely used in the social sciences to denote a typical representation of a social grouping that is neither correct nor a result of firsthand experience. It is usually a simplification and resistant to change, since people tend to perceive reality through stereotypes. They see what they expect to see. The concept of a stereotype is likely to be used to describe representations that are pejorative rather than positive.

The concept of gender was introduced in social sciences as there was a need to discriminate between biological sex and socially constructed sex, i.e., what is considered to be masculine or feminine. Feminists observed that physical differences between men and women were too often used to legitimate social differences, even when there was no obvious reason for this. There are few, if any, systematic sex differences that have any necessary social implications. Studies of sex differences consistently show that the overlap between the sexes is much larger than the mean difference, if any, between the groups. This means that people differ, but the differences are not systematically related to a person's physiological sex.

Masculinity and femininity are constructed as each other's opposites. The one is what the other is not, and the resulting *gender order* often reinforces male superiority. The psychologist Sandra Bem showed in 1981 that people in the United States thought that to be masculine meant to be self-reliant, assertive, forceful, self-sufficient, individualistic, dominant, aggressive, competitive, and ambitious. To be feminine was to be loyal, gentle, shy, yielding, gullible, childlike, affectionate, sympathetic, understanding, compassionate, warm, tender, and flatterable. These are examples of gender stereotypes.

Even if gender stereotypes have little basis in how people actually are configured, they still have social effects. Men and women, as they each learn how they and the other sex are supposed to be, try to live up to the norm in their thoughts and actions, and they expect others to do the same. People "think" and "do" gender, and thus reproduce a certain gender order. Even when people choose to do otherwise, their actions are still interpreted in relation to these norms. People who go against the norms therefore risk being seen as deviating and are labeled, for example, "tomboys," "sissies," or "iron ladies."

Organization scholars have shown that gender stereotypes affect organizing processes. In her now classic study, Rosabeth Moss Kanter found that people in token positions, i.e., those in which they were the only present representative of their kind, were seen not as individuals, but as representatives of their sex. Gender stereotypes influenced the way they were perceived and treated. A woman manager in a male-dominated management group not only had to act as a manager, but also had to deal with stereotyped expectations of what a woman is like—both those of her own and those of others. Due to its long tradition of male dominance, management is male gendered, and as femininity is perceived as its opposite, fulfilling both roles may imply great difficulties for a woman manager. She may find herself in a losing situation, no matter what she does. Conversely, a male manager who opts out of a management career to care for small children or to do something else considered female, may have his masculinity questioned.

Joan Acker shows that gendered expectations influence the opportunities for men and women in different ways. It is often assumed that work is separated from the rest of life, and that work should have priority for the worker. As women are expected to take the main responsibility for home and children, they are seen as a less dependable workforce than men, and therefore are not given the same career opportunities.

The effects of gender stereotypes are not always straightforward, however. They are different in different cultural contexts, and they vary over time. Professions may even change gender. One example of this can be seen in secondary school teachers in Scandinavia. This used to be an exclusively male profession, but is today dominated by women. Gender stereotypes may even work differently within any organization. Silvia Gherardi quotes an incident of potential sexual harassment that was seen and interpreted differently by different age groups, occupational communities, and at different hierarchical levels. She shows that women newcomers in organizations varied in how they were able to negotiate gender relations. Some of them were even able to use gender stereotypes as a resource. These women positioned themselves in their organizations in different ways, but there was no escaping the stereotypes—all of them had to deal with these in one way or another.

Researching gender stereotypes is therefore difficult, particularly as scholars often embody them themselves. Organization theory has largely been gender-blind, building on the assumption that members of organizations are men who have no obligations or interests outside their work. Moreover, research that includes women risks falling prey to stereotypes. Helene Ahl's analysis of research texts on women's entrepreneurship shows that even when no differences in entrepreneurial traits between men and women were found, such results could nevertheless be interpreted through a mental framework of differences. Women entrepreneurs were, for example, said to be self-selected, and different from ordinary women, even if there was no comparative data on "ordinary women." This interpretation served to protect the conception of men and women as different, and it demonstrates the pervasiveness of gender stereotypes.

Critical Commentary and Future Directions

Although the concept of gender has been of great use for feminist theorizing, it is also problem-ridden. The first problem is that it has been co-opted by daily language, and is today used in the same binary sense as sex. Whereas surveys used to ask people to indicate their sex, in English-speaking countries they today ask for people's gender. Thus, the original analytical distinction has been lost. This implies that "gender stereotypes" tend to be reduced to "misunderstandings about men and women."

A second problem is the question, what comes first, sex or gender? The sex/gender distinction assumes that there is a divide between that which is constant (nature, the body) and that which is variable (culture). But where does one draw the line? Judith Butler claims that the body should properly be regarded as socially constructed, just as much as all the meanings people attach to it. This does not mean that the body does not exist, but that it is not possible to understand the body without the confines of language and culture. According to Butler, gender/sex (same thing) is *performed*. Or rather, it is *co*performed, as any successful performance requires an accepting audience. Men and women sometimes go to great lengths in clothing, adornments, physical exercise, diets, and even surgery to produce socially accepted and distinctly different male and female bodies. Butler points out that this is done in a *heteronormative* way, i.e., it reproduces heterosexuality as the norm.

This touches upon yet another challenge. Postcolonial theory has criticized gender research for privileging white, middle-class, heterosexual women. That is, gender stereotypes have been questioned, but ethnicity, race, age, class, creed, sexual orientation, national origin, disability, and other forms of distinction that order and rank people have been ignored, rendering, for example, black women's subordination to white women invisible. Conversely, policies on, for example, racial discrimination have been accused of being gender-blind, treating color as the only basis for discrimination. The term *intersectionality* refers to how different sorts of stereotypes interact in positioning individuals and groups in relation to each other.

Assuming that gender is performed, however, means that the same goes for other types of distinction. One also "does" one's ethnicity, class, creed, and so forth, within the confines of what the audience expects or accepts. This means that instead of using gender, color, and the like as fixed variables in research, and in this way contributing to the reproduction of stereotypes, research should instead focus on *discourses* of gender, color, and the like, and how these impinge on or enable thought and action. The term *discourse* refers to stereotypes, but also to material and social practices that sustain stereotypes, such as the gendered division of labor with women in supportive occupations, such as nursing. By making such discourses visible and questioning them, other alternatives may open up.

Even if commendable, such an approach entails at least two difficulties. The first difficulty is cognitive: It is impractical, if not impossible, to question many categories at the same time. Language is built upon categories—they are necessary for people to be able to make sense of the world. Even if putting one or two under scrutiny, one needs to take most other categories for granted, in order to create and communicate an understanding.

The other difficulty is political: The wish to represent, for instance, women as a group, makes it difficult to argue for their common interests, if simultaneously assuming that gender is constructed, and that there is nothing that necessarily unites all women. This is why the concept of gender, as socially constructed, has met resistance from those feminists who claim that it is necessary to be able to speak from an oppressed group as if it were a group, when seeking a more positive identity.

Iris Young has a useful suggestion for how to come to terms with such a strategy intellectually. She introduces the concept of *gender as seriality*, borrowed from Sartre. She says that even if there is nothing essential that unites all women, they are still united in that they are *seen* as women. They all have to relate to gendered clothing, gendered spaces, gendered labor markets, gendered language, and to the circumstance that people around them label them as women. Women relate in infinitely many ways, but relate they must. And so must people who are labeled as men, or black, or working class, or homosexual, or any other category that classifies or orders people. Even if they do not identify themselves as such, others do it, and the categories will therefore have some repercussions on their lives. Thinking of gender as seriality allows the conceptualization of women and men as categories, without assuming that people in the same category have a common identity.

Research on gender runs the risk of misrepresenting people, but this risk does not mean that it is not worthwhile. There is still much work to be done in making the workings of gender stereotypes visible, and in questioning how dominant discourses contribute to organizational practices that marginalize certain groups. Discourses of management, leadership, and entrepreneurship were mentioned earlier, but the field of organization studies involves many other gendered discourses, such as human resources management, or even those concerning equal opportunities and diversity. One may, for example, ask if the business case for equality actually benefits equality, or whether equal opportunity practices are formulated within a discourse basically incompatible with the concept of equality. However, there is no final escape from the stereotypes, as they seem to be necessary for people to be able to make sense of the world, but one can always try to challenge them, ridicule them, and attempt to fill them with a different content.

—*Helene Ahl*

See also Gender Division; Masculinities and Management; Sexuality; Social Constructionism

Further Readings

Acker, J. (1992). Gendering organizational theory. In A. Mills & P. Tancred (Eds.), *Gendering organizational analysis*. London: Sage.

Ahl, H. (2004). *The scientific reproduction of gender inequality: A discourse analysis of research texts on women's entrepreneurship*. Copenhagen, Denmark: CBS Press.

Bem, S. L. (1981). *Bem Sex-Role Inventory*. Palo Alto, CA: Mind Garden.

Gherardi, S. (1995). *Gender, symbolism and organizational cultures*. London: Sage.

Kanter, R. M. (1977). *Men and women of the corporation*. New York: Basic Books.

Lippmann, W. (1997). *Public opinion*. New York: Free Press. (Original work published 1922)

Weedon, C. (1999). *Feminism, theory and the politics of difference*. Oxford, UK: Blackwell.

Young, I. (1995). Gender as seriality. In L. Nicholson & S. Seidman (Eds.), *Social postmodernism*. Cambridge, UK: Cambridge University Press.

GENEALOGICAL ANALYSIS

Genealogical analysis (GA) refers to a method of analysis of history that is written with the intention of critically questioning the present. It is an indispensable tool in conducting any Foucauldian analysis of power. GA seeks to write a varied history of the present by reconstructing such history in ways that make space for its marginalized aspects, hence questioning the sources of domination and exploitation.

Conceptual Overview

Michel Foucault borrowed the original idea of GA from Friedrich Nietzsche's philosophy. GA is a meticulous and patient documentary in the sense that it is concerned with a highly detailed and concrete exploration of history through locating words, actions, artifacts, and so on in their proper chronological order and contexts. In this way, GA seeks to obtain alternative understandings of how and why present-day organizational phenomena emerged. The researcher in GA is akin to a detective who traces the various clues that lead to the emergence of various projects, decisions, innovations, or other events. From this perspective, people are perceived as morally imprisoned by their own tacit and taken-for-granted ways of talking, acting, knowing, and being. By reconstructing history, GA seeks to make people conscious of who they are, where they come from, and why things are the way they are. This form of critical analysis provides researchers with the opportunity and means of reflecting on the self by using history to make the unconscious conscious, as noted by Mark Haugaard in 1997.

Genealogy relies on five basic concepts that are central to applying this method: contingency, descent, emergence, power, and archaeology. *Contingency* describes how events should be perceived, as noted by Gavin Kendall and Gary Wickham in 1999. Events are contingent on what came before; thus, events are always only a possible outcome of history—not the necessary or only outcome.

One must further distinguish between the concepts of *descent* and *emergence* in describing these contingencies, as noted by Foucault in 1984. *Descent* is linked to identity in the sense that values and perceptions of the self are historical constructs shaped in specific historical circumstances. The values behind choice and assessment are, in other words, not given; people are taught and socialized into how to behave and make value judgments in specific ways. *Emergence,* on the other hand, is a relation between forces that emphasizes that people's words and actions must always be viewed in relation to other actors and circumstances. In emergence, different identities and circumstances are in play. It follows that emergence is never finished or complete, as it moves through new relations, producing new objects, new actions, and new ways of speaking.

By describing the circumstances in which certain phenomena emerged, GA seeks to overcome, if only in part, the problem of moral imprisonment noted above, as it allows one to question the values embedded and embodied in societies, institutions, and organizations, as noted by Bent Flyvbjerg in 2001. This kind of knowledge is of critical importance because GA presumes that history is driven by unequal relations of *power* that are inscribed in ways of talking, acting, and being. They are also inscribed in the writing of history where contesting arguments, viewpoints, meanings, and actions are too often marginalized; it is most often the winners who write history.

Genealogical analysis seeks to challenge and overcome this problem by writing a more richly varied story of how certain phenomena emerged. To accomplish this, GA relies on a specific methodological procedure as the point of departure: *archaeology.* Archaeology is a systematic rewriting of history whereby events are organized in terms of chronology, actors, and contexts. Central to an archaeological rewriting of history are questions such as who is speaking, from which institutional site(s) does this speech gain its legitimacy and purpose, which positions are possible for the individual to occupy in relation to this speech, and so on.

Critical Commentary and Future Directions

GA approaches events as historical. The ordering in terms of who, where, and when is a basic tool through which phenomena are to be understood in GA. A main focus is on the relations between events. Less emphasis is paid to specific interactions between actors at discrete moments in time. This means that GA often overlooks how, specifically, reality is constructed interactively. GA is research at a distance; it does not have direct access to situations in which reality is constructed. A combination of GA with other approaches that focus more directly on the concrete interactions between actors can be very beneficial in terms of understanding emergence. This presupposes that the practice of GA in organization studies takes on a shorter time frame than originally proposed and used. Nietzsche and Foucault used GA in longitudinal studies of periods of several hundred years; in organization studies, GA is necessarily concentrated on much shorter periods of time, typically 5–10 years.

Finally, GA in practice relies on a combination of data sources. It differs in this respect from archaeology, which tends to rely solely on exploring historical texts and documents in the archive. GA combines the use of historical texts and documents with other sources such as interviews with key actors. These interviews serve to deepen, support, and validate interpretations of specific events and situations. It follows that the organization of the relationship between historical texts and documents and other data sources becomes crucially important to the quality of research output. A critical question to be addressed here is how the researcher influences data collection and thus how data are themselves influenced by the present.

—Kenneth Mølbjerg Jørgensen

See also Foucauldian Turn; Identity; Language and Organizations; Power; Social Constructionism

Further Readings

Flyvbjerg, B. (2001). *Making social science matter: Why social inquiry fails and how it can succeed again.* Cambridge, UK: Cambridge University Press.

Foucault, M. (1984). Nietzsche, genealogy, history. In P. Rabinow (Ed.), *The Foucault reader* (pp. 76–100). New York: Pantheon.

Haugaard, M. (1997). *The constitution of power: A theoretical analysis of power, knowledge and structure.* Manchester, UK: Manchester University Press.

Kendall, G., & Wickham, G. (1999). *Using Foucault's methods.* London: Sage.

General Systems Theory

General systems theory (GST) is an approach to inquiry that originated in biology. It emerged as a response to the perceived reductionism of analytical approaches to inquiry in science. GST seeks to provide a language and method to study phenomena across all disciplines. GST's focus is on holism; interconnectedness; understanding and articulating isomorphisms in all systems; and the application of systems principles, such as open system, equifinality, emergence, and equilibrium, across levels and disciplines. It has cross-pollinated with information theory and cybernetics, incorporating such key concepts as feedback and entropy, to become a cornerstone of holistic scientific approaches in the social sciences. It has had a continuing influence in sociology, organizational theory, and family therapy.

Conceptual Overview

GST originated in the 1940s in the work of the biologist Ludwig von Bertalanffy who initially sought to find a new approach to the study of life or living systems. More broadly, Von Bertalanffy envisioned GST as a way to address the increasing complexity of the world's problems. He believed that the dominant form of inquiry and way of thinking, reductionist analysis, was unable to address wholes, systems, and complexity. He argued that reductionism abstracts a subject of inquiry from its environment, and that by studying parts of a larger whole in isolation it is unable to account for systemic and emergent properties, and for the way relationships and interactions form the organization of the living. Von Bertalanffy saw GST as a new way of thinking that allows for the study of interconnections among systems, and accounts for the nature of open systems in their environments. He introduced key concepts such as *open and closed systems,* stressing the role and importance of context and environment; *equifinality* or the way systems can reach the same goal through different paths; and *isomorphisms* or structural, behavioral, and developmental features that are shared across systems.

GST presented itself as an interdisciplinary or generalist approach that went beyond the limitations of disciplines and specializations. GST would be the common language uniting diverse disciplines with the key concept of "system." GST also pointed toward a new worldview, a systems view of the world, which emphasizes such key concepts as every system's embeddedness in other, larger systems, and the dynamic, ever-changing processes of self-organization, growth, and adaptation.

In its early years, GST engaged in a fruitful exchange with information theory and cybernetics, most notably at the classic Macy conferences, integrating concepts such as negative and positive feedback, entropy, and self-organization. GST was quickly applied in sociology and organization theory. In sociology, the most important contribution was made by Talcott Parsons, whose work dominated the field in the 1950s and 1960s. Parsons's structural functionalism proposed that every system needs to fulfill certain functional imperatives. In organizational theory, Burns and Stalker, and Katz and Kahn made substantive contributions based on GST, introducing the concept of the organization as an open system. The open system presented an "organismic" alternative (reflecting von Bertalanffy's original concern with living systems) to more "mechanistic" approaches originating with Fayol and Taylor, that treated individuals, groups, and departments as machinelike closed systems.

Taylor's scientific management treated each individual worker as a closed system—performing his or her duty, but having as little contact as possible with coworkers and the rest of the organization. In the same way, departments were mostly isolated from each other. Traditional strategic planning is a classic example of closed system thinking that focused largely on organizational goals. It assumed the environment was "knowable." Consequently, the environment was thought to have little or no impact on the evolution of the organization's strategy.

Open systems tend to be far less stable than closed systems. The openness of the system with its ongoing exchanges with the environment leads to potential disequilibrium and the emergence of novelty. Open systems are stabilized by flow, but their structural stability is only relative because this structure is gradually, and sometimes quite rapidly, transformed by exchanges with the environment. The "organismic" metaphor saw organizations as open systems with goals, existing in a continuous interaction with their environment. Different environments require different organizational structures, and changing environments require organismic rather than mechanistic structures. Organismic structures are more flexible than mechanistic ones, which tend to be highly specialized and compartmentalized, with strict rules and rigid hierarchy. Organismic structures required decentralization, greater interdependence, more individual discretion, less formal tasks, and horizontal as well as vertical communication. The principle of equifinality showed that there was more than "one right way" to structure organizations and achieve organizational goals.

Attempts to organize the great diversity of "systems approaches" in management and organization theory recognize that there is perhaps more diversity than unity under the systems umbrella. There is substantial fragmentation and lack of communication between systems-based approaches, and there are often fundamental epistemological differences. "Hard systems," engineering-based approaches, are often characterized by mathematical models, rational decision making, objectivity, and uncertainty reduction. "Soft systems" approaches, typically informed by constructivist epistemologies, stress uncovering assumptions and worldviews, thinking about thinking (metacognition), consensus building, and participation.

Critical Commentary and Future Directions

After its initial successes in the 1960s, GST was criticized very strongly in the 1970s, largely because of its equilibrium orientation, considered to support the status quo and existing power relations. GST was also associated with social engineering. Although GST had introduced the notion of the open system, with the accompanying potential for disequilibrium, in social science much emphasis had been placed on the importance of maintaining equilibrium in the face of turbulent environments. Politically this was seen as an ideologically conservative support of the status quo, particularly in sociology. Systems-based functionalist approaches, and in particular the work of the leading German sociologist Niklas Luhmann, a protégé of Parsons, came in for criticism again in the 1980s, during the height of the postmodern debate, for being instrumentalizing, totalizing, and coercive. Postmodern critiques of modernity often portrayed systems approaches as the scientistic apotheosis of social engineering and technocracy. Against this trend, there was among different groups, and particularly in Europe, an explicit cross-pollination of systems approaches with the human sciences, a process that had been prefigured in the more philosophical works of von Bertalanffy.

The work of such systems thinkers as Ackoff, Churchman, and Mitroff in the USA; Maruyama in Japan; Checkland, Emery and Trist, and Jackson and Flood in Britain; Morin, Le Moigne, and de Rosnay in France; and Bocchi, Ceruti, and Manghi in Italy continued to enrich the systems discourse with a variety of approaches and perspectives. Churchman's "inquiring systems" focused explicitly on the inquirer's role and became an important precursor of the self-reflective, "soft systems" approach, which was more aligned with constructivist epistemologies. The work of the transdisciplinary maverick Gregory Bateson, who drew widely from GST and cybernetics and was a key figure in the legendary Macy conferences, had a profound influence in a variety of disciplines ranging from anthropology to cybernetics to ecology to family therapy. In organization theory, Bateson's work was particularly influential in the development of the concept of organizational learning.

In the 1990s, the term "systems thinking" made a comeback with Peter Senge's best-selling *The Fifth Discipline*. Senge tellingly did not refer to GST in this work, drawing instead almost entirely on systems dynamics with its use of feedback loops and circular causality. More recently, chaos and complexity theories have become closely linked with the holistic strain of thought associated with GST under the generic label of "new sciences." This term refers to the application of findings and perspectives drawn from cybernetics, quantum physics, evolutionary theory, and chaos and complexity theories. Senge's book coincided with the rising popularity of the new sciences, in turn popularized in the management literature by Wheatley's bestseller *Leadership and the New Science*. The popular works of Senge and Wheatley contributed to a renewed interest in systemic approaches.

GST was originally envisioned as a new worldview, what Ervin László called "the systems view of the world" in his work of the same name. It involved a different way of thinking, and a different way of organizing knowledge. GST's vision and goal was therefore "transversal," in the sense that it operated across disciplines, and proposed a different approach to and organization of knowledge. This goal of developing a new worldview was largely lost in the initial applications of GST, which were grounded in a more mechanistic, instrumental perspective, and seemed to promise the ability to control and predict more accurately and efficiently.

GST has not proved to be the single unifying breakthrough approach that von Bertalanffy envisioned. In some circles, GST is still viewed with suspicion as fundamentally scientistic. As a backlash against positivist social science, a substantial strain of "human science" and postmodern thinking has come to reject any attempt to apply perspectives and insights drawn from the natural sciences to the study of human beings, and systems approaches have for many years been held up as the worst offenders. The more philosophical, social constructionist management and organization theory discourse has also generally shied away from referring to systems concepts. Even in the management and organizational writings that draw on the popular new sciences, their diffuse origins, which can be traced back to quantum physics, evolutionary theory, information theory, cybernetics, and chaos and complexity theories, often overlook the specific and vital contribution of GST. While there is a definite movement toward antireductionistic, holistic approaches in management and organization theory, there is arguably often a lack of historical and theoretical coherence, and a tendency to reinvent the wheel.

One recurring theme in the more sophisticated discussions of complexity, whether in the sciences, management, or social sciences in general, is that reductive/analytic approaches to issues are unable to account for, and give an adequate understanding of, complex, interconnected phenomena. Reductive approaches isolate phenomena from their environment and operate with a disjunctive logic (either/or). This kind of thinking can be found writ large in the organization of knowledge in universities, with departments focusing studies in ever-greater specializations, with clear boundaries between one discipline or subdiscipline and another, but little or no effort to connect the knowledge gathered in the different departments, or to elaborate how the knowledge gained in different disciplines might be integrated in practical applications in the world. Popular pseudo-holistic approaches that define themselves in opposition to reductionism and reject "parts" in favor of "wholes," "analysis" in favor of "synthesis," and "control" in favor of "emergence" almost inevitably end up being vague and ineffectual feel-good New Age nostrums rather than serious efforts to address complexity, wholeness, and interconnectedness.

Edgar Morin and Mark Taylor have, in their reconciliation of the human and natural sciences, reemphasized the foundational importance of GST in today's movement toward complexity, arguing that any theory of complexity must also be a theory of systems. Morin has grounded a "method of complexity" in GST, information theory, cybernetics, and such key concepts as self-organization and recursivity. Coupled with the renewed interest in Bateson's epistemological sophistication, these developments point to the potential for a GST-inspired approach that can inform management and organizational theory in a way that is transdisciplinary, contextualizing, and relational, rather than scientistic and totalizing.

—*Alfonso Montuori*

See also Chaos Theory; Closed System Approach; Complex Adaptive Systems; Complexity Theory; Cybernetics; Organizational Learning

Further Readings

Bateson, G. (2002). *Mind and nature.* Cresskill, NJ: Hampton Press.

Burns, T., & Stalker, G. M. (1994). *The management of innovation.* New York: Oxford University Press.

Cavaleri, S., & Obloj, K. (1993). *Management systems.* Belmont, CA: Wadsworth.

Checkland, P. (1999). *Systems thinking, systems practice.* New York: Wiley.

Jackson, M. (1991). *Systems methodology for the management sciences.* New York: Plenum.

László, E. (1996). *The systems view of the world.* Cresskill, NJ: Hampton Press.

Morin, E. (1999). *Homeland earth: A manifesto for the 21st century.* Cresskill, NJ: Hampton Press.

Morin, E. (2006). *On complexity.* Cresskill, NJ: Hampton Press.

Senge, P. (1990). *The fifth discipline.* New York: Doubleday.

Taylor, M. (2003). *The moment of complexity: Emerging network culture.* Chicago: University of Chicago Press.

Von Bertalanffy, L. (1968). *General system theory: Foundations, developments, applications.* New York: Braziller.

GLASS CEILING

The *glass ceiling* is a term coined by the *Wall Street Journal* in 1986, and is a metaphor used to describe the condition that keeps women and minorities from reaching senior positions in both public and private sector organizations in America and across the globe. The term was rapidly picked up and has been used more recently, and more analytically, by Davidson and Burke in 2004, Powell and Graves in 2003, and Thompson and Graham in 2005. According to the International Labor Organization, who has adopted the glass ceiling nomenclature, women have more difficulty obtaining top jobs than those lower in the hierarchy. Thus, a rough rule of thumb is that the higher one looks in an organization's hierarchy, the fewer the women and minorities there will be. Thus, the term glass ceiling is used to reflect the ability of women and minorities to view the world above them, but the metaphorical ceiling prevents women and minorities from accessing the senior positions they can only view. This glass ceiling effect occurs when women and minorities with credentials that are equivalent to those of white men, i.e., those who traditionally occupy positions of prestige, authority, and power within organizations, are prevented from accessing top jobs simply because they are women or minorities, a usage that has been explored in Davidson's work of 1997; Powell's contribution of 1999; and Konrad, Prasad, and Pringle's 2006 publication. As the glass is clear, women and minority groups may be unaware at first that a barrier exists—because they can see through the barrier—but as they attempt to progress through the organization, the glass ceiling becomes a very real barrier to *their* career development, while seemingly not there for people from privileged male and nonminority statuses. In this respect, the metaphor of a glass ceiling, although now conventional, is not altogether apposite, as the ceiling varies in porosity depending on who tries to move through it, while glass does not.

Conceptual Overview

Does the Glass Ceiling Exist in Organizations?

The proportion of women in management has increased over the past three decades in almost all countries, and legislation in some countries (e.g., affirmative action legislation in the United States and Canada) has contributed to this trend, as Powell and Graves documented in 2003. Despite this encouraging increase, recent research by Catalyst in 2005 has highlighted that the glass ceiling is firmly in place. In the United States, women held 50.3% of all management and professional positions in 2005, yet only 7.9% of Fortune 500 top earners and 1.4% of Fortune 500 CEOs were women. In the United Kingdom, 78 Financial Times Share Index (FTSE 100) companies in 2005 had women directors, up 13% from the previous year. However, only 11 FTSE 100 companies had female executive directors, which was below the 2002 figure, and 22 of the FTSE 100 boards in 2005 were all-male (see the discussion and data in Singh and Vinnicombe's 2005 study).

These statistics largely reflect the experiences of white women. It is important to highlight that black and ethnic minority women across the globe often face significant barriers. Although there is a general lack of data on ethnicity and employment, black and ethnic minority women are underrepresented at senior and professional levels in the labor market, as the UK Commission for Racial Equality documented in 2006. In the United Kingdom in 2004, for example, 17% of ethnic minority men were managers or senior officials, compared to 10% of ethnic minority women.

The highest percentages of women and men in these positions were Indian and Chinese. Furthermore, in some countries such as South Africa, women of all races are disadvantaged and hardly any hold senior positions, especially in the corporate world, according to Mathur-Helm in 2005. Similarly, in China, 47% of the labor force is female, yet very few are in managerial roles, as Fang-Lee Cooke recorded in 2005. Thus, despite encouraging trends in some countries, women are still comparatively absent from managerial roles, and those who are in management tend to be in lower-level managerial positions.

The Pay Gap

Research shows that women leaders and women at all levels of the workforce are generally paid less than men with equivalent skills, training, and experience, for performing the same roles. In 2005, the percentage difference between the average hourly earnings of men and women working full time in Great Britain was 17.1%, according to the Equal Opportunities Commission in 2006. In the United States, women earn approximately 77 cents for every dollar earned by men, as Women's Bureau data from 2000, cited in Nelson and Michie's 2005 work, records. In 2005, the Equal Opportunities Commission in the United Kingdom highlighted three main reasons for this pay gap. First, there is discrimination in pay systems. Women are paid less than men for performing the same roles. Second, "occupational segregation" exists. Many women are concentrated in low-paid jobs such as cleaning, catering, and caring. Third, women assume caring responsibilities for children and other relatives/dependents, which affects their progression at work.

Why Does the Glass Ceiling Exist?

Authors have identified an array of complex factors that contribute to the existence and pervasive nature of the glass ceiling. Powell and Graves in 2003, for example, highlighted the lack of systematic promotional procedures when attempting to acquire top-management positions in organizations. Rather than being an open, fair, and just process, cases are handled on an ad hoc basis. As a result, biased decisions can be made without question. In addition, women often lack access to the informal networks that men occupy, and this can impact their access to resources, advice, and information, particularly regarding potential promotional opportunities. In contrast, promotional decisions in lower-level managerial positions tend to be based on clearly defined skills and characteristics, such as education, which women are equally capable of acquiring.

It has been argued that women are disadvantaged when promotional decisions are made for "top" jobs because decision makers tend to evaluate those they regard as similar to themselves in a positive way, whereas those they regard as dissimilar are consequently less likely to receive positive evaluations. This has been referred to as the "think manager, think (white) male" stereotype, noted by both Davidson and Burke in 2004 and Davidson and Fielden in 2003, among others. As most decision makers are men, they tend to gravitate toward maintaining the status quo. In *Men and Women of the Corporation*, a classic study from 1977, Kanter characterized the results of such a preference in top management ranks as "homosocial reproduction." She argued that organizations strive to minimize uncertainty. This is because uncertainty can be risky and may prove costly to the organization.

Other authors have confirmed this theory, reporting that women are more likely to be hired and promoted into a particular management level when women already occupy these positions. In these cases, the prospect of adding more women into positions of power is less fraught with uncertainty, as men are likely to be more accustomed to working alongside women. Thus, the main challenge is to get women into positions of power in the first place, as noted by Cohen and colleagues in 1998; Kanter in 1977; and Stroh, Langlands, and Simpson in 2004. Although female leadership characteristics such as interpersonal communication, nurturing, and mutual respect are beginning to warrant more value, they are yet to be regarded as important and effective, as Wilson argued at length in 2003 and which Still confirmed in 2006. For this to be achieved, men are required to reevaluate, in positive terms, behaviors of which they had previously been critical, as remarked by Peck in 2006.

Women's experience of the glass ceiling may impact their propensity to express an interest in top-management positions, making them less likely to apply for these jobs than equally qualified men, which is likely to create a self-fulfilling prophecy. The glass ceiling may, however, be weakened if some women and minorities make it to the top jobs. Research by Singh, Vinnicombe, and James, from 2006, has shown how this is important for aspiring female managers who view senior professional women as role models. Yet the low numbers of women at senior levels, particularly black and ethnic minority women, has meant that women face a potential burden associated with being "tokenized." Women may face pressures related to being a test case for the employment of future women in the company at senior levels, as suggested by Davidson in 2002. Frustrated by the glass ceiling, they may leave and start their own businesses, as Fielden and Davidson noted in 2005.

Research has highlighted that a glass ceiling exists even in occupations where women predominate. The number of women studying law in England, for example, now outnumbers men, according to Davidson and Burke, but partners in top law firms continue to be predominantly men. In Simpson's 2004 study of male workers in England from four occupational groups, primarily regarded as "female occupations"—primary school teaching, flight attendance (cabin crew), librarians, and nursing—the author found that while token women are severely disadvantaged by their minority status through negative stereotyping, the men in her study benefited from their minority status and were actually rewarded for their difference.

Managing Diversity

Affirmative action legislation in the United States and Canada has introduced mandatory measures to increase the number of women in management. While this legislation has had an impact on the number of women in management, there have been backlashes against affirmative action and consequently, glass ceilings still exist at senior levels within organizations. To counteract this, the business case for managing diversity has been highlighted. According to Davidson and Fielden in 2003, it consists of developing the potential of all employees and utilizing all their skills, irrespective of their social ascription, so as to understand and meet customer demand better, attract investors and clients, and reduce the risks associated with organizations that are open to charges of discrimination. The "bottom line" is that good diversity management leads to increased profitability, and this business case for managing diversity is gaining credibility. A survey of human resources (HR) professionals conducted by the Society for Human Resource Management (SHRM) and *Fortune* magazine reported that the majority believed their diversity initiatives had improved the organization's culture, employee recruitment, relations with clients, creativity, and productivity, as Bowl indicated in 2001.

Critical Commentary and Future Directions

How Can Women and Minorities Break Through the Glass Ceiling?

Although gender equality legislation and managing diversity initiatives have addressed sex discrimination across the globe, this alone is unlikely to change the current climate. For the globe to witness a substantial change, gender equality legislation and managing diversity initiatives need to be rigorously implemented and societal attitudes need to change. There are efforts being made to encourage women's participation in management positions and advances are slowly occurring. Changing family roles and expectations, as well as supportive company policies and practices including flexible work hours and improved labor market conditions, have all opened up new opportunities for women, as Davidson and Burke suggested in 2004.

Numerous initiatives have been implemented by organizations to combat stereotyping and discrimination. Catalyst, in 2005, advocated educating managers and executives about the negative influence of stereotyping and ways to override it. Furthermore, they suggest showcasing the achievements of women leaders, particularly those in traditionally male-dominated fields. Some organizations have implemented formal mentoring schemes as mentoring relationships increase awareness, knowledge, and communication between employees and have been shown to be particularly crucial to the career development of women, as mentioned in the contributions by Clutterbuck and Ragins from 2002 and Woolnough, Davidson, and Fielden's 2005 work. Individual strategies that women and minorities may employ to overcome barriers include tapping into networks, taking on more visible projects, and establishing informal mentoring relationships, as reported in Stroh, Langlands, and Simpson's 2004 publication. Eradicating the glass ceiling is a complex process that involves a commitment to changing the behaviors and stereotypes that are held by those in power and that permeate society as a whole.

The glass ceiling prevents women and minorities from reaching senior positions in both public and private sector organizations. Despite the existence of the glass ceiling, companies are increasingly recognizing the importance of employing the best people for the job and managing diversity initiatives are beginning to warrant value. Unless organizations take these active steps to eradicate bias, women and minority leaders will continue to be at a disadvantage, regardless of their skills and experience, and organizations will fail to utilize the talents of their entire workforce. There needs to be a shift in corporate culture from the think manager, think (white) male, to think manager, think "qualified person." By focusing on the positive opportunities eradicating the glass ceiling can offer, the economics of organizations will be dramatically improved.

—*Marilyn J. Davidson and Helen M. Woolnough*

See also Gender Division; Gendered Organization; Gender Stereotypes; Organizational Justice; Radical Feminism; Sociology of Work and Employment

Further Readings

Burke, R. J., & Nelson, D. L. (2002). *Advancing women's careers: Research and practice.* Oxford, UK: Blackwell.

Catalyst. (2005). *Women "take care," men "take charge": Stereotyping of U.S. business leaders exposed.* Available online at http://www.catalystwomen.org

Clutterbuck, D., & Ragins, B. R. (2002). *Mentoring and diversity: An international perspective.* Oxford, UK: Butterworth Heinemann.

Cohen, L. E., Broschak, J. P., & Haverman, H. A. (1998). And then there were more? The effects of organizational sex composition on the hiring and promotion of managers. *American Sociological Review, 63,* 711–727.

Commission for Racial Equality. (2006). *Factfile: Employment and ethnicity.* Available online at http://www.cre.gov.uk

Davidson, M. J. (1997). *The black and ethnic minority woman manager: Cracking the concrete ceiling.* London: Paul Chapman.

Davidson, M. J., & Burke, R. J. (2004). *Women in management worldwide: Facts, figures and analysis.* Aldershot, UK: Ashgate.

Davidson, M. J., & Fielden, S. L. (2003). *Individual diversity and psychology in organizations.* New York: Wiley.

Equal Opportunities Commission. (2005). *It's time to pay women fairly campaign.* Available online at http://www.eoc.org

Equal Opportunities Commission. (2006). *Facts about women and men in Britain.* Available online at http://www.eoc.org.uk

Fielden, S. L., & Davidson, M. J. (2005). *International handbook of women and small business entrepreneurship.* Cheltenham, UK: Edward Elgar.

Kanter, R. M. (1977). *Men and women of the corporation.* New York: Basic Books.

Peck, J. J. (2006). Women and promotion: The influence of communication style. In M. Barrett & M. Davidson (Eds), *Gender and communication at work.* Aldershot, UK: Ashgate.

Powell, G. N. (1999). *Handbook of gender and work.* London/Thousand Oaks, CA: Sage.

Powell, G. N., Butterfield, D. A., & Parent, J. D. (2002). Gender and managerial stereotypes: Have the times changed? *Journal of Management, 28*(2), 177–193.

Powell, G. N., & Graves, L. M. (2003). *Women and men in management* (3rd ed.). Thousand Oaks, CA: Sage.

Singh, V., & Vinnicombe, S. (2005). *New look women directors add value to FTSE 100 boards: The Female FTSE Index 2005.* Bedford, UK: Cranfield School of Management, Centre for Developing Women Business Leaders. Available online at http://www.som.cranfield.ac.uk

Singh, V., Vinnicombe, S., & James, K. (2006). Constructing a professional identity: How young female managers use role models. *Women in Management Review, 21*(1), 67–81.

Still, L. V. (2006). Gender, leadership and communication. In M. Barrett & M. Davidson (Eds.), *Gender and communication at work.* Aldershot, UK: Ashgate.

Stockdale, M., & Crosby, F. J. (2004). *The psychology and management of workplace diversity.* Oxford, UK: Blackwell.

Stroh, L. K., Langlands, C. L., & Simpson, P. A. (2004). Shattering the glass ceiling in the new millennium. In M. Stockdale & F. J. Crosby (Eds.), *The psychology and management of workplace diversity.* Oxford, UK: Blackwell.

Wilson, F. (2003). *Organisational behaviour and gender.* Aldershot, UK: Ashgate.

Woolnough, H., Davidson, M., & Fielden, S. (2005). *Challenging perceptions—leadership, career development and mentoring pilot programme for female mental health nurses in NHS Trusts: A report summary.* London: The NHS Leadership Centre.

GLOBALIZATION

The term *globalization* emerged in the social sciences in the late 1980s and early 1990s. Globalization refers to a new era of global interdependency. Risks arising from globalization are increasingly global and include the spread of avian flu, the impact of global warming, nuclear disaster, and the depletion of natural resources. These issues are not merely concerns for nation-states, but for all parts of the globe. Interdependency is also seen in the growing significance of international trade in goods and services, which link firms and individuals across locations into globally interconnected commodity chains. The collapse of these links could have a dramatic impact across the world, as they constitute a new stage of communicative ability between actors in different locations. The most obvious example can be seen in the technology of the Internet, which increases the actor's ability to communicate not just across national barriers but without the state actually being able to prohibit this (unless it is willing to undertake strong and expensive measures such as in China). This communicative ability is also central to the development of global financial markets, which depend on the instantaneous distribution of information. The interdependence arising from this makes the potential for financial collapse regional and even, potentially, global. Globalization also represents a new way in which individuals, firms, ethnic groups, epistemic communities, and social movements are organizing transnationally, often disregarding the boundaries constructed by states and instead developing forms of global organization and identity. It is in the interaction of these transnational communities that new understandings, practices, and policies are constructed in the global arena. Clearly, states are still of central importance in this but they are not the only actors.

Conceptual Overview

Scholte identifies what he terms four "redundant" concepts of globalization, i.e., ways of understanding this process that fail to recognize its distinctive character. First, this time period can be identified simply as a qualitative increase in the degree of internationalization, with nothing really distinctive from previous eras. Second, it might be identified with liberalization, in particular the deregulation of markets and the creation of an open, borderless world. Third, it can be identified as an increase in universalization—a transfer of objects, practices, and experiences to different parts of the world, implying growing homogenization, standardization, and convergence. Finally, it can be identified with Westernization—a particular type of universalization in which the values and practices of advanced Western societies are imposed on other parts of the world. Scholte argues that these redundant concepts fail to capture the distinctive characteristics of the current phase of globalization. Reducing globalization to internationalization fails to recognize the distinctive social character of the new period with the emergence of distinctive forms of community and communication. Similarly, to identify globalization with liberalization is to reduce it to a one-dimensional economic process when again it is the changing nature of social relationships that is crucial. Universalization and Westernization fail to capture the contested and diverse nature of globalization, the ways in which individuals, groups, social movements, and communities use the new possibilities open to them to contest and reshape particular Western and other practices. One alternative is to see globalization as consisting of multiple processes of translation between different arenas. An object or a practice taken from one setting to another is a process of translation where new and old meanings evolve, creating something new and different. Globalization should therefore be considered as something distinctive, sui generis, arising in a distinctive phase of human history.

On the other hand, it needs to be recognized that like all social science concepts, the idea of globalization is constituted as a discursive object by actors in particular circumstances. It can be argued that globalization has been talked into existence by people who wanted to undermine the powers of social democracies and enhance the freedom and power of capital. By constructing globalization as an external objective force that actors, organizations, and states need to adapt to, it is often assumed that therefore employment standards, wages, trade union rights, and welfare systems must be reduced. Similarly, from this perspective, taxation rates must be lowered in order to attract investment, and cultural distinctiveness will decline as global media and global brands spread. Thus, globalization as a way of seeing the world may be constructed to induce feelings of helplessness in the face of global capitalism.

Others have explored these issues further by showing how globalization as a discursive framing of economic and social problems is constructed differently in different countries. In France it is constructed as a threat, something that the political class opposes and mobilizes to strengthen its grip on society. In Germany, it is constructed in such a way that it becomes a means for managers and others seeking to challenge the German model of diversified quality production and codetermination with strong employee rights. It becomes, in effect, a discourse of modernization and change within Germany, a discourse that is resisted strongly by some groups but propounded by others. In the United Kingdom, globalization is treated as inevitable but also as something that should be welcomed because it brings new opportunities from the world market. These arguments suggest that it is very important to consider who is using the discourse of globalization, how they are using it, and why.

Allowing for this, however, we may ask the question as to how far globalization has developed. Held and colleagues make a simple but useful distinction between "hyperglobalizers," the "skeptics," and the "transformationalists." Hyperglobalizers assume that globalization is rapidly creating a new world order in which states are of declining significance and global movements of capital and a global liberal market order are in the process of emerging. The second perspective is that of the skeptics who suggest that globalization is exaggerated and is to be treated as an ideological construction designed to undermine state action and collective resistance and instead allow capital to have free rein. The transformationalists are defined as those who recognize that what is occurring is highly significant but, instead of identifying an end state, consider this a process with multiple sources and multiple sites of conflict and resistance. Globalization is seen as a long-term process full of contradictions that are shaped by specific events rather than unfolding teleologically. In other words, there is no final state of globalization but rather a set of processes that have been put in motion in a world where there are opposing and resisting forces of varying degrees of influence.

From this perspective, it is clearly more possible to explore both the unevenness of globalization processes and their potentially negative impacts. For example, it is obvious that resources remain distributed in a hugely unequal way around the world. What does it mean to most of the population of Africa or the rural populations of Asia and Latin America to talk of globalization? Many of them will not have access to the Internet, even if they are not illiterate. This reflects the digital divide that continues to exist within developed as well as developing societies. Furthermore, these social groups will certainly not have the money to travel, to access the products of cultural hybridity, or to buy imports. Their lives will continue to be bound to their locality and the fate of that locality in terms of nature and the environment. Inequality of wealth and income will continue to define a divided world. Indeed, it can divide the world more deeply as the rich get richer in the developed societies and the poor, in some societies, actually get poorer. In some cases, this enlarged financial difference is at least partly a result of the broader effects of globalization, such as global warming and environmental damage. Equally, however, transformationalists recognize that the impact of globalization on certain cities in places like India and China is not confined to the urban areas. Jobs from foreign direct investment or from the development of local enterprises can be linked into global commodity chains, bringing people in from the rural areas, often into appallingly bad employment and housing conditions. This leads to a difficult debate about the impact of globalization and how its worse effects might be mitigated.

Critical Commentary and Future Directions

With some exceptions, organization studies has not shown a great interest in understanding the dynamics of globalization. Clearly, there are a substantial number of management books extolling the significance of globalization, but most of these tend to fall into the trap of hyperglobalization, with authors acting almost as spokespeople for global capitalism. One significant strand of work around national models of capitalism is more in the skeptic camp, arguing that national business systems adapt in a path-dependent way to globalization. However, there is a remarkable lack of research on what have been identified as the key elements of globalization. First, the theme of interdependency and risk could be illuminated by closer studies of how the dynamics of firms and markets from the dominant economies create new uncertainties for localities in different parts of the world. For example, what does the struggle of a U.S. or UK company to create shareholder value mean in terms of how it invests in China or India and how it relates its investment to indigenous social institutions? Second, the increasing communicative intensity of globalization raises the issue of how technologies are constituted and distributed and with what effects. There are interesting studies of this in relation to financial markets but relatively little in terms of manufacturing multinationals, e.g., in terms of the information relationship between subsidiaries and headquarters. Finally, there is clearly much work to be done on the organization of new forms of transnational actors, such as addressing the question, how do they create networks and forms of activity out of the new resources and identities emergent under globalization? In conclusion, a stronger analysis of the organizational aspects of globalization will be a substantial contribution to the wider social scientific understanding of these processes.

—*Glenn Morgan*

See also Capital Markets; Digital Divide; Epistemic Communities; Information and Communication Technology; Transnational Corporations

Further Readings

Beck, U. (1992). *The risk society*. London: Sage.
Bhagwati, J. (2004). *In defense of globalization*. New York: Oxford University Press.
Bourdieu, P. (1998). *Acts of resistance: Against the new myths of our time*. Cambridge, UK: Polity.
Castells, M. (2000). *The rise of the network society: The information age: Economy, society and culture* (Vol. 1). Oxford, UK: Blackwell.
Czarniawksa, B., & Sevon, G. (2005). *Global ideas: How ideas, objects and practices travel in the global economy*. Malmo, Sweden: Liber & Copenhagen Business School.
Gereffi, G. (2001, June). Shifting governance structures in global commodity chains, with special reference to the Internet. *American Behavioral Scientist, 44*(10), 1616–1637.
Giddens, A. (2002). *Runaway world*. London: Profile Books.
Held, D., McGrew, A., Goldblatt, D., & Perraton, J. (1999). *Global transformations: Politics, economics and culture*. Cambridge, UK: Polity.
Knorr Cetina, K., & Preda, A. (2005). *The sociology of financial markets*. Oxford, UK: Oxford University Press.
Ohmae, K. (1990). *The borderless world*. London: HarperCollins.
Sassen, S. (1998). *Globalization and its discontents*. New York: New Press.
Schmidt, V. (2002). *The futures of European capitalism*. Oxford, UK: Oxford University Press.
Scholte, J. A. (2005). *Globalization: A critical introduction* (2nd ed.). London: Palgrave.
Whitley, R. (1999). *Divergent capitalisms*. Oxford, UK: Oxford University Press.

GLOBAL VILLAGE

Global village was a term coined by Marshall McLuhan to describe the disappearance of temporal and geographical barriers to communication brought about by advances in information and communication technology. Today, the global village is used to describe one of the possible outcomes of the use of information and communication technology—a world of interconnected individuals using the World Wide Web to share information and ideas and to coordinate action.

Conceptual Overview

Computer-mediated communication is often described as allowing close interaction among geographically dispersed individuals. Although earlier communication technologies such as the telephone and postal mail allowed such interaction, these media are comparatively less flexible and socially "thinner" than computer-mediated communication. Also, spaces for computer-mediated communication, especially the World Wide Web, allow people to have instantaneous access to detailed information about events everywhere across the globe. These three features of computer-mediated communication—close personal interaction, ease in establishing personal ties, and instantaneous information about everyday events—are evocative of the social experience in close-knit communities such as those that develop in villages. The collapse of geographical and temporal barriers allowed by computer-mediated communication gives these features a global reach.

For McLuhan, who first interpreted these features of computer-mediated communication as creating a global village, the use of these technologies ushered in a new era in human history. This historical period followed what he called the "Gutenberg Galaxy"—a time when the printed word, especially in the shape of books, was the dominant medium for exchanging ideas. McLuhan's views on the global village, however, were far less optimistic than the one this label currently evokes. McLuhan argued that the experience of the global village would be one of terror and oppression. Terror was the result of the access to information about events everywhere in the world. In a global village, every event has global repercussions. There are no independent places in which to find shelter. Everything affects everyone. Oppression is the result of others' access to information about one's action. The awareness of this heightened visibility leads to what Soshana Zuboff has termed "anticipatory conformity": individuals refrain from any behavior they interpret as deviant because of the constant fear of being detected. McLuhan also did not espouse the technological determinism that characterizes many of the current accounts of the global village. These accounts see technology as the driving force of human action.

The global village is, in this approach, an inevitable consequence of technological progress. For McLuhan, the changes brought about by the diffusion of computer-mediated communication triggered social change, but did not define its content. For McLuhan, the decisive factor for the consequences of the global village was agents' awareness of computer-mediated communication's effects. If agents were aware of the totalitarian, terror-inducing power of computer-mediated communication, then they could choose to use this technology otherwise, to create the current ideal of the global village—a global community of equals committed to social progress. When computer-mediated communication became more widespread, the global village started to be used to refer to the international use of computer-mediated communication, which had a number of positive features. This view espoused a fast-approaching future in which networked computers would be available to the vast majority of the world population. The world was seen as populated by agents with enough formal education to have a sophisticated understanding of world events in a variety of fields. These agents not only had the ability to follow world events but also the willingness to do so. What is more, they were not content with knowing what was happening in the world around them. They wanted to act on those events to promote a communal experience of everyday life.

Critical Commentary and Future Directions

The global village never became a part of people's everyday experience because one of its fundamental premises is, at best, very far away from becoming a reality—global access to networked computers. Many authors today speak of a global *digital divide,* separating the developed world from developing nations based on citizens' access to and use of computer-mediated communication.

People in developing nations not only lack the financial resources to acquire networked computers, but also lack the basic infrastructure needed to use this technology, namely wide-bandwidth Internet access and, in some cases, electricity to power their computers. Even in developed countries, the access to and use of networked computers is far from being universal. In fact, the term digital divide was first used to discuss differences in access to and use of networked computers between urban and rural areas in the United

States. The digital divide has also been found to exist among different economic strata and between different genders.

Global village is today used only occasionally in the literature. The phenomena that this label covered are now spread through the literature on globalization, the literature on the digital divide, and the social study of computer-mediated communication. Although the separation of these three aspects of the global village allowed each of them to benefit from more focused research, their relationship was de-emphasized. This led to a toning down of some of the earlier critical views of this label. Computer-mediated communication in particular earned a newfound power-neutrality. The oppressive nature of the technologies exposed by McLuhan was lost as scholars focused on technologies of surveillance. A critical view on the transnational pattern of computer-mediated communication and information technology use does not necessarily require a return to an umbrella term such as the global village. Instead, it requires taking the relationships among the different aspects of the global village seriously and seeking to understand the consequences of those relationships for issues of power and domination.

Doing so requires two efforts. The first consists of addressing the tension between the ideal of the global village and the reality of globalization. The purpose is to engage globalization critically from the standpoint of some of its espoused goals. The second consists of understanding the practices of the multiple agents in globalized power relationships. The purpose here is to understand the tensions between the local practices that on the one hand fulfill some of the promises of the global village and, on the other, pervert some of its ideals.

—*Joao Vieira da Cunha*

See also Communication; Computer-Mediated Communication; Digital Divide; Globalization; Information and Communication Technology

Further Readings

Castells, M. (2001). *The Internet galaxy: Reflections on the Internet, business, and society.* Oxford, UK: Oxford University Press.

Jones, S. (1995). *CyberSociety: Computer-mediated communication and community.* Thousand Oaks, CA: Sage.

McLuhan, M. (1969). *The Gutenberg Galaxy: The making of typographic man.* New York: New American Library.

McLuhan, M., & Powers, B. R. (1989). *The global village: Transformations in world life and media in the 21st century.* New York: Oxford University Press.

Norris, P. (2001). *Digital divide: Civic engagement, information poverty, and the Internet worldwide.* Cambridge, UK: Cambridge University Press.

Zuboff, S. (1988). *In the age of the smart machine.* New York: Basic Books.

Goal-Setting Theory

Goal setting describes the process whereby organization members engage in a dialogue about desired future states through the creation, assignment, and pursuit of goals. These goals help define and clarify these desired states. Over the past 35 years, goal-setting theory, a specific approach to goal setting, has been increasingly influential in organization studies.

Conceptual Overview

Goal-setting theory purports a direct link between setting achievable, specific, realistic, challenging, and measurable goals and increased performance among those participating, as noted by Edwin Locke and Judith Bryan in 1968. Resting on the premise that setting goals increases performance more than simply "agreeing to do your best," goal-setting theory is based on the argument that goals motivate individuals, groups, and organizations to perform at a higher level. Goal setting derives its motivational force through six fundamental motivators: participating, rewarding, supporting, clarifying, communicating, and challenging, as noted by Locke and colleagues in 1988.

Participating suggests that goals motivate when those pursuing them participate in the goal-setting process. Belief that participation in the goal-setting process motivates employees gained experimental validity through a series of studies released in the 1970s. Since that time, the direct connection between increased performance and employees' participation in the goal-setting process has become firmly established in the literature, as Gary Latham and Gary Yukl wrote in 1975.

Rewarding denotes the incentives, either psychological or material, given to motivate achievement of goals. Research reveals mixed support for the motivating power of rewarding. Researchers, including John Mowen and colleagues in 1981, originally presented rewarding as an absolute—rewards lead to increased performance in goal-related tasks. However, closer study revealed that rewarding must be linked to realistic goals. For example, the limits of rewarding came under question when looking at the impact of rate incentives on motivation, as noted by Manuel London and Greg Oldham in 1977. Locke wrote in 2004 that goal-setting theory advocates countered by creating four reward systems: (1) rewards assigned to the achievement of a goal, (2) rewards attached to step goals that ultimately lead to a final goal, (3) a reward scale corresponding to increments of achievement leading toward a final goal, and (4) performance-based rewards doled out after the achievement of a goal.

Supporting motivates organizational members through coaches, managers, and leaders expressing their confidence in the ability of these members to accomplish the assigned goals, as noted by Latham in 2004. Locke wrote in 1988 that this expression of confidence can be verbal, written, or include the commitment of time and resources toward achieving the goal. Another type of supporting occurs when employees support one another, especially in achieving a team or organizationwide goal. Lack of supporting behavior among employees can undermine the achievement of goals by reducing receptivity to suggestions, which in turn leads to inefficiency, as noted by Suzanne Scott and Reginald Bruce in 1994.

Latham and Yukl wrote in 1975 that *role clarity* motivates by creating confidence among organizational members in regard to what part they will play in the goal-achievement process. Without clarity, employees find it difficult to establish the clear purpose, challenge, and meaning that are fundamental to the success of a goal-based system. Furthermore, lack of clarity can lead to anxiety and can result in lackluster performance. At first, researchers believed responsibility for role clarity sat with supervisors. Recent studies, however, stress the importance of role clarity in the acceptance of, commitment to, and personal orientation derived from the goal-setting process.

Clear communication eliminates ambiguity relative to goals. Furthermore, as stated by Latham and Yukl in 1975, good communication helps avoid internal conflict and confusion. Clear employee-to-management communication clarifies the goal-setting process and establishes employee commitment. The motivating forces of clear communication have been among the most substantiated aspects of goal-setting theory, as Locke noted in 2004.

Challenging goals motivate organizational members if they believe the goal can be attained, but not too easily. Challenge, as originally suggested by H. Peter Dachler and William Mobley in 1973, entails establishing a realistic level of challenge. Later, self-efficacy theory absorbed challenge. Determining the correct level of challenge requires insight; indeed, it has been found that an absence of challenge can be detrimental to the goal-setting process, while too much can lead to failure, as noted by Locke in 1988.

Stretch goals closely relate to the creation of challenging goals. Stretch goals denote a specific difficult goal that is achievable, but only through exceptional effort, as noted by Steven Kerr and Steffen Landauer in 2004. By assigning stretch goals to employees, they can reach a high level of achievement. Lathan wrote in 2004 that when stretch goals are met, they enhance employees' sense of what they can achieve, which helps increase their sense of self-efficacy and commitment to future assigned goals. However, Lathan also noted recent findings showing that stretch goals may be tied to several negative consequences, including a focus on quantity over quality, ethical conflicts, and employee burnout.

Critical Commentary and Future Directions

Recent research has exposed several unintended consequences, beyond those already cited, that result from goal-setting theory. These include escalation of commitment to a failing course of action, encouragement of individual behaviors at the expense of the group or organization, and confusion in the face of ill-structured problems. Concerns about the limits of goal-setting theory have led to several studies that expose some of the negative consequences associated with goal setting.

The utilization of critical theory to critique goal-setting theory is based on questioning its overtly rational basis, as noted by D. Christopher Kayes in 2004. Critics believe that goal-setting theory rests on a set of underlying assumptions about the nature of knowledge that must hold true in order for goal setting to be predictive. Because of the underlying rationalist assumptions, critics argue that goal-setting theory will only predict future outcomes when it occurs under predictable and stable circumstances, which seldom occur in complex environments. Peter Berger and Thomas Luckmann wrote in 1966 that advocates challenge this fundamental rational outlook as a basic limitation to goal setting, instead embracing individual interpretations on goal setting. They state that, at the core of many of these problems, is goal-setting theory's apparent lack of focus on the human element inevitable in any goal-setting process. By ignoring the human element, goal-setting theory is drifting dangerously far into an unrealistically rational view of the world.

Furthermore, as noted by Berger and Luckmann in 1966, many critical theorists argue that organizational members hold their own internal goals that help shape their view of the external world in order to bolster their sense of identity. It is naïve to assume that these internal goals do not have an impact on organizational processes. However, goal-setting theory has yet to address these internal goals and their impact on the goal-setting process.

On an even more fundamental level, some researchers have questioned whether or not goals should be the focus of this process at all, as written by Karl Weick in 1995. For example, instead of forming a group whose end result will be to create a marketing plan for an organization, might a stronger end result be a unified marketing team who creates a marketing plan as a way of reaching a state of unity? Perhaps it is better to allow teams the option to converse through the project or let goals develop and encourage individuals to participate in their evolution.

The future of goal setting in organization studies includes seeking a better understanding of the link between motivation and incentives, a clearer definition of learning versus performance goals, and the development of the socially constructed nature of goals. As recent research has identified the certain conditions under which goal setting fails to be effective, future research should seek to set boundary conditions under which goal setting should or should not be encouraged. For example, the limits of self-efficacy on goal setting have already been exposed and deserve further attention, as noted by Pino G. Audia, Locke, and Ken Smith in 2000. Kayes write in 2004 that issues requiring further inquiry have been raised in research, including the role of stress overload brought on by difficult goals and the negative consequences that result from the overpursuit of narrow and idealized goals.

Task complexity and its impact on goal setting remains an issue. The response posed by goal-setting theory has failed to provide an adequately justifiable theory, beyond the promise of learning goals (or goals that emphasize generation of multiple strategies versus task completion). Questions remain regarding the constitution of learning goals, the process by which they are generated, when they are more useful than task-based goals, and problems involving measurement.

While studies generally support the motivational aspects of participation in goal setting in simple tasks, the motivational aspects of goal setting in the face of a complex task remain in question. Future research on goal setting may require a broader understanding of the internal social-cognitive processes by which goals are generated and pursued.

—*D. Christopher Kayes and Jonathan Raelin*

See also Critical Theory; Organizational Learning; Social Constructionism

Further Readings

Audia, P. G., Locke, E. A., & Smith, K. G. (2000). The paradox of success: An archival and laboratory study of strategic persistence following a radical environmental change. *Academy of Management Journal, 43*(5), 837–854.

Berger, P. L., & Luckmann, T. (1966). *The social construction of reality.* Garden City, NY: Anchor Books.

Dachler, H. P., & Mobley, W. H. (1973). Construct validation of an instrumentality-expectancy-task-goal model of work motivation: Some theoretical boundary conditions. *Journal of Applied Psychology 58,* 397–418.

Kayes, D. C. (2004). The 1996 Mt. Everest climbing disaster: The breakdown of learning in teams. *Human Relations, 57*(10), 1236–1284.

Kerr, S., & Landauer, S. (2004). Using stretch goals to promote organizational effectiveness and personal growth: General Electric and Goldman Sachs. *Academy of Management Executive, 18*(4), 134–138.

Latham, G. P. (2004). The motivational benefits of goal-setting. *Academy of Management Executive, 18*(4), 126–129.

Latham, G. P., & Yukl, G. A. (1975a). Assigned versus participative goal setting with educated and uneducated wood workers. *Journal of Applied Psychology, 60,* 299–302.

Latham, G. P., & Yukl, G. A. (1975b). A review of research on the application of goal setting in organizations. *Academy of Management Journal, 18,* 824–845.

Locke, E. A. (2004). Linking goals to monetary incentives. *Academy of Management Executive, 18*(4), 130–133.

Locke, E. A., & Bryan, J. F. (1968). The effects of goal-setting, rule learning, and knowledge of score on performance. *American Journal of Psychology, 79,* 451–457.

Locke, E. A., Latham, G. P., & Erez, M. (1988). The determinants of goal commitment. *Academy of Management Review, 13*(1), 23–39.

London, M., & Oldham, G. R. (1977). A comparison of group and individual incentive plans. *Academy of Management Journal, 20,* 34–41.

Mowen, J. C., Middlemist, R., & Luther, D. (1981). Joint effects of assigned goal level and incentive structure on task performance: A laboratory study. *Journal of Applied Psychology, 66,* 598–603.

Scott, S. G., & Bruce, R. A. (1994). Determinants of innovative behavior: A path model of individual innovation in the workplace. *Academy of Management Journal, 37*(3), 580–607.

Weick, K. (1995). *Sensemaking in organizations.* Thousand Oaks, CA: Sage.

GOVERNMENTALITY

Governmentality is a complex and polysemic concept. It was originally proposed by Michel Foucault with the intention of explaining the constitution of the modern subject. The concept expresses the effort made by the French philosopher to renew conceptual tools for understanding government practices and their modes of rationality. Foucault introduced the concept of governmentality to consider modes of government as an object of study.

The concept implies three related things: (1) the set of institutions, procedures, analyses, and reflections, and the calculations and tactics that allow the exercise of a very specific, albeit complex, power, which has as its target, the population, and as its principal form of knowledge, political economy, and as its essential technical means, apparatuses of security; (2) the tendency that, over a long period and throughout the West, has steadily led toward the preeminence over all other forms (sovereignty, discipline, and so on) of this type of power—which may be termed *government*—resulting, on one hand, in the formation of a whole series of specific governmental apparatuses, and, on the other hand, in the development of a whole complex of knowledges (*savoirs*); and (3) the process, or rather, the result of the process, through which the state of justice of the Middle Ages transformed into the administrative state during the 15th and 16th centuries and gradually becomes "governmentalized," as Foucault wrote in 2003. Governmentality may be seen in terms of the encounter between the technologies of domination of others and those of the self, suggests Foucault. However, Foucault did not elaborate a unified theory; considerations on governmentality are disseminated in his work from 1970 until his death in 1984. His courses at the Collège de France are a very important source to clarify the meanings of the concept and its theoretical relevance to understand different facets of the *conduct of conducts* in modernity.

After Foucault's death, this line of work was deepened by some of his disciples and colleagues. The contributions of Giovanna Procacci, Pasquale Pasquino, Jacques Donzelot, Francois Ewald, Robert Castel, Gilles Deleuze, and Daniel Defert are worth mentioning. This interest expanded rapidly and constituted, during the 1990s, ample development of the governmentality concept in the Anglo-Saxon world by authors such as Andrew Barry, Thomas Osbourne, and Nikolas Rose in 1996; Mitchell Dean in 1999, and Rose in 1999; and more recently, there have been similar developments in Spain and Latin America, such as J. Vázquez's contribution from 2005.

Foucault's work comprises 11 books, plus the fourth volume of his *History of Sexuality,* entitled *Confessions of the Flesh,* a carefully safeguarded text that remains unpublished, since Foucault did not want his work published posthumously. In addition to this body of texts, there is an incessant and meticulous flow of course reports, essays, interviews, and debates. His thought has been generally organized into three specific stages, as noted by Gilles Deleuze:

1. The archaeological stage (1961–1969), centered on examining the conditions of the possibility of discourses: What do I know? What is knowing?

2. The genealogical stage (1970–1979), in which power relations and practices are considered, as well as the formation of the institutions in which they can be found: What am I capable of? What is power?

3. The ethical stage (1979–1984), which examines the constitution of subjectivity based on the analysis of technologies and practices of individuation: What am I? What is oneself?

These stages, however, are only a resource for lending a certain order, and should be used cautiously, since they fade away when one observes the focal point around which the great Foucauldian project revolves. The preeminence of power only appears to be the focus, since the central problem he was concerned with can be found in the examination of relations between subject and truth.

In just over two decades, Foucault demonstrated the possibility of thinking in a different way, assuming theory as a local, not totalizing, practice that permits one to confront the events to which one is subjected. The task of characterizing his work implies unusual difficulties. His work is different, breaking with instituted disciplines, and removing itself from rules imposed by the will of truth from philosophy or history. Consequently, one can find another type of rigor in Foucault, the rigor of writing as a reflexive exercise of oneself that demonstrates vitality because it recognizes the normality of error.

One of the characteristics illustrated in his works is continuity, achieved, however, through leaps and jolts that demanded constant rewriting of texts that were always unfinished, with an absolute mistrust in that which might appear to be clear and true. This elusive character of thought in process, which never finishes correcting its initial versions, has led to highly diverse interpretations that have increased the density of his works. The authors of those interpretations outline a thousand faces of Foucault, since each one of them carries out a different process of assembling the highly diverse fragments, with different meanings, depending on the way they are joined together.

This gray tonality in Foucault's works indicates the essentially polemic pursuit of his thinking. Foucault cannot be identified as part of the left or part of the right, although he has been labeled as neoanarchist and as neoconservative. His place is next to events, singularities, and experiences, next to the breakdown in the evidence and truths upon which knowledges and practices of power are built. The production of a different way of thinking is based on the need to provoke effects that alter relations between forces, and that cannot be explained through the dual simplicity of good and bad forces, since both (and others) operate in a contingent manner, remaining trapped in the dilemmas of the dialogical game of their actions/reactions along the continuum of time.

Nevertheless, the problem is not a matter of knowing what Foucault said, but rather, of understanding the usefulness of his texts considering one's own practices. This is the necessary setting to discuss and reintroduce the Foucauldian formulations around governmentality, giving a fresh interpretation of the constitution of the modern subject.

Conceptual Overview

Governmentality can be reconstructed recognizing three traversed levels related with the three main forms of power from which the subject constitutes itself.

1. *Disciplinary power* refers to those relations that seek to influence control over the human body considered as a machine, for the purpose of strengthening its capacities and guiding its behavior. These are territories of power such as confinement and discipline. The body thus becomes an object of politics to produce economies through the subjection of individual will. This is a matter of power exercised over singularity

and details, and through surveillance and dressage (training), it can divide, specify, or differentiate individuals into particular categories of subjects, according to certain standards of normalization that represent economic aims or measures of efficiency. This is why it is referred to as the *political anatomy of the human body,* or in other words, as the useful, intelligible body.

Therefore, this form of power produces and operates an infinity of knowledges and technologies of the body that order, normalize, or prescribe particular modes of existence. These are knowledges that act immediately, in the moment. They are the know-how that will be systematized by "gray sciences," as the result of the observation, recording, and measuring of behaviors, or the "lesser knowledges" that assess and diagnose the normality of behaviors, by carrying out tests and experiments based on standards that allows for comparability. Knowledges like management and psychology facilitate the governance of individuals, through norms, technologies, and procedures that produce new economies, sustained by their capacity for individualization/differentiation.

This first form of power is extremely important for clarifying relations between the individual and the organization, and for understanding the modes of subjection that link the individual to material and symbolic spaces in which that individual produces, fabricates, or invents itself as a subject. These spaces are typically associated with behavior in the workplace, which is delimited by rules of calculation and procedures that govern the behavior of individuals and delimit their collective action.

2. *Biopolitics* corresponds to the art of governing populations regulating the social body from a certain reason of state, aimed at strengthening the population's productive capacities and at preserving life. It will be through the *science of police* that efforts will be made to strengthen the population in order to increase the state's power. Life thus becomes a matter of politics to be regulated and governed by the state. This biopolitics does not penetrate the human body, but is rather applied to the life of populations as a social body that represents the human species. State interventions and regulatory controls over populations are connected to an entire set of economic, social, and political problems, the solution to which is aimed at reinforcing the state's strength as a sovereign state.

The biopolitics conception calls for a different formulation from one in which the state is generally identified as a sovereign power sustained by a contract oppression scheme. According to Barry Hindess, this is not a matter of focusing analysis on the power of the state considered as a political universal on which a causal explanation for everything else is based. Instead, what is proposed is an examination of the art of governing under a certain reason of state and an institutional structure governed by intrinsic rational principles. In other words, what is involved here is examining the state's actions as a network of relations between very diverse forces and with goals of intervention or regulation, that is, as a governmentalized state that follows a political rationality based on management. Its practices are associated with bureaucracy and the designing of depersonalized disciplinary apparatuses that permit the regulation of behaviors indirectly or by steering at a distance.

With biopolitics, the idea of "society" appears with the emergence of the "social" field as responsible for its knowledge and systematization. The objectivation of what is social will initially take place through political economy, since it emerged as knowledge of populations, territory, and wealth, to support government actions. Alongside it, there are statistics—the *science of the state*—that have made it possible to quantify the population's phenomena, under specific rules of calculation related to a specific mode of rationality, as noted by Rose. This is the way that the governance of society is to be assured, acknowledging its problems, controlling its probabilities, and compensating for its effects: The formulation of strategies, programs, and goals of government is aimed at producing effects in very diverse reference groups, in order to preserve and increase their strength and energy, but also in order to diminish the economic costs of life (accidents, illnesses, ignorance, old age, death), thus demonstrating the capacity for power as totalization/aggregation.

Foucault links this second form of power with the first one, observing the double function of the shepherd who leads his flock but also each one of his sheep. One of the points of articulation can be found in state agencies and society's institutions, since they function as *spaces for governance* that also associate individualizing power that is exercised over bodies (the discipline organ of institutions), with totalizing power that is exercised over populations (the bioregulation through the state).

3. Finally, *ethics* refers to one's relation with oneself, to the operations carried out in relation to one's body and soul, as a practice of conscience and knowledge of oneself. Ethics refers to the modes through which one acts upon oneself to carry out transformations in one's behavior, with the aim of improving oneself and achieving one's personal realization. In this case, Foucault speaks of the forms and transformations of morality, and of the practices that lead to the *arts of existence*. These assume the establishment of certain rules of conduct, from which individuals seek to decipher themselves in their singularity and take on certain lifestyles.

Here individuals produce themselves through the *technologies of the self,* governing their own behavior. These technologies of self determine ways of being, both in the individual sphere as well as at the level of politics and society. Among these ways of being, there are two that are especially relevant for understanding the governance of conducts of the modern subject: first, *self-examination,* as an effort at self-[ac]knowledge[ment] and the objectivation of oneself in relation to oneself; and secondly, the *confession* that, supported by the will to know as expressed in the self-examination, assumes the obligation of verbalizing to others the truth regarding oneself.

Thus, under this third form of power, the individual is constituted as an ethical subject on the basis of self-ordering knowledge that permits one to discover oneself as responsible for one's own acts, and consequently, as a free individual that may shift the limits that define one's being, modifying certain behaviors in order to constitute oneself in another way.

This form of power is extremely important, since it holds the potential for transforming subjectivity and constituting a new ethics that permits the exercising of renewed practices of freedom. This is because knowledge of oneself crosses disciplinary power and biopolitics, forming part of them both. In this sense, from their reflexive singularity, individuals may encourage new forms of subjectivity that transform their particular modes of existence, thus affecting their relations with others and with the state.

Governmentality connects the three forms acquired by power linked to a complex network of relations, and to the strategies, programs, and goals of state intervention or regulation. In addition, governmentality implies the apparatuses of governance or control operated by society's institutions, but also the mentalities that nourish the projects, intentions, and wishes of individuals and groups.

Critical Commentary and Future Directions

Governmentality makes it possible to re-create the strategic significance of relations between knowledges, powers, and the constitution of the subject, reinvigorating the meanings of relations established in different spheres of social life. These spheres encompass disciplinary power, biopolitics, and ethics as distinct but connected levels from which the modern subject is constituted.

The ideas around governmentality clearly open up new theoretical possibilities, since they make it possible to recover the sense of management essentially as an act of government, and of organizations as spaces for relations between forces in which diverse modes of existence and ethical projects confront each other. Foucault's thought/experience represents an opportunity to develop theories in a different way, assuming academic work as a specific practice from which one can constitute oneself as a free subject. In this journey, one needs to listen to the silence imposed on certain voices, and to recover certain organizational problems that are not acknowledged as such, or that remain simply lost or ignored.

Thus, governmentality as a complex conceptual tool has been gaining relevance because it helps one to analyze management and organizations in a different way, reformulating research agendas within new contexts. Among them, it is important to highlight four fundamental areas:

1. Organizational problems cannot be viewed anymore as merely problems of structures. Organizations must be understood as spaces in which contingent relations and processes are verified, and from those relations and processes, subjects and their institutions are created and re-created. Therefore, organizations should be rethought as structures that govern processes and relations between forces that produce these structures. There is an urgent need to expand our approach beyond the limits of organizations, since they represent only one component of society's organization, specifically the device with which disciplinary apparatuses mediate relations between individuals and groups. As already explained, biopolitics and ethics should also be included to complete the network of relations from which what is social is produced, leading to diverse practices under a specific mode of rationality.

2. Governmentality makes visible the false dilemma related to the adoption of different levels of analysis jealously protected by positive knowledge. The fragmentation of knowledge, which exclusively assumes the analysis of reality from the micro, middle, or macro levels, actually operates as mechanisms for dividing the sense of realities that are presented to us broken up in pieces. The fact that there is only one complex reality can no longer be ignored, and it needs to be viewed simultaneously from its connections, that is to say, from the multiple contingent constitutions of the subject in relation to the state, to others, and to itself. In other words, an approach that simultaneously views down, straight ahead, and to the horizon is needed in order to address governmental actions as organizational problems in their multidimensional unity.

3. The mainstream approaches in organization studies have "forgotten" the subject; they are subjectless theories, centered on the analysis of structures with the aim of discovering universal laws that govern their behavior. To cover this absence, the formulations around governmentality can help as they place government action as a target, making it possible to observe the processes of conformation and changes in structures depending on those actions that are far from inevitable or already a given. In addition, it is important to explore the practical importance of management and organizational knowledges, since they have provided a very broad range of tools for the governing of behavior and the fabrication of identities.

4. Finally, disciplinary practices must be considered not only as practices with negative effects, recovering the link between discipline and desire. We must address not only the conditions of our own imprisonment but also those of our freedom. This leads once again to reproposing the study of organizations, not only as places of confinement but also as spaces in which a great variety of desires by distinct groups are produced, with codes and practices that we need to understand. The study of management and organizations will be, in this sense, a way of acknowledging the possibilities for the reconstitution of subjectivity and its effects.

—Eduardo Ibarra-Colado

See also Discipline; Liberal Technologies of Regulation; Panopticism; Power; Surveillance

Further Readings

Barry, A., Osborne, T., & Rose, N. (Eds.). (1996). *Foucault and political reason: Liberalism, neo-liberalism and rationalities of government.* London: UCL Press.

Bratich, J. Z., Packer, J., & McCarthy, C. (Eds.). (2003). *Foucault, cultural studies, and governmentality.* New York: State University of New York Press.

Burchell, G., Gordon, C., & Miller, P. (Eds.). (1991). *The Foucault effect: Studies in governmentality.* Chicago: University of Chicago Press.

Dean, M. (1999). *Governmentality: Power and rule in modern society.* London: Sage.

Deleuze, G. (1988). *Foucault.* Minneapolis: University of Minnesota Press.

Foucault, M. (2003). *The essential Foucault: Selections from essential works of Foucault, 1954–1984* (P. Rabinow & N. Rose, Eds.). New York: New Press.

Hindess, B. (1995). *Discourses of power: From Hobbes to Foucault.* Oxford, UK: Blackwell.

McKinlay, A., & Starkey, K. (Eds.). (1998). *Foucault, management, and organization theory: From panopticon to technologies of self.* London: Sage.

Rose, N. (1999). *Powers of freedom: Reframing political thought.* Cambridge, UK: Cambridge University Press.

Vázquez, J. (2005). "Empresarios de nosotros mismos": Biopolítica, mercado y soberanía en la gubernamentalidad neoliberal. In J. Ugarte (Ed.), *La administración de la vida: Estudios biopolíticos* (pp. 73–103). Barcelona, Spain: Anthropos.

Grand Narratives

Following the work of Jean-Francois Lyotard, grand narratives (also known as *grands récits,* master narratives or meta narratives) refers to all-encompassing bodies of knowledge that purport to offer general and sweeping explanations of history, nature, and every aspect of the human condition. These bodies of knowledge were a chief feature of modernity, though they also existed in earlier historical periods. They have a narrative character in as much as, like stories and myths, they have a time dimension, but their chief characters are abstract ideas or concepts rather than concrete people. Thus science, with reason as its protagonist, can be seen as a powerful grand narrative promising to emancipate humanity from superstition, poverty, disease, and suffering. Within a grand scientific narrative, disease, for instance, is viewed as caused by pathogenic agents (such as microbes, viruses, and genetic factors) rather than visited on people by divine caprice or bewitchment. It can be overcome and even eliminated through scientific knowledge, which has a universal validity and applicability, rather than prayer, exorcism, or traditional medicine. Socialism, communism, liberal democracy, fascism, but also Christianity and Islam, all count as grand narratives. Within the human sciences, all-inclusive doctrines such as Marxism, psychoanalysis, or positivism are also seen as grand narratives.

Conceptual Overview

A defining feature of the Enlightenment was its unflinching belief in progress coupled with a confidence that knowledge, in the form of generalizable scientific laws aimed at uncovering a universal truth, was the instrument that will deliver it. Modernity was built on the Enlightenment project to replace tradition, superstition, and irrational belief with grand narratives of incontestable rational authority. Confidence in the Enlightenment project has declined or even collapsed in what many scholars view as postmodernity. Lyotard and others have argued that grand narratives fragment and disappear, being replaced by *small stories,* through which people seek to make sense of their experiences and communicate them to others. Faith in progress is shaken, faith in reason dwindles, and faith in universal truths all but disappears as truth is revealed to be contingent on language, discourse, and power relations.

More particularly, it is argued that supposedly objective and eternal truths entail deeply enshrined power relations, including those rooted in colonial, race, gender, and sexual domination and subordination. Lyotard stages a powerful critique of the Enlightenment narratives of progress, science, reason, and absolute truth, arguing that they privilege certain discourses while silencing others and certain types of authority at the expense of others. Scientific reason, in particular, can be said to embody the values of patriarchy, aspiring, as it does, to explain, control, and dominate nature and providing the means whereby small sections of humanity can dominate, exploit, or oppress others (for instance, through military technology or the economics of aid).

Postmodernist theorists argue that a profusion of voices is now being heard where in the past there were sounds of choirs singing in unison. Where once everybody deferred to the power of the grand narrative (driven by universal reason, a universal aesthetic, and moral standards, universal regimes of truth), people are currently seeking to discover their own voice, based on their own experiences and forging their own individual identities. Even science is being challenged, when the voice of the expert scientist, for instance the physician, is questioned and contested by the voice of the patient, who is nonexpert and nonobjective, but has the authority of personal experience of an illness. Speaking with authority is no longer the exclusive privilege of the educated; it is the privilege of everybody who has an experience to narrate.

The view that postmodernity brings with it an end to all grand narratives has echoes of the earlier end of ideology thesis, proposed by Daniel Bell in 1960, and its more recent incarnation as the end of history thesis, proposed by Francis Fukuyama in 1992. According to these, faith in large-scale political and religious promises of salvation has collapsed in favor of a pragmatic embracement of pluralistic economic and political liberalism, which permits each person to discover his or her own identity and fashion his or her own life. But it goes beyond these theses, in that science itself is abandoned as a grand narrative. Thus, whether one looks at science, ethics, business, art, religion, politics, or economics, Lyotard argues that in postmodern culture the grand narrative in all its different forms—religious, philosophical, artistic, and scientific—has lost its credibility. Instead of grand narratives, postmodernity is characterized by a pluralism of voices, narratives, stories, and texts.

In the area of organizations, classical theories of bureaucracy by Max Weber, management practices such as Taylorism and Fordism, and a broadly empiricist mode of research are often described as grand narratives, within which smaller partial narratives nestle. Management, in the view of F. W. Taylor, ought to grow out of its prescientific phase, by adopting the philosophy, techniques, and methodology of science, aimed at maximizing productivity and reducing waste. Likewise, Weber viewed bureaucracy as the exercise of control on the basis of knowledge, stressing that this is the feature that makes it "specifically rational" and therefore indispensable for the needs of mass administration. Bureaucracy represented the triumph of the Enlightenment project in administration, sweeping away corruption, nepotism, and favoritism with the force of impersonal expertise and rational legal authority.

These views of management and organization are now coming into question at two interrelated levels. The suggestion is that grand narratives are no longer capable of explaining the phenomenon of organization, nor does this phenomenon meet the criteria of a grand narrative anymore. Martin Parker draws a distinction between postmodern theories of organization and postmodern organizations themselves. First, at the level of knowledge, it is claimed that a grand theory of organizations, approaching them as objective realities in their own right, is fundamentally flawed and should be replaced by a multiplicity of narratives, describing the organizational realities of different participants. Organizations are not things but social constructions, contested and challenged, emerging and constantly re-created through various discursive and nondiscursive practices. Managing people is not, as engineering might have been envisaged, the application of scientific knowledge, immutable generalizations, and universal principles. Instead, it is now seen more akin to the utilization of folk knowledge in ad hoc, opportunistic, and improvised ways, borrowing ideas, combining recipes, and adapting knowledge for new situations.

Second, as we move from modernity to postmodernity, the nature of organizing and organizations changes. While modernity featured solid buildings, solid organizations, solid relations, solid selves, and solid signifiers, current times are characterized by flux, mutation, reinvention, and flexibility. Flexibility, along with flux, fluidity, and flow, is one of the much-vaunted qualities of our times. It applies to individuals, organizations, and even entire societies, suggesting an ability and a willingness not merely to adapt and change but to radically redefine themselves, to metamorphose into new entities. Flexibility stands at the opposite end of rigidity, which, not accidentally, marks the chief quality of bureaucracy. The flexible organization (variously referred to as network, postmodern, post-Fordist, post-bureaucratic, shamrock, etc.) has emerged as the antidote to Weberian bureaucracy, a concept of organization that does away with rigid hierarchies, procedures, products, and boundaries, in favor of constant and continuous reinvention, redefinition, and mobility. Success, for such organizations, is not a terminus, a state of perfectly stable equilibrium, but a process of irregularity, innovation, and disorder, where temporary triumphs occur at the edge of the abyss and can never be regularized into rational procedures.

The influence of such postmodern thinking on theorists of organizations has been uneven. Many European scholars have, at least, recognized the limitations of objectifying organizations, their structures and their processes. They have turned increasingly to a study of language and discourse as a method of understanding the ways organizations are constituted or socially constructed. Numerous features of organizations, including change, leadership, performance, innovation, knowledge, learning, and so forth, have become problematized, or increasingly have come to be seen as ways of talking and describing the domain of organizations rather than as elements of this domain. By contrast, the broad majority of American scholarship on organizations (and its institutional expression in academic journals and conference papers) remains reasonably firmly attached to a positivist view of organizations and an empiricist mode of studying them.

Critical Commentary and Future Directions

While the prima facie case for the fragmentation of grand narratives is compelling, it has been contested. Defending the project of the Enlightenment and modernity, Jürgen Habermas has pointed out that the narrative of the collapse of grand narratives is itself a grand narrative (something that can also be said of the end of ideology and end of history theses). More importantly, it would appear premature to argue that all grand narratives have disintegrated. In spite of challenges and contests, science remains a widely embraced narrative in innumerable practices and discourses, ranging from providing solutions to environmental crises to providing the basis of technological breakthroughs to fueling entrepreneurship and innovation to providing the foundation of economic growth and prosperity. Economic growth itself continues to be the core of a grand narrative, embraced not only by Western economists but increasingly by governments and people throughout the world as the key to happiness and the good life. The supremacy of a market-driven capitalism along with unbridled consumerism as its cultural twin have emerged as formidable hegemonic narratives, scarcely touched by attacks from postmodernists and their allies. In medicine, for example, traditional, homeopathic, spiritual, and alternative treatments may offer complementary ways of dealing with many conditions, without displacing scientific medicine from its privileged position.

In academia itself and especially in the human and social sciences, the dominance of the economic narrative, increasingly expressed in numbers and highly abstract modeling, is scarcely contested, at least in Anglo-Saxon countries. In medicine, highly prescriptive randomized trials, based on a positivist methodology, are uncontested as the basis for development of new drugs and treatments. Physics, chemistry, and the biological sciences, along with the wide range of engineering and other applications, remain soundly grounded in the Enlightenment principles of absolute, incontestable truths and scientific methodology. In the light of such trends, as well as the resurgence of the grand narratives of religious fundamentalism, Eastern and Western, it seems premature to consign grand narratives to an obsolete past.

—*Yiannis Gabriel*

See also Bureaucracy; Ideology; Modernity; Narratives; Postmodernism

Further Readings

Bell, D. (1960). *The end of ideology.* Glencoe, IL: Free Press.

Clegg, S. (1990). *Modern organizations: Organization studies in the postmodern world.* London: Sage.

Czarniawska, B. (1997). *Narrating the organization: Dramas of institutional identity.* Chicago: University of Chicago Press.

Czarniawska, B. (1999). *Writing management: Organization theory as a literary genre.* Oxford, UK: Oxford University Press.

Fukuyama, F. (1992). *The end of history and the last man.* New York: Free Press.

Gabriel, Y. (2002). *Essai: On paragrammatic uses of organizational theory: A provocation. Organization Studies, 23,* 133–151.

Gabriel, Y. (2005). Glass cages and glass palaces: Images of organizations in image-conscious times. *Organization, 12,* 9–27.

Gray, J. (2003). *Al Qaeda and what it means to be modern.* London: Faber.

Habermas, J. (1981). *The theory of communicative action: Reason and the rationalization of society.* London: Beacon Press.

Habermas, J. (1984). *The philosophical discourse of modernity.* Cambridge, UK: Polity.

Lyotard, J.-F. (1991). *The postmodern condition: A report on knowledge.* Manchester, UK: Manchester University Press. (Original work published 1984)

Mintzberg, H. (2004). *Managers not MBAs: A hard look at the soft practice of managing and management development.* London: FT Prentice Hall.

Parker, M. (1992). Post-modern organizations or postmodern theory? *Organization Studies, 13*(1), 1–17.

Pfeffer, J. (1998). *The human equation: Building profits by putting people first.* Boston: Harvard Business School Press.

Pfeffer, J., & Sutton, R. I. (2006). *Hard facts, dangerous half-truths, and total nonsense: Profiting from evidence-based management.* Boston: Harvard Business School Press.

Taylor, F. W. (1911). *Principles of scientific management.* New York: Harper.

Tsoukas, H. (2002). Knowledge-based perspectives on organizations: Situated knowledge, novelty, and communities of practice—Introduction. *Management Learning, 33,* 419–426.

Tsoukas, H., & Hatch, M. J. (2001). Complex thinking, complex practice: The case for a narrative approach to organizational complexity. *Human Relations, 54,* 979–1013.

Weber, M. (1947). *The theory of social and economic organization.* New York: Free Press.

GROUNDED THEORY BUILDING

Grounded theory building (GTB) is a process of qualitative analysis that generates (builds) concepts and their relationships to explain and interpret patterns of social action (a theory) from rich data about a substantive domain of social action (the empirical ground). Grounded theory building is a style of doing qualitative analysis rather than a specific method, and quantitative data can also be used provided all data are used to discern core qualities of the social action under study. The three terms of GTB convey guidelines for the kinds of research topics and data to be gathered, the goal or expected outcomes, and the process of analysis.

Conceptual Overview

Grounded

GTB is "grounded" in the complexities of social life and in how people collectively think about, behave in, and make sense of their social situations. Social life is assumed to be inherently complex because people not only actively shape the world they live in, but also skillfully assess social situations, draw cues from them for proper behavior, retrieve details from experience, and create new knowledge with others, all in a situated manner. People routinely enact complex social activities (e.g., parenting, teaching, driving) without being told specifically how, as they go about everyday life. Thus, any observed instance of a construct is a contingent actualization of it, and the goal of GTB is to account for these contingent actualizations.

Research questions for GTB therefore concern social processes, social contexts, and situated interactions. Rather than study constructs that are abstracted from the complexities of social life, GTB explores their interactions with those complexities: what people actually do and think about the constructs, how and why they create and enact them in a certain way, why specific directions of change emerge, what shapes or enhances people's social skills, and why and how certain social understandings dominate. For organization studies, one might explore why and how hierarchy, work boundaries, or leadership styles affect how a particular kind of work gets done.

The data for GTB are rich in the sense that they must reflect these social complexities. Most GTB studies use textlike data such as observations, ethnographies, interviews, archives, photographs, and other symbolic artifacts, but can easily incorporate a variety of data sources and types, provided reasonable connections between them and the complexities of social action can be articulated. The categories that are discovered and honed by the study must, however, be in the data. A study that imposes constructs on the data is not GTB.

Theory

The purpose of GTB is to build theory, not to describe, illustrate, pilot test, or provide intuition. GTB seeks to achieve a better comprehension of a social phenomenon by generating concepts and their relations that explain, account for, and interpret the variation in the social action under study. A grounded theory gives a sense of understanding and control, and an access for action, just like any theory. The research may not create new ideas, but it should create new connections among ideas that shed new light on the social action being studied.

Developing a good theory requires *theoretical sampling* and *theoretical saturation.* Theoretical sampling refers to sampling on the basis of emerging concepts or categories. One captures the variation in the phenomenon by studying a diversity of settings for it and instances of it, but chooses those settings and instances to explore various properties of a category as these emerge in the analysis. Theoretical saturation means that no new information emerges about the category from additional data. When the researcher learns nothing new from additional data, he or she has enough data.

It is challenging to determine if a good theory has been produced by GTB. Barney Glaser recommends four criteria: (1) the theory must fit the realities under study in the eyes of the subjects, practitioners, and researchers; (2) the theory must work in that it should explain the major variations in behavior with regard to the main concerns of the subjects; (3) it must be relevant, which should be true if the first two criteria are met; and (4) it must be modifiable with more data. Anselm Strauss and Juliet Corbin rethink familiar criteria such as reproducibility, generalization, and how well the GTB process was executed, but their final point is that the theoretical findings must seem significant. One recommended rule of thumb is to be certain the theory really answers the research question. This criterion is fuzzy, too, however, for two reasons. On the one hand, good data reflect the "infinite profusion" of social life, so one cannot make enough sense of them to arrive at a good theory unless the analysis is guided by a clear research question. On the other hand, specific research questions for specific papers emerge from the analysis, so matching up questions and answers is part of the theory-building process. Arriving at a good question and a good answer comes out in the wash of writing each research paper. If a person cannot write a convincing paper about the theory, then he or she probably has not yet built that clear, simple, convincing theory.

Building

GTB is an active, ongoing, engaged, and subjective process (the researcher is interpreting people's social actions and discussions) of collecting data that are often about a subjective phenomenon (what people think, feel, and understand). These data are analyzed, sorted, fractured, and collected over and over again until a convincing theory emerges. In part because of all the subjectivity, GTB researchers work through the theory-building process very carefully and systematically, but never in a formulaic manner. GTB researchers engage in constant comparison across theoretically varying instances of the social action under study, always asking what is going on here in the data, and over time asking what is different about this instance versus that one and why that is useful or significant. GTB relies on coding, which refers to the analytical process through which data are fractured, conceptualized, and integrated to form a theory, according to Strauss and Corbin. GTB coding does not refer to cataloging data into predefined categories. That is called content analysis, which is a research technique that is often used for theory testing, not theory building.

GTB coding has three thrusts that occur together, although the emphasis shifts over time from the first to the third. The first is *open coding,* to develop many possible categories without premature closure. Open coding occurs as one closely reads the text a portion at a time (Strauss focuses on single words but others prefer paragraphs, going back in to pull out words), often with colleagues, to note different themes or ideas. Over time, some of these themes reoccur in different ways, so one begins to think about properties or dimensions for an emerging category and tries to articulate that category. The second thrust of analysis is *axial coding,* which looks at one emerging category across the data to refine it and define its properties, and to consider how it interacts with other categories. *Selective coding* begins when probable core categories are decided upon, and the researcher systematically examines how other categories relate to the core, with the intent of integrating and refining the theory.

Critical Commentary and Future Directions

One problem is that GTB is systematic but not codified—a troubling property in a field that focuses primarily on highly codified methods for theory testing. Strauss and Corbin try hard to explain how to do GTB, but the results are at times hard to follow. Glaser objects, saying that such detailed processes are forcing and imposing, but provides no alternate. The challenge is to develop some sense of how to do GTB well in organization studies without settling on a cookbook. Scholars can work this problem by debating three issues. First, GTB presumes a deep grounding in sociology or related fields, but organization studies comprise multiple disciplines in an applied field, so some researchers may have a limited grounding in any one discipline. How to incorporate a deeper sense of social science to either elaborate existing theories or create new understandings requires serious discussion. Second, while there is no one best way to display the underlying logic of GTB in published papers, dialogue is needed over how researchers can demonstrate that their analysis was done carefully and thoroughly. Researchers need to show how they continually juxtaposed emergent ideas about what might be going on in the data with existing theories and more data, in a kind of a spiral over time that iterates from the empirical to conceptual plane and back. Third, a GTB study should be compelling in the sense that an important, substantive issue is being clarified with rigorously developed theory. Thus it should be asked, is the question really vital and why, and does the answer really account for the social action? Researchers who do not want to build a compelling theory about complex social action should use another style of research.

Another problem is that the increasing popularity of qualitative research in organization studies is outstripping its comprehension. GTB is only one of many kinds of qualitative work, and it is important to elaborate the differences in research topics, outcomes, and processes among these diverse approaches and styles rather than lump them all together. More problematic is the tendency to equate qualitative data (defined as any data that are not strictly numerical representations) with qualitative research. Textlike materials such as archives, documents, photographs, observations, magazines, television shows, interviews, or responses to open-ended questions have often been quantified into metrics for constructs, and then used to statistically test theories. Using such data is not necessarily qualitative. By definition, empirical observations are based on real, apprehendable phenomena, which means that qualitative and quantitative investigations may be empirical, or not (modeling is not empirical). It is vital to sort out the different logics of theory testing and theory building, since a study that confuses the two is not useful. For example, imposing a priori constructs onto data is risky since this approach is not GTB and not proper theory testing.

One future direction is to combine qualitative GTB with quantitative approaches to really push theory development and refinement. How to do so is problematic, since combination studies for theory development are rarely published in organization studies. Instead, there are sequential studies that propose and then test the theory or pilot and then measure constructs. Integration would be useful, since researchers usually have ideas in their heads from the outset. Quantitative analyses push researchers to articulate those ideas well enough to measure them. These measures can be used to see if and to what degree the preliminary framework fits certain kinds of samples. Quantitative results help researchers to view their qualitative results critically, especially if the relationships are weak or not there, and to connect the constructs to outcomes that may not be captured in the qualitative data. Quantitative analyses also look at the apparent effects of macroscopic structures (e.g., the industry, location, organizational form, a scientific paradigm), and help overcome some biases, such as a holistic fallacy that all aspects of a situation are congruent, or a potential elite bias in the data, since fieldwork may overconcentrate on higher-status or more articulate people. Qualitative analyses complement quantitative ones by uncovering how and why a framework may fit or not; discovering possibly new limits, contingencies, or properties; and showing how people enact the structures in particular ways.

—*Deborah Dougherty*

See also Action Research; Clinical Perspective; Discourse Analysis; Ethnomethodology; Meta-Analysis; Qualitative Approaches; Quantitative Models and Methods

Further Readings

Bailyn, L. (1977). Research as a cognitive process: Implications for data analysis. *Quality and Quantity, 11,* 97–117.
Dougherty, D. (2002). Building grounded theory: Some principles and practices. In J. A. C. Baum (Ed.), *Companion to organizations* (pp. 849–867). Oxford, UK: Blackwell.

Glaser, B. (1992). *Basics of grounded theory analysis.* Mill Valley, CA: Sociology Press.

Glaser, B., & Strauss, A. (1967). *The discovery of grounded theory.* Chicago: Aldine.

Golden-Biddle, K., & Locke, K. (1997). *Composing qualitative research.* Thousand Oaks, CA: Sage.

Strauss, A. (1987). *Qualitative analysis for social scientists.* New York: Cambridge University Press.

Strauss, A., & Corbin, J. (1998). *Basics of qualitative research* (2nd ed.). Thousand Oaks, CA: Sage.

Guanxi

No single English word encompasses the full range of meanings of the Chinese term *guanxi* (*kuan-hsi* in older texts). It may be translated as "relations," "particularistic ties," "connections," or "to relate to"; the meaning is context specific. *Guanxi* refers to dyadic, interpersonal relations between people who can make demands on each other. *Guanxi* can be considered as a form of social investment, and developing and maintaining a *guanxi* relationship is akin to putting one's money into a bank account or purchasing an insurance policy so that it is available when needed.

Conceptual Overview

The use of networks and favoritism based upon particularistic considerations is scarcely unique to China. However, both the Chinese themselves and numerous outside observers regard extensive reliance upon particularistic ties as a major feature of Chinese societies. When contrasted with Western networking, Michailova and Worm remark that *guanxi* is viewed as being more pervasive, involving the rendering of more personal favors, and encompassing relationships that are more person specific and enduring.

In China, various historical factors encouraged the development of trust based upon particularistic relationships. For instance, the legal system provided little support to merchants or individuals and imperial officials exercised arbitrary rent-seeking powers. When the Communist Party took power in 1949, it sought to promote universalistic values such as comradeship that would supplant particularistic moral values such as nepotism, which were denounced as "feudal." However, recourse to *guanxi* continued in response to scarcity of goods in a system with bureaucratic allocation of resources.

During the post-Mao reform era, and especially since the early 1990s, China's economy has diversified and remonetized, engendering both the need and opportunity for a more diverse array of interpersonal connections. Meanwhile, despite improvements, key institutional features that support civil society and business in Western societies remain poorly developed in China. In an environment that lacks institutional safeguards and where societal support mechanisms are being dismantled and bases of trust between strangers are limited, whether people are seeking new opportunities, to minimize risk in some endeavor, or to tackle difficulties encountered, they routinely turn to their *guanxi*.

Guanxi is built upon various achieved and ascribed bases with the family as the inner core. Radiating outward in circles from this core are relatives and various relationships involving *tong,* meaning "sameness" or co-identification, such as classmates (*tongxue*); those from the same native place (*tongxiang*); and work colleagues (*tongshi*). Friendship, typically based upon some shared experience, plays a vital role in most people's lives and is an important form of *guanxi*.

In Chinese society, from the national to the familial level, distinctions are routinely drawn between in- and out-groups. Beyond the circles outlined are various categories of outsider such as foreigners and other strangers. To be "one of us" is to be bound by reciprocal rights and duties of mutual aid and support. Reciprocity is central both to Chinese family values and all forms of *guanxi*. In business circles, for instance, banqueting and inviting people to eat is a form of ritualized activity and gift giving that is crucial to what Yang calls the "art of *guanxi*."

The literature is divided on the importance of *guanxi* for foreign businesses in China. Some researchers such as Tung and Worm consider *guanxi* an integral component of doing business in China and required at all stages in companies' operations. Others consider *guanxi* beneficial for specific aspects of business operations or particular sectors. Several studies indicate that variables such as company size and form play an important part in determining the importance of *guanxi*. For smaller, private companies, Xin and Pearce observe that *guanxi* constitutes a substitute for the formal institutional support available to state-owned enterprises. Then, there are those such as Guthrie who see *guanxi* as either detrimental or of declining significance. These debates are explored further in the collection edited by Gold and colleagues in 2002. In addition, there is controversy over *guanxi*'s ethical status as outlined by Dunfee and Warren, and Gamble in 2006.

Critical Commentary and Future Directions

The future role of *guanxi* in China's economic affairs is a matter of debate. Wank reports that entrepreneurs in Xiamen were coming to perceive *guanxi* practice as dangerous and inefficient and to replace it wherever possible with reputational strategies. Pressures that will erode the institutional underpinning for *guanxi* use include the substantial measures being implemented to modernize and upgrade the legal system. The massive influx of foreign multinationals also poses a challenge to Chinese business culture. As Gamble shows in 2003, the fact that foreign firms operate by different rules can be attractive to local people; they might join such firms in part to escape the round of obligations entailed in *guanxi* norms.

Forces that will continue to militate against the decline of *guanxi*'s importance include China's entrenched regionalism. The one-party political system also stymies the emergence of powerful independent bodies such as a critical, watchful media and other organs of civil society. It is hard to conceive that *guanxi* will not continue to play an important role in China's developing economy for many years to come.

—Jos Gamble

Further Readings

Dunfee, T. W., & Warren, D. E. (2001). Is *guanxi* ethical? A normative analysis of doing business in China. *Journal of Business Ethics, 32*(3), 191–204.

Gamble, J. (2003). Transferring human resource practices from the United Kingdom to China: The limits and potential for convergence. *The International Journal of Human Resource Management, 14*(3), 369–87.

Gamble, J. (2007). *Guanxi* and business ethical issues in China. In S. Clegg, K. Y. Wang, & M. Berrell (Eds.), *Business networks and strategic alliances in China* (pp. 271–288). Cheltenham, UK: Edward Elgar.

Gold, T., Guthrie, D., & Wank, D. (Eds.). (2002). *Social connections in China: Institutions, culture, and the changing nature of* guanxi. Cambridge, UK: Cambridge University Press.

Guthrie, D. (1998). The declining significance of *guanxi* in China's economic transition. *China Quarterly, 154,* 254–282.

Michailova, S., & Worm, V. (2003). Personal networking in Russia and China: *Blat* and *guanxi. European Management Journal, 21*(4), 509–519.

Tung, R. L., & Worm, V. (2001). Network capitalism: The role of human resources in penetrating the China market. *International Journal of Human Resource Management, 12*(4), 517–534.

Wank, D. (1999). *Commodifying communism: Business, trust, and politics in a Chinese city.* Cambridge, UK: Cambridge University Press.

Xin, K. R., & Pearce, J. L. (1996). *Guanxi*: Connections as substitutes for formal institutional support. *Academy of Management Journal, 39*(6), 1641–1658.

Yang, M. M. (1994). *Gifts, favors, and banquets: The art of social relationships in China.* Ithaca, NY: Cornell University Press.

H

Hawthorne Studies

The Hawthorne studies were a series of human relations experiments conducted at the Hawthorne Works plant of the Western Electric Company in Chicago, Illinois, from 1924 to 1933. Major topics included employee productivity, satisfaction, motivation, and work group dynamics.

Conceptual Overview

In 1924 the National Research Council of the National Academy of Sciences along with researchers from the Hawthorne Works plant undertook the now-infamous experiments in illumination. The results of initial studies were quite puzzling, and the National Research Council promptly withdrew from the project, at which time Hawthorne researchers began collaborating with faculty from Harvard. The purpose of the investigation then changed from illumination studies to the investigation of factors leading to fatigue and monotony in the workplace. Near the end of the project, the focus again changed to understanding within-group social interaction and its effects on levels of effort and output.

Four major studies were conducted (experiments in illumination, the relay assembly test room, the interview program, and the bank wiring observation room) with two ancillary studies associated with the relay assembly test room (second relay assembly and the mica-splitting test room). The four major studies are briefly described below.

Experiments in Illumination (1924–1927)

Experimenters manipulated the quality and quantity of lighting to see whether changes affected employee efficiency. Increases in illumination resulted in increased output, but so did *decreases* in illumination—in both experimental and control groups. Because of the mixed results, researchers assumed that light was one variable among many that affected employee output, and experiments conducted on the shop floor had so many variables that it was nearly impossible to extricate the effects of one particular variable. The *Hawthorne effect* derived from the results of the illumination studies. That is, employee behavior during the course of an experiment can be influenced by a subject's knowledge of participating in the experiment. To isolate the effects of particular variables, researchers wanted to control extraneous variables, leading to the relay assembly test room studies.

The Relay Assembly Test Room (1927–1932)

Initially planned to be a brief study, this series of experiments lasted five years. A small group of employees was isolated in a separate room so that behavior could be systematically studied. Researchers attempted to control variables such as workload, changes in type of work, and the introduction of new group members. Five women assembling telephone relays were isolated in a room where their behavior could be carefully observed and their output measured. The longitudinal design of the experiment enabled researchers to vary the length of variables such as rest pauses, the workday, and the workweek. As the study progressed, researchers found that when work conditions improved (e.g., longer rest periods and shorter workdays and weeks), so did output. However, when favorable work conditions were removed, output remained at its higher level.

Once again, the studies produced mixed findings. The researchers concluded that the experimenter's behavior was very different from what the typical supervisor might display, and that employee attitudes were an important determinant of effectiveness. This conclusion led to the interviewing program.

The Interviewing Program (1928–1930)

The interviewing program was a distinct departure from the previous studies. In many ways it was a revolutionary idea in 1928, in part because researchers were concerned with employee feelings and attitudes. Scientists of that time were not equipped to measure attitudes. More than 20,000 interviews were conducted, leading to several notable findings: (1) some employees tend to complain regardless of the working conditions. These employees were labeled "chronic kickers," and the phenomenon may have been a precursor to what is now described as negative affectivity. (2) Being heard was an important component of job satisfaction. Some employees actually reported an increase in job satisfaction after the interview process even though no employee complaint had yet been addressed. (3) Attitudes were an important moderating variable in the relationship between an organization's attempt to increase employee satisfaction and the employee's response.

One important variable affecting employee attitudes was the social situation at work, involving satisfaction derived from other workers, supervisors, and the immediate work group. Individuals working collaboratively have shared sentiments that bind them together, and these shared sentiments covary with output. Output can then be thought of as a form of social behavior, a concept demonstrated in the subsequent series of studies known as the bank wiring observation room.

Bank Wiring Observation Room (1931–1932)

Here, researchers were intent on studying group process by observing group members without making changes to the group. The work group consisted of 14 workmen representing 3 occupational groups, wiremen, solder men, and inspectors. The work itself was highly interdependent and the men were paid in relation to collective piecework. The more they produced, the more they were compensated. They found that the workers regulated output to correspond with what they felt was a fair day's work. This was one of the earliest documented instances of group norms. For example, norms in this group determined that *ratebusters* worked too fast, *chiselers* worked too slow, *squealers* spoke ill of their colleagues, and *inspectors* were too critical of the quality of output. Researchers also found that the social pressure to conform to these norms was powerful.

The main findings of the Hawthorne studies as seen by the original researchers can be summarized as follows: (1) Human behavior in the workplace is multiply determined; direct cause-and-effect relationships rarely exist. (2) Work groups will develop norms, and these norms serve to mediate individual needs and the work setting. (3) A social structure exists in informal workgroups and is influenced by prestige and power associated with the job. (4) Employee satisfaction is multiply determined and perhaps best addressed by an attentive supervisor willing to listen to and understand the unique needs of each worker. (5) Resistance to change can be decreased through employee participation.

Critical Commentary and Future Directions

The Hawthorne studies have been criticized since Fritz J. Roethlisberger and William J. Dickson, Elton Mayo, and Thomas N. Whitehead published their results in the 1930s. Jeffrey Sonnenfeld reviewed much of the critical literature in 1985, as well as some of the actual participants, and found that most criticism can be condensed to ideological and methodological issues. A third area of criticism focused on the Hawthorne effect itself.

Ideological Issues

Much of the ideological criticism comes from the field of sociology, which may have felt the research had a decidedly promanagement bias and that the studies presented an inadequate view of society—both factors serving to manipulate the workforce, not help it.

One defender proposed that the timing and context of the criticism from sociologists was suspect. That is to say, the books written about the studies were the first of their kind, tackling issues traditionally related to sociology but applied to industry. The fact that a psychological perspective had addressed the organization and the worker first may have been perceived by some as a threat.

The ideological critics of the Hawthorne studies were emerging "social structure" sociologists who then had a vested intellectual interest in emphasizing systemic power issues in social structures and not levers for the individual. Scholars of this school minimized the "reductionism" of psychology, which suggested a significant influence of individuals and small groups despite social structure constraints.

Methodological Issues

Much of the methodological criticism focuses on the relay assembly test room data, almost to the exclusion of the other studies. It should be mentioned that most of the Harvard social scientists did not join in the design phases of the studies until the relay assembly test room studies were near completion. Specific complaints identified the small sample size, lack of a control, changes in the incentive plan, and changes in the number of subjects during the study, and finally, there were direct challenges to the integrity of the data themselves.

The criticisms of generalizing from small sample size appear well founded and were recognized by the researchers themselves at the time the results were published. Little or no factual evidence was leveled at the integrity of the data, and most if not all of the remaining criticisms are duly addressed in the literature.

The methodological critics acknowledge that the intervention of a new management approach led to an increase in production. The critics, like the Hawthorne studies writers themselves, never talked to the actual participants. Sonnenfeld's direct interviews with the surviving participants 50 years later confirmed that this new approach to management inspired them to work harder.

The Hawthorne Effect

At least two criticisms of the Hawthorne effect deserve mention here. The first deals directly with the definition, or lack of a consistently agreed-upon definition. This problem is in part due to multiple interpretations of the original work and reconceptualizations based on subsequent analyses of data. Although never more than an incidental finding at the time of publication, the original researchers held that a subject's awareness of participating in an experiment might alter his or her behavior.

Critics also question why many studies fail to find the same effect. Perhaps the best explanation is that it may not be omnipresent, and that the Hawthorne effect may depend more on the subject's interpretation of the situation than on the experimenter's interpretation. Researchers typically employ some type of check to verify the effectiveness of a manipulation. Sound advice is to ask the subjects directly via postexperimental interviews—a confirmatory technique utilized in the actual Hawthorne studies.

Conclusion

Despite scholarly debate over the contributions and criticisms of the Hawthorne studies, the conceptual impact on the study of organizations and the people within them is clear. Their influence on social and management science has been far-reaching and pervasive. The underpinnings of such topics as small-group behavior, organization theory, individual differences, job matching, employee participation, incentive plans, work design, and systems theory can all attribute, to some extent, their roots to the Hawthorne studies.

—*Terry Halfhill and Jeffrey Sonnenfeld*

See also Human Relations School; Job Satisfaction; Organizational Behavior

Further Readings

Jones, S. R. G. (1992). Was there a Hawthorne effect? *American Journal of Sociology, 98*, 451–468.

Mayo, E. (1933). *The human problems of an industrial civilization.* New York: Macmillan.

Roethlisberger, F. J. (1941). *Management and morale.* Cambridge, MA: Harvard University Press.

Roethlisberger, F. J. (1977). *The elusive phenomena.* Cambridge, MA: Harvard University Press.

Roethlisberger, F. J., & Dickson, W. J. (1939). *Management and the worker.* Cambridge, MA: Harvard University Press.

Sonnenfeld, J. A. (1985). Shedding light on the Hawthorne studies. *Journal of Occupational Behavior, 6*, 111–130.

Hegemony

Hegemony is the form of political leadership based on the skillful mix of force and consent. The consent of those being led is secured through a variety of material, discursive, and institutional apparatuses through which the worldview of the ruling class is rendered universal and accepted as common sense. Hegemony refers not only to the political and economic practice used to obtain dominance, but also to the outcome of such a process, or to the particular historic condition of class supremacy achieved through a balance of coercion and consent.

Conceptual Overview

The term *hegemony* (from the Greek *hegeisthai*, to lead) has been used since antiquity for describing the dominance of one nation over another. Its modern use, however, derives from the 1930s analysis by the Italian Marxist political leader and scholar Antonio Gramsci.

Deviating from the prevailing Marxist view of the time, which viewed ideology as a set of values and beliefs mechanically imposed for defending a specific economic order, Gramsci claimed that the organization of consent arises as a contingent accomplishment of strategic interventions and is based on the deployment of specific figures and apparatuses. A critical role is played in particular by the organic intellectuals, who perform the task of extending the range of consent by imposing the hegemonic views through prestige and intellectual seduction. An equally important part is played by the education system, the bureaucracy, the popular writers and filmmakers, and the media in general.

Because in any given historical moment more than one class of group aspires to impose its dominance, hegemony is necessarily a continuous exercise and an unfinished task: Maintaining a dominant position requires activity in the economic, political, and cultural spheres.

Gramsci's notion of hegemony had the historical merit of introducing a cultural and strategic dimension into the rigid, deterministic Marxist model of the time. In doing so, he provided a much more sophisticated account of domination, one in which hegemonic ideology mediates between social being and social consciousness. At the same time, he broadened the meaning of politics beyond the immediate struggle for control of the means of coercion to include the activities that organize (or disorganize) consent within the economy, state, and civil society.

Gramsci's idea that leadership relies on the cultural activity of social groups as much as on their political and economical influence attracted great interest during the cultural and linguistic turn in European social theory in the 1970s and 1980s. The idea of hegemony appealed especially to authors who were trying to rescue Marxism from its orthodox slumbers, but it resonated also with poststructuralists and postmodern scholars. The notion of hegemony, in fact, supported the idea of the historicity of cultural and discursive formations and their capacity to constitute at the same time the instrument, the arena, and the outcome of power struggles. Often deprived of its original immediate practical flavor (for Gramsci, who was one of the founders of the Italian Communist Party, hegemony constituted above all a political strategy), the idea was thus extended beyond the realm of concrete politics and became a general principle for explaining the relationship between identity, cultural formations, and domination. Authors such as Ernesto Laclau and Chantal Mouffe, for example, argued that hegemony is a generalized political strategy that operates at the level of the formation of personal identity. Hegemony is, in fact, the attempt to impose a dominant horizon of social orientation and action through discourse. A hegemonic discourse, such as capitalism or managerialism, aims thus at fixing meaning and identity in a context marked by antagonistic forces; it does so by imposing an ideology that is a totalizing horizon with its basis hidden from view and hence subtracted from scrutiny and dissent. All discourses, however, are unable to fulfill their will to totality and constitute by definition unfinished attempts to stabilize and condense social meaning around privileged signifiers. Hegemony is therefore a form of politics based on the continuous effort by both the dominant and the antagonist groups to occupy the spaces left undomesticated by the prevailing discourses. Hegemony, in this sense, signifies both the organization of consent around any dominant group and the possibility of constructing counterhegemonic formations by disarticulating the existing signifying relationships and constituting new ones.

Hegemony in Organization Studies

In organization studies, the concept of hegemony has been central to the work of critical management theorists, who have used it in exploring the multifaceted nature of the organizational manufacturing of consent. Advanced capitalist conditions of work, they argue, can be conceived as a hegemonic production regime. Starting from the 1930s, state interventions, such as social insurance and labor legislation, allowed in fact the establishment of a consent-based form of capitalist dominance based on the converging interests in a stable accumulation regime and economic security. This process has been supported by a variety of practices that weakened collective resistance and mobilized consent toward increased productivity. Workers have thus become actively involved in perpetuating their own subordination. In exchange for marginal local gains and constrained forms of autonomy, such as in quality circles, they effectively waive the possibility of pursuing their wider class interests, thus participating in the perpetuation of the hegemonic regime.

The concept of hegemony has also been used in the 1980s for critically reappraising the use of cultural perspectives and in the late 1990s for reappraising knowledge management discourses. From a hegemony-informed perspective, cultural engineering and knowledge management can be conceived as attempts at homogenizing norms, values, and discursive practices and at constituting work identities that prevent the emergence of antagonist perspectives and forces.

Critical Commentary and Future Directions

The notion of hegemony is central to the project of critical management studies and is likely to become increasingly relevant as the approach gains legitimacy and academic acceptance. Critical management studies stem in fact from a hegemonic reading of the project of corporate capitalism, bringing to the fore the supportive role played by management studies and business schools. It argues that business academics have often played the role of organic intellectuals both by manufacturing consensus-building tools and by naturalizing what is in fact a specific historically situated economic and organizational order. This hegemonic reading of their position in society in turn supports the effort of critical management scholars to find an alternative and less collusive position, which requires taking a critical and reflexive stance and denouncing the assumed objectivism and neutrality of mainstream management science as a masquerade that is already part of a well-formed project of domination.

While critical management studies have interpreted hegemony mainly as a kind of academic antagonist political practice, one that is aimed at contesting "from within" the consolidated views of modern capitalism and corporate society, the future of the notion of hegemony in management studies lies mainly in its still unexploited capacity to illuminate critical aspects of organizational life from a political angle. Once freed of some of the baggage deriving from its Marxist origin, the notion of hegemony becomes a powerful analytical tool for investigating the political dimension implicit in the performance of all aspects of organizational life. The concept of hegemony is not only a tool for understanding the accomplishment of any form or organization as the outcome of a struggle between diverging interests, but also a useful antidote to static and polar views of organizational life. For example, the notion of hegemony emphasizes that consent and coercion should not be conceived of as a polarity. Consent and coercion coexist in a complex and shifting dynamic based on complex tactics of attempted domination and clever local resistance, conflict and alliance, imposition of meaning through discourse and antagonism. The notion of hegemony becomes thus a powerful conceptual tool for exploring in detail the practices of domination and resistance, opening a still largely unexplored territory for future research.

—Davide Nicolini

See also Activism; Critical Management Studies; Domination; Identity; Ideology; Managerial Capitalism; Organizational Discourse; Politics of Organizational Culture; Power; Radical Feminism; Social Theory; Subordination

Further Readings

Grey, C., & Willmott, H. (Eds.). (2005). *Critical management studies. A reader.* Oxford, UK: Oxford University Press.

Laclau, E., & Mouffe, C. (2001). *Hegemony and socialist strategy: Towards a radical democratic politics* (2nd ed.). London: Verso.

Simon, R. (1982). *Gramsci's political thought.* London: Lawrence & Wishart.

HERMENEUTICS

The roots of the term *hermeneutics* lie in the Greek verb *hermeneuein,* meaning "to interpret," and the noun *hermeneia,* meaning "interpretation." These terms are associated with the god Hermes, the messenger of Zeus, god of commerce and patron of merchants and thieves (and a master thief himself). This association with Hermes as the messenger god implies for hermeneutics a function of bringing forth to understanding something previously foreign or unintelligible. Furthermore, there are three main meanings associated with the term *hermeneutics* in ancient Greek usage: first, to say or express something; second, to explain or clarify something drawing on context and preunderstanding; and third, to translate or mediate between two worlds.

Early usage of the term from the 17th century onward referred to principles and methods of biblical interpretation. Initially extended to obscure and specialized texts, subsequently *hermeneutics* was applied more broadly and referred, for example, to general rules of philological exegesis. Especially with the later development of philosophical hermeneutics by Martin Heidegger and Hans-Georg Gadamer, the meaning of *hermeneutics* was extended beyond the task of textual interpretation to the reflexive concern with the nature of understanding and interpretation itself.

Conceptual Overview

Hermeneutic streams of thought view language as constitutive of social reality rather than as merely representational. The groundwork for this social constructionist view was laid with the critiques of logical atomism and logical positivism represented by Bertrand Russell and the early work of Ludwig Wittgenstein (*Tractatus Logico-Philosophicus*). Logical atomism's tenets included the suggestion that elementary propositions are either true or false, they are mutually independent, the semantic names they are constituted of represent simple items in the world called "objects," and that worldly states of affairs are composed of combinations of these objects. Ordinary language philosophy, which included the later work of Wittgenstein (*Philosophical Investigations*), severely challenged these tenets. He suggested that there is no fixed essence denoted by words, as logical atomism held, but that rather words acquire their meaning through use, within particular language games (as Wittgenstein suggested) and within particular speech acts (as elaborated by J. L. Austin and John R. Searle).

Early Hermeneutics

Hermeneutics has had a rich and varied conceptual history. One of the early treatises on hermeneutics, Friedrich Ast's *Basic Elements of Grammar, Hermeneutics, and Criticism,* sets out the goal of hermeneutics as the understanding of the spirit of a text through three moments: historical understanding, grammatical understanding, and in relation to the text's author and the spirit of the age in which it was written. In this context, Ast proposed the principle of the hermeneutic circle: that to understand the spirit of an age, one can do so only through the individual works that exemplify that spirit; but these works can in turn be understood only through their relationship with the whole of which they are a part. Ast's three moments of understanding parallel three moments of *explanation*: the hermeneutic of the letter, of the sense, and of the spirit (referring to the life-world or controlling idea the text portrays). Friedrich August Wolf, also writing in the late 18th century, proposed that the goal of hermeneutics was to grasp the thoughts of the author by a "temperamentally suited" interpreter through dialogue with that author occurring through the medium of the text. Wolf, like Ast, believed that explanation must be grounded in understanding and also proposed three moments of interpretation: the grammatical, historical, and philosophical moments.

Believing that hermeneutics as a field had been specialized and fragmented, Friedrich Schleiermacher in the early 19th century sought to develop a general hermeneutics whose principles could serve as the foundation for all kinds of textual interpretation. He aimed to discover invariant, ahistorical laws governing interpretation that would constitute a science of hermeneutics. Schleiermacher distinguished between grammatical interpretation, concerned with analyzing the language of a text, and psychological interpretation, concerned with the effort to understand the mental processes, individuality, and style of the author. The underlying principle of understanding for Schleiermacher, building on Ast, is that of the hermeneutic circle. The hermeneutic circle involves a logical contradiction: If the whole derives its meaning from its parts, and the parts from the whole, and to understand one we must first understand the other, how do we start? Schleiermacher believed that the operation of understanding goes beyond logic, containing an intuitive and divinatory element; and it presupposes a shared preunderstanding within a community of meaning that enables the operation of the hermeneutical circle in the first place. In his later writings, Schleiermacher moved further toward psychological interpretation and further away from language as the central feature of textual interpretation, a move he was later criticized for.

Wilhelm Dilthey saw hermeneutics as the core discipline that could serve as the foundation for all humanistic studies, in opposition to the mechanistic reductionism of the natural sciences. Dilthey suggested that whereas the sciences *explain* nature, the human studies can *understand* expressions of life (such as texts) from a historical consciousness of lived experience. Dilthey's approach to interpretation privileged grasping this lived experience through its expressions. He viewed understanding as the comprehension of forms of life that open up possibilities for one's own experience, emphasizing the historicality of human self-understanding and human nature. Nevertheless, influenced by Schleiermacher, as well as by the positivist spirit of his time, Dilthey also sought to develop objectively valid interpretations and data, something not entirely in harmony with his efforts to grasp historically contingent lived experience.

Contemporary Hermeneutics

Moving away from questions of epistemology (the emphasis on developing valid rules and methods for textual interpretation) to questions of ontology, Heidegger was rather concerned with the ontological problem of being. Influenced by the phenomenological approach of Edmund Husserl, Heidegger, in *Being and Time,* developed a view of hermeneutics as the explication of human existence and as the process by which words bring about understanding. Gadamer followed Heidegger to develop *philosophical hermeneutics,* the encounter with Being through language. In common with Heidegger, Gadamer was interested in the nature of understanding itself, proposing that the hermeneutical experience is constituted by the aesthetic, the historical, and the linguistic spheres. He viewed understanding as historical and emphasized a process of conversation or dialogue in achieving understanding. In the research and hermeneutic process the interpreter's preunderstandings are crucial, for they make possible a context shared between the text and the interpreter that enables the very act of understanding to take place. Gadamer referred to these preunderstandings as prejudices, distinguishing between productive prejudices that aid understanding and unproductive ones that hinder it. According to Gadamer, people can become conscious of their prejudices and ideally become able to identify unproductive ones through encounter and dialogue with texts that challenge them.

Understanding is thus not seen as a one-sided process wherein the interpreter singularly grasps the meaning of an objective, unchangeable, and ahistorical text, but rather, as a conversation or dialogue between the interpreter and the text in the context of an acute sense of the historicality of both the text and the interpreter. An authentic understanding of texts through a dialogical process results in a fusion of horizons between text and interpreter, wherein the interpreter's horizons expand to gain an in-depth appreciation of the life-world of the text. Gadamer's views have thus challenged Schleiermacher's and Dilthey's earlier views that the ultimate goal of hermeneutics was to grasp the author's meaning, by providing a more relational, dynamic, and historical view of understanding and interpretation.

Jürgen Habermas's work, and in particular his exchanges with Gadamer, led to critical hermeneutics, the attempt to integrate ideological and emancipatory concerns with hermeneutics. This approach views language not simply as constructive, but also as surreptitiously embodying legitimations of existing social arrangements that are in the interests of dominant classes; hermeneutics thus becomes a committed form of emancipatory critique aiming to demystify debatable, taken-for-granted social arrangements.

Paul Ricoeur's work returned the focus of hermeneutics to its initial concerns with textual interpretation. Ricoeur defined hermeneutics as the art of interpreting texts, posing as a fundamental concern that once discourse is inscribed as text, it is severed from its author, and its meaning as interpreted by new audiences may not necessarily coincide with the author's original intentions. Thus, one key aspect of the hermeneutical task, according to Ricoeur, becomes the interpretation of texts in contexts different from that of the author and the original audience, with the ideal intent of discovering new avenues to understanding. Ricoeur noted that several interpretations of texts may arise from readers' preunderstandings and their particular interpretations of a text in relation to their own perceived situation.

Critical Commentary and Future Directions

Acknowledging the possibility of various textual interpretations, however, as Ricoeur and others have done, does not necessitate a lapse to relativism, the resignation to the idea that there is no way to arrive at certain textual interpretations that are more valid than other potential interpretations (a concern of the classical hermeneutics of Ast, Wolf, Schleiermacher, and Dilthey). In contrast to poststructuralist approaches, for example, which see the text as having a plurality of indeterminate and irreducible meanings and which, according to Roland Barthes, practice the infinite deferment of the signified, epistemologically oriented hermeneutic approaches assume that some meanings are more valid than others in the text's particular social-historical context. For Ricoeur, for example, a text displays few potential interpretations and is not a repository of potentially unlimited meanings.

Anthony Giddens, a hermeneutically oriented sociologist, suggests that the interpretive validity of texts can be improved through ethnographic inquiry into the settings in which the text was produced, the intellectual resources the author has drawn on, and the characteristics of the audience it is addressed to. He emphasizes the necessity of studying texts as the concrete medium and outcome of a process of production that is reflexively monitored by its author or reader. Inquiry into this productive process involves exploring the author's or speaker's intentions as well as the practical knowledge involved in writing or speaking with a certain style for a particular audience.

Even though hermeneutics, through the work of Heidegger and Gadamer, has expanded beyond epistemology to the realm of ontology, hermeneutically oriented empirical studies in organizational settings still need to employ clear and valid methodological directions. This applies both to textual analysis or, following Ricoeur, to any other types of phenomena that can be viewed and analyzed as texts (e.g., patterns of actions, organizations, or institutions). As noted above, a key concept in hermeneutics is the hermeneutic circle. In methodological terms, the hermeneutic circle implies an analytical approach to text seen as an iterative process of discovery, moving from a part to the whole and vice versa, each time further enriching the interpretations, and moving to progressively broader nested levels of context until an acceptable level of saturation is reached, when the researcher feels that he or she has gained sufficient understanding of the phenomenon under study.

Perhaps mirroring Ast's concern with understanding the spirit of a text, as a life-world or controlling idea portrayed by it, hermeneutically oriented researchers in organization studies tend to search for central themes in texts, for thematic unity (how central themes are interrelated in broader argumentations both within texts and intertextually), and they often relate the themes to patterns in ethnographic data over time in order to raise the validity of the interpretations.

The need for conscious attention to issues of preunderstandings and historicality of both the text and the interpreter has brought to the fore concerns of reflexivity in hermeneutic organizational research. The aim here is not to "sanitize" the process of research and understanding in the effort to grasp the objectively valid and immutable meaning of a text. This would indeed be impossible from the reflexivity perspective, since asserting an objective meaning would erroneously imply that the interpreter and the text can somehow stand outside time and history. Rather, the goal is to be conscious, in the process of understanding, of how one's own horizon encounters the horizon of the text, what prejudices or preunderstandings are involved, how they affect the nature of this encounter, and how the researcher-interpreter's own horizon develops as a result of the encounter.

Issues of appropriate method, the search for validity, the impact of historicality, and the impetus to reflexivity in hermeneutic organizational research have become more prominent and will continue to be so in researchers' ongoing search for deep understandings of the complex beast of organization.

—*Loizos Heracleous*

See also Interpretive Theory; Objectivity; Positivism; Reflexivity

Further Readings

Barthes, R. (1977). *Image, music, text.* London: Fontana.
Giddens, A. (1979). *Central problems in social theory.* London: Macmillan.
Giddens, A. (1987). *Social theory and modern sociology.* Cambridge, UK: Polity.
Heracleous, L. (2006). *Discourse, interpretation, organization.* Cambridge, UK: Cambridge University Press.
Kets de Vries, M. F. R., & Miller, D. (1987). Interpreting organizational texts. *Journal of Management Studies, 24,* 233–247.
Palmer, R. E. (1969). *Hermeneutics.* Evanston, IL: Northwestern University Press.
Phillips, N., & Brown, J. L. (1993). Analyzing communication in and around organizations: A critical hermeneutic approach. *Academy of Management Journal, 36,* 1547–1576.
Prasad, A. (2002). The contest over meaning: Hermeneutics as an interpretive methodology for understanding texts. *Organizational Research Methods, 5*(1), 12–33.
Ricoeur, P. (1991). *From text to action.* Evanston, IL: Northwestern University Press.
Ricoeur, P. (1997). Rhetoric-poetics-hermeneutics. In W. Jost & M. J. Hyde (Eds.), *Rhetoric and hermeneutics in our time: A reader* (pp. 60–72). New Haven, CT: Yale University Press.
Thachankary, T. (1992). Organizations as "texts": Hermeneutics as a model for understanding organizational change. *Research in Organization Change and Development, 6,* 197–233.
Thompson, J. B. (1981). *Critical hermeneutics: A study in the thought of Paul Ricoeur and Jürgen Habermas.* Cambridge, UK: Cambridge University Press.

HIERARCHY

Hierarchy originally meant rule by a priesthood, and the term was also used to refer to the ranks of heavenly beings, such as angels and archangels. Hierarchy today normally refers to an organizing principle that uses rankings and vertical links between superior and subordinate entities. Examples include taxonomic classifications of the natural world by species, genus, family, and so on and organizational structures like that of the Roman Catholic Church, where power passes down from the pope to archbishops, bishops, and the rest. In organizational terms, the emphasis of the term *hierarchy* may lie either on the source of authority residing with a single ruler or chief executive or on the ranked structure by which authority is then cascaded down through the organization. The term can be used to refer to the people within the organizational pyramid as well as to the organizing principle itself.

Conceptual Overview

Talk about organization usually centers on who is in charge and how decisions should be made. In the Western world, a long history of feudal political and social structures, as well as the usual ways of organizing religious and military bodies, has made hierarchy a familiar and comfortable habit. It has come to be seen as the obvious fallback, the default option. Plato, Thomas Aquinas, René Descartes, Thomas Hobbes, Immanuel Kant, and Georg Hegel have all relied heavily on the notion of hierarchy as the "natural" way of viewing the world, of structuring our thinking, and of viewing sociopolitical structures. Others have taken as evidence so-called hierarchical structures in the animal kingdom (pecking orders among domestic fowl, dominance hierarchies among gorillas and other primates).

The work of Max Weber and others in the field of organization studies, bureaucracy, and distribution of power has also tended to assume that a hierarchical structure is the most efficient way of regulating a decision-making body. Bureaucracies, in this definition, are driven by a top-down, command-and-control approach wherein managers have a strong directive role and considerable control over others who are accountable to them.

Challenges to the Hegemony of Hierarchy

As a result of these ways of thinking about organizations, hierarchy is frequently taken for granted as the inevitable way for humans to organize themselves, or to be organized. Hierarchy can also be comfortable, in that it frees the majority of people from the responsibility of decision making. In psychological terms, it can be said to appeal to the child in each person and is frequently easier than alternatives that demand an adult, independent stance. Though the hegemony of hierarchical thinking has been challenged by radical and revolutionary thinkers such as the Levellers, Tom Paine, Vladimir Lenin, and Che Guevara, critics draw attention to the tendency of hierarchical structures to reassert themselves (for example, in revolutionary France or in Communist Russia and China). The cooperative movement has challenged conventional Western capitalist patterns of ownership, but it often still employs hierarchical patterns of organization. In almost all cases, the modernist emphasis on efficiency and the hegemony of hierarchical thinking means that hierarchy is regarded as the de facto standard against which other systems and forms of organization must be measured.

Recent critics of hierarchy have included Peter Senge and Margaret Wheatley, who describe hierarchy as a whipping boy, something to blame for an organization's ills while forgetting that we are the ones creating it, or at the very least tolerating it. Rosabeth Moss Kanter says that hierarchies depend on fear and comfort: fear of powerful figures at the top and comfort with familiar patterns of relationships. These are factors that support the hegemony of hierarchy and echo W. Edwards Deming's exhortation to organizations to "drive out fear"—a fear rooted in a worker's incapacity to question and to act from his or her own experience.

Critical Commentary and Future Directions

Systems Theory, Contingency Theory, and Hierarchy

Because its hegemony leads people to think that hierarchy is the natural way to organize and be organized, people often feel that the only alternative to it is disorganization or anarchy. If that were so, then hierarchy would indeed be inevitable. Modern contingency theory, however—an outgrowth of systems theory—suggests that there is no single "best way" to organize and that, contrary to Platonic theory, individuals do not have a natural role or place in any organizational structure. Richard W. Scott points to the general orienting hypothesis that organizations whose internal features best match the demands of their environments will adapt most successfully. Walter Buckley was among the first to demonstrate the problems associated with a kind of social physics, whose central notion was that human beings were objects or advanced machines, whose behavior was subject to natural laws of the same kind as the laws of physics, and that humans in society could be analyzed and managed accordingly. Marxist visions of a series of inevitable social transformations made many of the same assumptions, even if the underlying analysis was more sophisticated.

Alternatives to Hierarchy

Current thinking about organization structure is focusing strongly on alternatives to traditional hierarchy. They include the following:

Self-organizing and self-managing team structures are designed to take advantage of economies of scale at the lowest levels of activity and to ensure the full involvement of employees at even the lowest levels.

Authority based on capability is designed to overturn systems in which authority is based on length of service and to ensure that the organization remains a means to an end rather than an end in itself.

Flatter organizations, with fewer middle managers, are designed to ensure that senior management work more closely with those people who actually provide products and services and work with customers (this is, of course, still a hierarchical structure).

Learning organizations are designed to ensure that knowledge is shared more effectively between employees and that an organization can quickly correct its own errors through a continuous feedback loop. In a learning organization, managers become facilitators who ensure that these processes occur appropriately and that other forms of learning (like adaptive and generative learning) are fostered.

Empowerment is an approach is designed to spread decision-making responsibility to a wider group of employees (especially those with direct customer contact), but still within a hierarchical framework.

Peer-to-peer working and networking approaches recognize and take advantage of new forms of working, communicating, and networking facilitated by the Internet, new communications technologies, and new media. In some cases, fear of the destabilizing outcomes of such working practices lead organizations to impose an even more rigidly hierarchical structure to manage networked employees.

Participative structures are designed to mirror bottom-up, participative political structures but often serve only to deliver more opinions between which senior management then have to choose.

Triarchy theory asserts that heterarchy and responsible autonomy should be combined with hierarchy to produce a more flexible, efficient, and humane organizational structure.

Heterarchy combines aspects of many of the above alternatives to distribute authority and decision making more widely within the organization and to encourage the parts of an organization to work together cooperatively while prioritizing a range of success criteria. In particular, heterarchy values multiple skills, working styles, and types of knowledge without privileging any one of them.

In an organization based on responsible autonomy, individuals and teams have autonomy to decide what to do and how to do it but remain accountable for the outcome of their decisions. This degree of accountability is what distinguishes responsible autonomy from anarchy. Responsible autonomy requires clearly defined boundaries at which external direction stops.

Many of these notions, in particular the notion of the flat or flatter organization (with correspondingly fewer hierarchical levels of control), are now well established among management and organizational theorists.

Nevertheless, as outlined above, the practical response to some of these developments, as well as to the trend toward decentralization and working remotely, has been to insist that a more rigid reliance on hierarchical structures is required to control the potential chaos of loosening conventional power structures. This is as true in the corporate world as it is politics and government.

Equally, it is often claimed that the more autonomous and heterarchical structures espoused by new technology, advertising, and media companies can work only in organizations with a highly educated and creative workforce.

It remains difficult to make an objective judgment about the value of hierarchy in organizations, and in society in general, because we will be able to make a balanced judgment about hierarchy's usefulness only when its hegemony stops and it comes to be seen as just one among several options.

Directions for Future Research

Future research in the field will clearly reflect developments in organizational theory and thinking as a whole. But other possibilities are now becoming clear.

Neuroscience. Coming at the subject from a biological viewpoint, neuroscientific research is increasingly informing our understanding of how individuals make decisions and balance priorities, how they have creative and innovative ideas, how they store and retrieve information, how they communicate with one another and work best with new forms of communication, and how they manage risk. These skills are highly relevant to questions about hierarchy, and future research may throw light on better organizational systems and procedures for fostering and enhancing those skills—especially in a world increasingly transformed by new developments in communication and knowledge management technology.

Behavioral research. Some of the most disputed current work on how individuals behave in groups covers the social behavior of primates and other animal groups. Its results may give us a clearer sense of what is "normal" and perhaps help to undermine the hegemony of hierarchy, but it is unlikely to offer clear alternatives.

Complexity theory. Complexity theory is a fruitful area for research into organizational design, especially since it combines results from many of the latest neuroscientific and behavioral research. While its underpinnings (including the idea that there is no one best way to organize) mean that it is unlikely to come up with clear guidance on how to organize better across the board, complexity theory is already strongly challenging the idea that a hierarchical approach is necessarily the best in most situations—or even any situation. As alternative forms of organizational design are recognized as more useful or effective, research in this area is likely to help to provide a significant challenge to the hegemony of hierarchy.

As this outline suggests, the future of hierarchy and its alternatives in organizational terms are unlikely to depend to any large degree on radical or inspirational thinking by researchers, academics, business leaders, and employees. As the hegemony of hierarchical thinking is slowly worn down, it is most probable that the changing economic, social, technological, and political environment will provide the major impetus for new developments in organizational design.

The economics and practicalities of doing business in a wireless-enabled, environmentally disabled world, subject to all kinds of unforeseeable upheaval, seem likely to become more and more the primary source of alternative management and organizational strategies. The usefulness of such new strategies as may emerge will be tested by experience and judged, as always, largely by the market and by the members of those emergent organizations.

—*Gerard Fairtlough*

See also Authoritarianism; Bureaucracy; Hegemony; Organizational Structure; Power

Further Readings

Bijker, W. E., & Law, J. (1992). *Shaping technology/building society: Studies in sociotechnical change.* Cambridge, MA: MIT Press.

Clegg, S. R. (1990). *Modern organizations: Organization studies in the postmodern world.* London: Sage.

Fairtlough, G. (2005). *The three ways of getting things done: Hierarchy, heterarchy, and responsible autonomy in organizations.* Bridport, UK: Triarchy Press.

Keidel, R. W. (1995). *Seeing organizational patterns: A new theory and language of organizational design.* San Francisco: Berrett-Koehler.

Lawrence, P., & Lorsch, J. (1967). *Organization and environment.* Cambridge, MA: Harvard University Press.

Malone, T. W. (2004). *The future of work.* Boston: Harvard Business School Press.

Mitleton-Kelly, E. (2003). *Complex systems and evolutionary perspectives of organisations: The application of complexity theory to organisations.* Oxford, UK: Elsevier Science.

Scott, R. W. (1987). *Organizations: Rational, natural and open systems.* Englewood Cliffs, NJ: Prentice-Hall.

HIGH INVOLVEMENT MANAGEMENT

High involvement management is a term coined by Ed Lawler for an approach to management centered on employee involvement. It entails providing employees with opportunities to make decisions about the conduct of their jobs and to participate in the business as a whole. Job-level involvement means increasing the decision making that people have in their work and is thus equivalent to work enrichment or role empowerment. Organization-level involvement, or empowerment, means giving employees a role in decisions on strategy, investment, and other major organizational matters. High involvement management is conceived as an alternative to a control model, which is founded on job simplification, tightly defined divisions of labor, rigid allocations of individuals to narrowly defined tasks, and minimal employee participation in higher-level decisions.

Conceptual Overview

High involvement management is, for Lawler, distinctive precisely because it includes organization-level empowerment and goes beyond a narrow concept of job redesign; it includes the organizational changes that are designed to support the job-level involvement. These include changes in supervisory roles and systems and in the allocation and determination of rewards. Without such organizational redesigns, job involvement may well fail, for example, if supervisors unilaterally usurp the decision-making authority that employees may have been given.

The underlying concept is that if workers are to be strongly involved in their organization and to care enthusiastically about its performance, then they need to be able to influence decisions. To do this effectively, workers also need to know about the goals and strategy of the organization, have the knowledge and skills to contribute to those goals, and be rewarded for using their skills to promote them. Consequently, Lawler's high involvement management model has four dimensions, respectively termed power, information sharing, developing knowledge, and rewarding performance. The power dimension is the fulcrum; it ensures that power is distributed to lower levels of the organization so that operational decisions are decentralized and employees have genuine opportunities to make suggestions and participate in strategic decision-making processes. The other three dimensions ensure that individuals have the right information, skills, and rewards to use their power in ways that contribute significantly to the organization's goals. Thus, high involvement management involves practices such as sharing information on quality, customer feedback and business results, organizational performance-related reward systems, and extensive training and development, the social and problem-solving skills required for high involvement working included.

In a similar vein, Richard Walton identified a high commitment approach to management centered on work enrichment, functional flexibility, and teamwork, and included the same range of supporting practices as those suggested by Lawler. Equally, employee involvement has figured prominently in more popular management writing, such as in Jeffrey Pfeffer's 16 best management practices. Indeed, high involvement management has been advocated as the approach most appropriate for the increasingly uncertain and competitive economy that many anticipate; the message of Lawler and Walton in the 1980s was that it was universally relevant and need not be confined to technologically advanced industries. Whether this was because it had superseded the control model as the best model for even stable situations, or that most organizations now faced an unstable environment, was not entirely clear. But the implication is that organizations that adopt it ought to perform better than those that do not.

Lawler and Walton were, however, mindful of the difficulties of implementing high involvement management and of the possibility that without certain conditions it was unlikely to produce the expected performance benefits. An important condition was that top management valued involvement and took a long-term perspective to employee relations and organizational strategy. They accepted that incremental development and transitional forms might be necessary if organizations were to realize the high involvement approach.

Governments, practitioners, and some trade union leaders have been attracted to the high involvement ideal. The notion of employee involvement became increasingly relevant to the performance requirements of organizations in what was taken to be a newly emerging political and economic era. It was this perspective that led the U.S. Department of Labor to relabel what was essentially the high involvement model as the "high performance work organization." This triggered a tendency to replace *high commitment* and *high involvement* terminology with *high performance management,* or at least to treat all the terms as synonymous. Formal definitions of high performance management typically present it in terms of three dimensions that mirror Lawler's four elements, with his knowledge and skills combined into one: work organization providing opportunities to participate, skills and knowledge, and motivational practices.

The high involvement approach built on work enrichment theory, but it also reflected observations that involvement was central to the pioneering management methods of leading-edge, often fast-growing, companies, particularly in the United States. Lawler initially associated successful implementations of high involvement management with new start-up companies or "Greenfield" sites, supporting his judgment that it was much easier to install it where a history of the control approach did not prevail. Yet he, and others, increasingly saw high involvement management as a natural accompaniment to new operational management methods, such as total quality management (TQM) and lean production, and hence anticipated that these would provide a major impetus for its development. The limited evidence, which is mostly from the United States, the United Kingdom, or Japan, is that there is indeed a tendency to use high involvement management in tandem with complementary practices such as TQM. Moreover, Lawler has embraced the high performance concept, but rather than treating it as synonymous with employee involvement, he considers high performance to be the consequence of a synergy between high involvement management and TQM; he argues that each is likely to have less effect on organizational performance in the absence of the other.

Within social theory, such new production concepts have been viewed as a vital part of a new social and economic order, subsumed under terms such as *post-Fordism* and *flexible specialization.* The contrast is made between a past economy, where expanding mass-production manufacturing industries based on an assumed rigid Fordist system of production were the bedrock, and an economy in which services become more dominant and operational management is based on a new set of more customer-focused, adaptive, just-in-time principles. As the control model of management was an integral component of the Fordist system, so the involvement model is central to the post-Fordist approach.

Similarly, within the industrial relations field, high involvement management was a core element in some theories of the transformation of employment relations in the last two decades of the 20th century. The extreme position is that high involvement management offers a substitute for trade unionism because it reduces the causes of unionism, that is, worker dissatisfaction. Less extreme versions place high involvement management at the center of managerial strategies that have radically altered the industrial relations scene. Among human resource specialists it is widely assumed that managers pursuing such strategies would prefer not to have a union, or even a work council, intervening in their relationship with employees. Nonetheless, Tom Kochan and Paul Osterman argue that, while high involvement management offers the prospect of a win-win situation for management and workers, it is more likely to succeed when implemented with union support. Certainly, some of the elements of high involvement management, such as work enrichment, job security guarantees, and priority for internal promotion over external recruitment, are not only compatible with trade union and workers' interests, but have been longstanding trade union demands.

Critical Commentary and Future Directions

A key question is whether the use of high involvement practices is in fact associated with superior organizational performance. In other words, does the evidence justify the high performance tag or is the approach best defended on the grounds of its benefits for employee welfare? The high involvement model gave a fresh impetus within organization and management studies to the quest to demonstrate a link between human resources and the overall performance of organizations, or more specifically the profits of businesses. This spawned studies testing the link between high involvement practices and organizational performance. Initial overviews of these tended to conclude that there is a strong positive link between high performance work systems and performance. But the results are not consistently positive, and the authors of some individual studies have inflated the support that their data gave to the high performance thesis. The measures of practices used across the studies are diverse and thus the constructs underlying them are more heterogeneous than reviewers imply. Moreover, studies are increasingly neglecting a key element of the original high involvement management model: work enrichment.

Few studies have tested whether the effects of high involvement are greater in unstable contexts, but those studies that have do not offer much support for the position that such contexts do show greater effects. Nor is there much solid evidence that a voice for the trade union enhances (or decreases) the impact of high involvement management. However, the few studies of the joint effects of high involvement management and TQM have been more supportive of Lawler's supposition that they are synergistically related. Studies that have examined the extent to which high involvement management affects employees' involvement, commitment, satisfaction, or attitudes toward work have been limited in number and scope, and the results have again been mixed.

Criticisms of high involvement management as a practice have centered on its authenticity as a source of genuine worker involvement or empowerment. The strongest argument is that the component practices are simply a means of intensifying the work effort and reducing employment levels, and that any attempt by management to implement high involvement management is a cover to give impression that the intensification of effort represents an increase in the influence that workers have. In these terms, it is not an alternative to the control model but another control strategy. It is true that many of the work organization changes associated with high involvement management do not provide the work enrichment envisaged in the model. Such methods, along with idea-capturing schemes such as quality circles, mean that management no longer monopolizes the procedures for determining work methods and processes; but despite this, simplified jobs that have been designed on Taylorist principles as under the control model may remain untouched. Complete high involvement management means that jobs are enriched. Consequently, any evaluation of the nature and effects of high involvement management should include work enrichment in the analysis, as well as measures of organization-level empowerment and employee voice.

Alongside criticisms of integrity have been concerns that high involvement management is replacing unionism. However, the few studies of this, again all in the United States or the United Kingdom, find no supporting evidence for such an association. If anything, it is marginally more likely to be found in unionized settings. However, there is some evidence to suggest that practices that may violate fundamental trade union principles, such as appraisal and performance-related pay, may be more prevalent in nonunion workplaces.

Most, but not all, of the studies of high involvement management have been based on cross-sectional or case study analysis, typically relying on interviews or questionnaires completed by managers for their data. More longitudinal studies are required that collect data on practices from multiple respondents or are based on independent audits of practices, including evidence of when they were first introduced within organizations, that can be matched with data on audited performance over many years. We need to further assess specific practices, so as to determine whether certain ones are crucial or whether it is management's general orientation toward involvement and participation that is decisive. Exploration of the many candidates for the mechanisms that explain the link between high involvement management and performance is also vital. Evidence from recent studies of work enrichment suggests that learning and proactivity are as likely to play this role as are the more often discussed job satisfaction and organizational commitment. High involvement practices need to be evaluated in the context not only of operational management practices such as TQM, but also alternative contributors to organizational performance and employee well-being, such as expenditure on research and development and managerial competence. Conventional indicators—profits, productivity, costs, and human resource measures such as labor turnover—are important. But the real gauge of high involvement management is whether it fosters innovation. Thus, it is the rates of change in these indicators that are most important rather than their absolute values.

Nonetheless, the quest to link high involvement management to performance should not mask the fact that, even if such a performance effect were not demonstrable, the use of practices that enhance employee involvement may be an end in itself. There is sufficient psychological evidence to suggest that empowerment, feedback, and well-designed reward systems are beneficial for employee well-being, though the effects of teamwork are less clear. High involvement management has an important role to play in social and organizational policies designed to provide justice, satisfactory work-nonwork balance, and equality of opportunity.

—*Stephen Wood*

See also Control; Decentralization; Empowerment; Human Resource Management; Japanese Management; Just-in-Time Management; Lean Production; Participation; Post-Fordist Economy; Scientific Management; Strategic Human Resource Management; Total Quality Management

Further Readings

Appelbaum, E., Bailey, T., Berg, P., & Kalleberg, A. L. (2000). *Manufacturing advantage: Why high performance work systems pay off.* Ithaca, NY: Cornell University Press.

Cappelli, P., & Neumark, D. (2001). Do "high performance" work practices improve establishment-level outcomes? *Industrial and Labor Relations Review, 54,* 737–775.

de Menezes, L. M., & Wood, S. (2006). The reality of flexible work systems in Britain using the workplace employee relations survey. *International Journal of Human Resource Management, 17*(1), 1–33.

Huselid, M. A. (1995). The impact of human resource management practices on turnover, productivity, and corporate financial performance. *Academy of Management Journal, 38*(3), 635–672.

Kochan, T. A., & Osterman, P. (1994). *The mutual gains enterprise.* Boston: Harvard Business School Press.

Lawler, E. E. (1986). *High involvement management.* San Francisco: Jossey-Bass.

Lawler, E. E., & Benson, G. S. (2003). Employee involvement: Utilization, impacts, and future prospects. In D. T Holman, T. D. Wall, C. W. Clegg, P. Sparrow, & A. Howard (Eds.), *The new workplace: A guide to the human impact of modern working practices* (pp. 155–173). London: Wiley.

MacDuffie, J. P. (1995). Human resource bundles and manufacturing performance: Organizational logic and flexible production systems in the world auto industry. *Industrial and Labor Relations Review, 48*(2), 197–221.

Machin, S., & Wood, S. (2005). HRM as a substitute for trade unions in British workplaces. *Industrial and Labor Relations Review, 58*(1), 201–218.

Pfeffer, J. (1994). *Competitive advantage through people: Unleashing the power of the workforce.* Boston: Harvard Business School Press.

U.S. Department of Labor. (1993). *High performance work practices.* Washington, DC: Author.

Wall, T. D., Wood, S. J., & Leach, D. (2004). Empowerment and performance. In I. Robertson and C. Cooper (Eds.), *International and organizational psychology* (pp. 1–46). London: Wiley.

Wall, T., & Wood, S. (2005). The romance of HRM and business performance: A case for "big science"? *Human Relations, 58*(4), 429–462.

Walton, R. E. (1985). From "control" to "commitment" in the workplace. *Harvard Business Review, 63*(2), 77–84.

Wood, S. J. (1988). Between Fordism and flexibility? The US car industry. In R. Hyman and W. Streeck (Eds.), *New technology and industrial relations* (pp. 101–127). Oxford, UK: Blackwell, 1988.

Wood, S. J. (1999). Human resource management and performance. *International Journal of Management Reviews, 10*(4), 367–413.

Wood, S. J., & Albanese, M. (1995). Can you speak of a high commitment management on the shop floor? *Journal of Management Studies, 32*(2), 215–247.

HIGH-RISK TECHNOLOGIES AND ORGANIZATIONS

The concept of high-risk technologies and organizations refers to the intersection of *risk,* the probabilistic chance of success; *technology,* a means of converting input to output; and *organization,* a structured purposeful collective. Together they describe the development and implementation of increasingly complex and indeterminate systems whose outcomes are difficult to predict. Today, organizations are challenged by a rapid advance of scientific knowledge and intensifying competitive pressures to innovate at greater speed, thus increasing both the promise and peril of their technological creations.

Conceptual Overview

Technology is the means by which organizations convert input to output. Inputs include raw materials, human labor, financial capital, and various skills and competencies. Outputs include valuable goods, products, and services. The conversion process might rely on simple procedures, such as youth squeezing fruit for their lemonade stand, or highly elaborate and interrelated systems, such as the production of advanced pharmaceutical or aerospace materials. The degree of technological sophistication employed by an organization has been modeled by theorists such as Joanne Woodward, in her studies of technological complexity, Eric Trist, in his studies of sociotechnical integration, Charles Perrow, in technological analyzability and variability, James Thompson, in technological interdependence, and Philip Anderson and Mike Tushman, in technological change. Technology is seen as riskier when it is more complex, disconnected, variable, and nonroutine, intensive, and radical. Together they sketch a multidimensional array of technological risk-facing organizations.

Risk is the probabilistic chance of success or failure in an endeavor. For example, wagering on the toss of a coin carries a 1-in-2 likelihood of success. Less risky endeavors have a greater chance of positive outcome whereas riskier endeavors, such as wagering on a long-shot horse or stock, have a lesser chance. Greater risks are often accompanied by greater potential rewards. Organizational actors do not, however, always consider risks from a purely mathematical choice-optimization perspective and frequently employ heuristics, or shortcuts, to make sense of risky situations. Daniel Kahneman and Amos Tversky showed that the manipulation of reference points or targets influenced tendencies toward risk-seeking or risk-averse behavior. James March and Zur Shapira showed that managers' attention influences their decisions. Philip Bromley linked strategic risk taking to past organizational performance. Gerte Hofstede reconciled risk-taking patterns with cultural values and posited that some societies are generally more comfortable with risk than others. Together these dimensions show that organizations and managers have subjective and imperfect approaches to managing risk.

Overall, technology presents organizations with various types of risk, such as

- Society-level and physical risk
- Industry-level and market risk
- Strategic and competitive risk
- Administrative and knowledge risk
- Level of product/process and profitability risk
- Level of individual and job risk

An example of a societal risk from high-risk technology that affects organizational environments would be the cases of nuclear, biochemical, or nanotechnological business. Charles Perrow and Scott Sagan contrast high reliability theory—predicting that redundancy, controls, safety checks, and learning mechanisms can mitigate risk—from the normal accidents theory—arguing that tightly coupled and increasingly complex systems cannot be completely controlled by boundedly rational and politically motivated actors and can even escalate small glitches into major failures. The thrust of the reasoning is that failure that can arise "normally" in systems by virtue of the interdependent nature of the components of the system itself, concluding that as technologies become more complex, the probability of tragic results increases. This logic has been subsequently extended to other organizational endeavors such as information technology, computer viruses, health care, large-scale construction projects, space exploration, and highway design and regulation.

Industry-level technological risk affects organizational markets, for instance, in the cases of industry standards. Disruptive or quantum technological shifts alter the dominant designs that are accepted in the marketplace, whereas sustaining or incremental advances in existing technology merely introduce improvements in its architecture or functionality. Scholars such as Clayton Christensen and Rebecca Henderson modeled this impact to show that emerging technology can displace whole industries such as vacuum tubes or traditional photography and that the leaders in an old technology, unless they reinvent themselves and adapt to the forces of change, likely fail to become leaders or even survive in the new context. Unfortunately, firms typically have many resources invested in the old technology to the extent that it is difficult for them to abandon historical areas of strength, and they are often less knowledgeable about newer technologies and lack the capability to learn how to use them. As a result, high-risk technologies may place an industry's viability in doubt. The Internet and digital imaging are recent examples of disruptive technologies that have revolutionized entire economic sectors as diverse as banking and finance, television, and publishing. In particular, information technology has changed the rules by which people communicate and collaborate, although the hoopla surrounding the paperless office has yet to be justified by any benefits that have materialized. Strategic alliances are a frequently used tool to mitigate technology-induced industry-level risk by providing firms with new sources of competitive advantage and access to emerging knowledge, technologies, and markets; however, alliances carry risks of their own. When organizations and institutions unnecessarily insulate themselves from outside information and technological advance, such as through the not-invented-here syndrome, this risk increases.

High-risk technology affects strategy and organizational competitiveness, for instance, in the cases of capabilities and requisite expertise. Technological innovations can be categorized according to how radical they are, or the degree of attempted advancement, where more radical innovation is relatively newer to the focal organization and represents a greater departure from existing practices. Strategically, it is more difficult to formulate and initiate radical change in the face of a major technological breakthrough. An organization's core competencies have been shown by Dorothy Leonard to act as core rigidities that work against the transformative process. Operationally it is more difficult to build a consensus for radical change because of the increased uncertainty and political instability. Internal transition is rarely smooth and almost always incurs resistance from employees who have been familiar, comfortable, and committed to the old way of doing things. As a result, high-risk technologies may place an organization's competitive position in doubt.

A separate danger of high-risk technology at the strategic level occurs when organizations act at the other extreme, radically overhauling their objectives and structures in too haphazard a manner. Because many organizations today are focused on quick growth and increasing profits, they have a natural tendency to be overambitious. This tendency can lead to disastrous results, particularly when ambition supersedes ability to the extent that the core organizational capabilities are outpaced and overextended, an outcome related to administrative risk.

At the administrative level, high-risk technology affects organizational knowledge in the cases of innovation, empowerment, and downsizing. Technological innovation introduces an internal source of uncertainty in an organization, necessitating structural and interpersonal governance mechanisms that absorb and manage the ensuing risk to organizations' knowledge and dynamics. Tom Burns and G. M. Stalker distinguished organic from traditional mode as the appropriate one to enable the creation and generation of new knowledge, which follows directly since a bureaucracy is coordinated on the basis of existing knowledge and technical requirements. More recent scholarship suggests that bureaucracies, if they are to survive and successfully leverage innovation, must be able to release creative activities and capture their inventions for integration into the larger system. This is an extremely complex and difficult process, as evidenced by the many failed attempts to manage this risk by implementing both value-based and administrative controls. As a result, high-risk technologies place administrative know-how in doubt.

Technology also presents high risk to an organization's administrative schema when it requires the diffusion of knowledge and decision-making power to increase employee involvement and commitment. This relates to the issue of empowerment, which is delegating decision making to the lowest level where a competent choice can be made. Empowerment necessitates the sharing of information and knowledge in order to ground people's decisions, the granting of authority to make these decisions, and the implementation of performance-based compensation systems to reward their decisions. When these principles are embraced, organizations can reap the advantages of a more committed, informed, proactive, and flexible workforce. However, many organizations have yet to realize the promise of empowerment because of faulty decision processes and remain vulnerable to risks of information overload, detached decision making, and poorly leveraged worker expertise.

Administrative risk is further perpetuated when technology outpaces existing organizational memory, resulting in increased exposure from a reduction in knowledge resources. An organization's memory is the stored information from its history that can be brought to bear on present decisions. As individuals share and integrate knowledge, the knowledge is stored in the organizational structure, systems, routines, and procedures. When individuals leave an organization, some of their knowledge also leaves, but, with sufficiently effective organizational memory, some also remains within the existing institutionalized practices of the firm. This is particularly true with tacit knowledge, which is difficult to codify and hard to articulate, so its memory is more sensitive to downsizing and turnover.

At the level of product, high-risk technology affects organizational revenue in the cases of profit windows and accelerated development paradigms. In general, there tends to be a positive bias for speed in technological development. The aura of being the first mover advantages pioneering and impels organizational efforts to accelerate technological development processes and produce what some might characterize as an obsession with speed. However, there are risks in pioneering new technologies, such as hidden costs, an increase in mistakes, heavy costs, and disruptions in workflow. Technological development speed should also be purposefully slower under certain conditions, such as when it affects the health and safety of users. In addition, rushing big projects is especially risky because they are often based on new, less familiar areas of technical expertise and, as Eric Kessler and Paul Bierly showed, it is often less advantageous to go fast if you can't see clearly and could be going the wrong way. As a result, high-risk technologies may place product success in doubt.

Product risk is further increased when there are poor feedback and communication systems. There are several guidelines for feedback that should be practiced in technology development. It should be continuous, it must be accurate and passed on to all key people, and it must build cumulatively to enhance learning in an integrated problem-solving process. Moreover, for successful technical development, an effective communication system must be implemented across vertical and horizontal levels as well as divisions and job descriptions. The use of cross-functional teams and concurrent practices to manage new technology is geared toward reducing this type of risk, although frequently they are misused or ill-implemented and actually increase associated risks to product and process success.

Technological risks to profitable organizational products and processes also include cost overruns and poor quality. Intensifying competition and increasingly turbulent environments with shorter product life cycles are forcing firms to improve the efficiency of their technological development activities. At the same time, the costs associated with new product innovation are rising steadily. Together, these forces are pushing firms to become more efficient in new product development by leveraging resources and reducing the risk exposure of single projects. For example, techniques to manage development costs are often employed under the rubrics of downsizing, total quality management, and reengineering. Moreover, with the modern business environment increasingly characterized by demanding customers, crowded markets, and intense competition, quality is even more important. Although technical quality is multifaceted, it can be defined as the degree to which a product's performance, attributes, or features satisfy customer requirements. This definition of quality can be traced back to management-philosophers W. Edwards Deming and Joseph Juran, who espoused a view that quality is derived from a product's "fitness for use." Just because a product is more technically elegant or high-powered does not mean that it is more successful in satisfying user needs, and thus technologies are high-risk when they aim at unclear, uncertain, or ill-established goals.

At the level of the individual, high-risk technology affects organizational jobs, for instance, in the cases of championing and downsizing. First, the process of introducing new technology to an organization is risky in and of itself. Alok Chakrabarti found that technology or product champions, who are typically highly committed and persistent individuals, take significant risks in that they demonstrate a willingness to sacrifice their positions and prestige. This notion is consistent with the classic yet seemingly timeless message that new ideas often encounter sharp resistance and that overcoming this resistance requires vigorous promotion. Second, the successful introduction of new technology often results in job loss on a broader scale. This is due to automation of work and the devaluation and displacement of human labor, technology trajectory advances and skill obsolescence, and market shifts and downsizing. As a result, high-risk technologies may place individual careers in doubt.

Critical Commentary and Future Directions

Among emerging technologies today, perhaps none represents a greater organizational risk than nanotechnology. Many predict that developments in the nanosciences or nanotechnology will be at the forefront of a new paradigm shift rivaling that of the computer or Internet. Nanotechnology is the ability to manipulate materials on the atomic and molecular level, changing their properties and creating new structures, devices, materials, and systems. The National Science Foundation estimates that this technological revolution could attain a market size of $1 to $2 trillion in the next several years. Therefore, whole industries and markets, organizations and strategies, administrative systems and knowledge resources, products and manufacturing processes, and individual jobs are all at risk. Nanotechnology also introduces risks to society at large. Scientists have warned of the ability of nanomachines to clone themselves or self-replicate. The *gray goo* scenario is the nightmare possibility of creating little machines—nanobots—that become uncontrollable, have a mind of their own, and can reproduce without restraint. Nanobots could also be used to replace human beings in many functions, such as medical sensors, drug delivery vehicles, and programmable machines. The normal accidents theory as well as the common law of unintended consequences—and as the concepts have been popularized in movies such as *The Terminator* and *The Matrix*—remind us that with high-risk technology something that can go wrong often does so. These and related concerns will force leaders to consider fundamental ethical questions, such as how far developments in high-risk technology should be taken.

There is also a technical but critically important process distinction that needs to be made, that being the conceptualization of technology risk versus technology uncertainty. New technologies more often than not bring uncertainty rather than risk. With risk, the probability distributions and the odds of success or failure are known. With uncertainty, the odds are indeterminate and, as in forecasting the weather, involves complex analyses of dynamic phenomena with a broad array of interdependent variables. Therefore, the more significant dangers lie not in high-risk technologies per se so much as in highly uncertain ones. Perhaps the greatest peril is not in what we can imagine going wrong but in what we simply cannot forecast.

Another important consideration is the definition of the success being subject to probabilistic risk calculations. As in agency theory, who is defining success and in what terms it is being defined must be considered. Success for power holders and control (as in George Orwell's fiction)? Success for stockholders and profitability? Success for workers and jobs? Success for society and life quality? These standards are often in conflict and therefore the political nature of risk must be considered. This recalls Eric Trist's arguments for joint optimization of the technological and human dimensions of organizations. Furthermore, adding to the descriptive consideration of high-risk technology, there is also a practical issue of interventions to reduce or manage the risk. This relates to the issue of what can and should be done, and at what level, to mitigate the risks of technology. Related discourses include societal regulation, industry standards, organizational strategy and ethics, administrative agency, innovation and technological process institutionalization, and individual decision making and motivation.

Then there is the deeper matter about the balance between the promise and the peril of high-risk technologies. This brings up the question of technological advance and its overall impact on humankind and society. Some might advocate a simpler, elementary approach to technology, as Thoreau did, whereas others would have us push outside of the envelope and embrace rapid, cutting-edge advancements that constantly transform how we live and interact. At the core is the issue of whether technology makes people happier, and research here is mixed. There is also a related reflection on the rationale for the very existence of organizations. Organizations are social constructions that, in theory, do more good than harm. If technological risks and rewards cannot be balanced, it calls into question the legitimacy of an organizational charter, as in the case of Enron and Chernobyl.

Finally, a proper discussion of high-risk technology leads the higher-order issue of knowledge versus wisdom. This gets at the fundamental differences between science and art, machine and man, and technology and humanity and gives rise to the realization that there is something greater than technological know-how. In the same sense that information transcends data and knowledge transcends information, wisdom represents the synthesis of technological potential with higher-order visioning and prudent judgment. In a way reminiscent of Albert Einstein's reconciliation of the scientific and spiritual, technology is concerned with what can be done, whereas wisdom also considers what should be done. The exponential advance of technological sophistication, the spotlight cast on ethical behavior and corporate social responsibility, the strategic complexity introduced by growing global integration, and rapidly developing product and service innovation across a broad array of industries have cast traditional models into question and call for new perspectives and approaches to the behavior within as well as the stewardship of organizations. Indeed, there is more and more evidence that success does not go necessarily to the organizations that have the best technology but to the firms that can make the best use of what they know. Therefore, as Eric Kessler and James Bailey point out, wisdom becomes increasingly important at balancing the promise and peril of high-risk technology and addressing the question of "should we?" as well as "can we?"

—*Eric H. Kessler*

See also Empowerment; Innovation; Risk Management; Technology; Uncertainty

Further Readings

Christensen, C. M. (1997). *The innovator's dilemma.* Boston: Harvard Business School Press.

Kessler, E. H., & Bailey, J. R. (2007). *Handbook of organizational and managerial wisdom.* Thousand Oaks, CA: Sage.

March, J. G., & Shapira, Z. (1987). Managerial perspectives on risk and risk taking. *Management Science, 33*(11), 1404–1418.

Perrow, C. (1999). *Normal accidents: Living with high risk technologies.* Princeton, NJ: Princeton University Press.

Trist, E. L. (1981). The socio-technical perspective. In A. Van de Ven and W. F. Joyce (Eds.), *Perspectives on organizational design and behavior.* New York: Wiley.

Tushman, M. L., & Anderson, P. (1986). Technological discontinuities and organizational environments. *Administrative Science Quarterly, 31,* 439–465.

Historical Analysis of Organization Theory

Max Weber's work in 1947 was initially influential in shaping the sociological analysis of organizations. It offered a unifying frame—the theory of bureaucracy—within which to research organizational processes and, unlike early management theory, did not offer prescriptive and self-contradictory principles. Weber focused on key features of an organization based on technical rationality hierarchy, written rules of conduct, promotion based on achievement, and a division of labor.

Conceptual Overview

Typically, researchers first started to interpret organizations using Weber's ideas, which they then revised as they attended to features of reality that were not captured in his model, producing an influential body of postwar work. Until the mid-1950s, the case study was the dominant method of research and Weber a central resource. These were based on substantive aspects of specific cases and thus their generalizability was low and hard to cumulate into a consistent body of interrelated theoretical knowledge.

In the 1950s, after the emergence of the journal *Administrative Science Quarterly,* the systems perspective came increasingly to dominate organization analysis. The perspective solved some problems inherent to the typological approaches. Systems approaches, modeled on the work of Talcott Parsons, promised a general approach to any organization conceived as a system of inputs, transformation processes, and outputs. General systems theory was scientifically influential, and organizations became a specialized domain of its analysis.

Emerging out of systems theory in the 1960s was the approach known as contingency theory. Organizations were still seen as systems, but organizations had to deal with contingencies that shaped their structure, such as their size, the key variable of the Aston School, led by Derek Pugh and David Hickson; technology, which was what Joan Woodward focused on; and environment, the variable that Tom Burns and George M. Stalker highlighted in 1962. Later, the idea of there being a national culture in which organizations were embedded was developed by Geert Hofstede in 1980 into a general theory of national culture as a contingency. While the earlier generation of researchers used case studies, contingency research was characterized by survey methods and larger samples, seeking to operationalize factors identified in the earlier literature, such as Weber's 15 dimensions of bureaucracy.

Population ecology was introduced by Michael T. Hannan and John Freeman in 1977, an approach that was influenced by general ecological theory, concentrating on populations of organizations and changes at the population level, typically dealing with big changes over large data sets, across significant periods of time, often using data sets that were not generated by the researchers themselves but that were already available or readily constructed. The approach was based more on the statistical testing of relations between constructs than upon intimate research knowledge. It was a sociological approach premised on biological models but one whose peak of influence seems to have passed.

From the 1970s onward, a number of new currents emerged. First, the influence of Harry Braverman's labor process approach, which he introduced in 1974, spawned a renewed fascination with case studies, such as the 1979 work of Michael Burawoy, and a series of multi-author monographs that represented the work of the labor process conference, held annually from 1983 onward, were produced. The labor process movement split into critical management studies (CMS) in the 1990s. It developed a broader, but usually oppositional and unconventional, perspective on organizations. Second, from the early 1980s onward, there was a renewed interest in Weberian theory, as a result of two related trends. One was the reemergence of institutional theory, after the seminal publication of Paul DiMaggio and Walter Powell's paper on the "iron cage"; the other was the popular success of George Ritzer's Weberian-inspired analysis of organizational rationalization as *The McDonaldization of Society.* There are some signs of synergies emerging between such approaches and CMS. More recently, since the 1990s, the influence of Foucauldian-inspired genealogical analysis has begun to make an impact on the field, perhaps best represented in the volume edited by Alan

McKinley and Ken Starkey in 1997. Closely related, but hotly contested, are more postmodern approaches, debates about which were collected by Ed Locke in 2003.

Critical Commentary and Future Directions

Increasingly, organization theory should be seen as a historical science, organized as a narrative structure in which proximate and ultimate causes can be identified. Its objects of inquiry do not constitute stable eternal forms but dynamic tendencies that play out in a highly competitive and political world, the outcomes of which is very difficult to predict. The fallacy of prediction as the hallmark of *all* science would be better abandoned in organization theory; instead the specificity of the historical sciences should be recognized. The appropriate explanation for historical science is a posteriori, explaining how it is possible that what is taken to have happened might have happened. This means sorting out an enormous number of variables, great complexity, unique actors, with no possibility of artful laboratory closure. Thus, the organization scientist has to adopt different strategies from that of covariation. The first injunction should be to respect the natural scene. That is, take seriously the lived experience and understanding of the action scenes that the participants make. Don't just go on a smash-and-grab raid with a questionnaire that might make sense to the researcher but not necessarily to the researched. Research is not just reportage: Theorize the data; don't just describe it. Be theoretically informed even when being descriptive. Hear the stories: People organize their lives through narratives, and research should adopt a narrative structure. Be reflexive: Always remember that you are the author of the fragments that these others author. There is unlikely ever to be a definitive account. The narrative is more likely to be a carefully crafted novel exposing different actors' perspectives on what might initially have been seen as the same scene but a scene in which the security of its definitive history slowly dissolves.

There is one great advantage when researching socially constructed phenomena, provided researchers are able to translate the language in use, researchers are able to interpret the understandings that the subjects have of themselves and the phenomena that they find salient. Ultimately, researchers can seek to understand interpretively the stories that people construct to explain reality for themselves. (While this is easier if researchers are able to be present and ask directly, historical traces can also yield great returns.) Essentially, the human condition is a narrative condition open to understanding, a work in progress paused to create spaces for interrogation, inquiry, and conversation. In the future, organization theory should strive to become a significant part of the conversation, rather than a narrow technical aping of covariation.

Scientific theories that are interesting draw inferences from many subject matters; for instance, in organization studies one might draw inferences from discourse analysis, business histories, ethnographic studies, and cross-sectional survey data. At present, these theories tend to be representationally embedded in each of these different forms of activity; in each one are assumptions that both predetermine the results of inquiry before data are collected and make assumptions that circumscribe what is to count as data, two obstacles to building scientific knowledge. For instance, in discourse theory using methods derived, say, from conversational analysis, the analysts will concentrate on discursively available and recordable data: That which is not discursively available—or is discursively available but for reasons of context is not recordable—will not feature. Contingency theorists using tried and tested instruments to collect their data already subscribe to a specific ontology of organizations before they cross any organization's threshold: The size of the organization is a function of its employment contracts. They may not know the outcome of any data-specific act of collection—but what data collection will occur is already prefigured by the assumptions that have been constituted in its instruments. It is therefore becoming increasingly evident that researchers need to draw on the rich pluralities available in organization studies to review reflexively the methods they choose and what they imply, by which we mean not so much an engagement with the confirmation of deductive logic, but an engagement that questions its auspices through reflections on those of other methods, approaches, and assumptions.

Research in the social sciences, such as organization theory, has to rely on the study of particular cases. Researchers need to approach these cases with a skeptical attitude to the strict object-subject divisions that have riddled conventional accounts of science. This division only admits two solutions: Objects determine what subjects objectively should think and the trick is to unravel nature's message; or subjects determine the nature of objects through intersubjective agreement. The subject-object split is a mistake: Objects only exist inasmuch as subjects perceive them to be, a perception that describes and categorizes them as being what they are taken to be. Organizations do not exist apart from people; how members articulate their experience of them through their own metaphors and categories is then translated through the filter of additional metaphors and categories that organization theorists use to make sense of their studies.

Methodological assumptions are inescapable, but they do not have to be hermetically sealed. To the extent that the metaphors and categories that researchers use fail to connect with the embodied experiences of those in organizations, they will lack realistic content. And of course, as complex stratified entities, there is a plurality of experiences with which to connect—or not connect. The broader these interactions are ethnographically and the deeper they are historically the more reflexive they will be. Reflexivity thus points to the limits of inquiry and pervades all concerns with theory, epistemology, methodology, and ontology, all of which are always bound up with any and every instance of practical research.

—*Stewart R. Clegg*

See also Critical Management Studies; Formal Organizations; Institutional Theory; McDonaldization; Narratives; Organizational Ecology

Further Readings

Bertalanffy, I. V. (1975). *Perspectives on general system theory: Scientific-philosophical studies.* (Edgar Taschdjian, Ed.). New York: Braziller.
Braverman, H. (1974). *Labor and monopoly capital.* New York: Monthly Review Press.
Burawoy, M. (1979). *Manufacturing consent: Changes in the labor process under monopoly capitalism.* Chicago: University of Chicago Press.
Burns, T., & Stalker, G. M. (1961). *The management of innovation.* London: Tavistock.
Clegg, S. R., Kornberger, M., & Pitsis, T. (2005). *Managing and organizations: An introduction to theory and practice.* London: Sage.
DiMaggio, P., & Powell, W. W. (1983). The iron cage revisited: Institutional isomorphism and collective rationality in organizational fields. *American Journal of Sociology, 48,* 147–160.
Hannan, M. T., & Freeman, J. (1977). The population ecology of organizations. *American Journal of Sociology, 82*(5), 929–940.
Hofstede, G. (1980). *Culture's consequences: International differences in work-related values.* London: Sage.
Knights, D., & Willmott, H. (Eds.). (1990). *Labour process theory.* London: Macmillan.
Locke, E. (Ed.). (2003). *Postmodernism in organizational thought: Pros, cons, and the alternative.* Amsterdam, Neth.: Elsevier.
McKinley, A., & Starkey, K. (1997). *Foucault, management, and organization theory: From panopticon to technologies of self.* London: Sage.
Parsons, T. (1951). *The social system.* London: Routledge & Kegan Paul.
Pugh, D. S., & Hickson, D. J. (1976). *Organizational structure in its context: The Aston Programme 1.* London: Saxon House.
Ritzer, G. (1993). *The McDonaldization of society.* Newbury Park, CA: Pine Forge Press.
Weber, M. (1947). *The theory of social and economic organization.* (T. Parsons & A. M. Henderson, Trans.). New York: Free Press.
Weber, M. (1978). *Economy and society: An outline of interpretative sociology.* Berkeley: University of California Press.
Williamson, O. E. (1985). *The economic institutions of capitalism: Firms, markets, relational contracting.* New York: Free Press.
Woodward, J. (1965). *Industrial organizations: Theory and practice.* London: Oxford University Press.

HUMAN-COMPUTER INTERACTION

Human-computer interaction is the study of the human factors associated with technology design, implementation, and use. While human-computer interaction has become a research subfield in the computer science and psychology disciplines, it has also emerged as a developing research agenda in organizational studies. In the last 20 years, a technological revolution has transformed the workplace and has produced rich contexts for examining human-computer interaction phenomena, including task design, service delivery, the Internet, and various communication platforms. The reliance on technology in the modern organization presents a unique opportunity for students and scholars alike to study computer information systems and related technological advances through a humanistic lens.

Conceptual Overview

Since the early days of Frederick Taylor and scientific management, technology's role in improving business processes has exponentially grown in both influence and quality with the advancements of the microcomputer, the Internet, and wireless technologies. While still considering the scientific aspects of technology development and delivery as a primary area of study, in the late 1960s researchers and practitioners began to acknowledge that the human factor could no longer be ignored. As Jonathan Grudin noted in a 2005 review of the field, there was a marked shift in examining the support systems for operations and management functions from solely a technical or engineering perspective to a more multidisciplinary focus on the organizational and human consequences of such technology.

Furthermore, John and Clare-Marie Karat noted in 2003 that since the first academic and industry conference devoted to human factors occurred in 1982, the human-computer interaction field has developed a broader net of topics and social settings that represent the multidisciplinary nature of studying the interaction between humans and computers. Among the numerous research streams devoted to human-computer interaction over the years, user-centered design and user acceptance have become central themes examined in organizational settings.

User-Centered Design

As the personal computer replaced the typewriter and no longer was a privileged tool for engineers and scientists, computer designers recognized that improving the human experience for all users should be a central theme in research and development. The concept of user-centered design in human-computer interaction refers to the extent to which the technology, including hardware and software, enables users to successfully complete their tasks. This involves both the interface and interaction aspects of design. First, with regard to interface design, software and Web site developers pay close attention to visual factors such as color, spatial display of objects, and text layout, as noted by Patricia Chalmers in her 2003 examination of interface design issues in human-computer interaction.

One of the most influential communication tools for organizations in recent years has been e-mail technology. Current research suggests that the design of e-mail software, and more specifically the way in which information is displayed, can have a positive effect on the usability and maneuverability within the e-mail program. Dov Te'eni and Zohar Sani-Kuperberg, in a 2005 empirical examination of e-mail software design, found that using levels of abstraction offers an alternative way for users to process information and provide greater discretion when reading e-mails. Using the level of abstraction is a strategy for presenting e-mails with various degrees of information specificity based on issues and topics identified in the e-mail by the software. Users essentially decide which information in the e-mail is most important to them and view the desired selection. Using a folding and unfolding communication structure that users can click to hide or show information, the initial level provides the most basic information, with the each level providing incrementally more detail on the topic. Te'eni and Sani-Kuperberg's innovative experiment with altering e-mail program design yielded relevant findings for usability concerns in human-computer interaction. The results indicate that using a level-of-abstraction design may provide ease of use and practicality for users who wish to choose which aspects of the e-mail to focus on more than others.

As Chalmers suggests, there is great benefit of incorporating the above-mentioned design considerations to ensure usability, learning, and accessibility. For example, timely task completion is more likely to result from the greater efficiencies of the information-processing characteristics of the design. Although the topic of user interface has been widely found to influence the user experience, Karat has argued that the research has begun to move beyond style alone and examine the actual interaction between the user and technology. An important issue is how the interaction itself satisfies the users' needs, including those design issues related to productivity. More specifically, researchers often question how interaction with the software or hardware affects users' task behavior.

A recent study sought to answer this question of technology usefulness and its related productivity implications (i.e., efficiency and quality control). In 2004, Jennifer Ockerman and Amy Pritchett investigated user interactions with task guidance systems in the context of conducting pilot preflight safety procedures. The task guidance hardware employed in this study was equipped with software that outlined specific procedural steps, connected with other devices (e.g., computers), and allowed for communication with other users. The researchers also incorporated location procedure context into the software design. This feature allowed users to clarify their location in the process of conducting preflight safety procedures. Essentially, the users can assess a current step in the process, such as checking fuel status or engine controls, and examine it in reference to previous or following actions and can engage in troubleshooting with the current action rather than using a general help function. In addition, the software provided a monitoring feature that reminded users of certain steps or any mistakes made during the safety procedure. The study revealed that the real-time assessment of their task using location procedure context provided greater engagement with the airplane in the form of more touches by pilots. This interaction with the location procedure context design and task guidance hardware prevented the pilots from losing focus or inadvertently skipping steps. The user-centered design presented in this study highlights the practical benefits of exploring the interaction between human and computer. In this case, the software had positive implications for user behavior and the quality of task completion.

User Acceptance

In line with the design considerations associated with technology use, the study of human-computer interaction is also concerned with the degree to which users accept the rapidly changing technology systems in today's workplace. User acceptance is important to designers, systems management, and those interested in task productivity. Resisting the technology advancements, and in many cases the change in the way work is conducted, can indicate to decision makers that alterations in design may not be the only area to address. Focusing on the individual and organizational factors associated with user interaction with technology, researchers in organization studies have found that acceptance and underlying usage intentions often relate to three factors: (1) inhibiting beliefs about the system and use, (2) user demographics, and (3) the involvement of both user and human resources managers in the development and implementation of technology products introduced specifically for work purposes.

Incorporating advancements in both software and hardware can be a costly investment for organizations interested in increasing performance and managing customer or citizen needs. Therefore, it is crucial to recognize the value in understanding what barriers exist that may inhibit user acceptance. In a 2004 field study, Ronald Cenfetelli examined what usage inhibitors exist and how such beliefs influence behavioral intentions. Using travel Web sites as the setting for the study, Cenfetelli discovered, for example, that users considered the quality of the system to be a significant factor inhibiting intentions to use the Web site. The system often required users to engage in redundant steps such as entering address information on more than one occasion. Another inhibitor was that users found the system requested information unrelated to the task at hand and often interrupted the user by offering unnecessary assistance with otherwise seemingly simple tasks. These findings indicate the adverse effects poorly designed systems can have and their negative impact on user attitudes toward technology.

The composition of the workforce and the demographic characteristics of those being served by the organization can also influence technology acceptance. Differences in age, as an example, may relate to the difference between those who accept and those who struggle with new technologies. Multidisciplinary research in cognitive psychology and computer science has found that the level of experienced anxiety is associated with age differences. In a 1997 study, Kerrie Laguna and Renée Babcock discovered that computer anxiety, which is a feeling of nervousness and apprehension about a specific digital device, is often greater for older users than for their younger counterparts. This is frequently linked to user confidence, exposure, and experience with computer technology. The study also found that anxiety had a negative effect on the time it takes to perform a task but did not influence the accuracy of completing tasks. For organizations that manage an age-diverse workforce, this research suggests that users asked to conduct time-sensitive tasks on a computer should be provided more training and sufficient time to complete the desired workload. Without considering the demographic differences of their consumers or employees, organizations may be faced with users who have a difficult time adjusting to any changes in software and hardware technologies.

Furthermore, human-computer interaction researchers have found that a strategy for encouraging user acceptance is to broaden the scope of involvement by both users and human resources professionals inside the organization. Inviting users' thoughts, concerns, and apprehensions with the technology during the production and implementation phases may provide users with a sense of ownership and satisfaction with the new systems, as Jane Carey noted in 1988. However, information technology staff alone cannot assure that users' needs will be effectively satisfied by allowing them to participate in the phases of development and during implementation. Maris Martinsons and Patrick Chong, in a series of case studies conducted in 1999, found that human resources managers are in an ideal position to buffer between the users and information technology staff. They argue that human resources managers are more in tune with direct issues with the technology and consequences of implementation. For example, users may be uncertain about the technology's effects on job security, adequacy of skills, and existing norms and values for work behavior (e.g., ingrained expectations on how to conduct certain tasks), to name a few. From the case studies, they found that the presence of human resources eased user concerns and raised awareness of the benefits of the new technology. Through training, communicating user needs in the product development phase and in follow-up assessments with users and technology staff, human resources managers had a positive impact on user acceptance and the overall assimilation of the new technology into the organization.

Critical Commentary and Future Directions

While there is an agreed-upon definition of human-computer interaction, there seems to be less consensus on the range of topics that encompass this field of study. Scholars such as Ping Zhang and Na Li, in their recent systematic review of the literature in 2004, have been critical of the limited focus on design and usability in much of the current research. They propose that future human-computer interaction research should also consider what has been learned from both the use and the impact of that technology in various social settings. Among the topics in need of greater attention are the antecedents to user acceptance, such as the emotional, less rational side of technology, and which workplace contexts are both timely and relevant for employees, managers, and information technology professionals. While this is not an exhaustive list of topics by any means, these examples point to the opportunities available for further human-computer interaction research in organizational studies.

Research on user-centered design and user acceptance has shown that affective-related phenomena, including anxiety, satisfaction, and attitudes, are central to understanding the human side of technology. However, as many researchers conclude, including Zhang and Li, attention must also be given to those factors underlying those affective experiences, mainly the existence of specific emotions. Users' interpretations of their interaction with technologies often lead to certain emotional responses, including fear, frustration, anger, joy, and even pride. The impact of that technology on user emotions is an important area of inquiry, especially since emotions are often correlates with satisfaction and indictors for certain behavioral responses.

For example, Cenfetelli and Izak Benbasat, in their 2003 study of online services, found that users often felt frustrated and displeased with their online shopping experiences. The frustration and displeasure correlated to a number of inhibitors associated with the Internet technology, including system unresponsive and a burdensome design that made it difficult to shop. The intolerance for such inhibitors led users to search out other Web sites or shopping options as a way to cope with their negative emotional interaction with the technology. This and other studies on emotions and technology point to the added value of gaining a deeper appreciation for user emotions, which contribute to stress, anxiety, and levels of satisfaction tied to technology use. More research is needed to examine the emotional effects of specific technology and how those feelings contribute to behavioral responses.

The study of human-computer interaction, regardless of the research focus, cannot happen solely within a vacuum or laboratory devoid of context. Much of the meaning associated with user interactions with technology are tied to the unique aspects of that experience. In a time when private and public organizations are capitalizing on various technologies to compete in the marketplace or to ensure quality service provision to the citizenry, numerous contexts for the study of human-computer interaction are available to researchers. For example, a current dilemma facing organizations is the use of electronic monitoring, which is often used to observe task performance and Internet usage. While there are obvious benefits to observing employee activities, such as ensuring quality customer service or addressing demands for information and network security, there are concerns that users may interpret that monitoring as a sign of distrust. How can the monitoring be designed to balance concerns of both the employer and the employees? How do users respond to instances of being monitored; what behaviors do they exhibit? These are just a few research questions that may be addressed.

Another related organizational context for researchers to consider is the growing use of the Internet at work for personal reasons. As some in organization studies have suggested, when using the Internet for personal benefit, called personal Web usage by Pruthikrai Mahatanankoon and colleagues in 2004 and cyberloafing by Vivien Lim in 2002, there is considerable threat to information security, in addition to placing the legal and fiduciary interests of the organization at risk. Current industry studies indicate that insider abuse of the Internet is on the rise. For example, a study by the Computer Security Institute and Federal Bureau of Investigation in 2005 found a 3% increase, from 53% to 56%, in organizations reporting unauthorized use of the Internet by employees since 2004. Researchers have begun to examine this aspect of human-computer interaction, but questions still remain. For instance, what are the benefits of personal Web use for employees; are there benefits to the employer? Does electronic monitoring successfully combat this behavior? Are there productivity implications from this new form of shirking in the workplace? Last, do differences in work environment, such as telecommuting versus traditional workspaces and the type of employment sector (i.e., public, private, or nonprofit), influence the frequency or variety of personal Web use?

For future research in human-computer interaction to continue its contribution to the field of organization studies, with both practical and theoretical relevance, a broader approach to issues and contexts will be required. Evaluating the complexities inherent in the interaction between technology and user will not only ensure a better understanding of design and implementation but also guide managers in preparing a diverse workforce for the technological changes of the future.

—*Micheal T. Stratton*

See also Computer-Based Learning; Computer-Mediated Communication; Information and Communication Technology; Organizational Change; Technology

Further Readings

Carey, J. M. (Ed.). (1988). *Human factors in management information systems.* Norwood, NJ: Ablex.

Cenfetelli, R. T. (2004). An empirical study of the inhibitors of technology use. *Proceedings of the Twenty-fifth International Conference of Information Systems,* 157–170.

Cenfetelli, R. T., & Benbasat, I. (2003). *Frustrated incorporated: An exploration of the inhibitors of IT-mediated customer service*. Paper presented at the ninth Annual Conference on Information Systems, Tampa, FL.

Chalmers, P. A. (2003). The role of cognitive theory in human-computer interaction. *Computers in Human Behavior, 19*(5), 593–607.

Dillon, A. (2001). Beyond usability: Process, outcome, and affect in human computer interactions. *Canadian Journal of Information and Library Sciences, 26*(4), 57–69.

Gordan, L. A., Loeb, M. P., Lucyshyn, W., & Richardson, R. (2005). *CSI-FBI computer crime and security survey.* Retrieved from www.gocsi.com

Grudin, J. (2005). Three faces of human-computer interaction. *IEEE Annals of the History of Computing, 27*(4), 46–62.

Karat, J., & Karat, C. M. (2003). The evolution of user-centered focus in the human-computer interaction field. *IBM Systems Journal, 42*(4), 532–541.

Laguna, K., & Babcock, R. L. (1997). Computer anxiety in young and older adults: Implications for human-computer interactions in older populations. *Computers in Human Behavior, 13*(3), 317–326.

Lim, V. K. (2002). The IT way of loafing on the job: Cyberloafing, neutralizing, and organizational justice. *Journal of Organizational Behavior, 23*, 675–694.

Mahatanankoon, P., Anandarajan, M., & Igbaria, M. (2004). Development of a measure of personal Web usage in the workplace. *CyberPsychology & Behavior, 7*(1), 93–107.

Martinsons, M. G., & Chong, P. K. C. (1999). The influence of human factors and specialist involvement on information systems success. *Human Relations, 52*(1), 123–151.

Ockerman, J. J., & Pritchett, A. R. (2004). Improving performance on procedural task through presentation of locational procedure context: An empirical evaluation. *Behavior & Information Technology, 23*(1), 11–20.

Te'eni, D., & Sani-Kuperberg, Z. (2005). Levels of abstraction in designs of human-computer interaction: The case of email. *Computers in Human Behavior, 21*(5), 817–830.

Zhang, P., & Li, N. (2004). An assessment of human-computer interaction research in management information systems: Topics and methods. *Computers in Human Behavior, 20*(2), 125–147.

HUMAN ENGINEERING

Human engineering is a field of study that aims to adapt work to human beings. Two objectives are usually associated with human engineering interventions: improvements in performance (e.g., efficiency, quality, efficacy) and the safeguarding of human values (e.g., safety, health, comfort, well-being). Human engineering is a multidisciplinary endeavor with influences from engineering, technology, medicine, and psychology, among others. That enriched and diversified background is generally associated with human engineering's broad range of interventions.

Conceptual Overview

Like other disciplines that have considered human performance at the workplace, the purpose of human engineering is to improve work systems by accommodating human characteristics, skills, and limitations. Human engineering evaluates and designs equipment, machines, jobs, products, environments, and systems in order to make them compatible with human needs, capabilities, and restrictions. Two main challenges emerge when trying to define human engineering: the term or name of the discipline and its definition. A variety of names have been used to refer to it: Human factors, ergonomics, human factors and ergonomics, human factors engineering, human engineering, and engineering psychology can all be found in the literature. Some authors use these terms as synonymous, while others associate the various names with different areas of study within the same field. Several factors can be identified, and have been, when explaining such a diversity of denominations. Concerns for human interaction with work systems can be traced to two distinct traditions: the Anglo-Saxon approach and those of Continental Europe. In the United States, a strong psychological influence can be identified very early, while in Europe only recently (e.g., 1980s) have experimental psychologists been involved with human engineering issues. The variety of denominations is also associated with the scope of the work developed. One way of presenting the areas of study in human engineering is to start with the definition of *engineering*: the practical application of scientific knowledge in the design, building, and control of machines, roads, bridges, and so forth. Human engineering considers human characteristics in this practical application, and therefore three areas may be considered: physical characteristics, cognitive specificities, and social or organizational issues. An emphasis on human physical capacities and limitations is usually associated with a focus on human-machine interaction, a perspective that highlights anthropometric and biomechanical issues as well as physiological processes (e.g., physical dimensions and movements of the human body, circadian rhythms). An emphasis on human cognitive characteristics is related to the study of human information processing (e.g., perception, analysis and decision making, learning processes, error analysis). Adapting work to human beings with a social emphasis involves the various forms of social organization one may find in work systems (e.g., group processes, leadership and supervision, communication, organizational structures and processes).

Critical Commentary and Future Directions

Today, human engineering faces two major challenges: a societal recognition of the science and the continual development of work systems. Although society recognizes the importance of the applied work developed by human engineering, difficulties still arise when trying to describe the field of study. In many instances, the multidisciplinary nature of the applied studies is viewed as evidence of a specific methodology and not as support for the uniqueness of the science. On the other hand, the development of human engineering is associated with its own applied nature, that is to say, the different areas of work are related with the emergence of technical developments or the use of integrative and multidisciplinary approaches to practical problems. Somehow, the bottom-up nature of human engineering has promoted the emergence of independent areas of work. By studying human physical characteristics, improvements can be achieved when designing equipments and machines (e.g., displays adapted to human perception processes and commands adjusted to human response), human physical comfort and well-being may be enhanced (e.g., adequate temperature and noise level at the workplace), and more adequate work schedules may be defined (e.g., work-rest cycles embedded in work schedules). An emphasis on human cognitive characteristics highlights the aptitudes, skills, and knowledge of work performance, complex psychological processes such as learning or mental models, and the important psychological consequences that may result from work performance, such as human errors and accidents, stress, satisfaction, and motivation, among others. Human social features are associated with interpersonal contacts developed at work, the shared nature of the tasks and jobs executed, the structure of the organization (e.g., work groups, organizational structure and power relations, participation in decision making), and the way work is organized (e.g., work methods, operational procedures, goal setting, work incentives).

Future developments in human engineering have, therefore, to balance these conflicting pressures favoring specialization and scientific integration for a more coherent scientific field and constructive applications to work systems. An example of such an endeavor may be found in Wilson-Donnelly, Priest, Salas, and Burke, who contend that traditional approaches like macroergonomics (top-bottom perspective) and microergonomics (bottom-up) must incorporate a third point of view, a middle-out perspective that focuses on optimizing human interfaces in an organizational setting, thus involving both micro and macro approaches.

—*Teresa C. D'Oliveira*

See also Ergonomics

Further Readings

Alcocer de la Hera, C. M., Martínez Iñigo, D., Rodríguez Mazo, F., & Domínguez Bilbao, R. (2004). *Introducción a la psicología del trabajo.* Madrid, Spain: McGraw-Hill.

Cañas Delgado, J. J. (2004). *Personas y máquinas: El diseño de su interacción desde la ergonomia cognitiva.* Madrid, Spain: Pirámide.

Dempsey, P. G., Wogalter, M. S., & Hancock, P. A. (2000). What's in a name? Using terms from definitions to examine the fundamental foundation of human factors and ergonomics science. *Theoretical Issues in Ergonomics Science, 1,* 3–10.

Herlander, M. G. (1997). The human factors profession. In G. Salvendy (Ed.), *Handbook of human factors and ergonomics* (2nd ed.). New York: Wiley.

Oxford advanced learner's dictionary (5th ed.) (1995). Oxford, UK: Oxford University Press.

Sanders, M. S., & McCormick, E. J. (1992). *Human factors in engineering and design* (7th ed.). London: McGraw-Hill.

Wickens, C. D. (1992). *Engineering psychology and human performance* (2nd ed.). New York: HarperCollins.

Wilson-Donnelly, K. A., Priest, H. A., Salas, E., & Burke, C. S. (2005). The impact of organizational practices on safety in manufacturing: A review and reappraisal. *Human Factors and Ergonomics in Manufacturing, 15*(2), 135–176.

Humanism

The term *humanism* implies a concern for the human and asserts the central importance of the human both as that which should be supported by our interests and activities and as that which provides the means to understand and further such interests. Humanism's central tenets are most pithily captured by the phrase *man is the measure of all things,* a quote often erroneously attributed to Leonardo da Vinci, the archetypical Renaissance man. More accurately, this quote can be attributed to the ancient Greek philosopher Protagoras, a somewhat villainous character in the texts of Plato because of his sophistry and its potential for relativism. As with other terms, *humanism* derives more meaning from what it opposes than from what it is. In other words, humanism is focused in opposition to overweening theisms and naturalisms that would seek to remove distinctive interests and means from humans and attribute them to one or more gods or to nature. In humanism's battle with these other isms, humanism has been particularly successful in the Western world. In fact, humanism has been so successful at this that its discourse organizes much of how we Westerners think about ourselves, our institutions, and our practices in the contemporary world. Further, humanism has become so successful that it has become a central strand of our common sense.

Conceptual Overview

Opinions about the emergence and meaning of the term *humanism* and about when and why it should be relied upon versus when, how, and why it should be qualified by other terms are manifold and interlinked. These differences of opinion can be productively approached if we consider the extent to which different notions of humanism distance themselves from the natural and the divine. For example, one of the senses one can discern in humanism's historical usage is that of a belief in the existence and humanity of Christ, but not in his divinity, a usage whose initiation is attributed to the English poet and philosopher Samuel Taylor Coleridge and one that is closely associated with the development of our contemporary understanding of the philanthropic notion of humanitarianism. Development of a system of thought and action as akin to that of a theist religion from a strictly human origin is a project most associated with August Comte, who both coined the term *sociology* and developed the philosophy of positivism. This "religion of humanity," in its development from Comte's positivism (as seen by the reliance on his term *altruism*), encapsulated much of the heart of the Enlightenment and was particularly influential on the writing of the English philosopher and political economist John Stuart Mill. Mill's utilitarianism, developed in the context of Comte, was in turn a key contributor to the secular liberalism that enabled the deep embedding of humanism in the common sense we currently inhabit.

Humanism's status as a quasi-religion continues to be a matter of debate today, with the capitalized form of the term being adopted by those who would choose it as self-descriptor. In this way, Humanism conveys adherence to an explicit, overarching nontheistic stance toward life (see, for example, the International Humanist and Ethical Union, the umbrella organization for Humanist groups worldwide).

Humanism's refusal to defer to the divine has a longer history, a history in which resistance of dogma through reason has a central role. Origins are claimed in the protoscience of the Ionian pre-Socratic philosophy of ancient Greece. Anaxagoras in the fifth century before the common era and his followers are key names here, through their role in bringing the ideas of the Ionians to the emerging central power of Athens. Still, it should be mentioned that earlier precursors such as Thales of Miletus, the so-called father of science, have also been invoked.

The Enlightenment project previously mentioned took its more proximal development, however, from the Renaissance (via the Reformation) that flowered in Europe from the late 14th century, following the Dark Ages. The Renaissance is where humanism, explicitly identified as such, makes its real power-play and begins to establish itself at the heart of our understanding and action. The "re" in Renaissance is instructive here, for at its core was a renewal and revival of learning via a rediscovery and revalorization of the texts of ancient Greece and Rome. This turn to antiquity, which enabled reflection on texts other than solely those of religion, was conducted by individuals who came to be known in the 17th century and beyond as the Humanists. Whilst the Renaissance coalesced in Florence in 1486 with the publication of Giovanni Pico della Mirandola's *Oration on the Dignity of Man*, exemplars of the movement could soon be found throughout Europe. Adherents sought to rebuild the achievements of the ancient world in the present, in the hope of reviving the virtues that were seen to have been lost since the fall of Rome (the practices of the liberal arts, such as art, music, poetry, history, oratory, and oratory's associated rhetoric), and their elaboration and enactment by the human (celebrated as a center of choice and origin of meaning). It is here that the distinction between humanism and an overweening naturalism is made clear. Whilst, for the humanist, all the objects found in the world have their own natures, they granted a tellingly unique nature to humans.

Seeing no immediate contradiction between the emerging humanist beliefs and those of religion, *Oration on the Dignity of Man* suggests that God has allocated man the particular duty to praise that which God has created; therefore, man must not condemn himself because he too is a creation of God. Pico has God inform Adam—the exemplary, original human—of the way in which he has been uniquely constituted. God tells Adam that, in nature, that which is not fixed, bound, and prescribed by laws that come from outside himself can be chosen. Adam is told that he is at the center of the world; as a result, he has the ability to survey its other contents. The human, he is informed, is neither made of the stuff of heaven nor the stuff of earth and is neither mortal nor immortal, but rather finds itself somewhere between these two materials and states. Only from such a position can the human possess the free choice and dignity with which to make itself into whatever it might choose. And the choice here is truly a free one: In Pico's account the human can choose to become reborn as a divine higher form or to degrade itself to the lower form, the beast.

Humanist doctrine does not, however, as we know, continue to live quite so comfortably with the divine, a tension most pronounced in the trial of Galileo Galilei, which displayed the contradiction that had emerged between the inquiry engendered by humanism and the established religious tradition in all its terrifying ferocity. Nevertheless, the self-realizing human subject became a central tenet of the Enlightenment, as the battle between theistic and nontheistic accounts of creation, creative potential, and their origins ebbed and flowed. The bridge between theistic and nontheistic accounts of the origin of the human's creativity is perhaps clearest in writings of the 18th–19th century German philosopher Immanuel Kant, who effectively enabled the displacement of God with and by reason, allowing rationalism to assert its centrality to humanism and creating a highly cerebral sense of what it means to be human.

Humanism was subsequently systematized within philosophy in the early 20th century by the German-British Oxford professor Ferdinand Schiller, more commonly known as F. C. S. Schiller. Schiller drew upon and reflected much of the pragmatism of the American philosopher and psychologist William James in the development of his humanism, which explicitly drew attention to the rational practice of comprehension and the attempted improvement of human experience as conducted by the actions of humans. However, his humanism particularly drew attention to the resources of the human mind. It is this strand of philosophy that is drawn upon and developed in the existential humanism of the French writer and philosopher Jean-Paul Sartre and its derivatives, including humanistic psychology. And it is in the relation to existentialism and its replaying of Pico's conceptualization of freedom and choice that the modern running sore of humanism is most vividly and painfully salted. For, if the human is both that which is served and the means by which it is served, the very being of the human is and must be thrown open to question.

Critical Commentary and Future Directions

The most immediate critique of humanism is likely its indictment on the grounds of "speciesism," a term coined by the British psychologist and animal-rights campaigner Richard Ryder in 1970. Speciesism indicates that by valorizing the human over and above other forms of life, one engages in a form of prejudice akin to that embodied by racism or sexism. Those negatively prejudiced by speciesism are species other than humans. However, the term has not been deployed just by the animal-rights movement, it has also been taken up by sociologists such as John Law, who see in the social science's lack of attention to the technical aspects of our world a similar overprivileging of the human.

Other critiques and articulations of potential future directions turn around the question of humanity, as alluded to above. For many, the rejection of humanism and its tenets is virtually outright. For example, the French Marxist philosopher Louis Althusser declared himself to be an antihumanist, distinguishing his more (post)structuralist understanding derived from Marx's later works from a humanism being pursued by those drawing their inspiration from early Marx's concern with alienation. Within the Marxist project, this differing conceptualization of humanism was, for Althusser, both misplaced and counterproductive. Others have adopted a less intransigent position. For example, the neohumanism of the Indian thinker Prabhat Rainjan Sarkar values the existential rights of both humans and animals, thus incorporating the concerns of speciesism. The notions of transhumanism and posthumanism are more contested. First usage of transhumanism is ascribed to the biologist Julian Huxley, who utilized it in 1957 to describe the human remaining human but simultaneously transcending itself by exceeding and transforming its (human) nature. Transhumanism was given further impetus along this path by the futurist philosopher Fereydun Esfandiary, who saw the term *transhuman* as referring to a transitory human: a being augmented by technology but insufficiently so to qualify as posthuman. The posthuman here is the human so transformed as to be a species different from the human. According to proponents of this direction of development, this evolved species will be realized through transhumanism as a philosophical doctrine. Such a doctrine shares the belief in reason and scientific progress seen to be characteristic of (some versions of) humanism and believes that this evolution can and should increasingly be realized through an improving of the human enacted by technological augmentation. This type of augmentation can generate a limitless development of both our intellectual capacity and the endurance and persistence of the individual and social life sustained by our bodies. In somewhat less scary formulations, posthumanism is less the desire for a novel technologically mediated species and more the collective name for the various critiques of humanism that have emerged from philosophy and critical and literary theory. These schools of thought enjoin humans to consider a somewhat more modest understanding of their answer to the question of human being than that offered by humanism. This project has been pursued with most vigor by the German philosopher Martin Heidegger, who insists that we must continue to think about, rather than merely answer, the question of (human) being.

—*Simon Lilley*

See also Actor-Network Theory; Dehumanization; Human Rights; Poststructuralism; Radical Humanism

Further Readings

Althusser, L. (2003). *The humanist controversy and other writings.* (F. Matheron, Ed.). London: Verso.

Badmington, N. (Ed.). (2000). *Posthumanism.* Basingstoke, UK: Palgrave Macmillan.

Davies, T. (1996). *Humanism.* London: Routledge.

Pico della Mirandola, G. (1965). *On the Dignity of Man.* Indianapolis, IN: Bobbs-Merrill. [A very readable translation of the opening of this text (paragraphs 1–7) is also available at: http://www.wsu.edu/~dee/REN/ORATION.HTM; a rather different but more extensive translation of the text can be found at http://www.cscs.umich.edu/~crshalizi/Mirandola/.]

Sartre, J-P. (2007). *Existentialism is a humanism.* New Haven, CT: Yale University Press. [Text also available at http://www.marxists.org/reference/archive/sartre/works/exist/sartre.htm]

Schiller, F. C. S. (1970). *Humanism: Philosophical essays.* Westport, CT: Greenwood Press.

HUMAN RELATIONS SCHOOL

The Human Relations School refers to an intellectual circle and research agenda based on the work of G. Elton Mayo (1880–1949) and his colleagues at the Harvard Business School from 1925 to 1947 and his direction of the Hawthorne Experiments at Western Electric Company (1928–1933), including the publications of that research (1933–1945). The Human Relations School focused on the "human" aspects of the workplace, as distinguished from Frederick W. Taylor's mechanistic and technical focus and from the rational actor theory of classical economics. The Human Relations School's key theoretical contribution was its articulation of the informal organization—relationships and interactions based on and perpetuated through affect, viewed as nonrational, as opposed to formal means of management control such as hierarchy. The Human Relations School considered informal organization at the group, organizational, and societal levels. It posited informal organization as the mechanism of larger social order. The Human Relations School's key practical contribution was the counseling interview, a technique to increase worker productivity through therapy. The Human Relations School has been fundamental in the development of organizational behavior, industrial relations, and personnel and human resource management.

Conceptual Overview

The Human Relations School drew from psychology (Sigmund Freud, Pierre Janet), political theory (Vilfredo Pareto), political psychology (Gustave Le Bon, Harold Lasswell), sociology (Émile Durkheim), anthropology (Bronislaw Malinowski), and contemporary political events and debates (labor movements and antimovements, capitalism versus communism, democracy versus fascism). In applied fields, it drew from industrial psychology and industrial relations (Hugo Munsterberg, Elmer Southard).

The Human Relations School originated in relation to a larger dialogue about the impact of the Industrial Revolution on individuals, families, communities, and society at large. From the early 19th century, the heavy noneconomic costs of industrialization were evident. In intellectual circles, sociology emerged in part to attack laissez-faire economics, which had been used to justify these costs. In the United States, the leading early sociologists were social reformers. Many were sons of clergymen, for churches founded and maintained the U.S. institutions of higher learning until the late 19th century. They earned their Ph.D.s in Germany in reform-oriented intellectual circles. They mounted campaigns addressing child labor, occupational hazards, and poverty-level wages. In companies, concerned executives established programs for employee welfare known as "industrial betterment." Discussion and experimentation ensued to explore how to humanize the workplace. Offerings ranged from lunchrooms and showers to political experiments, including profit-sharing, worker education, and joint decision-making. In the late 19th and early 20th centuries, the term *human relations* is found in such varied contexts as conflict resolution, immigration and diversity, and democracy and citizenship.

The Human Relations School developed in consort with the professionalization of business as a field, the growing view of managers as a class, and the acceptance of collegiate business schools as legitimate institutions. The Human Relations School was simultaneously a research agenda to lend credibility to the emerging science of management, a leadership program for elite young men of the nation, and a way to generate appropriate educational content for this elite.

Mayo grounded his approach in medicine. His family had expected him to become a doctor. He began medical studies but dropped out and decided to pursue psychology. His formative experience was as a clinical psychologist in a hospital, treating shell-shock victims of World War I. Through his lifetime, he considered verbal communication as a symptom of underlying disorders and conceived of his professional relationships according to the doctor-patient model.

Mayo transitioned to industry through his service on a committee to develop worker education and vocational training programs. He noticed similarities between angry workers and shell-shocked war victims; these workers were prone to organize and agitate. He wrote a series of articles on the psychological basis of labor unrest. He drew from Pierre Janet's theories linking physical and mental fatigue. Janet saw reverie, the reduced capacity for attention, as related to fatigue. Then Mayo developed his social argument through Durkheim and the view that industrialization produced alienated workers. In this dispossessed state, the fatigued worker was prone to obsessive preoccupations, leading to industrial and social unrest. Organizations were a socializing force, and work, thus, a process of psychological adjustment to society.

Mayo's work attracted the interest of Lawrence Henderson, an influential member of the Harvard faculty, who noticed that Mayo's ideas resembled those of Elmer Southard, who had headed the Boston Psychopathic Hospital until his premature death. Henderson helped bring Mayo to Harvard in order to continue Southard's work. In this, he was supported by a close circle of businessmen assembled by Wallace Donham, the dean of the Harvard Business School, who took the institution from a fledgling to a leadership status during his tenure (1919–1942). This group sought to protect capitalism from threats such as socialism. It also was antiunion, the most vehement voice being that of John D. Rockefeller and his son. The Rockefellers, through a social science foundation, paid Mayo's salary at the Harvard Business School and funded the Hawthorne studies.

Although Taylor suggested physical fatigue as an initial focus, he also called for studies of human motivation. Mayo began at Hawthorne, in 1928, with fatigue studies of workers doing repetitive tasks. (The studies, underway for two years when Mayo joined them in 1928, initially explored the effects of lighting on production.) Focusing on blood pressure, and later on menstrual cycles, Mayo sought an objective standard of workers' productive capacity—an exact replication of Taylor's goal.

At the Harvard Business School, Mayo was influenced by Pareto as interpreted by Henderson. He convened seminars and social clubs around Pareto's work (the "Pareto circle"). According to Lawrence's protégé, George Homans, Pareto gave the wealthy capitalist elite an intellectual defense against Marx. Henderson was particularly intrigued by Pareto's analysis of irrationality ("residues"), for he felt that the political left overemphasized rationality. Henderson took a special interest in Pareto's ideas about social equilibrium and the idea that elites lose power from excess sympathy for the lower classes. Mayo adapted the constructs of equilibrium and residues, which he called "non-logical sentiments," in designing and analyzing the Hawthorne research, particularly the counseling interview.

Mayo's role at Hawthorne was strategic and interpretive. Senior officers at Hawthorne had approached him to analyze the voluminous data from the Relay Assembly Test (a special room set up for the research, where a group of women assembled electrical relays). A consistent finding was a steady increase in production. Mayo focused on social and psychological factors (i.e., workers' solidarity as a group) as opposed to material ones, such as pay and physical conditions.

Mayo's contribution was most fully articulated from 1928 to 1930, when he designed and led an extensive interviewing campaign at Hawthorne. Mayo developed interviewing as a therapeutic as well as a managerial technique. Informants were encouraged to talk extensively and openly in a form of emotional release to discharge the mental attitude (irrationality) of the worker and enable social adjustment. This logic conformed to Mayo's earliest ideas about psychology as a tool to remedy discontent. The key elements were the counselor as expert, disregarding the literal level of the communication, identifying the underlying truth, and restoring the misled individual to normality.

Mayo's protégé, Fritz Roethlisberger, and William Dickson, head of Employee Relations Research at Western Electric, wrote the most extensive account of the research. They summarized the experiments chronologically, described the interviewing program and method, established a cause-effect relationship between the interviewing program and "personal equilibrium" (adjustment), posited the existence of the informal organization and described its workings, posited counseling interviews in the workplace as a means of social control, and proposed the management of the informal organization and the use of the counseling interview as the purview of the personnel management function.

The term Human Relations School also refers to extensions of Mayo's work. Because he focused on integrating the formal and informal organization and participated in the Pareto circle, Chester Barnard is often associated with the Human Relations School. The Human Relations School continued at Harvard through the work of Roethlisberger and others, notably T. N. Whitehead and Abraham Zaleznik. William Foote Whyte, trained at Harvard, moved to the University of Chicago and established that university also as a center of Human Relations School research in the 1940s. Whyte's interviewing practice emphasized data-gathering, not counseling; and he identified attitudes and sentiments held by management as well as by workers. In the 1950s, important Human Relations School work was done at Cornell, Yale, MIT, Princeton, and the University of Illinois. Kurt Lewin, Rensis Likert, and others at the University of Michigan also did significant work. Focus was on attitudes and their effect on productivity. The Human Relations School came under the influence of social, cognitive, and experimental psychologies. In the 1960s and 1970s, it was also influenced by humanistic psychology, particularly the work of Abraham Maslow and Douglas McGregor and the technique of the T-group.

Critical Commentary and Future Directions

The Human Relations School is of paramount importance in understanding management theory's attempt to transcend simplistic models of human nature and interaction. It represents the first major move by management thinkers to encompass the fuller human being, including the subconscious and emotions. The Human Relations School is fairly well understood as a phenomenon demonstrating these arguments, but it is not understood as one move in a larger series of moves. For example, historical studies of the relationship between the Human Relations School, industrial betterment, and social reform are lacking in local-cultural as well as cross-cultural contexts.

The Human Relations School has achieved dominance as the quintessential school of "human relations." However, this point of view obscures the competing visions of such an inquiry. "Human relations" is not owned exclusively and permanently by Elton Mayo and his colleagues. The competing visions, such as those of Mary Parker Follett, merit greater consideration.

In contemporary times, to what extent does the Human Relations School still have currency? Its major organizing principles include feigned neutrality and distance between the counselor (researcher, expert) and counselee (subject, worker), a privileging of the inner life of individuals over external contexts, a disregard of the literal level of verbal communication, a predisposition to regard the other (not the expert) as obsessive, and a belief that this relationship and interaction technique is constructive. To the extent that these tenets are subscribed to and practiced today in relationships and settings, the Human Relations School lives on. They are certainly operative in research. They are evident in practices of employee counseling. "Psychology" in the Human Relations School sense is still used as a means to adjustment. Their traces appear in training programs, team-building events, and retreats. "Active listening" is part of routine supervisory training. Thus has the Human Relations School experienced popularization along with the general field of psychology. However, the historical evolution and contemporary applications of these practices, both in local and in cross-cultural contexts, have not been examined. More important, their usefulness, their ethics, and above all their alternatives, in and for an ever-changing world, remain unexplored.

—*Ellen O'Connor*

See also Classical Management; Hawthorne Studies

Further Readings

Bourke, H. (1982). Industrial unrest as social pathology: The Australian writings of Elton Mayo. *Historical Studies, 20,* 217–233.

Gillespie, R. (1991). *Manufacturing knowledge: A history of the Hawthorne experiments.* Cambridge, UK: Cambridge University Press.

Hagedorn, H. (1958). A note on the motivation of personnel management: Industrial welfare, 1885–1910. *Explorations in Entrepreneurial History, 10,* 134–139.

Keller, R. (1984). The Harvard "Pareto circle" and the historical development of organization theory. *Journal of Management, 10,* 193–203.

Mayo, E. (1952). *The psychology of Pierre Janet.* London: Routledge & Kegan Paul.

Niven, M. (1967). *Personnel management, 1913–63.* London, UK: Institute of Personnel Management.

O'Connor, E. S. (1999). Minding the workers: The meaning of "human" and "human relations" in Elton Mayo. *Organization, 6,* 223–246.

O'Connor, E. S. (1999). The politics of management thought: A case study of the Harvard Business School and the Human Relations School. *Academy of Management Review, 24,* 117–131.

Roethlisberger, F. (1977). *The elusive phenomena: An autobiographical account of my work in the field of organizational behavior at the Harvard Business School.* Cambridge, MA: Harvard University Press.

Roethlisberger, F., & Dickson, W. (1939). *Management and the worker.* Cambridge, MA: Harvard University Press.

Trahair, R. (1984). *The humanist temper: The life and work of Elton Mayo.* New Brunswick, NJ: Transaction Books.

Human Resource Management

In its broadest sense, *human resource management* is a widely used term coined to encapsulate management policies and practices concerned with the supply and utilization of the labor resource required for the firm to meet its commercial objectives. To do so, the employer has to be able to compete within the labor market and meet basic requirements of social legitimacy relevant to the society in which the firm is located. The employer needs to be able to attract and keep labor and ensure that labor power is utilized for productive purposes relevant to its business objectives. It is by no means certain how best to proceed in this endeavor. This uncertainty in the context of inevitable resource constraints—whether financial, cognitive, or the capacity for control—make both the meaning and practice of human resource management difficult and ambiguous.

Conceptual Overview

Human Resource Management as a Function

Human resource management as a new label for the personnel function and as a descriptive term for labor policies was developed in the United States in the early 1980s. The work of Harvard academics was especially influential, as seen in the book by Michael Beer, Bert Spector, Paul Lawrence, D. Quinn Mills, and Richard Walton. The usage of the term spread rapidly in the Anglo-American world and beyond. At the same time, it attracted widespread criticism for its excessive managerialism and seeming exclusive concern with the management prerogative and the achievement of shareholder value to the neglect of other stakeholders. The critical question then, as now, is whether human resource management was a new approach to labor management or merely a new label on an old bottle. This relabeling of the personnel function is itself of interest, since it reveals one of the conceptual problems with the term and points to the long-running difficulty of the role and influence of the function. Criticism of professional personnel managers and departments for their lack of influence and inability to make meaningful contributions to the achievement of strategic objectives has been long running. The rapid spread of the nomenclature human resource management for professional labor managers and their departments can be seen as an attempt to gain legitimacy and respect from senior executives by downplaying the welfare image of personnel management and giving emphasis to the contribution to business strategy. By the early years of the 21st century the term *business partner* was widely adopted although not universally accepted.

This link between human resource management as a set of labor policies and the description of the function is one source of confusion whenever the term *human resource management* is used. Often the meaning of the term is bound by the policies and practices that are designed by the function itself and found within the human resource manual, or Web site. There are three major limitations to this way of defining human resource management. First, many of the human resource policies designed by the human resource function rely on other managers, especially line managers, to implement them. There is frequently a gap between the espoused and the enacted. To define human resource management as only those formal policies found in the manual is to severely limit understanding of how the human resource of the firm is managed. Second, not all firms have a dedicated human resource department or manager, yet they too, of course, need means of managing their human resources. Third, if we ask how the human resource in the firm is managed in the sense of how it is recruited and selected, trained, motivated, and deployed and how the aspirations and expectations of employees are dealt with, a much wider array of managerial behaviors have to be included. Increasingly the very broad term *people management* is used to cover this wider area of interest. *People* in this context includes managers themselves considered as employees, as well as others whose labor power is utilized by the firm, and rewarded for it, whether temporaries, labor agency staff, or the self-employed.

Human Resource Management as a Distinctive Approach to Labor Management

Leaving aside the problem of human resource management as the function, the other substantial, and long-running, debate is whether human resource management means a distinctive approach to labor management—a new way of managing labor—or whether it is a generic term covering all the many approaches adopted by employers to meet their needs for viability and, for some, competitive advantage, within the economic, social, and regulatory environment under which they operate. There is a great advantage in defining human resource management as a distinctive approach to labor management since we can ask what it is; what type of, or "bundle" of, policies are commonly used; how it is different from previous approaches; and what the outcome effects are both in terms of firm performance and employee well-being.

This distinctive approach, according to John Storey, is one that focuses on the development of a committed and capable workforce by using a whole range of cultural, structural, and human resource management policies to achieve competitive advantage. The component characteristics are clear. First, the purpose of human resource management is seen in business terms as the achievement of competitive advantage. Second, competitive advantage is promoted by having, and thus gaining, the commitment of employees to the firm, to its strategic objectives, and to it as a social entity. Third, the quality of the human capital is an important policy objective: to gain and keep a capable workforce. Fourth, these outcomes are achieved through the design and implementation of a set, or bundle, of human resource policies and practices that are integrated one with the other: what is termed *horizontal fit*. These techniques will be those that are necessary to have an impact on employee commitment and capability.

It is politically and practically highly attractive to adopt this distinctive approach to human resource management. It is psychologically or emotionally attractive for those practicing human resource management to place emphasis on workforce commitment rather than on more brutal or directive policies linked to command and control. It holds out the promise, or the illusion, of a win-win approach to labor management wherein both workers and employees are capable of achieving respective gains. David Guest sees this as a manifestation of the American dream. At the practical level, while the huge volume of research seeking to show a positive, causal relationship between this type of human resource management and firm performance has, as yet, never quite been able to come up with categorical proof, there is enough indication of a positive relationship. Even if we argue a reverse causality whereby it is successful firms that are more likely to adopt this type of human resource management, as opposed to human resource management causing high performance, the rational assumption remains that firms (or at least some firms) adopt human resource management because it is effective.

The distinctive approach discussed here has both led to, and been influenced by, interest in employee motivation, commitment, and productive behavior. This is reflected in growing interest in psychological contracts, organizational justice, trust and fairness, and organizational citizenship behavior. Behind all these is a recognition that most workers in most, but not all, jobs have the capacity and opportunity to engage in discretionary behavior. That is, managerial control is always partial, whether the control is exercised by power and command or whether through commitment-inducing policies. Discretionary behavior is not necessarily provided for the benefit of the firm as illustrated by numerous studies of employee resistance. Whether positive or negative from employers' perspective, discretionary behavior is a recognition of employers' reliance on worker cooperation and talent, and thus human resource management focuses on commitment and capability.

The distinctive approach to human resource management, and its attractiveness, led in the 1980s and 1990s to a search for a universal policy set of *best practices* that, it was implied, would benefit all firms and by implication all workers. The best-known of these was propounded by Jeffrey Pfeffer, who identified seven practices that would contribute to building profits by giving priority to people management. This rather idiosyncratic list included employment security, selective hiring, self-management teams or teamwork, high pay contingent on company performance, extensive training, reduction in status differences, and sharing information. What is notable here is the absence of any reference to employee voice or employee representation. This illustrates a wider problem that while, in general terms, distinctive human resource management is concerned with commitment and capability-related policies and practices, there is no agreement on quite what should be included and excluded in the list. There are distinct cultural and social differences. For example, it is more likely that American policy lists will include individual performance-related pay than Europe lists will, while outside the United States employee voice–related policies involving trade unions or employee representation will be more common. In some countries, for example, the Netherlands, as pointed out by Jaap Paauwe, legislation requires the adoption of labor management policies that are seen as innovative initiatives elsewhere.

Human Resource Management as a Generic Term

The search for a universal set of human resource management policies is seen by John Purcell as a cul-de-sac limiting and trivializing the analysis of human resource management and confusing ends and means. Even when different labels are used to indicate subsets of human resource management, like high performance work practices, high commitment management, and high involvement work practices, the lack of agreement on the policy mix remains. This, though, is inevitable, since varieties of economic and social contexts, business strategies, and the beliefs and values of dominant top executives will strongly influence the extent to which certain policies are considered relevant and will be adopted.

The distinctive commitment and capability of human resource management policy mix has always been susceptible to the criticism that if it really associated with better firm performance and worker well-being, why is it that so few companies adopt it? In general, the American and United Kingdom evidence indicates that less than one-fifth of companies with more than 25 workers adopt even half the policies usually found in the human resource management list. This diffusion problem has led to a neglect of other forms of labor management, for example, in developing and rapidly industrializing countries and in low-skill, price-sensitive firms where command and control labor management is frequently found. It is seriously misleading to focus on one type of labor management when the strategic contingencies that firms face vary so substantially. This line of thinking has had two consequences. First, instead of focusing on a list of best practices, attention has turned to the fit between human resource management and contingent and strategic circumstances faced by firms and chosen as goals. This is the so-called best-fit approach. Second, it has led to human resource management being defined, for example by Peter Boxall and Purcell, in generic terms as all those activities associated with the management of employment relationships. This allows for a different set of questions to be posed related to patterns of management styles and approaches and the contexts in which these approaches apply. This generic definition allows for the analysis of variances in employer approaches to labor management. It is equally logical to call command and control management human resource management, since this is one way, and quite a common one, to manage the human resource of the firms' nonmanagerial employees, for example, in transactional call centers and low-wage routine component-assembly factories. Here neither employee commitment nor employee capability is required to anything like the same extent as, for example, in knowledge-intensive firms. The danger with the particular form of human resource management sometimes called *developmental humanism* is that these other approaches to human resource management are simply ignored.

The best practices, best-fit dichotomy can be taken too far. There are clearly fundamental principles or guidelines for designing and implementing critical policies and practices. All firms have to recruit and select, and all pay employees for their labor. One way or the other there will be a relationship between effort and reward, and all employers have an interest in managing performance. Some form of training or the need for employees to learn the job is inevitable and many employees will be required to work collaboratively with others in teams. Beyond these fundamentals, every employer has to deal with discipline problems and organize work. Workers are not machines. They have views, interests, and values, requiring information and some form of voice collectively or individually expressed. It is in these latter areas of human resource management that legislation is most commonly found, as in the case of discrimination, to establish a floor of rights. It is here, too, that social legitimacy is relevant as a driving force for employer conduct. It is the precise form of these areas of policy requirement that varies, as does the manner in which they are implemented or, at times, ignored. Varieties of human resource management, like varieties of capitalism, allow for greater understanding of contexts and contingencies, and historical paths taken, in the choice employers make on how to manage their human resource. There is no one best way.

Critical Commentary and Future Directions

The high-commitment, high-skill particular model of human resource management has been subject to heavy criticism, especially where claims of high performance work systems have included mutual gains as an outcome effect, for example, as seen in job autonomy, empowerment, and teamwork. These are often illusionary, and there is evidence, well reviewed by Rosemary Batt and Virginia Doellgast, of work intensification, insidious forms of control exercised by teams over themselves and little empowerment of job autonomy. Not for nothing did Karen Legge subtitle her seminal book *Rhetorics and Realities*. It is also pertinent to note that it is extremely rare for studies in human resource management to consider restructuring, redundancies, and offshoring and their effects on employees. Not only does the particular view of human resource management lead to a focus on relatively few companies, ignoring the rest, it also, especially within the United States, treats the firm as a stand-alone, independent entity capable, through its management leadership, of determining its own future beyond invisible economic and social contingencies. It is a glass-half-empty-or-half-full problem. While critical management scholars find in the rhetoric of human resource management a new form of social control that is delusional in that workers do not experience new freedoms, human resource management research often finds counterexamples of growing worker satisfaction with their jobs and commitment to their employer. Worker satisfaction and commitment are associated with better performance. Maybe this is not surprising, since human resource management scholars often focus their research on the best firms, for example, those in the list of top 100 companies to work for, while critical management scholars often use a wider sample of firms (for example, the National Workplace Employment Relations Survey in the United Kingdom). Neither, of course, has a monopoly on the truth.

The biggest drawback of human resource management studies, especially those that seek to find evidence of performance outcomes, is that, until recently, they have concentrated on management policies and ignored the views of employees. This has led some to suggest that human resource management implicitly views employees as passive recipients of management initiatives who will, or certainly should, respond positively. This is where the trenchant criticism of human resource management as "unitarist," with unfettered management prerogative pursuing an individualistic agenda, originates. Employee collective voice and representation is neither considered in the policy mix in this form of human resource management nor included within classic, mainly American, studies.

The early neglect of employees within much of human resource management research is surprising, since it was at the heart of the *black box problem*. This is the difficulty of explaining, or showing, how progressive human resource policies feed through into positive performance outcomes. Apart from better recruitment and selection techniques, which may improve the quality of new starters, all other policies rely for their effect on the response of existing employees. If there is to be a performance outcome, it must be that these are influencing employee conduct and capability, especially the exercise of discretionary behavior related to productive work. Such limitations are not found in other subject areas within the broad canon of organizational behavior, for example, industrial sociology and organizational or personnel psychology. As Jacqueline Coyle-Shapiro, Lynn Shore, Susan Taylor, and Lois Tetrick show, there is now a growing interest is using social exchange theory within human resource management, since this focuses on aspects of reciprocity between employees and managers and the wider organization. This is where insights from studies of the psychological contract, perceived organizational support, organizational citizenship behavior, and organizational justice can usefully be deployed within human resource management. The specific contribution that human resource management can make is to explain how particular practices of performance management, communication, and employee involvement, for example, have an impact on, and are mediated by, employees. In turn, the definition of, or boundaries around, the subject have to broaden. If the interest remains management policies and practices concerned with the supply and utilization of labor, then an employee-centered approach would need to cover areas currently on the fringes of human resource management, although often included within management discourse, such as leadership, culture and climate, and line manager-employee relationship.

—*John Purcell*

See also High Involvement Management; Strategic Human Resource Management

Further Readings

Batt, R., & Doellgast, V. (2005). Groups, teams, and the division of labour: Interdisciplinary perspectives on the organization of work. In S. Ackroyd, R. Batt, P. Thompson, and P. Tolbert (Eds.), *The Oxford handbook of work and organization* (pp. 138–164). Oxford, UK: Oxford University Press.

Beer, M., Spector, B., Lawrence, P., Quinn Mills, D., & Walton, R. (1984). *Managing human assets.* New York: Free Press.

Boxall, P., & Purcell, J. (2003). *Strategy and human resource management.* Basingstoke, UK: Palgrave Macmillan.

Coyle-Shapiro, J., Shore, L., Taylor, S., & Tetrick, L. (Eds.). (2004). *The employment relationship: Examining psychological and contextual perspectives.* Oxford, UK: Oxford University Press.

Guest, D. (1990). Human resource management as the American dream. *Journal of Management Studies, 27*(4): 377–397.

Legge, K. (1995). *Human resource management: Rhetorics and realities.* Basingstoke, UK: Palgrave Macmillan.

Paauwe, J. (2004). *HRM and business performance: Achieving long-term viability.* Oxford, UK: Oxford University Press.

Pfeffer, J. (1998). *The human equation: Building profits by putting people first.* Boston, MA: Harvard Business School Press.

Purcell, J. (1999). Best practice and best fit: Chimera and cul-de-sac? *Human Resource Management Journal, 9*(4), 26–41.

Storey, J. (1992). *Developments in the management of human resources.* Oxford, UK: Blackwell.

Human Rights

Human rights, in the aggregate, is a universal moral standard of rights that stands above laws of any particular nation. These rights can be considered a basic entitlement for every human being or group, for example, a right to health, food, education, property, shelter, or freedom of expression and movement. A right, in contrast to a duty, is a justified entitlement to something from someone, and the "from someone" implies a duty from that "someone." Human rights originate in civil codes, not natural law; they are not granted from a deity.

Human rights include three types of rights: socioeconomic, fundamental freedoms or civil liberties, and ethnic and religious rights. The United Nations Universal Declaration of Human Rights, adopted in 1948 by the U.N. General Assembly, advocates the broadest definition of rights and includes freedom of expression, speech, and religion; a right to a viable standard of living and a healthy work environment; the right to organize and join a union; access to education, adequate health care, adequate housing, and due legal process; freedom from torture; freedom from slavery; freedom from discrimination based on race, religion, gender, or ethnicity; and freedom from economic exploitation.

Conceptual Overview

According to the historical record, human rights were first codified in approximately 2,000 BC when Hammurabi, the king of Babylonia, issued codes for how Babylonians were to treat each other, establishing fair wages, protection of property, and requiring charges to be proven at trial. Later Moses and Mohammed set standards for how their followers were to treat one another, and the Romans developed the concept of the rights of citizens. Over the past 800 years, the Magna Carta of 1215, the English bill of rights of 1689, the U.S. Bill of Rights of 1791, and the French Declaration of the Rights of Man and the Citizen of 1789 have provided precedents for more recent declarations and conventions of human rights. Before the 20th century, those codes were designated for particular groups of persons and excluded others, often women, children, and slaves.

The U.N. Universal Declaration of Human Rights is the best-regarded code of conduct, although not universally accepted by the corporate world. William Schulz, former executive director of Amnesty International, once noted that the U.N. declaration is taken variously as pragmatism, communitarianism, or postmodernism. The Global Compact, the International Labour Organization Conventions, the International Covenant on Civil and Political Rights, and the Convention on the Rights of the Child have had the most impact on business organizations. These universal codes and conventions abolish child labor and forced labor, establish rights to equal pay for equal work, to a living wage, to organize and form trade unions, and to safe working conditions, as well as protection against discrimination based on race, creed, gender, religious affiliation, union affiliation, and more.

One controversy surrounding a corporation's violation of human rights centers on the definition of a corporation: whether it has the same duties and responsibilities as a person. As an example, when corporations use child labor in manufacturing or agricultural operations, on occasion they defended their practices by claiming they do not have the same moral obligations as individuals and therefore are not required to abide by the same ethical or moral standards as individuals. Their position is founded on Milton Friedman's theory of free market capitalism, which argues that corporations do not have the same responsibilities nor should be held to the same moral standards as individuals. In practice, however, the more egregious the corporate behavior, the harder it is for corporations to defend violating human rights.

In addressing the role of business in upholding human rights around the globe, Shultz in 2002 cautions that the relationship between economic incentives and political reform is complicated. He counters the commercialist argument that claims that political freedom is positively correlated to economic growth, citing Singapore as a example of the opposite trend. With the second-highest standard of living in Asia after Japan, Singapore suppresses all political opposition, executes people for minor drug offenses, and bans Jehovah's Witnesses. Singapore's autocratic government fines a person $1,000 (U.S.) for chewing gum on the street and the act of ordering gum from a mail-order catalog is subject to one year in prison and a $6,173 fine.

Indonesia, Nigeria, Burma, Chile, Guatemala, and Sudan are examples where political instability and systematic violations of human rights resulted in economic crises, including billions of dollars in lost investments. Business cannot function without a free flow of information and equitable enforcement of contracts. Countries that suppress freedom of speech and the press, limit access to information and ideas, tolerate corruption and bribery, and have ineffective regulatory and judicial systems are not conducive to economic growth and development.

Under the universal codes of human rights and additional codes of conduct for corporations, businesses throughout the world face the challenge of compliance, regulation, and consequences. Outsourcing is a widespread corporate practice wherein human rights have consistently been violated, particularly in apparel manufacturing in developing countries. Sweatshops are synonymous with exploitation, and Sweatshop Watch, Corporate Watch, the Union of Needletrades, Industrial and Textile Employees (UNITE), and the International Labor Organization have pressured retail companies to comply with the human rights codes. In response, many companies have formed industrial trade groups such as the American Apparel Manufacturers Association to set up their own less stringent set of standards for monitoring factories. In the Mariana Islands, a U.S. territory, U.S. companies have avoided complying with the U.S. labor standards and instead have established sweatshops that primarily hire women from China who themselves pay labor contractors to give them jobs and the hope of earning money to send back home to their families in China. Living as indentured servants, these workers are paid substandard wages, work between 16 and 20 hours a week, pay back the labor contractors for transport from China, a work permit, food, and substandard living arrangements, with no means of saving money for their families or for their own return to China. Some of these unethical labor practices by U.S. companies have surfaced because of their ties to U.S. congressmen and prominent lobbyists.

Corporate violations of human rights often involve subcontractors and the host governments. In some cases Western corporate interests have partnered and profited with military-led dictatorships, while the host country workers are exploited, sometimes killed, and in the case of Burma, work as forced laborers, are frequently beaten, raped, and forcibly removed from their homes and villages, all under military orders. In the apparel industry, from Honduras to Indonesia, clothing manufacturers frequently contract with Korean subcontractors to operate sweatshops, hiring mostly young women under severe working conditions.

Critical Commentary and Future Directions

Since the beginning of the industrial era, corporations have violated human rights. The capitalist free market system privileges the elite few with the accumulation of shareholder wealth while exploiting workers as "human resources" and "human capital" to be used to maximize profits. Embedded within the systematic corporate violation of human rights is a worldview and structure based on race, class, and gender, seeing individuals as groups, and some groups as less human than others. The dehumanization of others, treating a person as an object or resource rather than a human being with dignity and rights, underscores the paradox, on the one hand, of constantly striving for increasing connections with others around the globe, aided through technology, and on the other hand, of increasing anomie, isolation, and loss of connection with the earth, as well as the readily available illusion of freedom and happiness through rampant consumerism. As globalization dominates the political, economic, and moral terrain, the gap between the rich and poor continues to widen. While street vendors in Bangkok may use cell phones, they lack clean air, water, adequate food, shelter, education, housing, and health care. Despite gains in some industries, unionization has struggled to maintain a significant presence throughout the world.

On the positive side, the movement for corporate social responsibility has gained a higher profile and support among consumers, perhaps because environmental destruction attracts followers out of pure self-interest. Some Latin American governments have seized control of natural resources in response to exploitive private foreign interests. The foreign exploitation was most glaring when multinational corporations grabbed water rights from indigenous people in Bolivia. Through grass-roots organizing, Bolivians forced Western corporations to leave. The example of Venezuelan oil is similar. Parts of Latin America are increasing state control of industries and opening democratic political and economic processes while discouraging the hegemonic presence of Western corporate interests. The fair trade movement has made strides in the last decade of the 20th and first decade of the 21st centuries, promoting fair working conditions and compensation for workers in several industries, including coffee, carpets, and chocolate. Technology has aided in the education and awareness of consumers on the conditions of workers and their environments around the world. Optimistically, Mary Robinson, the former United Nations High Commissioner for Human Rights, believes that throughout the world, from governments to civil society, a culture of human rights is growing, advancing the cause of dignity and freedom.

If Noam Chomsky is correct, war and corporate greed are primary causes of the decline of human rights, making a mockery of those very democracies that espouse implementing the will of the people. As corporations, with government support, genetically engineer seeds, outsource labor, build prisons, train private "security" forces, or sell consumerism as a panacea, human rights continue to erode. Scholars have unlimited opportunities to critically study the impact of corporate-government partnerships on human rights.

—*Judith A. White*

See also Corporate Social Responsibility; Dehumanization; Slavery; Sweatshops; Worker Rights

Further Readings

Chomsky, N. (2006). *Failed states: The abuse of power and the assault on democracy.* New York: Henry Holt.
Donaldson, T. (1989). *The ethics of international business.* New York: Oxford University Press.
Light, J. (1999, February 4). Repression, inc.: The assault on human rights. *CorpWatch.* Retrieved May 31, 2006 from http://www.corpwatch.org/article.php?id=911

Schulz, W. (2002). *In our own best interest. How defending human rights benefits us all.* Boston: Beacon Press.
Waddock, S. (2002). *Leading corporate citizens, Vision, values, value added.* New York: McGraw-Hill.

Humor

Humor is a ubiquitous, pervasive, universal phenomenon potentially present in all situations in which people interact. It is a complex, multifaceted phenomenon involving cognitive, emotional, behavioral, physiological, and social aspects that have a significant effect on individuals, social relations, and even social systems. Organizational settings are no exception to this; humor is an ever-present feature of organizational life, and research shows that it can play a part in a range of organizational behaviors and processes. There is a long and varied tradition of theory and research on humor across a range of disciplines, but humor research in organizations has been intermittent, lacking in theoretical coherence, and with a functionalist bias.

Conceptual Overview

Humor has been the subject of serious conceptualization, at least within the West, going back as far as Aristotle and Plato. Indeed, a diverse range of philosophers, from Søren Kierkegaard to Immanuel Kant, has offered a consideration of the phenomenon. The disparate perspectives articulated continue to be mirrored in the theoretical variety that persists in the field. This variety notwithstanding, it is common to consider three theories as dominant contemporarily: incongruity theory, superiority theory, and relief theory.

There are variants of incongruity theory, but it basically assumes that humor arises when two disparate, normally distant and unrelated, or even antagonistic, ideas, events, or worldviews are juxtaposed or framed in a surprising manner. It is perhaps better labeled incongruity-resolution theory, since many argue that it is not the incongruity itself that is funny but the resolution through which the strange and perhaps uncomfortable juxtaposition is resolved. An influential version of incongruity today is the semantic-script theory of Victor Raskin, which focuses on the linguistic incongruities in humor; a derivation is the general theory of verbal humor developed by Raskin with Salvatore Attardo.

Superiority theory, with roots in Plato's conceptualization, supposes that humor emerges from the perception of a hierarchical relationship wherein those who locate themselves in a superior position can feel good about their position relative to others and derive humor from the derision, misfortune, and malfunctioning of those in lowly positions. It is an aggressive conception of humor and has been discussed, for example, with respect to ethnic jokes, but also in relation to the establishment and maintenance of hierarchical relations in organizations.

Finally, relief theories are rooted in Freudian psychoanalytic conceptions. At its core it suggests that humor is the result of the pleasurable relief experienced when a humorous situation allows the release of energy normally used to suppress feelings, particularly sexual and violent ones. Humor and comedy provide a socially acceptable outlet for these repressed feelings and drives. Other, less psychoanalytic versions see humor as a relief from negative feelings such as pain or sadness.

This summary does not exhaust the theoretical perspectives on humor, and all three discussed have their variants. The diversity reflects a difficulty in the area—the sheer variety of humor as a phenomenon. The variety derives from both the multiplicity of forms that humor and comedy can take—as diverse as pratfalls, jokes, parody, and satire—and the range of contexts in which it occurs—whether formal, staged humor or spontaneous occurrence in everyday interactions—and in verbal, written, and graphic modes of presentation.

Research on humor in organizations specifically first appeared in studies of the effects of bureaucracy and industrialization in the 1950s. Studies such as that conducted by Donald Roy revealed the use of humor to alleviate the boredom and anomie encountered in the modern organization. The ethnographic approach adopted by Roy has been more the exception in studies, for most have adopted an individualistic, psychological perspective and deployed positivistic methods such as experiments. Indeed, the bulk of the research has been conducted within the functionalist paradigm with the aim of demonstrating a relationship between humor and various positively functional organizational outcomes. The focus has been on individuals or groups as the level of analysis, with rather less work on humor at the organizational level, even though the earliest investigations were at that level.

At the individual level, one particularly strong research tradition is that relating humor to stress reduction, coping behavior, or to general well-being. The positive effects of coping humor in relation to stress were particularly established by Herbert Lefcourt, Rod Martin, and their colleagues in the 1980s but are a continuing stream of research, within organizational contexts as well as others. In a related way, research has focused on the positive effects of humor on people's health and well-being, although Martin finds the evidence at best equivocal. This research has led to considerable experimentation and application of humor in at least one organizational setting, hospitals, where the stress-relieving and palliative effects of humor are investigated.

The individual focus on humor has meant that some conceive of humor, or really sense of humor, as a personality trait, leading to a significant amount of work relating humor as a disposition to a range of other attitudes and behaviors. For example, the work of Nicholas Kuiper reveals relationships between a sense of humor and such factors as positive affect and higher motivation in relation to tasks, positive self-concept, and above-average self-esteem. Humor has also been associated with other individual-level attributes such as mental flexibility and then related to phenomena like creativity. A number of measures have been developed in relation to such studies purporting to measure, for example, a sense of humor (e.g., the Overall Sense of Humor Index), the propensity to find things humorous (e.g., the Situational Humor Response Questionnaire), or people's reactions to humor (e.g., the Coping With Humor Scale).

There have been a few studies seeking to link humor to leadership effectiveness, but the evidence is limited thus far. There is rather more evidence related to the use of humor to enhance communication effectiveness—something leaders can draw upon—and substantial research on the use of humor in educational contexts to enhance educative communication and learning. It is also suggested that humor can facilitate the motivation of employees, but again neither the evidence nor the explanatory mechanisms are strong.

Another track of research explores humor in organizational groups and teams. In a general sense, humor is considered to be a type of social lubricant, smoothing and enhancing social relationships. For example, the work of Duncan and colleagues examined the role of humor in facilitating group formation processes and group dynamics such as cohesiveness, identification, and solidarity. Other work has explored the role of humor in enhancing group processes such as intra- and intergroup communication and conflict resolution. There are a number of studies relating humor to improvements in group problem solving, innovation, and creativity. More recently, humor has also been associated with the formation of organizational cultures and subcultures, although the evidence is again rather weak.

There have been some attempts, often informed by superiority theory, to research humor in relation to social structures and specifically to examine the role of humor in establishing status and hierarchical relations. Such approaches begin to consider the role of humor in power relations—between individuals, but also between groups and even between organizations. Such work shows how humor is used to generate in-group–out-group relations and hence to enhance in-group identification and a sense of solidarity. In some cases, this consideration of power has edged research on humor and organizations away from a functionalist agenda toward a more critical perspective by showing how humor can be used not only to maintain extant power relations but also to be part of resistance to them.

Critical Commentary and Future Directions

Although there is a growing body of research on humor in organizations, it remains patchy and fragmented, and despite the available array of theoretical perspectives, tends to remain undertheorized. Future research would be enhanced by clarity on what theoretical position informs the research: There is no indication at this stage, however, of theoretical convergence. That notwithstanding, the vast bulk of the research remains entrenched in the functionalist paradigm and increasingly tends toward a managerialist agenda wherein humor is examined for its possible application in enhancing organizational processes and outcomes of value to managers and their employing organizations—consequently, a significant practitioner literature and business has emerged. For some, a reliance on the epistemology and methods of the functionalist paradigm fails to do justice to the complex, contextual, relational, socially constructed nature of humor in organizations. Much of the research, especially experimental, is often decontextualized and, through an intra-individual focus, neglectful of humor's socially constructed nature. Future research would benefit from attention to context and to the social processes in which humor is produced. Furthermore, because the modes of humor are so diverse, research needs to be clear about what mode is being considered and, again, in relation to what context.

Organizational humor research, as noted, is slanted toward positively functional outcomes and viewed more generally as a positive process with positive effects. Not all humor can be viewed in this way; it also has aggressive, threatening, antisocial, resistive, and even subversive forms such as sarcasm and satire, and the functionalist slant has meant a relative neglect of these aspects of humor in organizations. However, the subversive potential of humor has always been recognized and is, indeed, inherent to its nature. Such recognition is signified by the persistent attempts throughout history and across contexts to control, manage, or co-opt humor. David Collinson and others have pointed to such attempts within organizations. A pervasive dynamic exists whereby humor instantiates a challenge to and potential subversion of the established order, leading to attempts by elements within the established order to control and co-opt it. However, humor is an ever-present, spontaneous, and sometimes chaotic, carnivalesque social phenomenon such that attempts to control, manage, and engineer it appear doomed, thus undercutting any managerialist agenda.

Some work considering humor in organizations in terms of its nonfunctionalist, resistive, and subversive capacities has emerged. For example, humor can serve as a counterpoint to the rhetoric of seriousness, order, and rationality pervasive in many organizations. More important, perhaps, humor has significance not because it has directly subversive and transformative capacities, but because it exposes the arbitrariness, paradoxes, inconsistencies, and absurdities inherent in organization. Such revelations may be the ground on which resistance and transformation can be initiated in an alternate, nonhumorous mode. Research also shows humor used more directly to challenge the established order, power hierarchies, and management regime. It is a type of symbolic resource used to challenge an organization's presumed ordering and meaning frames and interpolate an alternative. Part of humor's efficacy in challenging power and authority is its expressly nonserious mode, which provides a safer ground upon which to mount a critique. Challenge and critique in serious mode are easier to identify, more difficult to back away from, and more likely to generate negative reactions. There is again ambiguity here, inherent to humor, since it provides not only the basis for resistance and critiques to be mounted, but also the basis for it to be ignored or rejected, since it was "not serious."

The subversive potential of humor remains debated. Some argue that humor is a permitted and tolerated contraposition within social systems—a kind of safety valve—and hence it actually affirms the status quo rather than subverts it. Others argue that humor and comedy contain a genuine subversive potential. Further research is needed to examine the processes of humor in organizational contexts in order to better understand these dynamics. A step outside the functionalist paradigm is necessary for this to happen, as is greater attention to the specificities of context and forms of humor. More complex, contextually sensitive and ethnographic studies of humor in organization show it to be a multifaceted phenomenon capable of a range of forms and effects: affirmations of power, functional roles as social lubricant, and the facilitation of resistive solidarity and subversion of the established order among them.

—*Robert Westwood*

See also Control; Managerial Rationality; Organizational Misbehavior; Organizational Paradox; Paradox

Further Readings

Chapman, A. J., & Foot, H. C. (Eds.). (1996). *Humor and laughter: Theory, research, and applications.* New Brunswick, NJ: Transaction.

Collinson, D. L. (2002). Managing humour. *Journal of Management Studies, 39*(3), 269–288.

Critchely, S. (2002). *On humour.* London: Routledge.

Holmes, J. (2000). Politeness, power, and provocation: How humour functions in the workplace. *Discourse Studies, 2*(2), 159–185.

Martin, D. M. (2004). Humour in middle management: Women negotiating the paradoxes of organisational life. *Journal of Applied Communication Research, 32*(2), 147–170.

Morreall, J. (1997). *Humor works.* Amherst, MA: HRD Press.

Taylor, P., & Bain, P. (2003). Subterranean worksick blues: Humour as subversion in two call centers. *Organization Studies, 24*(9), 1487–1509.

Westwood, R. I. (2004). Comic relief: Subversion and catharsis in organisational comedic theatre. *Organisation Studies, 25*(5), 775–795.

HYPOCRISY

Organizations are often expected to display consistency among talk, decision, and action: to act according to decisions and presentations of its management. But organizations may also talk in one way, decide in another, and act in a third way. Organizational hypocrisy can be defined as a situation in which organizations act contrary to their talk or decisions.

Conceptual Overview

Hypocrisy is a response to a world in which values, ideas, or people are in conflict—a way in which individuals and organizations handle such conflicts. It is a way of trying to satisfy some demands by talk or decisions and others by action. For instance, a company could try to satisfy environmental concerns by producing visions or plans or make decisions about environmental protection while satisfying demands for profitability by continuing to use polluting production processes. To act consistently with what is said and what is decided would be to satisfy one interest while leaving the others completely unsatisfied.

According to standard administrative wisdom and traditional decision theory, management talk and decisions in one direction increase the likelihood for organizational action in the same direction. Situations of conflicting demands make it often easier to act in one direction if either the talk or the decision indicates the opposite, that is, the likelihood of an action decreases the more it is talked about and the more often clear decisions are made about it. Its likelihood increases if what is said and decided is in opposition to it. Talk and decisions in one direction compensate for actions in the opposite direction and vice versa. Talk, decisions, and actions are not "de-coupled" or "loosely coupled" but "coupled," although in a way other than is usually assumed.

Critical Commentary and Future Directions

Hypocrisy may be used as a conscious strategy by managers for whom the legitimacy of an organization is important. But organizational hypocrisy also arises without anyone having intended it. For example, a decision about a certain action can be the very impetus for the opponents to make active resistance that prevents the implementation of the action. And it is not unusual to set goals in areas where the organization is weak, in areas in which it has not succeeded in satisfying a certain interest through action. Such goals are, by definition, examples of hypocrisy, for they express what is not being done, but the purpose of setting goals may be the opposite of hypocrisy.

Hypocrisy is meaningful only if people value not only organizational actions but also organizational talk and decisions. Modern organizations produce a great deal of talk and decisions. Organizations are seldom secretive about their visions, programs, and important decisions; on the contrary, they are often published. Modern corporations have communication departments that specialize in explaining the what and why of current strategies and decisions to external and internal parties. Politics revolves, to a large extent, around ways of talking and of presenting decisions. And organizations rarely need to go begging for attention—mass media interest is high for organizational planning, strategies, programs, opinions, and decisions. Talk and decisions generally reach wider audiences than actions do.

One reason people pay attention to organizational talk and decisions is that they believe in traditional decision theory, and so they hope that talk and decisions about an action they like increase the likelihood of that action. Then hypocrisy will "work" precisely because people do not believe in it. For those who want to make their hypocrisy work, there is reason for "meta-hypocrisy": to propagate the view that their organization works according to the traditional model and does not produce hypocrisy.

Hypocrisy can be expected to be particularly common when conflicts are extensive or strong or when they are emphasized. Politics in democratic states tends to generate hypocrisy. But most other contemporary organizations are exposed to conflicting demands. For example, modern companies should be profitable, provide employment, offer a good working environment, provide their employees with decent wages, give good service to their customers, and contribute to a sustainable physical environment. It is popular to talk about "corporate social responsibility." Such responsibility is fertile ground for hypocrisy, and hypocrisy becomes an important source of legitimacy for organizations.

Organizational hypocrisy creates complications for those who expect to influence organizational actions by forcing the organization to make decisions about these actions. It may be difficult to know whether a decision stimulates or obstructs a corresponding action.

An important issue for further research to explore is when conflicts lead to hypocrisy and when conflicts are handled in other ways such as by domination by one interest (as in majority rule) or by finding actions that are compromises among different interests. A related issue is what influences the extent to which hypocrisy is tolerated. When is the norm for consistency between talk, decisions, and actions evoked and when is it less important? When organizations are viewed as one actor—as modern organizations often are—the norm seems more valid than when organizations are seen as assemblies of multiple actors.

Another issue to explore is under what circumstances hypocrisy is unstable and when it is stable. A superordinate hierarchical level that can sanction hypocrisy may increase instability. When this is lacking—as it is in international relations, for instance—hypocrisy can be expected to be more stable. Hypocrisy often involves talk and decisions about the future, promises that actions in the future shall reflect interests that are not satisfied by today's actions. What happens when the future becomes the present? Even in a distant future, people may refer to the decisions made long ago and demand that they should be implemented, and this could force belated implementation. On the other hand, old talk and decisions are sometimes forgotten or they are considered irrelevant in a new situation, and so there is no pressure for implementation.

—*Nils Brunsson*

See also Accountability; Action; Communication; Complexity of Decision Making; Conflict; Control; Corporate Branding; Corporate Citizenship; Corporate Social Responsibility; Corporate Values; Decision-Making Theory; Goal-Setting Theory; Institutional Theory; Loose Coupling; Management and Public Policy; Neoinstitutional Theory; New Institutionalism; Organizational Citizenship Behaviors; Organizational Communication; Organizational Environments; Organizational Image; Organizational Rhetoric; Organizational Rituals; Politics; Strategic Discourse; Trust; Truth

Further Readings

Brunsson, N. (2002). *The organization of hypocrisy. Talk, decisions, and actions in organizations* (2nd ed.). Malmö, Sweden: Abstrakt Liber Copenhagen Business Press.

Brunsson, N. (2003). Organized hypocrisy. In B. Czarniawska & G. Sevón (Eds.), *The northern lights* (pp. 201–22). Malmö, Sweden: Liber Abstrakt Copenhagen Business Press.

Edelman, M. (1971). *Politics as symbolic action.* New York: Academic Press.

Krasner, S. (1999). *Sovereignty: Organized hypocrisy.* Princeton, NJ: Princeton University Press.

Machiavelli, N. (1999). *The prince* (G. Bull, Trans.). London: Penguin Classics.

Meyer, J., & Rowan, B. (1977). Institutionalized organizations: Formal structure as myth and ceremony. *American Journal of Sociology, 83*(2): 340–363.

IDENTIFICATION

The increasing interest in identification within and to organizations can be seen as a response to two major organizational trends: (1) eroding employee loyalty to organizations due to changes in psychological contracts and a trend toward more self-managed careers, and (2) the desire to retain top performers (e.g., professionals, knowledge workers) to maintain a competitive advantage in a "knowledge economy." Given that compensation packages are fairly easy for other organizations to replicate, managers, leaders, and scholars are paying more attention to the role that binding an employee's sense of self with some aspect of the organization might play in motivating and retaining employees.

Conceptual Overview

Identification has a long history in the social sciences. Conceptualizations have ranged from a type of persuasion based on personal liking to a by-product of impersonal categorization based on one's membership in a social group. What unites recent conceptualizations is the implication of identity. To identify with a target (e.g., belief, person, collective) means that this target becomes self-referential. Thus, I identify with IBM when I see IBM as reflecting who I am. Historically, identification has been viewed primarily in cognitive terms. It has been argued to occur in at least two primary ways: (1) affinity, where I recognize a target (e.g., an organization) as reflecting who I am, and (2) emulation, where I strive to become more like a target.

Organizational identification is associated with a rather long list of antecedents and outcomes. With regard to the former, identification with an organization is most likely to occur when the organization is prestigious or otherwise attractive, when it is distinctive, when members are relatively homogeneous, and when the organization is salient when compared with other organizations. In general, these and related organizational antecedents help meet members' needs for consistency, self-esteem, meaning (e.g., serving a higher purpose), uncertainty reduction, and the like, and the more they do so, the more likely members are to identify with that organization. Identification with an organization may also be more likely when members are collocated and proximal than when they are physically dispersed, when one's affiliation with an organization is public and visible (versus private), when there is interpersonal attraction with other members, and when members have shared goals and/or shared history. However, it is important to note that identification is quite robust, and can occur even in the absence of some of these conditions. For example, Reicher, Spears, and Postmes's review of the social identity deidentification (SIDE) model shows how identification can form in the lack of physical proximity.

There have also been a multitude of advantages and disadvantages associated with having individuals identify with an organization. Traditionally, organizational identification has been linked with lower turnover, increased motivation and job satisfaction, and an increased willingness by employees to think and act in ways that are favorable to the organization. By contrast, more recent research has begun to examine the "dark side" of (over-) identification. Identifying too strongly with one's organization can result in high individual vulnerability (especially if the organization's reputation fails); distrust and paranoia; overdependence on and overconformity to organizational dictates; antisocial, unethical, immoral, and even tyrannical behaviors by both leaders and followers; decreased creativity and risk-taking; and the loss of an independent sense of self.

Critical Commentary and Future Directions

Identification scholars confront several conceptual issues. One of the biggest concerns conceptual boundaries. For example, early research on organizational commitment by Mowday, Porter, Steers—and later work by Meyer and Alan on affective commitment—each viewed identification as a facet of commitment. Thus, there has been considerable effort to disentangle these two constructs, notably by Ashforth and Pratt from the identification camp, and Meyer, Becker, and Van Dick from the commitment camp. One aspect of identification that clearly differentiates it from other "attachment" concepts, however, is the implication of an individual's identity.

A second conceptual issue involves the relationship between identification and identity. As evidenced in the review by Ashmore and colleagues, many psychologists view identification as synonymous with social identity. For conceptual clarity, it helps to differentiate the two. For example, from a social identity perspective, one's identity can be comprised of both idiosyncratic (e.g., I am smart) and social elements (e.g., I am a member of the bowling team). Identification, however, involves only social identities. Moreover, identification varies in magnitude—thus one can strongly or weakly identify with being a member of a bowling team. However, in both of these cases, the existence of the bowling team social identity remains invariant.

Thus, one might see identification as an indicator of how much one values and internalizes a particular social identity—and as an indicator of the degree to which the identity determines one's behavior.

A third conceptual issue concerns the relationship between identification and a collective-level "identity." For example, in the organizational literature, there has been some debate about the relationship between organizational identity and organizational identification. Foreman and Whetten, for instance, tightly bind the conceptualization of organizational identity—or what members view as central, distinctive, and relatively enduring about their organization—and member identification. However, other scholars point to the multivocality of organizational identity expressions, as well as the role of individuals' unique experiences and expectations in interpreting organizational identities, and call for a looser coupling between the study of organizational identity and organizational identification.

Beyond these controversies, research in identification is vibrant and growing. Emerging research has focused on further exploration of what identification is (and how to measure it), how identification occurs, the application of identification to "new" organizational contexts, and the management of identification.

First, there has been increasing interest in the extracognitive aspects of identification. Most organizational research on identification, such as Dutton, Dukerich and Harquail's foundational piece, has viewed identification solely as a cognitive construct. However, Tajfel and Turner's original conceptualization of the term describes evaluative and emotional aspects. Thus, researchers have begun exploring the affective side of identification. To illustrate, Elsbach proposed an expanded model of identification that notes that the cognitions in identification are infused with emotion, such as positive, negative, or mixed feelings. Moreover, Pratt has shown how various combinations of socialization practices (e.g., sensebreaking and encapsulation) can lead to positive, negative, or ambivalent identification among members. These differing understandings of identification are reflected in the field's ongoing attempts to measure the construct. Some scales view identification in terms of cognitive overlap, such as the Bergami and Bagozzi circle scale, while others also explore the emotional side, such as the Ashforth and Mael scale. Thus, with emerging work come new controversies.

Second, research has also begun looking at new antecedents for identification. For example, while identification is not a trait or stable individual difference (and should not be measured that way), there may be some traitlike predictors of identification. Glynn, for example, has argued for need for organizational identification (nOID). Other research has focused on identification motives or needs. Whereas early SIT research focused on the importance of organizational attractiveness on member self-esteem in engendering identification, others—such as Hogg and Deaux—have postulated a wider set of motives. The work of Ashforth and colleagues, in particular, challenges the notion of "attractiveness" by examining identification in occupations that are physically, socially, or morally tainted. Cardador and Pratt have taken a different slant on the genesis of identification by examining the various bases, or underlying mechanisms, scholars have used to explain the formation of identification: relationships (both personal and impersonal), behaviors, and symbols.

Third, research has begun to examine identification in new contexts. For example, social identity scholars such as van Knippenberg, van Dyck, and others have begun to explore identification dynamics in mergers, while others, such as Hogg and Terry have examined identification and leadership dynamics. Haslam's work on social identity in organizations chronicles such advancements. Organizational researchers, such as Wisenfeld, Raghuram, and Garud, as well as Rockmann and colleagues, are examining identification among distributed workers. And research in marketing, such as that by Bhattacharya, extends models of organizational identification to those that are chronically outside of the organization: customers. By examining how different types of individuals interface with the organization (e.g., "virtual" workers and customers), work in this area is beginning to unpack how the nature of someone's organizational affiliation (e.g., proximal versus not, paid versus not) influences identification.

Finally, emerging research has begun to examine how organizations might *manage* people's identification in an organization. Implicit in many perspectives on identification—such as rhetoric, social identity theory/self-categorization, commitment, and (role) identity theory—is that individual members have multiple potential targets for identification, and that such multiplicity needs to be "managed" in some way, either by the individual or by the dyads, groups, or larger collectives of which that person is a part. In organizations, the management of identification often involves getting individuals to identify with the "right" target of identification, which is usually the organization or an organizational subunit (e.g., department). Thus, work has arisen that discusses other identification targets that compete for attention. For example, in the field of communications, Scott and colleagues build from Cheney's classic work to examine how individuals identify with different organizational targets. Others have built from Gouldner's classic work and have honed in on professional identification and how it differs from organizational, group, and other types of identification. Still others are examining multiple identifications that involve nonwork targets such as demographic groups (e.g., race, gender, or culture) and how these can lead to the emergence of "fault lines" that can tear a group apart. In this regard, organizational identification research is revisiting long-standing tensions, such as those embedded in professional versus organizational attachment and organizational diversity.

While the field is maturing, two critical areas in identification have been underexplored. First, while interest is increasing in how organizations might manage identification, there has been relatively little work on the *morality* of this practice. What are the ethical ramifications of implicating employee identity with an organization—especially when organizations eschew lifetime job employment? Is the creation of such an organization-specific bond justified under these situations? Second, while the field has done a nice job of identifying antecedents and outcomes of identification, considerably more work needs to be done in exploring the *process* of identifying. How do identifications form and change over time? A focus on identifying over time is likely to bring new challenges, and to draw upon work on such disparate fields as collective-level beliefs, individual experience and expertise, and the meaning of work.

—*Michael G. Pratt*

See also Organizational Identity; Social Identity Theory

Further Readings

Ashforth, B. E., & Mael, F. (1989). Social identity theory and the organization. *Academy of Management Review, 14*, 20–39.

Cardador, M. T., & Pratt, M. G. (2006). Identification management and its bases: Bridging management and marketing perspectives through a focus on affiliation dimensions. *Journal of the Academy of Marketing Science, 34*(2), 174–184.

Cheney, G. (1983). The rhetoric of identification and the study of organizational communication. *Quarterly Journal of Speech, 69*, 143–158.

Dutton, J. E., Dukerich, J. M., & Harquail, C. V. (1994). Organizational images and member identification. *Administrative Science Quarterly, 39*, 239–263.

Elsbach, K. (1999). An expanded model of organizational identification. In R. Sutton & B. Staw (Eds.), *Research in Organizational Behavior, Volume 21* (pp. 163–199). Stanford, CA: JAI Press.

Haslam, S. A. (2004). *Psychology in organizations: The social identity approach* (2nd ed.). Thousand Oaks, CA: Sage.

Pratt, M. G. (1998). To be or not to be: Central questions in organizational identification. In D. Whetten & P. Godfrey (Eds.), *Identity in organizations: Developing theory through conversations* (pp. 171–207). Thousand Oaks, CA: Sage.

Tajfel, H., & Turner, J. C. (1979). An integrative theory of intergroup conflict. In W. G. Austin & S. Worchel (Eds.), *The social psychology of group relations* (pp. 33–47). Monterey, CA: Brooks/Cole.

IDENTITY

In basic terms, identity refers to the individual characteristics by which a person is recognized or known. Identity is central to how people recognize each other in the street and how they describe themselves when they look in the mirror. Identity is about sameness—it is the identification of how one sees oneself and others in relation to being the same as some types of other people. Perhaps more importantly, it is also about difference—to whom one is not the same. The sense of self that one has about oneself can refer to characteristics, personalities, images, and so forth and relies on self-knowledge in order for it to be expressed. Identity is about who a person is.

From an essentialist position—one that sees identity as being grounded in essential aspects of the person—identity is unitary in nature and refers to how people concretely describe "who I am"—white, female, working class, Welsh, hysterical, for example. This traverses identity descriptors of the skin, social identity categories, language, bodies, knowledge, and power practices. From a social constructionist perspective, identity is constructed between self and other and focuses, as Robyn Thomas and Alison Linstead suggest, both on "who am I" and "who am I becoming." However, if one moves from an essentialist position to one where the relation between attributes of the person and identity is more contingent, in keeping with a poststructuralist approach, identity can be regarded not only constantly changing but also as fragmented, multiple, and emergent.

Conceptual Overview

The study of identity has a long history in organization studies, with an intellectual lineage that traces back, inter alia, to George Herbert Mead's symbolic interactionist studies of self-making, the functionalism of Talcott Parsons, the development of role theory by Robert Merton, the dramaturgical sociology of Erving Goffman, and Harold Garfinkel's ethnomethodological studies of how social membership is achieved through talk.

Alison Pullen argues, after Garfinkel, that identities are changing but relatively stable, and moves toward the recognition of identity construction as a form of first order accounting that is characterized by paradox, fluidity, inconsistency, and constant emergence. However, in agreement with Hugh Willmott, it can be suggested that because of subjects' "equivocal positions," identity construction is not a matter of resolving ambiguity and making clear-cut choices, but is characterized by confusion and conflict within the individual, including how those identities constructed relate to the organizational context. Identity formation in and around organizations is not only embedded in the demands of the present, but is constructed in terms of the conjunction of past and future. Identities are formed through an explanation of previous events (as episodes in an unfolding narrative) in a way that positions the constructor of the account advantageously for future episodes—indeed it may be a rehearsal for them.

Goffman reminds us that identities can be seen as masks that are actively used, manipulated, and created as resources for participation in the performance of an ongoing masquerade. Within this process are particular events that significantly affect the shaping of identity and that may change its course dramatically. Identities as masks are created and/or mobilized as resources in a project of becoming. They are outfits for participation in an ongoing masquerade—a masquerade that protects and shelters their lack and/or loss. Masks are a resource for people to work out who they are and what they need to do to become it. Masks can also give prominence to certain characteristics so as to showcase and define the face. Masks are therefore simultaneously false representations of identity, and essential parts of the creation of selves. Masks, however, do not just protect and conceal the face but over time take the shape of the face. The natural features of the face die and give way, dissolving into the permanence of the mask—and one can question, after Pullen, whether this leads to both the death and resurrection of the self.

Pullen and Stephen Linstead develop the idea of identity as a process; that is, identity as a project rather than a product. By such an account, identity is a process that involves societal factors, psychological factors, interaction, reflection, practice, and performance. Pullen and Linstead discern three areas of identity formation, which are interconnected and recursive rather than sequential, and which are infused by power relations and suffused by reflexivity. These three areas of identity formation are *identity capital*, processes of subjective *identity formation*, and *identity performance* (or identity events) and are discussed below.

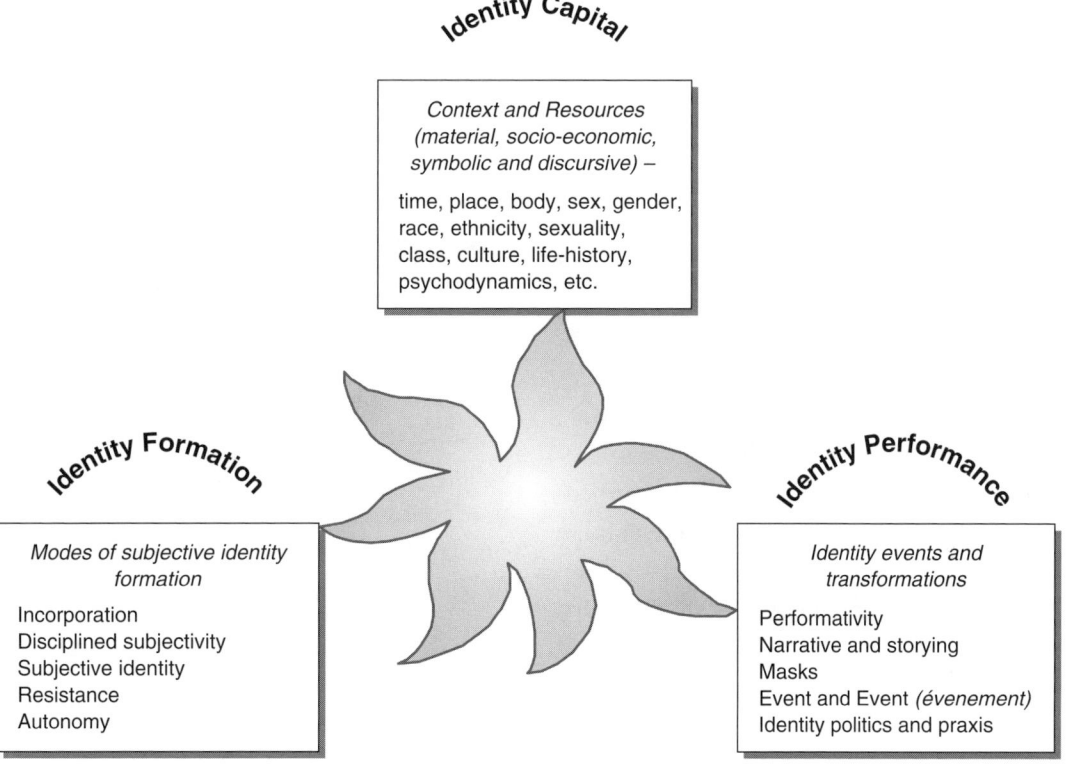

Figure 1   Processes of Subjective Identity

Source: Pullen, A., & Linstead, S. (2005). *Identity and organization.* London: Routledge. Used with permission.

Identity Resources and Identity Capital

Identity as a process rather than a product is a result of a response to the other (i.e., both particular other people, and the notion of other people in general). Such a process is grounded in ontological insecurity, rather than certainty. However, the meaning and symbolism of this notion of the other is complex when it is not embodied in specific interpersonal interactions. In such cases, the other against whom one defines the self is a manifestation of traces of one's past experiences with both oneself and other people, as well as projections of the existence of one's identity into the future. This identity process draws on, and relates to, contextual features that may be present, historical, or based on a shared expectation of the future. Pullen and Linstead argue that this makes for an identity that reaches forward and backward in ways that may be material, socioeconomic, symbolic, or discursive. Hence, identity will be a combination of all these phenomena, although not all may be given the same degree of attention.

These "resources" can be regarded as *identity capital*. Certain properties of identity capital often act so strongly as to "name" an individual or body, to convey a set of attributes and expectations that may be either an advantage or disadvantage to the change or creation of new identity. Indeed identity capital may represent both burden and opportunity for leverage. The contextual field too is dynamic, and identity capital may lose or increase value when shifted from one place to another—whether an individual changes organization, an organization attempts to operate in a different market, or both move to a new physical location. Identity also changes over time and in relation to prevailing interpretations of history and future projections. The immediate history of power relations in an organization or community, historical and prevailing class or caste relations, and familial dynamics that may be partly cultural or ethnically shaped may all have influence. Manuel Castells argues that the dominant groups in a society may have the power to institute legitimizing identities in order to extend this domination, and relatedly Mats Alvesson and Hugh Willmott identify forms of identity regulation.

Physically, where individuals are concerned, body, sex, and race, considered along with social constructions of ethnicity, gender, and sexuality may play a part. Also at an individual level, personal life-history and the ongoing (and intertextual) life-narrative form a structure, an interpretation, and often provide a teleology into which identity resources can be drawn and that affects those aspects of selection and deployment over which the individual has some exercise of agency. Finally, psychodynamic processes are also active in identity formation—for example, ego-defenses or narcissistic self-projection deploy identity resources and are a form of psychological skill or competence capital, even where this may be pathological.

Modes of Subjective Identity Formation

In considering how subject formation occurs, Pullen, influenced by Michel Foucault, identified five modes of subjective identity formation in her work on how managers were constructing their identities in restructuring organizations. These processes of identity construction are grounded in power, knowledge, and language. These are perhaps best conceived in terms of the five questions that they address:

1. Mode of Incorporation (the ways that individuals accommodate organizational goals in a climate of change and restructuring). The question here is how individuals align themselves with new organizational goals and objectives and accommodate visions that may be at odds with what they previously held or currently hold. These may range from enthusiastic embrace to attempts at avoidance. Examples include vision/advocacy (seduction), acceptance, accommodation, consent, citizenship, legitimation, and knowledge management. In subjective identity formation, what is acknowledged to be known is selective, and the unpalatable denied.

2. Mode of Disciplined Subjectivity (how individuals fit themselves into gendered organizational social systems/discursive structures). The question here is how individuals identify with new systems with different requirements of them and different means of controlling and evaluating them as organizational members. Where the mode of incorporation deals with values and beliefs, it will be more grounded in the praxis of membership and what sort of a member the subject becomes. Examples are social subject/team player (surveillance), leading subject, political subject, professional subject, and acting subject (performer of a role or roles).

3. Mode of Subjective Identity (the means by which individuals position, or see themselves positioned, within/identify with wider social discourses). The question here is how individuals weight organizational discourse in relation to wider discourses of which they may be a part. This deals with the subject in relation not just to the organization, but to whom they *see* themselves being in the world, and the tensions, strains, or opportunities that may ensue. Examples may be personal, familial, professional/careerist, ethical, and aesthetic.

4. Mode of Resistance (how individuals resist, transgress, and change established discursive structures or create new ones). Here the question is how individuals resist being colonized by discourses of which they do not approve or in which they do not believe, and how they resist having unacceptable identities inscribed upon them. Castells argues that collective resistance identities may be formed from common modes of resistance permeating a group or society. Examples both individual and collective can include political opposition, noncooperation, subversion, symbolic/discursive opposition, counterseduction, transgressive reinscription, reflexive critique, and dissent.

5. Mode of Autonomy (how individuals convert identity into agency and how praxis can thereby be enabled and realized). The final question is how individuals are able to create identities that they can use to establish some sovereign epistemological space that can become a resource for change and development. Examples are political agency, emancipation, empowerment, networking and alliances, bricolage/improvisation, play, and managing boundaries.

The modes of subjective identity formation described above may be thought of as involved in deploying different masks, at a tactical level, while simultaneously cohering to form different dimensions of a larger mask. Different masks may consequently be employed *within* different modes of subject formation to achieve a common objective or a specific combination of modes of subject formation may constitute one particular mask.

Identity Performance and Event

In her book *Gender Trouble,* Judith Butler argues (in relation to gender) that identity is shaped and constructed in time and space rather than through a stable identity. However, in *Bodies That Matter,* she extends this consideration to the ways in which bodies exceed the demands placed on them by discursive limits. As Butler argues, identity is a social temporality that accomplishes its own origin; it is *performative* in that in functioning as a label for a set of behaviors and styles it constructs those behaviors as the result of a *substantial* source of identity. For Butler, identity is performative because it is through one's actions and performances that one's identity is constituted, rather than a preexisting self being the originator of behavior. Pullen and Linstead recognize the lack of consideration that has been given to issues of performativity in studies of identity in organizations. They argue that how identity, or its appearance of substance, may be generated from acts or series of acts, stylized in harmony with the modes of subjective identity formation is critical to identity formation.

Narrative and story may become part of the performative dimensions of identity, as Barbara Czarniawska has outlined in the context of institutional theory. Identity performance may be enacted through the assumption of a succession of masks. Yet perhaps the most significant concept in Pullen and Linstead's model is one developed from Foucault by Gilles Deleuze—that of *évenement. Évenement* is an event that changes the way one experiences the world, the way one thinks about it, and signals the possibility of radical identity change—after an *évenement* happens things can never be the same again. The events of 9/11 were certainly *évenement* for many people.

Identity performances are often employed to attempt to permanently change the way people think of another person, to make his or her performance an *évenement*. But, as people are caught up in the events of others, they cannot rule out the possibility that someone else's *évenement* may envelop them and change who they "are" forever.

Finally, issues of agency and praxis come together in the consideration of identity politics, the paradigm case of which would be feminism. Castells attempts to capture this dimension in terms of what he calls *project identity*, whereby individuals draw on the cultural resources (identity capital) available for them to create new identities and effect social change (which could also be organizational change where conditions are appropriate). Pullen and Linstead argue that the concept of project identity is a form of purposeful collective identity performance that can achieve small and potentially large scale social change.

Critical Commentary and Future Directions

Doug Kellner has observed that identity has always been experienced as a problem, even though the postmodern condition has accelerated and fragmented the processes of identity formation. Studies of identity in organizations are now mainstream and the issue of identity has become an important aspect of organizations, both in terms of their members' identity and the identity of the organization as a whole. The concept of identity however requires thinking through from as many dimensions as possible, especially if the project is to explore the fragmentation, multiplicity, and fluidity of identity. How then can theorists interrupt and disrupt identity as sameness to incorporate identity as difference? There is a need here to consider whether the concept of identity itself is deeply constraining. The issue of *disidentity* posed by Nceku Q. Nyathi and Stefano Harney is seductive in this context. In positing this issue, the authors suggest that disidentity offers a critique that desires the superadequation of the person that might provide agency, and as such the individual would have no need of any category of identity and no basis on which identity struggles would occur. The remaining question then becomes whether there is mileage in thinking beyond identity. And, more important, what can we do about it?

—Alison Pullen

See also Alterity (Otherness); Authenticity; Narcissism; Organizational Identity; Social Identity Theory; Subjectivity

Further Readings

Alvesson, M., & Willmott, H. C. (2002). Identity regulation as organizational control producing the appropriate individual. *Journal of Management Studies, 39,* 619–644.

Butler, J. (1990). *Gender trouble: Feminism and the subversion of identity.* London: Routledge.

Butler, J. (1993). *Bodies that matter: On the discursive limits of sex.* London: Routledge.

Castells, M. (1997). *The power of identity.* Oxford, UK: Blackwell.

Czarniawska, B. (1997). Narratives of individual and organizational identities. In S. A. Deetz (Ed.), *Communication Yearbook 17* (pp. 193–221). Thousand Oaks, CA: Sage.

Garfinkel, H. (1967). *Studies in ethnomethodology.* Engelwood Cliffs, NJ: Prentice Hall.

Goffman, E. (1971). *The presentation of self in everyday life.* Harmondsworth, UK: Penguin. (Original work published 1959).

Kellner, D. (1992). Popular culture and the construction of postmodern identities. In S. Lash & J. Friedman (Eds.), *Modernity and identity* (pp. 141–177). Oxford, UK: Blackwell.

Nyathi, N. Q., & Harney, S. (2007). Disidentity. In A. Pullen, N. Beech, & D. Sims (Eds.), *Exploring identity.* London: Palgrave.

Pullen, A. (2006). *Managing identity.* London: Palgrave.

Pullen, A., & Linstead, S. (2005). *Identity and organization.* London: Routledge.

Thomas, R., & Linstead, A. (2002). Loosing the plot? Middle managers and identity. *Organization, 9*(1), 71–93.

Willmott, H. (1997). Rethinking management and managerial work: Capitalism, control, and subjectivity. *Human Relations, 50*(11), 1329–1359.

IDEOLOGY

Ideology refers to a collection of ideas and has been used as an analytical concept in both critical and mainstream approaches to organization studies. The critical approaches to ideology have their roots in Marxist theorizing but are increasingly drawing on post-Marxist and other discourse-based approaches to organizational analysis. Critical perspectives on ideology are interested in the nature and origin of ideas in relation to social and organizational structures and how these ideas serve the interests of particular groups. Mainstream perspectives define ideology more broadly as a set of beliefs or worldview and use it to conceptualize organizational culture. This approach places greater emphasis on consensus and shared meaning, which is the essence of culture. Whatever approach is taken, ideology remains a useful concept for understanding why and how employees consent to managerial authority in organizations.

Conceptual Overview

To understand the relevance of ideology for organization studies, it is first necessary to trace the origins of the term in social theorizing. The term *ideology* was first used by Destutt de Tracy at the turn of the 19th century to denote a "science of ideas" that could be employed to discover the "truth." The most well-known contribution to the ideology literature comes from Karl Marx. For Marx, ideology comes into existence with the development of a class-based society, which divides those who control economic resources (the bourgeoisie) from those whose are subordinated because they only have their labor to sell (the proletariat). Marx proposed a base/superstructure model of society, where the *base* refers to the means of production (e.g., technology, capital, materials). Ideology is part of the *superstructure*, which also includes religion, as well as the political and legal systems. In orthodox Marxism, the base determines the superstructure, meaning that ideology is determined by those who control the economic resources and is employed by the ruling group to further their interests. Marx viewed the ideologies of the ruling class as false and misleading because they served their own narrow interests.

The orthodox Marxist approach to ideology has been vigorously criticized for being grounded in an essentialist and deterministic conception of society. This critique has two aspects: the base/superstructure epiphenomenon and the notion of false consciousness. The first criticism is that ideological forms are seen to be directly determined by the economic base, with critics stating that social life cannot be explained purely in terms of people's position within a class structure. Antonio Gramsci rejected this determinism and provides an alternative understanding of ideology based on hegemony, which refers to a system of domination that elicits consent. Gramsci explained that in gaining hegemony, dominant social groups define the parameters of what can and cannot be said and who is considered legitimate and right. This "common sense" is ideology and is produced by agencies such as churches, schools, and the mass media.

Extending Gramsci's work, Louis Althusser sought to address problems with the Marxist theory of ideology as false consciousness. An example of false consciousness from a Marxist perspective would be the way in which the ideology of the market hides the fact that the production of goods involves the exploitation of labor. This concept is criticized for its objectivist assumption of the existence of a truth that lies behind ideology that agents can somehow access to become enlightened. Althusser argued that ideology plays a pivotal role in securing the subjective conditions required for the continuation of capitalism. Ideology interpellates or hails individuals as subjects, inducing people to identify with the dominant ideology. Ideology is a powerful force because the socially constructed nature of our subjectivity slips from view, making the dominant ideology appear pregiven and natural, and producing an illusion of freedom and self-determination.

The structural Marxism of Gramsci and Althusser inspired further critique of the Marxist theory of ideology from postmodernism and poststructuralism. From these perspectives, discourse and language should be a central focus of the study of ideology rather than being accorded secondary status behind matters of the economy. On the issue of false consciousness, Michel Foucault questioned the simplistic binary between truth and error and demonstrated that a number of discourses that had attained the status of *scientificity* remained linked with social and political forces. This turned attention away from the discovery of "truth" to the ways in which "truth effects" are produced within discourses.

To this point, the focus has been on ideology at the level of society. Within organization studies, a number of theorists have explored the ideological dimensions of workplace power and control. Typically, critical studies of ideology at the organizational level assume that the relationship between employee and employer is an unequal power structure that necessarily produces conflict. The challenge then becomes how to account for the active consent by employees to work arrangements that dominate and disadvantage them.

Reinhard Bendix's classic work in 1956 sets out to investigate Marx's proposition that collections of ideas are used by groups to advance their material interests. Bendix defines managerial ideologies as ideas espoused by or for those who seek authority in organizations and which attempt to legitimize that authority. Bendix contends that these managerial ideologies are a direct consequence of the internal bureaucratization of organizations and the need for command and control. For example, scientific management and human relations movement are both seen as ideologies that endeavor to invoke active faith in the necessity of managerial control. Scientific management justifies managerial authority by applying a "scientific" approach to work in place of tradition and worker control of the labor process, while the human relations movement legitimates managerial authority by promoting the idea that management is attending to workers' social and psychological needs and not merely their economic needs, as is considered to be the case with scientific management.

Michael Burawoy published one of the most important empirical applications of Marxist ideology theory in 1979. Drawing on an Althusserian approach, Burawoy conducted an ethnographic study of a machine shop to investigate the ideological apparatuses through which consent to an exploitative social structure is organized. Responding to the criticism that Marxist approaches underplay the importance of subjectivity in the maintenance of an exploitative labor process, Burawoy argues that ideology is something that is lived, emerging from concrete social practices. Consent is achieved through the organization of activities that appear to present employees with real choices, yet these choices are narrowly defined within the boundaries of the capitalist system. In the organization that Burawoy studies, the lack of obtrusive management control and this supposed capacity to choose ensures high productivity levels.

In 1980, Stewart Clegg and David Dunkerley expanded on Burawoy's influential findings by highlighting the role of management theories in maintaining a consenting workforce. Following Gramsci, Clegg and Dunkerley suggest that ideology at the organizational level is propagated by a cadre of management intellectuals and academics in the form of theories of leadership, motivation, and the like. When these ideological practices become hegemonic in the workplace, they act as the dominant lens through which employees understand and make sense of organizational reality. Further work on the generation of consent in the workplace was conducted by Dennis Mumby, who focused on workplace communication as a medium through which ideology generates consent. In 1988, Mumby argued that workplace communication structures operate ideologically by providing a medium through which managerial groups can establish their meaning systems as the only legitimate ones. The resulting hegemony is one way of explaining why workers often collude in their own domination.

In the 1980s, a new take on ideology emerged in the mainstream organization studies literature that defined ideology more broadly than its origins in social class. This perspective sees ideologies as ways of understanding that are based on shared values and beliefs, and therefore has a strong resemblance to the concept of organizational culture. Ideologies evolve out of specific contexts, influence interpretations, facilitate some actions while inhibiting others, and can be used to justify political interests. However, in this view ideologies are not necessarily or inherently political. Ideologies can relate to social classes but also to any social group, such as national cultures, professional groups, and organizational departments. Organization theorists adopting this view are interested in ideologies at the organizational level, with the aim of understanding and predicting behavior in and between organizations.

This attempt to subsume interest-based approaches to ideology is criticized by those of a Marxist persuasion. Weiss and Miller argued in 1988 that the focus of the mainstream ideology studies is the extent to which these ideas are shared, rather than on the nature and origin of ideas, which they believe is the essence of ideology. As with organizational culture, interest in the concept of ideology by the mainstream of organizational theory appears to have receded since reaching a peak in the 1980s and 1990s.

Critical Commentary and Future Directions

As with many concepts associated with the Marxist tradition, a concern with ideology appears largely out of fashion among today's sociologically inclined theorists of organizations, who have turned in increasing numbers to ideas associated with postmodernism and poststructuralism. This has resulted in some theorists rejecting their earlier views. Clegg, for instance, moved from fully endorsing the concept to later rejecting it on the basis of Foucault's rejection of the truth/falsity distinction. Scholars loyal to a Marxist theory of ideology accuse its critics of constructing a straw man by using a valid critique of one specific conception of ideology (the orthodox view) as justification to dismiss the entire project of ideology critique. They also note the paradox that in a world racked by ideological conflicts such as Islamic fundamentalism and Christian evangelicalism the notion of ideology has almost disappeared.

Looking to the future, theorizing on ideology is likely to proceed in two directions. First, some will wish to continue in the Marxist tradition of ideology critique on the grounds that it remains a powerful lens for analyzing contemporary work organizations in both developed and developing contexts. In this tradition, class will remain a central focus, although its theorization will need to avoid accusations of essentialism and determinism leveled by those committed to postmodernism and poststructuralism. This represents the second future direction for studies of ideology. Here, the focus will be on the use of language and discourse to secure hegemony, not only in relation to class, but to a range of identity-based political movements such as race, gender, or sexuality. Through this lens, ideology remains a valid concept for analysis, but its epistemological foundations in class are jettisoned. Writers such as Ernesto Laclau and Chantal Mouffe, for instance, retain the concept of ideology but employ it to describe the desire for total closure by hegemonic projects. The emphasis is on contingency, in contrast to the determinism of orthodox Marxism. Although Laclau and Mouffe have, to this point, received little attention from organization theorists, it can be expected that these and other post-Marxist approaches will receive growing attention.

—Todd Bridgman

See also Class; Conflict; Hegemony; Organizational Culture; Postmodernism

Further Readings

Alvesson, M. (1991). Organizational symbolism and ideology. *Journal of Management Studies, 28*(3), 207–225.

Beyer, J. M. (1981). Ideologies, values and decision-making in organizations. In P. C. Nystrom & W. H. Starbuck (Eds.), *Handbook of organizational design* (pp. 166–202). New York: Oxford University Press.

Burawoy, M. (1979). *Manufacturing consent: Changes in the labor process under monopoly capitalism.* Chicago: University of Chicago Press.

Clegg, S. R., & Dunkerley, D. (1980). *Organization, class, and control.* London: Routledge & Kegan Paul.

Deetz, S. (1994). The new politics of the workplace: Ideology and other unobtrusive controls. In H. Simons & M. Billig (Eds.), *After postmodernism: Reconstructing ideology critique* (pp. 172–199). London: Sage.

Laclau, E., & Mouffe, C. (1985). *Hegemony and socialist strategy: Towards a radical democratic politics.* London: Verso.

Mumby, D. (1988). *Communication and power in organizations: Discourse, ideology, and domination.* Norwood, NJ: Ablex.

Weiss, R. M., & Miller, L. E. (1997). The concept of ideology in organizational analysis: The sociology of knowledge or the social psychology of beliefs? *Academy of Management Review, 12*(1), 104–116.

Impression Management

Impression management describes the process of controlling, or attempting to control, how individuals are perceived by others. The intent of impression management is to influence the behavior and attitudes of others. The concept of impression management dates to the early 1960s and considerations of general patterns of social interaction, but over the past 30 years has been increasingly linked to interactions in the workplace.

Conceptual Overview

Impression management refers to self-presentation behaviors that individuals use to control the perceptions that others have of them, as noted by Edward E. Jones and Thane S. Pittman in 1982. Impression management occurs when individuals convey particular impressions of their skills and abilities, attitudes and emotions, or other personal characteristics to others in an attempt to influence them and obtain desired outcomes.

Researchers have identified five different types of impression management tactics that individuals use to influence others. First, individuals may flatter others, providing gifts and support to others, or do favors for them, seeking to *ingratiate* themselves. Alternatively, individuals may engage in *self-promotion,* making sure others are aware of their skills, status, and achievements, and that these are presented in the best possible light. Third, individuals may project themselves as organizational "citizens," always undertaking extra work and going far beyond what their job requires, in an attempt to influence others by providing a good example, engaging in what is termed *exemplification.* The fourth type of impression management, *supplication,* is the opposite of self-promotion and exemplification. In supplication, individuals are seeking to be perceived as weak and needy, and may beg for help or assistance. Finally, the most negative form of impression management involves threatening and bullying behavior resulting in *intimidation* of others. This final form of impression management causes the target to feel afraid not to comply, even though the actions taken may be subtle rather than overt, such as stressing the decision-making power or influence that the intimidating person has.

With the exception of intimidation, most impression management involves efforts to present a socially desirable impression. People are more likely to influence others if they are perceived as skilled, likeable, of high status and good character, or otherwise socially desirable. People are motivated to manage how others perceive them when they believe that these perceptions will affect their attainment of outcomes, such as rewards. Impressions are generally created through the behaviors that an individual displays, including his or her communication, nonverbal cues, and general demeanor. In addition to the behaviors themselves, others' perceptions are influenced by the timing, frequency, and consistency of an individual's presentation of himself or herself. Initial impressions can be particularly powerful. This is why people often hear advice to "create a positive first impression" in obtaining a job or meeting someone for the first time. Impression management has been linked to a variety of positive outcomes for individuals, including enhanced social attractiveness, so that the individual is seen as a good potential team member, coworker, or boss. Impression management, particularly its more positive forms, has also been linked to increased performance ratings and promotions, increased compensation and other rewards, and career success.

Impression management, however, is not just associated with an increased desire for success within an organization; to a greater or lesser extent it is a fundamental characteristic of social interaction, as people's attitudes, abilities, values, and emotions are largely invisible to others without efforts to organize and communicate them through self-presentation. Mark R. Leary and Robin M. Kowalski, in 1990, identified five contextual and individual characteristics that impact the likelihood and nature of impression management. The first characteristic is the roles people occupy and the social norms associated with those roles. That is, certain roles, such as the positional role of manager or the professional role of nurse, may trigger certain behaviors and presentations of self to others, to convey competence, caring, or authority. The second influential characteristic is the individual's self concept, which may cause people to project the image that they have of themselves and to maintain consistency with their self-perception. For example, someone with a very weak self-concept might present himself or herself as ineffective or of low ability. The third influential characteristic is the nature or role of the person who is the target of the impression management, as the individual may want to create an impression that is aligned with the values and expectations of the person the individual is trying to impress. For example, a job applicant may wish to create the impression that he or she is a loyal and reliable employee, to meet his or her perception of the expectations of a potential employer. The fourth characteristic that influences impression management is the need to dispel or address the way a person is currently perceived, and overcome negative and/or incorrect perceptions. This may be particularly relevant when stereotypes must be overcome, for example, when an older worker projects an impression of being receptive to change, when stereotypes might include that older workers resist change. Finally, individuals may project an image of themselves that is how they wish to be seen, and how they wish to be, creating a desired self in the presentation of themselves that challenges them to become more similar to the image they are creating.

Critical Commentary and Future Directions

To date, most research on impression management has focused either on how situational or individual factors influence the use of specific impression management behaviors or how certain impression management tactics influence outcomes. These are often treated as static or unchangeable behaviors. However, increasing attention is being devoted to the elaboration of the processes of giving and receiving perceptual cues, and interpretation of behaviors, particularly in a cross-cultural context. Future research may elaborate the interactive processes that allow complex impressions to be conveyed, understood, and altered over time, as well as the impact of culture and cultural similarity on effective impression management.

Future research may also pay greater attention to the intentions of those engaging in impression management. In some contexts, impression management has negative connotations, implying that it is deceptive or manipulative. This is not necessarily the case.

Individuals may engage in impression management to overcome perceptual biases and ensure that others perceive them accurately. Even where impression management biases communication by suppressing negative aspects of an individual's skills or personal characteristics, there is evidence that supervisors and other targets of impression management are sensitive to distortions in self-presentation and skilled at discounting self-promotion and exemplification behaviors.

—*Marie G. Wilson*

See also Attribution Theory; Influence; Organizational Citizenship Behaviors; Performance Appraisal

Further Readings

Bolino, M. C., & Turnley, W. H. (1999). Measuring impression management in organizations: A scale development based on the Jones and Pittman taxonomy. *Organizational Research Methods, 2*(2), 187–207.

Bolino, M. C., Varela, J. A., Bande, B., & Turnley, W. H. (2006). The impact of impression-management tactics on supervisor ratings of organizational citizenship behavior. *Journal of Organizational Behavior, 27*(3), 281–297.

Jones, E. E., & Pittman, T. S. (1982). Toward a general theory of strategic self-presentation. In J. Suls (Ed.), *Psychological perspectives on the self, volume 1* (pp. 231–262). Hillsdale, NJ: Lawrence Erlbaum.

Leary, M. R., & Kowalski, R. M. (1990). Impression management: A literature review and two-component model. *Psychological Bulletin, 107,* 34–47.

Schlenker, B. R. (1980). *Impression management: The self-concept, social identity, and interpersonal relations.* Monterey, CA: Brooks/Cole.

Tedeschi, J. T., (Ed.). (1981). *Impression management theory and social psychological research.* New York: Academic Press.

Improvisation

Organizations today face pressures to innovate in order to remain viable in globalizing markets that increase competition and reward continuous change. Add to this heightened stakeholder expectations that relentless advances in technology and organizational learning will lead to unending improvements in the quality of life worldwide, and it becomes clear why companies now find themselves perched precariously between their customers' demands for better and cheaper products, their shareholders' insistence on a constantly increasing return to their capital investments, and humanitarian desires for corporate social and environmental responsibility. In the face of greater innovation, rapid organizational adaptation, and more flexible work practices, is it any wonder that the days when stodgy bureaucracies ruled the world have come to an end? It is within this world that organizational improvisation researchers find their groove.

Organizational improvisation has sometimes been defined antithetically to organizational routines and structure: where routines establish regularity, improvisation promotes novelty; where structures stabilize patterns of behavior and relationship, improvisation challenges or disrupts existing patterns. However, pitting structure or routine against improvisation leads into false dichotomy because, without these constant companions to organizing, there would be nothing to improvise on. Structure and routine provide improvisational grist by framing expectations for improvisers to confront and ultimately alter. Organizational improvisation means playing in the empty spaces left by institutionalized expectations. Improvising means exploring the not yet said or done that existing structure enables but does not (yet) claim.

Conceptual Overview

Metaphor offers the most common method of applying the practice of improvisation to organizations. Interpretive organizational researchers, organizational development specialists, and management trainers make comparisons between organizing and the practices of jazz bands or comedy troupes like Second City in order to explain and encourage organizational, group, and individual learning, creativity, and change. Whether examined in terms of jazz, improvisational theater, or comedy, the metaphor of organizational improvisation emphasizes the nonhierarchical, unplanned, and emergent qualities of organized systems and develops experiential or aesthetic appreciation for them. Take the jazz practice of jamming as just one example. Jamming occurs when musicians get together to play informally (i.e., jam), at which time they may allow neophytes to test and improve their improvising skills by playing with more experienced musicians in a context that lies outside the pressures of formal (i.e., paid) performance. Such an idea suggests the value of engaging with others in mutual play and learning that do not take place within normal organizational contexts—the Japanese managers who perform Karaoke together, the management team that spends time repairing an orphanage. Informal get-togethers such as these are known to contribute to organizational learning and change, but these opportunities might be enhanced by reframing them as jam sessions.

Some applications of the organizational improvisation metaphor involve reconceptualizing classic concepts like strategy, structure, and performance. For example, Karl Weick used improvisation to reconceptualize strategy by combining it with newer ideas such as organizational learning and collaborative innovation. His aesthetics of imperfection, derived from his appreciation of jazz, instructs managers to treat errors as opportunities for learning rather than threats to the current system, and failure as an inevitable part of innovating instead of something to be stigmatized. This mind-set is apparent in organizations like 3M, which is famous for using one of its failures (it mistakenly produced a very weak adhesive instead of the strong bonding agent it was after) to create 3M Post-it Notes, one of the most successful products of all time.

In regard to structure, Mary Jo Hatch observed that jazz bands improvise by playing around musical structures to produce rhythmic appeals to their listeners' emotions and used this metaphor to stretch the definition of organizational structure to include openness, emotionality, and rhythm. Addressing structural openness, Frank Barrett, Shona Brown, and Kathleen Eisenhardt, among others, argued that the idea of minimal structure used by jazz musicians was applicable to organizations operating in high-velocity environments, and thus should be considered an organizational design option. Barrett emphasized the possibilities of using the jazz practice of shared leadership to redefine organizational hierarchy.

Reinterpreting organizational performance via the metaphor of improvisation suggests that organizational researchers move away from the discussion of profit or other measures of organizational output and focus instead on performativity. Examining the performative aspects of organizational improvisation requires finding organizational correlates for the performance practices improvisers use. Organizationally relevant jazz practices, for example, include *soloing* (taking the lead for one part of a performance, but not all of it), *comping* (accompanying and complementing other soloists by following their lead, while occasionally feeding them ideas to enhance their solos), *trading fours* (exchanging ideas in rapid succession to build excitement and intensity), *groove and feel* (finding and maintaining the rhythmic and harmonic patterns the group needs to perform at its best). All of these practices depend on the improvisational principle of *listening and responding* to others, a principle that is used in improvisational theater and comedy as well as jazz. Application of this principle involves expanding awareness (e.g., of your multisensory experiences of other improvisers and audience response) and the logic of both/and (i.e., building on the ideas others offer by accepting their premises and adding your own offer in a way that is responsive to theirs).

These jazz practices suggest directions researchers might usefully take in organizational improvisation studies. For example, in regard to the logic of both/and, it is worth noting that many of those who are gifted at improvising enjoy and use paradox. Many paradoxes are present in the discourse of jazz improvisation; for example, the simultaneous need to compose and perform a piece of jazz music, or the interrelationship between competition and collaboration that occurs when jazz musicians dare each other to perform ever more ambitions solos even as they work toward achieving a collective result in which they share one aesthetic fate. Other paradoxes improvisers confront include order/chaos and freedom/constraint. Used to describe the delicate balances all improvisational performers must achieve to realize their art, these paradoxes and the ways in which improvisers produce and/or handle them could hold important lessons for managers who also balance between poles of contradiction such as centralization-decentralization, integration-differentiation, and tight-loose coupling.

Early research relating to the performative aspects of improvisation brought the scholarship of organizational improvisation into contact with the activities and ambitions of management trainers, who adapted improvisational exercises from comedy schools and acting classes to help managers and other employees approach their work in a more spontaneous fashion. For example, Chicago's Second City comedy troupe created interactive performances to teach improvisational skills. They literally improvise to improve valued business outcomes such as creativity and customer satisfaction. While collaborating in Second City's management workshops, Mary Crossan and Marc Sorrenti defined intuition and spontaneity as crucial dimensions of organizational improvisation.

Empirical studies have found organizational improvisation in teams of customer support technicians and in new product development teams working within several computer companies, as well as in an electronic instruments producer and a food products manufacturer. Wanda Orlikowski found that improvisation significantly improved a software company's application of computer technology to its customer support process, and Shona Brown and Kathleen Eisenhardt showed that improvisation was a factor in distinguishing between the success and failure of teams operating within both hardware and software divisions of companies in the computer industry. Meanwhile, Christine Moorman and Anne Miner found that not all organizational improvisation was effective. In their study, otherwise negative effects of improvisation on product effectiveness, cost, and time efficiency were reversed by the timely use of organizational memory and real-time information about the environment. Respectively, these three studies used ethnography, comparative case study, and observation plus survey research methods, suggesting that the concept of improvisation is robust to these methodological differences. However, given the close association between the creativity of artistic improvising and that demanded by new product or technological innovation, research conducted in settings lying in other organizational domains will be necessary to establish the generalizability of the concept to other types of organizations and different functional specialties. In particular, research on the role and effect of improvising on management practices, leadership styles, teamwork, and organizational change outside the domains of new product development and information technology is needed.

Critical Commentary and Future Directions

Theory development outside the metaphoric understanding of improvisation has been minimal. Mary Crossan, Dusya Vera, Miguel Pina e Cunha, and Joao Cunha proposed two conditions—time pressure and uncertainty—under which they believed that improvisation would be beneficial. Drawing together the findings of empirical studies conducted thus far, these researchers also presented a causal model to explain why some improvisations are more successful than others. The differentiating factors they proposed are: experimental culture, communication of real-time information in real-time, organizational memory, expertise, and teamwork skills. The trouble with their approach is that this kind of theorizing is anything but improvisational. It is so structurally determined as to spark little of the imagination so essential to improvisation. According to jazz musicians, playing in the spaces between planning and spontaneous performance is where improvisation occurs, not by structuring, but by breaking through existing patterns to find out what else there is to do or say.

Most writers on organizational improvisation mention the need to specify boundary conditions for the theory. The efforts of Crossan and her colleagues attempt to do this in terms of discovering the conditions under which improvisation enhances desired organizational outcomes. One might also question the extent to which managers are willing or able to compromise existing control structures in order to take advantage of employee efforts to redefine rules and norms, or to trust them to improvise without narrowing their options to the point of frustrating their efforts to be creative or to innovate.

In regard to the metaphorical approach, some complain that jazz is gender biased because there are so many more male than female jazz musicians, thus its metaphoric use in organization studies might reinforce already problematic discriminatory practices in the business world. Applications of the organizational improvisation metaphor could offer case studies to examine whether introducing a new metaphor produces organizational change.

The most pressing need is for empirical research into activities that appear to benefit from being framed as improvisation that can support or deny the efficacy of the metaphor, and feed the theory development process in ways that move us beyond metaphoric representation into the domain of greater conceptual clarity without losing the aesthetics that improvising both demands and brings to organization studies.

—Mary Jo Hatch

See also Adaptive Learning; Aesthetics of Organization; Collaboration and Cooperation; Organizational Learning; Organizational Routines

Further Readings

Barrett, F. J. (1998). Creativity and improvisation in jazz and organizations: Implications for organizational learning. *Organization Science, 9,* 558–560.

Brown, S. L., & Eisenhardt, K. M. (1997). The art of continuous change: Linking complexity theory and time-based evolution in relentlessly shifting organizations. *Administrative Science Quarterly, 38,* 628–52.

Crossan, M., & Sorrenti, M. (1997). Making sense of improvisation. In J. Walsh & A. Huff (Eds.), *Advances in strategic management,* vol. 14 (pp. 155–180). Greenwich, CT: JAI Press.

Hatch, M. J. (1999). The empty spaces of organizing: How improvisational jazz helps redescribe organizational structure. *Organization Studies, 20,* 75–100.

Kamoche, K., & Cunha, M. P. (2001). Minimal structures: From jazz improvisation to product innovation. *Organization Studies, 22,* 733–765.

Moorman, C., & Miner A. S. (1998). The convergence of planning and execution: Improvisation in new product development. *Journal of Marketing, 61,* 1–20.

Orlikowski, W. J. (1996). Improvising organizational transformation over time: A situated change perspective. *Information Systems Research, 7,* 63–92.

Vera, D., & Crossan, M. (2004). Theatrical improvisation: Lessons for organizations. *Organization Studies, 25,* 727–749.

Weick, K. E. (1995). Creativity and the aesthetics of imperfection. In C. Ford & D. Gioia (Eds.), *Creative action in organizations* (pp. 187–192). Thousand Oaks, CA: Sage.

INCOMMENSURABILITY

The term *incommensurability* was used by Thomas Kuhn to indicate the cognitive inconsistency that occurs when one natural science paradigm gives way to another. For Kuhn, saying that one paradigm is incommensurable with another meant that the same objective phenomena were viewed completely differently through the lenses of the two different paradigms. Kuhn believed that there was no objective reference point, or God's-eye view, through which incommensurable paradigms could be reconciled. Building on this foundation, scholars like Andreas Scherer and Horst Steinmann and William McKinley and Mark Mone have used *incommensurability* to signify the absence of any objective standard through which the relative validity of two or more perspectives in organization studies can be judged.

Conceptual Overview

The issue of incommensurability has been the subject of considerable discussion in organization studies in recent decades. Opinions differ both about whether incommensurability between different organization studies schools of thought actually exists, and also whether it is desirable. On the question of whether incommensurability exists, scholars such as Gibson Burrell and Gareth Morgan, Norman Jackson and Pippa Carter, and McKinley and Mone have delivered a resounding answer of yes. Because Burrell and Morgan's arguments are extensively reviewed in the entry on *Paradigm Incommensurability*, the focus here is on other affirmations of the existence of incommensurability. In particular, McKinley and Mone gave an affirmative response to the question of whether incommensurability between organization studies schools of thought exists, and attributed that incommensurability to the ambiguity of the constructs that are routinely used in organization studies research. Because organization studies scholars do not agree on the definition and measurement of specific constructs, any empirical tests of schools of thought organized around those constructs are likely to be inconclusive. This makes the task of comparing different schools of thought with competing claims very difficult. McKinley and Mone therefore suggested that there is a *de facto incommensurability* (Charles Booth would call it a *weak incommensurability*) in contemporary organization studies that stems not so much from different ontological assumptions as from the failure to achieve consensus on how individual constructs are to be defined and measured.

The positions of the organization studies scholars mentioned above can be contrasted with those of another group of scholars who take a more nuanced (or perhaps noncommittal) approach. This latter group maintains that incommensurability between organization studies schools of thought exists, but that it can be bridged if the analyst can ascend to an appropriately abstract meta-level of analysis. For example, Graham Astley and Andrew Van de Ven make this argument, juxtaposing different organization studies perspectives as a way of highlighting their differences while simultaneously emphasizing their underlying similarities. Dennis Gioia and Evelyn Pitre attempt the same feat, pointing out that the boundaries between Burrell and Morgan's paradigms are not clear-cut, but rather characterized by blurred "transition zones" that can be sites for reconciliation of apparently opposed paradigms. They identify Anthony Giddens's structuration theory as one vehicle for potential integration of the functionalist and interpretivist paradigms. Finally, Mark Tadajewski and many others have suggested that incommensurability (in organization studies and other disciplines) can be overcome through an appropriate translation process. Thus, comparison of seemingly incommensurable paradigms is not impossible.

On the normative issue of whether incommensurability is desirable, the opinions are as diverse as those on the issue of whether incommensurability exists. At one extreme, Jackson and Carter see paradigm incommensurability in organization studies as desirable, because it protects budding nonmainstream perspectives from excessively harsh scientific scrutiny.

Jackson and Carter believe that deviant perspectives need time to develop, and incommensurability provides a protective barrier within which this development process can take place. Thus incommensurability is to be defended. At the opposite end of the spectrum, McKinley and Mone see incommensurability as a major problem, because it impedes the winnowing of organization studies schools of thought in favor of the more valid. McKinley and Mone (see also Lex Donaldson's work) are disturbed by the proliferation of organization studies schools of thought providing different explanations for the same phenomenon, and would like to overcome incommensurability to move toward an empirically valid, integrated paradigm.

Critical Commentary and Future Directions

If coherence is to be preserved in the discussion of incommensurability, the first step is to eliminate the incommensurability between different definitions of the construct *incommensurability*. For example, Kuhn's conceptualization of incommensurability as schematic incongruence seems different from Burrell and Morgan's or Gioa and Pitre's conceptualizations of incommensurability as differences in ontology, epistemology, and methodology. Those conceptualizations are, in turn, different from McKinley and Mone's conceptualization of incommensurability as lack of empirical comparability. If the discussion of incommensurability is to continue in organization studies, it might be worthwhile to consider how the conversants could come to consensus about what incommensurability means. Possible arenas for achieving such consensus would be a conference or special issue of a journal in which different interpretations of the construct are explicitly juxtaposed and debated and negotiations are begun to produce a common definition of the term.

If such negotiations suggested that incommensurability can be consensually defined, the next questions would be whether incommensurability, as defined, does exist in organization studies, and whether it is a desirable or undesirable phenomenon. The normative question would arguably be more difficult to resolve than the definitional question or the empirical question.

Some organization studies scholars will surely insist, with Jackson and Carter, that incommensurability is an important prophylactic that protects theoretical diversity in organization studies. Others, in the empiricist tradition of McKinley and Mone, will insist just as loudly that incommensurability is a problem for any discipline that wishes to function as a science—i.e., an enterprise that tests theories against data and eliminates those theories that do not adequately represent the phenomena captured by the data.

The resolution of the normative issue of the desirability of incommensurability could only take place in the context of a much broader normative debate about what the basic philosophical and epistemological commitments of organization studies are to be. Specifically, should organization studies move toward the epistemological model favored by the humanities, which embraces subjective, idiosyncratic behavioral and cognitive microstates? Or should organization studies follow the model of the natural sciences, which attempt to generalize beyond microstates by using idealized constructs? Authors like Bill McKelvey have alerted us to the differences between these basic epistemological orientations, but thus far a broad normative debate between representatives of these orientations has not taken place in organization studies. It may be time for organizational scholars to think about organizing such a debate.

—*William McKinley*

See also Epistemic Communities; Paradigm Incommensurability; Paradigms; Philosophy of Science; Relativism

Further Readings

Astley, W. G., & Van de Ven, A. (1983). Central perspectives and debates in organization theory. *Administrative Science Quarterly, 28,* 245–273.

Booth, C. (1998). Beyond incommensurability in strategic management: A commentary and an application. *Organization, 5,* 257–265.

Burrell, G., & Morgan, G. (1979). *Sociological paradigms and organizational analysis.* London: Heinemann.

Donaldson, L. (1995). *American anti-management theories of organization: A critique of paradigm proliferation.* Cambridge, UK: Cambridge University Press.

Giddens, A. (1979). *Central problems in social theory*. Berkeley: University of California Press.

Gioia, D., & Pitre, E. (1990). Multiparadigm perspectives on theory building. *Academy of Management Review, 15*, 584–602.

Jackson, N., & Carter, P. (1991). In defence of paradigm incommensurability. *Organization Studies, 12*, 109–127.

Kuhn, T. S. (1970). *The structure of scientific revolutions* (2nd ed.). Chicago: University of Chicago Press.

McKelvey, B. (1997). Quasi-natural organization science. *Organization Science, 8*, 352–380.

McKinley, W., & Mone, M. A. (1998). The re-construction of organization studies: Wrestling with incommensurability. *Organization, 5*, 169–189.

McKinley, W., & Mone, M. A. (2003). Micro and macro perspectives in organization theory: A tale of incommensurability. In H. Tsoukas & C. Knudsen (Eds.), *The Oxford handbook of organization theory* (pp. 345–372). New York: Oxford University Press.

Scherer, A. G. (1998). Pluralism and incommensurability in strategic management and organization theory: A problem in search of a solution. *Organization, 5*, 147–168.

Scherer, A. G., & Steinmann, H. (1999). Some remarks on the problem of incommensurability in organization studies. *Organization Studies, 20*, 519–544.

Tadajewski, M. (2004). HOT on the discursive limits of organization theory. *Ephemera: Theory and Politics in Organization, 4*(1), 21–39.

INDIVIDUALISM

Individualism, as defined by Hazel Markus and Shinobu Kitayama and Harry C. Triandis, is a cultural pattern in which individuals feel autonomous from in-groups, such as family, work group, political party, religious groups, educational group, geographic group, economic group, race, sex, nationality, and so on. When personal goals are different from in-group goals, the individual is most likely to choose the personal goals. Triandis found that in such cultures social behavior is a function of attitudes much more than of in-group norms, and people stay in relationships only if the costs of the relationships are smaller than the rewards.

When data are obtained across cultures, individualism is the one pole of a dimension and collectivism is the other pole. When data are obtained within culture these two tendencies are often orthogonal to each other, and for that reason it is best to use a different terminology for work within culture. Corresponding to individualism is *idiocentrism;* corresponding to collectivism is *allocentrism.*

All cultures have idiocentrics and allocentrics, but more idiocentrics are found in individualist cultures and more allocentrics in collectivist cultures. When culture and personality are consistent, the individual is well adjusted. When they are inconsistent, the individual is dissatisfied or even maladjusted. Thus, idiocentrics in collectivist cultures try to leave the culture and move to an individualist culture; allocentrics in an individualist culture try to join a variety of groups, but feel that they never have sufficiently intimate relationships with others.

Conceptual Overview

People in individualist cultures often feel proud or superior, are high in well-being, and easily move in and out of new groups. Thus they have less difficulty leaving a company than those in collectivist cultures. They emphasize the new and uncommon. They are curious and exploratory. They like to confront and debate. They make the fundamental attribution error (see the behavior of others as due to internal factors like attitudes and beliefs; while the others see it as due to external factors like norms and role definitions) more often than do collectivists. They socialize their children by emphasizing creativity, exploration, and adventure.

Idiocentrics

When asked who they are, idiocentrics give mostly personality attributes, and allocentrics give mostly social attributes, such as "I am a member of this work group" or "I am an uncle." In work relationships, idiocentrics show social loafing (the tendency to let others do the work) while in collectivist cultures workers working with in-group members do not show this tendency, though they do show it if they are working with out-group members.

Idiocentrics value personal effectiveness, achievement, and hedonism more than personal relationships. They tend to be direct, candid, and generally themselves, not paying too much attention to the feelings of others. When they break a norm, they tend to justify their actions rather than to apologize.

Idiocentrics see the world from the inside out. Thus, they see most entities according to their personal standards rather than according to the standards of other people. As a result they use their personal standards in judging their accomplishments rather than the standards of other people, such as their parents. They conceive success to be a function of their personal attributes rather than the help they have received from others. Their most frequent emotions are disengaged from others (e.g., superior, proud). They value privacy, and use abstract language more often than allocentrics. For example, they are likely to say "he is stubborn" rather than "on Monday when I tried to persuade him, he did not change his views."

Idiocentrics pay less attention to the context of stimuli or social behaviors and emphasize the context of communications (e.g., how was something said, gestures, tone of voice, position of the body) less than do allocentrics. In short, they focus on the content of the message. They are less concerned with saving the other person's face. They reject inconsistency, while among allocentrics the meaning of an entity depends on its context so that inconsistent entities are acceptable. Among idiocentrics, in-groups and out-groups are seen as not very different, but the person is seen as very different from in-groups. According to Jeffrey Sanchez-Burks, professionalism, for idiocentrics, means one is not supposed to engage in many social behaviors or discuss personal matters in work settings.

Idiocentrics tend to use linear (if something is good it will become even better), analytic thinking. They categorize by common attributes. For example, when given the triad "sheep, chicken, and grass" and instructed to identify which two entities go together, they are most likely to put sheep and chicken together, because they are animals, rather than sheep and grass together, because sheep eat grass. Allocentrics use circular (if something is good it will become bad, and then good again), holistic thinking, and categorize entities by function (sheep eat grass).

Idiocentrics have many in-groups, so they distribute their energies among many rather than just one or two in-groups. They conceive of behavior as due to internal factors such as attitudes, beliefs, and personality, rather than due to external factors such as norms, role definitions, or group pressures. They see the person as relatively stable and the environment as constantly changing; allocentrics see the environment as constant and the person ready to fit into new environments. When there is no fit between person and situation, idiocentrics believe that it is appropriate to change the situation (e.g., leave the job) rather than change the self. They are motivated by personal goals, rather than by group goals. They do not behave out of duty as much as allocentrics do. They want to be unique and different from others and prefer to have many choices. They work best when they decide what to do, rather than when other people tell them what to do; allocentrics often work best when a trusted source tells them what to do. Idiocentrics prefer individual rewards to group rewards, such as profit sharing. They help others based on liking rather than on duty. They do not feel very close to in-group members, so they know less about them than do allocentrics.

Horizontal and Vertical Varieties of Individualism

Horizontal individualism is a pattern in which people assume that they are equal in status to others. They emphasize self-direction and uniqueness. They are quite concerned with the environment and feel more like global citizens than do vertical individualists or collectivists.

Vertical individualism is a pattern in which people try to be the "best," competition is seen as highly desirable, and people have an unusually good opinion of themselves. Thus, in the United States the average response of a sample of a million high-school students indicated that 70% to 100% of them believed that they were better than the average high-school student on most desirable traits, such as leadership, competence, or driving ability. The mathematics tells us that no more than 50% should view themselves that way. In less individualistic cultures, the percentages are closer to 50. They emphasize achievement, status, and power and are enterprising.

Conformity to in-groups is higher in collectivist than in individualist cultures. Lying to save face is high in many collectivist cultures, but vertical individualists are also corrupt when they are in intense competitions. When dealing with in-groups, people in individualist cultures use equity (to each according to contribution), while people in collectivist (especially the horizontal) cultures are more likely to use equality of distribution.

The religions of individualists tend to be independent of groups (e.g., the church), and if they decide to change religion they do so alone, without expecting members of their in-group to join them.

In most American business and academic cultures, vertical individualism is high. In Sweden and Australia, the individualism is more horizontal, and people do not like those who "stick out." In fact, sticking out is considered in poor taste. Australians tend to seek to bring down "tall poppies."

Individualists try to be consistent in their behavior, so that if they are reminded of previous behaviors they are likely to try to behave in the same way. In recreation, they join different small groups or very large groups (e.g., cocktail parties) and can even have fun alone. Loneliness is an important clinical category in such cultures. Related to individualism is narcissism or self-absorption, which has been found to have increased between 1958 and 1998 in the United States.

The highest motive, in a hierarchy of motives, is self-realization, while in collectivist cultures the highest motive is service to the in-group.

Causes of Individualism

Triandis and David Trafimow found that individualism is high in affluent societies, and among young, much-traveled persons, who watch the mass media, are less religious, and among those who are socially mobile, or have changed cultures.

The more traditional the culture, the less individualistic it is likely to be. Most of the research on individualism has compared Western samples, especially in America, with East Asian samples. However, other studies contrast European-Americans with Latin Americans and East Asians in the United States, and the results are usually consistent with the Western–East Asian results. It is generally the case that Western cultures are more individualistic than the rest of the world.

Critical Commentary and Future Directions

This cultural pattern is very broad and needs to be broken down into many of its elements, as was done by Sanchez-Burks in 2005. Marilyn Brewer and Ya-Ru Chen have distinguished "relational" from "group" collectivism. Relational collectivism reflects the intensive link of individuals to groups. Group collectivism is the absorption of the individual into the group, so that personal identity fades away, and the individual thinks of self only as a member of the group.

Most of the empirical work was done by comparing North Americas and East Asians, and there is a need to extend it to other parts of the world, especially Africa.

—*Harry C. Triandis*

See also Attitudes; Collectivism; Personality, Five-Factor Model

Further Readings

Brewer, M., & Chen, Y. (2007). When (who) are collectives in collectivism? Toward conceptual clarification of individualism and collectivism. *Psychological Review, 114*(1), 133–151.

Markus, H., & Kitayama, S. (1991). Culture and self: Implication for cognition, emotion, and motivation. *Psychological Review, 98,* 224–253.

Sanchez-Burks, J. (2005). Protestant relational ideology: The cognitive underpinnings and organizational implications of an American anomaly. In B. Shaw & R. Kramer (Eds.), *Research in organizational behavior,* vol. 26 (pp. 267–308). New York: Elsevier.

Triandis, H. C. (1989). Self and social behavior in different cultural contexts. *Psychological Review, 96,* 269–289.

Triandis, H. C. (1995). *Individualism and collectivism.* Boulder, CO: Westview Press.

Triandis, H. C., & Trafimow, D. (2001). Cross-national prevalence of collectivism. In C. Sedikides & M. B. Brewer (Eds.), *Individual self, relational self, collective self* (pp. 259–276). Philadelphia, PA: Psychology Press.

Industrial Democracy

Industrial democracy is about how workers influence their working life through participation. The concept of *participation* holds many dimensions:

- Who is participating. *Exclusively* workers or are they participating *together with* the company owners and managers?
- Who of the workers are participating. Are they all participating *directly* or through elected representatives—*indirectly?*
- Degree of participation. Is the degree low in that workers have *information/consultation* (ranging from information, opportunity of protesting against decisions, make proposals to being ensured prior consultations)? Does it involve *codetermination* (ranging from temporary to permanent veto right to codetermination right)? Or are the workers granted the highest degree of *decision-making right?*
- How participation takes place. Through *negotiations, ballot,* or *dialogue?*
- In which decisions workers are participating. *Wage and working conditions* and/or *company decisions* (at operative, tactic or strategic level, respectively)?

Industrial democracy is sometimes juxtaposed with organizational democracy and workplace democracy, and the discussions are often overlapping, although the types of organizations and work practices subject to analysis may differ significantly. For reasons of space, the following solely focuses on industrial democracy. Industrial democracy is also often linked to economic democracy, and this linkage is, to a certain extent, discussed in the following six stories of industrial democracy. But many aspects of economic democracy are also neglected here.

Conceptual Overview

Focusing on the development since World War II, the discussions about industrial democracy can be divided into six different stories. Each of the stories emphasizes different forms of participation and how participation might strengthen influence on working life.

1. Pressure Groups

The pluralist idea of democracy that characterized Western politics since World War II was highly important for the development of pressure group democracy—also referred to as the *interest model* or *collective bargaining*. This model rejects the orthodox class struggle between exploiting capitalists and exploited workers. Alternatively, the company is viewed as consisting of many different interdependent groups of interests, and power is divided among several groups.

In the 1950s, H. A. Clegg argued that in pressure group democracy the important interests of participants were organized and represented in various interest groups. Not all desires could be met, but sufficient to make everybody feel that they were being treated fairly, making it possible to reach a situation of equilibrium. The way of achieving this goal was for the workers to put pressure on management through collective bargaining—under the condition that management was not weak. Industrial democracy requires both strong management (elite) and strong pressure groups among workers. Clegg defined three principles for industrial democracy: (1) unions should be independent of the state and the company management system; (2) only the labor movement could represent worker interests; and (3) ownership was irrelevant for good industrial relations. In general, labor representatives should minimize participation in company decisions in order to avoid cooptation.

The model in its purest form has primarily been practiced in the United States, Canada, and the United Kingdom. It has also played a role in other European countries, but here it has to a larger extent been combined with certain of the subsequent models.

2. Comanagement

Comanagement dates back to around World War I, developed first by the British and further developed by the Germans. The controversy raised by Clegg in the mid-1950s was an attempt to oust the idea of comanagement. The attempt failed, and in the 1960s comanagement came to play an important role in many Western countries in discussions of issues such as works councils, partly autonomous work groups, employee representatives on boards of directors, and worker directors.

Comanagement does not question the societal mixed economy and views ownership as secondary. Stronger employee participation and influence is not necessarily assumed to reduce the influence of management, but may add to the overall influence on the company.

The model focuses in particular on changes in company tasks and technology and discussions of who should participate in what have been extensive. In 1964, Thorsrud and Emery advanced the hypothesis that democratization should be bottom-up via direct worker participation moving upward toward, among other things, the level of board of directors with employee representatives. Others, however, found it necessary to start from the top, where important and far-reaching decisions were made that, among other things, determined the framework conditions for potential work groups further down the hierarchy.

3. Codetermination

Parallel with comanagement, codetermination democracy emerged and absorbed some of the same ideas about the positive effects of participation on safeguarding interests. This model has, however, maintained the conflict perspective of pressure group democracy: the workers' task is to frame management in situations that force it to choose between two evils: either to fight for excluding them from the process or to accept their involvement negotiating a political solution permitting workers some influence. The essential thing for the workers is to ensure that the costs of management opting to exclude workers from the process will be higher than including them. The way in which workers exploit their foothold in the processes is not irrelevant, as it does not suffice to count on workers possessing expert knowledge. Early in the decision process they must develop legal rights and use legal means of power.

According to the International Labour Office, Germany is the best known example of a country in which worker representatives participate in overall decisions through participating in industrial councils, boards of directors, and as worker directors. But also countries such as Austria, Spain, France, Denmark, Norway, Sweden, Luxembourg, and the Netherlands have formal arrangements that facilitate this form of democracy. The formal arrangements permitting codetermination can also be used for encouraging comanagement. In practice, participants are negotiating which type of industrial democracy the formal arrangement should include.

4. Collective Democracy

By the early 1970s, popular movements emerged in the United States and Europe in response to the impotent political climate in the Western countries where parliamentarism seemed sunk into a rut. These movements attempted, among other things, to organize collectively managed companies owned by the employees.

Joyce Rothschild-Whitt has formulated a theoretical foundation for the collective democracy starting from Weber's four types of rationality: the traditional, the affective, the formal (instrumental), and the substantive rationality. For each of the three former types of rationality, Weber identified specific structures of authority: the traditional, the charismatic, and the legal-rational authority, of which each type corresponds to specific organizations. But Weber did not develop any type of authority/organization for substantive rationality. Rothschild-Whitt has attempted this. She contrasts a bureaucratic and a collective democratic organization on eight different dimensions (authority, rules, social control, social relations, recruitment and advancement, incentive structure, social stratification, and differentiation), and describes the authority form as resident in the collectivity as a whole. Delegation is only temporary and subject to recall—if it is done at all. Compliance is to the consensus of the collective, which is fluid and open to negotiation.

Collective democracy does not imply a fundamental change of society that makes collective organizations assume the status of being "quite contrary" in Western economies, meaning that they can only survive given they are able to secure legitimacy from the surrounding society without imitating the dominant bureaucratic governance forms. In effect, it seems easier to make collective companies survive economically and collectively if they remain economically marginalized.

5. Representative Democracy

In the last part of the 19th century, labor movements emerged along with worker cooperatives established and owned by trade unions. The labor movement found that the inner dynamic of the organizing of work required hierarchy, and the external conditions, represented by employers' associations or a market, forced trade unions to opt for representative democracy. This was found to ensure fast, competent, and responsible decisions that would be impossible to obtain directly as the workers did not possess the skills for managing companies. Beatrice and Sidney Webb played an important role in the early 20th century with their studies of union democracy, which to them represented industrial democracy. The interest for democracy among trade unions and worker cooperatives has focused on understanding how members/workers could control representatives via compulsory empowerment, short election periods, frequent competition among representatives, and recruiting representatives from the same groups as they would represent, assuming that this would enhance common values. Another issue has been how representatives could control bureaucrats/managers.

Combining Collective and Representative Democracy

A special case of industrial democracy combining the collective and the representative democracy is the Mondragon group of almost 200 industrial firms in the Basque region of Spain that have emerged since World War II. A large network of institutions (e.g., banks, education, and research) supports the firms, which are economically successful. In each firm, workers would form a general assembly, although the management structure is hierarchical, and the management of the whole group is based on representative democracy.

Another special case is the kibbutz system in Israel, consisting of 267 kibbutz communities. Originally, the system was based on collective democracy and rotation of offices. However, in the past 20 years the system has suffered identity crises resulting from economic and social crises, and today stronger emphasis is placed on personal achievement and organizational efficiency resulting in a rapid change from collective democracy to representative democracy.

6. Self-Management

The five models of industrial democracy mentioned so far were developed under the conditions of capitalist market economy. Since World War II, however, a societal model *democratic socialism* developed in both Eastern and Western Europe. This model argued for the necessity of transgressing the capitalist market economy in order to achieve real industrial democracy.

Self-management usually presumes an ownership status granting the employees the right to manage the firm and to profit sharing. On the other hand, employees often do not have the right to sell the firm or hand it over to others. In this way, one could say that it is a combination of societal and employee ownership.

Even though capitalism has been abolished, the idea of the free market as a rational regulation of supply and demand has been retained. However, the idea of regulating the market through planning also prevails; that is, local units realize the need for mutual coordination that results in agreements on self-management. Since World War II and until its disintegration by the end of the 1980s, Yugoslavia was a unique example of an approximation to democratic socialism.

Critical Commentary and Future Directions

The six stories are systematized in Figure 1 on the dimensions of participation, societal system in which they operate, and ownership form.

The stories are based on different assumptions about the individual, the organization, and the society. It is not possible to discuss these assumptions further in this context but these differences imply that the stories often cannot communicate with each other as they are attaching different meanings to how worker

	Pressure groups	Comanagement	Codetermination	Collective democracy	Representative democracy	Self-management
Who participates?	Owners, managers, and workers in the firm	Owners, managers, and workers in the firm	Owners, managers, and workers in the firm	Workers in the firm	Workers and managers in the firm	Workers and managers in the firm and state representatives
Who participates among the workers?	Representatives	Representatives and all workers	Representatives	All workers	Representatives	Representatives and all workers
Degree of participation?	Codetermination is minimal	Consultations and co-determination	Codetermination	Full determination	Full determination	Full determination
Type of participation?	Negotiations	Dialogue	Negotiations	Dialogue	Dialogue and ballots	Dialogue and ballots
Participation in which decisions?	Wage- and working conditions	All decisions on which consensus is reachable	Strategic decisions	All decisions	All decisions	All decisions except sale and discontinuation of firm
Societal system?	Pluralist democracy with mixed economy	Pluralist democracy with mixed economy	Pluralist democracy with mixed economy	Pluralist democracy with mixed economy	Pluralist democracy with mixed economy	Socialist market and plan society
Form of ownership?	Capitalism	Capitalism	Capitalism	Worker ownership	Union owned and possibly worker ownership	Worker and state ownership

Figure 1 Six Models of Industrial Democracy

participation leads to influence on/power over working conditions. Despite these differences, the stories have one thing in common: putting into speech an active individual, meaning that they are not mere stories of structure. This does not imply that structures are unimportant for the individual's possibilities to act, but individuals are not imaged as mere structural puppets.

In the current Western economies, we primarily witness comanagement and codetermination, but there is reason to assume that they will both be subject to pressure. The international trend is toward short-term employment, and an increasing number of people are not even employed by the organization, but merely affiliated with it as temporaries and/or contractors. International tendencies also seem to point toward a growing number of employees working more closely with employees in client organizations than with people in their own organization. It is reasonable to assume a positive correlation between these forms of cross-organizational work practice and a more nomadic affiliation with organizations undermining known forms of industrial democracy.

—Ann Westenholz

See also Agency; Agency-Structure Debate; Authority; Bureaucracy; Classical Management; Collaboration and Cooperation; Collective Social Phenomena; Collectivism; Community and Organizations; Conflict; Control; Coordination; Corporate Citizenship; Decentralization; Decision-Making Theory; Dialogue; Domination; Effectiveness; Employment Relations; Empowerment; High Involvement Management; Industrial Relations; Influence; Leadership, Styles; Leadership Theory; Machine Bureaucracy; Mechanistic Organizations; Motivation; Negotiation; Organizational Citizenship Behaviors; Organizational Democracy; Participation; Politics; Power; Sociotechnical Systems; Team Leadership; Theory Y ; Trust; Unionism; Wage Inequities; Worker Rights

Further Readings

Crouch, C., & Heller, F. A. (Eds.). (1983). *International yearbook of organizational democracy,* vol. 1. Chichester, UK: Wiley.
Lafferty, W. M., & Rosenstein, E. (Eds.). (1993). *International handbook of participation in organization,* vol. 3. Oxford, UK: Oxford University Press.
Lammers, C. J., & Szell, G. (Eds.). (1989). *International handbook of participation in organization,* vol. 1. Oxford, UK: Oxford University Press.
Russel, R., & Rus, V. (Eds.). (1991). *International handbook of participation in organization,* vol. 2. Oxford, UK: Oxford University Press.
Stern, R. N., & McCarthy, S. (Eds.). (1986). *International yearbook of organizational democracy,* vol. 3. Chichester, UK: Wiley.
Szell, G. (Ed.). (1999). *Concise encyclopaedia of participation and co-management.* Berlin: de Gruyer.
Wilpert, B., & Sorge, A. (Eds.). (1984). *International yearbook of organizational democracy,* vol. 2. Chichester, UK: Wiley.

Industrial Relations

Industrial relations (IR), also called labor relations, refers to the relationships between employers and employees within an organization. Historically, the term was intended to cover all aspects of work; however, the field has narrowed its focus to collective bargaining, becoming largely orientated to management-union relations in general and collective bargaining in particular. In the minds of the general public, it has unfortunately been associated with conflicts between employers and employees. Contributing disciplines to industrial relations include sociology, history, law, political science, psychology, and economics.

Conceptual Overview

The origins of the field of industrial relations began with the industrial revolution to deal with the problems of labor and the threat posed to the fabric of society. The industrial relations community developed a reformist agenda to save capitalism by improving the quality of work life, with the United States as its original home, from where IR developed as a distinct subject. The reformist agenda had a focus on rule-making institutions, examining wage drift, procedural issues, unofficial strikes, labor utilization, and other labor issues, covering both procedural and substantive issues. IR developed a strong normative commitment to pluralism and trade unionism.

While there is no single disciplinary core, the IR paradigm emerged within the research subjects of organized labor and collective bargaining. The interpretative framework was based on institutional rule making with a focus on practical policy orientation. Research methods tended to be historical descriptions and case studies of institutions with an implicit epistemology and ontology of unreflective pragmatism and realism geared toward the discovery of critical but useful knowledge. In recent years, there has been a more quantitative bent as scholars look to measure outcomes and the contributions of labor economics. The field is genuinely interdisciplinary, relatively open to influences from the broader social sciences.

Critical Commentary and Future Directions

The golden age of industrial relations was in the two decades after World War II, when collective bargaining was the centerpiece, offering workers a voice to raise their concerns and grievances in the workplace. Trade unions were also seen as having a wider role in society. However, by the 1970s trade unions began to be identified as a contributor to economic malaise and were seen as contributing to inflation and low productivity because of restrictive practices and industrial action. By the 1980s, a deregulation and foreign competition in the United States and the United Kingdom helped legitimize an attack on unions. Collective institutions were seen as interfering with the market and inhibiting the development of an enterprise culture. As a result, much of the institutional structures of IR was dismantled. In addition, wider changes in society and the economy, particularly the decline of manufacturing and the changing demographics of the labor force (gender, atypical work, and so on) meant that the IR tools of previous times began to seem less relevant. As unions declined in influence and union density plummeted across much of the industrialized world with the labor problem apparently solved, the IR field was seen as rather outdated in its focus and assumptions. The traditional IR system was called into question as its boundaries were eroded. Even the label *industrial relations* came under threat, with *employment relations* seen as a more appropriate, modern alternative.

The 1980s saw the arrival of human resource management (HRM) as a field; further eroding IR by offering an alternative agenda and form of governance. High performance work systems and nonunion voice, pioneered in the United States and associated with best practices, potentially threatened the collective bargaining option preferred by IR specialists as the best form of conducting work relations. In practice, dualism seemed to be more apparent with HRM initiatives to be found in unionized settings.

The location of the IR field within business schools also made the field vulnerable as it sits uncomfortably alongside organizational behavior (OB) and economics, with the former incorporating labor relations management and the latter regarding labor as simply a commodity or assets to be utilized. However, issues of engagement, legitimacy, voice, and social justice are likely to remain prominent practical concerns. Linked to a growing interest in corporate governance, the field is also broadening to include new actors (customers, employment agencies, consultants, nongovernmental organizations), and its openness provides for insights from other disciplines. New developments included a greater emphasis on employer behavior and strategy, looking at IR within a political economy framework and examining multiple forms of voice. Partnership or mutual gains (a more cooperative approach to industrial relations) is becoming more in vogue with unions seen as partners in the business relationship, contributing increased performance or competitive advantage.

Taking a global perspective, industrial relations has spread widely across the world partly due to the work of the International Industrial Relations Association. As it widens the scope of the field to look beyond joint regulation and collective institutions for established economies, as well as examining new, emerging economies, the future and relevance of IR is likely to be assured.

—*Adrian Wilkinson*

See also Conflict; Employment Relations; Human Resource Management; Labor Relations

Further Readings

Ackers, P., & Wilkinson, A. (Eds.). (2003). *Understanding work and employment: Industrial relations in transition.* Oxford, UK: Oxford University Press.

Bacon, N., Blyton, P., Fiorito, J., & Heery, E. (2007). *Handbook of industrial relations.* London: Sage.

Budd, J. (2004). *Employment with a human face.* Ithaca, NY: Cornell University Press.

Kaufman, B. (2004). *The global evolution of industrial relations.* Geneva: International Labour Organization.

INDUSTRIAL REVOLUTION

The industrial revolution (IR) began in England around 1765, as a process characterized by the development of industrial methods of production and structural transformations. In less than a century, it expanded to France, Belgium, Germany, the United States, Japan, and other countries, continuing through the first half of the 19th century. According to Arnold Toynbee, the IR can be described as the substitution of competition for the medieval regulations that had controlled the distribution of wealth. This revolution signified the emergence and consolidation of the factory system, and it facilitated the development of an industrial bourgeoisie and the generalization of waged work, leading to the formation of a new social class. This process created both industrialists and wage earners, while promoting the establishment of a market for capitalist industry, thus allowing capitalism to turn toward foreign trade as a way of widely reproducing itself.

Conceptual Overview

The IR was possible due to the technological innovation that allowed for the development of machine tools, which in turn facilitated the manufacturing of other machines, with the steam engine as the most important innovation in industry and transportation. The manufacturing of these machines was made possible by developments in iron smelting and metal working, through the use of coke instead of charcoal. Subsequent inventions for the textile industry were highly important, from the flying shuttle invented in 1733, to the dressing frame developed in 1803, enabling England to become the leader in world trade in wool and cotton fabrics.

Nevertheless, the causes of the British industrial revolution extend beyond technological development, and in this regard an intense debate has emerged. Some of the factors that have been highlighted are the following: transformations in agriculture, growth in foreign trade, and an abundance of capital and credit, within a business framework in which, according to Max Weber, technical progress and the acquisition of wealth were considered to be desirable and legitimate. Other important factors were the ideas professed in various Protestant faiths with regard to austerity in spending and the virtues of saving and investing. It is also important to establish that a favorable climate for the development of the factory system was created by the individualism and rationalism in British society, its greater social flexibility, and its legislation that was more permissive than in other European countries in relation to trade associations and workshops.

The IR cannot be understood without the contribution made by modern political economics, emerging with the writing of Adam Smith dated 1776 and titled *The Wealth of Nations,* and in which the causes of wealth within a competitive system of industrial freedom are analyzed. When Smith, Ricardo, and other scientists from the same era proposed the market and free trade as regulators of the economy, they contributed to the forming of public and private policies promoting a new form of decentralized organization of the economy and of companies based on competition.

Critical Commentary and Future Directions

An important element incorporated beginning with the second IR consisted of *scientific administration,* completing the first major cycle of the rationalization of the internal operation of organizations. See Figure 1. It is important to highlight the importance of the organization of the first planning departments, as well as the standardization and differentiation of work through time and movement studies, and the implementation of wage incentive systems associated with productivity. Later, with the beginning of the scientific and technological revolution, Keynesian economics contributed knowledge for the fiscal and monetary regulation of the economy, and organizational theories moved away from an internal framework for analyzing companies, to incorporate structural explanatory elements. The liberation of flows of communication has played an increasingly important role in the successive industrial revolutions. The universe of communication networks has constituted the essential focus around which progress has developed, although it has also been known to play an important role in the generation of utopias, according to Armand Mattelart.

What continues to distinguish the first IR is its link to the change from feudal production to the capitalist mode, while other revolutions have only continued the development of capitalism, the system still in force. The first and second industrial revolutions, as well as the scientific and technological revolution, were linked to the technical principle of specialization—as proclaimed by Smith, and further developed with Taylorism, Fordism, and contributions from the theory of organization and administrative practice—facilitating the entrance into

Period	Revolutions	Major innovations	Further developments
17th century	Industrial preconditions	Machine tools made mainly with hand tools	Mining, salt, copper, tin, nail, and other industries in England on a partial factory basis
From 1765 to the end of the 1870s	First industrial revolution	Machine tools Steam engine Locomotive engine Iron rails	Metallurgy Textile industry Railroad transport Telegraph
End of 19th century and early decades of the 20th	Second industrial revolution	Political economy Electrical engine Gasoline engine Chemical developments Aviation	International trade theory Electromechanic industries Automobile industries Chemical industries Aviation industries
		Cost accounting Industrial psychology Scientific administration Institutional economics	Production control systems Human relations movement Administrative theory Keynesian economics
From 1940s to the end of the 1960s	Scientific and technological revolution	Nuclear physics Electronic development Chemical synthesis Bureaucracy theory Behavioral school Welfare economics	Military and nuclear energy Electronic industries Synthetic fibers Pharmaceutical industries Contingency movement New human relations Economic development
From 1970 on	Third industrial revolution	Microelectronics Computing Biochemistry developments Sprouting of new theories of organization Liberal monetary theories	Robotics, automation, telematics Information industries Biotechnology Space industries Postmodern organizations New economics
Periods and dates for some major innovations and further developments are debatable for some IR researchers.			

Figure 1 Industrial Revolutions

the era of mass production. In contrast, the third revolution has inaugurated the technical principle of productive flexibility, and has given birth to the new economics in which knowledge constitutes the engine for growth. Although flexible technology has allowed for greater adaptation to consumer preferences, as well as reengineering in companies, and a certain decrease in company size, the prediction made by Piore and Sabel regarding the disappearance of large productive units has not yet become reality. Rather, globalization, taking advantage of flexible technology, has animated new complex organizational forms, and as a political strategy of capitalism, it has favored the surging of a new global business class.

—*Víctor M. Soria*

See also Communication; Competition; Organizational Evolution; Reengineering; Technology

Further Readings

Ibarra-Colado, E. (2001). Los saberes sobre la organización: etapas, enfoques y dilemas. In E. Ibarra-Colado, *La universidad en México hoy: Gubernamentalidad y modernización* (pp. 161–245). Mexico: Universidad Nacional Autónoma de México y Universidad Autónoma Metropolitana.

Mattelart, A. (1996). *La mondialisation de la communication.* Paris: Presses Universitaires de France.

Piore, M., & Sabel, C. (1985). *The second industrial divide: Possibilities of prosperity.* New York: Basic Books.

Toynbee, A. (1884). *Lectures on the industrial revolution in England.* Retrieved March 4, 2007, from http://socserv.mcmaster.ca/econ/ugcm/3ll3/toynbee/indrev

Weber, M. (1958). *The protestant ethic and the spirit of capitalism.* New York: Scribner.

INFLUENCE

Influence is referred to as the purposeful set of actions that one exerts to change the attitude, belief, or behavior of another. *Influence* is a term that theorists have used, predominantly in the management literature, to describe behaviors using interpersonal power. Leadership research over the past 20 years has shifted from a focus on power in the abstract to a focus on specific influence behaviors, and influence is often written about from either the perspective of the influencer or the target of influence. In particular, influence does not have to have a successful or unsuccessful result, but it includes the notion of intentionality. Influence attempts are deliberate; these attempts are typically studied by examining the direction of the influence in the organization.

Influence occurs between the influencer and target in multiple directions within the organization's hierarchy, down the hierarchy or laterally, across the hierarchy. Upward influence occurs between an employee and a manager. Downward influence occurs between a manager and an employee, and lateral influence transpires between two peers. Other typologies have focused on influence as arising at the individual level, group level, organizational level, or societal level. Most studies of influence, however, converge on the interpersonal level between an influencer and a target.

Conceptual Overview

Organizations exist to control, dominate, and exploit the talents and resources of their human capital. Such control and domination allow organizations to generate profit, expand, and flourish. That is, organizations do not exist for the good of the individual to invest and develop the individual worker except where the organization can profit from the increase in skills that the worker attains after training. *Upward influence* is the mechanism by which workers contain the rampant exploitation and control by which they are subjected. Upward influence describes the organizationally sanctioned means to impose checks on the potentially rampant power of management. Other mechanisms to contain the power of management and not necessarily sanctioned by the organization include sabotage, public dissent, exiting the organization, enlisting the aid of an external regulatory agency, or spreading misinformation.

Upward influence is an intentional attempt to change the behavior, attitudes, or beliefs of a target higher on the organization's hierarchal structure than the influencer. A multitude of tactics tagged by researchers are referred to as upward influence tactics.

One researcher identified as many as 346 different influence tactics, but more conventional typologies cluster these tactics into six behavioral strategies, which will be explored shortly.

In downward influence, or manager-to-subordinate influence, the manager enjoys all sorts of decision-making freedoms and the formally sanctioned right to impose sets of tasks and ideology on subordinates. The manager has to employ some level of skill in persuasion to entice the subordinate to comply, but with the arsenal of organizational resources at the manager's disposal, such as promotions, demotions, overtime, compensation adjustments, bonuses, and other benefits, this is relatively easy to accomplish compared to the level of skill that subordinates must attain to influence up the hierarchy.

Max Weber, the influential sociologist, cautioned about managers who amass power to achieve personal goals in organizations. Organizations cannot function well and rationally when they contain organizational tyrants intent on achieving and sustaining their own personal agendas at the expense of their subordinates and ultimately the organization. Understanding the resources and tools that subordinates wield against this tyranny helps to promote the growth and viability of organizations. With an understanding of these interactions, people in organizations can begin to shift the power amassed by a few and counteract the effects of imposed control. That is, workers can learn how to sell their ideas, distribute resources, and transmit knowledge up the hierarchical structure of an organization.

Three major research trends have emerged within organizational studies. Each trend focuses on the (1) antecedents, (2) attempts themselves, or (3) outcomes desired.

The antecedents or factors that effect the influence process before the process occurs include the following:

- Choice of a specific influence strategy or a cluster of multiple strategies
- Decision process to attempt influence or to take another alternative
- Reason for influence as either benefiting the personal goals (personal agendas) of the influencer or the organization's goals
- Personal characteristics or demographic factors such as gender, personality, age, occupation, race, ethnic background, and experience
- Organizational characteristics such as the size and structure of the workplace, the type of industry, the type of organizational climate or culture, and workplace history and norms

The second category of research considers more fully the actual attempt at influence. This area of research considers the different types of strategies that workers use to gain resources, sell ideas, or accomplish objectives. As mentioned, early studies of influence identified more than 346 different influence tactics. More recent researchers have combined the multitude of tactics into six major clusters of influence strategies:

1. *Reason* is viewed as the use of logical arguments to persuade a target to achieve a task or an objective. The use of reason often involves preparation and presentation of data and facts. This strategy involves the use of self-control, and influencers using this strategy do not use strong emotion with targets.

2. *Assertiveness* is described as the use of demands or threats to gain compliance from a target. Assertiveness is often described in negative terms and can include anger, face-to-face confrontations, and real or implied threats. Most social scientists, however, have made a different distinction between assertiveness and aggressiveness. *Assertiveness* happens when an individual makes a clear statement of desires and preferences with no implication of threat if someone does not comply with the request. *Aggressiveness*, on the other hand, involves the capacity for pressure and threats.

3. *Ingratiation* is defined as the process of strengthening a relationship with a target or seeking the target's favor prior to launching a request. This strategy is designed for the influencer to become more attractive and likeable in the eyes of the target. Other behaviors in this category could include flattery, compliments, performing favors, giving gifts, feigning interest in the target's personal life or hobbies, and actively managing impressions. This strategy is described in particular as a low-risk and high-benefit strategy.

4. *Bargaining* is defined as the promise of resources or benefits in exchange for the influencer's request. Bargaining can imply fulfillment of the influencer's request at a future point in time and can also be termed "owing a favor." Bargaining can be an actual promise or an implied promise to exchange of favors, and favors can be tangible favors such as an improved work assignment, additional resources, or intangible favors such as knowledge or information sharing.

5. *Coalition* occurs when the influencer aligns himself or herself with other employees in order to exert a group influence on the target. This strategy is the most complex of the other strategies as it is dependent on other people to launch influence on a target. The breadth and depth of an influencer's network is also a factor in this strategy. A strong relationship maintained by the influencer within a large network has more potential on a target than weak relationships within a small network.

6. *Higher authority* is where the influencer deliberately sidesteps traditional hierarchical structure and makes a request of the target's boss or gains support from someone higher in the organizational hierarchy than the target of influence. The concept of higher authority seems to be least developed in studies of influence. This may be because of the conceptual overlap between coalition formation and alignment with others higher in the organizational structure.

The third category of research focuses on the outcomes surrounding the influence attempt. These studies look at the success or nonsuccess of the influence process and the impact influence has on other people and systems. These studies include discussions of results such as individual and organizational financial gain, performance review data and results, job promotions, implementation of ideas, and gain of resources, to include human, capital, technological, knowledge, sales results, and improved opinions of peers, customers, management, supplier, and the community.

Influence research occurs across all levels of the organization: upward, downward, and across levels. Studies that examine downward influence are the most abundant in the management literature and center on those individuals who have a stake in preserving their formal hierarchical position and access to institutional resources. In addition to studies of downward influence, theorists have examined mutual influence in groups and between peers. Finally, upward influence studies, although not as widespread as downward influence studies, hold a lot of promise relative to circumventing organizational structure to attain organizational goals.

Critical Commentary and Future Directions

The variety of influence strategies available to individuals is likely to change given the changing nature of the workplace. New organizational structures continue to emerge, notions of hierarchy are blurred, and customers, managers, and workers can be virtual, thousands of miles away or in the next office. In addition to the evolution of workplace hierarchy and structure, the global economy necessitates a new look at cultural considerations relative to influence. Although studies of influence have been in abundance for decades, they continue to occur in traditional workplaces or with traditional and well-recognized typologies of influence strategies. First, influence research aims to adequately capture the new blurry organizational hierarchy with all of the emerging geographical considerations. Studies need to reflect the complexity of the new workplace. In other words, are there new and different decision factors based on these new workplaces that affect the choice of influence strategy? As the workplace becomes more global, are multicultural studies of influence relevant?

Second, influence studies are still stuck in the rut of conventional clusters of behaviors. Human behavior is necessarily complex enough to warrant investigations into new and daring forms of deliberate behavior that could be termed *influence*. Recent studies on creativity in the workplace, sex in the workplace, and humor and storytelling are steps in this direction. Are there new combinations or clusters of tactics that researchers haven't bundled together to label a *strategy* yet? This question should prompt the next generation of researchers and practitioners to determine an adequately complex and evolving set of labels to describe the intentional behaviors exhibited in the workplace.

—Anna B. Kayes

See also Authority; Business Networks; Conflict; Cross-Cultural management; Hegemony; Leadership, Charisma; Leadership, Dispersed; Leadership, Servant; Leadership, Styles; Leadership, Transactional; Leadership, Transformational; Leadership Theory; Negotiation; Politics; Subordination; Trust

Further Readings

Gabarro, J. J., & Kotter, J. P. (1993). HBR classic: Managing your boss. *Harvard Business Review, 72,* 150–157.

Kipnis, D., Schmidt, S. M., & Wilkinson, I. (1980). Intraorganizational influence strategies: Explorations in getting one's way. *Journal of Applied Psychology, 65*(4), 440–452.

Mowday, R. T. (1979). Leader characteristics: Self-confidence, and methods of upward influence in organizational decision situations. *Academy of Management Journal, 22,* 709–725.

Schilit, W. K., & Locke, E. (1982). A study of upward influence in organizations. *Administrative Science Quarterly, 27,* 304–316.

Yukl, G., & Tracey, B. (1992). Consequences of influence strategies used with subordinates, peers, and the boss. *Journal of Applied Psychology, 77,* 525–535.

Informal Economy

The informal economy is the diversified set of economic activities, enterprises, and workers that are not regulated or protected by the state. Since its discovery in the early 1970s, the informal economy and its role in economic development have been hotly debated. Some observers view the informal economy in positive terms, as a pool of entrepreneurial talent or a cushion during economic crises. Others view it more problematically, arguing that informal entrepreneurs deliberately avoid regulation and taxation. Still others see the informal economy as a source of livelihood for the working poor. Each of these perspectives has merit in regard to specific components or aspects of the informal economy. Contrary to early predictions, the informal economy has continued to grow and has appeared in new forms. Today, it represents a significant share of the global economy and workforce.

Originally applied to self-employment in small unregistered enterprises, the concept of informality has been expanded to also include wage employment in unprotected jobs. The self-employed in small unregistered or unincorporated enterprises include: employers, own-account operators (both heads of family enterprises and single person operators), and unpaid but contributing family workers. Wage workers without worker benefits or social protection include: employees of informal enterprises, informal employees of formal firms, casual or day laborers, unregistered or undeclared workers, industrial outworkers (also called homeworkers), most domestic workers, and some temporary or part-time workers.

So defined, the informal economy comprises half to three-quarters of the nonagricultural labor force in developing countries. When informality in agriculture is also measured, the share of informal employment in total employment is higher still: as high as 90% in some countries in South Asia and sub-Saharan Africa. Although comparable estimates are not available for developed countries, evidence suggests that nonstandard jobs and self-employment represent a sizeable (more than 25%) and growing share of total employment in Western Europe and North America.

Conceptual Overview

Over the years, the debates on the informal economy have crystallized into four schools of thought regarding the informal economy. The *dualist* school sees the informal sector as comprised of marginal and survivalist activities—distinct from and not related to the formal sector—that provide income for the poor and a safety net in times of crisis. According to this school, the persistence of informal activities is due largely to the fact that not enough modern employment opportunities have been created to absorb surplus labor in developing countries. The *structuralist* school subscribes to the notion that informal enterprises and informal wage workers are subordinated to the interests of large capitalist firms, supplying cheap goods and services. Structuralists see formal and informal modes of production as inextricably linked and attribute the persistence and growth of the informal economy to the nature of capitalist development.

The *legalist* school, on the other hand, sees the informal sector as comprised of plucky microentrepreneurs who choose to operate informally in order to avoid the costs, time, and effort involved in formal registration. According to the legalists, cumbersome government rules and procedures create barriers to formalization and thus stifle the productive potential of informal entrepreneurs. The related *illegalist* school assumes that informal entrepreneurs deliberately seek to avoid regulations and taxation and, in some cases, to deal in illegal goods and services. According to this school of thought, informal entrepreneurs choose to operate illegally—or even criminally—in order to avoid taxation, commercial regulations, electricity, rental fees, and other costs of operating formally.

Given the heterogeneity of the informal economy, there is merit to each of these perspectives as each school reflects one or another "slice of the (informal) pie." But the informal economy as a whole is more heterogeneous and complex than the sum of these perspectives would suggest.

Critical Commentary and Future Directions

The recent renewal of interest in the informal economy stems from the recognition that the informal economy is growing and represents a feature of modern capitalist development, not just traditional economies. Given its size, significance, and permanence, several dimensions of the informal economy in today's global economy need further conceptualization and empirical analysis. First, the segmentation within the informal economy by employment status, sex, and other variables needs further analysis, including differences in average earnings, poverty risk, and other characteristics associated with different segments. Second, the continuum of employment relations between pure formal relations (i.e., regulated and protected) at one pole and pure informal relations (i.e., unregulated and unprotected) at the other, with many categories in between, needs further analysis. Also, the linkages between units and workers along this continuum need to be better understood. Finally, the costs and benefits of working at different points along this continuum need to be better measured and understood. Mainstream economists—particularly those who subscribe to the illegalist school of thought—tend to focus on the benefits of working informally to the relative neglect of the costs of doing so. However, recent studies have shown often substantial costs—many of which remain hidden—associated with working informally.

—*Martha Alter Chen*

See also Capital Movement, Migration, and Maquiladoras; Contingent Employment; Employment Relations; Entrepreneurship; Small and Medium-Sized Enterprises

Further Readings

Chen, M. A., Vanek, J., Lund, F., Heintz, J., Jhabvala, R., & Bonner, C. (2005). *Progress of the world's women 2005: Women, work, and poverty.* New York: United Nations Development Fund for Women (UNIFEM).

de Soto, H. (1989). *The other path: The economic answer to terrorism.* New York: HarperCollins.

International Labour Office. (1972). *Employment, incomes and equality: A strategy for increasing productive employment in Kenya.* Geneva: Author.

International Labour Office. (2002). *Women and men in the informal economy: A statistical picture.* Geneva: Author. Retrieved March 6, 2007, http://www.ilo.org/public/english/employment/gems/download/women.pdf

Maloney, W. F. (2004). Informality revisited. *World Development, 7,* 1–20.

Moser, C. N. (1978). Informal sector or petty commodity production: Dualism or independence in urban development. *World Development, 6,* 1041–1064.

Portes, A. (1994). The informal economy and its paradoxes. In N. Smelser & R. Swedberg (Eds.), *The handbook of economic sociology* (pp. 426–453). Princeton, NJ: Princeton University Press.

Tokman, V. (1978). An exploration into the nature of the informal-formal sector relationship. *World Development, 6,* 1065–1075.

INFORMATION

Information is that which informs. It can be any type of data that enlightens a person in some way so that he or she can better undertake a particular activity or make a decision. For the Massai Mara warriors of Kenya, marks in the dirt may provide information about the presence of a lion, because they have learned to interpret this data so that they know the difference between different types of marks. Based on this information they would then take appropriate action—be very wary as they move forward. This same data (the marks in the dirt) for someone else may not provide information if that person has not learned how to interpret the data. However, a Massai warrior can verbally communicate his interpretation to another, telling him or her of the presence of the lion. The communication would then provide information to others even if they could not "read" the original data, provided that they understand the language that the Massai warrior uses, whether verbal or nonverbal.

This makes it clear that what is information (as opposed to mere data) depends very much on a person's existing knowledge and so his or her ability to interpret the data; whether this is raw data (marks in the dirt or inflation figures) or the data that have been processed by another (a communication about the presence of a lion or a communication about remortgaging one's house to beat inflation). Even data that have been interpreted by an expert and passed on to others in the form of a written or verbal communication in order to provide others with information upon which they can act, may not inform, or not inform in the way that was intended by the expert, if the recipient of the communication does not share some kind of common understanding and knowledge with the communicator. For example, engineering experts produced data to try and stop the launch of the *Challenger* space shuttle because the data they had informed them that launching in very cold temperatures was very likely to lead to a fatal accident caused by blowby. However, for nonengineers this data informed them that there was no direct correlation between temperature and blowby problems, and so they decided that they could launch the shuttle, leading to the fatal tragedy. Data, knowledge, and information are thus inextricably linked. Information is the product of data plus knowledge, with the creation of information from data depending on one's existing knowledge that allows one to make sense of the data.

Conceptual Overview

The above definition makes it clear that data carry information if they convey some meaning to the recipient—clarify something, provide new insight about a problem, reduce uncertainty, and so on. Data do not convey meaning. Whether data convey meaning (and so constitute information) depends on the individual's existing knowledge and the use of this knowledge to make sense of the data. The link between data and information is thus knowledge—what is data to one person can be information to another. As a very simple example, take this encyclopedia that is written in English. To a person who cannot read English, the book contains meaningless data; to a person who can read and understand English it may contain information. However, a book written in English but about nuclear physics may contain only data even to the person who can read and understand English as he or she is unable to make any sense of the concepts and ideas being written about, so that it conveys no information.

A lot of common knowledge exists within an organization, so it is possible to convey information across people and places—data that will be interpreted by all to convey the same (or at least sufficiently similar) information that allows coordinated action. This is crucial because without the sharing of information it would not be possible for organizations to exist, since there would be no way to coordinate the activities of people in order for them to work toward the attainment of organizational goals. So, a lot of information exists within an organization that has been created and shared for specific uses—a mission statement defines the overall goals of the organization so that everyone has information about the purpose of the organization and so can make decisions and take action with this purpose in mind; rules provide information about what can and cannot be done in particular situations so that, for example, employees are all treated fairly; policies and procedures provide information about how different tasks will be undertaken so that consistent behavior is achieved; job descriptions set out the overall objectives of a particular job and provide information about the tasks and responsibilities of the person that will allow him or her to fulfill these objectives; sales orders are given to suppliers, providing them with information about what they need to deliver and when; and marketing campaigns are designed to convey product information to potential customers to persuade them to buy the product.

In a traditional, bureaucratic, top-down organization, those at the top of the organization create the information, those at the middle of the organization ensure that the information is communicated effectively, and those at the bottom carry out the instructions that the information conveys. For example, senior management may interpret data about competitor behavior to mean that the organization needs to invest in a more aggressive marketing campaign. They communicate this information to the marketing managers, who then develop tactics to implement this more aggressive strategy and so provide more information to potential customers about the benefits of this company's products over the competitors'. In more dynamic contemporary organizations, it is recognized that all organizational members can create information from the data they are exposed to so that information is communicated in all directions. Moreover, more contemporary organizational design recognizes that the lateral sharing of information is as important as the vertical communication of information.

The sharing or communication of information is thus crucial for organizational functioning. Nevertheless, many problems in an organizational context exist because data are interpreted in different ways—essentially convey different information. Part of the problem here can lie in the fact that the information that is provided is insufficient to convey the intended meaning. Information richness refers to the learning capacity of a communication—its ability to convey what was intended by the source to the receiver. Face-to-face communication is often considered to be a richer medium of communication than written communication because there is an opportunity to "read" nonverbal cues that can convey additional information. For example, the source can use hand gestures to convey the seriousness of the information being communicated and the recipient can use facial expressions to communicate that he or she has not fully understood and need more information.

Other information problems occur because of differences in knowledge and understanding between individuals and groups. Dorothy Dougherty, for example, talks about groups having unique *thought worlds* based on their different education and experiences. For example, engineers are trained to look very carefully at the risks associated with different design options and to try and avoid designs that are too risky in favor of designs that carry less risk. On the other hand, marketing specialists are trained to look at designs from the point of view of functionality and performance that will attract potential buyers. The same data on a new model car design sheet may then provide very different information to the engineer and the marketing specialist because of their different knowledge and sensemaking orientation—their different thought worlds.

These differences in the information gleaned from the same data cause many problems in organizations, in particular because it is often assumed that one's own interpretation of the data is the only rational one, and that other interpretations are therefore wrong. Rather than try and understand the information that is being received from the different point of view, effort is put into convincing the other of the rightness of one's own reading. In many situations, however, there is no right way to read the data because there is ambiguity in the situation and equivocality in the sense that there are several ways of interpreting a problem and several potential solutions, none of which is inherently best because what is best depends on one's viewpoint. *Karl Weick* refers to this as requisite variety, indicating that there are multiple meanings of action, and so of information.

These information-related problems in organizations are also reflected in the confusion that exists in the academic literature with respect to distinctions between data, information, and knowledge, which are often conflated. For example, there is much talk in both the academic literature and in practice about knowledge management. Knowledge management refers to practices that are focused on the more effective creation and use of knowledge within organizations, with knowledge management systems (KMS) described as systems that can encourage the storage and sharing of knowledge between individuals and groups; for example using intranets, databases, or e-mail. These KMS evolved from information systems, which in turn evolved from data systems. In reality, however, KMS only store and transfer data, not even information, since it is the interpretation of the data, based on the recipient's knowledge and sensemaking, that determine the information that is extracted. Ignoring and conflating the differences between knowledge, information, and data has left many organizations with very expensive but not very productive KMS.

Critical Commentary and Future Directions

The above makes it clear that data can be interpreted in multiple and often contradictory ways, so that there is always an equivocal quality to any communication that is intended to convey information between individuals or groups. Much organizational research fails to fully take this into consideration and so there is a burgeoning literature on knowledge management or best practices that assumes that communication of information is no different to shooting an arrow to hit a bull's-eye. The information will hit as intended, and produce the desired result, as long as one carefully communicates the message. Thus, in much of the noncritical knowledge management literature, it is assumed that knowledge (not even mere information) can be stored and transferred between individuals located in different locations using knowledge management systems. This completely ignores that information systems can only ever communicate data that will need to be reinterpreted and made sense of by the recipient, based on his or her own knowledge and sensemaking capacities. Similarly, information systems are supposedly designed based on best practices within a particular industry so that an organization adopting the information system will automatically be acquiring best practice. This ignores both that it is not possible to define what is best, given the requisite variety of organizational form, and that it is not possible for systems to produce organizational results.

Critical management research thus recognizes that different stakeholders have different, but potentially equally legitimate, agendas and purposes so that the communication of information has the potential to create divergence as well as convergence. Increased communication of information has as much chance of creating a vicious circle of distrust and divergent perspectives as a virtuous circle of trust and common perspective. Research that explores these viscous cycles of information communication, especially in the context of virtual information communication between individuals of diverse cultural background that is increasingly common, is thus important.

—Sue Newell

See also Actionable Knowledge; Bureaucracy; Classical Management; Communication; Complex Organizations; Conflict; Coordination; Critical Management Studies; Job Evaluation; Knowledge; Knowledge Management; Organizational Rules; Politics; Rational Choice Theory; Risk Management; Sensemaking

Further Readings

Banker, R., & Kauffman, R. (2004). The evolution of research on information systems: A 50th year survey of the literature in management science. *Management Science, 50*(3), 281–298.

Cross, R., & Sproull, L. (2004). More than an answer: Information relationships for actionable knowledge. *Organization Science, 15*(4), 446–462.

Dearstyne, B. (2005). The information enterprise: New challenges new dimensions. *Information Management Journal, 39*(4), 38–45.

Eppler, M., & Mengis, J. (2004). The concept of information overload: A review of literature from organization science, accounting, marketing, MIS, and related disciplines. *Information Society, 20*(5), 325–344.

Galliers, R., & Newell, S. (2003). Back to the future: From knowledge management to data management. *Information Systems and e-Business Management, 1*(1), 5–14.

Sambamurthy, V., & Subramani, M. (2005). Special issue on information technologies and knowledge management. *MIS Quarterly, 29*(1), 1–7.

Information and Communication Technology

Information and communication technology (ICT) describes the integrated use of physical equipment and computer software to store, retrieve, process, and transmit information. Known also as information technology (IT) or infocomm, ICT enables distributed work and collaboration, especially in large, multinational organizations. Over the past 20 years, advances in processor power, storage capacity, and global networks such as the Internet have allowed broader access to world markets while challenging conventional notions of organization.

Conceptual Overview

Information and communication technology implies both the processing and successful exchange of information. Though the structured expression and communication of information is thought to have begun with Mesopotamian cuneiform around 3000 BC, information theory was only recognized as a discipline with the publication of Claude Shannon's paper, "A Mathematical Theory of Communication" in 1948. This date closely parallels the creation of the Electronic Numerical Integrator and Computer (ENIAC) in 1946. As Weik notes, ENIAC was the first general-purpose computer to use vacuum tubes rather than mechanical instruments to perform calculations, making it the first electronic computer. The modern age of digital computing was thus begun, providing the foundation for ICT.

Also of note is the project that created ENIAC; slated to finish in 1943, the US$61,700 contract between the University of Pennsylvania and the U.S. Army required nine extensions before finishing in 1946 at a total cost of US$486,804.22, according to Weik in 1961. Thus began an alarming pattern of late delivery and cost overruns in ICT projects. This pattern of challenged projects has implications for both the project organizations that create and implement ICT projects and for the organizations that attempt to adopt them. Logan notes that the most frequently cited reasons for ICT project failure—poor communication, lack of clear objectives, and lack of senior leadership support—are organizational rather than technical in nature, and Wickenberg provides a more detailed analysis of the effects of formal and informal systems in project teams (see Logan's 2005 study and Wickenberg's 2004 study). In fact, Wickenberg points out that project management practices, long thought to remove uncertainty in the development of ICT applications, may actually prevent the learning and adaptation necessary for project teams to navigate the complexity of interdependent technologies and stakeholders. Any discussion of ICT in organizations must acknowledge the difficulties of creating and adopting such systems.

Since the advent of digital computing, ICT has attained astonishing breadth and depth in society generally and in organizations specifically. Global IT spending reached US$965 billion in 2004 and is expected to grow at a compounded annual rate of 6%, according to Gonsalves. The ubiquity of ICT can easily be taken for granted; e-mail, voice technologies, instant messaging, streaming video, digital audio players, and handheld messaging devices have become fixtures in daily life over the past two decades, with much of the technology transitioning from innovation to commodity in the past 10 years.

Kristula notes the significance of the 1957 launch of Sputnik, the first artificial earth satellite, in provoking the most profound societal application of ICT to date: the Internet. Launched by the Soviet Union to gain an advantage in the exploration (and subsequent militarization) of space, Sputnik shocked the American public with the possibility that the Soviets could launch ballistic missiles from a space-based platform. In addition to escalating the pace of satellite development, the United States also formed its Advance Research Projects Agency in the Department of Defense to lead the development of innovative military technologies. One of these technologies, ARPANET, was conceived as a means to communicate without interruption during a nuclear attack, and its underlying concepts produced the commercial

Internet. Begun in 1968, ARPANET enabled e-mail in 1972, listservs in 1979, the World Wide Web in 1992, and the online ordering of Pizza Hut pizza in 1994, as noted by Kristula in 1997. Most current applications of ICT make use of the Internet.

Innovation and progress in ICT are generally measured in size, capability, freedom of movement, and access. Among the significant recent advancements in ICT hardware are the steady replacement of desktop computers with laptops, more powerful processors, the near obsolescence of storage media such as floppy disks, the growing potential for solid-state technologies (such as flash drives) to replace fragile hard drives, and the frontierlike growth of wireless Internet access. These advances facilitate the broad expansion of software-based ICT applications such as instant messaging, file sharing, virtual communities, and social networking.

Outsourcing and offshoring of work, an application of ICT to increase organizational capacity while minimizing cost, has had a profound effect on the way work is organized, who is considered a member of an organization, and how an organization discusses and enacts its values. Morello notes the effects of stress toward weakening organizational productivity and performance, emphasizing that managers are often ill-equipped to address the organizational backlash created by the frequent job losses associated with offshoring. These losses are particularly felt in information technology organizations.

Vygotsky's social development theory offers compelling implications for the recent explosion of virtual communities and social networking portals such as MySpace and Friendster. These communities enable thousands—and sometimes millions—of strangers across diverse geographies to engage each other in various forms of interaction. In addressing the cultural context of social development, Vygotsky inadvertently anticipates the creation of a new cultural context in which geographically dispersed strangers develop ideas, communities, and even identities in a shared virtual space. While more recent works such as Rivers's have raised cautions about ontological freedom and intentionality in such communities, few dispute their increasing growth and prominence, especially among younger generations. These applications form the social vanguard of modern ICT.

Critical Commentary and Future Directions

ICT carries broad organizational implications, though relatively little research has been conducted nor theory established with regard to these implications compared with that of social construction theories such as appreciative inquiry. Some of the areas offering opportunity for study include centralization/decentralization of decision-making processes using ICT; team development in geographically diverse organizations, especially those with ambiguous boundaries such as offshore/outsource situations; the effect of rational-positivist concepts such as project support structures on the creators and recipients of ICT applications; and the implications of information and relationship ubiquity on intellectual property.

The decentralization of decisions was a necessary shift in establishing distributed organizations such as multinational corporations. Challenging conventional notions of command and control, most based in the works of Max Weber and Frederick Taylor, the decentralization of decisions enabled decisions to be made at the point at which the most information and the quickest response were available, according to Van Zandt. Recent trends toward more robust hardware and increasingly versatile communications software have challenged the premises of decentralization, yielding comparable speed and quality of information at many nodes throughout the organization, including its headquarters. Van Zandt's work with bounded rationality in decentralized processes is a useful start, and more research will yield a greater range of options in the design and management of organizations.

The outsourcing and offshoring of work to low-cost providers in locations such as India, China, and Singapore has challenged conventional ideas of where an organization's boundaries lie. Pfeffer and Salancik stated in 1978 that "the organization is the total set of interstructured activities in which it is engaged at any one time and over which it has discretion to initiate, maintain, or end behaviors . . . the organization ends where its discretion ends and another's begins." Given this definition, there is a case to be made that an outsourced offshore provider is within the boundaries of the organization. This view carries unique implications for motivation, alignment, diversity, and team development in such organizations. The maturing—and perhaps the effectiveness—of offshore outsourcing as a practice will benefit from investigation into these issues.

Wickenberg's work in investigating the relationship of project support structures to informal organizational entities is an unusual and useful approach to the project management teams that build ICT applications, and, by implication and collaboration, those who adopt them for use in their work. The rational-positivist stance often associated with technical professionals presents a barrier to acknowledging the existence of shadow organizations, which implies that they operate out of the awareness of ICT project teams. The very structures created to minimize risk in such projects would seem to preclude consideration of such shadow organizations, which paradoxically results in increased risk. As such teams create more and broader ICT applications, further research into critical theory will help expand awareness of nontechnical influences in the creation of ICT.

As the boundaries of organizations become more porous through the various uses of ICT, information—including intellectual property—becomes more broadly available and easily conveyed, both to those with lawful access and those with malicious intent. Predictably, most of the work in addressing this dynamic has occurred within the field of law. Benkler notes that organizations inclined toward tighter control of intellectual property may be less effective in more distributed organization forms. With intellectual property from medicinal compounds to film and music easily transferable within and between organizations, organization theorists must examine the implications of technology on information control and organizational governance.

Organization theory has been generally slow to take up the topic of ICT, with such notable exceptions as Zuboff reinforcing the paucity of study elsewhere in the field. More recent works by Boland and Tenkasi have taken up epistemological concerns in the creation and deployment of ICT, but the general absence of such treatments in organization theory points up a fertile field of study. As ICT becomes woven more thoroughly throughout the fabric of modern life, organization theorists have an opportunity to understand and explain the powerful influence of this force in the lives of individuals and organizations.

—*Joseph Logan*

See also Information Processing; Organizational Communication; Organizational Learning; Outsourcing; Project Management; Virtual Organization

Further Readings

Benkler, Y. (2002). Intellectual property and the organization of information production. *International Review of Law & Economics, 22*(1), 81.

Boland, Jr., R. J., Tenkasi, R. V., & Te'eni, D. (1994). Designing information technology to support distributed cognition. *Organization Science, 5*(3), 456–475.

Gonsalves, A. (2005, January 25). "Moderate" growth predicted in global IT spending. *TechWeb News.* Retrieved March 6, 2007, from http://www.techweb.com/wire/ebiz/57703348

Kristula, D. (1997). *The history of the internet.* Retrieved June 15, 2006. from http://www.davesite.com/webstation/net-history.shtml

Logan, J. (2005). Managing and practicing OD in an IT environment. In T. Torres-Coronas & M. Arias-Oliva (Eds.), *E-human resources management: Managing knowledge people.* Hershey, PA: Idea Group.

Morello, D. (2005). *The organizational implications of offshore outsourcing.* Stamford CT: Gartner.

Pfeffer, J., & Salancik, R. (1978). *The external control of organizations: A resource dependence perspective.* New York: Harper & Row.

Rivers, T. J. (2005). An introduction to the metaphysics of technology. *Technology in Society, 27,* 551–574.

Sertel, M. (Ed.). (1999). *Contemporary economic issues, vol. 4: Economic design and behavior.* London: Macmillan,

Shannon, C. E. (1948). A mathematical theory of communication. *Bell System Technical Journal, 27,* 379–423, 623–656.

Vygotsky, L. S. (1978). *Mind and society: The development of higher mental processes.* Cambridge MA: Harvard University Press.

Weik, M. (1961). The ENIAC story. *ORDNANCE: The Journal of the American Ordnance Association,* January-February. Retrieved March 6, 2007, from http://ftp.arl.mil/~mike/comphist/eniac-story.html

Wickenberg, J. (2004). *Exploring the shadows of project management.* Göteborg, Sweden: Chalmers University of Technology.

Zuboff, S. (1988). *In the age of the smart machine: The future of work and power.* New York: Basic Books.

INFORMATION PROCESSING

Information processing describes the means of converting data into meaningful information for an observer. The processing is generally understood as being carried out by an information system. This formulation originates from information theory, in which information is produced when a message is communicated or processed from a sender to a receiver.

Conceptual Overview

The following theories and disciplines traditionally associated with information processing are introduced below: the theory of information; cognitive science; the field of information systems and its definitional differences between data, information, and knowledge; systems theory; management information systems; and interpretivist approaches to information processing.

Claude Shannon and Warren Weaver formulated their *Mathematical Theory of Information* in 1949, and it has been widely applied in the design of communication systems. This theory of information as a message endows the word *information* with measurement. The information content of messages is measured for particular sending devices, for instance a technical communication relay. From this theoretical perspective, information does not have to be related to truth, communication, or representation, and signals, messages, or patterns to be transmitted may be devoid of meaning. When a pattern of something is processed into a pattern of something else, the latter is information. Information is any type of pattern that influences the formation or transformation of other patterns; for example, DNA. This concept of information, as seen by information theorists, has a very specific meaning not to be confused with the more common use of the word.

By contrast, cognitive approaches do not envisage information as mechanically constructed or presented by some sender, and communication as not automatically implying information processing or exchange of information. Someone has to interpret the information. *Cognitive science* aims to understand human thinking, and information processing is seen as involving conscious mind, either constructing the representation or interpreting it. Sampling and encoding result in constructing a representation, and interpreting it involves inference and decoding. The information-processing approach in psychology is allied to cognitivism and functionalism.

Information depends on but is separate from the media used to communicate it, but it is meaningless unless someone is present to interpret it. However, the terms *information, data,* and *knowledge* have come to be used interchangeably and often do not denote anything different from one another. They are ambiguous concepts with a wide range of connotations attached to them. In the technical-functional paradigm, the relationship between data and information is that information is data that have been processed in order to make them useful or meaningful. Data are basic facts, or raw material, already present and presumed to be true as corresponding to reality. Information is about processing, conversion, or transformation of data to a recipient and its understanding by a recipient. The purpose of information is to effect change in the recipient. Knowledge is deduced from facts and information through reasoning and logic. These definitions are central to the field of *information systems* in which data are recorded transactions transformed into information by data (computer) processing. The data represent thousand of facts, which presented as such would only confuse. Data are often defined as quantities, characters, or symbols on which operations are performed by computers and which may be stored. However, what constitutes information to one person may be data to another.

The action of informing is defined as communicating a piece of knowledge, news, occurrence, subject, or event, as contrasted with data. Informing means giving form; for instance, to the mind in education. In organizations, information processing is often conceptualized as supporting or informing the managerial decision-making process. This can be related to the notion of feedback in *systems theory,* where information systems process input data into outputs that can be used as feedback to rectify and refine decision making. *Systems theory* refers to information as patterns circulating in a system, and the system being the information processor as it changes the patterns and representations; for instance, for feedback purposes. Systems are composed of subsystems, subsystems interact with and transform one another, and the properties of the system as a whole result not only from the properties of its subsystems, but also from the interactions across them.

Systems theory has been a major contributor to information systems research and practice. Fred Emery and Eric Trist's ideas of sociotechnical systems of the 1960s have been applied to describe the information that an organization requires from an information system and to design, implement, install, and procure information systems so that they can deliver the information required. The premise is that, symmetrically, there are information requirements that the social system poses to the technical system, as well as organizational requirements that the technical system poses to the social system.

Information systems used to be called electronic data processing systems. They are used by people, organizations, and businesses for many reasons, including keeping records, processing transactions, communicating information, supporting business processes operations, decision making, and competitive strategies. Some examples are recording and storing sales, purchase, payroll, and inventory data; and processing these records into production schedules, inventory systems, sales activity reports, environmental scanning reports or financial portfolio models. They can be used to gain competitive advantage; for instance, using an extranet to integrate the supply chain or through electronic commerce. Information systems, sometimes also called *management information systems* (MIS), is the academic discipline concerned with the development, use, and impact of information technology-based processing systems in organizations and society as a whole. More broadly, many people speak of the information age, the information society, or information technologies— the latter more closely related to computer science. *Information technology* (IT) or *information and communications technologies* (ICT) are the technology required for information processing, in particular the use of electronic computers and computer software to store, protect, convert, process, transmit, and retrieve information. *Systems* has generally come to denote computer systems, and *information systems* often means the same as *information technology,* where both terms sometimes simply designate the computer.

Individuals, groups, organizations, and global communities use collections of hardware, software, networks, and data structures; these information systems are designed to support information processing, communication, and decision making. These help process, for instance, a firm's materials into the products and services that it sells. But this is an abstract model and many situations do not fit this ideal. It often implies new work roles and division of labor and undesirable organizational changes that may lead to resistance, opposition, and failure. The accepted wisdom in the information systems management community is that this is less likely to occur if the continually evolving requirements of both the social system and the technical system are regularly monitored and taken into account.

These traditional approaches to information processing have been questioned and expanded upon more recently. These understandings have limitations as they rely on hypothetico-deductive or technical-functional positions, and they have been critically assessed in the literature. Broadly, the still dominant positivist and functionalist views have progressively been complemented by inductive theories of information and knowledge and interpretivist approaches. Similarly to the field of organization studies, the study of information, information processing, and information systems has drawn on many bodies of knowledge, initially information theory, cognitive science and systems theory, and more recently hermeneutics, phenomenology, the sociology of knowledge, and the history, philosophy, and sociology of science and technology. The latter were gathered in a book edited by John Mingers and Leslie Willcocks in 2004. They adhere to different ontological, epistemological, and methodological perspectives and try to move away from explanations based on rational choice, as illustrated so far in the conventional understandings of information processing. On the subject of the connection between business requirements and IT management of an organization, an example is the perceived need for strategic alignment of information systems and business, seen as the domain of rational strategic choice. Many intended strategies may not be realized in practice, and this lack of success is often explained as due to "negative" perceptions about IT. An alternative standpoint is to examine the origins, motives, tensions, and contradictions of the strategic discourse on the competitive potential of information systems and of the beliefs in how "IT delivers business value."

Critical Commentary and Future Directions

Orthodox notions of information outlined above have been challenged for instance by Lucas Introna in 1997. He argues that the reasoning process from data to information to knowledge is acontextual, ahistorical, and aperspectual, and he offers a hermeneutic critique of the concept of information, particularly for management information. The hermeneutic perspective helps develop notions of understanding that take as its foundation the "always already involved manager." Facts are decontextualized through computer processing or management reporting. But through "appropriation" the interpreter renders information relevant to the local and contextual. Information is the referential network of significant relationships that we always already understand as part of "being in the world." We do not become informed, interpretation is the working out of the possibilities already given in our understanding of the world we are in.

Finding computer-generated reports useful or meaningful does not flow from sense emerging from the report. The technical-functional notion of information is based on the idea that someone does not know what to do and then receives the information and consequently knows what to do. Information received by managers "already in the world" simply becomes more explicit than that which they already understand. This type of analysis provides a more complex frame for understanding the nature of information processing.

More broadly, our society has an image of information that, although alluring, is counterproductive. It confuses the capacity to transmit raw signals with the capacity to create meaningful messages. It has focused too much on computers and too little on the people who use information in order to make sense of the world. The sociotechnical approach can also be criticized. It assumes a distinction between the social and the technical, which has been challenged by constructivist authors as socially constructed, for example in the chapter on "The Social Shaping of Technology" in Mingers and Willcocks's book. It states, for instance, that the hardware and software of an enterprise information system can pose the requirement that the organization must reengineer its manufacturing processes to fit the information processes that the software was programmed to manage. This division between technical information requirements and social arrangements cannot be dissociated from a technologically driven managerial agenda. A more productive notion is that of emergence of information systems, occurring as a result of the mutually transformational interactions between information technology and the organization. The information system is the result of an information technology intervening in an organization, as much as the result of an organization enabling an information technology.

A further critical stance developed by David Knights and Fergus Murray in 1994, two critical organizational theorists, is the degree to which organizational politics—for instance, resistance to change brought by information systems—is seen as disruptive but eradicable, or simply inescapable. They state that the development of software cannot be isolated from the social world, and information systems research has benefited from organizational analysis, for which technological change has been a constant concern. Critical discourse analysis, rationalities and knowledge claims, social and cultural capital, and the interplay between power and information-processing systems are some other critical themes investigated in another recent book edited by Debra Howcroft and Eileen Trauth in 2005 on critical information systems research. Their aim is to explore the social nature of activities associated with the development, implementation and use of information systems, and the management of people who carry out these activities, which leads to considerations of social and political power.

—Nathalie N. Mitev

See also Information; Information and Communication Technology; Knowledge

Further Readings

Emery, F. E., & Trist, E. L. (1960). Socio-technical systems. In C. W. Churchman & M. Verhulst (Eds.), *Management sciences, models, and techniques* (pp. 83-97). New York: Pergamon.

Howcroft, D. A., & Trauth, E. (Eds.). (2005). *Handbook of information systems research: Critical Perspectives on information systems design, implementation, and use.* London: Edward Elgar.

Introna, L. D. (1997). *Management, information, and power: A narrative of the involved manager.* Basingstoke, UK: Macmillan.

Knights, D., & Murray, F. (1994). *Managers divided: Organisation politics and information technology management.* Chichester, UK: Wiley.

Mingers, J., & Willcocks, L. (Eds). (2004). *Social theory and philosophy for information systems.* Chichester, UK: Wiley.

Newell, A. (1990). *Unified theories of cognition.* Cambridge, MA: Harvard University Press.

Shannon, C., & Weaver, W. (1949). *The mathematical theory of communication.* Urbana, IL: University of Illinois Press.

INNOVATION

Innovation is now commonly defined as the creation of novelty of economic value. This usually translates into seeing innovation as the creation of new products and services, as the processes of production of these and as the associated organizational changes, sometimes including the establishment of new work practices and skills.

Early discussions of innovation focused on the technological elements of new products and processes, especially on the way in which these new technologies contributed to overall changes in major areas of an economy, a change referred to as a technoeconomic paradigm shift. Many analysts now focus on the relationship between innovation, especially technological innovation, and economic growth and development. Many economists now view technological innovation as an endogenous factor in economic growth and see companies' growth trajectories as increasingly affected by their organizations' innovation strategies and activities. More and more firms in high-income countries depend on continuous innovation to maintain their competitiveness. How and in which ways organizational forms and strategies selected can assist or retard innovation success is thus increasingly important to companies, especially those operating in international markets; this concern has generated an important literature.

Innovation is not only about technology; there are many elements important to success. Because innovation is a highly risky activity and most candidate products for commercial markets do not succeed, most income from firms' innovation activities comes from very few products or product families.

What may be called the ingredients of innovation have come to be a more recent focus. Innovation surveys in many countries have established the levels of innovation activity undertaken by companies and assessed what is often the most important ingredient: expenditure on research and development. These surveys show significant differences in levels of innovation-related expenditure between sectors of economies, between firms of different sizes, and between countries. In many cases, high-technology firms, such as biotechnology, are innovation-intensive (knowledge-intensive) and spend up to 10% or more of turnover on research and development. Very new, science-based firms spend considerably more.

Innovations may be radical or incremental; they may change fundamentally the kinds of products produced—think computers or cars—or they consist of smaller improvements to existing products or processes of manufacture. Incremental innovations are much more common, both across industries and across size and age of firms, than radical ones as most firms stay on familiar trajectories and smaller changes are much less risky. Radical innovations, such as those in the information and communications technology fields, which start life as products may then push major process changes—think computer-aided design, computers in manufacturing, or new biological ways for dealing with waste matter. Economies mostly function with a mix of firms making radical and incremental innovations. In some cases, the same firms will move between radical and incremental innovation as the technologies used, for example, mature.

The so-called high-tech industries are often thought of as more innovation-intensive than their low-tech counterparts, but recent work in several countries has shown that the low-tech sectors often have leading edges where both product and process innovation are occurring. "Old" industries such as mining and agriculture are in fact highly knowledge-intensive and research and development–intensive, and increasingly constant innovators through the application of science.

International interest has recently turned to innovation in service industries, which rely less on new technologies, and to complex industries, which in their operations integrate many innovations from different sectors—new technologies, products, design processes, customization. A prime example of this is the building and construction industry.

Conceptual Overview

The different types of innovation and the highly diverse ingredients that go into making and marketing product and process changes have been the subject of much work by analysts in different disciplines, from economics to organizational theorists over the past few decades.

Evolutionary economists see innovation as occurring when technological or other changes enable or encourage firms to create new products and hence greater product variety. Consumers favor some new technologies and products over others, making some firms prosper while others die through a process of creative destruction. Eventually sectors mature and may stabilize or lower rates of innovation activity as dominant designs or paradigms develop and processes of production reach an agreed maximum efficiency. Then a new approach to product development and production processes, often from a different country or region, may radically transform, for a period at least, how an industry does its business. A well-known example of this shift is the transformation of automotive production by Japanese firms during the 1980s, which could make cars more quickly and cheaply than leading American and European firms. That case shows both that innovation in organization form can be critical to competitive success and that the lead achieved through innovation can be transitory as others copy the model.

Western analysts of the Japanese "miracle" suggested that innovation organization in given industries partly derived from the national context in which companies operate, a view that saw innovation organization as a product of complex patterns of relationships and institutions. National levels of innovation were determined partly by the characteristics of these relationships and levels of innovation varied according to the specific configurations of social institutions in national systems of innovation. The institutions concerned included legal systems, especially concerning the ownership and use of intellectual property, work organization, education and training systems, capital (especially venture capital), markets, the levels of science and technology available, and the skills and orientations of policymakers. Relevant institutions were also seen in economists' "rules of the game," shaping both public sector and private sector production choices and organization, and the diminution of the risks of (especially radical) innovation.

International work suggested that some innovation systems functioned better than others. The link between innovation and sustained competitiveness in world markets, especially among manufacturers, gave policymakers a keen interest in innovation policies, such as extra investment in sectors such as science and education. The debate over whether and how policymakers in any jurisdiction can affect levels of innovation is still current.

The national systems of innovation approach has been complemented by work on the differing innovation capacity of regions and even smaller localities, seeking to link innovation levels to local specificities, including organizational capacity. The organizational specificity of sectoral innovation systems has also recently attracted attention, with some work linking innovation in sectors across countries.

The fast-increasing internationalization of economic activity and growth of world markets and the globalized organization of companies (who often keep their research and development close to home as a core competence) mean that national authorities may have limited scope for reshaping the local organization of innovation, although many innovation ingredients are still subject to national direction.

Literature in the management and organization field has more usually focused on processes of innovation at firm or interfirm (supply chain or networks) level. At this level, analysis focuses on many internal aspects of organizational activity, leading to very detailed work on enterprise processes of innovation, the management of innovation, and the associated management of knowledge, on variations in innovative capacity in firms of different size and sector, and the innovation management skills and technologies required. Internationally, not all analysts agree on the critical factors in firms' innovation success; some, for example, focus on firms' research and development and technological absorption capacity, while others suggest that market and customer orientation and links with other research and development–intensive organizations are key.

While some authors suggest that most research and development–related innovations come from large firms, others suggest that new, small, knowledge-based technology firms are the most innovative overall. Large firms have the most research and development capacity, but may be reluctant to take the risks associated with innovation, especially radical innovation, and numerous studies concern potential internal reorganization to better use the knowledge they produce. Large firms also watch the ideas produced by their smaller competitors and merger and acquisition and collaboration figure large in some innovation strategies. Firms with large research and development departments have better technology and market environment–scanning ability, and hence greater absorption capacity, and the cash and personnel resources to produce the new product efficiently or to manage the inevitable risks.

Many firms obtain their innovation ideas from outside. International studies show the most important innovation knowledge source as existing customers, then suppliers and competitors. Close linkage with end-users lowers innovation risk and smooths the innovation process, especially where design assistance is available. Client-focused firms are less likely to develop links with public sector research organizations and to take up public innovation assistance programs.

Even characteristics such as size of firm, however, do not alone determine the degree and directions of innovation activity. There is evidence that the type of technology central to the firm, the stage of development of that technology, and the type of market in which the company is operating also shape innovation decisions and levels of investment in new products. Some recent studies attempt to specify more clearly what these packages of influences look like, but the field remains complex and highly variable.

There have been many models of the process of innovation. The linear model (knowledge-push) suggests that new knowledge moves more-or-less directly from its creators, usually in the public sector, into commercial hands. Over time this model has been modified to include market pull, feedback loops, and firm organization and management elements, such as cross-functional teams and computer-aided manufacturing, concurrent engineering, and manufacture and links with outside organizations. The most recent model, still emerging, is the fifth generation model, said to be typical of distributed or open forms of organizing innovation and integrating the knowledge and capabilities of several players through networks, some of which may be global and some local, some permanent and some transient, some of organizations, some of individuals with special skills. In fifth generation innovation processes, special new IT-based innovation technologies enable more effective simulation, rapid prototyping, team design, quick moves to manufacturing, and lower risks through a process of think, play, do. If these innovation technologies substantially reduce risk, more firms may organize for innovation for their competitive edge and contribute to faster change in the industrial and service landscape of 21st-century economies. Their successful adoption may mean that the organization of innovation and production is fundamentally altered.

Critical Commentary and Future Directions

There is still no overall theory of innovation that would bring together the diverse approaches currently taken. Little work links approaches that focus on macro (national, regional, or local) systems of innovation and factors encouraging or retarding innovative activity across firms of different sizes, locations, and sectors. The management and organization of innovation inside firms is still little understood. Although there is now a considerable mass of case studies of different elements of the managerial and organizational aspects of innovation, including notably the place of innovation in management strategies, these are far from cumulative and largely remain limited to factors relevant to firms working in particular technological fields, with differing resource capacities and risk tolerances. Similarly, the surveys of different innovation-related investments give an overall view but do not drill down to the factors behind the general picture and, more importantly, cannot indicate the key factors that make for change: innovation activities are by definition dynamic and their results fast-moving. Macro studies of innovation enable views of overall factors affecting performance and microanalysis the details of innovation processes in certain fields. Survey snapshots are not enough, however, and the field appears so complex that detailed studies cannot easily feed into the meso-level analysis that would link firms' activities to the many elements of the larger systems or framework that surround internal firm choices. While there has been some work on the linkage between organizations, institutions, and firms in the generation of innovation, there remain many gaps here. Future studies could usefully focus on developing methodologies for making the key links between levels of analysis so that both firms and policy players have a clearer picture of the dynamics of their fields and the relationships between these, the organization of their operations, and competitive success.

—*Jane Marceau*

See also Collaboration and Cooperation; Networks; Team Development; Technology

Further Readings

Coriat, B., & Weinstein, O. (2002). Organizations, firms and institutions in the generation of innovation. *Research Policy, 31*(2), 273–290.

Dankbaar, B. (Ed.). (2003). *Innovation management in the knowledge economy*. London: Imperial College Press.

Dodgson, M. (2000). *Management of technological innovation*. Oxford, UK: Oxford University Press.

Dodgson, M., Gann, D., & Salter, A. (2005). *Think, play, do: Technology, innovation, and organization*. Oxford, UK: Oxford University Press.

Freeman, C., & Soete, L. (1997). *The economics of industrial innovation* (3rd ed.). London: Pinter.

Hollenstein, H. (2003). Innovation modes in the Swiss service sector: A cluster analysis based on firm-level data. *Research Policy, 32*(5), 845–863.

Lester, R., & Piore, M. (2004). *Innovation: The missing dimension*. Cambridge, MA: Harvard University Press.

Lundvall, B. (Ed.), (1992). *National systems of innovation*. London: Pinter.

Marceau, J. (1999). Networks of innovation, networks of production, and networks of marketing. *Creativity and Innovation Management, 8*(1), 20–27.

Malerba, F. (2003). *Sectoral systems of innovation*. Cambridge, UK: Cambridge University Press.

Nelson, R. (2005). *Technology, institutions, and economic growth*. Cambridge, MA: Harvard University Press.

Organisation for Economic Co-operation and Development. (1999). *Managing national innovation systems*. Paris: Author.

Utterback, J. (1994). *Mastering the dynamics of innovation*. Boston: Harvard Business School Press.

Von Hippel, E. (1988). *The sources of innovation*. New York: Oxford University Press.

Whitley, R. (2000). The institutional structuring of innovation strategies: Business systems, firm types, and patterns of technological change in different market economies. *Organization Studies, 21*(5), 855–886.

Institutional Entrepreneurship

Institutional entrepreneurship refers to the process through which actors in an interorganizational field create new institutions, change existing ones, or tear down old ones. Actors to whom responsibility for new or altered institutional arrangements is attributed are called institutional entrepreneurs. In some instances, these are individuals; in others, they are collective actors such as organizations, coalitions, or social movements. Although the term *institutional entrepreneur(ship)* can be traced to earlier usages, Paul DiMaggio's elaboration of the concept in 1988 did much to highlight its importance for institutional theories of organization. By describing how actors are constrained by and conform to the expectations of their institutional environments—actors unreflectively adopt taken-for-granted practices and, in so doing, individually acquire legitimacy and collectively reproduce the institutional order—institutional theorists have had success explaining stability in fields but have been challenged by novel action and change. Institutional entrepreneurship is therefore an important concept; it helps to explain nonisomorphic change in fields and, in so doing, brings to the fore two concepts addressed problematically in much recent institutional theorizing—agency and interests. It is thus a promising concept for bridging what have come to be called, since DiMaggio and Powell's essay of 1991, the old and new institutionalisms in organizational analysis, and it serves as a key conceptual locus of efforts to advance the agency-structure debate.

Conceptual Overview

The Paradox of Embedded Agency

The theoretical puzzle is this: If actors are embedded in an institutional field and thus subject to the regulative, normative, and cognitive processes, which, like pillars, support institutions therein, how is it that they are motivated and able to envision new practices, then can subsequently get others to adopt them? Actors who are truly embedded are not supposed to desire, imagine, or realize alternative ways of doing things because institutionalized arrangements and practices structure cognitions, define interests, and, in the limit, produce actors' identities. Even if conceiving of alternatives becomes possible, those actors who are disadvantaged by or peripheral in a field and thus motivated to change institutions typically lack the power to do so. Several solutions to this puzzle have been proposed, relating to the sources of institutional entrepreneurs' (1) motivations, (2) ideas for change, and (3) ability to realize new institutional arrangements.

Motivations for Change

Motivations for changing institutional environments vary depending on whether a field is emerging, mature, or in crisis. In emerging fields, institutional entrepreneurs do not have to escape the so-called iron cages of existing institutions before building new ones. In these contexts—where actors are only beginning to recognize themselves as belonging to a common enterprise, relationships are fluid, meanings are heterogeneous, understandings are not widely shared, and multiple possible scripts for action exist—actors are motivated to stabilize relationships, meanings, and practices to reduce uncertainty for themselves and to facilitate development of the field in ways congruent with the realization of constructed interests that predate or are emerging with the field. Different actors will, however, prefer different relationships, meanings, and practices to become institutionalized.

In mature fields, motivations for change vary with actors' positions. Peripheral actors who are disadvantaged by existing institutional arrangements have a greater incentive to break with current practices, while more powerful central actors have less. With more to gain and less at stake, peripheral actors are more willing to experiment with alternative practices, as demonstrated in a 1991 study of U.S. radio broadcasting by Huseyin Leblebici, Gerald Salancik, Anne Copay, and Tom King. Historically, innovative departures from transaction conventions originated with peripheral players, and only once their merits were demonstrated were they adopted by central players and institutionalized as new conventions.

But powerful actors in mature fields can be motivated to change too. This is the case when, for example, current practices result in problems or prevent field elite from capitalizing on opportunities. Thus, the social construction of problems or opportunities from the perspective of powerful actors can weaken the grip of existing institutional arrangements and motivate change. This was the case, for example, when large accounting firms pioneered the multidisciplinary practice as a new organizational form because it brought with it opportunities for cross-selling other professional services in addition to accounting, as described by Royston Greenwood and Roy Suddaby in 2006.

In addition to these endogenous mechanisms, actors in mature fields can also become motivated to change as a result of exogenous shocks, such as natural disasters, social unrest, new technologies, regulatory change, or authoritative publications critical of the field, all of which can give rise to field-level crises. By generating problems and causing taken-for-granted assumptions to be questioned, environmental jolts disrupt field-level consensus and motivate institutional change.

Ideas for Change

What is the origin of institutional entrepreneurs' ideas? This is a particularly key question in mature fields where the repeated reenactment of institutionalized practices and iterated reproduction of institutions are supposed to reinforce cognitive structures that prevent field members from conceiving of alternatives. Empirically, several mechanisms have been identified, including transposition and translation of practices from other fields by less or multiply embedded actors, competing logics within a field, sensemaking, and contradictions within and among institutions.

Novel ideas in a field commonly originate in other fields, so the transposition and subsequent translation of practices are important mechanisms for initiating change. Whereas transposition refers to importation of practices, translation refers to how imported practices are tailored and adapted to make them fit, both materially and discursively, with other practices, values and meanings in the field. These changes are more likely to be initiated by actors who somehow avoid or resist a field's cognitive processes such that they are more open to and aware of alternative action scripts—by actors who are less embedded in the field, in other words. Thus, because new field participants, even those that take up highly institutionalized central roles, are initially less embedded and arrive with cognitive structures and norms learned elsewhere, they are important sources of ideas for change. In addition, longtime field participants can also serve as vectors of ideas for change if they are multiply embedded, which means that they are simultaneously socialized participants in other fields in addition to the focal one. In this way, even central actors can become aware of and open to alternatives if they occupy positions that bridge beyond the field's boundaries, as demonstrated by Greenwood and Suddaby in 2006.

But ideas for change can originate within a field as well. This becomes more obvious if fields are conceived as political arenas in which actors promoting different means-ends scripts compete. Although a single institutional logic tends to dominate in a field at any point in time, its stability, persistence, and hegemony is not guaranteed; the accumulation of events can shift power relations slowly until a truce-breaking threshold is crossed causing promoters of a long-available rival logic to openly rechallenge prevailing institutional arrangements. Similarly, but more speedily and dramatically, an exogenous shock can surface long-standing tensions and transform latent or covert conflict into the manifest or overt kind. Moreover, in addition to reviving old struggles, jolts to a field can also spawn new struggles as a result of sensemaking; because field-level crises give rise to ambiguity and confusion, a novel rival logic can emerge in the wake of a jolt as field participants make sense of their new situation.

Finally, institutional contradictions can also be the impetus for change. Contradictions, which are inconsistencies and incompatibilities among institutional imperatives within or across fields, are unavoidable by-products of institutionalization. As Myeung-Gu Seo and W. E. Douglas Creed explained in 2002, the development and deepening of contradictions within and between institutional fields—the accumulation of experiences of contradictions and associated tensions by greater numbers of actors—increases the likelihood of praxis, a concept comprising actors' self-awareness and critical reflexivity as well as their mobilization and subsequent collective action. Because contradictions give rise to ambiguity, they disrupt taken-for-granted enactment of a dominant logic; when more than one prescribed logics of appropriateness can be logically considered appropriate, field participants are presented, effectively, with choices or opportunities for sensemaking that can lead to change.

Realizing Institutional Change

Institutional change projects require the support of actors inside and, sometimes, outside the field, all of whom do not necessarily share the motivations and ideas of the institutional entrepreneur, so it is common to conceptualize institutional entrepreneurship as a political process. As a result, social movement theory has been influential, as with Hayagreeva Rao, Cal Morrill, and Mayer Zald's discussion in 2000 of institutional entrepreneurship to create and legitimate new organizational forms. Thus, resource mobilization, framing and rhetoric, as well as capitalizing on opportunity structures, are important components of the process. Research has also focused on the attributes and skills of institutional entrepreneurs that help them to lead collective action to realize institutional change.

Resources can be accessed and mobilized through material means such as bargaining and negotiation, exercising formal authority, or exploiting extant networks, associations, and coalitions in the field, depending of course on field organization and the institutional entrepreneur's position therein. In addition to mobilizing resources through preexisting interorganizational relationships, institutional entrepreneurs can also initiate new ones, and several studies suggest that field-level change often begins with new collaborations among a small number of actors in a field.

In addition, appropriate framing, rhetoric, and discursive strategies in institutional entrepreneurs' legitimating accounts of the changes they champion can result in more and different resources being accessed and mobilized. Persuasion is thus another important means by which actors motivate cooperation for institutionalization projects. Indeed, it might be said that institutional entrepreneurship involves, most generally, accessing and mobilizing material and symbolic resources in creative or even artful ways, a conceptualization suggestive of bricolage and consistent with William Sewell's 1992 theorization of agency as a capacity, through acts of communication, to reinterpret and harness resources using schemas not typically associated with them.

The collective action frames of institutional entrepreneurs constitute and legitimate change by constructing it as aligned with difficult-to-contest ideals that may be field-level or entrenched beyond the field as societal values. In addition to these rhetorical appeals to *dignitas* and *bonum* (i.e., the worthy and the good) to secure normative legitimacy, institutional entrepreneurship also involves appeals to *utilitas* (i.e., the useful or advantageous) to secure pragmatic legitimacy. For example, in their 2004 study of an emergent field, Steve Maguire, Cynthia Hardy, and Thomas B. Lawrence demonstrated how institutional entrepreneurs deployed not one but an entire array of arguments that translated the interests of a diverse set of constituencies in the field and showed how many goals would be realized via the institutionalization project. Thus, theorization of novel practices—the elaboration of a theory of the practices that, in abstract categories, links them in means-end relations to outcomes valued highly by field constituencies who are the targets of persuasive appeals—is required for institutional change. Because persuasion of field participants to support institutionalization projects is so important, the rhetorical and discursive strategies of institutional entrepreneurs are increasingly receiving researchers' attention, as with Suddaby and Greenwood's presentation in 2005 of five generic theorizations commonly drawn upon to legitimate institutional change.

Opportunity structures in a field are also important. For example, Maguire and Hardy, in their 2006 study of the emergence of a new global institution governing the chemical industry, show how norms of negotiating global treaties provided opportunities for nonstate actors such as environmentalist nongovernmental organizations and industry associations to influence the institution building process through the strategic production and distribution of texts, even though the actual negotiations included only state actors. In mature fields, professional associations serve as arenas for debate that may have reforming rather than conservative outcomes, and thus can provide for institutional entrepreneurs to champion ideas for change, as described by Greenwood, Suddaby, and C. R. Hinings in 2002. In other instances, institutional entrepreneurship may involve the creation of opportunities. Such is the case with convening: actors can initiate institutional change in the absence of clear alternative practices to be championed by bringing field participants together to begin to discuss some problem, as explained by Silvia Dorado in 2005.

Not all actors in a field are equally endowed or skilled to lead collective action projects as institutional entrepreneurs. In emerging fields, for example, research suggests that institutional entrepreneurs are actors who have wide legitimacy among, and who can thus bridge between, diverse constituencies controlling different resources in a field. Related research has underlined the importance of institutional entrepreneurs' trustworthiness, and how efforts at building trust among influence targets in the field may be required prior to initiating change. Finally, social skills are vital to success; Neil Fligstein argued in 1997 that institutional entrepreneurs are able to motivate cooperation because they can imaginatively identify with other actors and, in the legitimating accounts they offer for their institutionalization projects, provide those actors with common meanings and identities.

Critical Commentary and Future Directions

As an emerging locus of the agency-structure debate, the concept of institutional entrepreneurship is a promising one for social theorists and for critical management researchers in particular, given that many institutions have effects that disadvantage some social groups. To realize this promise, several research directions are suggested.

First, classification schemes for distinguishing and developing more nuanced theories of different types or modes of institutional entrepreneurship would be valuable. To give just one example, from a critical perspective there is a need to distinguish those instances of institutional entrepreneurship that reinforce power relations, consolidating or augmenting power among field elite, from those where power relations are transformed.

Second, solutions are required for the problem of bounding institutional entrepreneurship temporally and conceptually. As described above, change often occurs in response to a problem or opportunity or contradiction. However, these are not objective phenomena; they are socially constructed. Even jolts are not inherently disruptive but must be constructed as such to give rise to crises, as pointed out by Kamal Munir in 2005. It is unclear, therefore, whether institutional entrepreneurship begins with the construction of a problem, its proposed solution, or the mobilization of support for the solution. And once support has been generated, when does institutional entrepreneurship end? What degree of adoption and institutionalization of new practices is required before an old institution is declared changed or a new one declared built? In the limit, one may reasonably ask whether successful institutional change is required at all or whether simply entrepreneurial effort to change institutions is sufficient. Certainly, current research is characterized by a strong bias for studying only instances of success, depriving researchers and practitioners of lessons to be derived from systematic investigation of failed efforts to change institutions. Insights could be gained, for example, by researching how actors exercise agency to successfully resist institutional change and maintain institutional arrangements in the face of challenges. All in all, models that endogenously capture institutional stability and change would be welcome contributions.

Third, the roles of actors other than institutional entrepreneurs require more attention. Currently, there is a strong tendency to attribute responsibility for new institutional arrangements to only one or a few actors judged key by field participants or researchers as they narrate stories of institutional change. In singling out and focusing on only these actors, the critical roles played by others who participate in but do not lead institutionalization projects are overshadowed, leaving a distorted view of institutional change as a linear process motored directly by the activities of heroic individuals or organizations. This problem is compounded in research that, in foregrounding agency, presents actors as incredibly rational, opportunistic, strategic, and seemingly unconstrained by institutional arrangements or other actors. A more balanced and realistic approach to embedded agency within a context of collective action is called for.

Finally, organizational researchers, especially critical management scholars, should take seriously the idea that institutional entrepreneurship is a political process and develop theory accordingly. Bringing contemporary typologies, models and theories of power to bear in analyses of institutional entrepreneurship would go a long way toward bridging the old and new institutionalisms in organizational analysis.

—Steve Maguire

See also Agency; Agency-Structure Debate; Institutional Theory

Further Readings

Clemens, E. S., & Cook, J. M. (1999). Politics and institutionalism: Explaining durability and change. *Annual Review of Sociology, 25*(1), 441–466.

Colomy, P. (1998). Neofunctionalism and neoinstitutionalism: Human agency and interest in institutional change. *Sociological Forum, 13*(2), 265–300.

DiMaggio, P. J. (1988). Interest and agency in institutional theory. In L. G. Zucker (Ed.), *Institutional patterns and organizations: Culture and environment* (pp. 3–22). Cambridge, MA: Ballinger.

DiMaggio, P. J., & Powell, W.W. (1991). Introduction. In W. W. Powell & P. J. DiMaggio (Eds.), *The new institutionalism in organizational analysis* (pp. 1–38). Chicago: University of Chicago Press.

Dorado, S. (2005). Institutional entrepreneurship, partaking, and convening. *Organization Studies, 26*(3), 385–414.

Fligstein, N. (1997). Social skill and institutional theory. *American Behavioral Scientist, 40*, 397–405.

Greenwood, R., & Suddaby, R. (2006). Institutional entrepreneurship in mature fields: The big five accounting firms. *Academy of Management Journal, 49*(1), 27–48.

Greenwood, R., Suddaby, R., & Hinings, C. R. (2002). Theorizing change: The role of professional associations in the transformations of institutionalized fields. *Academy of Management Journal, 45*(1), 58–80.

Leblebici, H., Salancik, G., Copay, A., & King, T. (1991). Institutional change and the transformation of interorganizational fields: An organizational history of the U.S. radio broadcasting industry. *Administrative Science Quarterly, 36*(3), 333–363.

Maguire, S., & Hardy, C. (2006). The emergence of new global institutions: A discursive perspective. *Organization Studies, 27*(1), 7–29.

Maguire, S., Hardy, C., & Lawrence, T. B. (2004). Institutional entrepreneurship in emerging fields: HIV/AIDS treatment advocacy in Canada. *Academy of Management Journal, 47*(5), 657–679.

Munir, K. A. (2005). The social construction of events: A study of institutional change in the photographic field. *Organization Studies, 26*(1), 93–112.

Rao, H., C. Morrill, C., & Zald, M. (2000). Power plays: How social movements and collective action create new organizational forms. *Research in Organizational Behavior, 22*, 237–281.

Seo, M., & Creed, W. E. D. (2002). Institutional contradictions, praxis, and institutional change: A dialectical perspective. *Academy of Management Review, 27*(2), 222–247.

Sewell, W. H. (1992). A theory of structure: Duality, agency, and transformation. *American Journal of Sociology, 98*(1), 1–29.

Suddaby, R., & Greenwood, R. (2005). Rhetorical strategies of legitimacy. *Administrative Science Quarterly, 50*(1), 35–67.

INSTITUTIONAL ISOMORPHISM

Institutional isomorphism describes the process in which organizations gain increasing similarity in structure. This process is assumed to be driven primarily by a desire of decision makers to create organizations that conform and/or excel in their practice of social rules, ideals, and practices.

The term *isomorphism* originates from biology and describes the degree to which individuals of different genetic origins look similar to each other. In the 1960s, it was suggested that similar processes exist among populations of organizations. The idea was in essence that nonoptimal organizations are selected out, or that managers are able to skillfully redirect their organizations to fit the environmental conditions. In other words, a competitive mechanism for creating isomorphism was suggested. This grew into a school of thought called *population ecology*. Much like the idea of the survival of the fittest in biology, competitive isomorphism among organizations is thought of as weeding out the weak and poorly adapted. However, competitive isomorphism was soon considered a limited explanation for why organizations grow increasingly similar. Organizations in some environments in particular seemed to be strongly influenced by societal rules, culture, and history and less by market competition. Several researchers worked therefore to criticize competitive isomorphism and modify it. The concept of isomorphism was extended in the early 1980s to describe noncompetitive sources for isomorphism; i.e. institutional mechanisms.

Institutional theory has been pivotal in the development of organization studies, frequently used in prestigious journals all through the 1980s to the 2000s. Within institutional theory (within which institutional isomorphism is an essential part) is certainly one that has helped spur this development. Some texts even treat institutional isomorphism almost synonymously with the neoinstitutional perspective on organizations. The concept of institutional isomorphism has also been shown to play an important part in highly competitive environments. The fast spread of management concepts such as total quality management (TQM), the multidivisional form, and long-range planning has been fruitfully analyzed through an institutional framework.

Conceptual Overview

The three institutional mechanisms that influence organizations to grow increasingly similar are coercive, normative, and mimetic.

Coercive mechanisms include laws, rules, and sanctions. An organization gains legitimacy (i.e., credibility and status) through compliance with the rules set up by an institutional actor/source. A consequence of gaining legitimacy is external validation, which could improve the organization's access to resources.

Coercive isomorphism results in a desire to comply with coercive mechanisms, and self-preservation from organizations upon which the incumbent organization is dependent and by cultural expectations in the society within which organizations function.

Not complying with coercive mechanisms is often connected with sanctions, and in the worst case, leads to the death of organizations. In relation to exchange relationships with other powerful organizations, noncompliance to rules may sever the specific exchange. If the exchange is essential to the organization, it directly and significantly damages and threatens the survival of the organization. For example, Enron disobeyed accounting legislation and was found guilty of fraud in 2001. It ended up costing about 4,000 people at Enron their jobs, leading to its demise.

The *normative mechanism* relates to what is desirable and considered good and appropriate behavior. It influences appropriate goals, as well as the means that could be used to get them. For organizations, an example of an appropriate goal is to be prepared for environmental changes, and an appropriate way to deal with this is to plan ahead. For this reason, different versions of long-range planning have been central in the work tasks of many employees.

Normative mechanisms stress the moral aspect of legitimacy. It stems from an evaluation of whether the organization does the right thing and plays its role correctly, and it is viewed as an organization that does desirable things. This may result in two beneficial effects. First, the organization may gain pragmatic legitimacy that serves the organizations direct goals. Second, it may grant the organization moral legitimacy that enforces a belief that the organization serves a greater social good. Continuing with the Enron case, it did not only have consequences for Enron itself. In addition, it had severe consequences for several accounting firms not following the accounting rules properly. Most spectacular of those was the accounting firm Arthur Andersen, which also was practically destroyed because of the scandal. Andersen was never ruled guilty of any illegalities. However, not acting as the public saw fit for an accounting firm, such as destroying important documents before investigation, was enough for it to lose its credibility and legitimacy.

Modeling itself after other organizations that the incumbent organization feels similar to, and looks up to, is the *mimetic mechanism*. An organization that looks similar to others is likely to get a positive evaluation from the organizational environment based on improved comprehensibility. By modeling situations according to a well-established system, the organizational activity will be perceived as predictable, meaningful, and inviting. It also simplifies communication with other organizations. Modeling after other organizations is also a way of dealing with uncertainty. If an organization is uncertain as to what is the right cause of action, it may opt to do what a similar high-status peer is doing. Benchmarking is one common management tool in which mimetic isomorphism develops.

Organizations in general try to avoid uncertainty and maintain rules, and they prefer simple rules to difficult ones. To imitate preexisting models may reduce experienced uncertainty and often demands less effort than creating new models from scratch. To do something that deviates from the conventions in a field may be more unfavorably evaluated by the environment. Many good ideas are not accepted, such as the improved Dvorak keyboard, while others, including the electric light, are only accepted once it is sufficiently similar to previous technologies. Once a truly new innovation reaches the market, it faces a difficult situation, with very few consumers willing to buy it. However, once some consumers have opted for it, and evaluated it favorably, the uncertainty of buying this product is reduced, increasing mimetic pressures with rapid diffusion as a consequence.

Critical Commentary and Future Directions

It was noted in the earliest conceptions of institutional isomorphism that there may be potential empirical overlap between the three isomorphic mechanisms. The overlap complicates application of institutional isomorphism in empirical analysis, explaining the relatively few empirical investigations into the relative strength of the different mechanisms on isomorphism.

Perhaps more problematic is the empirical overlap between institutional isomorphism and competitive isomorphism. There are both conceptual and empirical problems of separating these two types. Consider coercive isomorphism: compliance to coercive isomorphic pressures is often in the self-interest of the incumbent organization, as noncompliance can come with a risk of costly penalties, or in extreme cases with termination of the business. On the other hand, we may expect companies to conform to coercive pressures regardless of if it is economically rational to do so or not.

Normative isomorphism enjoys a dual conceptual overlap. First, compliance to normative isomorphic pressures can be a very profitable business. Companies conforming to norms with respect to environmental concerns can be shown to be necessarily correlated. For instance, reduced energy consumption and reduction in waste production in companies potentially both reduces costs and improves the extent to which the organization complies to normative isomorphic pressures from environment-aware customers and suppliers.

Second, striving to become efficient and competitive can be considered a norm in itself in parts of the industrialized world. Organizations gain status and recognition by showing that they are efficient and by being competitive. Managers of efficient and profitable organizations, such as Jack Welch, Michael Dell, and Ingvar Kamprad, gain idolized attributes and legendary status.

Early imitators of successful practices seem to enjoy consistent and positive performance outcomes from their mimetic isomorphism, making it hard to distinguish between competitive and institutional at this stage. However, research indicates that this benefit diminishes at later stages. This indicates that the relationship between institutional isomorphism and performance is influenced by time of adoption.

The three isomorphic pressures have often been conceptualized as reinforcing each other in the process of institutional isomorphism. That is, we expect to find high degrees of isomorphism where mimetic, normative, and coercive pressures work in concert. However, as several researchers have pointed out, institutional isomorphism has dealt little with the cases where institutional pressures are ambiguous (e.g. when norms contradict the practices of the most successful firms). Detailed attention to institutionalization processes may yield a better understanding of the processes involved in institutional isomorphism, which could result in mechanisms that are empirically distinct and thereby easier to research.

Institutional isomorphism emphasizes the importance of how environments influence organizations. By focusing on the directional influence of the environment on the organization, institutional isomorphism has been criticized for lacking sensitivity to agency. It has been seen as promoting a weak view of organizational agency, not acknowledging that organizations can conform to institutional pressures in many distinctly different ways.

A bit exaggerated, it could be said that the proposition of early versions of institutional isomorphism has been that organizations need to conform now, rather than later, or run the risk of dying. Early conceptualizations of institutional isomorphism also assumed that changes to institutional pressures came from outside the institutional field.

Current theorizing in neoinstitutional theory often relaxes the assumptions of environmental determinism and allows interplay between organizational discretion and environmental determination, where actors create and recreate institutions and institutions imperfectly determine the behavior of actors. Future work along these lines is likely to improve our knowledge about institutional isomorphism, as well as it may disentangle the paradox of agency and environmental determinism.

Finally, institutional isomorphism is not well specified with respect to time. First, some indications suggest that early adopters of institutionalized tools reap greater benefits from conforming than later adopters. Second, increasing age of the incumbent organization may decrease its willingness to conform to any environmental change, including isomorphic change. New organizations, for instance, may have less power to resist institutional pressures; they may find themselves less able to conform to the more-rigid institutional demands due to the fluidity of their identity and structures. Old organizations may have well-developed internal structures and identities, therefore having power to resist. However, their stability may also make it easier for older organizations to conform. Take the pressures on organizations to engage in long-term planning for instance. Long-term planning could be very difficult for a new organization to engage in, as their goals and strategies still are in their formative stages. They may find themselves forced to write plans to gain access for the external capital they so dearly need. For an older organization, goals and strategies may be well established. However, long-term planning still is resisted, since there could be an assumption that everyone knows what to do anyhow, or that the planning is isolated to a planning department. Here additional empirical work is warranted to improve our understanding of the moderating effect of age of organizations with respect to institutional isomorphism.

—*Tomas Karlsson*

See also Organizational Structure

Further Readings

Abrahamson, E. (1996). Management fashion. *Academy of Management Review, 21*(1), 254–285.

Carroll, G. R., & Michael T. Hannan, M. T. (1989). Density dependence in the evolution of populations of newspaper organizations. *American Sociological Review, 54,* 524–548.

DiMaggio, P., & Powell, W. (1983). The iron cage revisited: Institutional isomorphism and collective rationality in organizational fields. *American Sociological Review, 48,* 147–160.

Farjoun, M. (2002). The dialectics of institutional development in emerging and turbulent fields: The history of pricing conventions in the online database industry. *Academy of Management Journal, 45*(5), 848–874.

Hannan, M. T., & Freeman, J. H. (1977). The population ecology of organizations. *American Journal of Sociology, 82*(5), 929–964.

Mizruchi, M. S., & Fein, L. C. (1999). The social construction of organizational knowledge: A study of the uses of coercive, mimetic, and normative isomorphism. *Administrative Science Quarterly, 44,* 653–683.

Oliver, C. (1991). Strategic responses to institutional processes. *Academy of Management Review, 16*(1), 145–179.

Scott, W. R. (2000). *Institutions and organizations.* Thousand Oaks, CA: Sage.

Suchman, M. C. (1995). Managing legitimacy: Strategic and institutional approaches. *Academy of Management Review, 20*(3), 571–610.

Westphal, J. D., Gulati, R., & Shortell, S. M. (1997). Customization or conformity? An institutional and network perspective on the content and consequences of TQM adoption. *Administrative Science Quarterly, 42,* 366–394.

Institutional Legitimacy

Legitimacy is the perception that an object (e.g., an organization, its structure, its procedures) is valid and appropriate. Multiple definitions of legitimacy exist that address how legitimacy facilitates the use of power and authority within organizations or provides access to resources controlled by others in a field. From the institutional perspective, Mark Suchman's work offers one of the most comprehensive definitions: a generalized perception or assumption that the actions of an entity are desirable, proper, or appropriate within some socially constructed system of norms, values, beliefs, and definitions.

Conceptual Overview

Legitimacy, in dealing with perceptions and assumptions of appropriateness, desirability, and validity, represents a necessary condition for organizations by enabling control internally and access to resources controlled by the organizational field externally. Internally, legitimacy justifies who (e.g., person, roles) has the power and authority that is a necessary condition for control and coordination. Externally, legitimacy is conferred on organizations, which allows them access to resources within their organizational field, which is particularly difficult for new organizations and accounts for the liability of newness identified by Arthur Stinchombe.

Both internal and external legitimacy have their roots in the work of Max Weber, who linked legitimated authority to rules that are rationally established by enactment, agreement, or imposition. These three aspects of authority foreshadow the multifaceted nature of legitimacy in both sociology and organization studies. Weber's influence is seen explicitly in the frameworks for and examination of legitimacy by Richard Scott, Robin Stryker, and Mark Suchman. Specifically, Weber's authority through imposition aligns with Scott's legal sanction as the basis for the regulative pillar, Stryker's behavior that undergirds instrumental mechanism of legitimacy by providing material benefits for compliance, and Suchman's pragmatic legitimacy based in both exchange and influence, to the extent that exchanges are transacted within the framework of behaviors that are legally sanctioned.

Weber's authority through *agreement*—what actors agree is appropriate—is the legitimating mechanism for Scott's normative pillar, encompasses Stryker's attitudinal orientation that underpins normative mechanism of legitimacy through internalizing rules of the game and creating loyalty and allegiance toward those rules, and Suchman's moral legitimacy concerned with appropriate ends, means, structures, and leadership.

Finally, Weber's legitimacy through enactment and what he terms traditionalism, or the belief in the everyday routine as a norm of conduct, aligns with Scott's cultural-cognitive pillar as the basis of legitimacy and shares the same label of cognitive dimension of legitimacy used in both Stryker and Suchman's typologies, all of which emphasize taken-for-grantedness and comprehensibility. These scholars use different labels and highlight distinct mechanisms and rationale; however, their underlying typologies are highly congruent.

Although research on legitimacy spans units of analysis from an individual act or position within an organization to the status structure of an entire organizational field, the source or sources of legitimacy invariably trace their roots back to Weber and to one or more of the three abstracted components identified by Scott, Stryker, and Suchman. In addition, as Cathryn Johnson in her introduction to legitimacy processes explains, despite the seemingly multiple definitions of legitimacy, they all share the same focus on legitimacy involving some consensus by a social audience.

Critical Commentary and Future Directions

Although there has been considerable work done in response to early criticisms that legitimacy was a poorly defined construct in institutional theory, the operationalization of legitimacy still lacks consistent or standardized methods of operationalization because of the situational nature of legitimacy itself: operationalizing legitimacy necessarily involves addressing the questions "legitimate for what?" and "legitimate for whom?" within any particular study. Considerable empirical research has advanced our understanding of the role of legitimacy in organizations; however, the inherent subjectivity of measures of legitimacy is problematic for reproducing and comparing findings and for building an integrated, cumulative research agenda.

One area in which comparison would be particularly beneficial is in the relative impact of different sources of legitimacy on theories of authority or power within institutions. Although there is some extant literature that compares different sources of legitimacy, most studies operationalize legitimacy as unidimensional. Future research employing a multidimensional operationalization of legitimacy can help expand our understanding of the complex means by which the various sources of legitimacy interact.

Another area relatively unexplored in the existing literature is individuals as objects of legitimacy. Although extant research considers individual positions, acts, groups, and many other aspects of organizations as potential objects of legitimacy, individuals are absent. However, consistent with most definitions of legitimacy, an individual's actions can be perceived or assumed as desirable, proper, or appropriate. In fact, the hiring process is designed to find individuals qualified for a specific position based on exactly such criteria—a perception that their actions within a specific role will be appropriate, proper, and desirable for that role. In addition, individual behavior that is perceived as inappropriate or invalid delegitimizes an organization. Recent scandals in corporate America, such as the actions of CFO Andrew Fastlow and CEO Kenneth DeLay, brought the downfall of Enron and the few errant employees of Arthur Andersen, who verified Enron's accounting practices, brought the demise of this once-Big Eight accounting firm. Future research should extend the construct of legitimacy to encompass both individuals and organizations, distinguish between the two, and attempt to identify when and how they interact and when they do not.

Finally, although the link between legitimacy and institutional theory is rooted in the legitimation process identified in Paul Berger and Thomas Luckmann's work on the social construction of reality, there is comparatively little work on legitimation processes, and even less that investigates the relationships between legitimation and legitimacy processes. Theoretical and empirical research that explores how legitimacy and legitimation processes interact would improve our understanding of both legitimacy and legitimation, as well as the evolution of institutions and authority.

—*Rich DeJordy and Candace Jones*

See also Authority; Institutional Theory; Organizational Field; Social Constructionism

Further Readings

Berger, P. L., & Luckmann, T. (1966). *The social construction of reality*. Garden City, NY: Anchor.

Johnson, C. (2004). Introduction: Legitimacy processes in organizations. *Research in the Sociology of Organizations, 22*, 1–24.

Powell, W. W., & DiMaggio, P. J. (Eds.). (1991). *The new institutionalism in organizational analysis*. Chicago: University of Chicago Press.

Ruef, M., & Scott, W. R. (1998). A multidimensional model of organizational legitimacy: Hospital survival in changing institutional environments. *Administrative Science Quarterly, 43*, 877–904.

Scott, W. R. (2001). *Institutions and organizations*. Thousands Oaks, CA: Sage.

Stinchombe, A. L. (1965). Social structure and organizations. In J. March (Ed.), *Handbook of organizations* (pp. 142–193). Chicago: Rand McNally.

Stryker, R. (1994). Rules, resources, and legitimacy processes: Some implications for social conflict, order, and change. *American Journal of Sociology, 99*(4), 847–910.

Suchman, M. (1995). Managing legitimacy: Strategic and institutional approaches. *Academy of Management Review, 20*(3), 571–610.

Weber, M. (1985). *From Max Weber: Essays in sociology*. (H. H. Gerth & C. W. Mills, Eds). Boston: Routledge & Kegan Paul. (Original work published 1948)

Zelditch, Jr., M. (2004). Institutional effects on the stability of organizational authority. *Research in the Sociology of Organizations, 22*, 25–48.

INSTITUTIONAL THEORY

Institutional theory, a building block of today's organization studies, drawing from sociology, social psychology, political science, and economics, offers explanations for social order, social action, and cultural persistence. It does so with regard both to the stability of social systems at various levels (i.e., organization, field, society, world) and to the effects of institutional processes in situations of change or of conflicting legal, cultural, or normative jurisdictions. Institutional theory highlights the role of rules, norms, and typifications (cultural beliefs and scripts) in constraining and empowering social action and giving meaning to social life. Earlier contributions emphasized the stabilizing role of institutions through the constitution of structures, organizational forms, fields, and social actors' identities. More recent contributions draw attention to the concurrent role of institutions in situations of change, where interests, agency, and power play their own role in reaching stability or domination.

Conceptual Overview

The aim of institutional theory is to explain the stability and persistence of social (inter)action in specific socially constructed contexts (ranging from the world system to the intraorganizational realm). Besides regularities emerging from the encounter of competitive processes with the bounded rationality of individuals, it is the presence of institutions, salient in the specific action context, that largely explains stability in (inter)action patterns among socially constructed actors (ranging from individuals to organizations, communities, or states). Institutions exist in the standardized behaviors of individuals and in the isomorphic displays of organizations and of nation states. They are settled habits of thought and of action, imperfect and pragmatic solutions used to work out past problems and to reconcile past conflicts.

Institutions, shaped by a set of cultural and historical forces, are considered as multifaceted, relatively self-activating social reproductive processes, made up of symbolic elements. According to Philip Selznick, to institutionalize is to infuse with value beyond the technical requirements of the task at hand. Institutions emerge when some symbolic element has attained a state of legitimacy; i.e., social acceptability and credibility. Legitimacy derives from the connections of social elements, such as goals, structures, artifacts, or actors' identities, to values, meanings, or rules that are wider and of a higher order than the action context under consideration.

Cognitive-cultural elements of institutions are taken-for-granted components of social reality grounded either in the stability of interpretation and of cognitive frames or in specific systems of cultural beliefs considered as constitutive rules. Constitutive rules define the very nature of social reality and of the actors legitimated to act in it. They are taken for granted because they emerge in a process, which Peter L. Berger and Thomas Luckmann defined as the succession of externalization, objectification, and internalization. *Externalization* is the production in social interaction of symbolic structures whose meaning comes to be shared by the participants. *Objectification* is the process by which, through the cultural transmission of such meaning to individuals other than their creators, this production comes to confront individuals as a facticity outside of themselves, as something out there, as a reality experienced in common with others. *Internalization* is the process by which the objectivated world is retrojected into consciousness in the course of socialization.

But taken-for-grantedness does not mean subconscious; it means that socially constructed realities are experienced as objective facts external to the consciousness of individuals, and their existence, although merely reliant on its production in human social interaction, is not questioned. Internalization, realized through socialization, can indeed constitute institutional elements within the subconsciousness of individuals, making them part of their selves or even their personalities, as emphasized in Talcot Parsons's view. But this is not a necessary precondition.

Normative institutions are conceived as values and norms. According to Richard Scott, values are conceptions of the preferred and the desirable together with the construction of standards, while norms specify how things should be done and define legitimate means to pursue valued ends. Norms and values, which emerge in interaction, become institutions when they are internalized or taken for granted.

Regulative institutions are conceived as accepted rules of the game (e.g., laws, operating procedures, rules) or as legitimate power (i.e., authority). Rules of the game and authority can be conceived as institutions only if they are legitimate and taken for granted, or if their existence gets internalized as an objective nonquestionable fact. Internalization can take place when the regulative pressures are not subject to reflective rational scrutiny. For instance, a red traffic light does not stimulate a rational decision process in a German driver, who would almost automatically stop and wait, but does so for a driver in some southern European cities, where a decision process starts regarding how meaningful a traffic light is at that crossroad (rational scrutiny), the probability of a policeman being around (probability of coercion), and how much the driver is in a hurry (interests). An institution exists when a sufficient number of people take for granted its definition and the action consequences that stem from it. Beliefs, scripts, norms, and rules need to be taken for granted or considered objectified constraints by a sufficient number of people for acquiring the property of institutionalization.

Social beliefs, norms, and rules have a stabilizing influence, both when they are internalized, when they are considered objectified constraints, or when they are imposed by others. But in the latter case they cannot be conceived as institutions. As clearly elaborated by Max Weber, the degree of reflexivity of individuals defines three possible state of consciousness. A high degree defines a purely instrumental or a value rational orientation of action: norms, rules of the game, and cultural categories represent in this situation constraints to be taken into account as any other. A middle degree of reflexivity defines a situation where action is based on nothing but actual practice, and norms, rules, and cultural categories are taken for granted. A low degree appears as ingrained habituation, which activates action almost automatically; this represents the internalization of social controls. Only in the latter two cases can one conceive institutions as relatively self-activating social reproductive processes, and therefore talk of the invisible hand of institutionalization. In the first case, institutions could only survive as equilibria in relational games.

Rational choice theorists have proposed the least strong interpretation of institutions as equilibria in relational games. Consider for instance a situation in which each presenter at an academic conference decides to use PowerPoint slides instead of other presentation techniques (e.g., blackboard, voice only), because each of them believes that all the others consider this technology the appropriate way to present and although each of them regards this specific presentation technique as an ineffective way to present. In such a case, the stability of the action pattern is neither based on ingrained habituation, which wouldn't allow the social actors to see an alternative to the legitimate option, nor on actual practice, but on the fragile assumption that PowerPoint is institutionalized for all the others: the assumption, and this kind of institutionalization, are fragile, because it is enough that one presenter breaks with the supposed norm, without incurring sanctions, that the institution as relational equilibrium vanishes.

Nevertheless, if social beliefs, norms, and rules are imposed by others, then power, agency, and interests emerge as additional stabilizing effects: resource dependence, rational choice, and competitive dynamics affect and support the attainment of social order and stability in interaction patterns. Therefore, the kind of guarantee to which norms, rules, and values are subjected is not constitutive of institutions. Departures from the (inter)action patterns of which institutions are made can be counteracted in a regulated fashion by repetitively activated, socially constructed controls (rewards and sanctions), which, according to Weber, range from the probability of coercion by an appositely appointed apparatus of people, as in the case of law, to relatively general and practically significant reactions of disapproval, as in the case of conventions. But such rewards and sanctions are not constitutive of institutions. The latter, as is evident in the case of customs, usages, or fashions, are not bound to any external guarantee. According to Berger and Luckmann, they are guaranteed by their very character; i.e., being typifications of habitualized actions. By the very fact of their existence, institutions control human action by setting up predefined patterns of conduct, which channel behavior in one direction as against the many others that would theoretically be possible, and this occurs prior to or apart from any mechanisms of sanctions specifically set up to support an institution. The actual use of sanctioning power is rather a signal of lacking or fading legitimacy of either laws, conventions, or authority.

Imposition (edict) or coercion (menace/violence) by some powerful actor, imitation in situations of uncertainty, or emulation within networks of professionally defined peers, the mechanisms described by Walter W. Powell and Paul J. DiMaggio as constituting the motives and forces that sustain the diffusion of isomorphic (similar) structural features within specific (inter)action contexts or fields, are the processes through which rules, categories, and norms are diffused. These are symbolic structures diffused in social interactions of different kinds (hierarchical, competitive, communitarian) whose meaning comes to be shared by the participants. Because of the sharing of meanings, coercive, cognitive, and normative isomorphism are processes similar to that of externalization; they differ from the latter because they do not produce but diffuse shared meanings. And as for the case of externalization, such meanings become institutions only if objectification takes place. For instance the rules of democracy can be diffused by war, and among affected individuals a shared understanding of what such rules mean can arise, but democratic rules do not become institutions unless they are objectified; i.e., they confront individuals as a facticity outside of themselves. For democracy to be characterized by the property of institutionalization, the objective facticity of arms needs to be replaced by the symbolic facticity of democratic rules, norms, and ideas.

As the previous example makes clear, institutions are made up of symbolic elements, but they are also inextricably accompanied by associated social activities and material resources. Activities and resources are not themselves institutions. But certain activities and resources, as well as the access to them, can be objects of institutionalization if a social objectified meaning is attached to them. Institutionalized activities (scripts, routines, rituals) are typifications of habitualized actions by certain types of actors. They are symbolic typifications, not the actual actions carried out by the specific individuals subsumed under the type of actor who has the right to enact such institutionalized activities. So, when enacted, bound to the practical constraints of any given activity, they may change and deviate from the institutionalized pattern and the reproduction of such change may institutionalize a new activity pattern in the constant unstable equilibrium that Anthony Giddens called *structuration*.

In the same sense, material resources are not themselves institutions, but they may become institutionalized. They become institutionalized as artifacts, for instance buildings, products, or technical tools, or because the access to them is regulated by institutionalized symbolic systems in the sense that their attachment to specific activities and actors becomes taken for granted. Altars in churches or pulpits in classrooms are spaces reserved for priests and professors. The programming of computer numerically controlled (CNC) machines in French manufacturing firms in the 1980s was preserved for staff-technicians and forbidden to workers, as a "natural" effect of the institutional system of qualifications (professional identities) in which social actors were embedded in that country—differently than in Germany where CNC-machine programming was performed by skilled workers and not by technicians. In actual post-bureaucratic organizations, individuals' private sphere has lost the sacred quality that characterized it in earlier times, and more of their resources and competences are required to enter the capitalistic production process. Moreover, the meaning of resources also may become taken for granted. Natural resources may be considered as scarce or not depending on how they are socially constructed and typified.

Institutions define rights of or taken-for-granted access to resources and activities. They do this through rules, norms, and typification, but also through the definition of actors' identities. Berger and Luckmann stressed the reciprocity of institutional typifications and the typicality of not only the (inter)actions but also the actors in institutions. Institutions posit that actions of types X, Y, and Z will be performed by actors of types X, Y, and Z, be these managers, technicians, the German *Meister*, organizations, or communities. Richard Whitley, the proponent of the *business system approach,* a European version of institutional theory, has extensively studied how the identities of the actor "firm," which he calls the nature of firms, vary in many terms—e.g., the degree of managerial discretion from owners, the specialization of managerial capabilities and activities within authority hierarchies, the extent to which risks are managed through mutual dependence with business partners and employees—due to different national institutional contexts.

At the individual level, identities are conceptions of appropriate goals and activities for specified social positions. The proponents of the *societal effect approach,* another European version of institutional theory, have thoroughly studied how qualificational identities, grounded in national institutions, shape the way work processes take place both at workers' and managers' level. Behavior is informed and constrained by the ways in which knowledge is constructed and codified. Skills are never simply a technical matter, because they are closely connected with commonly shared norms and values that are the reference points for the assignment of respect, status, and income.

Actual expectations, which define a role, are different from institutionalized expectations, which define an identity. Institutions, and therefore also institutionalized expectations and identities, are typifications. The latter, to varying degrees, may become internalized by individual actors as components of the self or may serve as taken-for-granted templates for structuring (inter)action in the specific context. Institutions construct actors and define their available modes of action; they constrain behavior but they also empower it.

Earlier studies in new institutionalism concentrated their attention on stability conceived as isomorphism within institutional fields; i.e., they were trying to discover why organizations' (formal) structures, mostly of public organizations, were becoming more and more similar. Students of the societal effect approach, to the contrary, concentrated their attention on industrial organizations and identified stability not in the spread of similarity but in the dialectic equilibrium of interdependence between different forms, such as the bureaucratic mass-producing giant with the small flexible deliverer of specialized machine tools.

Critical Commentary and Future Directions

Institutional theory has mainly placed its focus on explaining similarity and homogeneity, tending to assume institutional frameworks as monolithic and unified, downplaying agency and overstating deterministic effects. Indeed, not only some critics of institutional theory, but also some of its proponents, misunderstood the concept of stability of social (inter)action with that of invariance of the results of such (inter)actions. First, the background of habitualized activity opens up a foreground for deliberation and innovation. Second, highly institutionalized action contexts, such as science and the arts, but also innovative industrial districts such Silicon Valley, reach innovative results thanks to and not despite the high stability of interaction patterns. These patterns are based on procedural more than on substantive routines, and these procedural routines are such that they oblige individuals to constantly question both their own premises and each others' ideas, allocate authority ad hoc, and the like—they represent in some way the institutionalization of reflection.

Only recently, and following a disregarded position embedded in the foundational piece of John W. Meyer and Brian Rowan, a trend is recognizable toward considering the nondeterminant, interactive nature of institutional processes, recognized as multiple, overlapping, and offering competing alternative formulations and prescriptions. Institutional theorists are starting to explore competing and pluralistic institutional pressures, because the institutional context is far less coherent and homogenous than usually considered, and even contradictory determinants of social action coexist. Studies in areas of overlap, interference, and conflict among institutional influences, areas that are growing due to globalization, are helping to bring institutional theory further.

Moreover modern institutionalists tended to forget that ideas and ideology reflect and are attempts to justify material reality. Through the very process of objectification, structures of oppression and exploitation, involving the accompanying beliefs, norms, and power relations, appear to be external and objective to their participants, although they are product of human ideas and activity. Many structures persist and spread because they are regarded as appropriate by entrenched authorities, even though their legitimacy is challenged by other, less-powerful constituencies—cultural beliefs may be held by some but not by others. Once it is recognized that interests are also culturally constructed, future research should try to understand how far behavior reflects the pursuit of rational interests and the exercise of conscious choice, and how far it is shaped by conventions, routines and habits.

—Giuseppe Delmestri

See also Authority; Corporate Culture; Cross-Cultural Management; Deinstitutionalization; Diffusion; Discourse Analysis; Institutional Entrepreneurship; Institutional Isomorphism; Institutional Legitimacy; Knowledge; Neoinstitutional Theory; New Institutionalism; Open Systems; Organizational Field; Organizational Routines; Organizational Rules; Organizational Structure; Social Constructionism; Social Movements; Structuration; Values

Further Readings

Berger, P. L., & Luckmann, T. (1967). *The social construction of reality.* Garden City, NY: Anchor.

Campbell, J. L. (2004). *Institutional change and globalization.* Princeton, NJ: Princeton University Press.

Giddens, A. (1984). *The constitution of society.* Berkeley: University of California Press.

Maurice, M., & Sorge, A. (Eds.). (2000). *Embedding organizations.* Philadelphia: John Benjamin.

Meyer, J. W., & Rowan, B. (1977). Institutionalized organizations: Formal structure as myth and ceremony. *American Journal of Sociology, 83*(2), 340–363.

Powell, W. W., & DiMaggio, P. J. (Eds.). (1992). *The new institutionalism in organizational analysis.* Chicago: University of Chicago Press.

Scott, W. R. (2001). *Institutions and organizations* (2nd ed.). Thousand Oaks, CA: Sage.

Selznick, P. (1949). *TVA and the grass roots.* Berkeley: University of California Press.

Whitley, R. (Ed.). (1992). *European business systems: Firms and markets in their national contexts.* London: Sage.

INTEGRITY

Integrity is defined in two spheres: the physical and the moral. Its physical meaning is derived from the Latin *integritas* and the concept of *integer* or whole number. It is the physical state of completeness, of undivided wholeness. In the moral realm, integrity is defined as an unimpaired moral state, characterized by incorruptibility, innocence, honesty, and sincerity.

The two senses of integrity meet in the world of organizations. An organization is both a collection of individuals and a "thing" separate from its members. Whether integrity is conceived as a virtue of individuals or as an attribute of an organizational system, it implies an uncompromised whole.

Conceptual Overview

Scholars and practitioners have long sought to fashion a concise definition of integrity to guide action in their areas of concern. Contemporary business scandals have stimulated many efforts to develop a conception of integrity that would clarify the moral dilemmas in this context. It may be that the physical meaning of integrity reassures business practitioners that there is a comprehensible and achievable standard of morally appropriate behavior that can resolve unpleasant and painful uncertainties.

The notion of wholeness at the heart of integrity suggests its ethical meaning. An individual with integrity might be one who is morally consistent, who applies ethical rules in diverse contexts without partitions based on conditions. In doing so, he or she is whole and uncorrupted, not swayed by momentary passions or situations to abandon fundamental commitments. One may face conflicts among values but resolves them by appeal to more fundamental values. Harry Frankfurt's "fully integrated self" appears compatible with this notion of integrity.

The fully integrated self poses a problem in that it does not distinguish between the character of the commitments one pursues with consistency. On the other hand, Scott Peck's description of individuals fully experiencing the tug of conflicting interests, needs, and demands and seeking a sustainable balance suggests a conscientiousness and discipline that is in keeping with popular notions of integrity. In this view, integrity requires a conscious reconciliation of disparate concerns through nuanced and principled judgments.

Alternatively, integrity might be defined with respect to commitments so powerful that they are critical to one's identity. Bernard Williams calls these identity-conferring, and others call them ground projects. Integrity so interpreted is sharply distinguished from virtue, which incorporates judgments as to intentions. In fact, identity-conferring commitments may entail actions and beliefs that are widely condemned as immoral, as long as they are constitutive of identity. Authenticity is central, not the actual content of commitment and behaviors.

Integrity as a Social Virtue

Some scholars have followed Aristotle's lead and considered integrity in the larger context of virtues. This would imply that integrity represents a means or balance between extremes.

Robert C. Solomon, for example, has proposed a business ethics founded on a conception of integrity as a social virtue. Following Aristotle, Solomon defines virtue as a revealed disposition to act morally. Integrity constitutes a balance between institutional loyalty and moral autonomy, undergirt by moral humility. Solomon characterizes integrity as a supervirtue or complex of virtues, demonstrated in intent and action.

Similarly, Cheshire Calhoun sees integrity as a social virtue displayed in one's good judgment in relating to others, guided by respect for others and their judgments. Both Solomon's and Calhoun's perspectives ground integrity in such a way that a selfish consistency could not possibly qualify. Solomon's balance of loyalty and autonomy and Calhoun's regard for the deliberations of others have this effect.

Richard DeGeorge defines integrity as a realm of autonomous action constrained by a moral minimum of responsibility to others. Both self-determination and other-regard are required. DeGeorge suggests that this interpretation might be manifested in programs of continuous employment and profit-sharing for employees. He submits that multinational corporations can meet the standard of integrity through respect for human rights and by fostering human development.

Objectivism and Integrity

Objectivists like Ayn Rand and Leonard Peikoff have defined integrity as active loyalty to a moral code that promotes the long-term survival and well-being of individuals as rational beings. Objectivists regard capitalism as the social system most conducive to the exercise of self-interest, pursuit of individual rights, and practice of individual reason. Objectivist integrity is an interesting contrast to some of the other interpretations advanced above because it rejects the social dimension of integrity. Rather, integrity is presented as an approach to individual contracting with other individuals. Individuals may choose to practice a limited "benevolence" toward others in accord with rational self-interest, but this is merely a choice and it does not constrain self-interest. While few practitioners embrace the label *objectivist,* many construe integrity as a matter of fairness in contracting.

Pragmatism and Integrity

Several scholars have argued for the application of philosophical pragmatism in the construction of a framework for business ethics. David Jacobs has proposed a pragmatist approach to integrity that would require that individuals consider the objective social consequences of their actions. Unlike traditional utilitarianism, which focuses on a single quantitative measure of "happiness" as the measure of action, pragmatist integrity would require an iterative, case by case inquiry as to moral choices and their consequences. Moreover, pragmatist integrity would emphasize growth and experiential learning.

Corporate Integrity

Scholars and practitioners in business ethics continue to strive for a formulation of integrity that is highly practical and susceptible to implementation. Given managers' preoccupation with "systems" that render problems routine and soluble, there has been considerable experimentation with integrity systems. Many corporations have established ethical compliance systems characterized as "integrity management." At consulting firm KPMG, integrity management entails comprehensive systems to deliver compliance with laws, regulations, policies, and codes of conduct. Advocates of integrity management claim that it embeds legal and ethical principles in the strategic planning process of the firm. Lynn Sharp Paine has defined organizational integrity as a governance system for the corporation that supports ethical standards exceeding legal requirements. Implicit in all of these interpretations of integrity is a notion of uncompromised wholeness blended with systems thinking.

Unsatisfied with relatively vague definitions, Joseph Petrick and John Quinn have formulated the integrity capacity model. Integrity capacity stipulates that organizational members consider the balance of four ethical theories (analyzing questions of duty, consequences, virtue, and systems development) and apply disparate theories of the law (one embodying economic rationality while another mandates attention to social conditions) in proper balance to develop and institutionalize a system of continuing moral improvement in organizations. In Petrick and Quinn's view, imbalance leads to unethical behavior. However, the authors do not explain what constitutes balance.

Critical Commentary and Future Directions

Despite the hopes of many scholars and practitioners in business ethics, the concept of integrity does not illuminate an easy path through ethical terrain. Fundamental questions remain contested. While many views of integrity combine moral consistency with social concern, the character of this consistency and the content of social concern remain disputed. Only objectivism seems to produce crisp answers, and these are at the expense of attention to social consequences. Particularly unpromising are corporate integrity systems whose drive for routine and predictability magnify the illusion of simple solutions.

The hard work of developing a framework of ethical behavior in organizations is not a practical exercise constrained by the limitations of existing organizations. None of the definitions of integrity is self-sufficient; each derives from well-established approaches to ethical inquiry. Researchers have ample reason to return to first principles and address ethics without mechanical algorithms. Ethics cannot be separated from nuanced and holistic judgment.

—*David Carroll Jacobs*

See also Authenticity; Pragmatism; Virtue Ethics

Further Readings

Becker, T. E. (1998). Integrity in organizations: Beyond honesty and conscientiousness. *Academy of Management Review, 23*(1), 154–161.

Calhoun, C. (1995). Standing for something. *Journal of Philosophy, 92,* 235–260.

DeGeorge, R. (1993). *Competing with integrity in international business.* New York: Oxford University Press.

Dewey, J. (1920). *Reconstruction in philosophy.* New York: Henry Holt.

Frankfurt, H. (1987). Identification and wholeheartedness. In F. Schoeman (Ed.), *Responsibility, character, and the emotions: New essays in moral psychology* (pp. 27–45). New York: Cambridge University Press.

Halfon, M. (1989). *Integrity: A philosophical inquiry.* Philadelphia: Temple University Press.

Jacobs, D. C. (2004). A pragmatist approach to integrity in business ethics. *The Journal of Management Inquiry 13*(3), 215–223.

Paine, L. S. (1994). Managing for organizational integrity. *Harvard Business Review, 72*(2), 106–117.

Peck, M. S. (1987). *The different drum: Community making and peace.* New York: Simon & Schuster.

Peikoff, L. (1991). *Objectivism: The philosophy of Ayn Rand.* New York: Meridian.

Petrick, J., & Quinn, J. (2000). The integrity capacity construct and moral progress in business. *Journal of Business Ethics, 23*(1), 3–18.

Rand, A. (1964). *The virtue of selfishness: A new concept of egoism.* New York: Signet.

Solomon, R. C. (1992). *Ethics and excellence: Cooperation and integrity in business.* New York: Oxford University Press.

Williams, B. (1973). Integrity. In J. J. C. Smart & B. Williams (Eds.), *Utilitarianism: For and against* (pp. 108–117). New York: Cambridge University Press.

Intellectual Property

Intellectual property refers to the protection of products of human creativity or invention under national and international laws. Intellectual property comprises principally copyright, patents, and trademarks. Individuals and organizations can protect intangible assets in these three areas. The term *intellectual property* refers to rights of use, and not to physical property such as real estate.

Conceptual Overview

Copyright

The first copyright law was enacted in China in 1068. The concept and protection of copyright developed further in Europe beginning in the 16th century (for example, the Statute of Anne, 1710, in England) and was embodied in the U.S. Constitution in 1787. The writers of that document empowered Congress "to promote the progress of science and useful arts, by securing for limited times to authors and inventors the exclusive right to their respective writings and discoveries." In addition to promoting the progress of science (i.e., knowledge), the rationale for copyright was economic: writers needed to have exclusive rights to their works for a time in order to make a living. That time, originally 14 years, has been extended in the United States over the years to the lifetime of the creator plus 70 years. International treaties, such as the 1994 World Trade Organization Agreement on Trade-Related Aspects of Intellectual Property Rights (TRIPs), have harmonized the laws of different jurisdictions.

Copyright applies to many types of creative works, once they are fixed in a tangible medium, including written materials, sound recordings, and dramatic, musical, pictorial, graphic, architectural, choreographic, and audiovisual works. Computer software and works stored in any printed or electronic medium, including CD-ROMs and Web sites, are also protected by copyright.

Copyright protection does not extend to ideas, facts, principles, or business processes or systems. Copyright covers a particular expression of ideas, not the ideas themselves. Similarly, titles, short phrases, slogans, domain names, and lists of contents are not subject to copyright. Copyright implies an element of creativity: hence, for example, the compiler of an alphabetical list of names with telephone numbers cannot claim copyright in the list. Contrast bibliographies that involve a creative selection or arrangement of facts; such works may be protected.

Copyright vests automatically in a work upon its fixation. In other words, there is no need to "copyright" a work. Furthermore, when the United States became a signatory to the Berne Convention for the Protection of Literary and Artistic Works in 1988, effective in 1989, the U.S. government amended the Copyright Act of 1976 to provide that copyright notice is no longer required. Individual authors and organizations that wish to make clear their claim to copyright in a work, however, are still encouraged to use a copyright notice (which includes the copyright symbol, author's or organization's name, and year of publication). Registration of the work with the national copyright office, although optional, also provides an additional measure of protection. In the United States, a copyright owner may not sue for copyright infringement without such prior registration.

The owners of a copyright, whether they are individuals or organizations, hold a bundle of exclusive rights in a work: to (1) reproduce it, (2) prepare derivative works, (3) distribute copies by sale or rental, (4) perform it, (5) display it publicly, and (6) perform a sound recording by digital audio transmission. A *derivative work* is an adaptation or transformation of an original copyrighted work; derivatives may be translations, abridgments, motion pictures, dramatizations, or art reproductions. *Copyright infringement* is the violation of any of these rights, regardless of whether the infringer has acknowledged the source.

An organization may act as an author by commissioning a work, called a *work made for hire.* Such a work is either created by an employee in the course of his or her employment or prepared under an agreement with a consultant or other party. Under such an agreement, the copyright in the work initially vests in the employer or the commissioning party, not in the creator. A work for hire must fall into one of several categories, such as a contribution to a collective work. Works made for hire are covered by copyright for 95 years from publication, or 120 years, whichever is shorter.

Individuals and organizations that wish to use a copyrighted work—for example, to make photocopies of a book chapter for use in training—must request permission from the copyright holder. A work is in the public domain if it is no longer under copyright protection or if it is not copyrightable because it fails to meet the requirements for copyright protection. Works in the public domain may be used freely without the permission of the former copyright owner. Works posted on a Web site or funded by a government should not be assumed to be in the public domain without further investigation.

Organizations may also license specified rights in a work to other parties. A *license* may be exclusive (available to only one party) or nonexclusive (available to more than one party). A license may require payment of royalties or be royalty-free. A royalty is a fee that applies to each use or sale of the copyrighted material; for example, the retransmission of a television or radio broadcast.

The provisions of fair use in the U.S. Copyright Act of 1976 allow certain uses to be made of copyrighted material without permission or a license. The law specifies four factors to consider in determining whether a use is a fair use: (1) the purpose and character of the use, (2) the nature of the copyrighted work, (3) the amount and substantiality of the portion used, and (4) the effect on the potential market or value of the work. Quotation of short passages from a long work by a reviewer in a magazine or by a researcher in a book is a protected use. An organization could not, however, legally make photocopies of an entire copyrighted journal article to distribute to its clients or employees.

Patents

The term *patent* originated in 1292 with "letters patent," which were authorizations for a person to make, use, or sell an invention. The first U.S. federal patent act was enacted in 1790, although its roots, like those of copyright, are in the U.S. Constitution. A patent confers a right of exclusive exploitation; it is a form of monopoly that bars not only copying by others but also parallel or independent creation. Patents can be obtained for useful articles (which are not copyrightable)—these are called utility patents—designs, and plants. Some countries do not allow patents on medical or surgical goods, techniques, and procedures, but drugs are patentable throughout the world.

The four categories of subject matter of patents are: a new and useful (1) process, (2) machine, (3) manufacture, or (4) composition of matter (such as chemical compounds). A patent is much more difficult to obtain than a copyright, which comes into being automatically upon the creation of an original work of authorship by fixing expression in a tangible medium—even if that work's literary quality is very low. In U.S. law, a patent must meet several standards, including utility, novelty, and nonobviousness.

Utility means that an invention must do what its inventor claims it will do. It also entails a test of whether the invention has been made practical, in such a form that others can make and use it, or is pure science (which is not patentable).

The tests of novelty are whether an invention was previously known, used, or described in a publication (information accessible to the public, called *prior art*). An inventor cannot obtain a patent if his or her invention is already known or used by others in the United States or patented or described in a publication in the United States or a foreign country. A thorough patent search is required to establish the novelty of an invention.

A patent may be refused if the application describes something that is not substantially different from what has been used or described before. Meeting the standard of nonobviousness implies that the invention would not be obvious to a person having ordinary skill in the area of technology related to the invention.

A patent is a contract between the inventor and the U.S. government granting a monopoly for a term of years and is given only in exchange for a full disclosure of the technology in the patent application. A patent application, which is usually prepared by a patent attorney or patent agent, contains background, a summary and brief description of the invention, drawings (in almost all cases), a detailed description, and a series of claims, which determine the scope of the patent.

A patent may be issued or denied once the patent examiner has considered the application in light of the tests of utility, novelty, and nonobviousness, among others. In the United States, public use or sale of an invention more than one year before an application is filed is grounds for denying a patent, although most countries have no such grace period. Only the United States has a rule giving priority to the first to invent (that is, to the first person to have a complete idea, called the *conception of the invention*); other countries give priority to the first to file a patent application. The term of patent is 20 years from filing. The term *patent pending* has no legal significance, but it may deter competitors. Only individuals can apply for a patent, although organizations may become the owners of a patent by way of assignment of rights by the inventor(s).

In the United States, it is relatively costly to apply for a patent (there are filing, search, and examination fees), and the process is long and complex. Small organizations are eligible for reduced fees. If a patent is issued, there is an issuance fee in addition to maintenance fees. The U.S. Patent and Trademark Office receives more than 350,000 patent applications per year. Organizations, therefore, typically investigate the business value of potential patents before applying. Like a copyright, a patent may be transferred or sold only in writing, and it may be jointly owned. Licenses may also be agreed to.

Trademarks

Trademark protection can apply to a word, slogan, design, picture, or other symbol used to identify and distinguish the source or origin of goods and services. The term *service mark* applies when a word, slogan, design, picture, or other symbol identifies a service (for example, investment services) rather than a tangible object. Trademarks were first used in commerce to protect consumers against a particular kind of fraud (passing off; that is, representing one product as another).

There are four categories of marks. The first category, generic names (including surnames, geographical names, and commonly used designations such as raisin bran), cannot be protected as trademarks. The other categories are descriptive (for example, Post-it Notes), suggestive (for example, Greyhound), and arbitrary or fanciful names such as Kodak: all can be protected under federal trademark law and designated with the symbol ® once the mark has been registered. Like patents and copyright, a trademark is a kind of monopoly granting, in the case of patents, or creating, in the case of copyright, certain exclusive rights. It is easier to apply to register a trademark, however, and there is no limit to the period of protection so long as the trademark remains in use and does not become generic and no longer functions to designate the source of goods or services.

Critical Commentary and Future Directions

Some organizations, such as educational, charitable, or nonprofit institutions that aim to serve the public good, choose to share their intellectual property with others. New technologies such as the Internet enable sharing through various forms of open access, such as Creative Commons licenses, although an organization may still retain its copyright in a work. The organization can also specify the terms of use; for example, the work may not be altered, no commercial use may be made of it, and/or the organization must be credited.

Intellectual property rights will continue to fuel debates that reflect the push and pull between those for whom the concept of intellectual property is most beneficial and those whom it puts at a disadvantage. Among those who benefit are the manufacturers of pharmaceuticals, publishing conglomerates, and the entertainment industry, including individual authors and artists. Those who are at a disadvantage include consumers, when various forms of monopoly on knowledge restrict access to necessary products or information. This problem is illustrated by doctors and patients in developing countries, who need access to information and medicines, and by faculty and students around the world, who need materials for teaching and learning. Furthermore, it can also be difficult to research the copyright holder of a work, and in some cases, the estates of authors have impeded scholarship by claiming broad rights.

Current intellectual property laws have expanded the scope of exclusive rights and become increasingly difficult to enforce, and piracy of protected materials such as books, songs, and DVDs is common in many countries. New technologies and new media, as they make it easier to share protected content, however, also provide new market opportunities for copyright holders.

—*Barbara K. Timmons*

See also Cultural Capital; Information; Knowledge Creation; Knowledge Management; Law and Economics

Further Readings

Fishman, S. (2004). *The copyright handbook: How to protect and use written works* (8th ed.). Berkeley, CA: Nolo.

Kirsch, J. (1995). *Kirsch's handbook of publishing law for authors, publishers, editors, and agents.* Los Angeles: Acrobat.

McCarthy, J. T. (1996). *McCarthy on trademarks and unfair competition* (4th ed.). Stamford, CT: Thomson West.

Nimmer, M. B., & Nimmer, D. (1997). *Nimmer on copyright: A treatise on the law of literary, musical, and artistic property, and the protection of ideas.* New York: Matthew Bender.

Schechter, R. E., & Thomas, J. R. (2003). *Intellectual property: The law of copyrights, patents, and trademarks.* St. Paul, MN: West Group.

U.S. Patent and Trademark Office. (n.d.). *General information concerning patents.* Retrieved March 13, 2007, from http://www.uspto.gov/web/offices/pac/doc/general/index.html#faqs

Waxer, B. M., & Baum, M. L. (2006). *Internet surf and turf—revealed: The essential guide to copyright, fair use, and finding media.* Boston: Thomson.

Yale University Library. (2000). *Copyright resources online.* Retrieved March 6, 2007, from http://www.library.yale.edu/~okerson/copyproj.html

INTELLIGENCE

See CULTURAL INTELLIGENCE

INTERACTION ANALYSIS

Interaction analysis includes a host of quantitative, empiricist approaches that draw from studies of message functions and language structures to assess the frequency and types of verbal behavior in organizational interaction. The focus is on language use, interaction process, and the categorization of behavior according to a predefined set of codes. Such coding enables analysts to study the sequences and stages of interaction, their redundancy and predictability, and the link between interactional structures and the organizational context. Collectively, interaction analysis research constitutes a diverse array of topics, theories, and coding schemes. Its basic appeal is a process view of social interaction.

Conceptual Overview

There are six genres of interaction analysis common to the organizational sciences. First, Robert Bales's interaction process analysis (IPA) examined the task and socioemotional functions of group interaction, although the focus is on the distribution of individual acts rather than sequential patterns. More recent research adopts SYMLOG, a coding scheme that utilizes retrospective rating methods for coding group interaction.

Second, the behaviorist studies of Judith Komaki and colleagues draw from operant conditioning theory to study the impact of leader verbal behavior on employee performance. The operant supervisory taxonomy and index codes leader performance monitoring, antecedents, and consequents, which are correlated with organizational or team effectiveness measures.

Third, in systems-interaction research, the way in which people talk in everyday work conversations, is fundamental to the ongoing enactment of control within organizations as systems. Control dynamics are best understood by knowing how people act relationally, that is, how one's control attempts are met with acceptance or rejection by another. Gail Fairhurst and colleagues used relational control coding and sequential analyses (lag sequential, Markov chain) to study leadership interactions.

Fourth, negotiation research draws heavily from systems-interaction and focuses on understanding bargaining strategies and tactics, sequences of bargaining patterns, the stages or phases of negotiations, and the enactment of rules or norms in these contexts. Utilizing numerous coding schemes, it is a large and growing body of research including work by Linda Putnam and Laurie Weingart.

Fifth, adaptive structuration theory (AST) utilizes interaction analysis to study the mutual influence of technology (e.g., group decision support systems) and social processes on organizational change. AST researchers Scott Poole and Geraldine DeSanctis developed coding schemes for the appropriation of structures as they arise from and occur within the discourse. Such schemes are intended as heuristic devices to track ironic meanings associated with technology appropriations that depart from intended use.

Sixth, an emerging genre of interaction analysis addresses the effects of time on group behavior based on the work of Connie Gersick. This research codes attention to time, task activity, and transitions in task activity, focusing solely on the pacing of group task activity sans a concern for interaction.

Critical Commentary and Future Directions

Interaction analysts adopt a traditional view of text as a moment of interaction frozen in time, based on a coded version of an actual, taped (audio or video), and/or transcribed interaction. This textualization is not just a record of the interaction, but a translation to a coded form in which the observing-recording-translating system necessarily restricts the questions that can be asked of the data. Analysis focuses on the order, coherence, and the iterability of action. For the systems-interaction, negotiation, and AST genres, concerns for sequentiality are paramount; the context of any individual action is the sequence of behaviors that preceded it, with that action destined to itself become part of the context as it unfolds. These genres are particularly adept at accounting for the communicative context of an utterance.

Most interaction analysts treat the organization as context, despite constructs of interest that emphasize an organizing perspective. Key to an organizing perspective is that the system is constituted by, not divorced from, the influence of its parts. Constructs like leadership, negotiation, and technology appropriation evolve from message patterns and communication systems. Following Gregory Bateson, systems emerge over repeated interactions that evolve into multileveled orders of pattern (e.g., relationships, hierarchical levels/units, organizations). With the exception of AST, most interaction analysts focus solely on organizational relationships—casting the organization as an already formed entity that constrains relational processes. Nevertheless, this bottom-up approach shifts the emphasis away from the organization as a static entity to a dynamic view of organizing. The net effect of this shift is that phenomena like leadership, negotiation, and technology use are now intrinsic to organizations rather than epiphenomena. However, while interaction analyses reveal the ways that talk creates structure, order or pattern does not produce the complex social form "organization" according to Robert McPhee. Organizing can always take place in the absence of organization (i.e., an entity with formal properties). Thus, future research must better address the ways in which patterns of organizing scale up to organization.

The subjects of meaning and agency are complex and contested within interaction analysis genres. Most interaction analysis research (IPA, behaviorist, negotiation, and group time studies) has postpositivist leanings that emphasize structure over action. Communication is transmissional, and conceptions of meaning bypass actors' interpretations in lieu of coder-assigned meanings. However, systems interaction analysis ascribes constrained choice to actors but deemphasizes their active, interpretive role in making these choices. AST is the only genre that strives to integrate action and structure.

Despite its labor-intensive nature, Alan Firth argued that social meanings are more ephemeral, malleable, and negotiable than interaction analysis can depict. Many cognitive and interpretative researchers also react to the pragmatic or behaviorist underpinnings of coding systems by arguing that they must capture actors' intended meanings to be valid. Interaction analysts respond that there is much to learn in the patterns and temporal form of concerted behavior. To discern these patterns, they avoid making claims about the cognitive bases of discourse production or subjective levels of meaning, focusing instead on meanings that are culturally available to all members of a language community (including coders). They also note that a structure-in-action view of organizations operates from the assumption that organizations are patterned and recurrent across time, yet few discursive analyses are as equipped as interaction analysis to address such concerns. Thus, interaction analysts situate themselves in between researchers who study the microprocesses of text, such as the conversation analysts, and those who study discursive formations, such as the postmodernists. As such, it remains dedicated to the study of the patterns and temporal form of organizational interaction from a unique vantage.

—*Gail T. Fairhurst*

See also Agency; Agency-Structure Debate; Communication; Control; Conversation; Discourse Analysis; Language and Organizations; Leadership, Styles; Negotiation; Organizational Communication; Participation; Power; Quantitative Models and Methods; Technology

Further Readings

Bakeman, R., & Gottman, J. M. (1986). *Observing interaction: An introduction to sequential analysis.* Cambridge, UK: Cambridge University Press.

Fairhurst, G. T. (2004). Textuality and agency in interaction analysis. *Organization, 11,* 335–353.

McPhee, R. D., & Zaug, P. (2000). The communicative constitution of organizations: A framework for explanation. *The Electronic Journal of Communication, 10,* 1–16.

Poole, M. S., Folger, J. P., & Hewes, D. E. (1987). Analyzing interpersonal interaction. In G. R. Miller & M. Roloff (Eds.), *Explorations in interpersonal communication* (2nd ed.) (pp. 220–255). Newbury Park, CA: Sage.

Putnam, L. L., & Fairhurst, G. T. (2001). Discourse analysis in organizations. In F. M. Jablin & L. L. Putnam (Eds.), *The new handbook of organizational communication* (pp. 78–136). Thousand Oaks, CA: Sage.

INTERACTIONISM

Interactionism reflects a movement in the social sciences to rigorously apply the theories and principles of evolutionary thinking to human social systems and to the psychology of individuals. Interactionism is, broadly, the perspective of relationship. More specifically and in terms of human communities it is the study of symbolic or *languaged* relationships.

Conceptual Overview

Current application of interactionist thinking is consistent with the science of complexity and the phenomena of emergence. The historical antecedents of interactionism encompass the major threads in Western thought up to and including Georg Hegel, Immanuel Kant, and Charles Darwin. Interactionism has its roots in both pragmatism and activity theory. These schools, born respectively in the United States and Europe and Russia, explored the new landscape that post-Darwinian thought opened up in the social sciences. The most significant contributor to the body of ideas making up what is now called interactionism is George Herbert Mead.

Mead's work outlined the fundamentally reciprocal and interactive nature of human behavior and emergent human consciousness—enacting both gestures and responses toward the environment as a whole. His work on the development of the self (and consciousness) through and by language stands as the definitive theoretical foundation for interactionism. However the work of John Dewey and William James can also be interpreted through an interactionist lens. In Dewey's case, the work is indexed under the rubric of the "transactional." It is unfortunate that Dewey defined *transactional* in opposition to *interactional;* however, a close reading of Dewey's work reveals substantive ties with Mead. The similarities of the work of William James are noted in his general explication of radical empiricism.

Critical Commentary and Future Directions

Mead's work was a significant effort to link the evolution of biological forms with behavior in general. Specifically Mead argued that all forms exist in a social context that gives birth to individuality, specialization of function, and eventually, for humans, consciousness and selfhood. The processes of linked and coordinated behaviors in a social context define the core ideas of interactionism. Mead's early development of ideas associated with what is now called complexity is remarkable. Mead analyzed the emergent behaviors of ants, bees, and flocks of birds in his effort to make sense of human behavior, sociality, and language. His work anticipated the formal study of emergent behavior, self-organization, and complex adaptive systems.

Underlying the ideas of interactionism is the gesture-and-response cycle. The movement of the organism in the environment is considered the basis for the gesture. The intrinsic responsiveness of the environment to this movement is the basis for the fundamental response. Ecological psychology terms this interactive relationship the *affordance* and sees this phenomenon as central to the behavior of all organisms. Mead's particular interest was in how the universal gesture and response cycles of biological organisms evolved into significant symbols (language) and stable social acts. A significant element of Mead's thought involved taking into account the recursive nature of human development in the context of a preexisting social system. While individuals are partially formed by their social environment they, in turn, partially form it. This idea of the output of a process being part of the input to the same process (thought at a different time) is one of the central ideas of interactionism and, of course, a central tenet of nonlinear functions and dynamical systems of all kinds.

Later application of Mead's thought by Herbert Blumer and others has resulted in the work being appropriated by sociology and used primarily as a vehicle for explaining the creation and maintenance of identity, role, and the fitting into social contexts.

Symbolic interactionism is a term coined by Blumer and emphasizes the central place of language in Mead's thought. With the advent of the significant gesture (the symbol), human beings have created a world phenomenally independent from the physical matrix that supports bodies. A symbolic world exists that structures human development and behavior over and above the structuring of the physical world of space, air, surfaces, available nutrients, and so on.

A central task of symbolic interactionist is to describe and explain both social systems and individual psychology as a consequence of the symbolic interaction making up language and its resultant behavior. Mead pioneered this effort by exploring and theorizing in detail the ideas of the self, the social act, objects, and joint or cooperative action. His primary assumption in framing this work was that consciousness and the self were the consequence of society. This inversion of a common ontological assumption is probably the greatest barrier to accessing and appreciating Mead's thought. The implications of Mead's thinking displace human consciousness from its central position in the social universe just as Copernicus once displaced the Earth from the center of the solar system.

The self is understood by Mead as that function in human experience that renders the subject as an object to itself. In explaining the emergence of these phenomena, Mead had to rely on a stable system of historical acts or patterns that the human brain could internalize and then reflect back into the world.

Action, or the act, was for Mead the realization that human beings (like other organisms) are proactive energetic animals in constant meaningful engagement with their environment. Human beings are released into a world that has both spatial and temporal structures as well as symbolic structure. This gives the quality of human actions a profile not found in the rest of nature. In distinguishing between objects and social acts, Mead took the theory of action into territory similar to pragmatists and activity theorists.

Objects, from Mead's perspective, are created in use. While not denying the physical and energetic nature of an object as a substance, Mead further defined *object* from a human observer's point of view as a meaningful affordance or opportunity for action in the environment.

The social act is considered the mediating link between interlocutors and provides the opportunity for meaning. Meaning is defined as the social process of interacting in a known context. This mediating function of the social act serves as the primary motive for both consciousness and meaningful individual or joint activity. It is in the social act that Mead's thinking resembles and imitates the reflexivity of the human person. It is only through language that a self can be born and only through a self that language can be uttered. The social act is both the midwife of language and its constant framing background. Interactionism reflects the evolution of broad themes in human knowing. Current theorizing in psychology, sociology, information technology, economics, and anthropology finds many of its roots in the body of thinking advanced by Mead.

—*Chris Francovich*

See also Complex Adaptive Systems; Epistemology; Pragmatism; Reflexivity; Symbolic Interactionism

Further Readings

Blumer, H. (1969). *Symbolic interactionism: Perspective and method.* Berkeley: University of California Press.

Chaiklin, S., Hedegaard, M., & Jensen, U. J. (Eds.). (1999). *Activity theory and social practice.* Aarhus, Denmark: Aarhus University Press.

Dewey, J., & Bentley, A. F. (1949). *Knowing and the known.* Boston: Beacon.

Heft, H. (2001). *Ecological psychology in context: James Gibson, Roger Garlock Barker, and the legacy of William*

James's radical empiricism. Mahwah, NJ: Lawrence Erlbaum.

Mead, G. H. (1934). *Mind, self, and society: From the standpoint of a social behaviorist* (C. W. Morris, Ed.). Chicago: University of Chicago Press.

INTERGROUP CONFLICT

Intergroup conflict may be defined as a tension between groups that is rooted in perceived differences. In attempting to understand intergroup conflict, researchers have reverted to describing and investigating the conflict episode. Some limited knowledge exists on the important relationship between intergroup conflict and both the organizational context and organizational effectiveness.

Conceptual Overview

The starting point for understanding intergroup conflict varies across different social science disciplines like anthropology, political science, sociology, or psychology. Definitions of conflict often depend on the respective theoretical framework that is common in each discipline. For instance, within social psychology, conflict is often defined as some incompatibility of goals, beliefs, attitudes, and/or behavior. While there is evidence that conflict between groups has unique and different predictors than intrapersonal or interpersonal conflict, researchers agree that the conflict phenomenon itself is equal across layers.

Instead of attempting to define conflict more precisely, researchers such as Pondy in 1967 reverted to analyzing the conflict episode or process. In 1992, Thomas described the conflict episode as a process that starts with one party's *awareness* of a conflict. This awareness may involve a variety of concerns or issues (e.g., a threat of a group's interest or a perceived goal difference). It leads to diverse *cognitions* and *emotions,* which result in *behavioral intentions* regarding how to cope with the conflict. These intentions are the combined motivational forces produced by cognitions and emotions. Behavioral intentions in turn lead to observable *behavior,* reacted upon by the other party. This behavior itself likely affects and reshapes a party's thoughts and emotions in form of a feedback loop. Finally, behavior results in *conflict outcomes.* These outcomes conclude the episode, but may in turn launch a subsequent episode about the same or related issue.

Conflict Awareness

Conflict awareness has mostly been conceptualized in the form of conflict over issues, goals, and means.

Conflict Over Issues

Several conflict typologies distinguished substantive or realistic conflicts rooted in divergence of interests from conflict concerned with affective or cognitive aspects. For example, De Dreu, Harinck, and van Vianen in 1999 distinguished conflict over resources or interests from conflict over information. The former involves access to and distribution of resources. Examples may include a dispute between two team leaders about which health care team should cover a patient. The latter contains both intellective and evaluative issues. Intellective issues have factual solutions according to commonly accepted standards, such as what is the most cost-efficient PC equipment. For intellective issues, the task is to find the true or correct solution, and accuracy of resolution has priority over agreement. On the other hand, evaluative issues may involve ethical or aesthetic judgments for which there are no demonstrably correct answers. Thus, for evaluative issues, the "right" answer is achieved by reaching consensus. An example might represent a dispute about the dressing code within a consultancy company.

Conflict Over Goals

Many scholars distinguish goal conflict from cognitive conflict, the former involving disagreements that focus on competition for rewards or status. Studies examining the roots of individuals' conclusions about conflicting goals between groups and departments identified both a structural and psychological basis. For instance, research showed that reasons for employees' perceptions of competitive goals include a party's lack of concern for each other's interests, conflict defined as win-lose contests, and competition over scarce resources between departments.

Conflict Over Means

Even though two groups may share cooperative goals, they still can be (and often are) in conflict, suggesting that further conflict concepts are necessary to enhance our understanding of conflict. In 1995, Jehn investigated conflict within organizational groups using multiple methods and distinguished relationship conflict from task conflict. Relationship conflict mainly includes affective components, such as dislike and feelings of annoyance and irritations. Task conflict is characterized as an awareness of differences in viewpoints and opinions pertaining to a task *without* the personal animosities germane to relationship conflict. It may even coincide with animated discussions and personal excitement, but is void of the intense interpersonal negative emotions associated with relationship conflict.

Thoughts and Emotions

A strong contribution toward understanding conflict has been made by studies that investigated how individuals cognitively frame and make sense of the conflict they experience. Frames can be described as thematic perceptual dispositions that increase the salience of frame-irrelevant information and are related to both cognitions and emotions. Frames are perceptual sets of orientations that are pre- or metaschematic and serve to guide how information is perceived and interpreted in terms of these schemas. Research has identified outcome frames, which refer to whether outcomes are coded as gains or losses, and conflict frames, which refer to how people cognitively frame everyday conflicts they are involved in.

In 1990, Pinkley used multidimensional scaling to reveal three dimensions of conflict frames: The *task vs. relationship* dimension illustrates that people differ in the extent to which they attribute the conflict to problems in the relationship and, consequently, how concerned they are about the other party and maintaining the relationship. While disputants with a task orientation focus more on material aspects of a dispute, such as money or property settlements, relationship-oriented disputants rather focus on interpersonal concerns and the relationship involved. The second dimension was labeled *cooperate vs. win* and implied that a discrepancy exists in the attributions made regarding blame for the conflict. Some disputants attribute blame to both parties and seek a compromise solution. Others concentrate on winning the conflict, as the other party is to blame. The third dimension was labeled *emotional vs. intellectual* and emphasizes the variance in degree of attention paid to the affective component of conflict. Although some disputants focus on the feelings involved (e.g., anger and frustration), others seem to attend only to the specific behavior and thoughts involved.

Intentions (Motivation)

De Dreu and colleagues describe that conflict motivation is frequently concerned with the desired contribution of outcomes between the parties involved. The authors distinguish three motivations. A disputant's *competitive motivation* is characterized by reaching a relative advantage over the other party. *Individualistic motivation* is characterized by an ignorance of the other party's outcome, and disputants are concerned with their own outcome. Finally, *prosocial motivation* is characterized by disputants concern for both themselves and the other party. The authors found that even though social motives are partially rooted in individual differences, they may also be triggered by features of the situation, or may be adopted for genuine or instrumental reasons.

Conflict Behavior

Conflict behavior is a core aspect of the conflict episode, as captured by dual concern theory, which represents an extension of Blake and Mouton's managerial grid as published in 1964. The theory considers negotiation style as a function of the two motivations' high or low concern for themselves, combined with high or low concern for the other party. It suggests groups' negotiation behavior can be characterized by combinations of both concerns yielding five negotiation styles.

Contending refers to imposing one's will on the other party. Thomas explains that in goal conflicts the intention is to achieve one's goal at the sacrifice of the other's goal. In intellective conflicts, an attempt is made to convince the other party that one's conclusion is right and the other is wrong. During evaluative conflict, Thomas describes that one tries to make the offending party accept blame for some perceived transgression, together with any responsibilities attached to blame (e.g., guilt, punishment, restitution). The flip side of contending is *yielding,* which refers to accepting and incorporating the other's will. Thomas outlines that in goal conflicts this intention may represent an attempt to attain the other's goals at the sacrifice of one's own goals, and in intellective and evaluative conflict to support the other's opinion despite one's own reservations, or to forgive the other for a perceived transgression and to allow subsequent ones.

Avoiding involves active withdrawal and passive avoidance. By using this technique, one tries to avoid involving oneself in an issue, allowing events to take their own course without attempting to steer the outcome toward the concern of either party. *Problem solving* is characterized by an attempt of a party to achieve a settlement that satisfies the concerns of both parties. While during goal conflicts one attempts to find a win-win solution that allows both parties' goals to be completely achieved, in intellective conflicts the goal is to achieve a synthesis, a new conclusion or idea that incorporates the valid insights of both parties. In evaluative conflict, one might try to arrive at a shared set of expectations and an interpretation of the transgression in question that meets both parties' standards of what is proper in a given situation.

There is some disagreement in the literature as to whether *compromising* reflects a fifth negotiation style or rather a form of tentative problem solving. It involves attaining moderate but incomplete satisfaction of both parties' concerns.

Additionally, Walton and McKersie have made a crucial distinction between integrative and distributive dimensions. The distributive dimension seeks a particular allocation of outcomes and includes dominating, compromising, and yielding. The integrative dimension seeks the amount of integration of the two parties' joint outcome and embraces collaborating, compromising, and avoiding.

Conflict Outcome

Thomas concludes that consideration of conflict outcomes is largely dependent upon the respective evaluation criteria, which are widespread and complex. The author describes that the most obvious outcome of a conflict issue may be the decision (or lack of decision) that has been reached regarding the conflict issue. De Dreu and colleagues describe four types of such outcomes; integrative settlements, compromise, victory to one, and impasse. Integrative settlement refers to solutions that satisfy and embrace the interests of both parties. Integrative agreements have been assumed to be optimal outcomes, as they are more enduring and satisfying for the parties involved, even though this assumption has been questioned for information conflict. Irrespective of the outcome of the conflict episode, each aspect of the conflict episode separately can be theoretically linked to organizational performance and effectiveness as alternative outcome variables.

Critical Commentary and Future Directions

In order to better understand the phenomenon of organizational intergroup conflict, two aspects frequently not explicitly outlined in conflict models require further consideration: first, the relationship of intergroup conflict with the organizational context, and second, the relationship of intergroup conflict with organizational effectiveness.

Intergroup Conflict and Organizational Context

In organizations, intergroup relations do not happen in a vacuum, but are embedded within the organizational context, a complex network of interdependent vertical and horizontal relationships with other groups, teams, and departments. Management theorists have argued that functional interdependencies between and among groups, such as power relationships, need to be diagnosed to allow an understanding of the dynamics of intergroup conflict. Further, researchers have pointed out that an organization's reward structure is frequently set up such that group performance is rewarded, rather than the quality and effectiveness of lateral relationships. In fact, many organizations stimulate competition between groups, thereby fostering intergroup conflict. Finally, groups in organizations frequently compete over a pool of scarce resources, such as staff, status, or finances, which further stimulates hostilities between groups. Even though it is acknowledged that the organizational context shapes relationships between groups, too little is known about the mechanisms of this effect.

Intergroup Conflict and Organizational Effectiveness

Heretofore, our understanding of how intergroup conflict affects organizational effectiveness is limited. Intergroup conflict in particular is predominantly regarded as a destructive force in organizational life characterized by hostile attitudes and bargaining behavior between organizational groups, resulting in reduced satisfaction, effectiveness, and enhanced turnover. The acknowledgment that conflict does not necessarily have to be dysfunctional, but may also contain functional aspects (or combinations of both), has a long-standing history in conflict research. For example, Amason found in 1996 that conflict within top management teams can be a constructive and creative resource for enhancing the quality of decision making. In fact, little or no organizational conflict may result in stagnation, poor decisions, and ineffectiveness. Conflict may also result in enhanced system stability through channeled interunit contact, and motivation may be enhanced through intergroup competition. Further, group processes, such as group cohesion, group motivation, and a group's identity may be fostered.

In summary, intergroup conflict may be both positively and negatively related to organizational effectiveness, and further research is needed to specify conditions under which conflict is functional or dysfunctional.

—*Andreas W. Richter and Michael A. West*

See also Conflict; Effectiveness; Organizational Structure; Social Identity Theory

Further Readings

Amason, A. C. (1996). Distinguishing the effects of functional and dysfunctional conflict on strategic decision making: Resolving a paradox for top management groups. *Academy of Management Journal, 39,* 123–148.

Blake, R. R., Sheppard, H. A., & Mouton, J. S. (1964). *Managing intergroup conflict in industry.* Houston, TX: Gulf Publishing.

De Dreu, C. K. W., Harinck, F., & Van Vianen, A. E. M. (1999). Conflict and performance in groups and organizations. *International Review of Industrial and Organizational Psychology, 14,* 376–405.

Jehn, K. A. (1995). A multimethod examination of the benefits and detriments of intragroup conflict. *Administrative Science Quarterly, 40,* 256–282.

Pinkley, R. L (1990). Dimensions of conflict frame: Disputant interpretations of conflict. *Journal of Applied Psychology, 75,* 117–126.

Thomas, K. W. (1992). Conflict and negotiation processes in organizations. In M. D. Dunette & L. M. Hough (Eds.), *Handbook of industrial and organizational psychology* (Vol. 3, 2nd ed.) (pp. 651–717). Chicago: Rand McNally.

Walton. R. E., & McKersie, R. B. (1965). *A behavioral theory of labor negotiation: An analysis of social interaction system.* New York: McGraw-Hill.

INTERNATIONAL BUSINESS

International business (IB) is a generic term that describes any form of business transaction, whether undertaken by individuals or organizations, involving parties from more than one country. It includes trade in raw materials and finished goods, in services, investment and financial transactions, collaborations and joint ventures, and relocation of business units to capitalize on lower costs of doing business. Contemporary IB involves activities in the field of e-business: buying, selling, communicating, and cooperating using the Internet.

Conceptual Overview

International business has been conducted since national boundaries were formed, from the days of the Phoenician Empire to the present. Czinkota, Ronkainen, and Moffett point out how, throughout history, IB has been used as a tool of governmental policy; either as an enabler, or as a form of coercion and control. Though IB has a long history, its economic, social, and political importance has increased with phenomena such as industrialization, transportation, globalization, and the growth of *multinational enterprises* (MNEs). As Buckley outlines, contemporary theory of IB embraces elements of applied economics, finance, business policy and corporate strategy, organization theory, and of applied management fields such as marketing.

Early theories of IB assumed imbalanced power relationships between nations in relation to financial and physical resources. *Mercantilists* believed that the prosperity of a nation was dependent on its reserves of precious metals, which in turn would be increased through generating high exports and reducing imports. In the mercantile system, the state fulfilled an active *protectionist* role, through the application of selective tariffs to promote exports and minimize imports. Between the 16th and 18th centuries, protectionism was one of the key factors underpinning European imperialism and many European wars.

The 18th-century economist Adam Smith opposed the mercantilists' restrictive and regulated system and, in his book *The Wealth of Nations*, he argued that free trade, competition, and choice spur economic development, reduce poverty, and stimulate social and moral improvement. Using examples from across the world, Smith provided a new understanding of the wealth-creating process and paved the way for an era of free trade and economic expansion in the 19th century. Adam Smith's arguments were based on the concept of *absolute advantage*, whereby each nation should export goods that it can produce more efficiently than any other, and should import those for which another country holds absolute advantage.

It is possible for two countries to engage in exchange even where one holds absolute advantage over the other in relation to the production of all goods. This is explained by the theory of *comparative advantage*, which places emphasis on the relative efficiency of the utilization of resources both within and between countries. Robert Torrens first described the concept in 1815, but it became widely known following David Ricardo's explanation in his 1817 book, *The Principles of Political Economy and Taxation*.

Early theories of IB were concerned with the competitiveness of countries rather than companies, and with trade in products rather than services, seeking to explain how countries could achieve and maintain a positive *balance of trade*, and why particular countries offered suitable targets for exports within the *global supply chain*. In addition to a shift in the focus of exchange from products to services, the second half of the 20th century saw the growth of MNEs: those companies owning separate operations in more than one country, accompanied by a move away from country-based theories to development of firm-based theories and consideration of industries and products.

Key firm-based theories include *country similarity theory*. Developed by Swedish economist Steffen Linder, this theory suggests that trade in manufactured products should take place between countries with similar per capita incomes and be related primarily to differentiated goods: those for which brand names and reputation play a crucial marketing role. Raymond Vernon's *product life cycle* theory describes the three stages of the cycle: from new product development, through maturing, into standardization. Associated with these three stages are parallel developments of domestic production, export, and net import by the innovating firm's home country. From looking more closely at interorganizational competition, Paul Krugman and Kelvin Lancaster developed *global strategic rivalry theory*, which outlines the numerous ways in which MNEs can seek to gain competitive advantage over their rivals. These include the ownership of intellectual property rights, strong investment in research and development (R&D), achievement of global economies of scale or scope, and the successful exploitation of the experience curve, relating high-value new product innovation to reducing unit costs over time.

Finally, Michael Porter offers the *theory of national competitive advantage* and outlines four major components from the point of view of a potential investor: (1) factor conditions, the appropriateness of the factors of production and their continuous development; (2) demand conditions, and the health and competitiveness of the company's home market; (3) related and supporting industries and supply-chain relationships; and (4) firm strategy, structure and rivalry, and the supporting or constraining conditions of the home environment. In addition, he highlights the mediating roles of government and chance factors.

Though trade is the most obvious form of IB, *international investment* also plays a key role, through cross-border supply of capital. International investment takes the form of either *portfolio investment,* passive investment without active control or management, and *foreign direct investment* (FDI), where the intention is acquisition of assets with the purpose of control. There are several key theories of international investment. *Ownership advantage theory* states that ownership of a key asset that creates advantage in the home market can be used to penetrate foreign markets through FDI. *Internalization theory* considers why organizations employ FDI, where the transaction costs and associated risks of contracting exceed those of ownership. John Dunning's *eclectic theory* sees successful FDI as being based upon three conditions: (1) ownership advantage, of a brand or technology, for example; (2) location advantage, in terms of costs and tariffs; and (3) internalization advantage, where direct control offers benefits over contracting.

A number of supranational agencies play key roles in the field of IB, including the International Monetary Fund (IMF), World Trade Organization (WTO), World Bank, and the G-8 group of nations. The IMF serves to promote international monetary harmony, to monitor exchange rates and policies, and to provide support to economies in difficulty. The key functions of the WTO include the administration of trade agreements, acting as a forum for negotiation, addressing disputes between members, and monitoring the national policies of members. The World Bank is an agency of the United Nations, and its purpose is to fund development projects around the world. Finally, Canada, France, Germany, Italy, Japan, Russia, the United Kingdom, and the United States comprise the G-8. Its purpose is to review economic developments within the member states and across the global economy and to initiate international economic and financial policies.

Related to IB is the concept of *economic integration,* a process aimed at reducing barriers to trade between national markets. The extent of integration is usually classified under six stages that involve establishing: a preferential trade area, free trade area, customs union, common market, economic and monetary union, and complete economic integration. A number of trade blocs exist, with different degrees of integration; e.g., the North American Free Trade Agreement (NAFTA), the European Union (EU), the Association of South East Asian Nations (ASEAN), and MERCOSUR, the group of South American countries.

Critical Commentary and Future Directions

Early theories of IB related primarily to consideration of products, whereas in the 21st-century IB is to a large extent grounded in cross-border facilitation of services and investment and increasingly relies upon use of Internet and telecommunications technologies. Contemporary literature on IB presents a range of viewpoints on whether the activities of MNEs, the policies of governments, and the actions of supranational agencies are seen to be supportive of economic growth and development for all, or contributing to an ever-greater socioeconomic divide between a super-rich global elite and an impoverished multitude. Central to the discussion is the concept of *globalization* and separate consideration of the respective impacts of the globalization of markets and of production. The former implies a convergence of markets, and of consumer buying power and buying behavior, while the latter depends on differences in factors of production between countries to enable economies of scale from lowering the costs of doing business through country selection.

Creating advantage in the field of services requires consideration of labor skills and access to capital, and countries like China, India, and Mexico seek to combine high levels of technological capability with lower costs of labor than in the developed world. In relation to products, particularly those with low technical specifications, advantage is dependent primarily on low labor costs, and these are the subject of critical debate in terms of how and why they are maintained. A number of viewpoints exist in the literature. Mainstream IB textbooks aver to issues of environmental impact, slave labor, and political corruption, but the predominant discourse is one of guidance and information on how best to engage in international business, with an implicit assumption that the growth and development of IB are both necessary and inevitable. Likewise, the idea of economic integration is underpinned by the notion that free trade is good. The concept of free trade has been criticized on several grounds, and alternatives have been proposed, including Tobin Tax, fair trade, balanced trade, and international barter. There is a body of writings that challenge the fundamental principles of growth and development. George Ritzer critiques the process of global homogenization, most famously in his *McDonaldization* thesis. His arguments are, however, developed across a broader range of issues of consumption and its dematerialization.

Naomi Klein considers the inherent tensions between the unifying effects of global markets and the social fragmentation of global production as problematic, due to their different impacts on socioeconomic structures. For others, globalization offers the only solution to the problems of social and economic exclusion and impoverishment. Philippe Legrain considers that, subject to supranational constraints to eliminate the excesses of corporate and individual greed and exploitation, a totally free market is the only course for future development. For Klein, however, fundamental problems of inequality cannot be addressed by the free market approach.

Despite the range of views and opinions on the benefits and problems of IB, it is apparent that there will be ongoing growth and development in the use of the Internet and of e-commerce. Individuals and organizations undertake transactions at a global level in real time, with increasingly open communications and transparency of pricing and costing structures. This has led to the development of new forms of interorganizational collaborations and networks and to novel ways of doing business, such as the *reverse auction*, whereby an organization seeks the lowest price for the supply of a particular product or service from bidders across the globe. The future potential of such developments will be linked to concerns of global social, political, and economic stability and turmoil; to the outcome of issues of security and attack, both physically and digitally; and to the extent and impact of climate change.

—George Cairns and Martyna Sliwa

See also Capital Movement, Migration, and Maquiladoras; E-commerce; Globalization; International Management; Multinational Enterprises

Further Readings

Buckley, P. J. (Ed.). (2003). *International business.* Aldershot, UK: Ashgate/Dartmouth.

Czinkota, M. R., Ronkainen, I. A., & Moffett, M. H. (2005). *International business* (7th ed.). Mason, OH: South-Western.

Klein, N. (2000). *No space/no choice/no jobs—no logo.* London: Flamingo.

Legrain, P. (2002). *Open world: The truth about globalisation.* London: Abacus.

Ritzer, G. (2001). *Explorations in the sociology of consumption.* London: Sage.

Sutherland, J., & Canwell, D. (2004). *Key concepts in international business.* Basingstoke, UK: Palgrave Macmillan.

INTERNATIONAL HUMAN RESOURCE MANAGEMENT

International human resource management (IHRM) examines the management of human resources (people) across national borders. Two broad issues are addressed within the field of IHRM: first, human resource management (HRM) in multinational corporations (MNCs) with operations in multiple countries, and second, comparative analyses of HRM across countries. It should be noted that some scholars argue that comparative analyses of HRM should not be viewed as part of IHRM, the latter only encompassing HRM in MNCs. The focus here is on HRM in MNCs.

Conceptual Overview

To understand what is meant by IHRM, it is useful to examine the field from a historical perspective. Although the coining and spread of the term *international human resource management* only happened around 1990, the history of what is today viewed as IHRM covers a time span of more than 30 years. Much of the early work focused on staffing decisions in MNCs and how to manage expatriate managers from the corporation's home country. Howard Perlmutter's seminal article "The Tortuous Evolution of the Multinational Corporation," which was published in French in 1965 and in English in 1969, is arguably the first influential article published within IHRM. Perlmutter distinguishes among three different attitudes of MNC headquarters executives: ethnocentric (home country oriented), polycentric (host country oriented) and geocentric (world oriented). A fourth category was later added: regiocentric. In MNCs in which headquarters has an ethnocentric attitude, managers from the home country are seen as superior to those of the other countries in which the MNC has operations; therefore, top management positions in foreign subsidiaries are usually staffed with MNC home country nationals. This framework of MNC headquarters orientations has become a standard way to classify IHRM strategies, in particular staffing policies and practices, and the terms *ethnocentric, polycentric,* and *geocentric* are today widely used.

Research has identified different staffing patterns among MNCs from different regions, with Japanese MNCs consistently being most likely to use home country nationals in key positions overseas. U.S. MNCs seem less likely than European firms to staff foreign units with home country nationals. Other factors found to influence staffing decisions are the subsidiary host country, the age of the subsidiary, and the international strategy and experience of the MNC. Development of foreign country nationals through transfers to headquarters—labeled *inpatriation*—appears to have increased in importance in many MNCs.

Subsequent to Perlmutter's important contributions, two streams of work soon began to emerge: one focusing on the management of expatriates (persons sent abroad on long-term assignments), where the emphasis was on the adjustment of the expatriate; the second on the roles that the transfer of people across units played in the management of the MNC. The focus in expatriate management was for a long time on how to select, prepare, train, and support expatriate managers and their families so that they would adjust well to conditions abroad. Most of this research asserted that lack of general, interaction, and/or work adjustment on the part of the expatriate increases the likelihood that he or she fails to complete the international assignment. Therefore, rather than select persons because of their technical skills or proven performance in the home country, they should be chosen based on their ability to adjust, with cultural intelligence recently having been suggested as an important predictor. Several studies also indicate that a well-adjusted spouse increases the likelihood that the expatriate will be well adjusted and complete his or her assignment abroad.

More recently, the IHRM literature has adopted a wider view of international mobility, including more short-term assignments abroad and frequent traveling, both of which are associated with considerable challenges for both individuals and MNCs. Furthermore, it has been acknowledged that significant human and organizational issues are associated with the process of returning to the home country after a foreign assignment.

Anders Edström and Jay Galbraith's research on the motives for transferring managers across units became highly influential in IHRM. In their 1977 article, they describe three motives for international assignments: to fill positions when qualified local nationals are not available, as management development (to develop expatriates through the experiences they gain during international assignments), and as organization development (through socialization of the expatriate as well as through the development of interpersonal linkages across MNC units).

One of the management issues facing MNCs is the extent to which to transfer management practices across borders. It has been strongly argued that MNCs need to pay attention to host country cultural (and institutional) factors when deciding on HRM policies and practices in their foreign operations. However, potentially positive aspects are also associated with transfer of practices, such as the possibility to replicate HRM systems found to be efficient elsewhere to other parts of the MNC. Thus, strong opposing forces face MNCs, dualities that firms need to understand as they develop HRM policies and practices for their international operations.

The term *human resource management* emerged in the 1980s, and in this time period HRM also became a recognized field of study. A central aspect of HRM that distinguished it from the previously dominating personnel management was the link between HRM and strategy. HRM was seen as long-term, proactive, and strategic, and it constitutes an integrated approach to the management of people. The new HRM discourse originated in the United States and was focused on the domestic operations of U.S. corporations, but it did not take long until scholars based outside North America and researchers doing work on HRM within MNCs became influenced by the new HRM concept. This has led not only to a surge in studies examining how HRM is related to organizational performance in different countries but also to critical reactions toward the notion that there might be a universal model of HRM regardless of the context of the organization.

In this way, the new HRM discourse has contributed to reinvigorate comparative studies of industrial relations and personnel practices in different countries. National and local cultural and institutional factors have been found to be related with the HRM practices found in a particular country, while the thesis that there are significant cross-national processes of convergence in HRM across countries still is subject to extensive discussion and ongoing research.

However, the biggest impact of the HRM concept on the IHRM field may have been in terms of its influence on efforts to link HRM policies and practices to the organizational strategy of MNCs. Within this body of literature—sometimes called strategic international HRM and building increasingly on developments in strategy and organizational theory such as the resource-based view of the firm—scholars have among others developed comprehensive models of the causal factors influencing HRM policies and practices in MNCs.

The field of IHRM has also been expanded into a range of other topic areas. Management of people in alliances, mergers and acquisitions, global management development and performance management, knowledge transfer and organizational learning, management of change, global outsourcing, and organizational culture development are just some of the issues included in IHRM. Furthermore, the human resource function itself and the roles it plays in the functioning of the MNC have also received increased attention. There is also some work emerging on IHRM in companies as they internationalize and expand their foreign operations. In short, the field of IHRM has developed into a large, complex, and constantly developing field of study, the boundaries of which are difficult to delineate.

Critical Commentary and Future Directions

IHRM scholars have argued that IHRM involves the same activities and dimensions as domestic HRM but operates on a much larger scale, with more complex strategic considerations and more complex coordination and control demands. Additional human resource functions are considered necessary to accommodate the greater operating unit diversity, more external stakeholder influence, and more challenges in gaining necessary insights into employee's lives and family situations. Others have argued that HRM in MNCs differs from management in a domestic context not only in *degree* but also in *kind* because the challenges faced by individuals and the organization are qualitatively different from those faced in a domestic context. These demands include increased ambiguity surrounding decisions, wider and more frequent boundary spanning, a more challenging and expanded list of competing tensions that need to be balanced, a heightened need for cultural understanding, and more challenging ethical dilemmas relating to globalization. The extent to which theories and concepts from the generic HRM literature are appropriate for issues within IHRM needs to be critically examined as the field evolves.

With research on expatriate adjustment as the main exception, there is only limited research on the effects of IHRM on employee and organizational outcomes. Hence, although advice concerning IHRM often is offered, the empirical basis for suggestions made by IHRM scholars and consultants remains rather limited. For instance, there are compelling reasons for MNCs to adapt their HRM practices to fit with local cultural and institutional contexts. However, there are also persuasive arguments for integration of HRM systems across MNC units to reap benefits of scale and scope, to facilitate control and coordination of dispersed units, and to exploit insights concerning successful HRM practices. To date, there is a lack of empirical work shedding light on when and how to deal with the local adaptation-global integration challenge. Furthermore, relatively little is known about the mechanisms through which HRM practices are integrated across units. For example, recent MNC adoptions of enterprise resource planning systems such as those provided by SAP, and which commonly include human resource functions, have led to increased integration of HRM policies and processes across MNC units, but so far little reference is made to such developments in the IHRM literature.

Another area in which more conceptual development and empirical research are badly needed is on factors associated with expatriate performance. In contrast with much conventional belief, research has indicated that the level of expatriate adjustment is only marginally associated with work performance. In some instance, the challenges of working abroad may even spur superior performance on part of the expatriate. The relationship between expatriate adjustment and performance thus awaits further examination.

Although HRM in MNCs and comparative analyses of HRM in different countries may be viewed as distinct (sub)fields, they are obviously interrelated. The HRM found in foreign subsidiaries of MNCs constitute part of the HRM systems found in the host country, and MNC practices can be important sources of inspiration for local companies looking for ways to change how they manage people. For MNCs, innovative HRM tools and practices found in foreign subsidiaries may in turn influence how people are managed in the MNCs' home countries. Hence, there are likely to be clear benefits in trying to find ways to integrate our thinking about comparative and MNC HRM in the years ahead.

IHRM is still a relatively young field and our understanding of the complexity of factors and processes that affect the effectiveness of IHRM policies and practices is still relatively limited.

—Ingmar Björkman

See also Human Resource Management; Industrial Relations; International Management; Strategic Human Resource Management; Transnational Corporations

Further Readings

Brewster, C. (1995). Towards a European model of human resource management. *Journal of International Business Studies, 26,* 1–21.

Dowling, P. E., & Welch, D. E. (2004). *International human resource management* (4th ed.). London: Thomson.

Edström, A., & Galbraith. J. R. (1977). Transfer of managers as a co-ordination and control strategy in multinational organizations. *Administrative Science Quarterly, 22,* 248–263.

Evans, P., Pucik, V., & Barsoux, J. (2002). *The global challenge: Frameworks for international human resource management.* New York: McGraw-Hill/Irwin.

Hofstede, G. (1991). *Cultures and organizations: Software of the mind.* London: McGraw-Hill.

Perlmutter, H. (1969). The tortuous evolution of the multinational company. *Columbia Journal of World Business, 4*(1), 9–18.

Sparrow, P., Brewster, C., & Harris, H. (2004). *Globalizing human resource management.* London: Routledge.

Stahl, G. K., & Björkman, I. (Eds.). (2006). *Handbook of research in international human resource management.* Cheltenham, UK: Edward Elgar.

Taylor, S., Beechler, S., & Napier, N. (1996). Toward an integrative model of strategic international human resource management. *Academy of Management Review, 21,* 959–985.

INTERNATIONALIZATION SCHOOL

Management literature has developed several theories that focus on the activities of business firms in foreign markets. The internationalization school is an important part of this literature. This school of thought tries to explain the phenomenon of internationalization of production and trade. The most important questions this school asks are: Why are firms leaving their home countries and going into foreign markets? What are the different strategies that firms use to enter a new foreign market? What factors influence the decision of when and where to enter? What parts of the corporate value chain will be outsourced across firm or national boundaries?

At this point, there is no encompassing theory that integrates all these questions. As a result, economic activities in foreign markets can be explained in different ways. The historical point of origin for such explanations is the theory of external trade. This theory enumerates the advantages stemming from exchange of goods across national boundaries (imports and exports). By contrast, theories of international production analyze the conditions that encourage the transfer of capital and factors of production into foreign countries, (i.e. foreign direct investments).

Conceptual Overview

Theories of External Trade

Classical/neoclassical trade theory explains the trade activities of domestic firms under perfect market conditions. Problems such as market imperfections, intermediary products, and transaction costs are neglected. One of the first theories of external trade was developed by Adam Smith. His concept of absolute cost advantages explained external trade as follows: a particular country specializes in the production of goods that it can produce at lower costs than other countries. These goods are exported, while goods that the country can only produce at higher costs than other countries are imported. This theory was further developed by David Ricardo. He explained international trade with the help of relative cost advantages of countries and argued that there may remain an incentive for international trade, even if one country can produce all products more cheaply than other countries. Yet another theory was developed by Heckscher and Ohlin. They distinguished different factors of production (e.g., capital and labor). According to Heckscher and Ohlin, the factor endowments of each country explain the particular mix of goods that that country produces and exports.

Theories of International Production

Theories about international production depart from the macroeconomic perspective on exports and imports described above. Instead these theories focus on the business firm as the unit of analysis, bringing the organization into close focus. Theories of international production identify market imperfections such as uncertainty, risk, the cost of information, and transaction costs, considering those important causes of the internationalization of business firms. One can distinguish economic and behavioral theories of international production.

Behavioral Explanations of International Production

The *behavioral theory* was proposed by Aharoni in 1966. He describes the internationalization of the firm as the result of a collective decision process in which the firm gradually increases its international involvement. The theory takes into account information imperfections and bounded rationality, treating these as core assumptions. The theory assumes that the decision-making process is not completely rational; rather, it develops in an incremental manner. In 1997, Johanson and Vahlne proposed a variation of this theory, which they called a *learning theory* perspective. This theory argues that the internationalization of firms is based on experimental knowledge that companies acquire about foreign markets. Companies first expand their activities into markets that have similar culture and language to their own. These firms start with exports, and from exporting they begin to gain an increasing understanding of foreign markets. After this knowledge has been acquired, business firms may feel competent to manage manufacturing operations in the foreign markets on their own. At that point, the firms decide to engage in foreign direct investment.

Economic Explanations of International Production

Economic theories of international production are based on the assumption that foreign investments are determined by different cost structures and divergent potential for earning profits. One of the first such theories in this research strand was developed by Vernon in 1966. He introduced the *product life cycle theory* and maintained that the categorization of products into different development stages can explain the international engagement of business firms. In the innovation stage of a new product, there are no foreign activities. These are developed and intensified only in subsequent product life cycle stages when business firms are capable of managing the production and distribution process at lower costs.

Another economic explanation of international production was proposed by Porter in his *diamond model* in 1990. The model clarifies the competitive position of a branch or firm in global competition. Competitive advantage is determined by the following variables: firm strategy and structure, demand conditions, production factors, and related supporting industries. Two additional variables complete the diamond: chance and the state.

Yet another theory of international production is the *internalization theory* proposed by Buckley and Casson in 1976. According to internalization theory, firms have two possibilities for carrying out international transactions: either the market (licensing and trade) or internal hierarchy (foreign direct investment). This theory distinguishes between two types of costs: transaction costs, caused by market imperfections, and coordination costs, caused by imperfections in the internal coordination mechanisms of a firm. The type of international transaction adopted is explained by both these cost factors.

A more complex view is provided by Dunning in his so-called *eclectic paradigm*. Like internalization theory, the eclectic paradigm assumes that markets are imperfect. These imperfections influence the economic activities of firms both locally and internationally. The eclectic paradigm states that international engagement of firms depends on a variety of different variables such as ownership advantages, internalization advantages, and local advantages.

Critical Commentary and Future Directions

Virtually all the theories described above depend on a limited number of causal variables, based on either an economic or behavioral paradigm. As noted already, there is no integrative theory that explains all aspects, forms, and problems of internationalization. Some of the theories reviewed here are static and therefore are unable to account for the dynamics of the process of internationalization. Furthermore, most of these theories are based on a realist epistemological model, which explains the internationalization of business activities as a natural process that is determined by external factors in a lawlike manner.

By contrast, critical theories of internationalization and globalization emphasize the problematic outcomes of capitalist production and trade, such as uneven distribution of benefits, social and environmental problems, and the weakening of political institutions by powerful capitalist firms. Some of these critical theories highlight the interests that are served by the internationalization process and show how weaker social groups, people, or regions get marginalized in that process. Also, critical discussion has addressed the question of how to govern economic globalization by institutional reform of international politics or by socially responsible business behavior.

Today the theory of the firm is dedicated to the economic role of the firm exclusively. However, the impact of the business firm on social, political, and environmental issues has become a matter of vigorous public debate. At the same time, business firms have started to take responsibilities for social and environmental issues and engage in the production of global public goods that had once been considered as the sole responsibility of the state. Future theorizing upon the firm has yet to integrate these extra economic activities and has to develop a vision of the role of business in a just and democratic global society.

—*Andreas Georg Scherer and Andreas Butz*

See also Behavioral Theory of the Firm; Competitive Advantage; Globalization; Market-Based Theories; Neoclassical Economics; Transaction-Cost Theory

Further Readings

Barnet, R. J., & Mueller, R. E. (1974). *Global reach. The power of the international corporation.* New York: Simon & Schuster.

Braithwaite, J., & Drahos, P. (2000). *Global business regulation.* Cambridge, UK: Cambridge University Press.

Chandler, Jr., A. D., & Mazlish, B. (Eds.). (2005). *Leviathans: Multinational corporations and the new global history.* Cambridge, UK: Cambridge University Press.

Hennart, J. (2001). Theories of the multinational enterprise. In A. M. Rugman & T. L. Brewer (Eds.), *The Oxford handbook of international business* (pp. 127–149). Oxford, UK: Oxford University Press.

Hymer, S. (1976). *The international operations of national firms: A study of direct foreign investment.* Cambridge: MIT Press.

Jones, M. T. (2003). Globalization and the organization(s) of exclusion in advanced capitalism. In S. Clegg & R. Westwood (Eds.), *Debating organization* (pp. 252–270). Oxford, UK: Blackwell.

Kobrin, S. J. (2001). Sovereignty@bay: Globalization, multinational enterprise, and the international political system. In A. M. Rugman & T. L. Brewer (Eds.), *The Oxford handbook of international business* (pp. 181–205). Oxford, UK: Oxford University Press.

Prasad, A. (Ed.). (2003). *Postcolonial theory and organizational analysis: A critical engagement.* New York: Praeger.

Scherer, A. G., Palazzo, G., & Baumann, D. (2006). Global rules and private actors: Towards a new role of the TNC in global governance. *Business Ethics Quarterly, 16*(4), 505–532.

INTERNATIONAL MANAGEMENT

International management is the application of management concepts, techniques, tools, and skills in multinational corporations (MNCs) operating in cross-cultural environments. Specifically, international management applies organizing, planning, leading, and controlling techniques to achieve coordination and control the variety of operating contexts in which MNCs compete. International management is experiencing a dramatic growth in importance in response to the exponential growth of the global economy. MNC success relies on a basic understanding and foundation in international management.

Conceptual Overview

The practice of international trade is ageless. Archeologists document thousands of years of movement of goods and services between societies. In less than 50 years, the field of international management has moved into the foreground as international business has grown in importance relative to domestic business activity. In 2004, Fortune 500 companies experienced growth in employment in their foreign operations that was seven times higher than the growth in their domestic operations; European, Asian, and other firms around the world are experiencing similar dynamics. International management grapples with disappearing boundaries among functional business activities, between organizations and across nations; dynamic work environments characterized by rapid change; and entry of new international players like Haier and Lenovo from China, Cemex from Mexico, Embraer from Brazil, Gazprom from Russia, and Tata and Mittal from India. In addition, information technology is flattening the world.

Organizing

MNCs are very large companies engaged in international business activities. They may have manufacturing, service, sales, or research and development sites in different countries around the world and may be organized in a variety of ways. One common MNC structure is the miniature replica in which almost all of the home country headquarters functions are replicated in a stand-alone fashion in each country in which the MNC operates. This structure is typical of MNCs that produce personal care or food products. Other MNCs are organized in very centralized structures where functions like finance and research and development are retained in the home country and only production, service delivery, or sales occurs in the foreign country. This is more typical of MNCs producing standardized products like consumer electronics, telecommunications equipment, and computer products.

While almost all companies and all countries in the world are involved in international business, a small number of MNCs from a small number of countries dominate global trade. The 10 largest MNCs produced more than the total gross domestic product (GDP) of the 100 smallest countries. The diversity MNCs encounter in operating environments results in their need to understand and respond to these differences.

Operating environment complexity only increases as the number of host countries increases; thus, MNCs often have very complex organizational structure. In addition, the boom in use of information technology means that MNCs encounter networked, integrated work spaces that extend the need for international management into global, virtual, and even asynchronous work contexts.

To make matters worse, MNCs have entered into mergers four times more often in 2000 than just 3 years earlier, from 2,100 to more than 9,200 in a 3-year period: this pace continues. By 2000, more than 40% of all mergers were cross-border, a statistic that highlights the importance of international management. Almost overnight, the world has gotten smaller and bigger for international managers and the MNCs in which they work. It has gotten smaller because MNCs are so extensively networked and integrated with partners around the world. It has gotten bigger because MNCs enjoy significant business opportunities beyond the domestic corporation's organizational and national boundaries.

Planning

Regardless of their structure, MNCs must execute a sustainable strategy that amplifies the benefits of its resources and competencies. This is done through the MNC planning process that seeks fit between the operating context, the MNC's available resources, and the leadership vision. Operating context is what dramatically differentiates international management from domestic management. The operating context in which international management occurs varies along political, economic, regulatory, social, technological, environmental, and cultural dimensions. MNCs experience push and pull from all of the dimensions in their operating context. Operating context is so important that it attracts much attention from international management practitioners and scholars alike.

Planning begins with a PESTE analysis to understand the international operating context. PESTE is shorthand for political-regulatory, economic, sociocultural, technological, and ecological environments in which business occurs.

The *political-regulatory environment* influences potential risk. For example will the firm's intellectual property be protected? Is the political environment sufficiently stable to support uninterrupted business activity? Does regulation require a joint venture to enter the market? Does the legal system support the enforcement of contracts?

The *economic environment* influences financial resources available within a country through institutions like a developed banking system, and through economic dynamics like growth rates and inflation rates.

The *sociocultural environment* influences key resources such as the availability of a desirable workforce with appropriate levels of skills and abilities, language spoken, and general level of education. The cultural environment has significant impact on all people-related business activities, their tastes and preferences as customers, and values and beliefs as employees.

The *technological environment* influences infrastructure including the access to and availability of communication and information technologies, and basic infrastructure like roads, electricity, water, and shipping or logistic options.

The *ecological environment* influences air and pollution level regulations and corporate responsibility dynamics that may constrain or enhance business activities.

All in all, operating context influences the level of profitability a firm can achieve, risk that it encounters, the tastes and preferences of its customers, and the values and beliefs of its workers; thus they are key inputs to the planning process. Several of these dimensions are singled out for a more detailed exploration of their impact on international management.

Economic Environment

Economic competition transcends national borders. The patterns and influences of economic activity far outreach the boundaries of countries. Today more than half of the largest economic entities in the world are businesses, not countries. In the past decade alone, international flows of investment to developed countries increased by more than 300% and the international flows of investment into developing countries increased by more than 600%. Corporations contend with foreign competition even if they remain in their home country. From 70% to 90% of all United States headquartered corporations face some form of foreign competition at home, and this is even more dramatic for local firms in non-U.S. markets. Thus, international management is important even for domestic firms. Companies around the world must acquire international management skills and abilities to implement defensive or offensive strategies.

Political Environment

The political context is the most controversial dimension of the MNCs operating context. There is an ongoing debate about the impact of globalization on countries. One side maintains that globalization constrains the country by limiting its ability to set policy and protect domestic companies. This perspective contends that global institutions, including the MNCs described above, gradually will take over the functions and power of countries. The evidence is the proliferation of international economic institutions, such as the World Trade Organization (WTO) and the International Monetary Fund (IMF), that facilitate a relatively barrier-free flow of goods, services, and capital around the world. These powerful international organizations influence the operating context in which international management is practiced, often more than any individual country. In addition, regional treaties such as the North American Free Trade Association (NAFTA), the European Union (EU), or the Association of South East Asian Nations (ASEAN) drive economic integration within geographical regions and have the most immediate impact on local businesses and business opportunities for foreign competitors.

The other side of the globalization debate argues that countries become more important as they control the conditions for creating growth and are key players in organizations and treaties that address global problems. Robert Reich, former U.S. Secretary of Labor, contends that countries create and maintain economic opportunity for their citizens through ensuring that their citizens have world-class skills to attract interesting and well-paying jobs. Michael Porter, a thought leader on strategic management and planning, contends that countries have the ability to control factor conditions, including land, labor, capital, and infrastructure, that influence the development of globally competitive industries within their boundaries. Examples of this include Italy in fashion, Japan in automobiles and consumer electronics, India in information technology services, or the United States in entertainment. The political environment enhances or constrains a company's ability to control its operations and particularly matters in international management because it can influence the quality, cost, and availability of the factors of production available to manufacturers and service providers alike as they implement strategies.

Cultural Context

Culture is the operating context dimension that attracts the most attention because it drives the behavior of people—customers, employees, and even other stakeholders in the communities in which MNCs operate. Culture is learned knowledge, learned from families, from institutions such as schools and churches, at work, and from friends. Cultural knowledge drives the formation of beliefs and values about what is good and bad and leads to the creation of attitudes about what is fair and unfair, or moral and immoral. These beliefs and values in turn influence behavior under different circumstances. Culture and national differences strongly influence attitudes and expectations; consequently they influence on-the-job behavior of individuals and groups and the expectations that employees have of their leaders and control systems. Cultural differences influence communication—language, communication patterns, timing, protocol, content, and style; consequently they influence hierarchical relationships and control systems that MNCs use for feedback on strategy implementation outcomes. Culture is dynamic: it does change, but only slowly.

A criticism of globalization is that it leads to cultural homogeneity through mass media, and business interaction and integration that diminishes cultural differences. Specifically, global norms, ideas, and practices are overtaking local values. The response to this criticism is that global culture stresses the value of cultural difference itself and that global norms, ideas, and practices are always interpreted through the lens of local culture.

Leading

Leadership in MNCs is a culturally bound practice. There is an emerging consensus that international managers must understand both cultural similarities and cultural differences. In the groundbreaking GLOBE study, House and colleagues found that it is imperative to understand the culturally endorsed leadership profile of the culture cluster in which international managers work. In the pioneering international business culture study, Geerte Hofstede identified cultural differences and similarities in 40 countries and contends that differences in cultural values must be understood but that MNCs must resolve differences in practice, often through the efforts of its leaders, if their strategies are to be successfully implemented.

Christopher Early and Elaine Mosakowski recommend international leader development to increase cultural intelligence or CQ. Cultural intelligence comprises knowledge, rote learning about cultural aspects of foreign cultures; body language, adapting people's habits and mannerisms as evidence that you have entered their world; and "heart," which is the persistence to overcome the obstacles and setbacks encountered in cultures different from one's own. They have demonstrated that cultural intelligence can be developed. Management guru Peter Drucker advised that tomorrow's business challenges will be less technical than they will be cultural. He asserted that culture must be managed just like any other business phenomenon for successful strategy implementation.

The unprecedented global search for goods and services coupled with intense pressure on cost containment has driven businesses toward internationalization to compete or even survive. In the global economy resources—goods, services, technology, people, and capital—flow and move freely across national boundaries. Despite this ebb and flow, the MNCs fundamental resource is people; the human talent of any organization who plan and implement strategies and coordinate business activity and resource flows. Prominent international management scholars believe that globally competitive MNCs sustain their edge through the unique talent of their human resources that rests on international human resource management systems for managing a supply of cross-culturally competent global leaders and workers who are capable of coordinating the international efforts of the company. Consequently, international management is also concerned with trends in the world labor market. The MNC must contend with aging workers in industrialized countries like the United States, Japan, and Germany. MNCs experience a shift in workforce demographics that includes an increase in women and minorities in a traditionally homogeneous male workforce.

In summary, the single critical success factor in international management lies with the pool of competent international leaders supported by skilled global workers who have the knowledge of the MNCs production and service capabilities and an understanding of consumer demands around the world. These leaders are key to control in MNCs.

Controlling

The international management tools and skills that help MNCs control their far-flung operations are part of their international human resource management systems and practices. Cultural sensitivity in the implementation of these systems and practices are necessary to successfully implement strategy and maximize strategic alignment and control. Effective control requires that the international manager on expatriate assignment demonstrate dual allegiance—to MNC headquarters and to the local affiliate—as they execute their duties.

The literature offers some major recommendations for international business leaders as they endeavor to control MNCs. First among these is that there is no one way of doing things. International leaders must achieve their given objectives through a variety of methods and approaches. Second, there are similarities and differences among leaders around the world, and culture is considered the most important influencing variable. Here, deep cultural understanding is key to effective control. Third, the international leader is often responsible for managing the inherent tension between the MNCs desire for global standardization and local market needs and desires for responsiveness. Balancing this tension is a critical control function. Fourth, the international business leader bridges distance, culture, and time as he or she practices international management. Finally, leaders on expatriate assignments must demonstrate a dual allegiance, that is allegiance to the parent organization and allegiance to the local affiliate in which they work. They are truly the linchpin in MNC control.

Critical Commentary and Future Directions

There is no hiding place for MNCs or their leaders in the new, complex, integrated, dynamic, global business environment. More than ever it is essential that the international management field increasingly addresses the subtlety and nuance of challenges faced by international managers. The field is well developed when it comes to understanding the easily measured, the visible, or the obvious—trade flows, global strategies, political risk, legal and regulatory environments, or MNC structures, for example. Nevertheless, when it comes to more nuanced, sociocultural challenges like cross-cultural leadership, alliance effectiveness, multicultural virtual team management, international human resource management best practice, cross-border merger integration, local consumer behavior, or global human supply-chain development, much of the work in the field of international management appears to be biased toward context-free knowledge that is universal and not subject to specific contextual influences. There is consensus among international management practitioners and scholars that context matters and that contextualizing understanding is important to produce usable knowledge to guide international managers. This is easier said than done.

What is the "context" that should be used to contextualize understanding? Many scholars urge that context-embedded research ought to include social, cultural, legal, economic, and even institutional variables. Although such contextualization will strengthen our understanding of international management at, for example, the organizational, institutional, and national levels, this type of contextualizing reveals only one type of context—the context that can be historically verified, seen, or measured by the scholar. The contextualization descriptions that scholars typically provide tend to favor descriptors derived from a PESTE analysis with a bias toward demographic descriptors such as age, gender, or ethnicity. Despite the number of these demographic descriptors, these are all of a kind; they do not provide understanding of the cultural context. It is the cultural context that provides insights into the people-based challenges and opportunities core to effective planning, controlling, leading, and organizing, core dimensions on which international management rests.

The next frontier in international management must be a deeper and more nuanced understanding of the cultural environment and the psychological context or global mind-set that enables effective leadership, one of the key dimensions of international management. Culture and global mind-set are where the truly perplexing and persistent challenges in the international management domain reside. Consequently, scholars who produce useful knowledge about the multiple cultures and mind-sets within which MNCs operate will provide international managers with the keys to success in meeting contemporary challenges. International business leaders and the MNCs in which they work must develop a global supply chain of leaders with well-developed global mind-sets. In sum, global mind-set matters and deep understanding in this domain promises to guide international managers and the MNCs in which they work toward highly effective performance. Of equal importance, the cultural context matters and it must be made explicit and understood—in all its complexity, difficulty in observation, and messiness—to ensure international management effectiveness.

—*Mary B. Teagarden*

See also Cultural Intelligence; International Human Resource Management

Further Readings

Black, J., S., Morrison, A. J., & Gregerson H. B. (1999). *Global explorers: The next generation of leaders.* New York: Routledge.

Earley, P. C., & Mosakowski, E. (2004). Cultural intelligence. *Harvard Business Review, 82,* 139–153.

Evans, P., Doz, Y., & Laurent, A. (1990). *Human resource management in the international firm.* New York: St. Martin's.

Hofstede, G. (1980). *Culture's consequences: International differences in work-related values.* Beverly Hills, CA: Sage.

House, R. J., Hanges, P. H., Javidan, M., Dorfman, P. W., & Gupta, V. (2004). *Culture, leadership, and organizations.* Thousand Oaks, CA: Sage.

Javidan, M., & House, R. J. (2001). Cultural acumen for the global manager: Lessons from project GLOBE. *Organizational Dynamics, 29*(4), 289–305.

Porter, M. (1990). *Competitive advantage of nations.* New York: Free Press.

Reich, R. B. (1991). *The work of nations.* New York: Knopf.

INTERORGANIZATIONAL RELATIONS AND COLLABORATIONS

In its simplest form, interorganizational relations and collaboration (IRC) refers to any form of relationship between two or more organizations. This can include both formal collaborations such as alliances, joint ventures, and partnerships and/or formal or informal networks. IRCs are relatively new forms of organizations that have emerged in response to increasingly uncertain, ambiguous, and complex environments. Broadly defined, IRCs are any mode of organizing in which two or more organizations come together to pool and share resources, knowledge, risk, and rewards in order to deliver a service and/or product. As Barbara Gray argued almost 20 years ago, IRCs are a process through which actors explore solutions that go beyond their own limited representations.

Conceptual Overview

Through IRCs, organizations can share resources in order to pursue their strategic objectives. These resources can include information, knowledge, expertise and experience, financial resources, management and managerial control systems, and complex dynamic capabilities such as leadership, access to networks, governance structures, processes, and so on. As such, IRCs appear as alternative modes of organizational development to more traditional internal or external modes of development. Organizations involved in IRCs can gain access to and share resources without bearing the cost and risks of internal or external development.

The use of IRCs has grown during the past decades due to a number of drivers. The first driver is globalization; the opening of the world economy has brought with it the necessity to compete globally. Hence, many companies choose IRCs in order to reduce the scope and/or to outsource some of their activities. A second driver is the importance of fixed costs, such as research and development investments or market entry costs necessary in some industries. Such costs are usually associated with the rapidity of technological evolution and diffusion. A third important driver is that of economies of scale that are sometimes required when operating in narrow or uncertain markets. The pooling of resources, skills, knowledge, and expertise allows organizations to build upon and highlight their strengths and cover their weaknesses. This means that considerations such as joint developments and innovations between partners from different industries, or possessing and accessing complementary resources, are also strong drivers for IRCs. Industries such as the pharmaceutical industry or the computer industry are typically underpinned by such drivers; thus, it is not surprising that the level of IRC is especially high in these two industries. Another critical driver for IRCs is the constant development of information technologies and the Internet as a market, thus leading to increased possibilities of collaborative work and engendering interorganizational virtual networks through collaborative computer mediated communications.

Underpinning each and every one of these drivers is the attempt for organizations to reduce the risk, complexity, and ambiguity they face in an ever increasingly complex world. IRCs are, for the most part, a response to risk.

Typology of IRCs

IRC covers a wide range of interorganizational arrangements. IRCs can include formal hierarchical contract-based relationships of supply chains; for example, McDonald's has a vast supply-chain relationship with a range of large and small organizations held together by black letter contracts and by McDonald's size and power as a global organization. Other IRCs may be in the form of outsourcing in which an organization closes aspects of its noncore operations and outsources to another organization that can do it cheaper and more efficiently. IRCs can be more complex, as in the form of joint ventures between two or more organizations coming together to bid for a contract, produce a product, or provide a service. Similarly an IRC may be a strategic alliance with or without shared equity (i.e., ownership) or a relationship-based alliance in which risks and rewards are shared. In reality, almost any situation in which multiple organizations come together to achieve an outcome can be thought of as an IRC, be it a collaboration between local, national, and international organizations to bring foreign aid to a third world nation, or a partnership between private firms to build the world's largest cruise ship.

While there are many types of IRCs, the very nature of the relationship depends on the preexistence of potential market negotiation or competition between the organizations involved in the IRCs. As touched upon above, these preexisting market conditions lead to the distinction between alliances among competitors, vertical partnerships, and symbiotic cooperation between noncompetitors.

Alliances concern IRCs between members of the same sector of activity, be they in direct competition in the same markets or operating in different markets—be they marketing segments or countries. In alliances, competition is an inevitable specter that can at any time affect the mutual development of the alliance partnership. The main difficulty of entering into IRCs is in the need for members to be able to free themselves from blind short-term oriented opportunism. Hence, as argued by B. Garette and P. Dussauge in 2000, alliances must be analyzed according to their scope, the convergence of competencies, and the degree of remaining competition in the market in order to reduce the need or temptation for opportunistic behavior. In other words, IRCs require a high level of trust and cooperative behavior. In an alliance in which scope is limited to a very precise step in the value chain, the risk of opportunism is high because members are not engaged together in a project that mutually binds them. The stakes are limited to a single project and its contribution to the specific value chain. On projects in which partners share equity, risk, and rewards, it might be easier to organize the cooperation through a dedicated project team. Doing so is said to create the conditions for local commitment and shared identity required in IRCs according to Tyrone Pitsis and colleagues.

A similar line of argument can be developed regarding IRC competencies. Competencies refer to the skills, knowledge, and expertise each collaborative partner brings to the interorganizational relationship. When the competencies are different, the interest to cooperate is obvious—it makes sense to collaborate with people and organizations that add value in terms of differing skills, knowledge, and so on. Of course, the temptation to try and capture the competency of the partner so as to become independent might be high in such situations. Direct market competition obviously makes cooperation more difficult, especially when the scope of the alliance is important, creating a tension between the necessity to cooperate and the difficulty to generate some form of goal alignment. As such, trust becomes a critical factor of most IRCs, especially alliances.

Vertical partnerships correspond to cooperation between suppliers and customers. In many sectors, vertical partnerships have emerged as an alternative to a purely price-mediated relationship between buyers and suppliers. This evolution was driven by a combination of the core competency focus of major companies and the benefits associated by conjunctive innovation efforts where learning was a necessity for survival. Nonetheless, vertical partnerships are not exempt from tensions resulting from market mechanisms. Creating a spirit of cooperation oriented toward innovation between partners whose relationship history is one of confrontation and conflict during the harsh negotiation processes is not easy. Still, Christophe Midler described how Renault made it possible in the case of the design of the small car *Twingo*. First, co-contractors were selected at a very early stage on the basis of a clear cost target. Any cost improvement achieved beyond this target cost through the design-to-cost process was shared between partners. The result neutralized the negative impact of negotiation on innovative design based on knowledge-exchange and mutual learning. Second, all participants to the project were brought together at the same location so as to create a sense of belonging. By the edification of new boundaries specific to the cooperation, the objective was to break down interorganizational boundaries. The experience proved successful on key elements of the project.

Finally, symbiosis corresponds to alliances between partners that do not necessarily belong to the same industry. In such a case, the establishment of a real cooperative game is more likely to emerge, as there is no history of competition or competitive negotiation in the relationship. Moreover, symbiotic relationships are more likely to project the members into new environments that will foster coexploration. This is not to say that the temptation to profit from the benefits of such cooperation is absent in symbiosis. However, the basis for the negotiation of common meanings and objectives might be easier to establish in such relations, hence yielding the full benefit of a reasonably long-term relationship should be easier.

Through a combination of these typologies of IRCs, organizations can escape their boundaries and gain access to competencies and resources that can be used to leverage their own success. That is, the organization is no longer constrained by its own boundaries but rather the center of a web of resources and competencies accessible through various relationships and networks, both tightly and loosely coupled. Yet, if such conditions are to be realized, it would mean that partners would need to fully accept that they are players in a cooperative game. That is to say, players accept that their long-term commitment to the partnership will yield higher benefits than would otherwise be realized through short-term opportunism. Nonetheless, in the reality of IRCs, and their daily organization, such an excessively rational reasoning is not enough to ensure that such ideals will be realized—simply saying "we are in this together, and we trust each other" does not necessarily make it so. The strategic objective rationale behind cooperation cannot be separated from the actual behavior of actors that respond through their fears and values, among which individualism might come first. Hence, much of the success of cooperations resides in the strength of their organization and not only in the clarity of their strategic ambition.

IRCs in Context: Some Issues for Concern

IRCs cannot be isolated from their context, a context that is often challenging to the development of cooperation. Underlying context is the dominance of hierarchical power-based organizational relationships that typify most markets. Because IRCs represent the new boundaries of the organization, they constitute spaces of exchange located at the periphery of the hierarchies and bureaucracies they stem from and are thus under the influence of these organizational hierarchic and bureaucratic spaces. In that sense, they are confronted with a paradox whereby the organizational periphery is becoming central to the strategy but might be jeopardized by organizational bureaucracy and hierarchical control. Bureaucratic rigidity thus constantly threatens interorganizational cooperative efforts because a can-do culture where improvisation and flexibility are needed can become constrained by overly bureaucratic and hierarchical control.

In addition, because organizing can be an issue of power and control, some organizations, especially larger ones, might seek to be the center or hub of the relationships in order to control the lesser partners in the relationship and to ensure their own interests prevail. If obtaining this centrality within an extended network is the ultimate strategic objective, then the network becomes the place of power games. It means that the quest for a mutually beneficial and reasonably long-term cooperation is necessarily questioned by the temptation of opportunism. This contradiction inherent to IRC is also present across vanishing industry boundaries where companies are caught in shifting games of multiple cooperation alliances. That is, when several companies are involved in multiple alliances, how knowledge is shared across those varied alliances is complex and difficult, if not impossible, to control. To put it simply, in a pragmatic sense, organizations can never be monogamous, yet many go into relationships as if they can be or should be. Such ideas should be seriously questioned when forming or managing IRCs.

Game theory aims at constructing conceptualizations that show how cooperative games are rational. Unfortunately, such reasoning is not sufficient to attain a state that can be described as one of synthesis. Synthesis can only be reached if opportunism and self-interest are constantly counterbalanced by trust and openness between actors. Indeed, the dynamics of IRCs make it extremely difficult to maintain relations over time simply because at some point or another at least one partner will need to seek new relations. Moreover, the stakes, benefits yielded, and objectives of participants are constantly shifting, naturally putting pressure on the cooperation. Each time an imbalance surfaces, the cooperation can fall from a virtuous circle of trust characterized by behaviors in conformance with mutually shared interests to a vicious circle where mistrust leads to self-interested behaviors and opportunism. This is a normal and necessary safeguard against opportunism and possible leaks of strategic knowledge. In other words, protecting the partners against opportunism can limit or destroy the potential of the collaboration. IRCs are, therefore, complex spaces, and the balance between control and freedom in terms of contracts is a difficult game.

The question of trust and trust-infusing mechanisms thus appears as central to reaching a state of synthesis necessary for the long-term success of IRCs. Trust is definitely calculative, in the sense that it incorporates some form of probabilistic expectation that the other will act in accordance to specific expectations. More often than not, the probability calculation is hard to base on facts. Hence, in any emerging relationship, trust-infusing mechanisms have an important role to play. This is why contracts are an important foundation of IRCs. This is especially relevant to Oliver Williamson's discussion of credible commitment and hostages in which breaking contracts can have serious costs. Nonetheless, there is no such thing as a contract that can warranty against opportunism. The contract cannot come first in a relationship that aims at developing more than a simple market exchange. Trust is often established over time and necessitates the accumulation of an emotional experience shared between members of the partnership. This is a local construction that emerges from the local interactions of the actors and thus cannot be included in the actual contract but rather constitute what becomes the psychological contracts that binds members to the partnership and is crucial to its final success.

If trust is a local construct, IRCs might be conceived of globally but need to be constructed locally to ensure the notion of trust is shared. For example, at the global level if a number of organizations join together in the United States to do business in, say, Iraq, what chance of success is there if there is no locally constructed trust? The case is no different if a number of New York–based organizations sought to develop IRCs in Texas. This is also why organizational arrangements that favor the dedication of resources to a specific interorganizational entity, rather than one organization, are more likely to lead to successful IRCs. This is the case of dedicated project teams; project teams lead to the edification of new boundaries that achieve the necessary buffering effect and isolate a space of cooperation where trust is more likely to happen. In fact, it could be argued that it is the emergence of some form of cultural convergence that is sought. A quest for cultural convergence calls for adequate project leadership that can embody the vision of the IRC. Still, boundary-spanning activities are also necessary in order to maintain a connection with the organizations of origin. Such activities will of course happen through formal mechanisms, such as reporting, budgeting, or strategic planning, but also thanks to looser forms such as informal networks or communities of practices. It is only if such a balance between boundary buffering and boundary spanning can be achieved that IRCs can deliver their full potential.

Critical Commentary and Future Directions

Two major debates in the field of organization studies can orient future research on IRCs. First is the argument between the transaction-cost and the resource-based—and subsequently the knowledge-based—views of the firm. Second is that of the interplay between governance, governmentality, and culture.

Interorganizational Advantage

The century-old debate on market failure—and the organizational advantage—has not spared IRCs. For a long time, transaction-cost economics was the central approach to explaining so-called hybrid forms. IRCs were considered as an intermediary form between market and hierarchy. The argument was that, in order to reduce transaction costs, hybrid forms were to be avoided in case of uncertainty. Hybrid forms would thus be adapted only for reasonably certain environments.

The competitive theory in explaining the existence of the firm is the resource-based view of the firm and its associated development toward the knowledge-based view of the firm. This theory provides a much more satisfactory explanation of the fact that companies tend to resort to IRC in case of uncertain environment. It is indeed the capacity of IRC to offer new possibilities in terms of knowledge creation and combination that can explain the most outstanding results. It is not only the access to resources that is important in IRCs but also the capacity to combine resources held by two or more organizations into new capabilities thus allowing for innovations. Such relationships can give birth to an interorganizational advantage despite the possible increase of transaction costs. Consequently, when pursuing IRCs, cost control may need to be a lower order interest, especially where innovations are central to the objectives or aims. Put simply, some IRCs can be very expensive, and while this is not always the case, cost may be a poor indicator of success.

Future research might focus on tackling value in IRCs, such as innovation, knowledge, and so on, especially in the case of multiple companies simultaneously working on multiple alliances. Indeed, if there is such a thing as an interorganizational advantage, it lies in the capacity of partners to leverage and combine their knowledge so as to redeploy their resources dynamically in order to form new strategic capabilities. Current research is far from understanding such complex phenomena at the interorganizational level.

Governance, Governmentality, and Culture

Approaches to IRCs are also characterized by an excess of confidence on governance mechanisms, even though their success is mainly dependant on the construction of a local dynamic. The subject of governance structure is definitely an important one; governance structure shapes the relationships, behaviors, and intentions of IRCs. Individual actors involved in IRC necessarily position themselves toward the governance mechanisms ultimately connected with contacts at various levels (between organizations and between organizations and individuals). Nonetheless, governance structures constitute the background of IRC, but what happens in the foreground and the daily life of actors involved in the interaction is essential. This articulation between foreground and background structures is definitely an important object for future research.

The concept of governmentality introduced by Michel Foucault in 1979 sheds light on this articulation between formal governance mechanisms and the possible evolution of an IRC. Governmentality can be defined as consensual forms of subjugation. As argued by Stewart Clegg and colleagues, neoliberal forms of governance are premised on the active consent and subjugation of subjects rather than on domination or external control, which were the objective of modern bureaucratic modes of governance. Authenticity of empowering is certainly more efficient in order to achieve synthesis in IRCs than the vain attempt to control directly; there is no such thing as controlling the local construction of interindividual relationships. Hence, if IRCs are framed within governance structure, governmentality is definitely a key issue that still needs to be researched in more details. This implies to dig into the levels of individual psychology and interindividual relationship building if one is to really understand the stakes of IRC. It is only by combining multiple levels of analysis from the aggregate level of organizations and governance structure to the detailed one of individual interactions that future research can gain a thorough understanding of the connection between the background and the foreground of IRC, between the institutional facade of governance and the everyday relationship experience of the actors.

It is also through these types of thorough approaches that the illusion of a unitary culture can materialize. Indeed, it would be vain to try to force upon individuals, through official discourse, the illusion of a unified IRC culture. If, as argued in a critical perspective, culture is fragmented and composed of conflicting and contradictory elements, than the projection of such a culture is an exercise of power that can only be fruitful if all stakeholders are able to integrate a metamessage by which behind the unity of discourse a reassurance on the acceptance of differences is conveyed. This calls for an acceptance of otherness in the philosophical sense of the term by all actors and especially by management. It is only by recognizing the necessity and the illusion of a common identity that we can progress in our understanding of the complexity of the mechanisms involved at the individual and interindividual level in IRCs. Perspective such as emotional intelligence, to the extent that it contributes to establishing the empathy necessary in order to experience otherness, should thus be integrated to further research on IRCs.

—Emmanuel Josserand and Tyrone S. Pitsis

See also Alliances; Networks; Outsourcing; Social Capital

Further Readings

Blau, P. (1964). *Exchange and power in social life.* New York: Wiley.

Clegg, S. R., Pitsis, T., Rura-Polley, T., & Marosszeky, M. (2002). Governmentality matters: Designing an alliance culture of inter-organizational collaboration for managing projects. *Organization Studies, 23*(3), 317–337.

Foucault, M. (1979). *Discipline and punish.* Harmondsworth, UK: Penguin.

Garette, B., & Dussauge, P. (2000). Alliances versus acquisitions: Choosing the right option. *European Management Journal, 18*(1), 63–69.

Gray, B. (1989). *Collaborating: Finding common ground for multiparty problems.* San Francisco: Jossey-Bass.

Hibbert, P., & Huxham, C. (2005). A little about the mystery: Process learning as collaboration involves. *European Management Review, 2*(1), 59–69.

Josserand, E., Clegg, S., Kornberger, M., & Pitsis, T. S. (2004). Friends or foes? Practicing collaboration. *M@n@gement, 7*(3), 37–45.

Midler, C. (1995). Projectification of the firm: The Renault case. *Scandinavian Journal of Management, 11*(4), 363–375.

Pitsis, T., Clegg, S. R, Marosszeky, M., & Rura-Polley, T. (2003). Constructing the Olympic dream: Managing innovation through the future perfect. *Organization Science, 14*(5), 574–590.

Pitsis, T. S., Josserand, E., Clegg, S., & Kornberger, M. (2005). Inter-organizational alliances and networks, *M@n@gement, 8*(4), 69–72.

Williamson, O. (1983). Credible commitments: Using hostages to support exchange. *American Economic Review, 73*(4), 519–540.

INTERPRETIVE THEORY

Interpretive theory is constituted of a family of approaches rooted in the German idealist tradition, beginning with Immanuel Kant's emphasis on the importance of *a priori* knowledge of mind as preceding any attempt to grasp empirical experience. This tradition, which included theorists such as Wilhelm Dilthey, Max Weber, Edmund Husserl, and Alfred Schutz, provided the grounds for challenging sociological positivism. These challenges included the understanding that science was not (and could not be) as value free and as providing objective, unmediated access to universal truth as previously assumed and, second, that the nomothetic methods employed in the natural sciences in search of general laws and causal explanation were seen as unsuitable for the cultural sciences, aiming to understand human life, its processes, and products.

From an interpretive perspective, the subject matter of sociology is not a predetermined universe of objects, but one that is constituted by active agents. The constitution of the social world should be seen as a skilled accomplishment, rather than as a mechanical, determined series of processes. Agency in this view is intentional but not unbounded; it is historically located and both constrained and enabled by broader structures. These structures are not separate and overarching, but are constituted through agents' actions and social practices in the context of structuration processes imbued with dimensions of meanings, norms, and power. Nomological analysis, where behaviors are positivistically understood and analyzed, also has a place as an avenue for explaining the structural properties of social systems but is seen as unsuitable for gaining in-depth interpretive understanding.

As the sociologist Anthony Giddens suggests, from the perspective of interpretive theory researchers interpret social life through drawing on their own stocks on knowledge and preunderstandings; and to understand a form of life they have to immerse themselves in it, but taking care not to become uncritical natives. Researchers' descriptions are then mediated by the discursive categories of social science, obeying a double hermeneutic, involving the second-order interpretations by researchers of the first-order interpretations of agents.

Conceptual Overview

Interpretively oriented approaches aim to achieve a meaningful understanding of the actors' frame of reference, what Dilthey and Weber referred to as *verstehen*. Dilthey suggested that whereas the natural sciences explain nature, human studies can understand expressions of cultural life based on a historical consciousness of lived experience. Dilthey's approach to interpretation privileged grasping this lived experience through its observable expressions. He viewed understanding as the comprehension of forms of life that can open up possibilities for our own experience. Influenced by the earlier writings of Friedrich Schleirmacher, as well as the positivist spirit of his time, Dilthey sought to develop objectively valid interpretations and data, to embed in the method of *verstehen* the search for scientific objectivity. Furthermore, in Weber's view, the aim to achieve in-depth, interpretive understanding is what distinguishes the social from the natural sciences. He saw *verstehen* as a methodological approach that could lead to knowledge that would both be able to access subjective meanings, as well as be comparable in objectivity to knowledge derived from the positivist tradition, an assumption often seen as problematic or overly ambitious.

Language and Social Construction in Interpretive Theory

Interpretive theory embraces a view of language as constitutive of social reality rather than as merely representational. According to John Thompson, the critiques of logical atomism represented by Bertrand Russell and the early Ludwig Wittgenstein (*Tractatus Logico-Philosophicus*), and its associated doctrine of logical positivism, provided a foundation for the social constructionist view. Ordinary language philosophy argued that there is no fixed essence denoted by words, as logical atomism held, but that rather words acquire their meaning through use, within particular language games (as Wittgenstein held in *Philosophical Investigations*) and within particular speech acts (as elaborated by the philosophers J. L. Austin and John R. Searle).

As W. Graham Astley has argued, this view of language implies that organization theories, and knowledge in general, do not provide objective access to truth, but are rather forms of linguistic representation mediated by one's worldview, and reinforced by institutional mechanisms. As the sociologists Peter Berger and Thomas Luckmann suggested, language is the most important sign system of human societies, and as such objectifies, typifies, and institutionalizes social and perceptual categories. Such a view does not deny the existence of objective realities, but accepts that human understanding of these realities is always mediated and subjectively constructed. Accordingly, the view of science that arises from this conception is not as a cumulative enterprise moving ever closer to truth, but as a paradigm-dependent, pluralistic, socially constructed enterprise whereby scientists do not discover fixed immutable truths but rather assign contingent meanings.

As Thomas Schwandt has noted, even though a distinction can be drawn between constructivism and interpretivism, based largely on the historical development of the two streams of thought, this distinction is more analytical than substantive since interpretivists and constructivists now share common concerns and perspectives. The social construction view as outlined by Kenneth Gergen assumes, for example, that there is no necessary relationship of correspondence between the terms by which humans understand the world and the world itself, that human modes of understanding and explanation are not free standing but relational, that these modes are not merely descriptions but actively construct one's world, and that reflexivity on and critique of these modes are essential for actively creating better futures.

Generalization and Validity in Interpretive Theory

Interpretivism is often erroneously equated with subjectivism, a view that interpretivism lacks objectivity, instead affording primacy to the idiosyncratic, subjective meanings of single actors with no necessary relation to a shared, intersubjective, and verifiable reality. If interpretivism were to assume fully subjective properties, this would suggest a potential for unlimited interpretations of observations and research data, with no means of verification or validation. Some have suggested that interpretivists reject generalization since each instance of observed social interaction is unique and social settings are complex and indeterminate.

Interpretive understanding does not however equate with a degeneration to extreme subjectivism, unlimited interpretations, and the inability to make any kind of generalization. For Weber, the search for generalizations derived inductively from first-order data was both compatible with, and dependent on, meaningful understanding of social action. His ideal types were aimed to inductively derive second-order frameworks based on regularities and patterns of empirically observed and theorized phenomena. Umberto Eco further suggested that the potential for unlimited interpretations does not imply that all interpretations are equally likely or valid. Interpretations of texts (or other cultural manifestations), for example, can be informed or guided by the semantic meaning of the words, the internal coherence of the text, the cultural context, the interpreter's own frame of reference, and the interpreter's immersion into the life-worlds from which the texts or cultural artifacts arise from and refer to.

Furthermore, a distinction has been made by Malcolm Williams between total generalizations (deterministic laws or axioms), statistical generalizations (where the probability of a situation or feature occurring can be calculated from its instances within a sample representative of a wider population), and moderatum generalizations (where aspects of a situation are exemplars of broader sets of features). Williams suggests that interpretive research does not aim to make total or statistical generalizations, but can (and should) make moderatum generalizations, within the limits of the inductive problem (that one cannot unproblematically generalize from a small number of known cases to a large number of unknown ones), and the ontological problem of categorical equivalence (that generalizations within one category of experience of domain may not apply to other categories). Other discussions of generalizability in interpretive research have distinguished between statistical and analytical generalizability and have also proposed four types of generalizability, depending on whether it involves generalizing from or to empirical and theoretical statements.

As Jörgen Sandberg has proposed, criteria of goodness for interpretive research include various types of validity. *Communicative validity* can be achieved by establishing a fruitful community of interpretation between researcher and research participants, by striving for coherence in interpreting field data, and by research interpretations judged as credible by a peer group of researchers. *Pragmatic validity*, or the actionability of the knowledge produced, can be aimed for through means such as interviewing oriented to applied concerns, participant observation, or by actually employing such knowledge in practice. *Transgressive validity* can be achieved by such techniques as the use of irony to highlight preunderstandings or biases in research interpretations and by the search for differences and contradictions rather than for coherent patterns. Furthermore, *reliability* as interpretive awareness involves being clear not only about the steps and techniques employed in research, but also being conscious and reflexive about how one's own subjectivity influences the research process.

Critical Commentary and Future Directions

Interpretively oriented theories and approaches have been gaining ground in organization theory, serving as repositories of tools for empirical analysis, theoretical perspectives, and thoughtful commentaries on social life and the human condition. Organization theory over the years has been host to a wide variety of such theories and approaches, beginning with Egon Bittner's classic work on the concept of organization and David Silverman's critiques of functionalist sociology. Hermeneutics, phenomenology, symbolic interactionism, ethnomethodology, critical theory, storytelling analysis, metaphorical analysis, and rhetorical analysis have all constituted an interpretive repository of approaches that organization theorists draw on. While they have subtle differences, they are united by a voluntarist orientation, their acceptance of the social construction of reality through language and social practices, the importance of grasping first-order realities, the active nature of agency, and the historicality and situatedness of experience. These themes have been the focus of active studies and debates in organization theory, and this trend is likely to continue.

The assumption held by Weber and Dilthey, among others, however, that a method could provide both empathetic access to the ideational world as well as objective validity of the type sought in positivist science has been seen as problematic, and a contrast is often made (in Paul Ricoeur's work for example) between meaningful understanding of the type sought in interpretive theory on the one hand and explanation as the search for causal, lawlike deterministic regularities based on the natural science paradigm on the other. Others such as Richard Daft went further, viewing both interpretive and nomothetic research as forms of storytelling, characterized by the need to tell a plausible story effectively and believably linking the data, their interpretation, and research outcomes. Employing literary metaphors, he advocated designing research as a poem, containing just a few (two to four) research variables that cohere together and provide depth of meaning, rather than a novel that has numerous variables without all having tight interconnections within a meaningful whole.

Conceptual debates on method and validity have continued to this day and are unlikely to abate. They revolve around considerations of paradigm incommensurability, celebration of conceptual fragmentation and pluralism or attempts to banish it as destructive and unscientific, and the continuing search for integrative methodological approaches where understanding and explanation can operate in a complementary manner. *Verstehen* itself has moved from the methodological to the ontological plane, with Martin Heidegger's and Hans-Georg Gadamer's development of philosophical hermeneutics, concerned with the nature of being in and through language. According the Gadamer, the linguistic, aesthetic, and historical spheres acquire ontological status and constitute the hermeneutical experience.

—*Loizos Heracleous*

See also Critical Theory; Ethnomethodology; Hermeneutics; Language and Organizations; Metaphor and Organization; Phenomenology; Social Constructionism; Storytelling; Symbolic Interactionism

Further Readings

Astley, W. G. (1985). Administrative science as socially constructed truth. *Administrative Science Quarterly, 30,* 497–513.

Astley, W. G., & Van de Ven, A. H. (1983). Central perspectives and debates in organization theory. *Administrative Science Quarterly, 28,* 245–273.

Berger, P., & Luckmann, T. (1967). *The social construction of reality.* London: Penguin.

Burrell, G., & Morgan, G. (1979). *Sociological paradigms and organizational analysis.* Hants, UK: Gower.

Daft, R. L. (1983). Learning the craft of organizational research. *Academy of Management Review, 8,* 539–546.

Denzin, N. (1983). Interpretive interactionism. In G. Morgan (Ed.), *Beyond method: Strategies for social research* (pp. 129–146). Beverly Hills, CA: Sage.

Eco, U. (1990). *The limits of interpretation.* Bloomington: Indiana University Press.

Gergen, K. (1999). *An invitation to social construction.* Thousand Oaks, CA: Sage.

Giddens, A. (1993). *New rules of sociological method.* Stanford, CA: Stanford University Press.

Heracleous, L. (2006). *Discourse, interpretation, organization.* Cambridge, UK: Cambridge University Press.

Lee, A. S., & Baskerville, R. L. (2003). Generalizing generalizability in information systems research. *Information Systems Research, 14,* 221–243.

Prasad, A., & Prasad, P. (2002). The coming of age of interpretive organizational research. *Organizational Research Methods, 5,* 4–11.

Ricoeur, P. (1991). *From text to action.* Evanston, IL: Northwestern University Press.

Sandberg, J. (2005). How do we justify knowledge produced within interpretive approaches? *Organizational Research Methods, 8,* 41–68.

Schwandt. T. A. (1994). Constructivist, interpretivist approaches to human inquiry. In N. Denzin & Y. Lincoln (Eds.), *Handbook of qualitative research* (pp. 118–137). Thousand Oaks, CA: Sage.

Thompson, J. B. (1981). *Critical hermeneutics: A study in the thought of Paul Ricoeur and Jürgen Habermas.* Cambridge, UK: Cambridge University Press.

Williams, M. (2000). Interpretivism and generalization. *Sociology, 34,* 209–224.

Yin, R. (1994). *Case study research: Design and methods* (2nd ed.). Thousand Oaks, CA: Sage.

Iron Law of Oligarchy

Bureaucracy is an organizational form consisting of differentiated knowledge and many different forms of expertise, with its rules and disciplines arranged not only hierarchically in regard to each other, but also in a parallel manner. If moving through one track, in theory, one need not know anything about how things were done in the other tracks. Whether the bureaucracy was a public or private sector organization would be largely immaterial. Private ownership might enable one to control the revenue stream, but day-to-day control would, however, be done through the intermediation of experts. And expertise is always fragmented. This enables the bureaucracy to be captured by expert administrators, however democratic its mandate might be, as Michels argued in his famous *iron law of oligarchy*.

Thus, at its core the iron law of oligarchy argument, simply stated, suggests that professional organization, even in highly democratic organizations, will always end up being controlled by a small elite group. The reasons for this are quite simple: Michels's argument explicitly identifies structures of communication in the production and reproduction of oligarchy: first, there is an inequality of knowledge (between leaders and led), which, together with the existence of differential control over the means of communication, means that the constraints of limited time, limited space, and the relative lack of organizational energy of the led, outflanked as they are by the superior resources of those who presently rule, together with the uneven distribution of communicative skill (the arts of politics), means that the odds are weighted against the inequality being overcome.

Conceptual Overview

Oligarchy is located at the core of organizational power; it is the means of monopolizing and perpetuating resources of power through perfectly legal and rational processes. Michels's basic reasoning was that organization precludes democracy, because of immanent oligarchical tendencies. According to Michels, political leadership is incompatible with democracy. Organization necessitates oligarchy. Simply, any kind of association becomes more-or-less rapidly a minority of directors dominating a majority of those directed.

Power struggles are evident as the core process of internal oligarchization and thus create a paradox of democracy. According to Michels, organization necessitates delegation and dispersion of authority. Even organizations that are democratic in conception, in the goals they promote as inclusive reasons for membership, will fail to be democratic in the procedures and rules they design and use; they may be democratic in the plurality of interests they objectively and institutionally represent, rather than in the causes they actually promote through their strategies. Consequently, even if organizational forms end up transforming democratic regimes into oligarchic regimes, this influence will be exercised concretely through power struggles. It is simply the underlying arguments and criteria, deciding who governs, which are likely to evolve.

Oligarchy derives from the political process of the "professionalization of leadership" more-or-less directly, because the interests of the experts in leadership are expressed in a struggle between leaders, who, in striving to compete to solidify their own personal positions, clash with those of the "masses." Oligarchy stands diametrically opposed to democracy; thus, if we are to understand oligarchy we must understand debates about democracy in relation to organizations.

The work of Tocqueville, who presents a sophisticated theory of democracy through which we may see bureaucracies as associative rather than fragmenting and atomizing organizational systems, enables one to understand the dynamics of oligarchy and democracy. Democracy for Tocqueville is not restricted to popular government but is assimilated to a process of increasing social equality. Democracy is a way to cope with the ever-growing threats of modern times and the atomizing effects of modernization. It is a political and cultural cornerstone of institutions capable of sustaining political equality, despite the fragmenting and disempowering effects of modernity. Organizational democracies are settings in which every individual, in principle, might be an active participant if all individuals were formally equivalent in power and status. Equality is generated through the same types of processes as authority. It is a slow and often contested social construction involving power struggles. It is not the result of a discursive construct, but of political debates and contestation. For Tocqueville, this is the very essence of democracy, as a set of institutions whose engineering facilitates the emergence of intermediary forms of power, enabling conscious democratic decisions, and developing an individual and collective sense of responsibility. Democracy entails a whole set of moral values whose activation helps organizations both to avoid social isolation and the excessive domination of bureaucratic and centralized power. From a political point of view, Tocqueville usefully differentiates centralized government from centralized administration. The former refers to the concentration of power used to direct general interests of the whole community and is deemed necessary to the prosperity of any kind of collective. The latter refers to the concentration of power used to direct certain peculiar local interests, which, according to Tocqueville, is a threat to democracy.

To a certain extent, a neo-Tocquevillean theory would put forward the idea that reforms and redesigns of organizational forms should be carried out mostly by intermediary and associative groups. The treatment of equality within organizations, from a neo-Tocquevillean perspective, requires an understanding of power structures. In other words, the first meaning of democracy in the context of organizations is how to avoid different corporate oligarchies taking over from either rule-governed forms of expertise, or from custom-governed forms of aristocracy, and developing more or less legitimacy in the process. The problem for democracy is oligarchy, in other words, as Michels recognized. Political struggle is the very definition of democracy, the only outcome of which can be rule by one or other set of elites.

Critical Commentary and Future Directions

To sum up, whatever the origin of the analysis, the political continuum between, say, bureaucratic forms embedded in oligarchic regimes, and post-bureaucratic forms embedded in democratic regimes, inevitably displays the existence of central political antagonisms that cannot be concealed. The relationship between the dynamics of organizational forms along this continuum and the dynamics of organizational power is at the heart of the construction of the political performance of organizations and is absolutely central to any projects for designing a post-bureaucratic, new form of organization, as a more democratic inclusive space.

The political performance of organizations lies primarily in the patterns of authority encompassed in the political relationship of subordination and in the political relationship between rival leaders. To be brief, political performance is produced by the interactions between four characteristics of political systems. These comprise the model of leadership (what is the basis of the distance between the elite and the governed), the model of inclusiveness (degree of required-tolerated participation), the decision-making model (from open dialogue to monocratic forms of imposition), and the model of elite production (endogenously organized through career-functional types of backgrounds or exogenously generated through educational-familial-social kinds of backgrounds).

Figure 1 suggests the existence of diverse types of political performance. For instance, an organization producing its elite through internal mechanisms of career, making decisions through deliberative settings, privileging personality-based types of leadership and critical participation, would generate a specific type of political performance, a sort of intermingling between social resistance, avoidance, and the power of charisma. An organization recruiting its elites externally, making decisions from the center, valuing a leadership based on rules and a compliance-based model of inclusiveness, would resemble a bureaucratic type of political performance; i.e., a mix of structural and procedural stability and of externally generated forms of values and authenticity.

Usually, two categories of assumption help define the agenda when studying political performance. The first assumption is that the stability of governments is related to the way organizational forms are constructed (e.g., participative forms, decision-making processes and procedures, pathways to the top of organizations). A second assumption is that political performance does not depend primarily on the internal

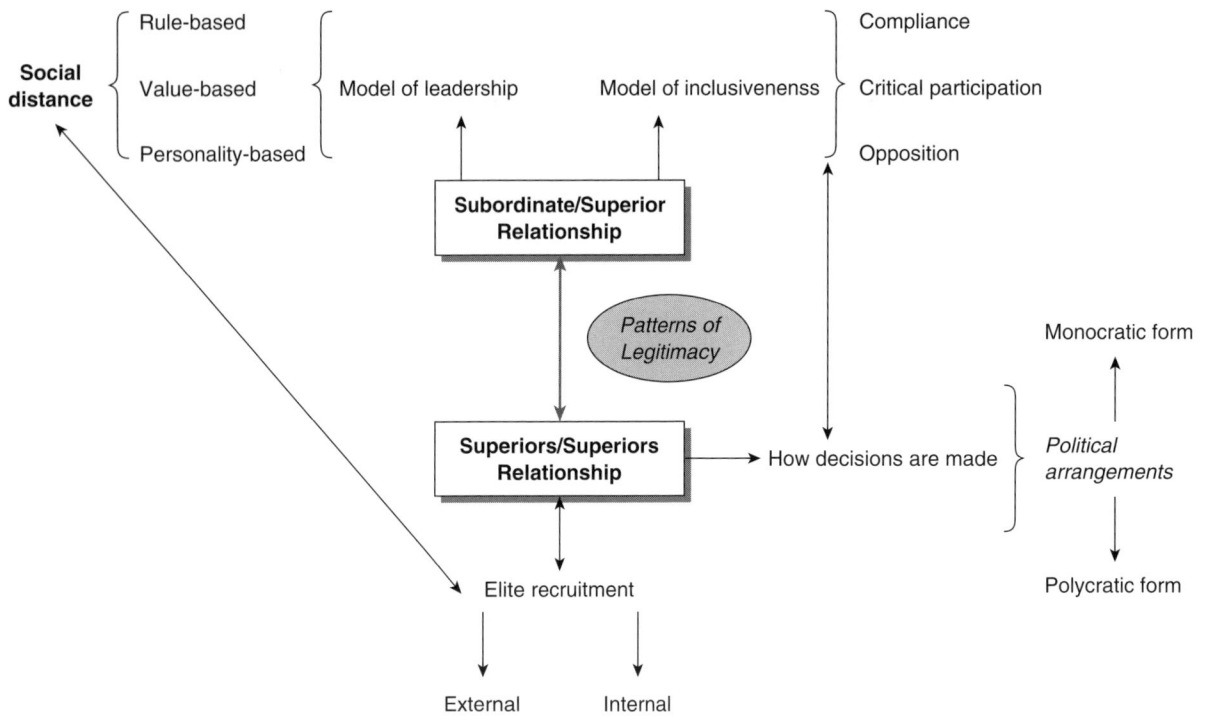

Figure 1 The Production of Political Performance

Source: S. R. Clegg, D. Courpasson, and N. Phillips. (2006). *Power and organizations.* Thousand Oaks, CA: Sage.

structures of powers, but on external ingredients, such as geography, education, social stratification, and so on. Both approaches have been largely recognized as insufficient in the attempt to elaborate a model for understanding the stability of organizational/political regimes. It is in the patterns of internal structures and relations of power that the stability and dynamics of [democratic and oligarchic] forms of organization can be better grasped. Political performance can be analyzed in terms of Eckstein's 1969 model according to the following items:

- *Durability,* or the persistence of a certain government without major change over time
- *Legitimacy,* or the ability of a certain government to command positive commitments in a society
- *Strife-avoidance,* or the ability of a certain government to avoid or minimize social violence directed at the structure of rule
- *Output efficiency,* or the ability of a certain government to arrive at directives pertinent to demands in a polity, especially intense and widespread ones
- *Permeation,* or the ability of the power holders to distribute resources and carry out reforms pertinent for the various segments of the social body
- *Authenticity,* which means that all these aspects should be accomplished without deviating from some sorts of implicit meanings (what does it mean to be a democratic leader for instance)

These dimensions relate to three political characteristics of organizational forms. Organizational forms are designed to generate certain kinds of rules, of subordinate-superior relationships, and certain patterns of elite production. In other words, organizational forms might be the major ingredient of a system of governance. From the perspective of the power holders, the political purpose of any government is to perpetuate itself. They do not do so when a dominant leader is ousted for whatever reason and organizational lives are affected, when the organization necessarily lives a drama symbolized by the transfer of power, such as in the context of changes in political regimes at the level of nations or a change of top management team or CEO.

Where the very essence of the legitimacy of leaders is contested and, as is often the case, ends up in unveiling of scandals or actual proof of incompetence, the lack of political performance is interpreted as a pivotal event and shatters the entire organizational edifice. In the upshot, it is the corporate elite as a "ruling class" that is affected, and that, therefore, strives to recover both the trust of destabilized subordinates and the dignity of uncorrupted leaders. Unobtrusively, one would expect that corporate elites will use the power of their interorganizational networks and slightly reorient the rules of their most powerful resource, the system of elite recruitment.

The iron law of oligarchy began its life with Michels's analysis of trade unions. In many countries, such unions have been declining in membership dramatically for at least the past two decades. Under siege, in terms of membership retention, they have had to turn to some new ways of organizing. In fact, some unions have been quite active in adopting new information communication technologies for popular, disintermediated, and decentralized communication. Development of such forms of communication holds out the promise of creating a more *distributed discourse*, one that would be corrosive of the centralized communication structures crucial for the construction and reproduction of oligarchy. It has been suggested that something like this began to emerge in the British Dockers' Trade Union during a major strike of the 1990s, by Carter and colleagues in 2003. At present, a more-generalized model of polyphonic—or multivoiced—discourse, one conceived as a more inclusive and less oligarchic mode of organization, is perhaps a possibility more implicit than a highly explicated reality, as Kornberger and colleagues wrote in 2006.

—*David Courpasson and Stewart R. Clegg*

See also Control; Coordination; Organizational Citizenship Behaviors; Organizational Design; Organizational Structure; Ownership and Control; Post-Bureaucratic Organizations

Further Readings

Carter, C., Clegg, S. R., Hogan, J., & Kornberger, M. (2003). The polyphonic spree: The case of the Liverpool dockers. *Industrial Relations Journal, 34*(4), 290–304.

Clegg, S. R., Courpasson, D., & Phillips, N. (2006). *Power and organizations.* Thousand Oaks, CA: Sage.

Courpasson, D., & Clegg, S. R. (2006). Dissolving the iron cages? Tocqueville, Michels, bureaucracy. *Organization, 13*(3) 319–343.

Eckstein, H. (1969). Authority relations and governmental performance: A theoretical framework. *Comparative Political Studies, 2*(3), 269–325.

Kornberger, M., Carter, C., & Clegg, S. R. (2006). Rethinking the polyphonic organization: Managing as discursive practice. *Scandinavian Journal of Management, 22,* 3–30.

May, J. D. (1965). Democracy, organization, Michels. *The American Political Science Review, 59*(2), 417–429.

Michels, R. (1962). *Political parties: A sociological study of the oligarchical tendencies of modern democracy.* (E. P. Eden & C. P. Paul, Trans.). New York: Collier.

Tocqueville, A. (1945). *Democracy in America.* (P. Bradley, Ed.; H. Reeve, Trans.). New York: Knopf.

Irrationality

Irrationality refers to decision making and behavior in the workplace that is emotion-driven and counter to the goals set forth by the organization. The act of irrationality is often associated with being illogical and less focused on the more rational alternatives for action. With the study of the irrational side of workplace behavior only recently becoming a prevalent and growing field in organizational research, many unanswered questions and areas for continued inquiry remain for students and scholars of organization studies.

Conceptual Overview

The study of irrationality in the workplace has been traditionally overshadowed by the emphasis on rationality. From the influential works of Max Weber and Frederick Taylor to Charles Barnard and Herbert Simon, the trajectory of organizational research has placed emotions and corresponding irrational behavior in a box, considering them problematic and troublesome for management. Organizations were structured and tasks were designed with the assumption that humans were rational beings with the ability to make choices designed to achieve a goal in the most efficient and logical fashion without influence from emotion. While Simon's seminal work in 1947 moved the Tayloristic focus on strict rationality to one of bounded rationality, there remained an enduring neglect for understanding the irrational side of humans. Simon argued that humans are incapable of being completely rational because they are bounded by the limited awareness of multiple alternatives and the potential consequences associated with decisions. Nonetheless, the preoccupation with the rational actor remained at the forefront of scholarly research until recent interest in emotions in the workplace began to surface.

Any examination of irrational behavior in the workplace must first consider the role of emotions, rather than judgment or heuristics, as Simon noted in 1987. Emotions are immediate positive, negative, or conflicted reactions to a social relationship, object, or event and are accompanied by physiological changes, interruptions to thought processes and alterations in behavior. In addition, there is an underlying appraisal process that defines the relative pleasantness or unpleasantness of the event, as Nico Frijda described in 1988. The direction of the emotional experience is based on certain factors that influence how individuals interpret and make sense of the event. Value and goal assessments pertaining to the event, in addition to social cues from the organization's cultures, often help define the type of emotional reaction and the ensuing decision and behavior. Factors relating to the event such as uncertainty, risk, ambiguity, known or unforeseen consequences, and dilemmas often lead individuals to act on emotions instead of reason.

For example, in a 2004 field study, Sarah Tracy examined how prison officials respond to conflicting organization policies guiding behavior and the contradictory realities of working in a correctional facility. The findings reveal that informants acted out their frustrated emotions in a variety of irrational behaviors that contradicted policy, such as placing emphasis on one rule over others and favoring select inmates while discriminating against others. In another study exploring irrational behavior in the workplace, Mark Stein found that narcissism, rather than lacking information or cognitive ability, can often result in organizational failure. In this 2003 field study, Stein found that feelings such as pride permeated throughout the organization under investigation, and as a result a sense of omnipotence overcame its members. The collective hubris also resulted in an irrational sense of immunity and independence from competition or challenges in the environment. These two studies represent a trend in organizational research for the inclusion of emotions and irrational behavior.

Critical Commentary and Future Directions

The recent shift from an overemphasis on rationality, bounded rationality, and judgment-driven behaviors to research on emotions in the workplace is a promising development for the study of irrationality. As with most phenomena in organizational studies, there is a great need for research to explore specific contexts and workplace settings that expose the dynamics, determinants, and consequences associated with the varying types of irrational behavior in today's workplace. Three specific opportunities for future research are presented here.

First, there exists an assumption in organization studies that irrational behavior is the antithesis of reason and often counterproductive to the organizational agenda. While emotions are indeed motivators for behavior and may interrupt an individual's attention toward goal satisfaction, Simon later admitted in 1997 that emotions might also play a more positive role. Emotions, positive or negative, can help focus individuals toward the goal. For example, the fear or embarrassment for goal failure and pride of goal attainment may direct individuals toward more rational behavior. Thus, emotions can be the basis for irrational behavior, but may also induce individuals to behave in concert with organizational demands as Theresa Domagalski and other emotion scholars have recently argued.

Second, the darker side of organizational behavior is often aligned with the concept of irrationality. The varying forms of misbehavior, including intentional acts to benefit self or endanger the organization, are considered by many as irrational responses to workplace injustices, peer pressure, or other events. A positive form of misbehavior, as presented in Yoav Vardi and Yoash Wiener's 1996 framework, is also a prevalent form of deviance in organizations. Individuals engage in positive misbehavior to benefit the organization while simultaneously violating organizational rules and/or societal norms or laws (e.g., fabricating accounting records). When individuals engage in this type of misbehavior, what emotions underscore the irrationality? Is this unique form of misbehavior actually goal-directed irrationality? While misbehavior itself requires further empirical investigation in organization studies, the concept of irrationality adds an additional layer of complexity that should be considered.

Lastly, organizations are frequently using monitoring devices to ensure that employees are adhering to policies and engaging in appropriate workplace behaviors. Monitoring, in its variety of forms, is a tool for organizations to control behavior. The underlying assumption for using monitoring systems, at least from an economic perspective, is that employees will respond by behaving in a rational manner. Essentially, employees will cease all shirking activities and return to sufficient effort levels to satisfy the task at hand. While individuals may react to monitoring in such a way, is it actually a rational response? Do employees rationally calculate the costs and benefits associated with continued shirking or rule adherence? Is their reaction to the monitoring, therefore, devoid of emotion? Recent research suggests otherwise. A study by David Holman in 2002 found that high levels of performance monitoring in call centers were negatively associated with employee well-being. In this study, employee well-being was operationalized using measures of anxiety, depression, and job satisfaction. The emotional consequences of monitoring, depending on the specific context, may be considerable. More research is needed to explore how the affective dynamics influence behavioral response and the degree to which it is indeed irrational or rational.

—*Micheal T. Stratton*

See also Affect; Bounded Rationality; Emotion; Organizational Misbehavior; Rational Choice Theory

Further Readings

Domagalski, T. A. (1999). Emotion in organizations: Main currents. *Human Relations, 52*(6), 833–852.

Frijda, N. H. (1988). The laws of emotion. *American Psychologist, 43*(5), 349–358.

Holman, D. (2002). Employee well-being in call centers. *Human Resource Management Journal, 12*(4), 35–50.

Simon, H. A. (1947). *Administrative behavior.* New York: Macmillan.

Simon, H. A. (1987). Making management decisions: The role of intuition and emotion. *Academy of Management Executive, 1*(1), 57–64.

Simon, H. A. (1997). *Administrative behavior* (4th ed.). New York: Free Press.

Stein, M. (2003). Unbounded irrationality: Risk and organizational narcissism at Long Term Capital Management. *Human Relations, 56*(5), 523–540.

Tracy, S. J. (2004). Dialectic, contradiction, or double bind? Analyzing and theorizing employee reactions to organizational tension. *Journal of Applied Communication Research, 32*(2), 119–146.

Vardi, Y., & Wiener, Y. (1996). Misbehavior in organizations: A motivational framework. *Organization Science, 7*(2), 151–165.

J

Japanese Management

Before Japan's miracle economic growth faltered in the early 1990s, Japanese management fascinated the West. During the 1970s and 1980s, Japan's manufacturing industries redefined global expectations about high-performance high-reliability products, notably in motor vehicles and consumer electronics. Almost overnight, Japan had asserted itself as a technological and economic superpower. Its economic expansion seemed unstoppable. Many believed that it had invented a new and superior form of capitalism. However, Japan's miracle growth faltered, just as America's long economic boom started to raise renewed faith in American-style liberal individualism, coupled to fluid labor markets for specialists. Global interconnectedness helped to spread the American model of flexible, market-rational entrepreneurship based on efficient, impersonal transactions. Entrepreneurs in developing countries could use the Internet to facilitate their participation in the global marketplace. Meanwhile, China presented the world with the biggest economic expansion in global history, reshaping the dynamics of international competition. New concerns about new patterns of global economic development eclipsed interest in Japanese management.

At the height of Japanese management's popularity, many imitators imagined that Japanese management could be reduced to universally applicable buzzwords. For example, the Japanese word *kaizen* (continuous improvement) became part of the management-speak lexicon in English-speaking countries. Applying *kaizen* to manufacturing, or any other form of collective activity, offered the allure of reproducing Japanese-style progress. Japan's Toyota Motor Corporation was seen as a paragon of perfection. Toyota was quick to realize that clogging-up the production process with things that were not being used did not make sense. It pioneered the use of signboards, or *kamban,* to manage the flow so that one got what one wanted when one needed it (just-in-time production); waste should be avoided (lean production) and people doing the job should contribute to discussions about improved quality (quality circles). Indeed, all employees should try to appreciate the way in which their contribution related to the total quality of what the organization, as a seamlessly integrated team, was trying to achieve (total quality management). Along with *kaizen* and *kamban,* five Japanese words beginning with the letter *s* were portrayed as the 5S model of Japanese management. English-speaking enthusiasts were quick to preserve the power of the alliteration, matching the 5S model with English edicts that began with *s*. Hence, people were required to sort and scrap (*seiri*), straighten and store (*seiton*), scrub and shine (*seisô*), standardize in a clean and neat manner (*seiketsu*), and sustain discipline (*shitsuke*).

Even after Japanese management ceased to be seen as a silver bullet, the idea of learning from Japan received a new lease on life with the publication of

The Knowledge-Creating Company: How Japanese Companies Create the Dynamics of Innovation, by two Japanese academics, Ikujiro Nonaka and Hirotaka Takeuchi in 1995. According to Nonaka and Takeuchi's model, tacit knowledge in the heads of employees could be converted into explicit knowledge that anyone could understand. This concept of tacit-explicit knowledge-conversion fueled the Western fashion for knowledge management, or KM, whereby the tacit dimension of personal knowledge is converted into explicit knowledge and managed.

Yet, not everyone subscribes to the view that Japanese management is a transferable commodity that can be captured in universally comprehensible words or initials (such as *kaizen,* the 5S model, or explicit knowledge) and used anywhere. An alternative view follows from the idea that the meaning of words depends on how they are used by specific people in specific contexts. Accordingly, appreciating the concepts that underpin Japanese management depends on appreciating how Japanese *insiders* use the terms. Such a perspective highlights the importance of the institutional processes that enable Japanese organizations to operate as tightly bounded, close-knit communities. Power, mediated by close community relationships among organizational insiders, underpins modes of communication and control that are often overlooked in Western management models according to Tim Ray and Stewart Clegg.

Conceptual Overview

Many Western approaches to organization studies assume that the management of an organization is analogous to controlling a machine: formal rules specify how the parts should fit together, while the levers of power control cause-and-effect relationships. Although the rise of the so-called knowledge economy and the importance of knowledge workers, who are paid to think for themselves, highlight difficulties with command-and-control management in which bosses tell subordinates what to do, most managers are reluctant to relinquish the reigns of authority. Techniques, ranging from F. W. Taylor's *scientific management* to the recent enthusiasm for *knowledge management,* help to satisfy the manager's desire to command and control. Nevertheless, securing the intelligent cooperation of knowledge workers typically involves a meaningful, two-way dialogue: the boss's *telling* has to be fused with *listening* and an ability to make sense of what is heard. On this account, informal processes (such as gossip among knowledge workers) become important to a manager's sensemaking processes: effective communication and factors affecting the capacity for control depend on getting to know the people involved. Managers have to engage with relevant communities of practice.

In contrast to the traditional Western model, Japanese management owes very little to formal rules. Rather, the power to guide practice within Japanese organizations is mediated—informally—by close-knit relationships among insiders who come to know each other well. The slightest nuance of body language or the significance of what is not said can convey important information to a fellow insider. Senior people are in charge, but their authority relies on acting and thinking in concert with the whole team. Consensus is important, and considerable efforts are devoted to ensuring that everyone has a hand in producing the plans that they have to implement. Enterprise-based unions are part of the organizational family and have a vested interest in the organization's long-term success. Ultimately, everyone is on the same side. Labor-saving production technology that increases productivity and makes things easier might be welcomed; it frees organizational insiders to help the team in other ways. In the course of a career, insiders can expect to do many different jobs within the organization.

Japanese writers ranging from the anthropologist Chie Nakane, writing in 1972, to the knowledge guru, Ikujiro Nonaka, writing with Ryoko Toyama and Noboru Konno in 2000, have used the Japanese concept of *ba* (which roughly means the *place* or the *frame of reference* for purposeful activity) to explore the implications of complying with insider norms. Activity within the *ba* is guided by the insider's implicit code, which shapes what ought to happen and is binding on members; as the Japanese aphorism cautions, "the nail that sticks out is hammered down."

Commitment to the organizational *ba* requires permanent employees to structure their lives around its requirements. Holidays should be short and "voluntary" overtime offered without question (it does not do to go home before one's boss); after-hours socializing with colleagues, along with weekend excursions to hot-spring resorts and similar destinations, helps to strengthen close community relationships among insiders. The sheer density of interaction encourages insiders to see things in similar ways. Like members of a football team that scores the winning goal, insiders position themselves automatically: they do not need to be told what to do next. Many activities that would require explicit instructions in, for example, an American or British organization, occur without anyone being told to do anything. In 1994, a distinguished English manager, John Harvey-Jones, whose team was outperformed by a Japanese organization, noted that the Japanese spent many hours in each other's company: they worked and dreamt together; anyone of them could cover for anyone else.

Japanese-style *intraorganizational communication* is a striking example of what Edward Twitchell Hall and Mildred Reed Hall referred to in 1990 as *high-context* communication. An extreme case might be twins who have shared a long life in close interaction with each other and can communicate in ways that would not be available to people from different cultures who have only just met. In contrast, low-context communication assumes that the other party knows very little about the background and has to be told almost everything. Transferring the reflexively automatic features of Japanese-style management to countries such as the United States and the United Kingdom, which rely heavily on low-context communication, is difficult. Simply telling people to strive for continuous improvement—*kaizen*—does not re-create the formidable peer-group pressure that is embodied in a Japanese workplace *ba*.

Embedded in a Japanese Context

Whereas the United States exemplifies the principles of a market-rational economy in which the government's main concern is with setting the rules of play for competitive innovation among rival firms, Japan's economic development has been *plan rational,* as Chalmers Johnson termed it in 1986. Japan's governmental bureaucracy has played an active role in guiding and coordinating the activities of leading firms. As well as promoting growth, Japanese bureaucrats have been important in ensuring egalitarian growth as organizations march forward in step and thereby preserve the existing economic structure. Unlike Joseph A. Schumpeter's famous image of capitalism advancing by the "perennial gale of creative destruction," as more advantageous ways of doing things displaced outmoded methods, Japan's economic growth, over the past half-century, has owed more to steady-state development: new technologies evolve from existing organizations. Despite the gales of globalization that have transmitted American business culture around the world, the principal pillar that supports Japanese management—*lifetime employment* (for selected employees in large organizations)—has not been whittled away.

By the mid-1950s, institutional conditions were in place whereby Japan's major employers could promise lifetime employment to a significant proportion of their employees, and once such promises became widespread, a route was paved for the age-related promotion of insiders and the effective prohibition of poaching, noted Ronald Gilson and Mark Roe. Permanent employees in upper-level Japanese organizations are the custodians of a tradition that is passed to successive generations. Senior employees routinely groom junior staff as "servants" who are expected to follow their "master" up the organizational ladder, with the result that master-servant relations (*shujû no kankei*) add historical momentum to the traditional, male-dominated status quo. Despite a law to allow equal opportunities for women employees (enacted in 1985) and the Child-Care Leave Law (enacted in 1992), the proportion of woman in positions of power remains low, as Yoshio Sugimoto documented in 2003.

As Japan's labor market for specialists weakened, the stable nature of the employer-employee relationship allowed organizations to trust their employees and invest in their long-term career development without the fear that they might defect to a rival Japanese organization. Graduates from the top-ranking universities could be offered a deal for life based on the guarantee of age-related promotion in an upper-level organization. In return to committing themselves to the organization, their rise on the age-related "promotion escalator" was assured. With the uncertainties of promotion removed, lifetime employees can act as team players (for example, by sharing information with subordinates) without the fear of being overtaken on the promotion escalator. The organization can ask them to do whatever expediency demands without raising concerns that less glamorous activities would undermine career prospects. Although those who are accustomed to non-Japanese contexts might see automatic promotion as a formula for laziness, Japan's limited labor market for specialists limits the scope for job-hopping. The ease of information flow among organizational insiders makes it remarkably easy for them to act collectively to retaliate against those who fail to meet expectations. Fear of ostracism and lack of alternatives encourage compliance.

Competitive rivalry among those who reach the very top of the organization hinges on demonstrating a capacity to cooperate: top people should be well versed in the art of consensus building. Unlike American organizations, in which outsiders—strangers—might be recruited to lead an organization and paid astronomical salaries, Japan's top managers are almost always insiders who know their colleagues extremely well and are paid a relatively modest premium for their responsibilities. Although the faltering of Japan's miracle economic growth prompted many organizations to experiment with performance-related promotion, many have back-pedaled as the effect on morale proved counterproductive.

The stable relationship between upper-level Japanese organizations and their permanent employees is complemented by stable relationships that the organization maintains with other organizations, such as its bank, suppliers, customers, and relevant sections of the governmental bureaucracy. There is an interlocking structure. For example, horizontal "families" of top-level firms in *keiretsu* groupings based on a common bank might be supported by vertically segmented supply chains (in which each firm is dependent on the one above for orders) that descend through lower tiers in the economic structure. When times are hard, each firm can demand more from its lower level suppliers. On occasions, firms at the bottom might be reduced to running at a loss, which is known as doing the *bicycle business*—because to stop would mean falling over (in the manner of an bicycle that loses momentum), making them incapable of responding when the upturn came.

Japan's nested stability, in which a stable population of upper-level organizations nests within a stable economic structure, embodies webs of self-reinforcing connections. For example, Japan's major organizations hire graduates from the top-ranking universities, which owe their reputations to the fact that top-level organizations hire their graduates. Because the status of the individual in Japanese society is shaped by the status of the organization to which he or she belongs, the ability of the best organizations to get the best people is sustained by the very fact that they are the best organizations. From an early age, education is oriented toward getting into the best possible university. The University of Tokyo is by far the most prestigious and has the hardest entrance examinations. After being selected for a top-ranking university, graduation and recruitment by a prestigious employer is relatively straightforward. Attending graduate school has been less popular than in other leading economies. Spending years studying for a PhD is at the opportunity cost of rising on an organization's promotion escalator.

Critical Commentary and Future Directions

Japanese institutions enable the loyalty of permanent employees to be taken for granted, which is diametrically opposed to American expectations about liberal individualism and a fluid labor market for specialists. The two approaches have different strengths and weaknesses. While the American model is vulnerable to key people leaving, recruiting new staff can allow the rapid acquisition of expertise in new areas. In principle, the profile of organizational activities can change quickly; although there is a risk that new staff will fail to fit in with the "way that things are done around here," which is not normally a problem amid the peer-group pressure associated with a Japanese organization. In the Japanese model, cohesion and continuous improvement—*kaizen*—are woven into the fabric of daily life; they are fundamental to sustaining steady-state innovation and the virtues of Japanese management. But it takes time for Japan's organizational insiders to learn how to do radically different things and rapid shifts in direction—the hallmark of American flexibility—are difficult.

The question of whether Japanese management can survive the gales of globalization is complex and controversial. Although the "company as family" model is associated with Japan's transformation into the world's second largest economy, critics have argued that the institutional stability of Japan Incorporated has outlived its usefulness. Certainly, the increased penetration of American business culture has given rise to an increase in market-rational activity—as illustrated, for example, by the growing volume of trading on the Tokyo Stock Exchange. Suddenly, providing value to shareholders has become a much-talked-about issue. Nonetheless, the embedded nature of the status quo tends to exclude sudden or dramatic changes. Those who have struggled to enter top-ranking universities and served their time in upper-level organizations might resist practices that undermine their positions of power (as the example of equal employment opportunities for women illustrated, new possibilities do not necessarily translate into new practices). A switch to Silicon Valley's hire-and-fire model would undermine the trust relationships that support Japanese management's distinctive modes of communication and control.

While there has been increased interest in American management practices and speculation about the evolution of new form of Japanese management, for instance by the U.S. management guru, Michael Porter, together with Japanese colleagues Hirotaka Takeuchi and Mariko Sakakibara in 2000, this would require the coevolution of new institutions. For example, an increase in the use of legally enforceable agreements suggests a need for more lawyers. Compared to the United States and other leading Western economies, Japan has comparatively few lawyers (trust-based relationships rarely require recourse to the law). Change implies extensive readjustments as more lawyers are trained and assimilated into the rhythm of everyday business life. Possibly, the addition of market-rational principles to Japan is akin to adding a modest amount of oil to a significant amount of water: the oil is in the water, but not dissolved. While the *tatemae* (façade) of Japan's market-related reforms could signal the death of Japanese management, the *honne* (true voice) of tomorrow's Japan might have a strangely familiar feel.

—Tim Ray

See also Communities of Practice; Knowledge Management; Scientific Management; Tacit Knowledge

Further Readings

Gilson, R., & Roe, M. (1999). Lifetime employment: Labor peace and the evolution of Japanese corporate governance. *Columbia Law Review, 1.1*(2), 508–540.

Hall, E. T., & Hall, M. R. (1990). *Understanding cultural differences.* Yarmouth, ME: Intercultural Press.

Harvey-Jones, J. (1994). *Managing to survive: A guide to management through the 1990s.* London: Mandarin.

Johnson, C. (1986). *MITI and the Japanese miracle: The growth of industrial policy, 1925–1975.* Tokyo: Tuttle. (Original work published 1982)

Nakane, C. (1972). *Japanese society.* Berkeley: University of California Press. (Original work published 1970)

Nonaka, I., & Takeuchi, H. (1995). *The knowledge-creating company: How Japanese companies create the dynamics of innovation.* Oxford, UK: Oxford University Press.

Nonaka, I., Toyama, R., & Konno, N. (2000). SECI, ba, and leadership: A unified model of dynamic knowledge creation. *Long Range Planning, 33*, 5–34.

Porter, M., Takeuchi, H., & Sakakibara, M. (2000). *Can Japan compete?* Basingstoke, UK: Macmillan.

Ray, T., & Clegg, S. (2005). Tacit knowing, communication, and power: Lessons from Japan? In S. Little & T. Ray (Eds.), *Managing knowledge: An essential reader* (2nd ed.) (pp. 319–347). London: Sage.

Schumpeter, J. A. (1976). *Capitalism, socialism, and democracy.* London: Allen & Unwin. (Originally published in the U.S., first UK publication 1943)

Sugimoto, Y. (2003). *An introduction to Japanese society* (2nd ed.). Cambridge, UK: Cambridge University Press.

Job Evaluation

Job evaluation is a process designed to measure the relative value of different jobs in an organization. Job evaluation plays a central role among human resource management systems, and for decades it has been considered the basis for determining pay structures in large companies.

Conceptual Overview

Although precursors can be traced at the end of the 19th century, modern job-evaluation systems developed at the beginning of the previous century and spread in large American companies after World War II. In Europe, it occurred later than in the United States, in line with its later industrialization. Job evaluation differs from any other evaluation process (e.g., skill evaluation, performance evaluation, or potential evaluation) as it rates jobs and not persons. The principal purpose of job evaluation is to promote internal pay equity (e.g., to meet the "equal pay for equal work" obligations), designing a compensation system that pays the most for the jobs with most worth. Job evaluation is the process through which the relative worth of jobs in an organization is set.

The development of a job-evaluation system requires the commitment and sponsorship of the top management and the definition of participants to the project, which normally include compensation specialists, managers, supervisors, and job incumbents. Once the system has been developed, it is necessary training in the use of the system. Results of the evaluation process need revision from higher levels; approved results need to be communicated to managers, supervisors, and incumbents. The cost for the development of a job-evaluation system can be very high and varies according to the different methods depicted below; the more analytical the method, the more costing the development.

Job evaluation begins with job analysis, followed by job description. Job descriptions are the basis for the assessment of the relative worth of jobs or a group of jobs. The assessment refers to the content of a job—skills, knowledge, and abilities required, level of education, working conditions, and responsibilities—and to the value or contribution of each job to the company's goals.

Of several job-evaluation methods, the most common are ranking, classification, factor comparison, point factor, and hybrids methods. Ranking involves comparing whole jobs with one another and arranging them in a hierarchy. Classification starts with the definition of grades into which jobs will be placed according to the characteristics expressed in the description and in the grade. Jobs are assigned to the best-fit grade. Factor comparison evaluates and compares jobs on the analysis of a number of defined factors. The point-factor method, the most common around the world, was developed by Edward N. Hay and marketed through his consulting firm. The point-factor method starts with the selection of the compensable factors and the definition of the relative weight of each factor. Each job is rated on each compensable factor using job descriptions, questionnaires, and/or interviews. Total points are counted for each job or job class. The last step assigns a specified point score to a specific wage level using salary scales, which usually results from wage surveys and benchmarking. Internal and external equity are also considered.

Critical Commentary and Future Directions

Recently, job evaluation has been criticized on many aspects. The presumed objectivity and equity of wages based on the relative worth of jobs has been questioned and received disconfirmation from empirical research. As an example, after the development of job-evaluation systems, wages for women continue to be lower than those for men as companies continue to practice discrimination through occupational segregation by gender. Once jobs are segregated, evaluators can value a factor only when it is found in male-oriented jobs or ignore factors found in female-oriented jobs. Moreover, factors used to evaluate jobs reflect societal weightings of job characteristics. In point-factor job-evaluation systems, factors often overlap or factors are ambiguously defined, or jobs at the highest hierarchical level are most valued because of their hierarchical level and not because of their intrinsic worth.

From a class perspective, job evaluation was criticized as it was a not so subtle way to reduce the bargaining power of unions, as job-evaluation systems were providing the objective (or the supposed objective) metrics to define salaries. Other concerns relate to the validity of job evaluations in today's organizations that do not resemble the ones from the beginning of the previous century and have moved far away from mass production. Today's organizations are flat, based on teams and more oriented to quality. These characteristics require multiskilling and the possibility to pay the person, to pay horizontal moves, and to pay performance more than jobs. On the contrary, job-evaluation systems reinforce bureaucratic and hierarchical organizational structures. For these reasons, in contemporary organizations, compensation theorists are emphasizing skill-based pay more than job-evaluation-based pay. Moreover, the development of job-evaluation systems in dynamic context could be too expensive and, to a certain extent, useless as jobs and roles change quickly.

Nevertheless, the need for internal equity and pay equity is important, and job evaluation remains a significant basis, although not a perfect one, to ensure it. Unions, especially in European countries, can express their voice quite strongly. Companies could adopt and empower diversity management practices to avoid discrimination if job-evaluation systems could not eliminate it.

What would be important for the future is the development of a more contingent approach to job evaluation, able to capture differences among industries, among companies in the same industry, and among departments, functions, and job families within a single company. A more contingent approach to job evaluation would allow companies to tailor compensation systems to different types of organizations or jobs, calibrating job-based pay, skill-based pay, or performance-based pay.

—*Silvia Bagdadli*

See also Gender Division; Human Resource Management; Industrial Relations; Organizational Design; Organizational Justice

Further Readings

Armstrong, M., & Stephens, T. (2005). *Employee reward management and practice.* London: Kogan Page.

Figart, D. M. (2001). Wage-setting under Fordism: The rise of job evaluation and the ideology of equal pay. *Review of Political Economy, 13*(4), 405–425.

Gupta, N., & Jenkins, G. D. (Eds.). (1991). Special issue on job evaluation. *Human Resource Management Review, 1*(2), 91–162.

JOB SATISFACTION

Job satisfaction, defined as an attitude toward one's job, is an internal state that is expressed by affectively and/or cognitively evaluating an experienced job with some degree of favor or disfavor. The internal state referred to is a tendency that predisposes positive or negative evaluative responses, which can be either covert or overt.

Conceptual Overview

For decades, job satisfaction has stood at the center of the study of organizational behavior. In 1976, Locke counted more than 3,300 studies on job satisfaction, and that figure rose to more than 12,400 in the late 1990s. As the most studied variable in organizational behavior research, several relationships have been uncovered between job satisfaction and other organizational variables, such as organizational citizenship and role withdrawal behaviors. Job satisfaction has implications for both individuals embedded within organizations and also for higher, collective levels of analyses (i.e., groups and organizations).

Past definitions of job satisfaction have focused on affective reactions toward an individual's job; these affective, or emotional, conceptualizations presumably capture how employees *feel* about their jobs. Such definitions of job satisfaction mask the differences between its distinct affective and cognitive components. More recent definitions of job satisfaction as an attitude toward one's job do not limit consideration to affect alone, but also include cognitive appraisals formed by individuals about their jobs.

Theoretical attention has focused on the determinants of job satisfaction. *Person-environment (P-E) fit* models have dominated the way in which organizational scientists have thought about the causes of job satisfaction. The underlying assumption of these models is that environments that fulfill employees' important needs are considered satisfying, reflecting an appropriate "fit" between what the environment has to offer and what the person needs. The Work Adjustment Project at the University of Minnesota, which yielded the Minnesota Satisfaction Questionnaire, was perhaps the most systematic and sustained program of research addressing the relationship between P-E fit and job satisfaction.

Various theories have been advanced that specify the *needs* employees seek to fulfill through their work. These include Maslow's need hierarchy theory; Alderfer's existence, relatedness, growth (ERG) theory; and Herzberg's motivator-hygiene, or two-factor, theory. The cumulative evidence in support of such needs theories is not compelling, primarily indicating the lack of a consistently verified taxonomy of needs that can be linked to specific job elements, goals, or outcomes.

Characteristics specific to the job have been considered influential sources of job satisfaction as well. Hackman and Oldham, in the *job characteristics model,* proposed that employees' perceptions of a set of task attributes, such as skill variety and autonomy, are associated positively with satisfaction. Empirical support has shown that the relationship between these task perceptions and satisfaction is reciprocal, such that task perceptions contribute positively to satisfaction and vice versa. Satisfied employees see more task variety, autonomy, and so on in their jobs, and these job characteristics positively influence perceptions of job satisfaction.

Salancik and Pfeffer, in their *social information processing* approach, also emphasized the importance of work environments. As in the job characteristics model, this approach posits that employees form perceptions about the job and its tasks. Jobs are considered ambiguous stimuli, with the potential to be interpreted in multiple ways. Where the social information processing approach departs from the job characteristics model is the way in which perceptions about the job are formed. This approach suggests that the interpretation of the job and work environment is influenced greatly by the information gleaned from coworkers about the work itself. As such, social cues contribute to the production of job attitudes.

Dispositional approaches to job satisfaction essentially assert that satisfaction, at least in part, is a product of personality. Empirical evidence supports these approaches and also indicates that genetic factors even may influence such relationships. Additional individual difference approaches to job satisfaction include a highly cognitive orientation wherein reported job satisfaction is a function of the memories employees retrieve about the positive and negative events in their work environment. Certain null results regarding individual differences also are worthy of mention. For example, sex and race are not reliably associated with job satisfaction, despite instances of salary inequalities along these demographic lines. Consistent findings, however, show an age-satisfaction relationship, with older employees reporting higher levels of satisfaction.

More recent, integrated models of job satisfaction incorporate both dispositional and situational factors. Brief and his colleagues' *integrated model of job satisfaction,* for example, posits that satisfaction is influenced directly by how employees interpret their jobs, and that these interpretations are influenced by objective job circumstances and global personality dimensions; i.e., extroversion, or positive affectivity (PA), and neuroticism, or negative affectivity (NA). Also supportive of an integrative model is Weiss and Cropanzano's *affective events theory* (AET), which recognizes that affect levels fluctuate through time. An individual's pattern of affective experiences is influenced by both endogenous factors, such as affective disposition (e.g., PA and NA), and exogenous factors, which create shocks to existing patterns. According to AET, job satisfaction is directly a product of this pattern of affect.

Job satisfaction—or the lack thereof—has many consequences, with important implications for how organizations function. In work environments, role withdrawal includes both psychological and behavioral forms, such as turnover, absenteeism, and reduced organizational commitment. Theories addressing turnover have included job satisfaction as a determinant, although empirical studies have demonstrated a somewhat modest relationship between the two constructs. However, job satisfaction is linked more strongly to thoughts of quitting, intentions to search for a new job, and intentions to quit. Physical withdrawal from an organization is influenced largely by exogenous variables, such as the presence of acceptable employment alternatives.

Employees who are not presented with acceptable alternatives might exhibit dysfunctional manifestations of job dissatisfaction, such as absenteeism, tardiness, the use of work time for personal tasks, taking long breaks, stealing, aggression, or undesirable coping methods (e.g., drug use). The relationships between job satisfaction with absenteeism and tardiness often are regulated by organizational policies, whereby standards establish acceptable amounts of these behaviors (e.g., vacation time, sick days). Behavioral adaptations to job dissatisfaction (e.g., turnover) should be accompanied by supportive thoughts, such as reduced organizational commitment; empirical evidence shows that organizational commitment and turnover are associated strongly.

Intuitively, job satisfaction should increase task performance, or the proficiency with which people perform role-prescribed tasks. The empirical evidence, however, shows a very weak relationship between the two, with job satisfaction explaining only 2% of the variance in task performance based on average observed and uncorrected correlational coefficients. Perhaps this weak relationship is partly a function of which satisfaction component (e.g., affective or cognitive) is measured, and the degree to which that variable aligns with the affective or cognitive nature of the tasks performed.

Despite the lack of a direct relationship to task performance, satisfied workers have been shown to engage in more collaborative efforts and are more likely to accept organizational goals. More consistent relationships between satisfaction and performance may exist when considering other types of performance and at higher levels of analyses. For instance, organizations populated by satisfied workers may exhibit higher levels of contextual performance than those employing less-satisfied people. Contextual performance, such as organizational citizenship behaviors and prosocial organizational behaviors, refers to the spontaneous and innovative contributions employees make to their work environment, which are not prescribed by their jobs. These behaviors, such as helping coworkers, protecting the organization, and making constructive suggestions, are considered more voluntary and have been shown to be more sensitive to differences in job satisfaction than is task performance.

Critical Commentary and Future Directions

Despite decades of research, inconsistencies in the job satisfaction literature remain, likely because of different conceptualizations and measures of the construct. For example, researchers often have been interested in identifying how satisfied employees are with different elements of their jobs, such as tasks, relationships, and pay. Largely because these dimensions, called *facets of satisfaction*, are easily identifiable, they have been attended to. Theory, however, generally has failed to address which facets of job satisfaction ought to be studied, how their relative impact varies across individuals and settings, and how their roles may vary as different antecedents and consequences are considered.

Facets of job satisfaction typically have been gauged by two instruments: the Job Descriptive Index (JDI) and the Minnesota Satisfaction Questionnaire (MSQ). Respondents to the JDI indicate the degree (*yes, uncertain,* or *no*) to which they agree with adjectives describing their coworkers, pay, promotion opportunities, and the work itself. Presumably, more positive answers (e.g., *intelligent,* in reference to coworkers) are associated with more satisfaction. However, responses do not explicitly represent how an individual *feels* about the indicated facet. A more comprehensive measure of satisfaction, the MSQ, asks respondents directly to rate their level of satisfaction with 20 different facets. Thus, how satisfaction is measured with the JDI and MSQ may differ markedly and in ill-understood ways. Theoretically driven measures of job satisfaction and its facets are sorely needed.

Relationships among facet satisfaction and *overall* (e.g., global) satisfaction are poorly understood. For instance, the correlation between the sum of the MSQ facets and a single-item measure of general satisfaction has been reported to be .32, indicating much is missing. Apparently, measures of overall job satisfaction tap something different from a summation of facet scores. Until there is a theory-driven measure of satisfaction addressing its dimensionality, it cannot be assumed that current measures accurately reflect the overall construct.

Organizational scientists claim to have addressed the affective component of job satisfaction, yet empirical investigations have been cognitively laden. Conventional methods of assessing job satisfaction—mostly self-reported paper-and-pencil ones—have failed to gauge the ways employees feel about, or affectively evaluate, their jobs. The MSQ, for example, seems to capture little affect, just cognitions; the JDI captures some positive affect, but mostly cognitions. The mismatch between the conceptualization and measurement of satisfaction is troublesome, considering that affective and cognitive components of attitudes may have different causes, that these components may not align, and that they might differentially predict the same criterion variable. All in all, it is time to recognize that job satisfaction is a poorly understood attitude construct in need of new ways of thinking about its meaning than its measurement. Ideas, not empirical tools, should drive its future.

—*Flannery G. Stevens, Arthur P. Brief, and Alexis N. Smith*

See also Affect; Attitudes; Fit; Organizational Citizenship Behaviors; Organizational Misbehavior; Personality, Five-Factor Model; Work-Family Balance

Further Readings

Brief, A. (1998). *Attitudes in and around organizations.* Thousand Oaks, CA: Sage.

Brief, A., Butcher, A., George, J., & Link, K. (1993). Integrating bottom-up and top-down theories of subjective well-being: The case of health. *Journal of Personality and Social Psychology, 64,* 646–653.

Brief, A., & Weiss, H. (2002). Organizational behavior: Affect in the workplace. *Annual Review of Psychology, 53,* 279–307.

Hackman, J., & Oldham, G. (1975). Development of the job diagnostic survey. *Journal of Applied Psychology, 60,* 159–170.

Locke, E. (1976). The nature and causes of job satisfaction. In M. D. Dunnette (Ed.), *Handbook of industrial and organizational psychology* (pp. 1297–1349). Chicago: Rand McNally.

Salancik, G., & Pfeffer, J. (1978). A social information processing approach to job attitudes and task design. *Administrative Science Quarterly, 22,* 427–456.

Weiss, H. (2002). Deconstructing job satisfaction: Separating evaluations, beliefs, and affective experiences. *Human Resource Management Review, 12,* 173–194.

Weiss, H., & Brief, A. (2001). Affect at work: A historical perspective. In R. L. Payne & C. L. Cooper (Eds.), *Emotions at work: Theory, research, and applications for management.* West Sussex, UK: Wiley.

Weiss, H., & Cropanzano, R. (1996). Affective events theory: A theoretical discussion of the structure, causes, and consequences of affective experiences at work. In B. M. Staw & L. L. Cummings (Eds.), *Research in organizational behavior: Volume 18* (pp. 1–74). Greenwich, CT: JAI Press.

JOINT STOCK COMPANIES

A joint stock company (or corporation) employs capital on an ongoing basis for the benefit of its owners. Ownership rights are vested in shares, which represent the value of the enterprise, that are held by individual or institutional owners. After evolving over three centuries, by the 19th century the joint stock enterprise reached a fully developed form that has provided the foundation for the modern corporation throughout the world. Today, this business structure is the subject of debates concerning governance, sustainability, and social and environmental responsibility.

Conceptual Overview

In its mature form, the joint stock company has four characteristics that distinguish it from other business structures. First, shares in joint stock companies are freely transferable; that is, they can be bought or sold at any time without any restriction. Second, the liability of shareholders (owners) is limited to the amount they have invested. They are not personally responsible for losses or debt incurred by the company. Third, the joint stock company is a distinct legal entity separate from its owners, and it can sue or be sued at law without its owner's private wealth being impacted. Fourth, management is centralized and divorced from ownership. These features made the joint stock framework a more stable and sustainable platform, than the partnership or the trust, for developing large-scale business.

Traditionally, most business was organized as a partnership, which constituted a contract among individuals. It was used in antiquity, developed further in Europe during the Middle Ages, and was then imported into England. In contrast, the trust, which concerned joint use of assets (usually land) by common law proprietors, was of English origin. Trustees controlled these organizations, which had allowed for joint holding and continuous association. Despite its flexible features, the trust did not prove to be the institutional form through which business subsequently developed.

In comparison to the corporation, the partnership had several limitations as noted by Cottrell in 1980 and Harris in 2000. First, the law restricted the number of partners and therefore the size of their personal wealth placed a limit on the amount of capital that the venture could mobilize. As a result, it was difficult to form businesses, like railways, that needed large amounts of capital using this framework. Second, partnership shares were not freely transferable; they could only be sold with the permission of all partners. Third, unlike corporations, partnerships were not immortal; when one partner died, the partnership was dissolved. Fourth, partners were personally liable for debts incurred by the partnership, and they therefore played an active role in the business, which meant that management was not centralized or separate from ownership. (France, however, permitted limited partnerships in which active partners were exposed to unlimited liability while sleeping partners were protected by limited liability.) Fifth, the partnership did not have a separate legal personality. If a suit against a partnership was brought to court, the partners were personally exposed. These features made the partnership a risky and unstable framework.

As noted by Boyce and Ville in 2002, the joint stock company appeared in different countries at different times. In the United States, the federal government did not have jurisdiction over incorporation; rather, individual states assumed this power, the earliest being New York in 1811. By 1860, all states had enacted general incorporation laws. In 1863, France passed laws granting limited liability. Prussia allowed incorporation from 1870, and under German Imperial laws passed in 1884, limited liability privileges were permitted but strictly regulated. Japan passed general incorporation legislation in 1893.

The evolution of the joint stock enterprise in England was protracted. The Crown and later parliament) had the right for grant charters creating joint stock companies that had fixed capital (as opposed to funds mobilized temporarily for example to support a trading or shipping venture of finite duration) with freely transferable shares and monopolistic privileges. Early examples, like the Muscovy Company (1555), the Levant Company (1581), and the East India Company (1600), did not enjoy limited liability, which was not a fully articulated concept until the 18th century. Some companies acted as administrative and military agents of the government. Charters were costly to obtain and therefore feasible for only large ventures.

The literature has viewed the Bubble Act of 1720 as a debilitating constraint on the spread of large-scale business based on the joint stock principle. However, Harris argued in 2000 that this legislation was intended neither to hinder the proliferation of corporations nor strengthen the government's franchise in selling charters. Rather, it was designed to support the South Sea Company, which restructured the national debt, by removing other companies that absorbed market liquidity. It was the stock market crash that *followed* the act's passage, other legal measures, and a change of government policy that discouraged the formation of joint stock companies. Nor was there a pronounced increase in new companies after its repeal in 1825.

During subsequent stock market booms, unincorporated entities proliferated without state sanction, and in response the government passed an act in 1844 to require the registration and regulation of all unlimited liability enterprises with more than 25 investors and freely transferable shares. Finally, in 1855 and 1856, England passed acts granting general limited liability protection, and in 1862 a consolidating act followed. As Cottrell indicated in 1980, from 1856 onward English company law became the most permissive in Western Europe. Nevertheless, the spread of limited liability companies proceeded slowly, mainly because investors considered this form of enterprise to be unstable and open to abuse. Such attitudes eroded slowly and, as Hannah observed in 1983, large-scale, publicly owned companies did not become a prominent feature of industrial organization until the 1920s and 1930s.

Critical Commentary and Future Directions

Since the appearance of joint stock companies, concerns have been voiced regarding the principal-agent problems created by the separation of ownership and management. The collapse of Enron and other major corporations in the 1990s accentuated these concerns and precipitated legislation, such as the U.S. Sarbannes-Oxley Act, designed to increase executive accountability and raise ethical standards. Corporate governance has also been extended to include issues of long-term sustainability regarding the social, cultural, and environmental impact of business operations. Thus, the corporation is now seen as an institution with wide responsibilities.

—*Gordon Boyce*

See also Complex Organizations; Corporate Governance; Formal Organizations; Managerial Capitalism; Ownership and Control

Further Readings

Boyce, G., & Ville, S. P. (2002). *The development of modern business.* Basingstoke, UK: Palgrave.

Cottrell, P. L. (1980). *Industrial finance, 1830–1914.* London: Methuen.

Hannah, L. (1983). *The rise of the corporate economy* (2nd ed.). London: Methuen.

Harris, R. (2000). *Industrializing English law.* Cambridge, UK: Cambridge University Press.

JUSTICE

See Organizational Justice

JUST-IN-TIME MANAGEMENT

Just-in-time management refers to a production management philosophy based on producing only what is needed, when it is needed, and in the quantity that is needed. Just-in-time production is also referred to as *lean manufacturing, demand flow manufacturing, stockless production,* or *pull-system manufacturing.* The result of just-in-time production is that no goods are produced without demand. Just-in-time is the name commonly used to describe the Toyota Production System.

Conceptual Overview

The creator of the just-in-time production management system, Taiichi Ohno, believed that traditional mass production is inherently inefficient and produces wastes at every stage of the production process. He identified *seven wastes* of mass production systems:

1. Waste arising from overproducing
2. Waste (time) arising from waiting
3. Waste arising from transport
4. Waste arising from processing itself
5. Waste arising from unnecessary stock-on-hand
6. Waste arising from unnecessary motion
7. Waste arising from producing defective goods

Mass production often generates overproduction, produces bottlenecks in the flow of production, moves work back and forth across the manufacturing plant, retains inefficient processes, maintains large levels of stock-on-hand, permits nonvalue adding movement across production lines, and produces defective goods because of production pressures. An important goal of just-in-time production management is the elimination of these wastes.

Traditional mass production management is based on a *push system,* whereby marketing forecasts tell the factory what to produce and in what quantity. Raw materials and parts are purchased based on these forecasts, stored and forced into the front end of the production process, and subsequently pushed through each succeeding step of the process. Push-mass production systems produce significant inventories of work-in-progress goods, as well as finished goods. Contrary to traditional mass production, just-in-time production management is a *pull system.* The just-in-time production schedule does not exclusively originate in market forecasts, but from the customer: the demand is made on factory assembly by pulling finished products out of the factory.

Production control in pull manufacturing systems is provided by the use of a *kanban,* a visual signal, card, or signboard that controls the movement of materials between workstations, as well as replenishing those sent downstream to the next workstation. The Toyota Production System uses two types of *kanban* to regulate production: a production *kanban* signals the need to produce more parts, while a conveyance *kanban* signals the need to withdraw parts from one work center and deliver them to the next workstation.

Just-in-time production management attempts to drive inventory levels to zero. Although this is impossible in practical terms, its real objective is to minimize raw materials and work-in-progress inventory to the maximum possible extent without shutting down production. Proponents of mass production systems believe that excess inventory levels are beneficial because one does not have to worry about on-time materials delivery and permits manufacturing to continue during machine breakdowns. However, holding excessive inventory carries significant costs: the cost of warehousing raw and work-in-progress materials and finished goods, as well as the costs associated with spoilage, deterioration, and obsolescence of goods. Producing and holding excessive inventory is wasteful and does not ultimately provide value to the customer. A major drawback of holding excessive inventory levels is that it acts to mask production problems that go unnoticed and unresolved, repeated over and over, while consuming resources and delaying process and product quality improvement. Unmasking the production system's problems through the elimination of inventories is a major strength of just-in-time production management.

The reduction of process cycle time is a fundamental goal of just-in-time production. Production cycle time is defined as that period bounded by the time that materials are sent to the manufacturing floor for the making of a product and the time the finished goods are dispatched from the manufacturing floor to a customer. Production cycle times are reduced in three ways: (1) by reducing lead times for production and delivery, (2) by reducing (or eliminating) setup times, and (3) by reducing lot sizes.

Production lead times are reduced by moving workstations closer together and by using cellular manufacturing concepts. The traditional manufacturing plant is structurally organized around the assembly processes that are used—goods are sent from one process location to the next process location. The just-in-time manufacturing plant is organized by product rather than by process. All the necessary processes for a given product are collocated in a single area and laid out in a compact manner so as to minimize unnecessary worker movement. By organizing work processes in this way, queue length is reduced, while coordination and cooperation between successive processes are enhanced. The just-in-time factory is visual: quality defects become immediately apparent and require people to stop their work. A "quality at the source" (*jidoka*) program is implemented to give workers the personal responsibility for the quality of work performed. While work stoppage is not acceptable behavior in a mass production factory; in a just-in-time plant it is both encouraged and expected.

Workers in a just-in-time factory are organized into semiautonomous work cells composed of natural work teams. The team is responsible for the total product, from the first production process to the shipping dock. Workers are multiskilled and cross-trained to operate several machines, perform quality inspections, and perform maintenance tasks. The just-in-time production line operates very close to capacity for every process with little tolerance existing for machine failure. Total productive maintenance (TPM) is routinely and regularly done by production workers during their normal shift. This allows the operators to develop a sense of ownership for the machines they use. The Toyota Production System concept of "respect for people" contributes to a good relationship between workers and management.

Just-in-time management is characterized by shorter production setup times, accomplished by better advance planning and through process and product redesign. In a mature just-in-time plant, setup times take only a few minutes, whereas in the traditional mass production factory, the same setups are measured in hours and days. Reducing setup times also allows for the economical production of smaller, more-customized lot sizes. Uniform plant loading (*heijunka*) acts to smooth daily production and buffer fluctuations in production. Just-in-time production management requires closer relationships with suppliers necessary to achieve these reductions in lot sizes. This requires more frequent, closely timed deliveries from suppliers, who are often located closer to the just-in-time factory. Suppliers are active partners in managing the raw materials inventory of the just-in-time plant. The just-in-time plant works in strong partnership with a smaller number of superior suppliers, requiring them to continuously improve their quality of supply.

Critical Commentary and Future Directions

Just-in-time production management requires robust process capability, statistical process control, and continuous improvement to work effectively. Just-in-time production is enhanced when it is part of a total quality system. The just-in-time plant is fragile: processes must work exactly as designed. There are no warehouses to buffer stock, with little excess capacity to mitigate breakdowns. Although just-in-time is compatible with automation, it is possible to use just-in-time principles with very little automation. The primary goal of just-in-time production is to improve product quality with minimal wastage and lower costs.

Just-in-time production management system requires developing durable, more continuous, and longer-term relationships with a small number of key suppliers. In its extreme formulation, suppliers are to be single-sourced. Achieving this may give individual suppliers considerable market power in negotiating better prices and conditions—a situation that could ultimately lead to an abuse of power whereby suppliers extract concessions from manufacturers. To avoid this, high levels of trust and respect must be developed between the supplier and manufacturer.

Some commentators on the just-in-time production management system suggest that its effectiveness is heavily dependent on the organizational culture in which it is established. Just-in-time principles and practices, as incorporated in the Toyota Production System, originated in postwar Japan and ostensibly reflect value systems that are unique to Japan. To date, its performance record over more-traditional mass production systems has been decidedly mixed when independently implemented in Western industrial settings. Nevertheless, the application of just-in-time production management practices achieves optimality in organizations that have more highly advanced total quality approaches in addition to a corporate culture that enables and supports its practices. While many Western manufacturing companies have adopted some type of "lean" initiative, the just-in-time movement has preceded beyond the manufacturing shop floor to white collar and service industries. Unfortunately, many of these efforts at implementing just-in-time practices are often disjointed, fragmented, and piecemeal approaches, motivated to achieve quick fixes aimed at reducing waste or lowering lead times. To be effective, lean applications require a longer-term change perspective, one coupled with a corporate culture that integrates people, processes, and technology. Ostensibly, its philosophy needs to go beyond the shop floor so as to enlighten thinking and practice in both the office and boardroom.

—Kent Rondeau

See also Lean Production

Further Readings

Flynn, B. B., Sakakibara, S., & Schroeder, R. E. (1995). Relationship between JIT and TQM: Practices and performance. *Academy of Management Journal, 38*(5), 1325–1360.

Liker, J. K., & Morgan, J. M. (2006). *The Toyota product development system: Integrating people, processes, and technology.* New York: Productivity Press.

Ogawa, E. (1984). *Modern production management: A Japanese experience.* Tokyo: Asian Productivity Organization.

Ohno, T. (1990). *Just-in-time for today and tomorrow.* Cambridge, MA: Productivity Press.

Walleigh, R. C. (1986). What's your excuse for not using JIT? *Harvard Business Review, 64*(2), 38–54.

Womack, J. P., & Jones, D. T. (1996). *Lean thinking.* New York: Simon & Schuster.

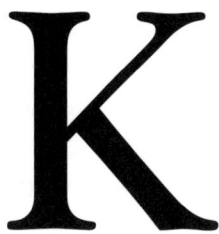

Karoshi

When a number of high-ranking Japanese business executives died without any previous sign of ill-health in the 1980s, the phenomenon was labeled *karoshi,* literally "death from overwork," or death caused by stress and fatigue consequent on long and intensive hours on the job. The most common medical causes of *karoshi* are cerebral and heart disease and mental distortion. The term became popularized in Japan after the Karoshi Hotline was set up by lawyers and doctors in 1988. The hotline estimates that more than 10,000 workers suffer from work-related cardiovascular disease each year.

Conceptual Overview

Because of the continuous high growth of the Japanese economy from the late 1960s, and the speedy recoveries from oil shocks in the 1970s, Japanese management techniques, symbolized by the just-in-time (JIT) logistics system, were studied with keen interest by Western business analysts. While these techniques contributed to their success, at the same time management was placing increasing demands on workers—not only financially, but physically and mentally as well. The phenomenon of *karoshi* became increasingly topical in such an employment environment.

During the bubble economy of 1990s, many Japanese workers increased their dependency on, and allegiance to, their corporate employers. The rapid rise of land prices made them rush to accept enormous and burdensome loans for purchasing their homes. While there were many bankruptcies, generated by the large number of bad loans that followed the bursting of the bubble economy, Japanese companies, faced with accelerated global competition, had to find still greater improvement in productivity, not only those involved in manufacturing, which were already highly controlled, but now also those of the nonmanufacturing sectors.

The financial big bang also resulted in the wide-scale bankruptcies of Japanese financial institutions, which had been bearing the kernel of the corporate grouping in Japan. Frequent amalgamations in this sector changed the shape of the Japanese corporate world. Japanese labor processes, once praised for their efficacy in producing loyal workers, were restructured. Companies introduced systems of promotion based on merit to replace promotion based on seniority and early retirement recommendation systems—schemes based on the presumption of lifetime employment with a single employer. Some companies resorted to bullying and harassment of middle-aged employees to force them to voluntarily resign. Such actions drove many dedicated employees to despair and suicide. The number of deaths by suicide increased sharply during the course of the prolonged period of recession. Particularly noticeable among the statistics were suicides attributable to *karo jisatsu* (overwork and stress among workers aged in their 40s and 50s).

While large numbers of middle-aged workers had become jobless, some workers, especially those of the younger generation, started to question the need to devote their working lives to a single company and began periods of long-term casual employment. As these conditions cut the high fixed labor costs associated with permanent employees, companies welcomed those seeking casual work. This resulted in the further dismantling of the traditional Japanese management style.

The remaining tenured workers faced increasingly excessive demands, such as the common expectation of them to work massive amounts of unpaid voluntary overtime. One of the leading Japanese financial institutions reported that male workers worked an average of 3,000 hours per year, including 700 hours unpaid work. This forced excessive workload is often represented as though it were performed at the workers' choice, by cloaking it under descriptions such as merit recognition systems and flexible working conditions. The unrealistic goals workers set themselves in response to these pressures exacerbated their stress and frustration.

Critical Commentary and Future Directions

Victims of *karoshi* are seldom compensated under the Japanese workers' compensation system. Claimants face considerable procedural difficulties, including the time-consuming nature of the proceedings, a lack of access to evidence, and a biased selection system for referees and compensation hearing board members. The coverage formula for cases of death from overwork, established by the Ministry of Labor in 1987, provides that before compensation may be awarded, it must be objectively recognized that there was a heavier psychological and physical overload or burden than that caused by the employee's usually specified hours worked in the week before the fall. One in-house policy stipulated that just one day of absence during the week preceding collapse ruled out compensation. This formula was revised in 2001, and the number of claims for *karoshi* compensation increased to 819 in 2002, from 466 in 1998. The number of claims for suicides resulting from overwork compensation increased to 341 in 2002, from only 42 in 1998. The number of young people (especially those 29 years old or younger) claiming compensation has also increased.

Nevertheless, the success rate for workers' accident compensation claims has remained pegged at about 30% because of concerns over establishing the legitimacy of *karoshi*, and they are confined to the measurement and compensation issues surrounding the condition. The *karoshi* conditions require that the family of the victim *prove* that long working hours were the cause of the accident. This is extremely difficult to achieve as in most cases the defendant companies can choose not to release vital information, or else to manipulate it in their own favor. The current arrangements are iniquitous, and governments should be obliged to make fairer outcomes possible.

While the labor unions and the government need to be empowered to achieve real compensation for *karoshi* victims, they should also be more proactive in *preventing karoshi*. The number of labors standard inspectors stands at about 3,500, and they monitor and regulate around 4.6 million workplaces in Japan. Clearly, this provision is inadequate.

The direct nexus between unemployment rates and suicide in Japan is due to the poor safety net provisions in the social security system. When an employee who has worked for a company for well over 20 years is laid off through corporate restructuring, that person can receive unemployment insurance for less than a year. Because career change is often not morally or socially acceptable, and vocational training systems to prepare for it are in any event inadequate, many middle-aged workers who find themselves unemployed would not hold much hope for their futures.

Some companies have started to reconsider their promotion-by-merit policies, for which the criteria have often not been made clear and open. Instead they have begun to take into account both seniority and merit when making decisions about wages and promotion. They have sought to restrict head hunting and to more intensely research the suitability of targets to their company. At the same time that some companies are taking back workers they had previously discarded.

Japan, with its rapidly aging society, must largely abandon lifestyles that have been predicated on the presumption of a lifetime's employment with a single, paternalistic employer. It must also enhance its social security system.

—*Keiko Morita*

See also Psychological Safety; Violence; Worker Rights; Working Time

Further Readings

Herbig, P. A., & Palumbo, F. A. (1994). Karoshi: Salaryman sudden death syndrome. *Journal of Managerial Psychology, 9*(7/8), 11–17.

Meek, C. B. (2004). The dark side of Japanese management in the 1990s: Karoshi and ijime in the Japanese workplace. *Journal of Managerial Psychology, 19*(3), 312–331.

Morita, K. (2000). Knowledge and control in the Japanese workplace. In J. Garrick & C. Phodes (Eds.), *Research and knowledge at work: Perspectives, case-studies, and innovative strategies* (pp. 102–116). London: Routledge.

National Defense Counsel for Victims of Karoshi. (1990). *Karoshi: When the "corporate warrior" dies.* Tokyo: Madosha.

KEIRETSU

Keiretsu are corporate conglomerates that originated in Japan after World War II. They are characterized as a network of businesses that hold equity interest in one another, generally as a means of ensuring long-term security. Keiretsu are often found between large manufactures, forging relationships in the supply-chain process.

Conceptual Overview

Keiretsu grew over decades by creating specialized firms with strong ties and relationships with other firms in the group. These groups of firms are sometimes connected by family relationships. The groups are classified as horizontal or vertical.

The major horizontal keiretsu include Mitsui, Mitsubishi, Sumitomo, DKB, Fuyo, and Sanwa. The firms in the horizontal keiretsu have cross-shareholding linkages and interlocking directorships that create a network of firms from a wide variety of industries. *Cross-shareholding* is the practice of one firm holding stock in another and vice versa, thus giving them mutual interests in the success of each firm. *Interlocking directorships* refers to the fact that executives of firm A are on the Board of Directors of firm B and executives of firm B are on the Board of firm A. However, no single firm controls the others, each firm may also have a network of subsidiaries, and those subsidiaries may have their own subsidiaries. The result is a very large network of associated companies. The horizontal keiretsu are similar to what we identify as conglomerates in the United States.

The vertical keiretsu are created by extensive vertical integration, both backward incorporating suppliers and forward through distribution. In other words, the company controls the inputs to production (raw materials, for example) by owning its suppliers, and the distribution channels by owning wholesalers or retailers of the products. These vertical keiretsu include Toyota, Hitachi, and Matsushita. A key difference between the two forms is that the vertical keiretsu typically are related to the primary industry of the leading company, for example automobiles for Toyota and consumer electronics for Matsushita (Panasonic). In the vertical keiretsu, in addition to equity (stockholder) connections, the companies are connected via technology transfer, financial assistance, and human resource assistance. Firms in a keiretsu grow independently but also understand that intragroup competition should be avoided. At the core of each keiretsu is a bank to provide financial resources and a general trading company to serve as an agent for transactions of member firms.

Benefits

Keiretsu offer several benefits to the member firms. They are more able to exercise market power due to their size and/or control of inputs and distribution and use common resources such as technology, brand names, or distribution systems. The association of the many firms also helps to compensate for informational imperfections in capital and labor markets and allows for more leverage in lobbying the government. Additionally, the firms in a keiretsu gain from the sharing of knowledge, trust, and the development of core competencies. The cultural norm of collectivism in Japan contributes to the establishment of trust, which, in turn, leads to reduced transaction costs and increased information sharing about product development and design and technological innovations. Another potential benefit is the ability of smaller firms in the group to have ready customers in the larger, successful firms. This ready access to strong customers stimulates the growth of the smaller firm.

Costs

The interfirm relationships among keiretsu can create a barrier to entry into the Japanese market. By trading within the group, keiretsu are engaging in anticompetitive practices. Thus, the capital requirements for entry are very high. A weakness of the keiretsu system is the static nature of membership in the keiretsu. Entry and exit from a keiretsu are difficult because of the inter-relatedness of their business activities. Though this enables consistency of membership, it also leads to inflexibility and challenges coping with emerging businesses and markets. Although the smaller firms may benefit from selling to the larger members of the keiretsu, those larger members may be receiving acceptable but not optimal resources. High exit barriers present a challenge also. Member firms that find opportunities in new sectors may not have the option of responding to that opportunity while in the keiretsu because of its linkages to the other firms. This challenge is particularly significant when the firm is operating in a mature or declining industry or business sector.

Critical Commentary

Miwa and Ramseyer question whether keiretsu actually exist. In a study entitled "The Fable of the Keiretsu," they present an exhaustive study of the previously discussed intragroup equity and financial connections by examining financial and shareholder records. They conclude, "If the keiretsu financial firms systematically coordinate their loans, that coordination does not appear." In other words, statistical analysis of the evidence regarding the assumptions of keiretsu and intragroup cooperation has been elusive. Miwa and Ramseyer go on to state that among nonfinancial firms the intragroup shareholdings of any sort are minimal. They also maintain a strong view that *keiretsu* are not losing economic power, as suggested by some business journalists and scholars, and therefore are not "unraveling" since, in fact, keiretsu may be figments of the imagination of academic and business journalists.

—*Robert E. Ledman*

See also Organizational Culture; Organizational Design; Organizational Economics; Organizational Structure

Further Readings

Ito, K., & Rose, E. L. (2004). An emerging structure of corporations. *Multinational Business Review, Special Edition, 12*(3), 63–83.

Miwa, Y., & Ramseyer, J. (2002). The fable of the keiretsu. *Journal of Economics & Management Strategy, 11*(2), 169–224.

Porter, M. E., & Sakakibara, M. (2004). Competition in Japan. *Journal of Economic Perspectives, 18*(1), 27–50.

KNOWLEDGE

The term *knowledge* refers to the ability to discriminate within and across contexts. As a field of study, it denotes the varied ways in which actors in particular social situations understand and make sense of where they are and what they are doing.

Conceptual Overview

The definition of knowledge above is broad enough to encompass both the cognitive aspects of knowledge as well as its essentially social nature. It is evident from many years of debate that *knowledge* is an intrinsically ambiguous and equivocal concept. Debates about the nature of knowledge have appeared in philosophical literature since the classical Greek period.

Thus a whole branch of philosophy, *epistemology*—from the Greek words *episteme* (knowledge) and *logos* (word/speech)—deals with, and debates on, the nature, origin, and scope of knowledge.

While there are many strands to these debates, two contrasting views of knowledge have come to the forefront, at least in the organization studies area. These have been usefully summarized as the *epistemology of possession,* which treats knowledge as something that people have, and the *epistemology of practice,* which treats knowledge (or, often the preferred term is *knowing*) as something that people do. Much current work on organizational knowledge and knowledge management reflects one or other of these views, although there is still a lack of agreement as to whether they are fundamentally opposing or could in fact be complementary.

The epistemology of possession emphasizes the cognitive aspects of knowledge—knowledge is seen as a possession of the human mind. In this view, knowledge is often treated as a resource—a mental capacity, or "high value form of information"—that allows people to understand where they are and make decisions about what to do next or to imagine the likely consequences of their actions. Theorists adopting this perspective have attempted to identify the different kinds or forms of knowledge that individuals and groups possess. For example, drawing heavily (and some might argue inappropriately) from Polanyi's earlier work on personal knowledge, a major distinction is often made between *tacit* and *explicit* knowledge. Tacit knowledge is associated with the skills or know-how that people develop through their own experience in specific contexts (e.g., knowing how to ride a bicycle) and has an essentially personal quality that makes it hard to formalize or communicate. In contrast, explicit knowledge can be "spelled out" or codified, making it more communicable across contexts (e.g., knowing what components a bicycle needs to have to make it work and how they should be put together).

Reflecting a Cartesian view that has tended to dominate Western thinking—where objective "truth" is valued over subjective "opinion"—tacit knowledge is often treated as a highly subjective, idiosyncratic, insecure, and uncontrollable type of knowledge that is "owned" by individuals. This has led to an emphasis, by many theorists, on converting this tacit knowledge into more reliable, accessible, systematic, and useful explicit forms in order to control and deploy it for the collective good of the organization. For example, Nonaka—who draws from Plato's widely quoted definition of knowledge as "justified true belief"—observes how the ability of organizations to create and use knowledge depends on their ability to externalize individual, tacit knowledge into more readily communicable, explicit forms. This view, coupled with proclamations in recent decades that knowledge is a—if not the—key organizational resource, underpins many studies of *knowledge management,* which focus on the exploitation or reuse of individual knowledge created in one part of the organization by its conversion into more explicit forms (e.g., new routines or databases) that can be applied in other parts of the organization. An underlying assumption in these kinds of studies is that knowledge can be taken out of, or abstracted from, the social context in which it was produced (e.g., by individuals doing their work), objectified, and transferred to other parts of the organization where it can be reapplied. Knowledge is therefore treated as an objective entity or "thing" that has particular characteristics in its own right and that, like other resources, can be moved around and managed.

The idea that knowledge can be extracted from live social interaction to be possessed (stored, shared, and distributed) by organizations and individuals has been widely criticized by proponents of the epistemology of practice. Starting from the premise that knowledge is socially constructed, some see knowledge as emerging from the social practices that groups are engaged in, not as something that stands outside those practices. In studies that began as a critique of cognitive assumptions (be it in relation to schooling or to artificial intelligence), writers embracing the epistemology of practice showed how the knowledge enacted by different groups was inextricably bound up with the way these groups worked together and developed shared identities. Their studies showed that social groups as diverse as photocopier technicians, tailors, and alcoholics did not spend their time converting tacit knowledge into explicit knowledge, but rather created norms, stories, and representations that enabled the individual's experience to be related to the knowledge of the wider community. Some studies in this area prefer to use the term *knowing* rather than *knowledge* precisely to underline this interweaving of what people know with who they are and what they do.

The epistemology of practice also stresses the need to take seriously the materiality of everyday life as both constitutive of, and constituted by, social activity. Objects such as technological artifacts, for example, are not merely deployed by individuals and groups to achieve particular ends, they are also an essential part of practice and so set limits around what change in practice is possible. For example, Orlikowski describes the ways in which material entities (e.g., laptop computers, Internet connections, phone lines, cables, connectors, pens, mute buttons on telephones)—or in her terms, the "stuff" of everyday life—act as "scaffolds" for social activity (in her case, an online business meeting). This attention to the role of artifacts has also been extended to understanding the way different communities of practice are able to collaborate through the use of what have been termed *boundary objects*. For example, in product development settings, objects such as design prototypes, blueprints, and drawings may serve as boundary objects between designers and product engineers. Where Nonaka described such objects as a way of codifying knowledge, in the practice-based view their role is to enable collaborating groups to represent their different ways of knowing to each other.

When applied to the organizational arena, this concern with ways of knowing directs our attention away from the accumulation and analysis of experience that is a feature of much work in the field of organizational learning. Instead, it highlights the way in which organizational structures and processes shape social practices and the communities that develop around them. This helps to explain the persistent findings of a strong horizontal dimension in organizational knowledge. As studies have shown, when knowing is distributed among a social community, it may readily span internal and external organizational boundaries, but it cannot be easily abstracted upwards as rules or routines.

Critical Commentary and Future Directions

The conflict between possession and practice as ways of viewing knowledge is not easily resolved. As noted, these views are deeply rooted in philosophical and research traditions that have developed in open opposition to each other. To the extent that these conflicting views expose new and hitherto unsuspected aspects of knowledge, their differences can be seen as productive. At the same time, however, this conflict creates a fulcrum for debate that may ultimately limit its scope and relevance to contemporary questions. This is not only because centering the debate on knowledge per se risks recycling long-held and incommensurable differences. Equally important is the tendency for such a debate to become self-sealing, to marginalize or exclude other facets of knowledge (technology, for example) and why it has become important to contemporary societies. Indeed, it is clear that a concern for epistemology on its own may lead to the neglect of several key aspects of social reality.

Here one can cite, first, the influence of information technology. This has undoubtedly helped to problematize knowledge, in the sense that people no longer take for granted the way it is produced, or validated, and the forms that it takes. Numerous examples from the Internet ecology show how knowledge has been problematized in this way. Consider, for instance, the emergence of Wikipedia an online encyclopedia produced and maintained by millions of volunteer contributors worldwide—or the spread of Linux and other open source communities, which apply the same principles to software production. In these examples, one finds some archetypal forms of knowledge—canonical academic knowledge and IT software—being produced and validated in radically different ways. The ways of knowing that such examples illustrate are a far cry from the more conventional expert-based and hierarchical forms that they help to substitute for—namely, the arcane and slow-moving procedures of, say, the *Encyclopedia Britannica,* or the research and development function of an IBM.

Developments such as these have promoted the perception that knowledge is a productive resource. At the same time, where such IT-based systems have failed, they have also highlighted that knowledge is sticky and not easily shared through systems alone. Now, these issues have certainly helped to fuel the debates on the nature of knowledge (and help to explain their emergence in fields such as organization studies and information systems). Yet, beyond critiquing the assumptions that underpin technology-based approaches such as knowledge management (and explaining why they sometimes fail), the epistemological debate outlined above tells us little about how these new technologies foster new ways of knowing (and why, with examples such as the Internet communities described above, they sometimes succeed).

Second, the epistemological debate also tends to gloss over the question of power. Although the work of Foucault and others makes the power-knowledge nexus central to that perspective on contemporary society, writers in both the possession and practice camps have been criticized for neglecting the political origins and effects of knowledge. We do not need to subscribe to the Foucauldian perspective to recognize that the ability to discriminate—to be a connoisseur of fine wines, for example, but equally to be an expert in the open source community—is bound up with the way in which societies and social groups allocate power and status to certain activities and refuse it to others.

Third, and finally, we need to ask whether a concern with the finer points of epistemology is not actually masking a wider shift in the way societies produce and consume knowledge. Many commentators, some pro, some anti, have argued that the production of knowledge is increasingly about solving society's problems—and therefore less about knowledge for its own sake, or ivory tower knowledge as it is sometimes known. Both pro and anti camps are able to cite widespread evidence for such a shift—be it in the growing links between business and universities, or in the rise of knowledge-intensive sectors such as management consultancy firms. It is also reflected in the rhetoric of the "knowledge economy" that has helped to justify the adoption of more neoliberal economic policies by governments in the United States, the United Kingdom, and elsewhere.

The knowledge economy rhetoric has probably helped to silence political debate about the implications of these changes in the way knowledge is produced. However, this is no argument for the same silence within academic debate. To argue for our conflicting epistemologies without some attention to the wider context for our debate may mean abetting, albeit indirectly, an increasingly instrumental attitude to knowledge. This view of knowledge as justifiable only in terms of solving immediate problems—and usually business problems—is an attitude that is ultimately hostile to academic debate itself.

—*Jacky Swan*

See also Actionable Knowledge; Knowledge Management; Organizational Knowledge; Power; Tacit Knowledge

Further Readings

Cook, S. D. N., & Brown, J. S. (1999). Bridging epistemologies: The generative dance between organizational knowledge and organizational knowing. *Organization Science, 10*(4), 381–400.

Foucault, M. (1980). *Power/knowledge: Selected interviews and other writings, 1972–1977.* Brighton, UK: Harvester.

Nonaka, I. (1994). A dynamic theory of organizational knowledge creation. *Organization Science, 5*(1), 14–37.

Orlikowski, W. (2006). Material knowing: The scaffolding of human knowledgeability. *European Journal of Information Systems, 15*(5), 470–472.

Polanyi, M. (1962). *Personal knowledge.* Chicago: University of Chicago Press.

Tsoukas, H., & Vladimirou, E. (2001). What is organizational knowledge? *Journal of Management Studies, 38*(7), 973–993.

KNOWLEDGE CREATION

Organizational knowledge creation can be defined as a process that organizationally amplifies the knowledge created by individuals and crystallizes it at the group level through dialogue, discussion, experience sharing, or observation. Most organizations recognize the deliberate creation of new knowledge as the cornerstone of innovation, a key factor of competitive advantage. While knowledge per se cannot fuel innovation, knowledge creation does.

Conceptual Overview

Knowledge that an organization gains and did not have in its repertoire before is termed *new organizational knowledge*. The emergence of such new knowledge can result from a serendipitous event, in which knowledge is discovered unintentionally. One example is the discovery of penicillin, which resulted from observing the antibiotic effects of some molds during an unrelated experiment. However, firms can and do not rely on this. A firm can work several ways in order to gain new knowledge intentionally. On one hand, knowledge is recruited by acquiring experts or organizational units or by cooperating with partner firms, thus accessing and gaining new knowledge (exploitation of knowledge that exists outside the organization). On the other hand, firms engage in a process of creating new knowledge (exploration of knowledge) by building upon the existing intraorganizational knowledge, utilizing impulses and sparks from the outside. The concept of organizational knowledge creation pertains to the latter way, the exploration of knowledge, as knowledge exploitation utilizes knowledge that has emerged by previous knowledge creation.

A theory of knowledge creation was introduced by Nonaka in 1994. It is based on Polanyi's introduction of tacit knowledge in 1966. According to Nonaka's theory, knowledge is created through the conversion between tacit knowledge, which is personal and context-specific, and explicit knowledge, which is easily expressed and codified. This assumption allows the postulation of four different "modes" of knowledge conversion: socialization (tacit to tacit), externalization (tacit to explicit), combination (explicit to explicit), and internalization (explicit to tacit).

Socialization comprises the conversion of tacit knowledge. Because tacit knowledge cannot be communicated or passed on to others easily, it is characterized by an intense interaction between individuals. Moreover, socialization occurs through an exchange of tacit knowledge that is based on common mental models (knowledge structures held by members of a group) and abilities and—at the same time—contributes to the enhancement of them. Without some form of common experience, it is extremely difficult for people to exchange and create new tacit knowledge.

Externalization is a process of articulating tacit knowledge and therewith transforming it into explicit knowledge. It then takes the shapes of descriptions, concepts, or hypotheses. The explication of tacit knowledge allows us to share it with others, and as the knowledge loses its tacit quality, it often becomes more commonly available. An act of codifying or converting tacit knowledge into explicit knowledge is writing.

Combination consists of three steps: First, explicit knowledge is acquired or collected from inside and outside the organization. Management figures or technical information from all over the company are examples for (firm-)internal knowledge, while published literature or material about competitors' sales, markets, or products provide external knowledge. Second, the collected bodies of existing explicit knowledge are synthesized. They are sorted, combined, edited, and processed to form new, more complex and systematic sets of explicit knowledge. In the third step, the new explicit knowledge is disseminated among the members of the organization.

Knowledge *internalization* is the process of absorbing explicit knowledge, such as accumulated explicit organizational knowledge, into individually held tacit knowledge. This conversion or manifestation of explicit knowledge can be done by actually applying that knowledge, thereby absorbing and embodying it. There are two different routes: (1) through personal experience in which knowledge is generated from real-world *experiences* (e.g., day-to-day work) and (2) through simulation and *experimentation* in which knowledge is generated from the "virtual" or "simulated" world.

While each of the four knowledge conversion modes creates new knowledge independently, the theory hinges on a dynamic interaction between all modes. It states that organizational knowledge creation takes place when all four modes of knowledge creation form a continual cycle.

Nonaka's approach explains the creation of organizational knowledge theoretically and substantiated, and thus, is widely acknowledged. The number of other scholars who have investigated the subject matter in detail is very limited. Moreover, authors who have dwelt on a theoretical explanation of knowledge creation have largely built on the contributions of Nonaka, merely modifying and/or adding single aspects, which underlines the theory's contribution and value.

Critical Commentary and Future Directions

Critics and their empirical research challenge Nonaka's assumption of a full cycle, in which socialization would be followed by externalization and so forth. While they operationalized, empirically observed, and even identified the four modes as influential on innovativeness (e.g., in the setting of new product development), they did not find them appearing in a cyclical manner.

Further, there is no creation of organizational knowledge without the creation of knowledge by individuals. Knowledge emerges because individuals learn. Considering this, the theory of organizational knowledge creation takes the contributions of traditional individual (behavioristic, cognitivistic, social) and collective (participative, cooperative, team) learning theories as a departure point. For example the mode of combination focuses on cognitive respective thought processes and involves cognitivistic learning theories. Also, team learning processes, where the knowledge available in the group is combined to new knowledge, have similarities to combination in Nonaka's sense. However, the link from individual and collective learning theories has merely been made transparent. Further research is needed to investigate the linkage (e.g., revealing whether there are additional organizational knowledge creation activities that are essential or contributing to understand the knowledge creation modes more in depth).

Another area of concern is the lumping together of organizational knowledge creation and organizational learning by a number of researchers, as there are major differences. For example, the core concern of organizational learning is the development of social knowledge, including a collectively shared repertoire of behavior that enables the organization to improve its understanding and adaptation to the dynamic environment. Organizational change is in focus, involving the whole organization, fostered by the management means of organizational development. On the contrary, organizational knowledge creation centers on the creation of technical or scientific knowledge (e.g., for the purpose of developing new products). Knowledge management is in focus, involving only parts of the organization, such as R&D or marketing. Consequently, further research is necessary to clarify the boundaries as well as the link between the concepts and theories of knowledge creation and organizational learning.

—*Anja Schulze*

See also Knowledge; Knowledge Management; Learning; Organizational Knowledge; Organizational Learning

Further Readings

Argyris, C., & Schön, D. (1978). *Organizational learning: A theory of action perspective*. Reading, MA: Addison-Wesley.
Kogut, B., & Zander, U. (1992). Knowledge of the firm, combinative capabilities, and the replication of technology. *Organization Science, 3*(3), 383–397.
Nonaka, I. (1994). A dynamic theory of organizational knowledge creation. *Organization Science, 5*(1), 14–37.
Polanyi, M. (1966). *The tacit dimension*. London: Cox & Wyman.
Von Krogh, G., Ichijo, K., & Nonaka, I. (2000). *Enabling knowledge creation*. New York: Oxford University Press.

KNOWLEDGE-INTENSIVE FIRMS

Knowledge-intensive firms are distinguished from other kinds of firms in that they are said to contain unique qualities; they claim to produce qualified products and/or service, and even generate new and unique knowledge. Knowledge-intensive firms are not bound to specific fields of practice. Organizations as diverse as law and accounting firms, management, engineering and computer consultancy companies, advertising agencies, research and development units, and pharmaceutical and high-tech companies are often seen as typical knowledge-intensive firms.

Conceptual Overview

The ideas of knowledge work, the knowledge worker, and knowledge-intensive firms are quite recent. Although one can argue that knowledge work has always been around, as has the knowledge worker, the categories have emerged as analytical tools in organization analysis the past 10 to 15 years. In particular, the recent explosive interest in knowledge management has fueled the interest in the rather awkward combination of knowledge and organization.

The concept of the knowledge-intensive firm is not unproblematic. The idea of knowledge-intensiveness is vague and tends to encourage interpretations of knowledge that erase the distinction between knowledge and other forms of human capacity, in particular if one considers so-called embodied and encultured versions of it. It is difficult to substantiate knowledge-intensive companies and knowledge workers as distinct, uniform categories. Nevertheless, differences exist between professional service and high-tech companies on one hand and more routinized service and industry companies on the other (e.g., in terms of broadly socially shared ideas about the significance of a long theoretical education and intellectual capacities for the work).

Typically, the literature suggests that the concept applies to organizational settings that share the following common denominators:

1. The personnel are highly qualified and have academic background or other comparable preemployment training and education.

2. Products and services are complex and/or nonstandard.

3. Product, market, and personnel development are significant activities within the organization.

The literature on knowledge-intensive firms generally pictures knowledge-intensive firms as a departure from the bureaucratic form, to the extent that bureaucracy sometimes operates as the antithesis of knowledge-intensive firms. The difficulties of employing valid and reliable rules and performance measures lead many authors to emphasize cultural-ideological or clan control instead of bureaucratic or marketlike (output) forms of internal control.

One central dimension of knowledge-intensive firms is ambiguity—persistent uncertainty (not easily reduced through more information), confusion, and contradiction. Ambiguity is present in several ways for knowledge-intensive firms. The concept of knowledge is, for example, highly ambiguous, thus making both the product in knowledge-intensive firms (knowledge) and its production processes (knowledge development and maintenance) ambiguous in character. The very idea of sophisticated knowledge—scarce expertise in a socially legitimated area—means that complexity and uncertainty prevail. This concerns the very nature of knowledge, calling for theoretical thinking and the exercise of judgment rather than the providing of objective facts. Because the results of knowledge work frequently are difficult to assess, this calls for subjective judgment—where variations among experts are not infrequent.

Critical Commentary and Future Directions

Knowledge-intensive firms are typically engaged in complex and difficult tasks, which cannot be perfectly converted into standardized work procedures and regulations. Thus, knowledge-intensive firms are forced to attract and retain qualified people who can adapt their repertoires to meet the demands of the task. As a consequence, to manage them strictly through a focus on behavior is difficult due to the nature of the work, as self-organization is necessary. Applying Blackler's terminology on knowledge forms means that the most important organizational knowledge is dislocated from the *embedded* form, typically present in the assembly line or the machine-bureaucracy, to the *embrained* form. In contrast to the bureaucratic form, mission-critical organizational knowledge is thus not "stored" or manifested in procedures and processes in knowledge-intensive firms, but rather in qualified individuals.

The claim that knowledge-intensive firms break with or substitute the bureaucratic form is sometimes linked to general societal and organizational trends and development. These are frequently described as increasing the significance of knowledge, flexibility, networking, and innovation—all features making bureaucracy and its standard elements (hierarchy, stability, standardization, and rules) less relevant as key organizational mechanisms. There is currently an interest among organizational practitioners and academics in highlighting "knowledge" as a key dimension in management and organization. "Exemplary" organizations are claimed to have shifted from capital-intensive industries, such as steel and automobiles, to information-intensive industries, such as financial services and logistics, and innovation-driven industries, such as computer software and pharmaceutical companies. In the latter, knowledge and the ability to apply it—competences and capabilities—are seen as vital.

Scholars also claim that entrepreneurial orientations of highly qualified personnel are more and more central for the operations of companies. Certain trends are claimed to have characterized organizational evolution for quite some time. First, more and more organizational members are expected to develop the ability to self-organize around operational, market, and partnering tasks. Second, an increase in the number of personnel expected to perform entrepreneurial tasks—identifying customer needs and then finding and focusing resources on them. Third, there are increased membership opportunities to experience psychological ownership of particular clients, markets, customized products and services, and so on.

Other authors talk about the need for the employees to develop and learn new knowledge. It has simply become more knowledge-intensive to do business. Those authors suggest that organizations are knowledge systems.

These authors emphasize general trends regarding organizational types, forms of management, and the significance of knowledge. Although the scope and depth of environmental changes sometimes are criticized, there seems to be a consensus that environmental pressures play an increasingly important role in shaping organizational action. Organizations aspire to be customer oriented. They are increasingly adapting flexible and decentralized work schemes. Taken together, these shifts favor organizational structures often associated with knowledge-intensive firms, such as the adhocracy.

As mentioned, the significance of knowledge and its adjunct learning are strongly emphasized in contemporary writings on management. As advocated by Senge, the manager is no longer a boss but rather a teacher, primarily concerned with knowledge development and learning. Although the manager-as-teacher phenomenon may lack strong empirical support, several intellectual currents push forward the idea that changes in technology, business environment, and society have redefined the managers' role. Most notably, these currents are visible in the related ideas of organizational learning and knowledge management. Organizational learning is typically associated to the idea of *communities of practice*. The vocabulary in use—*community, sharing, caring, nurturing social relations*—breaks radically with conventional ideas of bureaucracy. Management is rather a matter of coping with and encouraging diversity and of facilitating knowledge sharing. As Carla O'Dell and Jackson Grayson observe, sharing is difficult if not impossible to cultivate through the use of formal reward systems, but calls for intrinsic motivation—that is, knowledge sharing needs to be self-rewarding and thus largely outside the scope of influence of an external actor such as management, as conventionally understood.

Typically, texts on knowledge management explicitly or implicitly claim that the assistance of the creation, maintenance, and dispersion of knowledge is the manager's most important job. For example, Ikujiro Nonaka explicitly links managerial practices and knowledge creation in an attempt to provide ideas on how to manage knowledge creation. In the context of knowledge creation, Nonaka claims that managers are best viewed as catalysts. This breaks with conventional ideas of managers as mainly operating based in and through the means of bureaucracy.

To summarize, knowledge-intensive firms typically deal with tasks that require intellectual capacities, rather than financial capital or manpower. They tend to invalidate and break with bureaucratic modes of operation: hierarchy, division of labor, formalization, and standardization. The literature on contemporary organizations in general and knowledge-intensive firms in particular suggests that bureaucratic modes of operation are substituted for more organic and flexible forms of organizing. This seems to be a general trend: markets are more turbulent, customer preferences are more differentiated, and production systems are more knowledge-intensive.

—Dan Kärreman

See also Knowledge; Knowledge Creation; Knowledge Management

Further Readings

Alvesson, M. (1995). *Management of knowledge-intensive companies.* New York: de Gruyter.

Blackler, F. (1995). Knowledge, knowledge work, and organizations. *Organization Studies, 16*(6), 1021–1046.

Davenport, T., & Prusak, L. (1998). *Working knowledge.* Cambridge, MA: Harvard Business School Press.

du Gay, P., & Salaman, G. (1992). The cult(ure) of the customer. *Journal of Management Studies 29*, 615–633.

Miles, R., Snow, C., Mathews, J., Miles, G., & Coleman, H. (1997). Organizing in the knowledge age: Anticipating the cellular form. *Academy of Management Executive, 11*(4), 7–24.

Mintzberg, H. (1998). Covert leadership: Notes on managing professionals. *Harvard Business Review, 76*(6), 140–147.

Nonaka, I. (1994). A dynamic theory of organizational knowledge creation. *Organization Science, 5*, 14–37.

O'Dell, C., & Grayson, J. (1998). If only we knew what we know: Identification and transfer of best practices. *California Management Review, 40*(3), 154–173.

Senge, P. (1996). The leader's new work: Building learning organizations. In K. Starkey (Ed.), *How organizations learn* (pp. 288–315). London: Thomson.

Starbuck, W. (1992). Learning by knowledge-intensive firms. *Journal of Management Studies. 29*(6), 713–740.

Wenger, E., & Snyder, W. (2000). Communities of practices: The organizational frontier. *Harvard Business Review, 78*(1), 139–145.

Wikström, S., & Normann, R. (1994). *Knowledge and value.* London: Routledge.

Knowledge Management

The term *knowledge management* (KM) denotes the explicit strategies, tools, and practices applied by management that seek to make knowledge a resource for the organization. The field of KM is concerned with the development of concepts that illuminate or enhance the application of these practices.

Conceptual Overview

As this definition indicates, the theory and practice of KM encompasses multiple levels of analysis, ranging from overall organizational strategies through the development of different tools and ways of representing knowledge, to more microlevel practices of management. Equally, knowledge may be constituted as a resource in a variety of different ways—including a legally defined form of intellectual property, an accounting-based intangible asset, and valued lessons for practice. As such, KM is really an umbrella term to designate a number of different strands of managerial activity that seek to improve firms' exploitation of knowledge. These include strategies for managing knowledge-based organizations, for representing knowledge assets or "intellectual capital" in accounting, and for capturing and distributing organizational learning.

Although some authors claim that KM is a timeless activity—that organizations have always done it—it is clear that the self-conscious attempt to exploit knowledge in this way is a relatively recent phenomenon. Many of the conceptual foundations were laid by a small group of writers in the early 1990s. This group included Ikujiro Nonaka, whose work has been especially influential as a way of explaining the conversion of the tacit knowledge of organization members into the explicit form, which can be widely applied by the organization. The notion of tacit knowledge was originally developed by the philosopher Michael Polanyi to highlight the importance of knowledge that cannot be easily verbalized—as Polanyi, put it, "we know more than we can say." The distinction between tacit and explicit knowledge is often equated with the difference between "know-how" and "know-what."

Thus the classic example of tacit knowledge, as described by Polanyi, is knowing how to ride a bike.

Drawing on this account, Nonaka describes four stages of knowledge creation that he terms *internalization* (explicit to tacit), *socialization* (tacit to tacit), *externalization* (tacit to explicit), and *combination* (explicit to explicit). Nonaka argued that this cycle was central to the process of innovation within firms and applied it to analyzing the development of a new bread-making machine. The (re)discovery of tacit knowledge and its practical application to innovation did much to spark initial interest in KM. It seemed to offer businesspeople a new, hitherto hidden resource to be mined and exploited and gave academics a new focus for theoretical debates.

A further contribution to the debate on KM came from writers in the organization studies field who were not so much concerned with the functional outputs of knowledge, as with the diverse sources of knowledge within organizational settings. An important influence here was the work of Frank Blackler, who drew on a range of sociological studies to identify five different types of knowledge. These he termed *embrained* (conceptual skills and cognitive abilities), *embodied* (action oriented and only partly explicit), *encultured* (shared understanding through the development of an organizational culture), *embedded* (resides in systemic routines) and *encoded* (information conveyed by signs and symbols) knowledge. This and similar taxonomies extended the debate around organizational knowledge, but also implicitly extended the scope and opportunities for KM by highlighting new arenas for exploitation.

A similar trajectory—making knowledge manageable by breaking it down into components—is evident in the work of another influential writer, Karl-Erik Sveiby. Sveiby's contribution was to advocate the development of accounting measures to give some recognition to the knowledge-based intangible assets of the firm. Sveiby's work reflected the contribution that Scandinavian writers and firms, notably the financial services firm Skandia, made to pioneering attempts to evaluate the different components of a firm's intellectual capital. By defining the firm's knowledge-base as, at least metaphorically, akin to financial capital, these pioneers sought to demonstrate that traditional accounting methods radically undervalued key capabilities of the firm. More specifically, Sveiby and others argued that intellectual capital was an enduring resource for the firm and could be broken down into several contributory components: *human capital* (the skills of employees), *structural capital* (the learned operating routines of the firm), and *customer capital* (relationships with customers). By highlighting the difference between the book value (i.e., given by conventional accounting for assets) and market value (the firm's valuation by the stock market) of companies, these pioneers were able to develop a strong critique of existing accounting methods as inappropriate to the emerging knowledge economy. Although the collapse of the dot-com bubble poured cold water on some of these ideas (suggesting that market values were sometimes wildly inflated), the persistent inability of accounting methods to adequately represent the key drivers of economic value within firms provides continuing support for the basic argument.

While the work of writers such as Nonaka and Sveiby highlighted the exploitation of knowledge through innovation and business strategy, others have been more skeptical about the manageability of knowledge. In particular, one important strand in the literature on KM (which also overlaps with debates on organizational knowledge) has to do with embeddedness of knowledge in specific social and organizational contexts. This strand can be traced back to the important ethnomethodological work of Lave and Wenger on the acquisition and sharing of knowledge within informal social and occupational groups. Where other KM studies framed knowledge within a business life-cycle model of creation, development, and diffusion, the work of Lave and Wenger drew on noncorporate examples such as alcoholics and tailors and located knowledge at the hub of daily life within particular social groups. Their work was originally presented as a rejoinder to existing views in the education field, especially narrowly cognitive views that saw learning simply as a transfer of information from the teacher to the learner in classroom settings. In contrast, Lave and Wenger sought to take learning out of the classroom and relocate it within everyday life at work and home. They argued that the acquisition of knowledge came from participating in what they termed the *community of practice*. The latter they saw as representing the strong ties between work and community created by shared identities, understandings, and meanings.

Subsequent writers sought to apply this original concept of the community of practice to the debate around KM. An important contribution here came from the work of John Seely Brown and Paul Duguid, who translated communities of practice into the business arena by relating the concept to Julian Orr's ethnographic study of Xerox photocopier repair people (customer service reps). In this study, Orr had discovered that the Xerox rep's working day typically revolved around informal meetings with other reps over breakfast, lunch, and coffee. At these meetings, the reps would continuously swap war stories about malfunctioning machines that could not be repaired simply by going through the know-what of the repair manual. Orr found that one of these informal conversations would be worth hours of training. While chatting, the reps posed questions to each other, offered solutions, laughed at mistakes, and generally kept each other up to date about what they knew and what they'd learned on the job. As a result, knowledge was shared extensively among the community about ways of dealing with unusual glitches and problems that simply were not covered in the photocopier repair manual. Significantly, Xerox management was unaware of this informal community and its value to the business. They believed that the reps worked independently and that any socializing during the day was therefore inefficient. When Xerox management attempted to stop the coffee-break sessions, however, they discovered that the reps' *efficiency* (number of calls made) increased, but their *effectiveness* (number of calls required to complete a repair) was reduced. Brown and Duguid's retelling of the story of the Xerox reps' community and management's response became one of the iconic stories that helped to stimulate both theoretical and practical interest in KM. They used this and similar stories to suggest that while communities of practice were not on organization charts, and were not officially sanctioned, they were nonetheless an important ingredient in business performance.

Since the seminal works of the early and mid-1990s, the volume and complexity of academic debate on KM has expanded hugely, making it, as Linda Argote notes, much more difficult to develop a holistic or integrated account of the field. However, while it is impossible to identify the many ways in which, the theory and practice of KM have evolved in recent years, it seems clear that the different strands of thinking outlined above are linked to the emergence of two major approaches to KM tools and practices, which, though variously labeled by different writers, can be briefly summarized as the cognitive versus the community approach.

In the cognitive approach, KM involves extracting, storing, and reusing the valuable knowledge located inside employees' heads or in successful organizational practices via the use of IT tools and other artifacts. Tacit knowledge is codified into more explicit forms. "Lessons learned" exercises and "after action reviews," for example, attempt to codify and capture experience in project and work activities. Typically, then, this form of KM involves *centralizing* knowledge that is currently scattered across the organization to make it more accessible by a variety of groups according to business needs. The development of centralized databases and corporate intranets is one example of this approach.

As outlined above, the community approach is a more recent development. This draws on workplace studies that have highlighted the socially constructed nature of knowledge within communities of practice. Such communities are seen as critical to the sharing of tacit knowledge within the organization, providing, as they do, a forum for the swapping of stories and experience. The community model thus highlights the importance of shared work practices and understandings to the acquisition and sharing of knowledge. KM initiatives drawing on the community model have often focused on the development of virtual or online communities aimed at promoting knowledge-sharing between geographically dispersed groups of practitioners.

Critical Commentary and Future Directions

Relevant background for explaining the emergence of KM is the combination of rising global competition with the increased availability of information systems and tools that enable new forms of virtual collaboration across and between organizations. These factors, and the associated restructuring of business sectors, have created new sources of uncertainty about the sources and drivers of economic value. This uncertain environment seems to have prompted many firms to seize on KM as a way of speeding up and extending their ability to exploit knowledge—either by improving the throughput rate of R&D and innovation processes, or by spreading best practices in operations.

Against this kind of background, KM became a profitable label to apply to many IT-based systems and the offerings of consultancy firms. These firms, and other business intermediaries such as business media, publishers, and professional associations, seem to have played an important part in the diffusion of KM ideas and tools. Many consultancies, for example, were persuasive advocates of KM because they were at the forefront of early applications within their own practices. Equally, the discovery of KM's business potential prompted a huge growth in the number of books and articles on the topic, even extending to a *Complete Idiot's Guide to Knowledge Management.*

The success of KM has not been without its critics, however. The sheer scale of KM's diffusion into business arenas, for example, has lead researchers such as Scarbrough and Swan to dub it a *management fashion.* This is not necessarily a criticism because such fashions are a powerful way of spreading new ideas. In this respect, at least, KM has been very successful. Much of this success can be attributed to the ambiguity of the concept—the very fact that it can support the many different interpretations outlined above. In addition, as a new area of management thinking, KM has seen a contest for territory with a number of different professional and management disciplines trying to stake their claims and in the process further escalating the level of interest. Although these different forces promoting KM have sometimes created confusion rather than understanding, the continuing debate on KM's scope and purpose has helped to create a valuable space for interaction between social science research and organizational practices, which is not found in some more established disciplines.

Against these positive aspects of KM's spread, however, one negative implication of the management fashion tag must be recognized—namely, that KM's implementation in practice has lagged a long way behind its diffusion. Despite the highly publicized success of a small number of firms in applying KM, adoption in practice has been much more limited than the spread of KM thinking would suggest, and many KM initiatives have run into major roadblocks. Many of the early KM initiatives, for example, were based on a cognitive approach to knowledge. Failure here often had to do with their tendency to equate knowledge with information, frequently overstating the potential benefits of IT systems. As Michael Polanyi pointed out, knowledge, unlike information, is personal—that is, it involves a knowing subject. It follows that knowledge tends to be embedded within the social contexts of individual action. Moreover, some writers, following Polanyi, have argued that the notion of converting tacit knowledge into explicit knowledge, which is axiomatic to many KM practices, is misguided. Hari Tsoukas, for example, argues that the terms *tacit* and *explicit* are not different *forms,* but simply coexisting *dimensions* of knowledge.

Although the community perspective avoids some of these pitfalls, it is also increasingly subject to criticism. In translating the concept of communities of practice to their own operations, managers have frequently neglected or ignored many of the original implications of the concept—for example, its informal, nonpurposive nature, and the importance of socialization, identity, and participation in practice. Instead, they have used the term as a label for new cross-functional or cross-national units, which are designed to encourage participation in collective problem-solving activities. As a result, writers such as Alessia Contu and Hugh Willmott argue that communities of practice have become "social objects" that extend managerial exploitation of the workforce.

This critique points to the need for the KM literature—both theoretical and practical—to be more sensitive to the role played by management in KM. Up to this point, much of the focus has been on the mechanisms of exploiting different types of knowledge. The active role of management, and indeed of management knowledge, has not been fully explored. Yet managers are not simply the passive recipients or executors of the concepts and tools of KM. They may apply them for political purposes, as noted by Contu and Willmott, or for reinforcing existing structures of control. They may equally be applied to programs of change and restructuring. In this sense, understanding the way in which existing forms of management knowledge mediate and shape KM ideas is critical to addressing their outcomes for different stakeholder groups. One example of this is the link that has emerged between the spread of KM ideas and the active role of IS professionals in using such ideas to justify investments in new IT systems. This link helps to explain the popularity of cognitive approaches to KM and the association with IT.

It follows that from the point of view of better understanding KM's progress into practice, and even in attempting to speed up that progress, there is a need for greater attention to the active role that managers play in shaping its application to organizational practices. Addressing that role may lead in several different directions. For example, it may lead to greater interest in the *economic* evaluation of KM activities. If knowledge is indeed a valued resource for business, what are the barriers posed by existing accounting systems to adequately recognizing this value? And what are the implications for managers seeking to justify investments in KM?

A second approach might involve focusing on the role of *discourse* in KM. Because stories and language are crucial both in the sharing of knowledge—as highlighted by Orr's study—understanding the way in which the discourse of KM develops is relevant not only to understanding its diffusion, but also to its application in practice. This approach would take the interest in the concepts around knowledge and KM as a function of organizations' willingness and ability to be reflexive about their practices. It is ironic, for example, that an idea such as *tacit knowledge* has real consequences for organizational practices when managers begin to talk about it and apply it to their own business strategies.

In addition, an *organizational* perspective on KM might explore the dilemmas that managers face in explicitly constituting knowledge as a resource within organizations based on bureaucratic and Taylorist models. In organizations that are designed to minimize knowledge and that view it primarily as a cost to production, the reworking of KM may struggle to be anything more than cosmetic. While some writers have predicted the demise of such forms in an age of outsourcing and business networks, other evidence suggests that standardization, specialization, and deskilling remain the bedrock of many organizations. In this context, the aspirations of KM to make knowledge a resource may actually be a symptom of a wider struggle between old and new forms of organization and management.

—Harry Scarbrough

See also Actionable Knowledge; Communities of Practice; Intellectual Property; Knowledge; Organizational Knowledge; Organizational Learning; Tacit Knowledge

Further Readings

Argote, L., McEvily, B., & Reagans, R. (2003). Managing knowledge in organizations: An integrative framework and review of emerging themes. *Management Science, 49*(4), 571.

Blackler, F. (1995). Knowledge, knowledge work, and organizations: An overview and interpretation. *Organization Studies, 16*(6), 1021–1046.

Brown, J. S., & Duguid, P. (1991). Organizational learning and communities-of-practice: Towards a unified view of working, learning, and innovation. *Organization Science, 2*, 40–57.

Contu, A., & Willmott, H. (2003). Re-embedding situatedness: The importance of power relations in learning theory. *Organization Science, 14*(3), 283.

Nonaka, I., & Takeuchi, H. (1995). *The knowledge-creating company.* New York: Oxford University Press.

Orr, J. (1990). Sharing knowledge, celebrating identity: War stories and community memory in a service culture. In D. Middleton & D. Edwards (Eds.), *Collective remembering: Remembering in a society* (pp. 169–189). London: Sage.

Polanyi, M. (1958). *Personal knowledge: Towards a post-critical philosophy.* Chicago: University of Chicago Press.

Scarbrough, H., & Swan, J. (2001). Explaining the diffusion of knowledge management: The role of fashion. *British Journal of Management, 12*(1), 3–12.

Sveiby, K., & Lloyd, T. (1987). *Managing knowhow: Add value by valuing creativity.* London: Bloomsbury.

Tsoukas, H. (2003). Do we really understand tacit knowledge? In M. Easterby-Smith & M. A. Lyles (Eds.), *The Blackwell handbook of organizational learning and knowledge management* (pp. 410–427). Oxford, UK: Blackwell.

L

Labor and Offshoring

Offshoring refers to the setting up of a firm's business function in a foreign country for reasons of competitive advantage. A firm may offshore in order to enter a new market or to secure low-cost labor. When firms offshore, they substitute foreign for domestic labor, and if they contract with a local vendor in the foreign country, the process is further defined as *offshore outsourcing*. Offshore outsourcers can be third-party vendors, or they can be *affiliates,* local firms in which the parent company has directly invested. Lastly, offshoring often entails the explicit hiring of women for export production and service labor.

Conceptual Overview

The trend of offshoring arises out of profound changes in the world economy. Since the late 1960s and early 1970s, the United States, for example, has engaged in de-industrialization whereby manufacturers relocated "shop floors" to regions in the domestic south and to international locations in order to profit from low-cost labor and nonunion workforces. Supported by shifting U.S. and world political and economic ideologies, multinational corporations' (MNCs) cost-cutting efforts were heralded as part of the natural evolution of market capitalism and were facilitated in conjunction with international financial institutions' (IFIs) push to liberalize (or even eliminate) trade and labor laws in developing countries of the global South. The establishment of free trade or export processing zones (EPZs) in indebted countries further institutionalized a ready pool of cheap labor for MNCs seeking to offshore business functions.

The microelectronics industry was one of the first to employ offshore labor in EPZs. As early as the 1960s, South Korean and Taiwanese workers were employed by U.S.-based firms to produce integrated circuits, while other high-tech firms, also lured by the benefits of doing business in a free trade zone, set up *maquiladoras* along the U.S. and Mexico border. Over the past four decades, networks of offshore production have developed across manufacturing, textile, service, and finance sectors.

The latest development in offshoring stems from what some have labeled the third industrial revolution or the Information Age. With the advent and proliferation of information and communication technologies (ICTs), the trade of services is now facilitated through wire or wireless connections across the globe. Digitized information assists, for example, Indian call center workers in Bangalore serving UK and U.S. customers seeking to make purchases from catalogues, contest parking tickets in their local communities, or manage their credit reports. Other services include data entry and other back-office business-processing tasks.

Importantly, the varied types of offshore labor—from production to services—challenge traditional analytic categories of high-skill and low-skill employment. For instance, while child care providers and doctors' jobs demand face-to-face interaction (often referred to as "personal services"), radiologists', accountants', and even security guards' work can be offshored, because the tasks do not demand a physical presence (a.k.a., "impersonal services") and can be easily delivered electronically. In fact, jobs across the education, health, business, hospitality, financial, information, and utilities services have already been offshored. Some commentators argue that the practice of offshoring labor has yet to come to fruition, and many more formerly deemed personal services can and will be subject to global electronic commence and trade. Take for instance American fast-food establishments that use call center workers abroad to take drive-thru customer orders in the states; alas, face-to-face contact has been deemed nonessential for the provision of burgers and fries. The challenge thus arises for researchers and practitioners trying to paint a representative picture of offshore laborers who are diverse within and across occupation, industry, and nationality as well as race, class, and gender.

Critical Commentary and Future Directions

The offshoring of labor is a politically charged issue. While proponents support decreased governmental interventions aimed at full employment, regulation, affirmative action, unions, and progressive taxation in favor of market-based, macroeconomic policies such as offshoring, critics of these neoliberal trends maintain that privatization of the state, liberalized trade, and other restructuring trends only further reproduce global inequities of nations and populations. For detractors, the practice of offshoring labor is simply another opportunity for business to circumvent social responsibility and workplace justice—of both home and foreign workers alike.

One criticism entails the displacement of jobs from a company's home nation to a foreign one. While opponents point to American job losses, for example, other research suggests that while compression exists, particularly in manufacturing, total losses are small and are actually surpassed by gains in service sector employment. Still other research examines offshoring to industrialized (as compared to developing) countries as a means of breaking into foreign markets, thus not necessarily affecting labor in a firm's home country.

The transfer of white-collar service sector jobs overseas has further exacerbated the offshoring debate. While the transfer of manufacturing work evoked public criticism, the displacement of U.S. white-collar workers, in particular, has led to larger class-infused, political fury about the effects of offshoring on the American workforce and economy. Partly in response, Thomas Friedman sought to document "the other side of offshoring" in his 2004 film titled the same. He provides footage that explores the cultural, economic, and social changes experienced by Indians working for MNCs in Bangalore. He depicts how workers, particularly young women, are not only learning how to serve customers on the phone, but are also learning to become consumers in their own right as a result of the wages from their offshore jobs. The women are shown shopping for American products from Gap and Nike in newly built malls as well as eating American exports, including the fare of McDonald's and Pizza Hut. Friedman's portrayal celebrates call center work as not only a means for consumption, but as a means for young women to circumvent traditional cultural expectations as well.

While Friedman stops short of a critical analysis, the call center workers' narratives clearly demonstrate the gendered, raced, and classed tensions that arise in offshoring labor. The women negotiate complex cultural identities daily. For example, they are required to assume an American name and accent when engaging in customer service interactions at work. And the demands on worker's "selves" do not stop at the offshore workplace door. As other researchers have noted, women working in offshore production often have to manage or balance their MNCs' (often American) prescribed work identity with existing cultural expectations. Carla Freeman's oft-cited study of pink-collar data entry processing in Barbados identifies how young Afro-Caribbean women reconstruct meanings of professionalism, particularly through aesthetics such as dress, and in turn reshape the offshore employer's understanding of the ideal worker as a result. As it does with Friedman's subjects, consumption of the aesthetics of professionalism (e.g., designer clothes, products) also fuels these women's desire for offshore employment via ICTs. What can be garnered from the research on the gendering of offshore labor is not only how women are subject to but are also subjects of offshore production; they are shaped by and in turn, shape the meanings, practices, and even policies of offshore labor.

Feminist literature in management, development, and globalization studies provides further insights into the gendering of offshore labor. For example, researchers are examining how the social construction of gender shapes the arguments and justifications for firms' recruitment (and governments' promotion) of women laborers within and across Asia, South America, and the Caribbean. Here, women are sought for their "naturally feminine" agility, flexibility, and docility; the last of which implies that women as a group are less likely to resist poor working conditions and low wages than men.

To be sure, feminist researchers are also committed to challenging the injustices experienced by women and children in offshore work. Long hours with few breaks, unhealthy environments, constant monitoring, and harassment are well-documented forms of workplace discrimination. Furthermore, the precariousness of offshore production employment is well noted. For example, if women do organize for improved conditions, MNCs may employ new technologies to reduce labor needs, further subcontract business functions, actively suppress worker demands, or ultimately leave and offshore elsewhere.

In the end, the research on offshoring demonstrates a strong ambivalence regarding the potential and lived perils and promises of women's participation in offshore labor. While these arrangements do provide the economic means to resist rigid gender roles, practices, and expectations that may be otherwise unavailable to women, offshore labor comes with its own price tag of cultural change, dependency on foreign firms, and in worst cases a return to poverty.

—*Nikki C. Townsley*

See also Capital Movement, Migration, and Maquiladoras; Competitive Advantage; Outsourcing

Further Readings

Blinder, A. S. (2006). Offshoring: The next industrial revolution? *Foreign Affairs, 85,* 113–128.

Freeman, C. (2000). *High tech and high heels in the global economy: Women, work, and pink-collar identities in the Caribbean.* Durham, NC: Duke University Press.

Friedman, T., & Levis, K. (Producers). (2004). *The other side of offshoring* [Documentary]. (Available from the Discovery Channel, http://shopping.discovery.com)

Nash, J., & Fernandez-Kelly, M. P. (Eds.). (1983). *Women, men, and the international division of labor.* Albany, NY: SUNY Press.

Pyle, J. L., & Ward, K. B. (2003). Recasting our understanding of gender and work during global restructuring. *International Sociology, 18,* 461–489.

Taylor, P., & Bain, P. (2005). "India calling to the far away towns": The call centre labour process and globalization. *Work, Employment, and Society, 19,* 261–282.

LABOR RELATIONS

Labor Relations (LR), or Industrial Relations as it is often designated in Europe, is the interdisciplinary study of (a) work and employment, and (b) of the institutions, actors, rule-fixing processes, and outcomes in the labor market, often with a focus on the relationship between employers and employees and between their respective organizations of collective action.

Conceptual Overview

Originally, the core subject matter of LR was the study of work and conditions of work, both in connection with a project to democratize working life. This also was the idea behind studying collective bargaining, that is, the processes by which workers and their organizations (mainly trade unions) negotiate with employers, either at the workplace level (single-employer bargaining) or with employers' associations (multiemployer bargaining). These processes have many facets, including centralized formalized negotiations at the industry or national level versus local and informal bargaining at the workplace, and they include mediation and arbitration and the prevalence of industrial conflict (strikes and lockouts).

LR cannot be considered an academic discipline on a par with economics or law with its own set of theories. It is rather a well-established field of study, in which social scientists apply theories from their respective backgrounds, including sociology, economics, history, political science, organization studies, psychology, and law. In the Anglo-Saxon world, however, LR has become more of a distinct discipline, embedded in academic departments and with established academic journals. In continental Europe, LR has developed into a subdiscipline of the various more general academic disciplines, as in industrial sociology, industrial psychology, labor history, labor economics, and so forth.

Subject matter in LR research also includes wage formation and pay, equal pay and gender issues, industrial conflict, the role of shop stewards in the workplace, working time, skills and training, involvement and participation of employees at work, workplace democracy, and so forth. In most cases, the emphasis has been to explore how collective actors and rules for negotiation and mediation may influence and improve the conditions of employees or the productivity of companies or avoid industrial conflict. Authors have, however, given different priorities to these varying goals. In fact, the theoretical purposes of LR studies have been both varying and at variance, and the area is, perhaps especially it was, characterized by a significant degree of controversy, possibly reflecting the varying interests of the two opposing parties in LR, employers and employees. In a classic heuristic, it became usual to distinguish between three theoretical perspectives.

- *The unitary perspective,* which sees the purpose of LR studies and research as the avoidance of unnecessary conflict and the enhancement of superior collective communication toward the common goal. In this perspective, arbitration, mediation, the clear communication of management goals to employees, and the avoidance of all conflict are the main issues. Originally, this perspective was closely tied to Dunlop and to the functionalist perspective in sociology (especially Parsons) and to the human relations school (see the pioneering Hawthorne studies). Today, this same approach may be found in the theories of human resource management (HRM, see below).
- *The pluralist perspective,* which sees the LR arena as consisting several actors each pursuing their own goals and agendas, and where bargaining and mediation bring about constantly renegotiable compromises. Here, the processes of negotiation, of bargaining, of inclusion and involvement of employees, the generation of rules for arbitration, and the mutual understanding by the actors of the other parties' legitimate goals are the main focus.
- *The radical (Marxist) perspective,* which views and depicts LR as endemically conflict-ridden due to the inherently antagonistic interests of the respective collective actors. Here, the main points of interest are industrial conflict more than conflict resolution, exploitation of workers more than fair pay in wage bargaining, and issues of labor deskilling.

In unitary LR (or systems theory), it was usual to distinguish between (1) collective actors, (2) processes, and (3) outcomes, as originally in Dunlop. Collective actors are, first, employers and their associations; second, trade unions and their members; and, third, the relevant institutions of the state. Actors operate in economic and national *contexts;* they are under the influence of a consensual *ideology* tying the parties together, despite their differences. The parties enter into various types of *processes,* which may be viewed as (a) bilateral negotiations or bargaining, (b) mediation or arbitration, often with the assistance of outside parties, for example, agencies of the state, and (c) participation or involvement of employees at the workplace level, directly or via various forms of cooperative committees. The outcome of this may be either substantive or procedural, substantive when it concerns rights or rates, such as rates of pay and working hours, and procedural when it concerns rules for mediating and conflict resolution. Outcomes in the form of rates or rules feed back into the economic and social system and thus back to the collective actors as input.

This model has been criticized for its consensual approach, and it was challenged both by pluralist and by radical critics in the 1970s. One critique focused on the increasing tendency in LR theory to focus solely on the rule-making processes, thus ignoring the broader context of work and the changes in the nature of work taking place. Labor Process Theory (LPT) was one such challenge, which brought back the interest in how work itself was organized to the LR field. Although some of LPT's original conjectures did not stand up to closer scrutiny, the revival of the interest in labor processes and how they evolve has been an enrichment of the field, as can be seen, for example, in the studies of call center labor from the recent decade. One outcome of this was perhaps that the narrower focus on the institutions of collective bargaining, which was clear especially in the 1960s and 1970s, became challenged in the 1980s also by studies focusing on work and employment in both union and nonunion sectors. This led to the reemergence of studies of high-involvement and high-commitment work practices and companies and studies of how novel individualistic management strategies could be combined with good and dynamic working conditions for employees. In the eyes of radical LPT adherents, this might appear as the return to the unitary or the HRM orthodoxy, but the focus in this literature does uphold the understanding of interests at variance between actors, individual as well as collective.

In the recent decades, the above heuristic has been partially replaced due to the waning of the interest especially in the radical perspectives and in the face of the challenges from novel disciplines that have been moving into this field: the subject areas of HRM and of employment relations. These novel approaches or paradigms have—contrary to traditional LR theory—taken the perspective of the employment relationship vis-à-vis the individual employee, and this has forced LR scholars increasingly to include not only collective actors in their study but to consider more broadly the labor market from the perspective of the individual employee and to consider the interaction of the individual and the collective of, for example, employees not only from a moral but also from a rational action perspective. Thus, contemporary LR research may more usefully be characterized as coming in other trends, inspired by theoretical developments in the social sciences.

Sometimes these novel perspectives are characterized as "the new institutionalism," and one may helpfully distinguish between two tendencies. On the one hand, there is *sociohistorical institutionalism,* where the understanding of the establishment and evolution of LR institutions, and the role of these institutions in the shaping of broader societal outcomes, are the main focus. LR institutions and processes are studied either in their national contexts or, more and more often, in comparative studies, many of which have provided novel insights as to the understanding of labor market dynamics comparatively. Studies often combine historical and comparative approaches. Especially, comparative LR studies are becoming much more prevalent as a corollary to globalization challenges and an increase in the interest in studying strengths and weaknesses of national models of labor market regulation.

On the other hand, there is *rational choice institutionalism,* where the existence and conduct of both individual and collective actors are viewed as resulting from transaction cost types of reasoning, enabling the understanding of comparative or dynamic variances in, for example, propensities to organize (union density), to take up vocational training, to enter into collective arrangements at the workplace, and to take up industrial conflict.

The controversy between LR theorists has receded somewhat, but the theoretical understandings of the mechanisms of LR institutions and their impact on broader societal conditions still vary. Rational choice institutionalism, on the one hand, employs a relatively individualist understanding of actor motives and thus tends to view LR institutions as the outcome of micro-to-macro processes based on lines of argumentation taken up from transaction cost economics. Sociohistorical institutionalism, on the other hand, emphasizes the dynamo-historical and also sociological factors at play (macro-to-micro). This involves not so much individual rationality, but rather reflexive and normative factors in interaction with tradition and institutional embeddedness of LR institutions and their impact on present levels of economic output, on equality of pay, on unemployment, on industrial conflict, on participation, and so forth. In both theoretical tendencies, however, the role of LR institutions is viewed as crucial in the understanding of societal economic performance, unemployment and labor market policies, and their degrees of equality and welfare.

In both, issues of membership, participation, and coverage and take-up of collective action opportunities are central issues, implying that we have today a much better understanding of how collective action and collective institutions have a bearing upon generalized labor market and welfare outcomes.

Critical Commentary and Future Directions

The traditional focus in LR may be said—caricaturing only slightly—to focus on the male, white, full-time manual, unionized worker in a large manufacturing company. This employee type, however, represents a declining section of the workforce, not least due to the increase in female employment in the service sector, in part-time and in temporary employment, and in the increasingly multiethnic composition of the workforce. Manufacturing employment, conversely, now represents only 10–20 percent of aggregate employment in the advanced market economies. Therefore, although LR is a well-established area of study, it has in recent decades been challenged both by a number of real-world factors, which have seemingly minimized the importance of LR and of a LR perspective on labor market matters, and also by the emergence of novel academic disciplines, covering to a large extent the same empirical field as LR; these include, among others, human resource management, personnel economics, and employment relations.

Taking the real-world factors first, many of the advanced industrialized nations have experienced considerable decline in union density levels, especially so in the United States, the United Kingdom, France, and New Zealand, while at the same time only a small number of countries (e.g., the Scandinavian ones) have hitherto by and large been exempt from this trend. Also, the coverage of collective bargaining and of its institutions has become reduced, although this latter trend is less marked than the former one. At the same time, the incidence and prevalence of industrial conflict has been dramatically reduced since reaching its peak in the 1970s; in fact, today's levels of industrial conflict (measured as number of working days lost) are only 10–15 percent of what they were then. Thus, more employees work in nonunion workplaces, and the role of unions and of collective action more generally, both at the workplace level and at the broader societal level, is very much reduced.

There are several factors that LR authors have shown may have contributed to this change. The structural change of the labor market from manufacturing to services (where unions have a much smaller foothold) is one factor, and the role of international trade and globalization is another. Some forms of collective action (e.g., strikes) have become much more of a risk phenomenon for employees now that, in many cases, production may be moved to low-pay countries, or deliveries may simply be taken over by companies in other countries. In other words, the institutional protective barriers once created by national customs and tariffs have been (at least partially) removed, implying that collective interest organizations must adapt to completely different political and economic environments in order to survive. Yet another factor is that, politically and ideologically, trade unionism suffered serious setbacks, especially in the 1980s, in countries that became ruled by governments openly introducing legislation intended to curb union influence: New Zealand, the United Kingdom, and the United States figure especially prominently here. These factors (and others) have implied that fewer scholars and students see LR as an important issue now than earlier. In fact, the restrictive delimitation of LR as the study of rule-making processes through collective bargaining leads to a marginalization of the subject itself, and this has been part of the explanation why LR researchers increasingly are taking up issues of work and of employer/employee relations, including the individual aspects of this relationship.

More theoretically, in the academic disciplines, LR courses and LR and IR journals have been challenged by HRM and employment relations as novel ways of viewing what was once the preserve of LR. The individualization of the employment relationship has been a major challenge for LR theory, and especially the wide teaching and increasing research into HRM has become a challenge.

It is perhaps also striking that the conceptual apparatus of LR theory, especially in the Dunlop systems theoretical version, led to predictions about the evolution of LR systems that were irreconcilable with real-world developments. In some countries, including the United States, the problems LR systems were supposed to solve, such as recurring industrial conflict, have been solved not through the evolution of this system, but through its abolition. Such problems were inexplicable using Dunlop's theoretical framework, because the collective action problem, that is, why workers join unions in the first place, was not considered a problem at all. Instead, some of the more recent contributions have been able to make more sense of it.

On the other hand, however, the discipline of LR has adapted to these novel trends, while at the same time in HRM the collective aspects of the employment relationship have come to play a greater role. In today's LR and IR journals and textbooks, the individualist/collectivist dimension and issues of how, for example, unions can reconcile the individual interests of each individual member (and each potential member) play a much larger role than before. Also, although trade unions have become weakened and industrial conflict has very much disappeared from the public and news agenda, these institutions and occurrences still have a role to play: Collective bargaining still prevails in significant sectors of many of the advanced market economies, and even industrial conflict has not been wiped out; only the strike weapon appears to be used much more sparingly. Understanding collective action issues and problems in the labor market and understanding how institutional arrangements and their dynamics impact upon the capability of societies and of labor markets to adapt to both local and global challenges are still important issues for today's policymakers and administrators and for practitioners in personnel departments and trade unions. The internationalization of LR research—which was earlier much more a tradition of presentation and analysis of national models—in the form of theoretically inspired comparative research is one significant step here.

LR and IR both were and are not only fields of academic study but also areas of professional practice conducted by employees in personnel departments, by union representatives and employees, and by employees in the designated areas of state administration. The main challenges to theory and research into LR and to its concomitant professional practitioners would therefore seem to be how one can integrate the novel real-world issues of individualization, feminization, part-time work, globalization, and the multiethnic workforce into the existing theoretical framework and empirical understandings and also how one can integrate the study of work, of work processes, and of the evolution of high-commitment workplaces better into the study of LR.

—*Steen Scheuer*

See also Collectivism; Employment Relations; Goal-Setting Theory; Hawthorne Studies; Human Resource Management; Industrial Relations; Transaction Cost Theory

Further Readings

Clegg, H. A. (1976). *Trade unionism under collective bargaining: A theory based on comparisons of six countries.* Oxford, UK: Blackwell.
Commons, J. R. (1924). *Legal foundations of capitalism.* New York: Macmillan.
Crouch, C. (1982). *Trade unions: The logic of collective action.* London: Fontana.
Dunlop, T. (1958). *Industrial relations systems.* New York: Holt.
Hyman, R. (1975). *Industrial relations: A Marxist introduction.* London: Macmillan.
Hyman, R. (2001). *Understanding European trade unionism.* London: Sage.
Kochan, T., Katz, H., & McKersie, R. (1986). *The transformation of American industrial relations.* New York: Basic Books.
Marsden, D. (1999). *A theory of employment systems. Microfoundations of societal diversity.* Oxford, UK: Oxford University Press.
Webb, S., & Webb, B. (1897). *Industrial democracy.* London: Longmans.

Lacanian Psychoanalysis

This entry outlines the work of French poststructural psychoanalyst Jacques Lacan. One of Lacan's contributions to organization studies was a reconfiguration of

Freud's notion of the ego based on symbolic and linguistic theory. Lacan's work and major intellectual influences are explored, and his concept of human action as a tripartite of need, demand, and desire is explained.

Conceptual Overview

Lacan was interested in the therapeutic relationship between the analyst and the patient, or the *analysist* and the *analysand,* as he referred to them. These terms demonstrate his rejection of the traditional therapeutic model of the sick patient working toward an idealized mode of health. In contrast, Lacan saw the therapeutic process as one in which the individual worked to find an acceptable and manageable relationship to the social symbolic world.

Post-Freudian Lacan

In rejecting the notion of an ideal self as embraced by the humanists, Lacan clearly rejected the idealism of the humanist project, which he saw as necessarily connected with North American optimism. Although a self-proclaimed Freudian, Lacan also diverged from the traditional Freudians of his day. For example, Lacan held a different view on the prescribed length of therapy sessions, which he thought should be open-ended rather than fixed at 50 minutes. Also, Lacan focused on language as the key element of human change and development rather than the notion of ego and the unconscious. Another key distinction between Lacan and the Freudian tradition lies in institutional intent. Freud aimed to legitimize psychoanalysis as a science by developing acceptable and replicable methods that institutionalized the process of psychoanalysis. Specifically, Freud sought to outline a coherent theory of the relationship between the conscious and the unconscious. In contrast, Lacan saw his role as one of institution challenger and tester, seeking to obscure the theoretical relationship between the conscious and the unconscious.

Post-Lacanian Freud

These and other differences eventually led Lacan to leave the dominant Freudian organization of his day, the prestigious International Psychoanalytic Association. Yet, despite criticism that Lacan had abandoned his Freudian roots, Lacan continued to call Freud his primary intellectual influence and confirmed his commitment to Freudian psychoanalysis throughout his career.

The distinction between Freud and Lacan based on institutional grounds provides a theoretical demarcation point between structural and poststructural analysis. Freud's theories might best be considered to represent a structural approach to human nature. Freud believed in a single metanarrative, one overarching set of beliefs about the nature of human behavior. Thus, Freud can be seen as a structuralist in the sense that he believed that human behavior was subject to a set of universal underlying structures that applied across cultures. In contrast, Lacan was heavily influenced by the French intellectuals of his day who were considering alternative models of human behavior. Lacan's influences included the linguist Ferdinand de Saussure, the philosopher Maurice Merleau-Ponty, and the novelist-philosopher Jean-Paul Sartre. These French intellectuals were more interested in discovering local, relational truths, usually embedded in language and social circumstances. In contrast to the structuralists, these thinkers have been called poststructuralists. Some have argued that Lacan's work serves as a transition from the structural to the poststructural theory of human nature in organizations because of his belief in the subjectivity of language and its relationship to the unconscious.

According to Edith Kurzweil, one central theme of Lacan's work is that the unconscious is structured like a language. Here one can see the influence of linguistics and literary theory in Lacan. He believed that human behavior was subject to a set of unstructured yet somewhat predictable relationships between emotion, language, and relationships with other people. Because these relationships lacked any specific or consistent structure, understanding their causes or predicting behavioral outcomes often eluded both the individual acting in the world and the specialist seeking to diagnose the problem. Yet, despite the subjectivity of language, in the end language and its structure offered a better way to see these relationships coherently than other structures. Lacan believed it was the person's relationship to language that constituted the essence of human development.

Human Change and Learning

An important point of discussion for organizational studies lies in Lacan's view that change and learning are best described as a process of indoctrination into the symbolic world. Human development, beginning at birth and continuing into adulthood, occurs as individuals express inner needs in symbolic terms. Lacan's view of human development, then, is constructivist in that the individual constructs his or her own reality, yet it is also poststructural in that it does not assume that this construction is either rational or progressive. Lacan conceived of change as a complex process of self-deception, imaginary relationships with projected selves, and unattainable goals met only half way by internalized others. The purpose of change was for an individual to increase awareness of these self-deceptions. Greater awareness could be found in understanding that language and its use was deceptive and inhibitory in human affairs.

Lacan's view sharply contrasted with conventional theories of organizational change, such as those of the social constructionists. Lacan began not with a socially constructed world, internalized by the individual as the sociologist would suggest, but rather with the inner motivation of the individual, externalized in the available symbolic world.

Taking Lacan's ideas seriously challenges conventional thinking about the nature of individual change in organizations because it suggests that change is not a function of biology (as the behaviorists might suggest), nor is change to be understood as an evolution through a series of career or life stages (as the cultural theorists suggest), nor is it to be understood as a progression through a series of higher developmental stages (as the humanists would suggest). Rather, change is best described as an ongoing process of coming to terms with a continuous set of disruptions, disturbances, and scattered experiences and placing these experiences within the dynamic world of human experience. In this sense, change is a transitory process characterized by mitigating circumstances and the collision of circumstances with inner desires. These three elements—inner desires, circumstances, and their collision—are an important element of Lacan's theory and the tripartite of need, demand, and desire.

Need, Demand, and Desire

The basis of Lacan's theory can be found in the three interwoven concepts of need, demand, and desire. *Need* is the basic drive of all human activity and is the closest an individual can come to an unmediated experience. While need implies a state of natural, instinctual, or biological drive, need can never be conceived separately from its manifestation in an external object. If need is the term applied to the underlying drive for all human activity, it quickly becomes consumed under demand. *Demand* represents need in symbolic form. Through a complex and often unconscious process of internalizing the extant symbolic world, individuals begin to mistake demand (symbolic expression of need) as need itself. In other words, need in its purity is not something that can be represented directly. Need, which is often considered akin to emotion, essentially can be known only by the individual, but through its symbolic representation it quickly takes the form of demand. Demand transforms need into a symbolic command or action, displayed in the form of a word or communication. Demand is not demand for the thing demanded; it is demand for the underlying need. Thus, demand is only an unsatisfying substitute for need. *Desire* emerges in the space between need and its satisfaction in demand. Desire is an irresolvable tension that seeks fulfillment of need through demand, but that always falls short of satisfaction.

Postmodern Lacan

Contemporary French existentialists (postmodernists), including the father of French postmodernism, Jacques Derrida, have attacked Lacan's idea of need because it suggests an underlying existence, independent of its contextualized symbolic representation. While Lacan believed in something real that he called the Real, he believed this real could never be empirically placed. In other words, many have placed Lacan in contrast to postmodern thinking because he believed in an essence of human experience. However, others have placed Lacan within the postmodern project because he believed this essence was elusive, contextual, relational, and fleeting. Further complicating the matter, this essence could never be replicated, although it was often continuous. The elusive nature of this essence is reflected in Lacan's well-known phrase, "I speak the truth, but not the whole truth because that is impossible."

Critical Commentary and Future Directions

This section suggests ways that Lacanian psychoanalysis may influence or has influenced organizational studies. Lacan's contribution to organizational studies can be found in the view that organizations are a linguistic enterprise embedded in the social and political discourses of society. As such, Lacan provides a means to develop a new role for language and emotion in the study of organizations in three distinct areas.

A major contribution of Lacan's work is that it challenges prevailing notions of the ego in organizations. Lacan attempted to shift the discussion of his day from the Freudian idea of ego to the symbolic process of signifying inner needs. Similarly, Lacan's work can refocus current obsessions with ego and its manifestations in concepts such as narcissism and leadership to examine the processes by which leaders seek to express their needs in symbolic terms. This suggests two areas for critical study. First, the language used by leaders to influence followers can be viewed as expressed inner needs of the leader. Second, the leader's role is to help followers arrive at a better understanding of the relationship between their inner needs and their outward demands.

The second contribution of Lacan's work lies in a better understanding of the process of setting and pursuing goals. Consistent with the dominant view in organization studies, the Lacanian perspective views goals as future desired states. However, as seen from a Lacanian perspective, the pursuit of goals is not just a future desired state but represents a form of justification for pursuit. From the viewpoint of Lacan, the focus of study should be the actual pursuit of the goal and the emotions experienced by the individual during its pursuit. The goal itself simply serves as a justification for the pursuit. Said in Lacanian terms, desires (pursuit of goals) emerge because demands (goals) can never fulfill the needs (inner emotional drives) of the individual. This same logic can be applied to organizational goals and provides a fruitful theoretical basis for future reconceptualization of goal setting.

A third influence of Lacan lies in his concept of self, which he always defined in the context of the other. The self is not something that an organization constructs or develops without consideration of the others. Rather, identity construction results from a process that is imagined and objectified by others bound by a kind of imaginary order. From a Lacanian standpoint, organizational identity formation emerges as a constant process of development and change, characterized more by relationships with others and through the organization's interpretations of itself as represented by symbolic others.

—D. Christopher Kayes

See also Adult Learning; Clinical Perspective; Critical Management Studies; Critical Theory; Gendered Organization; Gender Stereotypes; Identity; Individualism; Language and Organizations; Modernism; Modernity; Postmodernism; Poststructuralism; Symbolic Interactionism

Further Readings

Bennington, G., & Young, R. (1987). Introduction: Posing the question. In D. Attridge, G. Bennington, & R. Young (Eds.), *Post-structuralism and the question of history* (pp. 1–11). New York: Cambridge University Press.

Grosz, E. (1991). *Jacques Lacan: A feminist introduction.* New York: Routledge.

Harland, R. (1987). *Superstructuralism: The philosophy of structuralism and post structuralism.* New York: Methuen.

Jardin, A. (1993). The demise of experience: Fiction as stranger than truth? In T. Docherty (Ed.), *Postmodernism: A reader* (pp. 433–442). New York: Columbia University Press.

Kurzweil, E. (1996). *The age of structuralism: From Levi-Strauss to Foucault.* New Brunswick, NJ: Transaction.

Lacan, J. (1978). *The four fundamental concepts of psychoanalysis* (J.-A. Miller, Ed.; A. Sheridan, Trans.). New York: Norton.

Ragland-Sullivan, E. (1986). *Jacques Lacan and the philosophy of psychoanalysis.* Urbana: University of Illinois Press.

Rubin-Suleiman, S., Nadja, D., & Lol, V. (1987). Stein: Woman, madness and narrative. In S. Rimon-Kenan (Ed.), *Discourse in psychoanalysis and literature* (pp. 124–151). New York: Methuen.

Wright, E. (1984). *Psychoanalytic criticism: Theory in practice.* New York: Methuen.

LANGUAGE AND ORGANIZATIONS

Among organizational scholars, it is increasingly recognized that language is more than merely a means of communicating information. Instead, language is understood as being fundamentally implicated in the social construction of organizations and in all of the related issues of power, knowledge, and meaning that lie at the core of organization studies. Language is complex and dynamic in form and effect, allowing organizational members to communicate while simultaneously providing an arena for the processes of organizing upon which organizations depend. Linguistic approaches to organizations focus attention on the socially constructed and processual nature of organizations and on the actual processes through which organizations are produced, maintained, and changed. Given this complexity, language warrants particular attention within organization studies and has received ever-increasing attention as researchers explore this important aspect of organizational phenomena.

Conceptual Overview

In the humanities and social sciences, the 20th century heralded a radical departure from views of language as a simple mirror of nature. Traditionally, language was seen as a passive descriptor of objects that preexist the development of appropriate labels to facilitate effective communication about them. Language from this viewpoint is "true" when it correctly reflects reality and "false" when it does not; reality is always the arbiter of claims to truth.

A number of philosophers spent considerable time and effort developing philosophical frameworks that explained this relation of language and reality. This view arguably reached its zenith with the development of logical positivism by the group of European philosophers often referred to as the Vienna Circle in the 1920s and 1930s. Work in this vein also led to the perspective that has had perhaps the greatest impact on social science of any work in philosophy of science, Karl Popper's work on falsificationism.

The postwar era saw a decisive shift in focus with language increasingly seen as performing a very different role: Rather than just reflecting a preexisting reality, it began to be understood to have a profound role in the production of social reality. From this point of view, humans do not encounter a preorganized reality to which they attach labels but rather actively construct reality through meaningful interaction. Meaningfulness is a characteristic of human interaction, not a characteristic of reality itself. This change in perspective in Western philosophy, which subsequently swept across the humanities and social sciences more broadly, has come to be known as *the linguistic turn*. This fundamental change in understanding initiated a new era in the humanities and social sciences in which social reality is increasingly understood as being dynamically constructed through the production of texts that are themselves subject to a constant process of mediation and negotiation.

The work of linguistic philosopher Ludwig Wittgenstein played a key role in this radical shift. Of particular note is his seminal volume *Philosophical Investigations,* published posthumously in German in 1953. In it, he addresses the conceptual complexity of language and semantics. Wittgenstein engages the reader in a series of "thought experiments" through which he shows that linguistic meaning and definition are inherently variable and socially constructed. Other important, early works that highlight the role of language as constitutive of social reality include writings by Alfred Shutz, Peter Berger and Thomas Luckmann, and Peter Winch. All of these writers continued the development of a theory of social construction based on this new view of language.

The analysis of the role of language in social construction was particularly influenced by various versions of structuralism, a philosophical framework that became very influential beginning in the 1960s. Structuralism emphasizes the way in which systems of meaning, such as those inherent in language, are centered on relationships between words and their terms of reference. This was the essential premise of the work of the structural linguist Ferdinand de Saussure, who was highly influential in the development of a structuralist approach to semiotics. The nature of language was also a key focus for poststructuralists in the 1960s and 1970s such as Michel Foucault and Jacques Derrida.

There are various methodological approaches to the study of language and organization that have been developed following the linguistic turn. While the effects of the linguistic turn took some time to find their way into organization studies, they have now had a significant impact on thinking about the nature of organizations. Linguistic methods in organizational studies reflect the basic premise that organizations are linguistically created and shaped and therefore draw on the whole range of available forms of language-based analysis. The most significant of these include the analysis of tropes, various forms of discourse analysis, narrative analysis, and conversation analysis, although other approaches such as semiotics and hermeneutics have also been drawn upon to some extent. This entry will consider each of these approaches in turn and provide a brief outline of their central principles, applications, and contribution to organization studies.

Tropes

One of the earliest forms of linguistic analysis in organization studies was the analysis of metaphor—a figure of speech whereby one thing is described in terms of another. Early work by Gareth Morgan focused attention on the critical way in which metaphors shape one's understandings of organizations and showed how different metaphors revealed different aspects of organizations while simultaneously hiding others. This work led to the development of whole range of related studies based on the importance of metaphor in organizations and organization studies.

But while metaphor has received the lion's share of attention, there are other tropes that have been used to good effect in analyzing organizations. The four master tropes identified in literary criticism are metaphor, metonymy, synecdoche, and irony. These four tropes are referred to as the master tropes, as they are the four tropes from which other figures of speech are derived. While the definitions of the master tropes remains contested, in general, metonymy is defined as using language to substitute for particular relationships, such as the cause for the effect or the sign for the thing. Synecdoche, on the other hand, is generally used for instances in which a part is used to represent a whole. Finally, irony refers to the use of language to depict something in a contradictory way; it is, like metaphor, about mapping across domains but in this case in a juxtaposition of opposites.

Tropes are used by organizational researchers in three primary ways. First, researchers sometimes study how the figures of speech are used by organizational members to understand and construct organizations. In this research, the focus of attention is the language-in-use of organizational members and how figures of speech are used. Second, researchers can use figures of speech as analytical tools for understanding organizations. This generally involves an empirical study of organizing framed as the application of one of the figures of speech. Finally, tropes can be used in the structured analysis of organization studies itself. Different schools within organization studies, as well as different constructs such as organizational identity or career ladders, can be recast using the tropes.

Discourse Analysis

Discourse, in general terms, refers to an interrelated set of texts and the associated practices of production, dissemination, and reception that bring an object into being. Discourse analysis, by extension, is the study of discourse and the social reality that it constitutes. Discourse analysis is therefore both a method and a methodology in that it makes explicit claims about the nature of the social world and provides a set of tools for studying it. From an organization studies perspective, organizational phenomena are produced and made real through discourse, and organizational phenomena cannot be fully understood without reference to the discourses that constitute them. Discourse analysis provides the tools for the study of organizational discourse.

It is important to point out that discourses can never be found in their entirety. Discourse analysts are therefore limited to examining selections of the texts that embody a particular discourse. Derived from linguistics, *text* is used to refer to various forms of language, based on either the spoken or the written word. Texts may take a variety of forms, including written texts, spoken words, pictures, symbols, and artifacts. At the same time, discourse analysts cannot simply focus on individual texts; rather, in analyzing discourse researchers must refer to *bodies of texts*, because it is the interrelations between texts, changes in texts, new textual forms, and new systems of distributing texts that constitute a discourse over time. Similarly, discourse analysis requires researchers to make reference to the social context in which texts are found and in which the discourses of which they are a part are produced. It is this connection between discourses and the social reality that they constitute that makes discourse analysis a powerful method for studying social phenomena.

Discourse analysis has become an increasingly accepted and popular approach to the study of organizations. It provides a powerful method for examining the social construction of organizational phenomena and an increasingly developed set of methods for carrying out organizational research. At the same time, it is important to emphasize that organizational discourse analysis is not a coherent body of literature. There are, for example, more micro-oriented approaches that focus inwards on the analysis of texts while others are more macro-oriented and focus on understanding the social context in which discourse is embedded. Another important difference is in their approach to power. Some approaches to discourse analysis are more concerned with power as a focus than others. While all of the different forms of discourse share an interest in social construction, they vary widely in terms of their exact focus of interest, and this should be kept in mind when thinking about organizational discourse analysis.

Narrative Analysis

As a specific type of text, a narrative or story involves a plot—that is, a sequence of actions or events in time, and characters whose actions drive the plot forward. Notions of temporality and sequencing are thus central to the nature of narrative, and these facets distinguish it from other forms of organizational texts. Researchers interested in narrative use these features, and any of a set of well-developed methodologies, to deconstruct their use, meaning, and purpose for organizational members.

In organization studies, narratives appear in at least four ways. First, there are accounts of organizational research that are written in a storylike fashion. These stories are often ethnographies or case studies seeking to communicate some aspect of organizational reality. Second, some organizational researchers collect organizational stories and analyze them. These stories could be the official narratives of management or the unofficial narratives of employees or other organization members. Third, some organizational research conceptualizes organizational life as story making and organizational theory as story reading. Finally, sometimes organization studies itself is taken as a set of stories and the field subjected to some form of literary critique.

Conversation Analysis

Conversation analysis is one of the most systematic sociolinguistic methods and is used to analyze speech as a broader facet of processes of social interaction. Proponents of this approach also commonly use the term *talk-in-interaction* rather than conversation analysis to capture the essence of the method. It can be applied to the examination of sequential patterns of interaction in everyday conversations or those found to be naturally occurring within organizations and the workplace.

It has defined principles and procedures that permit researchers to obtain reproducible results of naturally occurring talk and interaction. The basic premise of conversation analysis is to uncover the manner in which social action is organized and ordered in order to find the rules and structures that produce and constitute that orderliness. It assumes that social action is ordered by those responsible for its production and that repeated attributes—such as turn taking and the format of the turn-by-turn sequential organization of conversation—can be identified and subjected to analysis. Interest is centered on the mechanics of the interaction per se rather than the actors, settings, and organizations giving rise to those data. By focusing on the structure and order of talk, speaker utterances, and the syntactical components of naturally occurring speech, conversation analysis retains the data in their original form.

Conversation analysis has its roots in the tradition of ethnomethodology and was developed by, among others, the sociologist Harvey Sachs in the late 1960s. Technological developments at the time allowed Sachs to collate data from taped telephone recordings and other interactions. He sought to determine how the organization of talk yields important insights into the organization of social actions and how this affects the meanings and understandings of those engaged in the interaction. The role of the analyst is therefore to ensure that everyday meanings are retained alongside the examination of form and structure. A verbatim recording, audio or video, is vital for conversation analysis, as it enables transcription and repeated playback of the audiovisual data. Data collected by other means, such as field notes, observations, or recollections of conversations after their occurrence, are therefore precluded from the application of conversation analysis. An additional methodological constraint is the requirement that original data and transcripts be made available to others for scrutiny using a commonly used standard of notation comprehensive to all researchers in the area. This adds to its rigor and the replicability of research outcomes.

Critical Commentary and Future Directions

The growing literature on language in the study of organizations provides an important counterpoint to the historical focus on positivist and realist approaches in organization studies. The recognition that organizations are socially constructed, and that this construction takes place primarily through various forms of language broadly defined, has allowed a much deeper understanding of organizing processes than was previously possible. This perspective highlights the complex accomplishment that underlies organizations and points to a whole new research project focusing on how organizations come to be in the first place and how they then are maintained or disappear. Understanding how organizations are produced provides a much deeper understanding of organizational phenomena that is complementary to much of the work in organization studies that preceded it.

The range of research articles in organization studies employing a linguistic approach of some form is now quite large. This would appear to indicate that these now compose an established interpretative school of approaches to organizational theory and analysis. Despite this, proponents of these approaches still argue that they warrant a more central and considered place in organization studies. While there is more and more work being done from these perspectives, it is common to hear that organization studies is still predominately focused on positivist and realist studies of organizations, and even a brief look at the top journals confirms this. One major challenge for researchers working from a linguistic perspective, therefore, is to continue to gain ground in increasing the impact of the linguistic studies.

One reason for the lack of impact of the developing linguistic perspectives may be that the research and theorizing that make up this growing perspective are so fragmented and diverse. While the various approaches discussed in this entry all arise from the linguistic turn and the same basic observations about the production of social reality, they approach the theoretical understanding and empirical investigation of organizations very differently. In fact, the resulting work is so diffuse that there is a danger that the overall research program will fail to develop a critical mass. As a result, these approaches have remained marginalized and have not had the impact on the broader study of organization that similar approaches have had in other areas of social science.

Finally, there has been a tendency in all of the approaches that we have discussed for researchers to focus on the dynamics of language at the expense of engaging with more substantive topics in organization studies. In other words, researchers tend to focus narrowly on language in organizations, rather than focusing on the linguistic aspects of organizational topics. This tendency may be partly a function of the newness of the research stream or simply the enthusiasm of researchers for the study of language. In either case, it has the unfortunate consequence of reducing the overall impact of work done from this perspective on organization studies more generally. One major challenge, then, for organizational scholars working from a linguistic perspective is to connect more directly into existing discussions in organization studies. For example, it is important that researchers studying organizations from a discursive perspective not just study the production of organizations through discourse but connect directly to related discussions already well underway in the broader organizational literature, such as discussions of organizational identity. Unless scholars working from these perspectives engage directly with the broader field, they run the risk of creating areas of highly specialized academic activity with little or no broader relevance.

—*Nelson Phillips and MariaLaura Di Domenico*

See also Conversation; Discourse Analysis; Ethnomethodology; Narratives; Poststructuralism; Social Constructionism

Further Readings

Berger, P., & Luckmann, T. (1966). *The social construction of reality: A treatise in the sociology of knowledge.* London: Penguin.

Czarniawska, B. (1998). *A narrative approach to organization studies.* London: Sage.

Gergen, K. J. (1999). *An invitation to social construction.* London: Sage.

Oswick, C., Keenoy, T., & Grant, D. (2002). Metaphor and analogical reasoning in organization theory: Beyond orthodoxy. *Academy of Management Review, 27*(2), 294–303.

Phillips, N., & Hardy, C. (2002). *Discourse analysis: Investigating processes of social construction.* London: Sage.

Psathas, G. (1995). *Conversation analysis: The study of talk-in-interaction.* London: Sage.

Sacks, H. (1995). *Lectures on conversation.* Oxford, UK: Blackwell.

Westwood, R., & Linstead, S. (Eds.). (2002). *The language of organization.* London: Sage.

Winch, P. (1946). *The idea of a social science.* London: Routledge & Kegan Paul.

LAW AND ECONOMICS

Law and economics is a theory of law based on the proposition that legal rules can be interpreted as a system of incentives aimed at inducing people to behave in certain socially desirable ways. Underlying this view is a presumption that people are rational; that is, they respond to perceived costs and benefits in ways that further their self-interest. While such an assumption is standard in the analysis of market behavior, it is less obvious that it should also operate in the legal realm, especially in such areas as the common law of torts, family law, and criminal law, where financial or material gain are not necessarily the primary objectives. The application of economic analysis to these and many other areas of law has nevertheless proved extremely successful.

The so-called "new" law and economics is of relatively recent origin, emerging in the 1960s. Prior to that, the application of economic analysis to legal issues (the "old" law and economics) was primarily limited to the field of antitrust law, or the legal regulation of markets. But when Ronald Coase published a classic article on social cost in 1960, Guido Calabresi applied economic principles to tort law in 1961, and Gary Becker developed an economic analysis of criminal law in 1968, the stage was set for the application of economic theory to an ever-expanding array of legal fields not obviously economic in nature.

Conceptual Overview

Regardless of the particular area to which it is applied, economic analysis of law is aimed at answering two kinds of questions: What is the effect of a particular legal rule on human behavior? And, is that effect socially desirable? Examples of the first type of question, referred to as *positive analysis,* include questions such as these: Will enactment of a three-strikes rule deter more crimes? Does an increase in manufacturer liability lead to safer consumer products?

A stronger and more controversial version of positive analysis asserts that the common law—that body of law made by judges—tends to be efficient in the sense that it promotes an efficient allocation of resources. Advocates of this view qualify this claim in two ways: First, efficiency is not the conscious goal of judges but instead emerges as an unintended outcome of the legal process (much as efficiency emerges from the ordinary operation of competitive markets), and second, not all laws are efficient at any point in time. This second point suggests a role for economic analysis in making the law more efficient. This is the purpose of *normative analysis,* which relies on the proposition that economic efficiency is a valid social norm for evaluating and improving the law.

The Coase Theorem

Many scholars date the origin of the new law and economics to Coase's analysis of the role of legal rules in promoting efficiency in the presence of market failure. Prior to Coase, economists assumed that external costs like pollution could only be corrected by direct government regulation of markets, a tradition linked to Arthur Pigou. Coase's analysis changed that by emphasizing the role of property rights and bargaining in determining the ultimate allocation of resources. In particular, Coase argued that as long as property rights are well defined and transaction costs are low, bargaining among the parties to an external harm can result in an efficient abatement of the harm. Further, the efficient outcome will be achieved regardless of how property rights are initially assigned (that is, whether victims have the right to be free from harm or injurers have the right to impose it). This result, known as the Coase Theorem, suggests that market processes potentially eliminate the need for government intervention in the presence of externalities.

Coase recognized, however, that this conclusion rested on the assumption of low transaction costs, which is not realistic in many actual cases of external harm. When transaction costs are high, legal rulings take on a greater role in achieving efficient outcomes. The broader implication of Coase's analysis, then, is that transaction costs are key in determining whether markets or laws are better suited to addressing the problem of social costs. When transaction costs are low, markets are superior, with the law relegated to the subordinate role of protecting property rights and enforcing contracts, but when transaction costs are high, the law becomes central, in essence serving as a substitute for markets in forcing the efficient allocation of resources.

Property Rules and Liability Rules

The role of the law in this framework is made more explicit by considering the distinction between *property rules* and *liability rules,* a distinction first drawn in a classic article by Guido Calabresi and A. Douglas Melamed. These authors argued that the law can protect property rights in one of two ways. Under property rules, owners can refuse any offers to acquire their property, thereby forcing would-be buyers to bargain with owners until a mutually acceptable price is found. In this sense, property rules represent the legal basis for market transactions.

In contrast, under liability rules, owners cannot refuse efforts to acquire their property as long as purchasers are willing to pay an amount of compensation set by a court. Liability rules therefore permit nonconsensual (legal) transfers of property. An example of a liability rule is when the government uses its constitutional power of eminent domain to acquire a piece of property for public use, in return for which it must pay the owner just compensation. (Thus, private property is protected by a liability rule with respect to the government but by a property rule with respect to private parties.)

The Coase Theorem, along with the distinction between property rules and liability rules, provides a general framework for understanding the interaction between markets and law in allocating resources. As noted, this framework can be applied to a wide range of legal areas. For example, it suggests that much of property law can be understood as providing legal protection of property rights so as to encourage the efficient exchange and development of property. In this way, the law (through property rules) serves as a stable legal background in settings where markets are expected to function well. However, in cases involving external harm like pollution, automobile accidents, and dangerous products, efficiency often cannot be achieved by market processes due to high transaction costs. In these cases, property rules must give way to liability rules as the primary means for organizing exchange.

Broadly speaking, the switch from property rules to liability rules represents the boundary between property law and tort law. Under tort law, victims of harm are entitled to seek monetary compensation for their losses, and injurers, if found responsible, must pay that compensation. From an economic perspective, however, compensation of victims is not the sole (or even the primary) function of tort law. Instead, it is aimed at providing injurers and victims with efficient incentives to invest in precautions to *avoid* accidents in the first place. This function of liability rules can be illustrated by noting that if injurers are forced to pay the external damages that their actions cause, they have an incentive to invest in any cost-effective means to prevent those damages (or to refrain from engaging in the dangerous activity altogether if the expected harm exceeds the benefits). In this way, imposing liability on injurers simultaneously serves the twin goals of compensating victims and inducing efficient accident avoidance.

A problem with a rule of strict injurer liability, however, is that it does not provide *victims* with a proper incentive to avoid harm, which in many cases will be an effective way to prevent accidents. (For example, pedestrians can wear bright clothing, and consumers can follow directions when using dangerous products.) Tort law solves this problem with the rule of negligence. Under a negligence rule, injurers are only liable for damages if they fail to invest in reasonable (efficient) precautions—that is, if they are negligent. This provision gives injurers a powerful incentive to be careful, because by doing so, they avoid liability. At the same time, because victims anticipate that injurers will take efficient precautions, they expect to bear their own losses and hence have an incentive to invest in precaution to minimize those losses. The outcome is therefore efficient regarding the behavior of both injurers and victims. The predominance of some form of negligence as the applicable legal rule for most accidental harms is evidence that tort law is primarily concerned with establishing efficient incentives for accident avoidance.

Criminal Law

Criminal law also imposes legal sanctions for certain harms, but it is generally limited to those acts involving intent by injurers. The economic theory of criminal law as developed by Becker nevertheless views criminal fines as serving the same function as tort liability: namely, to deter unreasonably dangerous behavior. In many cases, however, injurers have insufficient financial resources to pay the victim's losses. This represents one economic justification for the use of imprisonment as an additional form of criminal punishment when fines provide inadequate deterrence. Another is the potential need to incapacitate especially dangerous offenders who would be likely to commit additional harmful acts if unrestrained.

Economic theory, however, is not entirely successful in explaining many aspects of actual criminal law. For example, one of the principal conclusions of Becker's analysis is that fines should be used to the maximum extent possible (that is, up to the defendant's wealth) before any prison time is imposed. The logic behind this prescription is obvious: While prison is very costly, fines can be imposed and raised with little or no cost. Thus, to the extent that both forms of punishment serve as deterrents, fines should be used first. The fact that this policy is apparently not followed in practice suggests that the criminal justice system embodies goals other than efficiency. (For example, the constitutional requirement of equal treatment before the law precludes an efficient punishment scheme that would fine the rich while sending the poor to prison for the same crime.)

Critical Commentary and Future Directions

Despite its success, law and economics is not without critics. Most critics focus on the use of efficiency as the primary norm for evaluating law. This criticism is most relevant for positive analysis—the claim that the law embodies an economic logic—but it also applies to proposals for making the law more efficient in those areas where efficiency is not its primary goal (as the example from criminal law illustrates). A related criticism is that individuals do not respond to legal rules in a rational manner, making economic analysis of law irrelevant. This criticism, which amounts to saying that economics should be limited to the study of markets, is largely refuted by the fruitful application of economic analysis to wide areas of nonmarket behavior, including law.

Finally, even if one believes that economics cannot explain the law as it exists, that does not invalidate its role in improving the law in those areas that are explicitly economic in nature, such as the law of contracts and antitrust and corporate law. And even in those areas of law where efficiency is not the primary goal, economic analysis is nevertheless useful for revealing the social cost of pursuing alternative values like justice or fairness.

—*Thomas J. Miceli*

See also Coase Theorem; Neoclassical Economics

Further Readings

Becker, G. (1968). Crime and punishment: An economic approach. *Journal of Political Economy, 76,* 169–217.

Calabresi, G. (1961). Some thoughts on risk distribution and the law of torts. *Yale Law Journal, 70,* 499–553.

Calabresi, G., & Melamed, A. D. (1972). Property rules, liability rules, and inalienability: One view of the cathedral. *Harvard Law Review, 85,* 1089–1128.

Coase, R. H. (1960). The problem of social cost. *Journal of Law and Economics, 3,* 1–44.

Miceli, T. (1997). *Economics of the law.* New York: Oxford University Press.

Posner, R. (2003). *Economic analysis of law* (3rd ed.). New York: Aspen.

Shavell, S. (2004). *Foundations of economic analysis of law.* Cambridge, MA: Belknap. Press of Harvard University Press.

LEADERSHIP, CHARISMA

Charismatic leadership has become an important theoretical approach to explaining leader effectiveness since the concept was most fully described in a 1977 article by Robert House. Prior to House's work, charismatic leadership theory was only loosely articulated, and the research that was done tended to follow ethnographic, qualitative forms. Since then, the theory has been more explicitly articulated and has permitted the use of other, more quantitative methods to be used. Based in part on Max Weber's conception of personal power, charismatic leadership theory rests on the notion that a leader's influence on his or her followers is often beyond the legal and formal authority structure of a group or organization and relies instead on the leader's personal charm, attractiveness, and persuasive communication. According to Weber, charismatic leaders are able to influence followers by articulating a compelling vision for the future, arousing commitment to organizational objectives, and inspiring commitment and a sense of self-efficacy among followers.

The unique and compelling traits that are attributed to charismatic individuals are often regarded as gifts granted from higher powers. Many of the most prominent charismatic individuals in human history are those that have been influential in the spiritual domain, such as Buddha, Jesus, Mohammed, and Moses. To others, charisma is associated with persuasion, power, and political leadership, with personal charisma regarded as the unique quality of exceptional heads of state (e.g., Winston Churchill, Mohandas Gandhi, Adolph Hitler, Franklin D. Roosevelt, Ronald

Reagan, and Mao Zedong). Finally, charisma finds itself as an important aspect of business leadership, as executives who are visionary, agents of organizational change, and capable of arousing commitment among employees tend to be described as charismatic. The most popular charismatic business leaders, such as GE's Jack Welch and Apple's Steve Jobs, have separated themselves as particularly attractive to stakeholders both inside and outside of their respective organizations.

Conceptual Overview

With its origin in the Greek language, *charisma* is regarded as a unique gift granted to a few, special individuals. One of the first approaches to the examination of charisma in the social sciences was offered by Weber in 1947, who described charismatic individuals as those with exceptional powers or qualities, such that these individuals are set apart from ordinary people. Charismatic individuals are those who maintain extraordinary individual traits (e.g., confidence and optimism), are attractive to others, and are often characterized as inspirational and eloquent communicators. Very often, charismatic individuals are cast into positions of power due in part to their abilities to inspire and persuade the masses. In reference to the unique capabilities of charismatic individuals, Weber suggested that certain abilities were of divine origin and otherwise inaccessible to the ordinary person. Contrary to the popular models of power and influence of the time, Weber introduced the notion that willing followers could be influenced beyond legal authority structures, reward systems, or traditional, bureaucratic systems. Instead, truly exceptional leaders inspire followers to higher levels of cognitive functioning and encourage high levels of productive behavior.

Charismatic Leadership Theory

Charismatic leadership theory asserts that exceptional leaders create a connection with followers, attend to their individual needs, and inspire followers to achieve beyond personal limits. By appealing to higher-order individual values and magnanimous ideals, charismatic leaders enhance the commitment of followers to an eloquent vision and arouse followers to develop new ways of thinking about problems. While tests of the theory have proposed a number of mechanisms by which charismatic effects are realized, a common set of behaviors generally characterize charismatic leadership. Charismatic leaders articulate a compelling and often innovative vision of the future, take personal risks, emphasize ideological aspects of the organization's mission, show sensitivity to followers' needs, and communicate in an emotional and enthusiastic manner. These leaders are personally attractive to stakeholders both internal and external to the organization, and they are able to arouse emotion among followers and inspire commitment to organizational change.

In the last several decades, research on charismatic leadership theory has used a wide variety of testing methods, research settings, organizational scenarios, leadership profiles, data sources, and attitudinal and behavioral outcomes. Many of the theory's major assertions have been supported across measure and method. Indeed, J. B. Fuller and colleagues in 1996 conducted a comprehensive quantitative analysis of studies that considered aspects of the charismatic approach and concluded that charismatic leadership was positively related to follower performance, follower assessments of leader effectiveness, and follower reports of satisfaction with the leader. More important, charismatic leaders tend to be particularly effective when outcomes are examined at the group or organizational level of analysis.

Charismatic Leadership Process

Beyond a collection of traits or specific behaviors, charismatic leadership is often described as a process that evolves in three distinct stages. An important illustration of the leadership process was presented in a 1998 book by Jay Conger and Rabindra Kanungo.

In stage one, charismatic leaders recognize shortcomings of the existing status quo and effectively articulate the need for serious organizational change. Ronald Reagan, for example, in his early speeches as the newly elected U.S. president, described the dangerous and constrictive nature of the American economy, the deficiencies in foreign and domestic policy decisions by the Carter administration, and the need for reform in the structure and size of the federal government. President Reagan attempted to clearly highlight the need for change in policy and organizational structure, a common attribute of charismatic leadership. Similar ideas about the status quo were expressed by then-Governor Bill Clinton during his announcement for a U.S. presidential run in October of 1991. Clinton pronounced that the upcoming election was about change—in the Democratic Party, in national leadership, and in the country overall. Beyond their extraordinary individual qualities and personal charm, both Reagan and Clinton had the ability to recognize shortcomings in the existing status quo and to describe the need for change in a compelling and convincing manner.

In stage two, charismatic leaders identify opportunities in the environment and communicate a vision for a vastly improved future state. Perhaps the most profound example of this is Martin Luther King, Jr.'s "I Have a Dream" speech, in which Dr. King identified an idealized future state, shifted attention among followers to lofty, higher-order values, and used powerful images of attractive future possibilities. A charismatic leader's vision for the future is expressed in stage two. Another relevant example can be found in the computer business, where Apple's Steve Jobs saw computers as a way to unleash human creativity and enjoyment and introduced new products designed to revolutionize higher education or solve the most important problems people face.

Finally, in stage three, charismatic leaders arouse commitment to expressed goals and inspire confidence among followers in their own abilities to carry out the leaders' vision. Stage three is characterized by the leader's expression of self-efficacy, personal risk taking, and selfless leadership, all in an attempt to empower followers to participate fully in the accomplishment of organizational objectives. In that vein, a research study conducted by Boas Shamir and colleagues in 1993 examined follower reactions to charismatic leadership and argued that leaders achieve their desired results by enhancing the confidence and self-efficacy of followers. Evidence of stage three charismatic leadership can be found in interviews with GE's Jack Welch, who regularly suggested that his vision for GE would be realized when employees were excited about their work and felt empowered to create and to grow. Welch not only recognized opportunities for GE's global development, but created a sense among employees that they each had the ability, resources, and support to achieve the CEO's grand vision.

Charismatic and Transformational Leadership

Charismatic leadership theory is often introduced with other modern approaches such as transformational leadership theory, which provides a description of effective leadership that depends heavily on the charismatic appeal of the individual leader. The transformational model suggests that exceptional leaders are intellectually stimulating, provide inspirational motivation, are considerate of individual needs and talents, and are charismatic. As such, the charismatic and transformational theories of leadership are complementary in that each describes leadership as a process by which leaders have an influence on the attitudes, beliefs, and perceptions of followers. The two formulations of leadership essentially study the same phenomenon only from different vantage points.

Worth noting, some leadership scholars regard charisma as a communication style, such that transformational leadership consists of (a) communicating a vision, (b) having a plan to implement the vision, and (c) demonstrating a charismatic communication style (speaking with a captivating voice tone, making direct eye contact, showing animated facial expressions). Still, it is fair to say that most researchers continue to see transformational and charismatic leadership as functionally equivalent concepts.

Recent Examinations of Charismatic Leadership

Recent studies of charisma have sought to critically examine the assumptions in charismatic leadership theory, with a particular emphasis on the role that followers play in the emergence and effectiveness of charismatic behavior. One such study examined the values and personality traits of followers in an attempt to determine which traits were particularly open to the influence of charisma. Followers who were achievement oriented, had high self-esteem, and valued autonomy preferred charismatic leadership styles to task- or relationship-oriented alternatives. Thus, followers' values and judgments of self-worth seem to facilitate the effectiveness of charismatic appeals.

Another trend in leadership research is the evaluation of charisma at the highest levels of executive leadership. Several studies have measured the charismatic behavior of corporate CEOs and extended the reach of charismatic leadership theory beyond intracompany boundaries. Two separate studies found that charismatic CEOs were able to garner high levels of support from securities analysts and external stakeholders, while three additional studies estimated the impact of charismatic leadership on accounting and market measures of organizational performance. In all five cases, charismatic CEOs were able to negotiate higher compensation packages, garner higher levels of support from external stakeholders, and outperform their noncharismatic counterparts in the short term. However, no significant differences in organizational performance were observed over time. That is, the impact of charisma on performance was short lived. Whereas charismatic leaders are particularly effective during times of transition, uncertainty, and organizational change, the long-term value of charisma at the executive level remains relatively unknown.

Critical Commentary and Future Directions

While charismatic leadership theory has been supported across a variety of research methods and designs, the underlying processes that explain leader effectiveness remain relatively ambiguous. In part, this ambiguity may be the result of the diversity by which charismatic leadership is described. Weber, for example, regarded charisma as a collection of extraordinary traits that exceptional individuals are granted from divine sources. However, research on charisma during the 1990s tamed the Weberian concept of charisma to make it more common and less extraordinary. House, in 1977, described charismatic leadership as a set of specific behaviors, while others regard charismatic leadership as a unique connection between leaders and followers, one in which effectiveness is attributed to the leader's ability to shape the values, emotions, and cognitive patterns of committed followers. Lastly, Conger and Kanungo regarded charismatic leadership as a process by which leaders identify shortcomings in the status quo, articulate a compelling image of the future, and arouse commitment and trust among followers. Thus, future studies of charisma should attempt to identify the cognitive processes that underlie the attitude and behavioral changes among followers and continue recent efforts to use a follower-centered approach to understanding the emergence and long-term effectiveness of charismatic leadership.

—*Ronald F. Piccolo, Timothy A. Judge, and Henry L. Tosi*

See also Emotion; Empowerment; High Involvement Management; Job Satisfaction; Leadership, Styles; Leadership, Transformational; Leadership Theory; Motivation; Organizational Behavior; Power; Storytelling; Values

Further Readings

Bass, B. M., & Stogdill, R. M. (1990). *Bass & Stogdill's handbook of leadership: Theory, research, and managerial applications* (3rd ed.). New York: Free Press; London: Collier Macmillan.

Conger, J. A., & Kanungo, R. N. (1998). *Charismatic leadership in organizations.* Thousand Oaks, CA: Sage.

Fuller, J. B., Patterson, C. E. P., Hester, K., & Stringer, D. Y. (1996). A quantitative review of research on charismatic leadership. *Psychological Reports, 78,* 271–287.

House, R. J. (1977). A 1976 theory of charismatic leadership. In J. G. Hunt & L. L. Larsen (Eds.), *Leadership: The cutting edge* (pp. 189–207). Carbondale: Southern Illinois University Press.

Howell, J. M. (1997). *Organization contexts, charismatic and exchange leadership.* (KLSP: Transformational Leadership, Working Paper). College Park, MD: Academy of Leadership Press.

Kirkpatrick, S. A., & Locke, E. A. (1996). Direct and indirect effects of three core charismatic leadership components on performance and attitudes. *Journal of Applied Psychology, 81,* 36–51.

Shamir, B., House, R. J., & Arthur, M. B. (1993). The motivational effects of charismatic leadership: A self-concept based theory. *Organization Science, 4,* 577–594.

Yukl, G. (2001). *Leadership in organizations* (5th ed.). Upper Saddle River, NJ: Prentice Hall.

LEADERSHIP, DISPERSED

Dispersed leadership is a collective form of organizational governance in which leadership tasks are widely distributed amongst the organizational members.

Conceptual Overview

"Dispersed leadership" sounds like an oxymoron: Leadership is about the concentration of power and responsibility in one leader, not its dispersal amongst many. This probably reached its apotheosis in the Prussian armies of Frederick the Great, where extraordinary discipline facilitated centralized control over huge armies of foot soldiers whose very size had hitherto inhibited control. However, the defeats of the Prussian army at Jena and Auerstadt in 1806 by Napoleon's troops demonstrated the limits of concentrated leadership and initiated a series of changes in the Prussian army that coalesced under von Moltke's leadership (1857–1888) into the philosophy of *Auftragstaktik*—mission command. This approach, embodied in the subsequent German armies but later undermined by Hitler, required a dispersed leadership where subordinates were made aware of the superordinate's goal but given the training, resources, and freedom to develop the tactics necessary to achieve that goal.

The shift away from assumptions about individuals "leading" organizations toward some form of collective alternative has increased markedly at two historical junctures. The first was during the mid-19th century under the influence of anarchists ("anarchy" means "without government," from *arkhos* meaning "sovereignty or ruler" and *an* meaning "without") like Kropotkin (1842–1921) and Proudhon (1809–1865). The second was during the 20th century within business, from McGregor's theories X and Y in the 1960s through to the semiautonomous workgroups of the sociotechnical systems and the worker-director experiments in the 1970s in Britain and thence to the current concern for enhancing worker participation through various boards, European works councils, and other representative channels. Even formidably successful capitalists have engaged with the problem—as Ricardo Semler's no-one-in-charge experiments at SEMCO in Brazil demonstrate, enormous energy can be realized when bosses let the followers lead. In fact, the largest number of cases of dispersed leadership has tended to occur within the educational establishment; this is often linked to the assumption that the leadership of professionals is more conducive to this philosophy and practice.

Although dispersed leadership takes many forms, it is instructive to note what Weber might have called an "ideal case":

- *Collective Responsibility:* Organizations are replete with leaders, they are leaderful, full of ordinary people carrying out modest leadership tasks, not dependent on the heroic individuals doing daring deeds beloved of Carlyle. Within this aspect, it is worth distinguishing between what Gronn calls *concertive action*, where a synergy is derived from collaborative leadership, and *numerical action*, where many individuals are leading—but only as individuals.
- *Collective Flexibility:* Traditional organizations maintain unyielding hierarchies of power, resources, and rewards. Such structures, however, impose limits on the flexibility of the incumbents to office. Dispersed leadership implies a shift toward *heterarchy*—a flexible structure that retains the necessary degree of coherence and coordination but does not require the roles or incumbents to operate within strictly defined limits. For example, an emergency medical team might switch leadership as the situation and the shift systems require. Similarly a rowing eight operates as a heterarchy, not a hierarchy: At different times the coxswain, captain, coach, and stroke all lead.

Critical Commentary and Future Directions

Dispersed leadership is both a process and a philosophy. The latter often implies for its supporters that dispersed leadership is necessarily preferable to traditional leadership, because it embodies decentralization, social responsibility, and collective learning. All of these appear either progressive or liberal or collectively beneficial. But because it is also a process that encourages subordinates to learn to lead, it means that it is possible to consider it as a neutral system that can be deployed for good or evil. In particular, the distribution of responsibility and leadership are also means by which profoundly undemocratic and illiberal organizations can distribute risk and confound those seeking their elimination.

These core ideas may seem attractive to people inhibited by idiosyncratic individual leaders or suffocated by stultifying bureaucracies, but dispersed leadership is an alternative method of leadership, not a utopian alternative to it. And therein lie two paradoxes:

- Traditional individual leadership brings with it not just the potential for corruption but also a mechanism for effective decision making. Thus, simply wishing away leadership through dispersal, rather than facilitating the structures and processes to make it work, may merely result in grossly inefficient and ineffective organizations and the potential for "decisive leaders" (authoritarians) to step in and offer a "solution" to the apparent indecision. In effect, dispersed leadership may be a cover for the derogation of duty rather than the delegation of responsibility.
- Dispersed leadership offers a potential alternative to the problem of authoritarian leaders, but it also generates the means by which liberal democratic societies can be destabilized by small and unrepresentative groups or even individuals. For example, part of the success of al-Qaida relates to the difficulty of democratic states penetrating and dealing with terrorist groups that have little in the way of a formal hierarchy.

Future research in this new area will need to provide a much greater level of empirical support for the claims of its supporters, but also a much more robust and critical analysis of its limitations. For there lies the greatest paradox of dispersed leadership—it provides some with a blueprint for *inhibiting* authoritarian leaders, but it also provides terrorists with a blueprint for *cohabiting* with what seems to be leaderless authoritarianism.

—Keith Grint

See also Leadership, Charisma; Leadership, Servant; Leadership, Styles; Leadership, Transactional; Leadership, Transformational; Leadership Theory

Further Readings

Bennett, N., Wise, C., Woods, P., & Harvey, J. A. (2003). *Distributed leadership.* Nottingham, UK: NCSL.
Grint, K. (2005). *Leadership: Limits and possibilities.* Basingstoke, UK: Palgrave Macmillan.
Gronn, P. (2003). *The new work of educational leaders: Changing leadership practice in an era of school reform.* London: Sage/Paul Chapman.
Harris, A. (2005). Leading from the chalkface: An overview of school leadership. *Leadership, 1*(1), 73–88.
Raelin, J. (2003). *Creating leaderful organizations: How to bring out leadership in everyone.* San Francisco: Berrett-Koehler.

Leadership, Servant

While the concept of servant leadership is relatively new to the field of organization studies, many argue that it has been in practice for thousands of years. By way of definition, servant leadership places the good of those led over the self-interest of the leader. That is, servant leaders lead by serving their followers. Central to servant leadership is the valuing and development of people, the building of community, and the practice of authenticity; it also promotes the sharing of power between leaders and followers as means to benefiting each individual, the total organization, and the broader community.

Conceptual Overview

Greenleaf's 1977 essay entitled the "The Servant as Leader" is accredited as the foundation work from which the theory of servant leadership has emerged. In his essay, Greenleaf credits Herman Hesse's *The Journey to the East* as the source of his ideas about servant leadership. For Greenleaf, servant leaders begin with the natural feeling that they want to serve first; then they make a conscious choice to lead. He argues that such a leader is sharply different from one who is a leader first; the difference is manifest in the care taken by the servant leader to make sure that other people's highest priority needs are being addressed. Greenleaf adds that the test of success for servant leadership is to ask, do those served grow as persons? Do they, through the service of the leader, become healthier, wiser, freer, more autonomous, more likely themselves to become servants?

While serving first is the defining characteristic of servant leadership, Greenleaf proposed several other attributes that are necessary for successful servant leadership; these included

- *listening*—servant leaders are able to listen to followers while at the same time directing them;
- *empathy*—they always maintain a sense of empathy toward followers;
- *imagination*—they have the ability to imagine and have the innovative capacity to provide vision;
- *intuition*—they must have a honed sense of intuition; and
- *foresight*—they must have the foresight necessary to make decisions that their followers will respect and benefit from.

The ideas that Greenleaf puts forth in his essay have idealistic, moral, and religious overtones. In regard to religion, other writers in the field suggest that even though Greenleaf was accredited with the founding work in servant leadership, he was not the first individual to introduce the concept; these writers attribute this to Christianity's founder, Jesus Christ. They argue that from narrative accounts of Jesus's life in the Bible, it is evident that he taught and practiced servant leadership more than 2000 years ago. These writers go further by asserting that since then the practice of servant leadership has been echoed in the lives of ancient monarchs. For centuries, monarchs have consistently espoused that they are in the service of their people; even modern coronation ceremonies and inaugurations of heads of state indicate a service to God, country, and the people, as noted by Sendjaya and Sarros in 2002. Interestingly, the servant leadership literature offers little by way of critique in regard to the disparity between the words and the deeds of such monarchs, a disparity that is echoed in history.

In the years since Greenleaf's work was published, numerous writers have attempted to extend his ideas and develop a particular model of servant leadership for organization contexts. Bass suggests that rather than having a religious grounding, the concept of servant leadership has its heritage in the theory of charismatic leadership, which can be traced back to the work of the German sociologist Max Weber. But he adds, in comparison to charismatic leadership, the theory of servant leadership is virtually nonexistent in organization studies. He and other writers observe that while the work that has emerged on servant leadership establishes it as a distinct leadership style in which the leader's focus is on the follower rather than on the organization, the literature lacks specific details that may help to identify clear definitions and models of the concept.

More recently, Russell and Stone, along with Sendjaya and Sarros, have attempted to address this problem by synthesizing the variety of definitions and models of servant leadership found in the literature. Collectively they identify 10 key functional characteristics of servant leadership. These are

- *listening*—servant leaders are seen by their followers as active listeners;
- *empathy*—they display an understanding and genuine sense of empathy toward their followers;
- *healing*—they are recognized as having the ability to heal both themselves and their followers by generating a sense of well being and helping their followers achieve a balance between mind, body, and soul;
- *awareness*—they are attributed with a general sense of awareness of the contextual issues pertinent to the success of their followers and their organization;
- *persuasion*—they have personal power, they influence their followers through persuasion rather than relying on positional authority;
- *foresight*—they display the ability to foresee the potential outcomes and consequences of emerging situations;

- *conceptualization*—they use their imagination and conceptualize their dreams into meaningful missions and strategies that benefit their followers and organization alike;
- *stewardship*—they first and foremost display a commitment to a form of leadership that focuses on the needs of others;
- *commitment to the growth and emancipation of people;* they display a commitment to the personal, professional, and spiritual growth of each of their followers; and
- *community building*—they genuinely seek to develop a sense of community and commitment to each other among the people they lead.

In their review of the literature, Russell and Stone point out that in addition to the functional characteristics mentioned above, the literature identifies a series of attributes that, while common to other forms of leadership, are central to servant leadership. These include a fundamental *appreciation for others;* a desire to *serve* these others; an ability to *influence* and, through this, shape their followers' values and behavior; an ability to provide *vision* while serving others; and an ability to *communicate* their vision. Central to these communication skills is also the ability to *persuade*.

The literature also indicates that followers will not follow servant leaders who lack *honesty* and *integrity;* this indicates that servant leaders must also have *credibility,* and along with honesty, integrity, and credibility, *trustworthiness* is central to servant leadership. Followers must consider their servant leader to be *competent* as a leader in regard to organizational key goals and core business operations. Servant leaders also need to influence their followers through an ability to *model* behavior and relationships. *Visibility* in the form of a charismatic presence is essential; as a part of this charismatic presence, followers need to see their servant leaders as *pioneers* who shape new approaches to old problems and emerging challenges. Servant leaders constantly *encourage* their followers; *delegating* responsibility and nurturing participation are central to service leadership. Delegation, participation, and the entrustment of others involves the *empowerment* of these others; and finally, leaders who want to empower their followers must also be *teachers*.

Summarizing these functional characteristic and attributes highlights that servant leadership begins with the recognition of the other; that is, first and foremost in the mind of servant leaders is the well being of their followers. Servant leaders dedicate themselves not only to serving but also to striving to develop their followers, so that these followers can reach their full potential. In an organizational context, the leadership objective is to channel this service and development in a way that realizes the organization's mission and goals. Somewhat paradoxically however, servant leaders, while serving and maintaining a commitment to the development of their followers, also exercise a charismatic influence over them.

Critical Commentary and Future Directions

By way of critique, first and foremost, as acknowledged by Bass (2000), the existing literature on servant leadership is primarily conceptual and lacks empirical verification. Furthermore, by putting the follower first and committing to the emancipation of followers, servant leadership somewhat paradoxically proposes the reversal of the power relationship between leaders and followers. In the past, this relationship has been one in which the leader is clearly differentiated from the follower on the basis of the leader's superior power. Changing such a power relationship is problematic in a number of ways. The most obvious is that followers may not accept a servant as their leader; it is highly likely, based on the historical theory and practice of leadership in an organizational context, that followers will expect leaders to behave in a manner contrary to the behavior that the theory of servant leadership projects. For most organizational members, the idea of leaders as servants will be quite alien; in fact, the expected behavior may be quite the opposite. In such cases, servant leaders will find it difficult to influence their followers.

Servant leadership is also subject to the same critique that more contemporary shared leadership theories are subject to; that is, when addressing empowerment, the theory neglects the paradox of emancipation, as noted by Benton in 1981. Benton illustrates that it is impossible for a person to emancipate another; he argues that the paradox of emancipation in its simplest form suggests that in order to be emancipated, a person must have autonomy, but if the autonomy of a subordinate is to be respected, then emancipation is out of the question; whereas if emancipation is to be brought about, it cannot be self-emancipation. In other words, to be truly emancipated, people need complete autonomy in the process by which emancipation is achieved; such autonomy leaves no space for leadership of any kind.

In light of this paradox, some people would argue that to assert, as the theory of servant leadership does, that followers can be emancipated by the altruistic actions of the servant leader is sociologically vacuous, not to mention politically naïve. From a practical perspective, such a suggestion neglects the fact that when persons are in leadership positions, they are in positions of power; followers are well aware of this power and act accordingly, which, in most cases, is an act of deference to the leader. From a conceptual perspective, people who believe they can emancipate others run the risk of adopting a self-acclaimed position of intellectual superiority by assuming that they know the best interest of these others better than these others do themselves. Whether on altruistic or completely self-centered grounds, adopting such a position hints of arrogance and in a cultural sense is ethnocentric. This hint of arrogance flies in the face of the servant concept.

Reflecting on the practical and theoretical consequences of this paradox, some would argue that servant leadership may result in the opposite of what its theory espouses; that is, those who practice servant leadership may quite unwittingly reinforce a dominant position of power, which is anything but emancipatory and service oriented. There is no acknowledgment, let alone empirical verification, that provides insight into whether or not any such consequences are at play in servant leadership scenarios; this area would be a particularly fruitful for future research endeavors. The key focus of such research would be on how, in both a sociological sense and cognitive sense, a leader can be in a position of power and serve at the same time.

—*Raymond Daniel Gordon*

See also Empowerment; Influence; Leadership, Charisma; Power

Further Readings

Bass, B. M. (2000). The future of leadership in learning organizations. *Journal of Leadership Studies, 7,* 18–40.

Benton, T. (1981). "Objective" interests in the sociology of power. *Sociology, 15*(2), 161–184.

Greenleaf, R. K. (1977). *Servant leadership: A journey into the nature of legitimate power and greatness.* New York: Pluralist Press.

Manz, C. C., & Sims, H. P. (1991). Superleadership: Beyond the myth of heroic leadership. *Organizational Dynamics, 19,* 18–35.

Russell, R. F., & Stone, A. G. (2002). A review of servant leadership attributes: Developing a practical model. *Leadership and Organization Development Journal, 23*(3), 145–157.

Sendjaya, S., & Sarros, J. C. (2002). Servant leadership: Its origin, development and application in organizations. *Journal of Leadership and Organizational Studies, 9*(2), 57–65.

LEADERSHIP, STYLES

Leadership style refers to the research that focuses on the behavior of leaders—what they do and how they act. Leadership style is the behavior pattern by which a leader interacts with and influences subordinates. The two most studied behaviors associated with leadership style are task behaviors and relationship behaviors.

Conceptual Overview

Research into leadership style marked a shift in leadership research focus during the 1950s and 1960s from personality traits to actual leader behaviors. A series of studies undertaken at The Ohio State University found behavior clusters called *initiating structure* and *consideration.* Other studies at the

University of Michigan identified two patterns of leadership behavior called *production orientation* and *employee orientation*. Although the two dimensions of behavior in each study have different names, they are strikingly similar. *Task behaviors* in both studies included behaviors such as facilitating goal accomplishments, helping a group get organized, and giving directions. *Relationship behaviors* included items such as taking an interest in workers as human beings and recognizing accomplishments.

The next stage of research, called the *situational approach,* examined which of four leadership styles based on task and relationship behaviors were effective in specific situations. The best known model is Hersey and Blanchard's situational theory of leadership, in which leadership style is linked to the readiness or maturity of subordinates. The readiness level of subordinates is reflected in their education level, professional skills, work experience, and work attitudes. Each leadership style is effective when associated with the proper level of follower readiness.

The *high task–low relationship* style is the most directive or autocratic behavioral style. This style is appropriate when followers are at a low level of readiness because of poor ability, few skills, low experience, or unwillingness to take responsibility for their own task behavior. The leader has to tell followers exactly what to do, how to do it, and when.

The *high task–high relationship* behavioral style includes both a concern for goal achievement and personal support to help employees reach their goals. This style is most effective when followers are at a moderate level of readiness. For example, followers might lack some education and experience for the job but demonstrate confidence, ability, and willingness to learn. Thus, the leader gives some direction but also welcomes ideas from followers rather than merely giving detailed instructions.

The *high relationship–low task* leader style is a participative or supportive approach to leadership, and it focuses on developing followers' confidence and skills, consulting with followers, and giving praise and feedback. The high relationship style works best when followers are at a high level of readiness and have significant education, skills, and experience. The leader primarily guides followers' development and acts as a resource for advice and assistance.

The *low task–low relationship* style is considered the most delegative and has been called free rein leadership. A leader with this style is quite hands-off, with little personal encouragement or involvement in detailed planning or goal clarification. This style lets subordinates work the way they see fit with little intervention and little social support. This style is effective when followers have very high levels of education, experience, and readiness, such as lawyers, social workers, and college professors who can perform tasks as they see fit.

Critical Commentary and Future Directions

Task behaviors and relationship behaviors represent two core dimensions of leadership style. Much research validates these basic dimensions of leader behavior. Leaders may naturally display one style or the other, both, or neither. A large body of research has been undertaken to search for the best leadership style. The research findings have been inconclusive, with no single style considered superior. There has been no consistent pattern of findings about how leadership style influences performance outcomes, morale, productivity, or job satisfaction. One general conclusion has been that the high task–high relationship style is somewhat better, but there is no conclusive proof that this is so.

Other criticisms cite the concept's narrow, overly rational approach to leadership and the ambiguous conceptualization of subordinates' readiness. Leadership is an intuitive dynamic among people that cannot be reduced to two types of behavior or a brief checklist of what do in complex situations. The two dimensions of task and relationship behavior are a simplistic view of leader behavior. And the notion of subordinates' development has not been clarified and tested systematically.

A study by Yukl, Gordon, and Taber proposed that a three-dimensional model was a more appropriate description of leader styles. They proposed that change-oriented behavior was a third significant category of leadership style. Their findings supported the third dimension, which included behaviors such as developing innovative new strategies and implementing major changes. This extension of the two-dimensional model is promising for a world characterized by rapid change and innovation.

Future research also can broaden the notion of leader styles to assess leader impact on macro organizational behavior. Task behavior could be extended to include the articulation of a strategy for the team or organization and the design of a suitable organization structure. Relationship behavior could be expanded to include the shaping of an organization's corporate culture. New research that refines or extends the building blocks of task and relationship behaviors will certainly be welcome in the literature on leadership style.

—*Richard L. Daft*

See also Leadership, Charisma; Leadership, Transformation; Leadership Theory; Participation; Team Leadership

Further Readings

Bass, B. M. (1990). *Bass & Stogdill's handbook of leadership: Theory, research, and managerial applications* (3rd ed.). New York: Free Press.

Hersey, P., & Blanchard, K. H. (1993). *Management of organizational behavior: Utilizing human resources* (6th ed.). Englewood Cliffs, NJ: Prentice Hall.

Northouse, P. G. (2004). *Leadership: Theory and practice.* Thousand Oaks, CA, Sage.

Stogdill, R. M. (1974). *Handbook of leadership: A survey of theory and research.* New York: Free Press.

Yukl, G., Gordon, A., & Taber, T. (2002). A hierarchical taxonomy of leadership behavior: Integrating a half century of behavior research. *Journal of Leadership and Organizational Studies, 9, 15–32.*

LEADERSHIP, TRANSACTIONAL

In transactional leadership, leaders influence the behavior of their followers through a process of exchange, as noted by Yukl. Transactional leaders engage their followers in a relationship of mutual dependence, in which the contributions of both are acknowledged and rewarded. Stated more simply, transactional leaders give followers something they want in exchange for their compliance.

Conceptual Overview

While the roots of transaction leadership theory can be traced back to earlier motivational exchange theories, Burns's 1978 work on political leadership is recognized as a seminal piece in regard to the theory's development. Burns illustrated that the process of leadership was political in nature and that leaders achieved compliance from followers not only through emotional or charismatic forms of influence but also through transactional exchanges between themselves and their followers. These exchanges involve leaders offering tangible rewards to their followers in return for the achievement of performance criteria. In short, Burns argued that leaders could shape the behavior of their followers by appealing to the self-interests and expectations of these followers.

In 1985, Bass applied Burns's ideas to management contexts and explained that the study of leadership as an exchange process in organizations emphasizes a transactional relationship in which followers' needs can be met if their performance measures up to contracts with their leaders. He added that transactional leadership includes "supervisory and subordinate relations in which leaders: (1) recognize and obtain resources that followers need for effective performance; (2) exchange rewards for effort; and (3) are responsive to their followers' immediate self-interests if these interests are related to the completion of work" (p. 11).

Much of the literature on transactional leadership discusses the concept in relation to transformational leadership. The comparison invariably presents transactional and transformational leadership as occupying opposite ends of a perceived leadership spectrum: Transactional leadership would occupy the rational end of the spectrum, because it grounds the influence of leaders in concrete rational exchange processes; transformational leadership would occupy the irrational end of the spectrum, because it grounds the influence of leaders over followers to the intangible, irrational, and, in most cases, charismatic qualities of leaders. In general, this comparative approach is aimed at ascertaining the organizational context in which either transactional or transformational leadership, or a certain mix of the two, is appropriate. These studies also focus on how to recognize and train transactional and transformational leaders. Some contributors to these studies include Kuhnert and Lewis in 1987, Howell and Avolio in 1993, and Wofford, Goodwin, and Whittington in 1998.

Critical Commentary and Future Directions

Reflection on the broader debates that were occurring in organization studies when Burns first published his work suggests that what he had to say about the transactional nature of leadership correlated with the attempt by organizational theorists to distinguish between leadership and management (see Yukl's 1989 study). Burns's work, however, subtly illustrates that these debates may have been somewhat misguided, because the transactional nature of leadership suggested that leadership necessarily has a management dimension. Further, his discussion of the need to recognize the role that exchange processes played in the politically oriented nature of leadership also suggests that, at the time, the literature had a preoccupation with the irrational side of leadership.

Many writers still argue that the distinction between transformational and transactional leadership is ill-founded, instead suggesting that transactional leadership, because of its focus on tangible forms of exchange, has more to do with management than leadership. For these writers, management and thus transactional processes, while being part of a leader's job, are not the essence of what makes a person a leader. They suggest that leadership has a necessary subjective or emotive dimension, because grounding the influence of leaders to concrete forms of exchange, as transactional leadership does, in effect suggests that anybody who is in a position to offer something in exchange for behavioral compliance can also be a leader. A number of transactional leadership theorists have attempted, some would argue with mixed levels of success, to engage with this critique by arguing that the nature or level at which the exchange process takes place enables one to differentiate between leaders and nonleaders. In short, these theorists argue that transactional leaders engage in exchange processes that have key significance to the leadership of an organization.

In recent times, research into transactional leadership appears to have attracted a renewed interest (see, for example, Judge and Piccolo's 2004 work and the Shivers-Blackwell study of 2004). This interest appears to coincide with the widespread introduction of new organizational forms by organizations across the globe. These organizational forms are characterized by flexible structures, autonomous work systems, and the empowerment of lower-level workers. Future research in the field might focus on the effect of the introduction of structures and systems such as these on the transactional exchanges between leaders and followers. The implementation of such structures and systems results in the differential in power between leaders and followers being usurped, at least theoretically. Consequently, leaders may face challenges from their (empowered) followers and find a greater need to resort to exchange strategies to secure compliance.

—*Raymond Daniel Gordon*

See also Empowerment; Influence; Leadership, Charisma; Leadership, Transformational; Power

Further Readings

Bass, B. M. (1985). *Leadership and performance beyond expectations.* New York: Free Press.

Burns, J. M. (1978). *Leadership.* New York: Harper and Row.

Howell, J. M., & Avolio, B. J. (1993). Transformational leadership, transactional leadership, locus of control, and support for innovation: Key predictions of consolidated-business-unit performance. *Journal of Applied Psychology, 78*(6), 891–902.

Judge, T. A, & Piccolo, R. F. (2004). Transformational and transactional leadership: A meta-analytic test of their relative validity. *Journal of Applied Psychology, 18*(5), 755–768.

Kuhnet, K. W., & Lewis, P. (1987). Transactional and transformational leadership: A constructive/developmental analysis. *Academy of Management Review, 12*(4), 648–657.

Shivers-Blackwell, S. L. (2004). Using role theory to examine determinants of transformational and transactional leader behaviour. *Journal of Leadership and Organizational Development, 10*(3), 41–50.

Wofford, J. C., Goodwin, V. L., & Whittington, J. L. (1998). A field study of a cognitive approach to understanding transformational and transactional leadership. *Leadership Quarterly, 9*, 55–84.

Yukl, G. A. (1989). *Leadership in organizations.* Englewood Cliffs, NJ: Prentice Hall.

LEADERSHIP, TRANSFORMATIONAL

Transformational leadership is the process whereby a leader fosters group or organizational performance beyond expectation by virtue of the strong emotional attachment with his or her followers combined with the collective commitment to a higher moral cause. For the past 30 years, transformational leadership has been the single most studied and debated idea within the field of leadership studies.

Conceptual Overview

While the term *transformational leadership* was originally coined by James Downton in a 1983 paper on rebel leadership, it was James MacGregor Burns who brought the term to wider parlance in his 1978 classic study of political leadership in the book simply entitled *Leadership*. Burns made an important distinction between transactional leadership, which he suggested was the way that most politicians led their followers on the basis of reciprocal exchange leading to the satisfaction of both the leader's and the follower's self-interests, and transformational leadership, which was practiced by those political leaders who were able to engage their followers not only to achieve something of significance but also to morally uplift them.

Seven years later, industrial psychologist Bernard Bass expanded on this important distinction and brought it to the top of the agenda for both leadership researchers and practitioners alike. While commencing with four factors, the Full Range Leadership (FRL) model that Bass and various others have elaborated currently contains nine factors. Within this model, the transformational leadership factors include idealized influence (both attributed and behaviors), inspirational motivation, intellectual stimulation, and individualized consideration. The second set of factors, transactional factors, include contingent reward and management-by-exception (both active and passive). Finally, the laissez-faire leadership factor indicates an absence of leadership (i.e., a nontransaction).

Focusing on the transformational leader factors, leaders with idealized influence become role models that followers want to identify with and emulate. These leaders are admired, respected, and trusted and are perceived to have extraordinary capabilities, persistence, and determination. Leaders who possess these qualities are frequently described as having charisma. Leaders who create inspirational motivation paint a clear vision for their followers' future state as well as provide the momentum to reach that vision through the arousal of team spirit. These leaders also provide meaning, challenge, clearly communicated expectations, and a commitment to set goals. Leaders who exhibit intellectual stimulation encourage followers to be innovative and creative in redressing old problems in new ways and regularly examining old assumptions to see if they are still viable. Finally, leaders showing individual consideration treat all followers as individuals and consider their individual needs, abilities, and aspirations. These leaders help individuals to develop their strengths and spend time coaching and guiding people.

For Bass, the ideal approach for leaders to take exhibits both transformational and transactional forms of leadership. Transactional leadership involves an exchange wherein the leader offers rewards in return for compliance and performance by his or her followers. The transaction usually takes the form of contracts, employment agreements, performance management systems, and service-led agreements. Attention is often drawn to the importance of the augmentation effect that transformational leadership has over and above the effect made by transactional leadership. Indeed the distinction that is drawn between transactional leadership and transformational leadership as well as the crucial role that transformational leadership plays in generating optimal performance parallels the widely discussed distinction that has been drawn between management and leadership.

Transformational leadership is arguably the most well researched and most widely applied leadership concept of the latter half of the 20th century. In accounting for its continued popularity, Jay Conger points to the desperate desire on the part of American businesses to develop a heroic response to the threat of international competition during the 1980s and the need to foster empowerment in the context of organizational restructuring and an increasingly demanding educated workforce.

Interest was further fueled by the publication of popular leadership books that celebrated well-known transformational leaders in the corporate and not-for-profit sectors. The most highly celebrated exemplars of transformational leaders from the world of politics include Mahatma Gandhi, John F. Kennedy, and Nelson Mandela. From the corporate world, Richard Branson, Anita Roddick, and Jack Welch have been frequently pointed to as exemplars of transformational leaders, though not without either debate or dissension.

Considerable confusion exits between transformational leadership and charismatic leadership. Some researchers do indeed see that charisma is a component of transformational leadership, while others feel that charismatic leadership is the ultimate form of transformational leadership. Charismatic theories and research have tended to measure leadership from the standpoint of perceived leader behavior, whereas transformational theories have largely concerned themselves with follower outcomes. In this regard, the formulations of both charismatic and transformational leadership are highly complementary.

Another reason for the enduring popularity of transformational leadership has been the Multifactor Leadership Questionnaire (MLQ), which was originally developed in 1990 by Bass and Bruce Avolio but has been subsequently refined on a regular basis. The MLQ has a self-rating version, a team version, and a conventional leader-rating version. In addition to its extensive research application, this instrument has been widely used as a practical tool for assessing leadership effectiveness and potential within corporations. Most survey studies that have used the MLQ and similar questionnaires find that transformational leadership is positively related to indicators of leadership effectiveness such as subordinate satisfaction, motivation, and performance. By contrast, too much corrective avoidant leadership (i.e., laissez-faire and management-by-exception) will result in reduced performance and goal attainment.

Some aspects of the transformational leadership model have, however, shown lack of empirical support due to conflicting evidence concerning the factor structure as well as the detection of strong relationships among the leadership factors. In response to this, several revisions and extensions have been made to the FRL Model. For example, John Antonakis and Robert House added another dimension, instrumental leadership, which characterizes the significant strategic and follower work-facilitation leadership role that was not covered by any of the transformational, transactional, or laissez-fair leadership dimensions. Others have developed their own questionnaires that identify related but different factors.

Critical Commentary and Future Directions

While transformational leadership continues to inspire theoretical refinement and spawn innumerable empirical studies the world over, several concerns have been raised as being problematic to this theory. First, transformational leadership research has tended to concentrate excessively on top leaders. While a switch toward the examination of the leadership *of,* rather than *in,* organizations has proven to be a useful counterweight to the small-scale, group-level preoccupation of earlier eras, this change in focus probably has gone too far, so that many lower-level leaders have subsequently been ignored. Similarly, as with earlier phases of research, transformational leadership studies have generally had little to say about informal leadership processes, choosing instead to focus their attention on formally designated leaders.

Second, there has been a tendency by leadership researchers to emphasize the exploits of successful leaders. Consequently, we know a lot more about how leaders acquire their transformational attribution than about how they lose it. This preoccupation with success has led to unrealistic expectations being placed upon transformational leaders as well as a missed opportunity to learn from leadership failure. Moreover, insufficient attention has been paid to identifying the negative effects of transformational leadership. This shortfall has, in part, been rectified by a few widely read expositions of overly narcissistic behavior on the "dark side" of transformational leadership. On the flip side of this psychodynamic coin, two of transformational leadership's most influential pioneers, Bass and Avolio, have initiated a promising line of research into authentic and inauthentic leadership that explicitly builds in an ethical and moral dimension.

Third, there is still considerable ambiguity regarding the exact nature of the underlying influence processes associated with transformational leadership. In other words, researchers might be fairly clear about how transformational leadership is manifested, but they still do not really know how it actually works. To move forward with this may require taking a more follower-centric view of transformational leadership. To this end, researchers might profitably examine followers' leader-identification processes, paying particular attention to how individual and collective identification have an impact on individual and group motivation and performance.

Fourth, and related to this, in the most trenchant critique of transformational leadership, Gary Yukl has argued that researchers have placed an inordinate amount of emphasis upon the dyadic processes of transformational leadership (i.e., between a leader and a follower) when, in fact, a more distributed leadership perspective is required. This perspective would recognize the influence of relationships among followers as well as the possibility of shared or coleadership. Fifth, a number of factors have been identified in the literature that can act as substitutes for transformational leadership in generating exceptional performance, such as transformational teams, professional associations, subordinate education, computer technology, and special policies and procedures.

Sixth, there has been an underlying assumption among transformational leadership researchers that the leadership process and its outcomes are essentially the same in all contexts. Recognizing this shortfall, a great deal of effort has been put into testing the situational validity of transformational leadership as well as endeavoring to build contextual variables into the transformational leadership model. There is growing evidence that situational constraints or contextual factors (e.g., technology, industry structure, the international trading environment, national public policy, and social and cultural transformation) may be much more important in restricting the transformational leader's room to maneuver than is generally appreciated. On the other hand, Bass has remained insistent that transformational leadership works in almost any situation but that the way in which it works is very definitely situationally contingent.

Finally, there is some question about whether or not the complete range of leadership behaviors has yet been recognized. While, as noted above, the phenomenon continues to be refined with the addition of new dimensions and new instruments, the theory's reach has ultimately been constrained by its reliance on the inductive process of theory building. This tendency has been further compounded by the fact that the theory has been developed largely by American researchers using American data. The GLOBE project led by House, involving 127 investigators from 62 nations, has endeavored to address this geographic bias. While the study has given some support to the belief that transformational leader behavior might be universally acceptable and effective, researchers still know relatively little about its behavioral manifestations in a wide variety of national and intranational cultural contexts.

—*Brad Jackson*

See also Leadership, Charisma; Leadership, Dispersed; Leadership, Transactional; Leadership Theory

Further Readings

Antonakis, J., & House, R. J. (2002). The full-range theory: The road ahead. In B. J. Avolio & F. J. Yammarino (Eds.), *Transformational and charismatic leadership: The road ahead* (pp. 3–33). Oxford, UK: Elsevier JAI.

Bass, B. M. (1985). *Leadership and performance beyond expectations.* New York: Free Press.

Bass, B. M. & Avolio, B. J. (1990). *Multifactor leadership questionnaire.* Palo Alto, CA: Consulting Psychologists Press.

Burns, J. M. (1978). *Leadership.* New York: Harper & Row.

Conger, J. (1999). Charismatic and transformational leadership in organizations: An insider's perspective on these developing streams of research. *The Leadership Quarterly, 10*(2), 145–179.

Downton, J. V. (1973). *Rebel leadership.* New York: Free Press.

Gardner, W. L., Avolio, B. J., & Walumbwa, F. O. (Eds.). (2005). *Authentic leadership theory and practice: Origins, effects and development.* Oxford, UK: Elsevier JAI.

House, R., Hanges, P., Javidan, M., Dorfman, P., & Gupta, V. (Eds.). (2005). *Culture, leadership and organizations: The GLOBE study of 62 societies.* Thousand Oaks, CA: Sage.

Tichy, N., & Devanna, M. A. (1986). *The transformational leader.* New York: Wiley.

Yukl, G. (1999). An evaluation of conceptual weaknesses in transformational and charismatic leadership theories. *The Leadership Quarterly, 10*(2), 285–305.

LEADERSHIP THEORY

Leadership is a term used to describe the act of transforming, inspiring, mentoring, coordinating, and managing people toward an individual's, a group's, an organization's, a community's, or a nation-state's vision, goals, and objectives. In organization studies, leadership is acknowledged as an important concept, but there is great debate about what leadership actually is and how it occurs and evolves. Typically leadership theory in organization studies is spread across a wide spread of perspectives. These perspectives offer differing views and underlying assumptions about leadership, including leadership as a genetic ability or trait that one is born with, leadership as a specific form of behavior, leadership as process or a way of thinking that is socially acquired, and leadership as a contingent product of environment. Within these perspectives, there are debates about the very need or existence of leadership. For example, dispersed leadership theory argues that leadership is a form of power that is everywhere and always present. Conversely some contingency-based notions of leadership argue that leadership can be substituted for and made obsolete or redundant.

Irrespective of what leadership theory one might believe in, the fact remains that leadership is a large and complex domain within organization studies. The field is overburdened and growing with old and new models of leadership, and little attempt has been made to debate or critique the very existence and validity of so many leadership theories and models.

Conceptual Overview

Leadership can be broadly defined as the process of inspiring, directing, coordinating, motivating, and mentoring individuals, groups of individuals, organizations, societies, or nations toward certain goals or outcomes. Such a simple definition hides the reality that leadership as a concept is rife with complexity and debate. More important, leadership as a field of study is vast and can be a daunting domain of study for newcomers to the field. Part of the challenge for people studying and researching leadership is the high volume of leadership theories and perspectives available. A simple search of the word *leadership* on http://www.google.scholar.com will yield several thousand articles and publications on leadership written by academic scholars. As such, any attempt to define and summarize leadership will be a complex endeavor that will never fully capture and account for the concept of leadership. The aim of this encyclopedic entry, therefore, is to provide a general overview of leadership specific to organization studies for the novice reader.

Origins and Key Concepts

The origins of leadership as a field of interest can be traced back to ancient times in China, when Taoist scholars roamed the country to espouse the virtues of good leadership and government. However, it was the ancient Greek philosophers, such as Plato, Socrates, and Aristotle, who sought to define leadership and plan for leadership development. For the ancient Greeks, the role of leadership was to foster and sustain excellence through the development of virtues such as aesthetics, justice, love, physical fitness, strategy of war, and democratic government. Plato, especially, was clear that leaders should be drawn only from the strongest and most intelligent members of Greek society. It did not matter whether leaders were male or female, only that they were able to progress through a series of complex and grueling tests. Those left were perceived to be the cream of the crop and suitable for leading the nation and its institutions and organizations. From their time of birth, new leaders were mentored and developed for the future leadership positions of ancient Greece and its satellite states.

Despite the ancient origins of the concept, it is only relatively recently that scholarly attempts have been made to understand, operationalize, and conceptualize leadership within the field of organization studies. Interestingly, however, current debates and arguments vary little from those espoused by the ancients. Many modern theories and models of leadership continue to espouse the need for intelligent, capable, and knowledgeable leaders, either born or developed as such, to run nations and their organizations. In terms of understanding leadership within the field of organization studies, an appropriate place to begin is with German sociologist Max Weber.

Weber's concept of leadership relies on subordinates (i.e., workers) understanding and accepting bureaucratic authority and its rules. In other words, leaders are afforded certain rights, responsibilities, control, and power over others by virtue of their position and role within an organization. As long as people accept and respect the bureaucratic system of hierarchy and subordination, then leadership maintains power. Weber identified three general typologies of leadership in bureaucracy: charismatic, traditional, and legal. Charismatic leaders are attributed powerful qualities by those who follow them, as is the case with Virgin's Richard Branson. Traditional leaders are powerful by virtue of hereditary wealth or peerage, as was the case with the peerage system in the United Kingdom. Legal leadership draws its power from professional knowledge and technical expertise, as is the case with a company's chief financial officers and other people with key technical and professional knowledge and skills. As such, leadership is legitimated by subordinates' understanding of and respect for rules and authority.

Weber's notion of leadership comes from a sociological perspective. Sociology is the study of society and its social systems emerging out of social structures, such as a society's institutions, organizations, and so on. While relevant, Weber's ideas are quite dated. It is in the field of psychology that the contemporary scholarly study of leadership research and theory is embedded. Interestingly, much of the psychological interest in leadership emerged from the United Kingdom during World War I, where a lot of time and money was invested in understanding the psychology of war. It should not be surprising that a remnant of the British peerage system was that it was assumed that leaders were born to lead because they possessed certain traits passed down through generations of selective breeding. It was common to find that British officers were wealthy aristocratic men, while the poorer classes emerged as infantrymen. Such an approach to identifying and allocating leaders and subordinates is more-or-less a trait-based approach.

From the 1940s onwards, researchers in the field sought to use trait-based approaches to distinguish leaders from nonleaders by systematically attempting to identify specific biological and genetic personality traits of leaders, rather than identifying leaders by virtue of their family name and socioeconomic status. Using tests such as personality inventories, trait theorists surveyed and tested individuals in a bid to identify those traits that belonged to leaders. A trait is a stable and consistent genetic characteristic passed on from one generation to the next through breeding. Traits such as honesty, integrity, intelligence, strength of character, and confidence were argued to be critical to leadership performance. Unfortunately, much of the research conducted by trait theorists is, at best, mixed. The key issue for the trait approach was that leaders proved no more likely to possess special traits than did nonleaders. As a result, the behavioral school gained strength, especially in the United States, because it argued that what distinguished leaders from nonleaders was not so much their traits but rather their observable behaviors. A leader, therefore, is what he or she does.

The behavioral school emerged out of the learning theories of psychologists such as Ivan Pavlov and

B. F. Skinner. For example, Pavlov conducted experiments on dogs to show that animal behavior could be shaped toward certain outcomes via learning. A dog could be taught to salivate at the site of a light or the sound of a bell if that bell or light was earlier paired with food. The dog learned that the bell or light meant food was coming. Similarly, behavioral leadership theorists suggested that if one were to study what leaders do, leadership behaviors could be isolated and taught or developed in others.

While behavioral theory no longer maintains the credence it once had, it did identify two important aspects of leadership that continue to be relevant in contemporary leadership theory. Studies of leadership showed that leaders displayed two styles of leadership behavior. The first style was a concern for people, where the key concern for the leader was the nature of the relationships at work, how people got along, and how they were being motivated and fostered. The second style of leadership behavior was a concern for production, where the key concern for the leader was the means of production, such as production targets, appropriate technologies, infrastructure, scheduling and planning, and work design. These two factors continue to underpin almost all modern leadership models.

As mentioned, despite its early popularity, behavioral notions of leadership dominated only until the 1970s, when arguments emerged stating that effective leadership was contingent on certain situational factors. If leadership was about how one acts, then a leader would have to act the same way all the time. Contingency-based situational leadership theory, like all contingency theory, argued that a number of factors determine whether a person is a leader or not. In other words, leadership ability is contingent or dependent on matching a person's skill, abilities, knowledge, and attributes with the demands of a situation. Thus, a person may emerge and succeed as a leader under one condition, yet fail under different conditions. Modern contingency theories see leaders' ability to influence performance as a function of their cognitive capacity to deal with situational stressors and the organizational environment.

More recently a range of leadership concepts has emerged that integrates, more-or-less, all the previously mentioned approaches. The study of charismatic, transformational, and transactional leadership has dominated the leadership landscape. Charismatic leaders, as the name suggests, exhibit certain characteristics that followers are attracted to. Through their charisma, these leaders have the ability to inspire and build dreams and sell their vision to those around them. Transactional leaders attend to all the necessary functional aspects of management, such as coordination, control, and budgeting. The emphasis on transformational leaders emerged out of the sociological work of James A. Burns on political leaders. The concept was later borrowed and extended by Bernard Bass and Bruce Avolio. Transformational leaders set examples through inspirational performance, inspire change and innovation, and deal in abstract concepts, such as vision and mission. While there is a certain degree of overlap between transformational and charismatic leadership, charismatic leaders tend not to transform followers into future leaders and do not see people and organizations through to completion of the changes they initiate. Most modern theorists and researchers tend to concentrate on transformational and transactional leadership.

Other contingency-based situational leadership approaches emphasize the important relationship between leader and follower. There are a number of these theories, but the most common is leader-member exchange theory. Leader-member exchange theory argues that leadership is a function of a two-way relationship between leader and subordinate. The appropriate leadership style to be used will depend on the readiness and willingness of followers. The concept is quite simple; if a subordinate is well skilled, knowledgeable, responsible, and autonomous, a more democratic or participatory leadership style can be used. If the subordinate is a novice and lacks skills and confidence, clearly a more controlled and monitored approach to managing this staff member is required.

Most recently a number of newer—or recycled older—approaches to leadership have emerged, most notably from a positive psychological perspective but also from postmodernist conceptions. Positive psychology seeks to investigate those factors that lead to positive personal, organizational, and social outcomes—such as strength of character, resilience, hope, happiness, positive psychological well-being, meaningfulness of life, quality of life, and so on. The positive psychology of leadership draws upon Bernard Bass's and Bruce Avolio's notions of transformational leadership with some additions. Current work on positive leadership concentrates on a person's ability to create social as well as psychological capital. Authors such as Fred Luthans and Carolyn Yousef see positive psychological capital as an integral part of leadership. Positive psychological capital refers to the social and psychological connections, networks, shared knowledge, skills, resources, and psychological support that a leader creates within organizations and communities. Through positive psychological capital, people are better able to achieve both their own and their organization's objectives, because their work is psychologically meaningful and has a positive outcome. What characterizes a good leader, then, is the ability and commitment to build strong communities through principles of economic, social, and environmental sustainability.

Leadership: Substitutable or Dispersible?

A number of key leadership approaches have been presented. These approaches are to be found in various forms in almost all models of leadership taught in universities and management colleges today. Two more interesting concepts of leadership that are increasing in popularity are leadership substitutes and dispersed leadership theories. Leadership substitutes are those things that replace or make a leader obsolete. For example, the empowerment of teams and the use of self-managing work teams are believed to make the requirement for individual leaders obsolete. Dispersed leadership, however, analyzes leadership as a form of power, and addresses how leadership power is transferred to structure, rules, procedures, and technologies. Interestingly, some argue that leadership substitutes, such as empowerment, are advanced and ingeniously designed forms of dispersed leadership power, and so leadership is never obsolete.

In a postmodern sense, leaders do not exist to lead but to be servants; they are servants to the frontline people who are, in turn, servants to customers. In essence the postmodern leader provides running commentary on how the organization is doing and how people fit within it; they construct the stories and rituals around life in organizations and determine where the organization will and can go, and they identify how one can become a better servant of the consumer.

Leadership Versus Management

A common discussion that the novice to leadership studies will eventually come across is the conceptualization of leadership and management as two distinct concepts. The debate on the leadership versus management distinction is indicative of the disjointed and disorganized conceptualization of leadership. There is no real right or wrong answer as to whether leadership and management are distinct concepts, but the majority of literature treats them as if they are. Management is typically defined as a specific role, often formal in terms of position and title. Managers essentially operates in the very same way that transactional leaders operate. They schedule work, allocate staff and resources, do budgeting, and reward or punish people for desired or undesired behaviors. Leaders, however, are to some extent deified when being compared to managers. For example, team leaders are not deemed leaders but rather managers because they are simply performing a formal managerial role. The CEOs of Virgin or of Google, however, develop hero status because of the transformational qualities that they represent. They may be seen as brave, intelligent, fun, exciting, wealthy, and powerful. As such, management refers to a role, whereas leadership is typically referring to a human quality or potential.

Critical Commentary and Future Directions

It might now be obvious to the reader that there is a wide and diverse set of perspectives on leadership. Within organization studies, there has been no attempt made, as yet, to synthesize, make sense of, critically compare and contrast, or debate the viability of so many different leadership theories and perspectives.

The need for debate, and even the rationalization of leadership models and theories, is a critical challenge for organization studies scholars. This challenge may prove too big, and perhaps leadership studies will continue to expand in an unconsidered and uncritical way.

More important, many leadership theories and concepts, even those discussed in this encyclopedia entry, lack support through scholarly research. Irrespective of the research methods used to investigate leadership, or the type of leadership theory under investigation, empirical research continues to be weak in terms of linking leadership traits, behaviors, styles, and contingencies to performance. No field within organization studies has managed to grow at the phenomenal rate that leadership studies has grown without scholarly empirical evidence.

Another issue related to the nature of research surrounding the study of leadership is how the role of the subordinate is downplayed in the leadership equation. For example, leader-member exchange theory assumes that ultimate power rests with leaders, and that they will decide when a subordinate is able, or not able, to follow. In reality, new organizational designs have transformed the role of leadership, and increasingly, concepts of self-leadership and autonomy have become popular. As such, how leadership works to influence others becomes even more problematic. Even within critical management studies, a similar bias toward the power of the leader exists. As a subordinate, the worker is always under the control and surveillance of leadership because that is how society is structured. Those in power have absolute control over those without power, and workers are always in an inferior position. The leader-subordinate relationship is much more complex than some of the leader-member exchange and critical management scholars claim.

A final issue or challenge to leadership theory is centered on the idea of gender. A number of studies have sought to establish that a discernable difference exists between the styles of leadership exhibited by males and females. Some of these studies come from a trait-based approach and others from a behavioral styles approach. The argument is that women, because of the feminine nature of mothering, communicating, caring, and listening, are somehow better equipped for leading organizations and teams where such virtues are in demand. For this reason, some leadership positions are said to be better suited to women. Conversely, some industries are seen to be more masculine oriented and less receptive to female leadership. There are many articles, book chapters, and publications that make such arguments with great conviction. However, once again there is little conclusive evidence to support such ideas. Despite this fact, gendered leadership and notions of feminine versus masculine leadership styles continue to flourish.

—*Tyrone S. Pitsis*

See also Authority; Bureaucracy; Contingent Workers; Positive Psychology; Postmodernism

Further Readings

Avolio, B. J., & Bass, B. M. (1988). Transformational leadership, charisma, and beyond. In J. G. Hunt, B. R. Baliga, H. P. Dachler, & C.A. Schriesheim (Eds.), *Emerging leadership vistas* (pp. 29–49). Lexington, MA: Lexington Books.

Boje, D., & Dennehey, R. (1999). *Managing in a postmodern world.* Retrieved March 18, 2007, from http://cbae.nmsu.edu/~dboje/mpw.html

Bryman, A. (2004). *The Disneyization of society.* London: Sage.

Burns, J. M. (1978). *Leadership.* New York: Harper & Row.

Clegg, S. R., Kornberger, M., & Pitsis, T. S. (2005). *Managing and organizations: An introduction to theory and practice.* Thousand Oaks, CA: Sage.

Donaldson, L. (1996). *For positivist organization theory.* London: Sage.

Fiedler, F. E. (1995). Cognitive resources and leadership performance. *Applied Psychology: An International Review, 44,* 5–28.

Greenleaf, R. (2002). Servant *leadership: A journey into the nature of legitimate power and greatness.* New York: Paulist Press.

Luthans, F., & Youssef, C. (2004). Human, social, and now positive psychological capital management: Investing in people for competitive advantage. *Organizational Dynamics, 33*(2), 143–160.

Meindl, J. (1995). The romance of leadership as a follower-centric theory: A social constructionist approach. *Leadership Quarterly, 6*(3), 329–341.

Parry, K. W., & Meindl, J. R. (Eds.). (2002). *Grounding leadership theory and research: Issues, perspectives and methods* (Volume 1 in Research in Leadership Horizons). Greenwich, CT: Information Age.

Seligman, M. E. P. (1999). The president's address. *American Psychologist, 54,* 559–562.

Sewell, G. (1988). The discipline of teams: The control of team-based industrial work through electronic and peer surveillance. *Administrative Science Quarterly, 43,* 397–428.

Weber, M. (1947). *The theory of social and economic organization* (T. Parsons & A. M. Henderson, Trans.). New York: Free Press.

LEAN PRODUCTION

Lean production is a manufacturing system that operates in a repetitive manufacturing environment. The objective of lean production is to streamline the flow of production while simultaneously seeking to reduce the resources required by production (including labor, equipment, materials, and floor space). Wallace Hopp and Mark Spearman proposed in the mid-1990s that operations could be classified according to their capacity utilization, inventory buildup, and system variability. According to this classification system, lean production calls for operation with a high capacity utilization and low inventory, requiring a minimization of all system variability (e.g., the variability arising from downtime, quality problems, or demand).

Conceptual Overview

Lean production is based on the Toyota Production System, developed by Taiichi Ohno and Shigeo Shingo to permit Toyota to compete against globally dominant automakers in spite of lower economies of scale and general access to resources. Mass production as practiced by these dominant players at the time called for high resource utilization, considered process variability as normal, and consequently built up large in-process inventories. In 1990, James Womack, Daniel Jones, and Daniel Roos published the book *The Machine that Changed the World,* in which the Toyota Production System concepts were extended to the global context under the new name of *lean production.*

Shifting from mass to lean production is accomplished through a set of practices that are geared to give management control over inventory levels and variability. These practices do not define lean production, however: Lean can be implemented in other ways, and the deployment of the practices does not automatically result in leanness.

Through lean production principles, Toyota gained substantial market share in a way that violated most traditional assumptions about competitive strategy. (Toyota's change in competitiveness through learning how to run lean can be considered as one of the motivations for the development of the resource-based view theory of firm competitiveness.)

A key breakthrough of the Toyota Production System was the concept of just-in-time manufacturing (JIT), in which goods were to be produced only as needed rather than to keep machines busy or to cover for any quality problem or unplanned downtime that might arise. Extra production was viewed as waste rather than value added. JIT and the Toyota Production System resulted in a new emphasis on setup-time reduction to eliminate the overproduction caused by large production batch sizes.

Waste in the form of quality problems was attacked through practices that include statistical process control, analysis by teams of workers, and an emphasis on continuous improvement (*kaizen*). The combination of practices used to attack quality problems is often referred to as *Total Quality Management.* Downtime was attacked through practices under the banner of *total preventive maintenance.*

Traveling between workstations (prevalent in job shops) was reduced through reorganizing workstations into cells. Workers in cells or on a production line are organized into teams, with some decision-making authority shifted to the team level.

A lean production practice entitled *heijunka* calls for sequencing production so that items requiring more work are systematically alternated with those requiring less work. The objective of heijunka is to minimize the impact of demand variability on the production line.

Over time, it was discovered that many of the problems faced in manufacturing were best eliminated during the design phase, leading to a practice called *design for manufacturing and assembly.*

Leanness carries with it an element of fragility. In a lean operation, an employee who is absent or unmotivated will stop the line. The developers of the Toyota Production System recognized from the beginning that worker commitment and motivation were essential to lean production effectiveness, leading them to place great emphasis on demonstrating respect for workers. Lean production theory calls for worker involvement in process development and problem solving, with workers being treated as valuable members of the team. Workers are often cross-trained, which both increases task variety and reduces repetitive strain injuries (although the incidence of repetitive strain injuries tends to be high in lean production). This attitude toward workers contrasts dramatically with the common attitude under mass production that workers were incompetent and of low value. (This attitude is demonstrated in Frederick W. Taylor's recommended separation of planning from execution, for example.)

Critical Commentary and Future Directions

There is general agreement that lean production is a powerful and logically coherent production system that outperforms traditional mass production in repetitive production environments. Because of its successes and its conceptual attractiveness, however, lean production has moved from being one of several effective systems to being synonymous with effective production. Lean is considered to be the answer to every operation (including service operations), and anything that makes an operation perform better is described as making it leaner.

Recall that this entry has classified lean production as having high capacity utilization, low in-process inventory, and low variability. There is increasing recognition that some variability can be strategically valuable and that profiting from such strategic variability may require a bit of extra "fat."

Lean production has been criticized as not living up to its promises to workers. Jobs under lean production continue to have short cycle times and low task variety even with cross-training and job rotation. As operations becomes leaner, workers have less time available to participate in problem-solving teams. Kaizen activities can degenerate into efforts to pass work content to a colleague rather than seek true improvement. Finally, although serious worker injuries are lower under lean than mass production, the lean's intense work pace has been observed to result in high levels of repetitive strain injuries.

—*Suzanne de Treville*

See also Empowerment; Japanese Management; Just-in-Time Management; Total Quality Management

Further Readings

Adler, P. S. (1993). Time and motion regained. *Harvard Business Review, 71*(1), 97–108.

Adler, P. S., Goldoftas, B., & Levine, D. I. (1999). Flexibility versus efficiency? A case study of model changeovers in the Toyota production system. *Organization Science, 10*(1), 43–68.

Schonberger, R. J. (1982). *Japanese manufacturing techniques: Nine hidden lessons in simplicity.* New York: Free Press.

Womack, J. P., Jones, D. T., & Roos, D. (1990). *The machine that changed the world.* New York: HarperCollins.

LEARNING

Learning describes the acquisition, processing, dissemination, application, and creation of knowledge that can occur at the individual, group, and organizational level. There is general agreement that learning involves a change that can come in the form of behavioral, cognitive, or social change. Although it is generally assumed that learning involves a positive change, there is some recognition that learning may not necessarily be for the better. According to many learning theorists, it is impossible to separate learning from its underlying epistemology; thus, learning and all attempts to define learning assume an underlying epistemology or theory of knowledge.

Conceptual Overview

Learning theories include behavioral, constructivist, sociocultural, cognitive, and experiential approaches. Each of these views on learning considers (1) the importance of learners' behavioral and internal reactions to stimulus, (2) the importance of context in knowledge creation, (3) the rational decision process in learning, and (4) the importance of learners' experience and subsequent reflection on that experience as well as relevant barriers to reflection.

Behavioral Theories

Behavioral theories of learning view learning as a change in a learner's behavior, short term or long term, as the result of external stimuli. Early theories of behaviorism advocated that learning was an involuntary process, such as simply salivating to the sound of a bell. Modern theories of behaviorism have expanded on this, and modern theorists believe that learning can be engineered by the right set of positive or negative reinforcements. These reinforcements can strengthen or weaken the motivation to learn and the outcomes of learning. For example, one type of reinforcement, providing praise to an individual when he or she engages in the right learning behavior, strengthens the motivation to learn, but focusing negative attention on individuals might decrease their motivation to learn something new.

Constructivist and Sociocultural Theories

The constructivist approach focuses on how learners will internalize and organize new knowledge based on the experiences that they have. There are several subcategories of sociocultural learning theory. According to the constructivists, learners create their own knowledge. In the constructivist view, the individual is fundamentally independent of his or her surroundings. Although the individual interacts with context and is affected by it, the individual's meaning still exists in his or her head regardless of the particular context. The sociocultural approach, in contrast, emphasizes the role of the participant in a particular social context. That is, the sociocultural approach focuses on how individuals are embedded in particular sociocultural practices. The constructivist and sociocultural approaches assume that learners need to be actively engaged with their environment and that individuals draw on their existing knowledge base, beliefs, and experiences in order to learn. The distinction between the two positions rests in which sets of beliefs are privileged. The constructivists privilege internal knowledge structures, where the sociocultural perspective privileges culturally bound knowledge. Essentially, each of these views rests on a rival view of human nature.

Other theories, such as Albert Bandura's social cognitive theory and Malcolm Knowles's adult learning theory, have attempted to bridge the constructivist and sociocultural perspectives. The social cognitive theory of learning reconciles the constructivist and sociocultural perspectives by theorizing that the quality of the learning experience is based on the integration of existing knowledge within a specific context. Knowles's contribution to learning was that he described adult learning in constructivist and sociocultural terms. Adult learning focuses on how an adult changes as part of the learning process and on how change can encompass a skill, a behavior, a knowledge level, or attitude. This theory included the internal motivation (constructivist) and the context in which the learning is to be applied (sociocultural).

Cognitive Theories

Like the constructivists, the cognitive theorists focus on the internal mental strategies necessary for creating new knowledge. These structures are often referred to as mental models or cognitive maps. The cognitive approach is more concerned than other approaches with how these existing mental maps limit or constrain learning. The cognitive approach posits that mental maps guide people's actions and that these maps constrain how people integrate and act upon new knowledge and process information. Cognitivists concern themselves with what knowledge is stored, how it is stored, and what variables facilitate its storage. Chris Argyris and Donald Schön describe the process of acting upon these mental maps as *single-loop learning. Double-loop learning,* in contrast, describes the situation where people critically analyze these underlying mental maps and question and reconfigure their rules, guidelines, values, and plans. Cognitive theorists describe learning as starting with a concrete experience; then the learner integrates this experience using symbolic representation.

In trying to help the learner uncover these mental structures, cognitive theorists have reasoned that the best approach to effecting mental models includes devising structures that will help learners process information efficiently into current mental models and then using metaphors, narratives, and analogy to bridge mental structures. In Argyris and Schön's case, they advocate uncovering the barriers in mental models or variables that impede new knowledge integration. In organizations that are undergoing change, this process of uncovering will allow learners to redesign their mental maps to be more efficient.

Experiential Learning

Experiential learning theories are similar to cognitive theories in that they also describe how learning starts with a mental map or a concrete experience. This concrete experience is transformed through reflection into a refined mental model and then acted upon; thus it generates a new experience. This has been described by David Kolb as a cycle of learning. Kolb can't be classified simply as a cognitive theorist, as his theory of conversational learning takes into consideration the transformative nature of conversation or a social interaction with the internalized mental model of the individual. These mental models are changed into shared mental models based on the process of conversation.

History of Learning in Organization Studies

Learning and its relationship to organizations remained largely marginal to the study of organizations until the 1990s. Early in the development of organizational studies, learning was conceptualized at the individual level. In the United States, learning theory was largely influenced by education theory. The popularity of group dynamics, influenced by the work of Kurt Lewin, examined learning as a group process. Two of the most influential learning theorists in the United States, Argyris and Kolb, both independently play tribute to the group dynamics movement. Despite the popularity of work by Kolb, Argyris, and others, the concept of learning remained largely marginalized in mainstream organizational theory, although there was strong support for the idea among some scholars and practitioners. Such marginalization did not occur in the United Kingdom, where the concept of management learning has gained a strong institutional standing as demonstrated by the emergence of management learning departments in business schools and of chaired professorships that focus on learning.

Until the 1990s, references to learning in organizations was relegated largely to more functionalist approaches to organizational-level learning such as the work of James March and Herbert Simon. In economics, Garry Becker's work on social capital also gained some traction. Both Simon and Becker deserve some attention, because they both won Nobel Prizes in economics for work that is based on the notion of learning.

Since the 1990s, however, learning has taken a primary role in the study of organizations, and the literature began to include work that showed an increased awareness of the importance of learning for organization studies. Over the past few decades, not only has the number of articles devoted to learning increased, a number of journals have been published that are devoted specifically to the topic of learning. Most notable are the journals *Management Learning,* a United Kingdom–based journal, and *The Academy of Management Learning and Education* in the United States.

There are several reasons for this surge in popularity. The growing knowledge-based economy certainly played an important role. As organizations became more knowledge intensive, learning provided a natural tool to help both understand and manage the increased knowledge.

One reason that research and practice have been slow to adopt the learning framework is that the research and thinking on learning has been fractionalized by levels, theories, and applications. The literature on learning is ripe with complex and often contradictory notions of what it means to learn. The current trend in learning, however, seeks to overcome this fractionalization by integrating various epistemologies into a more comprehensive understanding of learning. Beginning perhaps with Kolb's integrative theory of experiential learning as well as the Gestalt approach, there has been a significant increase in interest in integrating theory across epistemological boundaries. Learning theorists have begun to work across epistemologies to understand learning from a more holistic perspective that integrates cognitive, behavioral, and social dimensions of learning.

Critical Commentary and Future Directions

It should be noted that, despite the growing interest in integration, there are still those who believe that there are irreconcilable differences between epistemologies, because their assumptions are incompatible. For example, the humanist approach of Kolb and Gestalt is not compatible with the critical approach of the Frankfurt School; the humanist school believes in the innate potential of the individual and free will, while the Frankfurt school believes in the inevitable constraints of social class and political elites. One doesn't have to move too far beyond this argument to recognize the cultural biases of both positions relative to their geographic histories.

While there seems to be increasing interest in working across epistemological stances in conceptualizing learning, there seems to be little enthusiasm for understanding learning as a holistic process across organizations. Researchers continue to embrace the false distinction between individual, team, and organizational learning. While there are some efforts underway to understand learning more broadly, the distinction between levels of learning seems to be difficult to break. For example, efforts to understand organizational learning don't often consider the role of the individual and, despite the obvious links between individual and team learning, there remains little conceptual work that links the two in a sophisticated way. One reason for the continued distinction may lie in the fact that research on learning continues to be dominated by logical-positivist assumptions about learning. Thus, while there are continued integrative contributions at the theoretical level, these approaches may be hard to operationalize and study.

In summary, while there is a growing interest in learning in organization studies, there remains significant disagreement as to the nature of knowledge and the nature of change that takes place. After many years of marginalization in mainstream organization studies, the ideas behind learning are beginning to take center stage and have been influential in a number of subareas of organization studies, including the study of disasters, complex organizations, and knowledge management.

—*Anna B. Kayes and D. Christopher Kayes*

See also Absorptive Capacity; Actionable Knowledge; Action Learning; Adaptive Learning; Adult Learning; Behaviorism; Constructivism; Emotional Intelligence; Epistemology; Experiential Learning; Explicit Knowledge; Frankfurt School; Humanism; Knowledge; Knowledge Creation; Knowledge Management; Learning, Double-Loop; Learning Organization; Logical Positivism; Management Learning; Operant Conditioning; Organizational Knowledge; Organizational Learning; Reflexivity; Tacit Knowledge

Further Readings

Contu, A., Grey, C., & Örtenblad, A. (2003). Against learning. *Human Relations, 56*(8), 931–952.

Kayes, A. B., Kayes, D. C., & Kolb, D. A. (2005). Experiential learning in teams. *Simulation & Gaming, 36*(3), 330–354.

Kayes, D. C. (2002). Experiential learning and its critics: Preserving the role of experience in management learning and education. *Academy of Management Learning and Education, 1*(2), 137–149.

Knowles, M. S. (1980). *The modern practice of adult education: Androgyny versus pedagogy.* New York: Association Press.

Kolb, D. A. (1984). *Experiential learning: Experience as the source of learning and development.* Englewood Cliffs, NJ: Prentice Hall.

Mezirow, J. (1996). Contemporary paradigms of learning. *Adult Education Quarterly, 46*(3), 158–173.

Piaget, J. (1966). *The psychology of intelligence.* Totowa, NJ: Littlefield, Adams.

Reynolds, M., & Vince, R. (2004). Critical management education and action-based learning: Synergies and contradictions. *Academy of Management Learning & Education, 3*(4), 442–456.

Schön, D. A. (1983). *The reflective practitioner.* New York: Basic Books.

Vygotsky, L. S. (1978). *Mind in society: The development of higher psychological processes.* Cambridge, MA: Harvard University Press.

LEARNING, DOUBLE-LOOP

Double-loop learning is generally defined as learning on a deeper level. Double-loop learning means questioning the underlying assumptions of actions and thinking outside the existing frame of reference in contrast to responding to a stimulus in a predetermined or habitual manner (i.e., learning more of the same). Double-loop learning is a highly cognitive concept, whereby any action being performed always rests upon some kind of cognition. People always act on the basis of their mental models. More precisely, double-loop learning can be described as the second of two feedback loops; the second loop is initiated when the first feedback loop—feedback on present action provides answers on how to perform the task at hand—for one reason or another is no longer sufficient. In the second learning loop, the focus shifts from learning *how* to better accomplish tasks within a particular frame of reference to learning *what* to do by questioning the present frame of reference. Feedback needed for double-loop learning to take place derives from inquiries into the current frame of reference (for instance the prevailing norms, values, policies or theories) on which present action is based. Although double-loop learning does imply the questioning of an individual's or an organization's frame of reference, it does not necessarily imply that these are changed. The inquiry may conclude that the belief in the present frame of reference is confirmed.

The term *double-loop learning* was coined by Chris Argyris and Donald Schön in the 1970s, and it has an important role in the subject of organizational behavior and in particular organizational learning.

Argyris and Schön certainly succeeded in focusing attention on organizational processes that question underlying assumptions and dominant frames of reference for action.

Conceptual Overview

In understanding double-loop learning, it is important to first dissect the elements of the construct. *Double* means two—or more than a single response, and *loop* refers to a circular feedback figure—where information informs future action. Learning of this type, therefore, includes both cognition and action. Double-loop learning takes place when one realizes that single-loop learning is not enough, meaning the underlying frame of reference for action is questioned. Through inquiries, that is, feedback on present actions and theory of action as well as hypothetical questions about potential future needs, one can get feedback on the present theory of action, which then is evaluated and reflected upon. Taken together, the process can either generate changes in the present theory of action or result in a confirmation of the present theory of action. In either case, present action can be left unchanged—but perhaps looked upon from a new perspective—or might be significantly altered. The key for double-loop learning is the questioning (but not necessarily the change) of the frame of reference. The returning point is, metaphorically speaking, located somewhere other than the starting point—as in a loop.

When one tries to understand Argyris and Schön's choice of the loop metaphor, it is also important to bear in mind that in the 1970s, when Argyris and Schön presented their loop learning theory, other authors of the time described learning in circular terms, such as Kolb's learning cycle, in which both behavior (action) and cognition (reflection) were a part of the learning process. Even the action part, in terms of inquiries being made, actions being changed, and changed action being performed, belongs to the learning loop, and is consequently part of the learning process.

The concept of double-loop learning has several synonyms or related constructs, including second-order learning and higher-level learning. These siblings to double-loop learning are also more-or-less cognitive forms of learning, and represent, along with double-loop learning, one specific level of learning, and as such are part of a set of learning levels or types. Most sets consist of two or three levels. In Argyris and Schön's case, double-loop learning is complemented by single-loop learning and deutero-learning (i.e., double-loop learning).

In addition, there is some disagreement regarding the underlying definitions that are used to describe what it is that is under consideration for change in double-loop learning. Some authors speak about values, others about insights or ways of seeing. For the purposes of this entry, the underlying definition focuses on the concepts of frame of reference, theory of action, and underlying assumptions. These concepts include several aspects that may be considered, including norms, values, and policies.

In spite of the variances in conceptual use, it seems that most authors agree that double-loop learning (and similar concepts) means that one questions the basis for action in order to learn what one *should* be occupied with. Through inquiries, feedback on the frame of reference behind present action is examined, so that the appropriateness of the frame of reference is questioned. This creates a full feedback or learning loop.

Double-loop learning can be either individual or organizational. An example of double-loop learning at the individual level could be a parent who begins to question the underlying philosophy that informs the child-rearing practices that the parent currently applies. Instead of simply taking small, steady steps at improvement (single-loop), there is a reexamination of the frame of reference. The inquiry might result in a change of philosophy or a stronger belief that the present philosophy is sound.

At the organizational level, one can see organizational learning loops as individual learning loops whereby the results of the inquiries become institutionalized within the organization as a whole; that is, the knowledge is stored in the organizational memory (for instance, as new routines). Alternatively, one can look at learning loops at the organizational level from a cultural or collective perspective, in which the organization as a collective learns to modify its current frame of reference or to confirm it. For example, in the 1970s a mechanical calculator manufacturer reevaluated its frame of reference by examining future markets and competitor practices, resulting in a realization that it needed to shift to an electronic calculator product line. However, some companies did not succeed at double-loop learning, and, accordingly, did not survive.

Critical Commentary and Future Directions

Double-loop learning, together with single-loop learning, is often regarded as an either-or concept rather than one based on degree. Because it appears impossible to be constantly within a double-loop learning mode, the concept may need adjustments to reflect a trend of being more or less double-loop oriented.

Another issue concerns the specific term and metaphor of double-loop learning. Double-loop learning has become associated with various types of deeper level learning in general rather than as a specific type of learning that may occur. Therefore, it is perhaps time to at least question the present term and metaphor—that is, to double-loop learn a bit—in order to either confirm the value of it and keep it or change it into a more comprehensible and up-to-date term and metaphor that would avoid the problems of understanding that afflict double-loop learning.

In regard to the content of the double loop, scholars describe double-loop learning in a more positive light than single-loop learning, leaving the impression that double-loop learning is generally superior, even suggesting that organizations incorporate double-loop learning into the organizational culture. Double-loop learning organizations are, thus, seen as more modern, thoughtful, and responsive than their outdated, inefficient, and unresponsive single-loop learning cousins. However, Argyris and Schön argued—explicitly or implicitly—that most organizations are much better at single-loop learning than at double-loop learning and that most organizations would be healthier if they would double-loop learn more, but they have never written that double-loop learning should be a permanent state that individuals or organizations should be in. Future research may need to readdress the implicit frame of reference that double-loop learning is always more appropriate or useful for any individual or organization regardless of context. It might not, in fact, be better—at least not from a societal point of view—that as many organizations as possible survive; it might be better instead that the many are replaced with new, fresh organizations. And survival is a logical consequence from an increased rate of organizations that double-loop learn.

It is easy to get the impression that double-loop learning is a completely conscious activity. The present definition of double-loop learning seems to necessitate conscious thought, at least in the activities associated with recognition that single-loop learning is not enough and the questioning of the present frame of reference. However, those processes may be continuous and unconscious, and more research is necessary regarding the actual loop learning process that occurs in individuals and organizations. Furthermore, double-loop learning may be a less harmonious process than described. Many different solutions for improvement might be presented by different stakeholders and different employees, and conflicts are inevitable. Future research should include the potential unconscious nature of learning as well as the potential conflicts associated with learning.

Some criticize double-loop learning, as well as single-loop learning, especially Argyris and Schön's version, for being too focused on error; Argyris and Schön did in fact express (double-loop) learning in terms of error detection and correction. The critics argue that this might result in reducing (double-loop) learning to nothing but a question of error. Instead, (double-loop) learning can, for instance, also mean experimentation and exploration, which seem to be far away from error correction.

Finally, much of the current critique against organizational learning in general from some scholars can also be applied to double-loop learning. In fact, double-loop learning might demand more from the employees than organizational learning in general, because the employees must be willing to question the frame of reference that sets the agenda for action and the resulting conflicts that would potentially arise. (And there are even employees who would not prefer to learn whatsoever, if they have a choice.) Accordingly, even if double-loop learning demands that somebody question the frame of reference— which would seem to require a pretty open-minded workplace—this must be done at the demand of the organization, and the employees are thus restricted in their learning by their organization. Double-loop learning would accordingly demand that employees learn for their organization, be strongly committed to their workplaces, and probably often make efforts that at least sometimes go outside their original contracts of employment. The employees might feel obligated to do so. This can lead to problems, for instance, in the employees' private lives and especially in their relations with their families. Future research could take a look at the research that has criticized organizational learning in general, take these findings as a starting point, and look more closely at double-loop learning, also from a critical point of view. Is there, for instance, any way that organizations' double-loop learning and individual interests could harmonize, so that burnouts among employees can be avoided or at least be reduced in the future?

—*Anders Örtenblad*

See also Action Learning; Experiential Learning; Organizational Behavior; Organizational Learning

Further Readings

Argyris, C., & Schön, D. A. (1978). *Organizational learning: A theory of action perspective.* London: Addison-Wesley.

Argyris, C., & Schön, D. A. (1996). *Organizational learning II: Theory, method, and practice.* Reading, MA: Addison-Wesley.

Contu, A., Grey, C., & Örtenblad, A. (2003). Against learning. *Human Relations, 56,* 931–952.

Cook, S. D. N., & Yanow, D. (1993). Culture and organizational learning. *Journal of Management Inquiry, 2,* 373–390.

Crossan, M. M., Lane, H. W., & White, R. E. (1999). An organizational learning framework: From intuition to institution. *Academy of Management Review, 24,* 522–537.

Fiol, C. M., & Lyles, M. A. (1985). Organizational learning. *Academy of Management Review, 10,* 803–813.

Kolb, D. A. (1984). *Experiential learning: Experiences as the source of learning and development.* Englewood Cliffs, NJ: Prentice Hall.

Lipshitz, R. (2000). Chic, mystique, and misconception: Argyris and Schön and the rhetoric of organizational learning. *Journal of Applied Behavioral Science, 36,* 456–473.

Örtenblad, A. (2002). Organizational learning: A radical perspective. *International Journal of Management Review, 4,* 87–100.

Swieringa, J., & Wierdsma, A. (1992). *Becoming a learning organization: Beyond the learning curve.* Wokingham, UK: Addison-Wesley.

LEARNING ORGANIZATION

The learning organization (LO) is an idealized vision of an organization where the structures, routines, and working practices are open to continuous adaptation and improvement, where the individuals and teams engage in continuous learning, where the norms and values are supportive of continuous learning, and where strategic decision making is informed by and responsive to relevant data analysis and feedback.

Conceptual Overview

The literature on the LO is a colorful mosaic of diverse perspectives from academics and practitioners. The essence of LOs is effective organizational learning, but relevant academic disciplines, such as economics, anthropology, and social psychology, all entail different assumptions about what this might actually mean. Assorted analytical approaches such as population ecology and sociotechnical systems theory offer distinctly different vocabularies for describing what the LO might be or what it might do. The various business functions such as operations management, marketing, information systems, and human resource management, along with the field of strategic management, all emphasize different aspects of the LO.

Despite there being so many different perspectives on the LO, practitioners, consultants, and change agents tend to converge upon a common set of ideals and aspirations for the LO. They typically seek to create learning climates that are characterized by experimentation, risk taking, collaborative inquiry, dialogue, and open sharing of feedback, expertise, knowledge, and ideas. They tend to prefer that organizational structures be flat and organic and based on the principles of teamwork, flexibility, empowerment, and an absence of boundaries. They acknowledge the roles of human resource development and Total Quality Management in driving continuous improvement of all the organization's operations. They tend to regard company strategies as adaptable and provisional in the light of environmental scanning and timely market intelligence.

Ideas about the LO first developed during the 1960s and 1970s as optimistic, humane, and dynamic alternatives to traditional bureaucracy and hierarchy, aspiring to offer all organizational members opportunities for participation and development.

David Philip Herbst's pioneering account of crew organization on board the Norwegian ship M/S Balao was written in 1974 and was subsequently reprinted in 1993 under the title "A Learning Organization in Practice." The M/S Balao experiment was guided by the Tavistock Institute's sociotechnical systems theory and involved a reversal of several standard characteristics of traditional hierarchical and compartmentalized work organization. Features included total crew member involvement in the organization of change; the planning, implementation, and evaluation of organizational change as a learning process; participative planning of work tasks, taking into account impacts on other tasks and other persons; sharing the lessons of experience; development of a learning community with mutual respect between the ranks; and creation of open and joint territory throughout the ship.

Bob Garratt wrote in 2000 that the origins of the LO may be traced to a still earlier source—the work of scientists at the Intelligence Unit of the National Coal Board in the United Kingdom following the Second World War. Among them, Reg Revans developed the idea of action learning, which Garratt describes as the engine that drives the LO. In 1969, in a paper that was subsequently published in *The Origins and Growth of Action Learning,* Revans envisaged some conditions under which an enterprise could develop as a learning system. The CEO would assume major responsibility for bringing this about and would have an approachable style. Maximum authority would be delegated to subordinates within parameters that would be clarified through ongoing dialogue with superiors, and there would be good quality information systems to inform decision making. Experimental deviations from standard procedures would be encouraged and would be framed as learning opportunities. Subordinates would not be allowed to refer a problem to their superiors without (a) explaining why that problem could not be resolved at their own level and (b) proposing how systems should be changed to rectify the problem or prevent its recurrence. All teams would be encouraged to make regular proposals to investigate and reorganize their own systems of work, and such proposals would lead to discussion with other teams up, down, and across the organization.

Although a less visionary concept of the LO was encouraged in Britain during the late 1980s via the Charter Group Initiative, backed by the national government, which focused on opening access to training courses, the LO movement there continued to be led by a group of consultants and academics who aligned with action learning approaches. Among them, Mike Pedler, John Burgoyne, and Tom Boydell published *The Learning Company: A Strategy for Sustainable Development* in 1991, in which they defined a learning company as "an organization which facilitates the learning of all its members and continuously transforms itself." (p. 3) They believed that the foundation of the LO was individual and organizational self-development, rather than formal training, and they drew eclectically on various functional perspectives, especially information systems and human resource management, along with strategic management. Several of the 11 LO characteristics that they identified reflected the respective historical influences of Revans and the Tavistock Institute. For example, the LO characteristic "internal exchange" denoted the prevalence of manager-subordinate, peer-peer, and cross-departmental relationships that were based on candor, cooperation, mutual service, and give-and-take rather than on manipulation or command and control. "Enabling structures" represented flexible career paths, permeable job boundaries, and provisional rules and procedures, all subject to constant review and improvement, in contradistinction to the chains of rigid bureaucracy. "Informating" referred to arrangements for ready access by decision makers to databases containing relevant, up-to-date, and properly contextualized information.

While LO advocacy and practice originated in Europe, it was *The Fifth Discipline,* a book authored in 1990 by United States–based theorist-practitioner Peter Senge, that provoked a wave of mainstream interest through which the LO became a boardroom buzzword, especially in the United States. Senge argued that in order to kick-start the process of bringing about the LO, consultants should be invited to run developmental workshops to help leaders understand, appreciate, and adopt five disciplines (practices) of organizational learning.

Senge derived much of his vision of the LO from the tradition of systems modeling, but he, too, was eclectic in his approach. He termed one LO discipline *personal mastery,* an individual-level practice involving the development of learning capacity and the strengthening of commitment to ongoing self-development. He labeled a second discipline *working with mental models* and intended that through this practice, which was based on the work of Chris Argyris and Donald Schön, members would learn to recognize and rethink implicit and possibly dysfunctional assumptions about working together. This practice would also enable members to become better at detecting and refraining from defensive reasoning and would learn to engage in double-loop learning. Senge's third discipline was *team learning,* involving practice in suspending assumptions, engaging in open-minded dialogue, and working toward common goals. He labeled his fourth discipline *shared vision,* which entailed allowing and facilitating members' ideas and aspirations to surface, evolve, and eventually cohere into a common understanding of the organization's strategic direction that could serve as a driving force for change. The fifth discipline, which Senge regarded as the foundation for the other practices, was *systems thinking,* which included techniques for representing and understanding linkages between causal events across organizational boundaries and tools for detecting self-fulfilling assumptions and latent barriers to change.

Critical Commentary and Future Directions

There are three fundamental problems that future work on the LO will need to address. The first problem is that there is a state of confusion regarding what is meant by the learning that is associated with the concept of the LO. This entry will consider three possible responses to this problem of ontology (meaning). One response would regard "the LO is good at organizational learning" as a metaphorical statement that refers to various excellent learning-like organizational processes, such as the storage of information for common access. A second response would regard the LO as an ideal environment for individual learning processes, such as skill development, while acknowledging that it is not the organization itself that is engaging in that learning. A third response would regard organization members as agents of learning on behalf of their organization, and would therefore regard the LO as a consequence of the learning achieved by a set of highly effective individual learners. Advocates of the LO, such as Senge, tend to gravitate from one assumption to another, resulting in a patchwork quilt of models of the LO that are based on different, and possibly inconsistent, assumptions. Further theoretical work is needed to clarify, and if possible reconcile, the underlying assumptions about the nature of the learning that is undertaken by, in, or for the LO.

The second problem is that the ideals of the LO may be abandoned because they are judged to be unrealistic and unattainable. Advocates of the LO acknowledge that although becoming a LO may be formidably and maddeningly difficult, the effort is nonetheless worthwhile. Graeme Salaman argued in 2001 that conventional hierarchical and bureaucratic organizational structures inexorably produce negative and all-too-familiar phenomena such as power struggles, information distortion, inertia, and closed-mindedness, which are completely at odds with LO ideals and assumptions. Salaman pointed out also that these barriers to the LO are reinforced by a general tendency for managers not to question ingrained ideologies about how organizations must be managed. Argyris and Schön found that that both the sponsors and clients of LO-type consultancy interventions habitually engaged in defensive reasoning, through which they anchored themselves and their organizations to the status quo. Lars Steiner has described what may be a typical failure case, where the top management said that they wanted to create a LO but where change efforts encountered various roadblocks, such as preoccupation with meeting short-term goals, inadequate communication skills, reluctance to hold meetings, and general incomprehension. It is important to keep in mind that the LO is a vision, not a quick fix, and that the case of the M/S Balao demonstrates that the ideals of the LO can successfully be implemented.

The third problem, as pointed out by Victoria Marsick and Karen Watkins, is that notwithstanding the humane values underpinning the core ideals of the LO, ethically questionable policies and practices have nonetheless been carried out or justified in the name of the LO. For example, employees might be told that they will remain employable only if they use their own unpaid time to undertake studies during evenings and weekends and that they must pay any fees themselves, or workforces may be told that downsizing is the first step toward becoming a LO. It is therefore important that the foundational role of moral awareness and ethical reflection becomes more explicitly recognized as an essential element of LO theory and practice.

—*Robin Stanley Snell*

See also Action Learning; Learning, Double-Loop; Organic Organizations; Organizational Democracy; Organizational Learning; Sociotechnical Systems; Total Quality Management

Further Readings

Argyris, C., & Schön, D. A. (1996). *Organizational learning II: Theory, method and practice.* Reading, MA: Addison-Wesley.

Garratt, B. (2000). *The learning organization: Developing democracy at work.* London: HarperCollins Business.

Herbst, D. (P. G.) (1993). A learning organization in practice: M/S Balao. In E. Trist & H. Murray (Eds.), *The social engagement of social science: A Tavistock anthology; Volume II, the socio-technical systems perspective* (pp. 409–416). Philadelphia: University of Pennsylvania Press.

Marsick, V. J., & Watkins, K. E. (1999). Looking again at learning in the learning organization: A tool that can turn into a weapon! *The Learning Organization, 6*(5), 207–211.

Örtenblad, A. (2001). On differences between organizational learning and learning organization. *The Learning Organization, 8*(3), 125–133.

Pedler, M., Burgoyne, J. G., & Boydell, T. (1991). *The learning company: A strategy for sustainable development.* Maidenhead, UK: McGraw-Hill.

Revans, R. W. (1982). The enterprise as a learning system. In R. W. Revans (Ed.), *The origins and growth of action learning* (pp. 280–286). London: Chartwell-Bratt.

Salaman, G. (2001). A response to Snell: The learning organization: Fact or fiction? *Human Relations, 54*(3), 343–359.

Senge, P. M. (1990). *The fifth discipline: The art and practice of the learning organization.* New York: Doubleday.

Steiner, L. (1998). Organizational dilemmas as barriers to learning. *The Learning Organization, 5*(4), pp. 193–201.

LIBERALISM

Liberalism originally referred to a political system, or to a contending side within a political system, that is committed to free markets, cultural freedom, and democracy. That classical meaning of liberalism is still the predominant one in Europe. In the United States, though, liberalism as a political tendency has come to be associated with support for egalitarian regulation of markets rather than support for free markets. Both in the broad sense of an overarching political system and in the narrower sense of a political tendency with multiple strands, liberalism is influential in organizational studies. However, the overt liberal-conservative competition that characterizes democratic politics is usually latent rather than expressed in organizational studies and organizational life.

Conceptual Overview

Liberalism is a protean term, even more so than its great rival conservatism. Unlike conservatism, liberalism can be used to mean the entire contemporary democratic political system, with its emphasis on party competition and other forms of checks and balances. Relatedly, the term can be used to refer to a worldview that believes in the competition of interests and values in democracies with market economies as the culminating stage in human historical development, as envisioned in Fukuyama's work. In these overarching senses, liberalism as a system or worldview is opposed not to conservatism but to various forms of authoritarianism or utopian radicalism, such as Marx's, that find capitalist democracies fundamentally lacking in organic community or untrue to their own principles of liberty and creativity.

When it is used in juxtaposition with conservatism, four major meanings for liberalism need to be distinguished. Classically, liberalism referred to a political stance that favored changing society through free (or freer) markets in economics and also in culture, especially with respect to religion. Early 19th century English liberals, with their support for free trade, reduced regulation of business, and nonconformist approaches to religion, epitomized classical liberalism, which was once a powerful political contender in England and elsewhere in Europe but which lost support when the vote was extended from the middle and upper classes to a wider electorate.

A second major type of liberalism, which is largely opposed to the classical meaning, began to surface in late 19th century England but rose more clearly to the fore in the United States during Franklin Roosevelt's New Deal and remains significant in the United States and elsewhere. This type of liberalism, which may be called New Deal liberalism or egalitarian liberalism, accepts markets but holds that government needs to be active on behalf of workers and other underdog groups who are relatively disadvantaged by markets and other prevailing social institutions. With the abandonment in recent decades of the anticapitalist, socialist politics once widely professed by European left of center parties, egalitarian liberalism has become a significant presence in Europe as well as the United States. However, such a politics is generally described as social democratic or leftist rather than liberal in Europe and other democracies outside the United States.

A third major type of liberalism rose to prominence in the United States and other Western democracies in the 1960s and later decades. Associated with a shift among some members of increasingly affluent populaces toward postmaterialist values, as chronicled by Ronald Inglehart, this new type of liberalism cobbles together egalitarian liberalism's support for regulating economic markets with classical liberalism's support for freer, more flexible cultural markets in areas such as marriage and religion. Because support for regulating economic markets tends to be stronger among working-class people, while support for freer cultural markets tends to be stronger among more educated people as noted by Clark and Lipset, this new kind of liberalism lacks a clear class base of support. It also lacks the ideological coherence associated with both classical and egalitarian liberalism. In spite of, or perhaps because of, its lack of a coherent ideology and class base, it is this new type of liberalism, which may be termed modern liberalism, that has become dominant in affluent, stable democracies over the past few decades, along with a similarly heterogeneous modern conservatism (see Conservatism).

Finally, there is a fourth contemporary meaning of liberalism as opposed to conservatism that relates to the manner in which authority is exercised by figures such as managers, parents, and teachers. Liberalism in this sense refers to authority exercised in a way that disfavors the use of rules and punishment and favors efforts by authority figures to empathize with the group over which they exercise authority and to have that group share commitment to the values of the enterprise. Liberalism as a manner of exercising authority is not usually denominated as such, in keeping with the modern reality that liberalism is a term generally applied to the arena of democratic politics rather than to personal behavior. Instead, other terms are used, such as "student-centered learning" and "permissiveness" (the latter by detractors). This fourth meaning of liberalism as one approach to exercising authority relates significantly to liberalism as a modern political ideology. One of the major points of differentiation between the modern liberalism of the American Democrats or British Labor and the modern conservatism of the American Republicans or the British Tories lies in modern liberalism's preference for an approach to managing, parenting, and teaching that can be termed "tender-minded," in contrast to modern conservatism's preference for an approach that can be termed "tough-minded," to use Eysenck's terminology.

Critical Commentary and Future Directions

Some have attempted to elevate the stylistic contrast between tender-mindedness and tough-mindedness into the master key or Rosetta Stone for explaining the difference between liberalism and conservatism. For example, a prominent contemporary liberal analyst, George Lakoff, claims that the basic difference between the two worldviews lies in the contrast between the "nurturant parent" framework of liberalism and the "strict father" framework of conservatism. Similarly, a prominent contemporary conservative analyst, Thomas Sowell, claims that the central difference between the ideologies lies in the contrast between liberalism's utopian faith in the benevolence of human nature and conservatism's tragic vision of the fundamental flaws of human nature. Such efforts to offer a master key to the worldviews can be supported through an examination of the work of historical figures who have articulated either liberal tender-mindedness or conservative tough-mindedness about human nature. At the same time, given that liberalism as a contemporary political belief system can embrace many positions not readily derived from a "tender-minded" bent (such as support for abortion, skepticism about an afterlife, and support for striking workers), caution in endorsing the tender-mindedness explanation as a master key to liberalism is warranted.

If, as appears to be the case, modern liberalism and conservatism are not readily explicable in terms of an overarching value, or perhaps even of a set of values, it is worth considering whether the two value systems are explicable in other terms, such as their function in providing benefits to society from their competition. Here, however, there is a theoretical lacuna. Positive and normative political theorists have made many subtle arguments and derived some interesting theorems, but no functionalist theory of liberalism and conservatism has emerged (see Politics). Instead of being explained by political theory, liberalism explains political theory. The theory of justice advanced by Rawls is influenced by egalitarian, modern, and classical liberalism; that of Nozick is influenced by classical liberalism; that of Sandel is influenced by egalitarian and modern liberalism. Their work and that of other normative political theorists has elevated the discourse of liberalism but has not provided a scientific explanation of liberalism. Because rational choice political theorists also have not done so, an antipositivist understanding of liberalism and conservatism now prevails.

Although liberalism as an overarching system and rival of conservatism is usually taken to apply to electoral politics rather than to the personal or organizational spheres, its multiple major meanings can be usefully applied to organizations. For example, economically derived approaches to corporate governance, such as Williamson's, that assume the desirability of checks and balances to restrain opportunism can be contrasted to an authoritarian or a radical, utopian view of the firm. Similarly, approaches to management theory that assume the value of procedural justice as a check on managerial power or of culturally oriented, value-driven management as a complement and rival to cost-benefit-driven management are liberal rather than authoritarian or utopian in their support for the presence of diverse, competing values in the firm.

The across-the-board support for markets and innovation characteristic of classical liberalism no longer constitutes a major political position that wins elections in modern democracies. But it resonates strongly in economic theories of organization. It also resonates strongly in popular management literature, which is replete with advice to managers to flatten hierarchies and foster creativity. Although such popular literature may be criticized for lack of intellectual rigor, it is a revealing indication of the power in the organizational context of classical liberalism's opposition to hierarchy and support for change.

Just as liberalism better explains political theorists than it is explained by them, so too with organization theorists. Compared to political theory, where liberalism in its different forms typically manifests itself in the substantive doctrines of theorists, in organization theory the influence of liberalism as a worldview opposed to conservatism is less evident in the ideologically opaque doctrines of theorists like Herbert Simon than it is in methodological matters. The classical liberal skepticism of the absolutes of religion has broadened in one version of modern liberalism into a skepticism of the absolutes of science. This antipositivist or postmodern aspect of the modern liberal temper has become a strain in management theory. Here, as in other respects, there is a question to be raised about the coherence of modern liberalism, because there is no clear logic that dictates that a liberal on substantive politics should be a methodological skeptic. Nevertheless, the presence of a methodologically skeptical wing of organization theory that is identified perforce with modern liberalism, even though some of the skeptics are themselves apolitical, centrist, conservative, or radical, is a contemporary reality, manifested in the encyclopedia of which this entry is a part as well as elsewhere.

—*Wayne Eastman*

See also Conservatism; Politics

Further Readings

Bobbio, N. (1997). *Left and right*. Chicago: University of Chicago Press.
Clark, T. N., & Lipset, S. M. (2001). *The breakdown of class politics*. Baltimore: Johns Hopkins University Press.
Clegg, S. (1990). *Modern organizations*. Newbury Park, CA: Sage.
Eysenck, H. J. (1954). *The psychology of politics*. New York: Routledge, Chapman & Hall.
Fukuyama, F. (1992). *The end of history and the last man*. New York: Free Press.
Inglehart, R. (1989). *Culture shift in advanced industrial society*. Princeton, NJ: Princeton University Press.

Lakoff, G. (2002). *Moral politics* (2nd ed.) Chicago: University of Chicago Press.

Marx, K., & Engels, F. (2004). *The communist manifesto.* London: Penguin. (Original work published 1848)

McGregor, D. (1960). *The human side of enterprise.* New York: McGraw-Hill.

Nozick, R. (1974). *Anarchy, state, and utopia.* New York: Basic Books.

Rawls, J. (1971). *A theory of justice.* Cambridge, MA: Harvard University Press.

Rousseau, J. J. (2006) *The social contract.* London: Penguin Books. (Original work published 1760)

Sandel, M. (1998). *Liberalism and the limits of justice* (2nd ed.). Cambridge, UK: Cambridge University Press.

Simon, H. A. (1947). *Administrative behavior.* New York: Free Press.

Sowell, T. (2002). *A conflict of visions.* New York: Basic Books.

Williamson, O. (1996). *The mechanisms of governance.* London: Oxford University Press.

LIBERAL TECHNOLOGIES OF REGULATION

Liberal technologies of regulation is a term used to capture particular features of post-Fordist management techniques and organizational forms. They include human relations management, worker empowerment, the enterprising worker, project management, Total Quality Management, devolved budgets, performance appraisal, flat instead of hierarchical management structures, internal organizational markets, contractualism, and the use of audit mechanisms and key performance indicators.

The use of the concept of liberal technologies of regulation broadens one's understanding of organizational power to include the subjectivity, aspirations, and aims of individuals as well as the formation of subjective identity in the social world outside the organization. Studies of organizations working with this concept move the understanding of the operation of power beyond a simple opposition between discipline and resistance, or between power and freedom, to an understanding of the ways in which power operates through freedom, autonomy, and agency. A central concern of such approaches is to identify and analyze the techniques of management characterizing market-oriented and neoliberal organizational forms.

Conceptual Overview

Most theories of organizations agree that the exercise of power in modern organizations has a psychological dimension, depending on the formation of suitably disciplined forms of organizational subjectivity. The roots of the analysis of liberal technologies of regulation lie in the linkage of this idea with the observation that this takes place outside the organization, in the realm of culture and society, as well as inside it. Organizational theory has had an ambivalent relation to this linkage. On the one hand, Max Weber, for example, saw religion as playing an important role in the formation of a psychology suited to modern organizations in his analysis of the "spirit of capitalism." On the other hand, he also ended up seeing social life being taken over by formal-legal rationality and virtually swallowed up by the bureaucratic organizational form. In this sense, he seemed to see the psychological dimension of organizational power as determined entirely within the organization.

Key examples of this kind of attentiveness to the human dimensions of organizational power, what David Courpasson has called soft constraint, are the move away from Taylorism and Fordism toward human relations theory and the study of the informal dimensions of organizations. The French philosopher Michel Foucault used the term *techniques of the self* to refer to the ways in which individual psychology is shaped and acted upon in order to encourage particular kinds of behavior within organizations and society. What is specifically liberal about them is that they combine the exercise of power with the facilitation of what is usually regarded simply as the primary source of resistance against power, autonomous subjectivity. In his discussion of Chicago School economics and the neoliberalism of Ronald Reagan and Margaret Thatcher, Foucault himself spoke of liberal governmentality—that is, a range of liberal rationalities of government.

Such an approach to the operation of power within contemporary organizations does not see it as based on the issuing of commands that are obeyed to a greater or lesser extent, but as constituting a more subtle and supple mode of shaping individual and group conduct. The liberal governance of conduct presumes that individuals act and make choices and that the aim of organizational regulation is to set a particular framework for action and attach greater or lesser risks to different possible choices to make some pathways easier or more difficult.

The theorists who have been especially influential in developing the concept of liberal organizational power include Luc Boltanski and Ève Chiapello, Paul du Gay, and Peter Miller and Nikolas Rose. The central features of their analyses are, first, the concept of alliances being formed between individuals and those with authority over them. Rather than simply controlling and managing their members, organizations work through individual creativity and autonomy. Individual autonomy is approached as an ally of the operation of organizational power rather than being something to be tamed, controlled, or managed.

Second, they stress the importance of the development of shared modes of perception and cognition and the significance of producers of knowledge and expertise. Common vocabularies, normative positions, ways of seeing the world, and forms of explanation help establish flexible forms of coordinated association between a variety of individual, group, and organizational actors while all of them retain their formal autonomy. Expertise and knowledge have a central place in liberal forms of regulation, both because of the contribution knowledge makes to the ability to establish such coordinated associations and because expertise serves as a central nodal point around which perceptions and explanations can be organized.

Third, regulation increasingly takes place at a distance rather than through direct bureaucratic command. Important examples here are the mechanisms of audit and devolved budgets. Liberal organizational power operates through the establishment of rules and frameworks of action, such as legislation, constitutions, rules of association, and so forth. Audit mechanisms allow individual and organizational actors to be accorded considerable operational autonomy while also being disciplined at regular intervals according to rules that ensure their continued linkage with other apparatuses of regulation. Organizations are increasingly characterized by a combination of flatter structures (less hierarchy) and internal markets, with economic costs and benefits drilled down to ever-lower and smaller units of the organization. Each unit's self-regulation of its own efficiency and effectiveness then becomes increasingly important for its very survival. Central authority is strengthened rather than undermined through control over internal resource allocation and pricing.

Fourth, such technologies inherently entail a certain degree of risk as to the exact outcome of the operation of organizational power. By relying as much as they do on autonomy and choice, liberal approaches to regulation are open to shifting balances of power, and they often rely on chance, contingency, and conjuncture for the alignment and coordination of strategies, projects, and desires. This makes the management of the risks attached to this mode of organization a central element of its structure and dynamics.

Fifth, it is possible to see a line of historical development in the operation of liberal technologies of regulation. They move from a form of liberalism, which operates through social forms such as the family, the community, and the corporation, department, or firm, to a type of neoliberalism that places more emphasis on the concept of individualized but regulated choice. Rose understands the transition as one from liberalism to advanced liberalism. Boltanski and Chiapello refer to it as a transformation spanning three different spirits of capitalism—the first (1800–1930) was that of the adventurous capitalist enterprise led by the Promethean bourgeois entrepreneur. The second spirit of capitalism (1930–1967) was that of the large hierarchical organization with fixed career pathways. The current, third spirit (1968–present) is that of the flexible, lean, consumer-oriented organizational network populated by self-maximizing, but also self-regulating, enterprising workers.

These analyses draw attention to the ways in which there is an increasing emphasis on individual self-responsibility and autonomy in contemporary political, social, and economic life, generally heading toward the construction of the enterprising self.

Humans appear to be increasingly constructed as entrepreneurial, self-maximizing, organizational actors making responsible choices within a relatively loosely structured complex of actors, strategies, technologies, and goals. The moves in contemporary organizations toward individual empowerment, rewarding risk taking, autonomy, and agency can thus be seen as consistent with a particular strategy of governance, in which the costs of the failure of individual strategies are shifted from the organization to the individual or work group. Project management and devolved budgets are key examples of this form of organizational power, in which increased autonomy and potential reward is coupled with increased vulnerability and exposure to risk.

One useful example of liberal technologies of regulation at work is the study by Stewart Clegg and his colleagues of a major construction project during the lead-up to the 2000 Sydney Olympic Games. The construction industry was normally characterized by ongoing regulatory problems, the product of competing interests requiring continual surveillance, policing, arbitration, and litigation. This project's O-Team established clear alliances between all the participating actors and enterprises and a risk/reward system that made timely completion of the project a central concern for all the participants. A shared cognitive scheme was deliberately created, focused on what was called a "what's best for the project" culture. Every player's goals were linked to each other's, meshing all their aspirations and aims so as to converge around the operations team's central goal of timely completion.

As an exercise in organizational power, however, it also had limitations, in that its management of the external community interests remained imperfect, ultimately requiring the imposition of more basic forms of political power against the objections of parts of the local community affected by the project.

Critical Commentary and Future Directions

There remain a number of unresolved issues and problems in this understanding of current trends in organizational power. First, there appears to be an emphasis on the coherence of such strategies of regulation at the expense of a sensitivity to internal contradiction and paradox. When questions of contradiction, instability, uncertainty, or conflict within liberal strategies of regulation arise, they are often addressed in terms of a resistance to power rooted in some kind of recalcitrance in individual subjects, despite a parallel insistence on the social construction of identity. The sources of instability or disorder in a given organizational setting are located more in this individual unruliness than in contradictions or tensions internal to the organization itself.

Second, the concern with what is distinctive about the new forms of organizational power characterizing liberal technologies of regulation can obscure the continuities with previous forms of organizational power. Rather than bureaucracy having been entirely overtaken by networks, for example, some observers see the coexistence of these different organizational forms. Part of this issue is the question of the extent to which the expansion of individual autonomy in contemporary organizations can be regarded as real or illusionary. It is also not always clear that there is sufficient sensitivity toward the ongoing violence characterizing liberal modes of management, or toward the destructive effects of the new capitalism on people's psychology and everyday life. Richard Sennett's work on the corrosion of character in 1998 and the dynamics of the new capitalism in 2006 has had an important influence here.

Third, there remains some uncertainty about the way in which human agency is conceived, in essence the question of the authenticity of the space given to individual autonomy, and its position within relations of power. According to Barry Hindess, this conceptual problem arises from the ambiguity in liberal conceptions of individual autonomy—whether it is to be understood as somehow natural and presocial, or as socially created; a given part of the raw material with which organizational power works, or one of its outcomes.

For example, Bruno Latour has suggested that the dominant model of power in social theory is a diffusion model, in which persons, groups, or organizations are regarded as containing power that they diffuse through the surrounding social space, and the objects of that power act only to distribute or resist it. Latour argues, in contrast, that the supposed objects of power actually shape it according to their own aims and aspirations, which constitute the actual substance of the operation of power. From this perspective, organizational power is the consequence rather than the cause of human action. The important shift in perspective to which Latour's formulation leads is that it encourages us to look for the actions pursued by human beings in generating this effect rather than simply assuming it is there in organizational structures.

Among the more important insights accompanying the analysis of liberal technologies of regulation is a sensitivity to the danger of remaining caught in a dichotomy between individual and organization. It suggests that the central question may not be the possibility for emancipation from organizational domination. What may be as important is the problem of comprehending how freedom and liberty are mobilized by liberal techniques of regulation in alliance with one's own aspirations, hopes, and desires. Foucault and others have emphasized the impossibility of escaping the operation of power not, as is often assumed, because of a pessimistic or nihilistic orientation, but because attempts to produce power-free organizations tend simply to disguise the mechanisms of power. This is not to say that practices of freedom and ethical organizational action are not worth pursuing but that such a pursuit is hindered by the hope that such practices can operate outside power relations.

—*Robert van Krieken*

See also Actor-Network Theory; Governmentality; Liberalism; New Public Management; Post-Fordist Economy

Further Readings

Boltanski, L., & Chiapello, È. (2006). *The new spirit of capitalism.* London: Verso.

Burchell, G., Gordon, C., & Miller, P. (Eds.). (1991). *The Foucault effect: Studies in governmentality.* London: Harvester Wheatsheaf.

Clegg, S. R., Pitsis, T. S., Rura-Polley, T., & Marozzeky, M. (2002). Governmentality matters: Designing an alliance culture of inter-organizational collaboration for managing projects. *Organization Studies, 23,* 317–337.

Courpasson, D. (2006). *Soft constraint: Liberal organizations and domination.* Copenhagen, Denmark: Liber and Copenhagen Business School Press.

du Gay, P. (2000). Enterprise and its futures: A response to Fournier and Grey. *Organization, 7,* 165–183.

Foucault, M. (2000). Governmentality. In J. D. Faubion, (Ed.), *The essential works of Foucault 1954–1984, Vol. 3: Power* (pp. 201–222). New York: New Press.

Hindess, B. (1996). Liberalism, socialism and democracy: Variations on a governmental theme. In A. Barry, T. Osborne, & N. Rose (Eds.), *Foucault and political reason* (pp. 65–80). London: UCL Press.

Latour, B. (1986). The powers of association. In J. Law (Ed.), *Power, action and belief: A new sociology of knowledge?* (pp. 264–280). London: Routledge & Kegan Paul.

Latour, B. (2005). *Reassembling the social: An introduction to actor-network theory.* Oxford, UK: Oxford University Press.

Martin, L. H., Gutman, H., & Hutton, P. H. (Eds.). (1988). *Technologies of the self: A seminar with Michel Foucault.* London: Tavistock.

Miller, P., & Rose, N. (1990). Governing economic life. *Economy & Society, 19,* 1–31.

Power, M. (1997). *The audit society: Rituals of verification.* Oxford, UK: Oxford University Press.

Punch, M. (1974). The sociology of the anti-institution. *British Journal of Sociology, 25,* 312–325.

Rose, N. (1999). *Powers of freedom: Reframing political thought.* Cambridge, UK: Cambridge University Press.

Rose, N., & Miller, P. (1992). Political power beyond the state: Problematics of government. *British Journal of Sociology, 43,* 173–205.

Sennett, R. (1998). The corrosion of character: The personal consequences of work in the new capitalism. New York: Norton.

Sennett, R. (2006). *The culture of the new capitalism.* New Haven, CT: Yale University Press.

Weber, M. (1930). *The Protestant ethic and the spirit of capitalism.* London: George Allen & Unwin.

LIFE CYCLE

Organizational life cycles are the stages through which an organization progresses as it grows, develops, matures, and, sometimes, declines and dies. Based on the ideas of biological and ecological models of life, organizational life cycle stages can be described by the various activities, structures, and leadership demands characterizing them.

Conceptual Overview

The idea that organizations have a life cycle has been around for more than 40 years. With a foundation in biological and evolutionary models, early approaches to organizational life cycles paralleled organismic life cycles: birth, growth, death. However, unlike organisms, organizations are, hypothetically, able to maintain themselves in perpetuity. Therefore, the focus of life cycle models had concentrated more on the birth, growth, and development of organizations and less on their decline and death. Only more recently has a different literature emerged focusing on the processes of organizational decline and death. The combination of these two literatures, organizational life cycles and decline and death, leads to the identification of a common set of life cycle stages: (1) founding, (2) growth, (3) maturity, (4) renewal, (5) decline, and (6) death.

Life Cycle Stages

Founding, also called birth or the entrepreneurial or formation stage, is the creation of the organization. There are many ways an organization can be formed, including entrepreneurial start-ups (e.g., an Internet start-up), legislative actions (e.g., a new government department), breakaways (e.g., an airline CEO leaves, takes key personnel along, and starts a new company), and spin-offs (e.g., a conglomerate sells off various divisions that become new organizations). Common to all of these examples is an environmental need for a new organization. That is, the environment in which the organization exists has available resources, demands that are not being met, and a supportive setting (government, regulatory, competitive, etc.) that sets the stage for a new organization to emerge and fill that need. The prime concern of the organization and its leadership during this stage is to acquire the resources it needs to ensure its survival.

Growth is the next stage, also called collectivity and direction. It is the stage when the organization begins to establish rules and procedures to manage its growth while trying to continue to operate in a start-up, resource acquisition mode. In this stage, the organization is beginning to transform itself into a mature, established organization. The challenge during growth is to create rules and procedures that continue the organization's success and expansion now that survival is no longer the main concern.

Maturity, sometimes called formalization, bureaucratization, or transformation, is when the organization has established itself and has formal rules and procedures in place guiding its actions. In this stage, the earlier successes have been institutionalized, but the organization may also begin to be constrained by those same rules and procedures. Often, the organization has reached a certain size such that it can no longer be run in a strict, hierarchical manner. Here, organizations and their leaders face the challenge of remaining flexible enough to respond to inevitable environmental change but formal enough to allow for the governance of a large and complex organization.

By this stage, the organization also may be diversified in terms of its purpose, products, services, or geographic location. The organization may need to begin to grant decision-making and management authority to lower levels in the organization—those closer to the customers, clients, suppliers, and distributors—while top leadership focuses on long-term strategy and interactions with the external environment. Formal rules and procedures are still in place, but they are modified to allow the organization to better deal with its varied environments. The difficulty in this stage is for organizational leaders to find the balance between controlling the organization and trusting lower-level managers to make key decisions.

Renewal, or revitalization, is the next stage. Because the environment in which organizations exist is constantly changing, the organization will inevitably face some dramatic shift in the availability of resources, the level or kind of demand for the organization's outputs, or the setting's level of support. For example, such a change might include a new competitor entering the market, a new technology replacing an existing one, or a new governmental regulation that changes the way the organization has to operate. Key to this stage is how the organization and its leaders respond to the change. If the organization responds appropriately, it can be revitalized or renewed. If the response is inappropriate, too late, or absent, the organization can begin to decline and may eventually die.

Decline and *death,* the final two stages, are actually a series of substages in which a series of events, if not checked or corrected, eventually leads to the death of the organization. As noted above, an inappropriate organizational response to environmental change may lead to decline. If the leadership of the organization does not recognize the decline or continues to make additional mistakes, the organization may reach a point where the environment will no longer provide resources, demand output, or support the organization. Without resources and demand, the organization dies.

Death might come in two forms. First, an organization might completely disappear, with the people dispersing, the assets sold, and the name ceasing to be used. Second, an organization may be bought in whole or in part and merged into an existing organization, with or without a name change. In both cases, the identity of the organization and its culture, structure, and processes are inevitably changed and the organization, as it was known, dies.

Life Cycle Research

Turning to the research supporting life cycle models and their impacts, researchers have identified environmental characteristics that facilitate the founding of new organizations. Variables such as demographics (e.g., an abundant labor pool), political turbulence (e.g., scandals lead to demand for new media outlets), and market competition (e.g., many small competitors in a fragmented market actually lead to even more organizations) have been shown to lead to increases in organizational foundings.

The growth, maturity, and renewal stages have also been the focus of research. Assuming the organization has survived its first few years, it will now be faced with a never-ending series of environmental changes and challenges. This dynamic environment, as described by Howard Aldrich in 2000, can be characterized by four principles drawn from evolutionary models: variation, selection, retention, and struggle.

Briefly, there is a variation in the environment (e.g., a new competitor), the environment selects an organization to address the variation (e.g., customers buy the competitor's new high-tech product), that variation is retained and diffused across similar organizations (e.g., other organizations come out with a similar product), and the organizations struggle with their competitors to attract and retain the resources necessary to survive.

Based on these evolutionary principles, researchers from a range of disciplines have investigated related phenomena. For example, marketing researchers have looked at how organizations stay in touch with and track changes in their environments, leadership researchers have examined how leaders select appropriate responses to environmental changes, strategy researchers investigate how organizations identify and adopt best practices, and economists research micro- and macroeconomic principles that guide the acquisition of capital.

Finally, researchers have tried to figure out what types of environmental situations and organizational processes lead to decline and death. Several researchers, such as Donald Hambrick and Richard D'Aveni in 1988, argue that organizational decline and death is a downward spiral that, once started, gets progressively harder and harder to reverse. They argue that many organizations' initial response to environmental change is maladaptive and actually leads to further miscues, missed opportunities, and poor responses. These in turn lead to even more decline and, eventually, death.

Organizational life cycle research has benefited other areas such as leadership, strategy, and decision making. One area of particular focus and importance is that of leadership. If organizations exist in a constantly changing environment, then, according to the life cycle approach, in order to survive, the organization must recognize the change, respond to that change, and evaluate the response and modify future responses accordingly. This final step is particularly important to avoid a downward spiral if the response is inappropriate. Leadership researchers have argued, appropriately, that it is the organizations' leaders who are responsible for monitoring the environment, developing and implementing responses, and evaluating those responses.

Critical Commentary and Future Directions

The idea of organizational life cycles has guided a great deal of research and thinking about the nature, kind, and roles of organizations as well as research in related areas such as leadership, strategy, decision making, and other areas. That said, there remain uninvestigated issues about life cycle stages, how they are evidenced in different types of organizations, and the interaction between life cycle stages and a variety of organizational phenomena. Further, while the "founding, growth, maturity, renewal, decline, and death" framework adopted from biology and ecology is useful, it is only partially applicable to organizations.

As noted above, organizational life cycle stages are generally agreed upon. Across multiple models and researchers, the basic stages of birth, growth, maturity, renewal, decline, and death appear repeatedly. However, specific models have suggested three, four, five, and up to nine different discrete life cycle stages. Furthermore, many of the earlier life cycle models did not even address decline and death. Only by combining various models and approaches has a comprehensive model of life cycles more recently emerged.

The last two stages, decline and death, are covered primarily in a subset of the life cycle literature that has not fully addressed questions regarding what organizational death means. The challenge with all models of organizational death is defining death itself. Unlike organismic death, which is well defined, organizational death takes many forms and has many definitions. Is the organization dead when the name is changed? When all the people leave but the name and function remain? If two organizations merge, are they both dead, and a new organization is formed in their place? There is no single definition of organizational death that incorporates these various conceptualizations.

Beyond the stages themselves, many life cycle models were hypothesized and based on traditional organizations such as banks, newspapers, government agencies, and manufacturing companies. In light of trends toward newer organizational forms, such as virtual, multiteam, and technology-based organizations, it remains to be seen if these same life cycle stages and models will apply to these new types of organizations. In the least, these models may be applicable on a much accelerated scale. For example, some high-technology firms have progressed through the founding, growth, and maturity stages in as little as 10 years, while older, more established manufacturing firms may have taken 30 to 50 years to reach the same stage of maturity.

Finally, although biologic and evolutionary conceptualizations have been helpful, one needs to be careful not to wholly accept the analogy. Unlike organisms, organizations have multiple ways of being "born," are able to extend their organizational lives beyond the lifespans of their members, and may not die at all. If they do die, there are several different ways of ceasing to exist, including some that split an organization into parts that continue on independently. Thus, when using the terminology of life cycle models, one needs to be careful with the biologic analogy.

Future research in organizational life cycles will need to focus on the changing nature of organizations as well as extend existing work on the impact of life cycle stages to a variety of related areas of organizational research. First, as the nature of organizations change, so too must the life cycle models that describe their growth and development. Researchers will need to reevaluate these models in light of changes in organization types, structures, technologies, and locations. The increasing globalization of organizations raises many questions about varying environments, cultures, and organizational forms that life cycle models do not yet incorporate.

Second, as richer and more complete life cycle models emerge, research will need to look at the interaction between life cycles and organizational phenomena such as leadership, group processes, decision making, and strategic planning. While researchers have used the life cycle framework to study a variety of phenomena, much more needs to be done on the interactions of these phenomena with life cycle stages and on tracking changes over time. For example, research has looked at how leadership demands change as a function of life cycle stage throughout an organization's existence. Such longitudinal approaches should be applied to other areas of organizational research as well.

—David P. Costanza and Rebecca L. Fraser

See also Decentralization; Deinstitutionalization; Downsizing; Environmental Determinism; Evolutionary Theory; Organizational Development; Organizational Evolution

Further Readings

Aldrich, H. (2000). *Organizations evolving.* London: Sage.

Cameron, K. S., Sutton, R. I., & Whetton, D. A. (1988). *Readings in organizational decline: Frameworks, research, & prescriptions.* Cambridge, MA: Ballinger.

Cameron, K. S., & Whetton, D. A. (1981). Perceptions of organizational effectiveness over organizational life cycles. *Administrative Sciences Quarterly, 32,* 222–240.

Greiner, L. E. (1972). Evolution and revolution as organizations grow. *Harvard Business Review, 50*(4), 37–46.

Gupta, Y. P., & Chin, D. C. W. (1994). Organizational life cycle: A review and proposed directions. *The Mid-Atlantic Journal of Business, 30,* 269–296.

Hall, R. H., & Tolbert, P. S. (2005). *Organizations: Structures, processes, & outcomes.* Upper Saddle River, NJ: Pearson.

Hambrick, D. C., & D'Aveni, R. D. (1988). Large corporate failures as downward spirals. *Administrative Science Quarterly, 33,* 1–23.

Lester, D. L., Parnell, J. A., & Carraher, S. (2003). Organizational life cycle: A five-stage empirical scale. *International Journal of Organizational Analysis, 11,* 339–354.

Tushman, M. L., Newman, W. H., & Romanelli, E. (1986). Convergence and upheaval: Managing the unsteady pace of organizational evolution. *California Management Review, 29,* 29–44.

LIMINALITY

Liminality is the condition of being "in-between," at the limits of existing social structures and where new structures are emerging. In organization studies, liminality is being used as a metaphor to explore the shifting relationship between work and organization as organizations seek to become more flexible in response to global competition. The drive for organizational flexibility is altering employment relationships as they are restructured to become more transitory and individualized.

Conceptual Overview

The term *liminality* originates from anthropology where it is used to describe the intermediate stage in rites of transition from one social status to another. The term liminal is derived from the Latin word for threshold, *limen.* The term *liminal* was originally used by the French anthropologist Arnold van Gennep in 1909 in his book *Les rites de passage.* The work of van Gennep was developed by another anthropologist, Victor Turner, to capture an in-between state or place, for example, the ritual of transition experienced by young people between adolescence and adulthood. Turner studied ritual processes by living with the Ndembu people in Africa from 1950 through 1954. For van Gennep, ritual progression consisted of a tripartite process: separation from the everyday flow of activities and one's social position, transition (liminality) whereby individuals are separated from their previous social group or position in an ambiguous state, and reaggregation or incorporation whereby individuals are accepted back into the social structure. Liminality can be a journey to status elevation, for example, for the novice in transition to competent practitioner, or it can go to status reversal. The transition phase characteristic of liminality could be short-lived or prolonged as, for example, in the case of either the institutionalization of liminality in monastic life or the marginal world of the artist.

The liminality of transition removes the rights of liminal individuals over others but at the same time frees them from structural obligations based on formal roles and status. Liminality can be conceptualized as both a phase and as a state, in that it is used to capture a time and place of withdrawal from conventional social action and interaction, allowing liminal persons the space to scrutinize the values and norms of the culture from which they are marginalized. For Turner, liminality could be applied to the betwixt and between states that for him characterized the culturally alternative lifestyles being embraced by some in the West during the 1960s and 1970s. Turner believed that societies needed the dialectic of moving between structure and liminality. Too much emphasis on social structure as the basis for organizing in society could lead to rebellion. Liminality was associated with *communitas,* whereby the focus was interpersonal connection and a heightened sense of community and equality between people freed from normal social life. However, too much communitas may lead to political reactionism and structural rigidity. So in this sense, liminality provided a balance in society against overemphasis on structure.

Liminality has been applied to a growing range of contexts. In health, Warner and Gabe note that liminality has been applied to the ambiguous states arising from medical conditions such as cancer or schizophrenia, whereby the threat posed by such conditions leads to a liminal state of disorientation and uncertainty. Liminality has also been applied to professions, for example, to social work, in which professionals mediate between public policy and the private worlds of family groups. Liminality has also been applied to place, for example, to the symbolic importance of the street as a liminal place associated with mental health service users who (in service terms) exist in a liminal place between hospital and community. In terms of the democratizing of space, Tambyah noted in 1996 that the Internet provides enacted liminality for its users, whereby interaction between individuals can be potentially more democratic when anonymous online users are stripped of status trappings, enabling them to be evaluated for their ideas rather than their status in society.

The 1980s saw metaphors from anthropology being applied to the field of management. From the 1990s, liminality began to be applied as a metaphor to organization studies to capture a range of in-between places and states found in or at the margins of organizations. For example, liminality was applied to work organizations by examining temporary workers in Sweden and the United States by Garsten in 1999, management trainees by Eriksson-Zetterquist in 2002, management consultants by Czarniawska and Mazza in 2003, and flexible workers and organizational learning by Tempest and Starkey in 2004.

Liminality has been used as a lens to consider the shifting nature of the relationship between work and organization as firms seek greater organizational flexibility in response to global competition for customers and talent. As organizations seek to become more flexible, permanent and stable employment patterns are being replaced by greater use of flexible and marginal workers at all levels of organizations. Firms may look to flexible workers in the form of temps to undertake fairly standardized and low-skilled roles, but increasingly specialized roles may also be filled by flexible contract workers, consultants, or interim managers. Liminality provides a metaphor to capture the social limbo experienced by such workers, who operate in a marginal space—not fully members of their host organization or its community.

Czarniawska and Mazza noted in 2003 that organizations are experienced differently by liminal workers than by permanent employees. Liminality can be both liberating and daunting for workers. Liminality potentially frees people from the controls and the social rigidities of organizations, thereby opening the door to enhanced creativity, but equally it places them in a marginal place removed from the benefits of permanent employment with the uncertainty that this creates. Flexible workers have, theoretically, freedom to choose when and where to work and when and where to think. For professional contractors released from permanent employment, liminality can provide access to a diverse range of learning opportunities and the potential to capitalize on the value of their special competitive competencies and professional relationships. However, not all temporary workers are self-motivated specialists. Liminal workers are often denied permanent employment perks such as holiday pay, pensions, training, and access to firm information and status, and they face the stress of continually having to perform well with implications for their self-esteem and identity. For employing organizations, liminal workers may lack loyalty and commitment, challenge the processes and social capital needed for organizational learning, and create challenges for the maintenance and development of both organizational memory and service continuity as outlined by Tempest and Starkey.

Critical Commentary and Future Directions

Debates about the role and status of liminal workers and the implications for organizational forms and learning are ongoing and warrant further research. Some commentators are critical of a shift away from the stability of people having steady jobs with fixed salaries to more liminal workers and flexible employment patterns as problematic for workers and organizations alike—see, for example, March's 1995 work. Other commentators suggest that liminal workers interacting in more flexible organizations raises the possibility of new ways of organizing work that may promote innovation building on individual mobility and organizational fluidity. Garsten suggests that, rather than seeing these flexible employment relationships as inherently exploitative or utopian, more research needs to be done to explore their ambiguous character.

As well as reflections on the challenges of liminal work roles for individuals from a human resource management and personal identity perspective, questions remain about the strategic learning issues arising from the shifting patterns of work, career, and organization for firms that are emerging from a more individualized world of work in the 21st century. This leads to crucial emerging debates about where, in a world of flexible employment relationships, do responsibilities lie for individual and organizational learning, where does learning occur, and how is competence developed and leveraged?

In practice, there are various ways in which the relationship between a liminal worker and an organization can develop. For example, liminal workers may be permanently peripheral to the organizations they work for, or they may enjoy an ongoing relationship with the organizations they work with through latent network forms of organization that reconfigure on a recurring project basis. They may in time become core employees, or they may relish an independent and arm's length relationship, and these preferences have implications for organizing and experiencing work and the boundaries of organizational learning. More research is needed to look at the detail of different career paths and the implications that each has for effective organizational forms and learning processes.

Another challenge for organizations is finding ways to connect with workers who are not permanently employed. One solution may be to offer inclusive ideological cultures to forge allegiance with liminal workers as advocated by Garsten in 1999. However, will this become harder to achieve or sustain as more workers recognize their condition as individualized, liminal workers at the margins of the organizations to which they notionally belong? An alternative strategy may be for firms to try to offer career development opportunities via stretching projects and roles that encourage ongoing knowledge sharing. More empirical findings are needed to explore the value and implications of different approaches to foster ongoing connection with key talent.

The debates about liminality in organization studies have focused on what are claimed to be post-bureaucratic forms of organization and the changing character of work and organization. This begs the question: Will the closed boundaries of our traditional, industrial organizations with their stable, long-term workforces be conceptualized as a temporary aberration in the history of organizing human endeavor? Perhaps individualized workforces facing competitive labor markets are the norm for how work and organization come together for humans; this appears to capture the agrarian model of mobile farm workers, the medieval age of individualized craftsmen, and the early age of market economies driven by entrepreneurs employing itinerant workers as and when required. To develop the concept of liminality in organization studies, we may find it helpful to investigate the lessons of the history of work and organization as well as the future of new organizational forms.

—*Sue Tempest*

See also Learning Organization; Network Society and Organizations; Organizational Learning; Social Capital

Further Readings

Czarniawska, B., & Mazza, C. (2003). Consulting as a liminal space. *Human Relations, 56*(3), 267–290.

Eriksson–Zetterquist, U. (2002). Gender construction in corporations. In B. Czarniawska & H. Höpfl (Eds.), *Casting the other: Production and maintenance of inequality in organizations* (pp. 89–103). London: Routledge.

Garsten, C. (1999). Betwixt and between: Temporary employees as liminal subjects in flexible organization. *Organization Studies, 20*(4), 601–617.

March, J. (1995). The future of disposable organizations and the rigidities of imagination. *Organization, 2*(3–4), 427–440.

Tambyah, S. (1996). Life on the net: The reconstruction of self and community. *Advances in Consumer Research, 23,* 172–177.

Tempest, S., & Starkey, K. (2004). The effects of liminality on individual and organizational learning. *Organization Studies, 25*(4), 507–527.

Turner, V. (1969) *The ritual process: Structure and anti-structure.* Chicago: Aldine.

Turner, V. (1982). *From ritual to theatre: The human seriousness of play.* New York: PAJ.

Van Gennep, A. (1960). *Rites of passage* (M. Vizedom & G. Caffee, Trans.). London: Routledge and Kegan Paul. (Original work published 1909)

Warner, J., & Gabe, J. (2004). Risk & liminality in mental health social work. *Health Risk and Society, 6*(4), 387–399.

LITERARY THEORY

Literary theory has joined organization studies several times under various guises, the three most common being literary theory as a guide to fiction, as a repertoire of analytical tools, and as an aid to disciplinary reflection.

Conceptual Overview

Literary Theory as a Guide to Literature

The idea that social sciences can be enriched through close contact with literary fiction can be traced to the very beginnings of the social sciences and, more recently, to Lewis A. Coser's book *Sociology Through Literature from 1963.* Fiction, Coser claimed, is social evidence and testimony, a commentary on events and morals, more likely to be a source of sociological insights than the random comments of untrained informants. Recourse to literature cannot replace systematically collected scientific knowledge but can complement and enhance it. The social sciences stem, after all, from the humanities. Although Coser did not state it explicitly, quotes from literary theorists show that they were his guides in his search for excerpts to illustrate central sociological topics.

In 1968, Dwight Waldo published *The Novelist on Organization and Administration.* His argument was similar to Coser's in the sense that fiction is to be complementary to science, but he was more interested in a psychological complement. Fiction can add to scientific writing that which was removed in the first place: the concrete, the sensual, the emotional, the idiosyncratic. He also called attention to the gains emphasized later by narratologists: Novels are a source of vicarious experience. Similarly, he was the first to indicate the possibility of genre analysis conducted from the point of view of organizational knowledge.

In 1989, the *Harvard Business Review* published an article entitled, "Reading Fiction to the Bottom Line" by the literary theorist Benjamin DeMott. DeMott chose a story by Lionel Trilling from 1945, and another by Donald Barthelme from 1980, to show how they captured the social character of their times and how they presaged metaphors and concepts that emerged much later in the social sciences. This claim had been made before: Mikhail Bakhtin, the Russian postformalist whose works have become posthumously influential, claimed that the novelists had a keen sense for emerging processes, partly because they did not have to be cautious like the scientists. Milan Kundera, novelist and literary theoretician, pointed out that the novel dealt with the unconscious before Freud did, discussed the class struggle before Marx did, and practiced phenomenology before the term was even invented.

From such a perspective, novels are not a source of information, but a source of meaning. They are among texts to be taken into account while scientific texts are produced; they are models—not for imitation, but for inspiration. They are versions of the world, relevant and valid not because they match the world exactly but because they might contain appealing categories. It is the power of creative insight rather than documentary precision that makes novels both a potential competitor to and a dialogue partner for organization theory.

It was in this spirit that Barbara Czarniawska and Pierre Guillet de Monthoux edited a collection called *Good Novels, Better Management;* David Knights and Hugh Willmott collaborated on the collection *Management Lives! Power and Identity in Work Organizations;* and Martin Parker and his colleagues edited a special issue of the journal *Organization* dedicated to science fiction. Fiction, in their eyes, accomplishes feats that organization theory often misses. It combines the subjective with the objective, the fate of individuals with the fate of institutions, and micro events with macro systems. Interest in fiction continues, and organization theorists are looking for inspiration in literary theory but also trying their hand in the literary theory of organizing.

Literary Theory as an Analytical Tool: Deconstruction and Narratology

Deconstruction is a technique and a philosophy of reading that is characterized by a preoccupation with desire and power. Used by Jacques Derrida for reading philosophical texts, it is a kind of philosophy itself; used by gender scholars, it is a tool of subversion; used by organization researchers, it is a technique of reading by estrangement. As a technique of reading, it earned an excellent introduction in Joanne Martin's article "Deconstructing Organizational Taboos." Martin attended a conference at which one of the participants, the CEO of a large transnational, told the participants a story. Martin deconstructed and reconstructed his story from a feminist standpoint. (Alternative standpoints could have been, for example, the political leftist or the rationalist standpoint.)

Marta B. Calás and Linda Smircich, following the suggestion of Jean Baudrillard, juxtaposed the notions of leadership and seduction and actually used three poststructuralist approaches—Foucault's genealogy, Derrida's deconstruction, and feminist poststructuralism—to reread four classics of organization theory. Martin Kilduff deconstructed other classical texts by Chester Barnard, James G. March, and Herbert Simon. His deconstruction of March and Simon's *Organizations* demonstrated that this famous text contains a simultaneous rejection and acceptance of the traditions the authors sought to surpass. Kilduff ended his deconstruction with yet another loan from literature—a confessional tale that analyzed his motives in undertaking such an enterprise.

Heather Höpfl uses deconstruction as the primary method of addressing organizational issues. In this way, she demonstrates the heterogeneous character of organizational texts, the significance of the interpretation, and the varying status of different interpretations. These interests are common to organization scholars who use deconstruction (and other poststructuralist devices) and narrative analysis, although their ways of treating the field material might be different.

Interest in narrative came to organization theory from the humanities and social sciences. Historian Hayden White postulated as early as 1973 that there can be no discipline of history—only of historiography—as historians emplot the events into histories rather than finding them. He became interested in the modes of emplotment, of turning simple chronological narratives into stories with a point, and he discerned clear traces in history of the traditional narrative forms: tragedy, comedy, and romance. The Swedish organization scholar Kaj Sköldberg discovered that different representations of organizational change, which he was studying, were emplotted with the use of these classical plots, thus resulting in different versions of the same sequence of events.

William Labov and Joshua Waletzky espoused and improved upon Russian folklorist Vladimir Propp's formalist analysis, suggesting that sociolinguistics should concern itself with a syntagmatic analysis of simple narratives, which will eventually provide a key to understanding the structure and function of complex narratives. Inspired by their work and by ethnomethodology, David Boje investigated the occurrence of stories in conversations that took place in work organizations. He found out that storytelling in contemporary organizations rarely follows the traditional pattern of a narrator telling a story from the beginning to the end in front of an enchanted and attentive audience. Narrators tell their stories in bits and pieces, and are often interrupted, sometimes for the purpose of completing the story and sometimes for aborting the storytelling. As to uses to which stories were put, Boje classified them into pattern finding, pattern elaboration, and pattern fitting—all steps on the way to sensemaking, the process charted so well by Karl Weick.

Yiannis Gabriel treats stories and storytelling as a part of organizational folklore. The stories he elicits differ from those spontaneously occurring in the conversations recorded by Boje: They have been told before, tested, and are of significance to the organization. These stories highlight the atypical, the critical, or the extraordinary, giving the listener or the reader access to what lies beyond the normal and the mundane. In this sense, they are reminiscent of Greek myths—another interest of Gabriel's—which also help living the mundane life by resorting to the extraordinary.

Barbara Czarniawska has tried several approaches borrowed from literary theory on the material collected through her studies of public administration in different countries. Her special interest lies between Boje's and Gabriel's in the very process of the fabrication of actual stories from the disjoined fragments observed by Boje, in the combat between various modes of emplotment as a way of playing out organizational politics, and in the shaping influence of popular culture on organizational plots.

Literary Theory as a Help in Disciplinary Reflection

Social science is a kind of writing, and its various disciplines can be best compared to literary genres. Organizational scholars thus attempt a genre analysis (following the example of anthropologists, e.g., John Van Maanen) in order to renew the reflection on their own discipline.

Czarniawska used the concept of genre suggested by Elizabeth Bruss: Genre is a system of (literary) action that became institutionalized and is recognizable by repetition. The meaning of genre stems from its place within symbolic systems of literature and culture, and it acquires specificity by elaborating a difference from other genres. Organization science is a system of literary action that became institutionalized and recognizable. All writing—of science and of fiction alike—involves a choice of style or subject matter, of a search for novelty or perfection in a genre already existing. The name of the genre does not dictate the style or the construction of a text, however; it tells the reader what to (legitimately) expect from a given text.

But genre is only a space within which one can position various works, and it would be their distance from other works that would establish their genre. Genre analysis in literature places most works between genres; disagreement thus remains as to where the genre borders should run and if it makes sense to draw them at all. The best known attempt at genre analysis within organization theory, Gibson Burrell and Gareth Morgan's classification of main paradigms, revealed its heuristic power in provoking massive protests and reclassifications.

Such reflection, or self-reflection, makes a genre more distinct and more elaborate. The analysis of a genre is one of its main constitutive forces. Social scientists busy themselves constructing the institutions they describe. Describing what they do, organization researchers can increase the legitimacy of their own genre.

Carl Rhodes chose Bakhtin as his guide to genre analysis, assuming at the outset that organizations are heteroglossic (multivoiced) universes, which makes generic choices difficult. Should one silence the multiplicity of the voices, giving priority to the omniscient narrator, as in the classical genre of scientific writing? Or is it possible to re-present the heteroglossia in a manner different from cacophony? This question has been posed by most, if not all, organization scholars, who find different answers to it, contributing to the heteroglossia of the discipline. Rhodes's choice was to mix genres and to retell the stories from the field in several different genres, including the traditional science and pure fiction. A comparison of different stories is the source of most interesting insights.

Critical Commentary and Future Directions

The encounter between organization studies and literary theory has barely begun. Many experimentations are taking place, and keeping the experimentation going might be more fruitful than solidifying the merger by some static combination. While the practice of using literary work in teaching is already well established, one would hope that many other venues will open. One obvious possibility lies in close readings of literary texts from the perspective of organization theory; another is a wider use of various techniques of text analysis to scrutinize organizational texts; a third is to imitate and take inspiration from literary texts. All these must, however, remain within the limits of organization theory. The challenge is not to turn organization theory into a branch of literary theory, but to use the latter as an aid in making organization theory a distinct and appealing genre.

—Barbara Czarniawska

See also Dramaturgy; Grand Narratives; Hermeneutics; Metaphor and Organization; Narratives; Organizational Rhetoric; Popular Culture

Further Readings

Boje, D. (2001). *Narrative methods for organizational & communication research.* London: Sage.
Calás, M. B., & Smircich, L. (1991). Voicing seduction to silence leadership. *Organization Studies, 12*(4), 567–601.
Coser, L. A. (1963). *Sociology through literature.* Englewood Cliffs, NJ: Prentice Hall.
Czarniawska, B. (1999). *Writing management: Organization theory as a literary genre.* Oxford, UK: Oxford University Press.
Czarniawska, B., & Guillet de Monthoux, P. (Eds.). (1994). *Good novels, better management.* Reading, UK: Harwood.
DeMott, B. (1989). Reading fiction to the bottom line. *Harvard Business Review, 67*(3), 128–134.
Gabriel, Y. (2000). *Storytelling in organizations.* Oxford, UK: Oxford University Press.

Höpfl, H. (2003). Maternal organization: Deprivation and desire. In H. Höpfl & M. Kostera (Eds.), *Interpreting the maternal organization* (pp. 1–12). London: Routledge.
Kilduff, M. (1993). Deconstructing organizations. *American Management Review, 18*(1), 13–31.
Knights, D., & Willmott, H. (1999). *Management lives! Power and identity in work organizations.* London: Sage.
Martin, J. (1990). Deconstructing organizational taboos: The suppression of gender conflict in organizations. *Organization Science, 1*(4), 339–359.
Parker, M., Higgins, M., Lightfoot, G., & Smith, W. (1999). Amazing tales: Organization studies as science fiction. *Organization, 6,* 579–590.
Rhodes, C. (2001). *Writing organization: (Re)presentation and control in narratives at work.* Amsterdam: John Benjamins.
Sköldberg, K. (2002). *The poetic logic of administration.* London: Routledge.
Waldo, D. (1968). *The novelist on organization and administration.* Berkeley, CA: Institute of Government Studies.

Locus of Control

The concept of locus of control, developed by Julian Rotter in 1966, was devised to assess the extent to which individuals can deal with or control events that affect them. A type of personality analysis, locus of control refers to the way individuals perceive the outcome of their efforts. People with external control feel there is no personal control of outcomes, while people with internal control anticipate that they have control over the outcome of their efforts.

Conceptual Overview

The Internal-External Locus of Control Scale (I-E) forces choices between statements conveying internal locus of control and those conveying external locus of control. People with a strong internal locus of control believe they have a command over their environment. They see a reasonable chance of success and are not troubled by change. Even if change is seen as arising from external causes, they believe they can influence the impact of change and feel confident with their coping skills. Those with a strong external locus of control are more inclined to believe that success arises from luck, accident, or coincidence. Psychologists expect a person's locus of control, or general outlook on life, to play a primary function in developing his or her conception of self. Links have been found between locus of control and behavior patterns in a number of different areas. The Locus of Control Scale, which has a more economic perspective than the I-E, was developed by Spector to assess behavior in employment and organizational situations.

According to Jungian psychological theory, information is received and processed differently by individuals with different personality temperaments. Personality types have been linked to decision making and are correlated with the social dimension of market exchange as noted by Wright, Kacmar, McMahan, and Deleeuw. Determining people's personality types gives some insight into how they will react in certain situations; how their temperament, character, and personality are configured; and how they are predisposed to certain actions and attitudes. An individual's personality determines communication practices, through which individual needs are shaped and decisions are made.

Critical Commentary and Future Directions

In a review of more than 40 years of research, at least 4,600 citations of the term *locus of control* have appeared in the social and psychological literature. Clearly, the construct has drawn a great deal of research interest. Rotter notes that in American culture, internal locus of control is associated with the most successful managers, and research points to the same conclusion, in that people are handicapped by an external locus of control.

Research on managers high in external control suggests that they are more alienated from their work environment than internals, are less satisfied with their work, and experience more job strain and less position mobility than do high internals. Similarly, high externals tend to perform less effectively under stress than high internals. Externals are also less likely to pursue entrepreneurial activities than internals.

Other studies point to similar results. For example, Hammer and Vardi noted that externals are less active in taking charge of their own careers than internals. As noted by Orpen, externals tend to have lower levels of job involvement than internals, and externals are less satisfied with a participative management style than are internals. However, high externals are more likely to help provide structure and role clarification and to show consideration for others than are high internals. Similarly, high externals are more likely to follow directions from leaders and are more accurate in processing feedback about successes and failures than are internals. Externals have less difficulty making decisions with serious consequences for someone else than internals do.

As more and more workers move from manufacturing to services employment, it is more difficult to quantify external indicators of effort that can be used to determine motivation. Meaningful measurements of workers performing knowledge work are still theoretical.

Finally, to keep things in perspective, some research has shown that locus of control is not necessarily a fixed dimension. It can shift over time. For example, as noted by Harvey, locus of control orientation is partly a function of the position one holds in an organization. That is, low-level personnel who have external control orientations tend to develop expectancies of internal control orientation as they move to higher-level organizational positions. Likewise, an external locus of control orientation does not prevent an individual from reaching top organizational positions.

—*Martha C. Spears*

See also Behaviorism; Control; Job Satisfaction; Morale; Motivation; Politics of Organizational Culture

Further Readings

Hammer, T., & Vardi, Y. (1981). Locus of control and career self-management among nonsupervisory employees in industrial settings. *Journal of Vocational Behavior, 1,* 13–29.

Harvey, J. (1971). Locus of control shift in administrators. *Perceptual and Motor Skills, 33,* 980–982.

Orpen, C. (1992). The work locus of control scale as a predictor of employee attitudes and behavior: A validity study. *Psychology: A Journal of Human Behavior, 29,* 35–37.

Rotter, J. (1966). Generalized expectancies for internal versus external control of reinforcements. *Psychological Monographs, 80*(1), 1–28.

Rotter, J. (1990). Internal versus external control of reinforcement: A case history of a variable. *American Psychologist, 45,* 489–493.

Spector, P. (1988). Development of the work locus of control scale. *Journal of Applied Psychology, 77,* 251–260.

Wright, P. M., Kacmar, K. M., McMahan, G. C., & Deleeuw, K. (1995). P-F(M x A): Cognitive ability as a moderator of the relationship between personality and job performance. *Journal of Management, 21,* 1129–1139.

LOGICAL POSITIVISM

Logical positivism asserts that philosophy should adopt the logical and empirical rigor of natural science as exemplified by physics. It views traditional philosophy concerning metaphysics, theology, and ethics as meaningless speculation, because any such statements are neither logically nor empirically verifiable by the strict standards of scientific proof. Logical positivism was a historically important European intellectual movement of the early 20th century that attempted to subordinate philosophy to science and then further to create a unified science modeled on physics. Although, as John Passmore commented in 1967, logical positivism is dead as a philosophical movement, it has left a significant legacy still broadly influencing the methodology of today's social sciences.

Conceptual Overview

The essential feature of logical positivism is a strict principle of scientific verifiability concerning all statements about ideas or real phenomena. Acceptable proof may be logical or empirical, hence the label logical positivism. Scientifically meaningful statements must be either logically true (i.e., analytic) or empirically verifiable (i.e., synthetic). An analytic statement about an idea or concept can be demonstrated logically (i.e., through a priori reasoning) to be true or false independently of any empirical experience. The Latin term *a priori* means deductive reasoning from cause to effect based on theory. For example, in plane geometry, a line can be defined as the distance between two points. This definition is analytically true. A synthetic or empirical statement about real phenomena must be verified by observation or other sensory experience. The Latin term *a posteriori* means inductive reasoning from effect to cause based on observation or experience. For example, by verifiable observation, the moon rotates about the earth, which rotates about the sun.

Logical positivism asserts that any other statements, being neither analytically true nor empirically verifiable, are meaningless. Metaphysics, theology, and ethics therefore must fall within this meaningless category. Today's philosophers believe that critical and speculative inquiries can prove useful independent of strict scientific proof.

Logical positivism also has been called or treated as synonymous with variously consistent empiricism, logical empiricism, logical neopositivism, rational empiricism, and scientific empiricism. This variable terminology reflects intellectual roots in both 18th century British empiricism and the positivism of the 19th century French sociologist Auguste Comte. British empiricism asserted that all knowledge must be experiential and cannot come from reason alone. Logical positivism did not accept this position, as there can be logical arguments. Comte applied scientific observation and experimentation (i.e., positivism) to a new science of sociology aimed at reform of society along strictly scientific principles. Comte viewed sociology as a third and scientific phase of social development beyond earlier, outmoded theological and metaphysical stages; it absorbed philosophy and all other sciences. Hence logical positivism is neopositivism but not strictly pure empiricism on the British model. Logical positivism asserts scientific unification but attempts to combine deductive theory and inductive observation.

In 1931, Albert E. Blumberg and Herbert Feigl gave the name logical positivism to the set of ideas advanced over time by what became known as the Vienna Circle. The logical positivism movement began in 1907 when a mathematician, an economist, and a physicist at the University of Vienna began informally to discuss philosophy of science. They were reacting to strongly empiricist views, akin to British empiricism and Comte, of the experimental physicist Ernst Mach, who argued that science describes experience. These academics felt that Mach, who was also antimetaphysical in his views, did not give sufficient importance to mathematics, logic, and theoretical physics. Modern physics combines mathematical theorizing and empirical verification. This Vienna group looked to the new positivism of French mathematician Henri Poincaré. From 1922, when the group stimulated his invitation to join the University of Vienna, a larger Vienna circle organized around Moritz Schlick. In 1926, Rudolf Carnap joined the university and became the leading exponent of the circle's views. Ayer stimulated appreciation for the Vienna Circle in the English-speaking world through his book *Language, Truth and Logic* (1936). The title succinctly linked the logical positivism of the Vienna Circle (truth and logic) with the language philosophy of Ludwig Wittgenstein and George E. Moore.

Wittgenstein and Karl Popper, not formally part of the circle, interacted with its members. Wittgenstein's *Tractatus Logico-Philosophicus,* published in Germany in 1921 (under a different title), greatly influenced the circle. Wittgenstein argued that metaphysical statements cannot be verified. This verifiability principle, also formulated by Schlick, treated the meaning or sense of a statement (or proposition) with the method of verifying the meaning. The truth of a proposition is equivalent to the relevant set of experiences. Logical and mathematical propositions, or expressions, are in contrast tautologies empty of empirical content. The economist Otto Neurath, one of the original group members, argued that the Vienna Circle should operate like a political party to destroy traditional metaphysics as a source of reactionism.

Circle members published a collection of monographs aimed at promoting a unified science. World War II suspended publication, but the works were later published in translation as *Unified Science: The Vienna Circle Monograph Series* (1987). In 1938, the circle began publishing an *International Encyclopedia of Unified Science,* also disrupted by World War II and never completed. Two volumes including 20 monographs were published during the period 1938–1969. Thomas Kuhn's influential *The Structure of Scientific Revolutions* (1962) was one of the 20. The Vienna Circle also published a collection of *Monographs on the Scientific World-Conception* (1928–1937), including Karl Popper's influential *The Logic of Scientific Discovery* (1934, in German).

Critical Commentary and Future Directions

Logical positivism left an important legacy because the movement focused on unified scientific methodology and was deeply skeptical of theological and metaphysical assertions. The continuing scientific problem involves how to relate logical (a priori) theory and empirical (a posteriori) verification. A difficulty with the skepticism was that it tended to group all nonempirical reasoning with meaningless metaphysics. This skepticism extended for some circle members to all ethics, aesthetics, and speculation. Tracing the influence of logical positivism is quite difficult, because there were disagreements among members of the Vienna Circle. Discussions ranged broadly at the fuzzy boundaries of a priori theorizing, empirical verification, language analysis, and antimetaphysical philosophizing. Intellectual influences on circle members included mathematicians Gottlob Frege (whose terse style of expression Wittgenstein adopted) and Bertrand Russell, whose logical atomism conception posited that the universe breaks down into ultimate logical parts (atoms) that can be studied independently of the whole universe. (The alternative view that no part can be understood without understanding the whole is monism).

Logical positivism is concerned with epistemology (the theory of knowledge of the real world), while tending to eschew metaphysics, ethics, and theology as meaningless expressions. In addition to verifiability, logical positivism promoted unification of science. A difficulty in unification is that the approach tends to treat all social sciences as it treats physics and thus to eschew both evolutionary biology and complexity theory.

Social sciences are in a postpositivistic era in the sense that logical positivism is a dead philosophical movement. Modern social sciences remain, in effect, stuck between pure empiricism and scientific relativism. On one hand, social scientists today emphasize empirical verification and realism. On the other hand, they lack an independent standard (such as logic) for scientific objectivity. Human behavior is arguably neither fixed nor easily described, and scientific researchers themselves have barely understood biases.

The methodological views of Milton Friedman and Paul Samuelson—both Nobel economics laureates—are instructive. Friedman emphasized empirical research; Samuelson advanced mathematical economics. Friedman argued that realism of theoretical assumptions is irrelevant; what matters is empirical validity of testable implications (or consequences) of assumptions. Verifiability of implications is equivalent to validation of a theory's usefulness or relevance. This pragmatic position on positive economics is not necessarily logical positivism. As Samuelson noted, the difficulty is that Friedman tended to argue further that the more unrealistic the assumptions were, the better they were in reducing complexity to predictability. Samuelson argued that the reality of the assumptions is precisely the key matter. He commented that the profit maximization hypothesis is a mixture of truism, truth, and untruth. Behavioral economics seeks to improve predictability by reuniting economics with psychology to study real behavior and motivations.

—Duane Windsor

See also Analytical Empiricism; Objectivity; Philosophy of Science; Positivism; Social Constructionism

Further Readings

Ayer, A. J. (1959). *Logical positivism.* Glencoe, IL: Free Press.

Camerer, C. (1996). Behavioral economics: Reunifying psychology and economics. *Proceedings of the National Academy of Sciences, 96,* 10575–10577.

Friedman, Michael. (1999). *Reconsidering logical positivism.* New York: Cambridge University Press.

Friedman, Milton. (1953). The methodology of positive economics. In M. Friedman, *Essays in positive economics* (pp. 3–43). Chicago: University of Chicago Press.

Passmore, J. A. (1967). Logical positivism. In P. Edwards (Ed.), *The encyclopedia of philosophy* (Vol. 5, pp. 52–57). New York: Macmillan.

Samuelson, P. (1963). Problems of methodology— Discussion. *American Economic Review: Papers and Proceedings, 53*(2), 232–236.

LONG-WAVE THEORY

Long-wave theory is a family of theories that explain societal trends with reference to decades- or centuries-long historical cycles. History is filled with repetitious economic, political, social, and demographic patterns—it tends to repeat itself. Organizational analysts and strategists are aware of the short-term repetitiveness of societal trends and often use better-known, short-term cyclical theories—like classic (Juglar) business cycles or electoral cycles—in their analyses and planning. Long-wave theory is similar to these better-known theories and can be used for similar purposes in long-term planning and analysis. If history does repeat itself in ways identified by a particular long-wave theory, then researchers can look at history to anticipate how today's economic, political, or social environment will change in the upcoming decades.

Conceptual Overview

The best-known long-wave theory is that of *Kondratieff waves.* Soviet economist Nicolai Kondratieff theorized that economies undergo (roughly) 50-year economic supercycles. There are many versions of this theory, but most follow at least part of the following outline: Long-term growth is spurred by the coalescence of minor technological innovations that produce a new sector that propels general prosperity (e.g., railroads, automobiles, telecommunication, and information technology). Innovation and investment activities overconcentrate on this new technology, which eventually becomes widely adopted and loses its enormous growth potential. Disproportionate investments in this innovation may create overcapacity, making the economy vulnerable to downsizing. Businesses are expected to have been reluctant to change or innovate during prosperous times, and their old operational models will be strained to find new markets or improve productivity. When the leading sector's life cycle reaches maturity and declines, the economy will have lost its underlying engine of growth. Stagnation will begin and it will continue until a new technology is found.

Typically, analysts argue that the capitalist system entered a downturning phase of a Kondratieff wave in the 1970s (approximately the time of the stagflation crises and developing world debt crises) and an upturn in the early 1990s. Many observers argue that a sustained period of economic decline is ahead.

A second well-known long-wave theory is *Kuznets swings*. Simon Kuznets proposed 20- to 25-year cycles in long-term production and price levels, although the focus of his work was on industries rather than the aggregate economy. Like Kondratieff waves, these swings were attributed to the introduction, growth, and saturation of a new technology, market, or resource in specific industries and to corresponding cycles of reinvestment.

Kondratieff waves and Kuznets swings offer two examples of long-wave economic theories, but the use of long-wave theory extends well beyond predicting periods of economic prosperity or stagnation. Just as short-term economic fluctuations are often linked to changes in the political, social, and demographic environment, so are long-term ones. Many historians and social scientists have attempted to show how long-term economic cycles cause and are caused by other long-term societal cycles.

Many political historians have linked the interaction of economics and demography to cycles of social conflict and political stability. This theory begins with the observation that population and prices have risen in tandem historically. The world system begins the cycle with a low population relative to the physical and social infrastructure available to absorb human resources. Populations begin to recover, as the disease, economic, or social conditions that caused the last population recession abate. Population growth raises aggregate demand and prices, drives down the purchasing power of wages, spurs trade and migration, and ultimately results in an abundance of humans relative to society's capacity to absorb them. These kinds of theories generally see the population boom as being punctuated by war or revolution (which can result from too many people, especially elites, becoming frustrated and mobilized by decreased social opportunities) or plague (resulting from overpopulation and the international transmission of disease). David Fischer and Jack Goldstone offer noted examples of this tradition.

These cycles have been shortening as time passes; they took hundreds of years at the beginning of the last millennium and have a range of 50 to 100 years in the modern era. The current cycle began with the end of World War II, after which the world's population exploded. According to this theory, the postwar era should eventually see sustained inflation, the erosion of wages, urban overcrowding, increased trade and migration, and increasing disaffection with a political-economic system that fails to integrate more and more of the population (all of which it has seen). The hazard of war or plague is supposed to rise with the population, which is predicted to eventually puncture the cycle.

A fourth prominent long-wave theory concerns changes in the balance of power in international relations and how economic life changes with this balance. The dominating world power is usually at the center of these theories, generally referred to as theories of *hegemonic cycles*. When a particular country comes to dominate the world economy—as did the early 17th-century Dutch, 19th-century British, or 20th-century Americans—international systems of finance and trade tend to flourish. Ultimately, these dominant countries act as regulators and guarantors of the international system and enjoy substantial rents and international bargaining leverage as a result of their position. However, the costs of maintaining a hegemonic position in international affairs rise as the dominant power's society becomes more affluent, the costs of maintaining the military rises, challenging powers develop more effective competitive strategies, increasing interconnectedness creates more opportunities for conflict, and increasing disparities between the powerful and the powerless prompt rebellion. Ultimately, hegemonic power collapses or faces challenge in a hegemonic war, after which the dominant world power is reestablished or replaced.

Critical Commentary and Future Directions

The United States is generally agreed to be the world's dominant power since World War II, and it has overseen a flourishing of globalization in trade, finance, and migration, especially since the collapse of its primary competitor, the Soviet Union. The United States enjoys a range of benefits for its privileged position, some of which are economic (e.g., foreigners' practice of holding dollars in reserve acts as interest-free loans to the U.S. economy) or political (e.g., the United States holds a disproportionate number of votes in many multilateral institutions). This theory would suggest that the costs of maintaining this international order will increase for the United States, especially in terms of military costs. It should become embroiled in foreign conflicts at a time when defense costs become increasingly burdensome. This theory predicts that the United States will progressively tie itself to debt and foreign conflict, until the international economic and political system it espouses is abandoned or, more likely, openly challenged.

These four examples of long-wave theory illustrate their use as tools in long-range planning and comprehending organizations in their big picture historical contexts. History generally does not unfold in a progressive manner; it is replete with tipping points and critical junctures. Long-wave theory offers cues about when these tipping points and junctures might occur and what might happen when they do occur. In many ways, history repeats itself, and these theories sensitize us to those recurrent facets of history, or at least the possibility that there are *some* long-run, recurrent phenomena to be considered in any organizational problem.

—*Joseph Nathan Cohen*

See also Historical Analysis of Organization Theory

Further Readings

Abramovitz, M. (1961). The nature and significance of Kuznets cycles. *Economic Development and Cultural Change, 9*(3), 225–248.

Fischer, D. H. (1996). *The great wave: Price revolutions and the rhythm of history.* New York: Oxford University Press.

Goldstone, J. A. (1991). *Revolution and rebellion in the early modern world.* Berkeley: University of California Press.

LOOSE COUPLING

There are three increasingly sophisticated definitions of loose coupling. Weick initially defined loose coupling as a situation in which elements are responsive, but retain evidence of separateness and identity. Weick later wrote that loose coupling is evident when elements affect each other suddenly (rather than continuously), occasionally (rather than constantly), negligibly (rather than significantly), indirectly (rather than directly), and eventually (rather than immediately). Orton and Weick later revised the elements, writing that loose coupling is not one end of a unidimensional continuum but is instead a dialectical perspective that emphasizes simultaneous coupling and decoupling, which generates the paradoxical, chaotic, and unpredictable character of loose couplings. If there is neither responsiveness nor distinctiveness, the organization is not really a system, and it can be defined as a *noncoupled system*. If there is responsiveness without distinctiveness, the organization is a *tightly coupled system*. If there is distinctiveness without responsiveness the organization is a *decoupled system*. If there is both distinctiveness and responsiveness, the organization is a *loosely coupled system*.

Conceptual Overview

The loosely coupled systems perspective emphasizes the evolution of organizational forms and organizational strategies from simplistic monolithic firms to complex adaptive systems (see Complex Organizations). In organizational theory, this can be seen in the movement during the 20th century from tightly coupled firms to moderately coupled bureaucracies to loosely coupled networks. In strategic management, this can be seen in the movement from business strategies to corporate strategies to network strategies. As noted by Baum in 2002, there are currently 10 clusters of theories in organization and strategy that are built around 10 specific "motors" or explanations: economics, technology, power, institutions, learning, cognition, ecology, evolution, networks, and complexity. All 10 of these theoretical approaches have captured a movement from presumptions of organizations as tightly coupled firms to presumptions of organizations as loosely coupled networks.

The loosely coupled system perspective is a product of the Herbert Simon agenda to shift attention away from organizations as things toward organizations as arenas in which complex processes take place. Research in the Simon-March-Weick tradition on strategy making, decision making, and sensemaking processes required a reformulation of organizations from monolithic, tightly coupled firms toward chaotic, loosely coupled networks. The loosely coupled systems perspective has facilitated the development of theories of change, culture formation, organizational identity formation, strategy making, decision making, organizational learning, knowledge creation, new product design, and innovation.

Critical Commentary and Future Directions

Orton and Weick described loose coupling as a "linguistic Trojan horse" that served to pry researchers away from simplistic assumptions of organizations as rational, monolithic, predictable actors and to move researchers toward more complex models of organizations. The horse has been rather tame lately because the concept of loose coupling (1) continues to be simplified into merely a sexy synonym for decentralization, (2) is disconnected from the larger and more important theoretical project of understanding equivocality-reduction processes in organizations, and (3) gravitates toward horizontal and vertical loose coupling rather than procedural loose coupling.

More Research on Dialectical Interactions Between Coupling and Decoupling

Despite Orton and Weick's 1990 reminder that loose coupling is not a unidimensional variable ranging from loose coupling to tight coupling but is instead a dialectical concept that emphasizes complex patterns of simultaneous coupling and decoupling, most researchers continue to siphon the unpredictability out of loose coupling by translating it into variables such as fragmentation, modularity, division of labor, or decentralization. One solution to this problem is to retroactively cast Weick's 1976 article on loose coupling as a chapter in March and Olsen's *Ambiguity and Choice in Organizations* of 1976 in order to emphasize the link between garbage-can decision processes and loosely coupled systems.

More Research on Causal Indeterminacy and Equivocality

The general driver of loose couplings and loosely coupled systems is causal indeterminacy, or unclear means-ends connections. Simple, comprehensible, visible, well-known, objective, explicit cause maps lead to tightly coupled firms; complex, incomprehensible, unknown, enacted, tacit cause maps lead to loosely coupled networks. Orton and Weick identified five different research traditions that explore the problem of causal indeterminacy: (1) bounded rationality, (2) selective perception, (3) uncertainty, (4) ambiguity, and (5) knowledge heterogeneity. The expansion of the resource-based view of the firm, the knowledge-based view of the firm, and the dynamic-capabilities–based view of the firm in strategic management, and the expansion of learning theory and cognitive theory in organization theory, have—in combination—improved organizational scholars' understanding of causal indeterminacy. Weick's theory of sensemaking, and the applications of sensemaking theory to high-reliability organizations by Weick and his colleagues, Sutcliffe and Obstfeld, suggest that the study of loose coupling may be part of a larger theoretical project: explaining organizations through sustained study of the recognition, exploitation, and reduction of equivocality.

More Research on Procedural Loose Coupling

There are three increasingly complex categories of loosely coupled relationships in organizations: horizontal loose couplings, vertical loose couplings, and procedural loose couplings.

Horizontal loose couplings exist at multiple levels of analysis within organizational contexts. Individuals can be seen as parts of loosely coupled networks of relationships, identities, or roles—a "parliament of selves" as Weick calls it. Teams can be seen as loosely coupled networks of individuals, as noted by Ibarra in 1992. Subunits can be seen as loosely coupled networks of teams; organizations can be seen as loosely coupled networks of subunits; corporations can be seen as loosely coupled networks of organizations; industries can be seen as loosely coupled networks of corporations; and communities can be seen as loosely coupled networks of industries, as noted by Saxenian in 1994. Horizontal loose coupling is a familiar problem for organization and strategy researchers, dating back to Adam Smith's discussions of division of labor and Georg Simmel's observation that wholes are composed of parts.

Vertical loose couplings are more complicated, because they introduce the concepts of control, influence, adaptation, and interaction between levels of analysis. The loose coupling between environment and organization is a foundational premise of institutional theory, according to Meyer and Rowan's 1977 work, and it has led to a large number of insightful studies about how organizations manage to maintain simultaneous distinctiveness and responsiveness to their environments. New research on network strategies is helping to clarify how network centers can influence other organizations in the network (see Dyer and Singh's 1998 study). There is a long tradition of research within organizations on how corporate headquarters can better control subsidiaries (domestic and international), how top management teams can better control divisions, how division leaders can better control subunits, and how subunits can better control teams, and how team leaders can better control individuals (see Ouchi's 1978 writing).

Procedural loose couplings range from the relatively simple question of sequence to the much more complex questions of causality, prediction, and intentionality. The general term "procedural" is chosen here for its linkage to "processes," not its linkage to "procedures," and it is more complicated than either horizontal couplings or vertical loose couplings because it introduces the concept of chronology. One example of research on sequential loose couplings is Andersson's research on distribution networks as loosely coupled systems. One example of research on causality, predictability, and intentionality is Salancik's research on loose couplings between intentions and actions. Shifting attention away from horizontal and vertical loose coupling toward procedural loose coupling would help revitalize the study of organizations as loosely coupled networks.

—*James Douglas Orton*

See also Complex Organizations; Historical Analysis of Organization Theory; Strategic Management

Further Readings

Andersson, P. (1992). Analysing distribution channel dynamics: Loose and tight coupling in distribution networks. *European Journal of Marketing, 26*(2), 47–68.

Baum, J. A. C. (Ed.). (2002). *The Blackwell companion to organizations.* Oxford, UK: Blackwell.

Dyer, J. H., & Singh, H. (1998). The relational view: Cooperative strategy and sources of interorganizational competitive advantage. *Academy of Management Review, 23*(4), 660–679.

Ibarra, H. (1992). Structural alignments, individual strategies, and managerial action: Elements toward a network theory of getting things done. In N. Nohria & R. G. Eccles (Eds.), *Networks and organizations: Structure, form, and action* (pp. 165–188). Boston: Harvard Business School Press.

March, J. G., & Olsen, J. P. (1976). *Ambiguity and choice in organizations.* Bergen, Norway: Universitetsforlaget.

Meyer, J. W., & Rowan, B. (1977). Institutionalized organizations: Formal structure as myth and ceremony. *American Journal of Sociology, 83*(2), 340–363.

Orton, J. D., & Weick, K. E. (1990). Loosely coupled systems: A reconceptualization. *Academy of Management Review, 15,* 203–223.

Ouchi, W. G. (1978). Coupled versus uncoupled control in organizational hierarchies. In M. W. Meyer et al. (Eds.), *Environments and organizations* (pp. 264–289). San Francisco: Jossey-Bass.

Salancik, G. R. (1975). *Notes on loose coupling: Linking intentions to actions.* Urbana: University of Illinois Press.

Saxenian, A. (1994). *Regional advantage: Culture and competition in Silicon Valley and Route 128.* Cambridge, MA: Harvard Business School Press.

Weick, K. E. (1976). Educational organizations as loosely coupled systems. *Administrative Science Quarterly, 21,* 1–19.

Weick, K. E. (1979). *The social psychology of organizing* (2nd ed.). Reading, MA: Addison-Wesley.

Weick, K. E. (1982). Administering education in loosely coupled schools. *Phi Delta Kappan, 63*(10), 673–676.

Weick, K. E. (1995). *Sensemaking in organizations.* Thousand Oaks, CA: Sage.

Weick, K. E., & Sutcliffe, K. M. (2001). *Managing the unexpected: Assuring high performance in an age of complexity.* San Francisco: Jossey-Bass.

Weick, K. E., Sutcliffe, K. M., & Obstfeld, D. (1999). Organizing for high reliability: Processes of collective mindfulness. *Research in Organizational Behavior, 21,* 81–123.

Index

Abductive inference, **4:**1299
Aborescent networks, **3:**974
Abrahamson, E., **3:**848, 849, 850, 868
Absolute advantage, **2:**702
Absolute objectivity, **3:**993
Absorptive capacity, 1:1–4
   components of, **1:**2–3
   influences on, **1:**3
   knowledge transfer costs, **1:**1–2
   overview, **1:**1–2
   potential, **1:**3
   research issues, **1:**2–3
Abstract conceptualization (AC) learning mode, **2:**488, 490, 491
Abstract thinking, **1:**36
Academic procrastination, **4:**1306
Academy of Management, **3:**1015, **3:**1016
Accountability, 1:4–8
   balanced scorecard, **1:**6
   corporate social responsibility and, **1:**5
   ethnomethodology and, **2:**475
   external, **1:**4
   internal, **1:**4
   interpersonal, **1:**6
   national competitive advantage theory, **2:**702–703
   of formal organizations, **2:**516
   organizational, **1:**5–6
   research issues, **1:**7
   societal, **1:**4–5
Accounting, impact on organizations and society, 1:8–11
   balance sheet, **1:**9
   Committee on Accounting Procedure, **1:**9–10
   Federal Accounting Standards Advisory Board, **1:**10
   financial statements, **1:**8–9
   generally accepted accounting principles, **1:**8, 9
   global standards need, **1:**10–11
   Governmental Accounting Standards Board, **1:**10
   history of, **1:**8
   income statements, **1:**8–9
   International Accounting Standards Board, **1:**10, 11
   managerial accounting, **1:**10
   Securities and Exchange Commission, **1:**9
   statement of cash flows, **1:**9
   statement of stockholder's equity, **1:**9

Acker, J., **4:**1571
Action, 1:11–13
   analyst relation to, **1:**13
   analytic *vs.* subjective meaning of, **1:**12
Actionable knowledge, 1:14–17
   cocreation models, **1:**16
   consumption models, **1:**16
   knowing-doing gap on, **1:**15
   knowledge-action relation, **1:**14–15
   Model I and Model II theories-in-use on, **1:**14–15
   organization complexity and, **1:**16–17
   overview, **1:**14
   production models, **1:**15–16
   reflexive critique research need, **1:**15
   theory-practice relation, **1:**14
   translation process and, **1:**16
Action anthropology, **1:**22
Action ethnography, **1:**22
Action frame of reference, **1:**13, **3:**996
Action inquiry, **1:**22
Action learning, 1:17–20
   as learning-in-action, **1:**17
   as reflection-in-action, **1:**22
   business-driven approach to, **1:**18
   components of, **1:**17–18
   critical approach to, **1:**18
   current issues in, **1:**18–19
   individualistic focus of, **1:**18
   political issues in, **1:**18
   reflective action learning sets, **1:**19
   sensemaking and, **1:**38
   traditional approach to, **1:**18
Action research, 1:20–24
   history of, **1:**21–22
   indirect reporting of, **1:**23
   organizational view on, **1:**20, 21
   relation to practice, **1:**14
   research-oriented, **1:**22, 23
   social action view on, **1:**20, 21
   validity of, **1:**22–23
   widespread use of, **1:**23–24
Action science, **1:**14, 22
Active experimentation (AE) learning mode, **2:**488, 490, 491

Activism, 1:24–27
   criticism, **1:**25–26
   evolution in Western world, **1:**24–25
   globalism effects on, **1:**25–27
Actor-network theory (ANT), 1:27–31, 261
   agency-structure debate and, **1:**48
   epistemic relativism in, **1:**30
   generalized symmetry principle and, **1:**28
   new sociology of science and, **1:**30
   nonhuman agents in, **1:**28–29, 30–31, **3:**970
   on diffusion research, **1:**384–385
   on technology, **4:**1541
   on truth, **4:**1580
   origins of, **1:**27–28, 30
   power relations in, **1:**31
   punctualization in, **1:**29, 30
   social agents in, **1:**28–29
   translation in, **1:**29
Actor-observer effect, **3:**861
Actual participation, by employee, **4:**1228
Act utilitarianism, **4:**1594–1595
Adaptive instability, **3:**1083
Adaptive learning (AL), 1:31–33
   generative learning and, **1:**32
   learning organization theory and, **1:**32
   organizational learning theory and, **1:**32
   stages in, **1:**32
   uses of, **1:**32–33
Adaptive organization, **1:**170
Adaptive structuration theory (AST), **2:**694, **4:**1483
Adhocracies, 1:33–34
   administrative, **1:**34
   bureaucracies *vs.,* **1:**33, **1:**34
   operating, **1:**33–34
Adjectival ethnography, **2:**473
Administrative adhocracy, **1:**34
Administrative organizational science, **3:**1013
Adolphus, G., **3:**904
Adorno, T., **1:**84, 263, 330
   See also Frankfurt School
Adult learning, 1:35–38
   andragogy and, **1:**35
   behavior theory on, **1:**35–36
   cognitive theory on, **1:**36
   constructivist theory on, **1:**36
   humanist theory on, **1:**36
   sensemaking and, **1:**37–38
   social learning theory on, **1:**36
   theoretical bases of, **1:**35–36
Adult learning theory, **2:**802
Adverse selection, **3:**1061
Aesthetic labor, **2:**433
Aesthetics of organization, 1:38–41
   aesthetic categories, **1:**39
   aesthetics approach to, **1:**40, 41
   anaesthetizing aestheticism, **1:**39
   archaeological approach to, **1:**40
   empathetic-logical approach to, **1:**40
   external environment and, **1:**39

   future, **1:**40
   organizational life and, **1:**39
   overview, **1:**38–39
   practice concept in, **1:**39
   volition concept in, **1:**39
Affect, 1:41–43
   cognition *vs.,* **1:**42
   criticism/future, **1:**42
   definitional issues, **1:**41
   emotions and, **1:**41
   mood and, **1:**41
   overview, **1:**41–42
Affective commitment, **2:**628
Affective events theory, **2:**738
Affective labor, **3:**1101
Affirmative action, **1:**121, 375, 394, 399, **2:**552,
   554, 764, **4:**1359, 1360
Affluenza, **3:**1073
Agency, 1:43–46
   authority *vs.,* **1:**44
   bounded rationality of agent, **1:**43
   economic modeling of, **1:**43–44, 45
   information asymmetry and, **1:**43
   in interpretive theory, **2:**720
   monitoring concept in, **1:**43–44
   overview, **1:**43
   principal concept in, **1:**43–44
   social structure *vs.,* **1:**260
   Taylorism and, **1:**44–45
   voluntaristic, **1:**46, **1:**47
   workplace design *vs.,* **1:**44–45
   See also **Agency-structure debate; Agency theory**
Agency problem, **1:**360, **3:**1061, 1211
Agency-structure debate, 1:46–49
   action determinism and, **1:**46, 47
   actor-network theory on, **1:**48
   bounded rationality of agents, **1:**47
   contingency theory on, **1:**47
   critical-realist theory on, **1:**48
   environmental determinism and, **1:**46
   ethical intervention and, **1:**48
   neoinstitutional theory on, **1:**47
   poststructuralist theory on, **1:**48
   sovereignty and, **1:**46, 48
   structuration theory on, **1:**47–48
   voluntaristic agency and, **1:**46, 47
Agency theory, 1:49–50
   agency costs, **1:**49, **3:**1061
   behavioral theory of the firm and, **1:**97
   bonding costs, **3:**1061
   critical theory *vs.,* **1:**50
   ethics and, **1:**50
   limitations to, **1:**50
   monitoring costs, **3:**1061
   on corporate governance, **1:**297, 298, 300
   on economic rationalism, **2:**418
   on formal organizations, **2:**515
   on organizational economics, **3:**1061
   overview of, **1:**49

residual loss, **3:**1061
self-interest and, **1:**49, 50
uncertainty and, **4:**1583
Agent-based simulation, **1:**244
Albert, S., **3:**939, **3:**1077
Alchian, A., **3:**879, **3:**1060
Aldrich, Howard, **2:**819
Alienation theory, **1:**284–285
Alliance governance, **1:**53
Alliances, 1:50–54
alliance governance, **1:**53
alliance organization, **1:**52–53
alliance performance, **1:**52
definitional issues, **1:**51
equity, **1:**51
explicit contracts, **1:**53
forms/types of, **1:**51
implicit contracts, **1:**53
joint ventures (*See* Joint ventures)
leadership and, **1:**53
lifecycle of, **1:**51–52
nonequity, **1:**51
Allocative wage discrimination, **4:**1627–1628
Allocentrism, **2:**645
Alterity (otherness), 1:54–55
alterity construction, **1:**54
attributed, **1:**54
corporations and, **1:**54–55
differentiation of difference as, **1:**54
ICT effect on, **2:**665–666
identity free of, **1:**55
identity paradigm and, **1:**54
identity *vs.*, **1:**54
incorporated, **1:**54
negativity *vs.* true, **1:**54
overview, **1:**54–55
self-marginalization and, **3:**875
tyranny of identity and, **1:**54
Althusser, L., **1:**391, **2:**609, 635
Altruism, **1:**197, **2:**482, **3:**1025
Alvarez, J. L., **3:**851
Alvesson, M., **3:**848, 1083
American Institute of Certified Public Accounting (AICPA) Committee on Accounting Procedure, **1:**9–10
American Society of Mechanical Engineers (ASME), **1:**164
Anaesthetizing aestheticism, **1:**39
Analytical empiricism, 1:55–57
applied social statistics and, **1:**56
concept theory and, **1:**56
criticism/future, **1:**56
future, **1:**57
fuzzy set theory and, **1:**57
hermeneutics and, **1:**57
mathematical criticisms of, **1:**56
neoinstitutional analysis and, **1:**57
organizational literature on, **1:**56
philosophical criticisms of, **1:**56

roots of modern, **1:**55–56
type theory and, **1:**57
Andragogy, **1:**35
Animal superexploitation, **2:**497
Antenarrative, **4:**1458
Anthropology, 1:57–60
cognitive approach and, **1:**185
cultural translation concept in, **1:**58
culture concept in, **1:**57–58
fieldwork in, **1:**58
human diversity concept in, **1:**57
hybridization/creolization concept in, **1:**58
mirroring concept in, **1:**58
on organizational ethnography, **3:**1066–1067
organizational theory relation with, **1:**58–60
overview, **1:**57–58
Antiperformativity, **1:**322
Antirationalism, 1:60–64
bounded rationality and, **1:**61
ecology theory and, **1:**62
feminist epistemology and, **1:**61–62
future, **1:**64
irrationalism *vs.*, **1:**63–64
overview, **1:**60–63
postcolonial theory and, **1:**62
postmodern theory and, **1:**63
poststructural theory and, **1:**62–63
rationalism *vs.*, **1:**61
satisficing and, **1:**61
Antirealism, 1:65–67
deconstruction and, **1:**66
definition of, **1:**65
overview, **1:**65–66
Antisweatshop campaign, **4:**1495–1496
Antonakis, J., **2:**793
Aperspectival objectivity, **3:**993
Applied psychology, **1:**184
Applied social statistics, **1:**56
Appraisal-anxiety-avoidance model of stress and coping, **4:**1306–1307
Appraisal theory, **2:**429
Appreciative inquiry (AI), **1:**307, 382
Apprenticeship, **1:**210–211, **4:**1417
Aquinas, T., **2:**586
Arab Organization for Administrative Development (AOAD), **3:**1105–1106
ARA model, **3:**968
Archaeology, **1:**40, **2:**548
Archetypes, 1:67–68
Golden Shadow, **1:**67
myth relation with, **1:**67–68
organizational design, **3:**1047
overview, **1:**67–68
Shadow, **1:**67
weaknesses of concept, **1:**68
See also **Configuration theory**
Architectonic dialogism, **3:**1000, **4:**1456
Architecture and organizations, 1:68–72
criticism/future, **1:**70–71

functional approach to, **1**:71
generative possibilities of architecture, **1**:70
interaction-promotion facilities, **1**:69
organizational culture and, **1**:69
organizational needs and, **1**:69–70
overview, **1**:69–70
panoptical space, **1**:70–71
postmodernism influence on, **1**:69–70
power of space, **1**:70
Archival data, **4**:1346
Argote, L., **3**:1017–1018
Argyris, C., **1**:279, **2**:802–803, 805, 806–807, 809, 810, **3**:1015, 1088, 1096, **4**:1587
Aristotle, **2**:462, 795–796, **4**:1624
Arms length outsourcing, **2**:1210, **3**:1209
ARPANET, **2**:664–665, **3**:974
Arrow, Kenneth, **1**:156, **3**:974, **4**:1252
Arrow core template, **4**:1374–1375
Artifacts, as organizational symbolism, **3**:1192
Artificial intelligence, **1**:184
Arts and organizations, 1:72–74, 3:1134
   aesthetics and, **1**:72–73
   artistic actions and, **1**:73
   artists, **1**:73–74
   dark side of, **1**:73
   defining organizational art, **1**:72–73
   globalization and, **1**:73
   leadership and, **1**:73
   overview, **1**:72–73
Ashby, R., **1**:351, **1**:352
Asset specificity, 1:74–76, 3:1004, 1209
   competition and, **1**:76
   dedicated asset specificity, **1**:75
   discriminating alignment hypothesis on, **1**:75
   firm captial structure and, **1**:76
   human asset specificity, **1**:75
   physical asset specificity, **1**:75
   site specificity, **1**:75
   transaction-costs economics theory and, **1**:74–75, 176
   uncertainty and, **1**:76
Ast, Г., **2**:583, 584, 585
Aston studies, **1**:13, 115–116, **2**:598, **3**:1114, 1186, 1197, 1201, **4**:1443, 1540
Atomistic conception of reality, **3**:995
Attitudes, 1:76–79
   attitude change, **1**:78
   attitudinal baggage, **1**:79
   attitudinal components view on, **1**:77
   behavioral sources of, **1**:77
   elaboration likelihood model and, **1**:78
   evaluative nature of attitude construct, **1**:77
   formation of, **1**:77–78
   functions of, **1**:78
   heuristic-systematic model and, **1**:78
   job satisfaction/performance and, **1**:78
   latent process view on, **1**:77
   moods *vs.*, **1**:77
   negative attitudes toward groups, **1**:79
   of top management, **1**:79

persuasion research and, **1**:79
socialization influence on, **1**:77–78
unconscious, **1**:77
Attitudinal baggage, **1**:79
Attitudinal components perspective, **1**:77
Attributional explanation, **1**:80–81
Attribution theory, 1:79–82
   achievement model of motivation and, **1**:80
   criticism/future, **1**:81–82
   error/actor-observer bias in, **1**:81
   false consensus bias in, **1**:81
   hedonic relevance bias in, **1**:81
   hostile attribution bias in, **1**:81
   Kelly's cube and, **1**:80
   on managerial/organizational cognition and, **3**:861
   overview, **1**:79–81
   self-serving bias in, **1**:81
Audit society, **3**:869
Auftragstaktik, **2**:784
Authenticity, 1:82–84
   overview, **1**:82–83
   relative, **1**:83
   self-actualization and, **1**:83
   self-values and, **1**:83
Authoritarian domination, **1**:402
Authoritarianism, 1:84–87
   autocratic-democratic continuum and, **1**:85
   charismatic domination, **1**:84–85
   creative class and, **1**:85
   criticism/future, **1**:85–86
   emotional intelligence and, **1**:85
   in large corporation, **1**:84
   in small-/medium-sized enterprise, **1**:84
   overview, **1**:84–85
   post-bureaucratic organizations and, **1**:85–86
   rational-legal domination, **1**:85
   traditional domination, **1**:85
   women managers and, **1**:85
Authority, 1:87–90
   agency *vs.*, **1**:44
   charismatic, **1**:87, 88
   feminist critique of, **1**:89
   legitimacy of, **1**:87, 88
   overview, **1**:87–89
   patriarchy and, **1**:87, 89
   postmodernism and, **1**:89
   power and, **1**:88–89
   rational bureaucracy and, **1**:87
   rational-legal authority, **1**:88
   traditional, **1**:87
Authority based on capability, **2**:587
Autopoiesis, 1:90–92
   autopoietic system, **1**:90
   biological roots of, **1**:90–91
   heteropoiesis *vs.*, **1**:90
   knowledge and, **1**:91
   model of, **1**:91, 92
   organizational closure and, **1**:90
   self-sustainable system, **1**:91–92

structure concept in, **1:**90
sustainable system, **1:**91–92
Autopoietic system, **1:**225, **4:**1437
Avolio, B., **2:**793, 794, 797, 798
Axial coding, **2:**572

Babbage, C., **1:**56, **4:**1540
Backlash, **3:**928
Backstage behavior, **1:**406
Baker, A., **2:**492
Bakhtin, M., **1:**382, **3:**1000, **4:**1456
Balanced scorecard (BSC), 1:6, **93–95**, **3:**1151
    causality hypothesis, **1:**93–94
    customer perspective, **1:**93
    financial perspective, **1:**93
    future, **1:**94
    learning and growth perspective, **1:**93
    process perspective, **1:**93
    scientific management and, **4:**1393, 1395
    shortcomings of, **1:**94
    strategy translation, **1:**93
Balance of trade, **2:**702
Balance sheet, **1:**9
Bales, K., **4:**1418–1419
Balmer, J. M. T., **3:**1082
Banana time, **4:**1551
Bandura, A., **2:**802, **3:**920, 924
Bapuji, H., **3:**1095, 1096
Baran, P., **3:**972
Barney, J., **4:**1380
Bar-On, R., **2:**434
Barth, F., **2:**469
Barthes, R., **2:**584, **3:**944, **4:**1286
Bartlett, C., **4:**1566
Basel Convention, **4:**1493
Basic statistical methods, **4:**1347
Bass, B., **2:**780, 792–793, 794, 797, 798
Battle of the sexes game, **2:**533
Baudrillard, J., **4:**1281
Bauman, Z., **4:**1336
Beck, U., **3:**1090
Becker, G., **1:**393, **2:**777
    economic theory of criminal law of, **2:**779–780
    human capital theory, **4:**1558
    on social capital, **2:**803
    tastes and preferences approach of, **1:**393
Beckhard, R., **3:**1048
Beer, M., **4:**1468
Beer, S., **4:**1616, 1617
Behavior
    maximizing, **1:**98
    See also **Behavioral theory of the firm;**
        Opportunistic behavior; Organizational behavior
Behavioral analysis. *See* **Operant conditioning**
Behavioral cultural intelligence, **1:**346, 347, 348
Behavioral decision research, **2:**481–482
Behavioral theory
    on adult learning, **1:**35–36
    on hierarchy, **2:**588

on leadership, **2:**796–797
on managerial/organizational cognition, **3:**860–861
See also **Behavioral theory of the firm;**
    Operant conditioning
Behavioral theory of the firm (BTF), 1:95–99
    agency theory and, **1:**97
    bounded rationality and, **1:**108–109
    contingency theory on, **1:**99
    contract theory and, **1:**97
    criticism/future, **1:**95–99
    definitions of firm and, **1:**96
    economic theory and, **1:**95
    economic theory of the firm *vs.*, **1:**95
    evolutionary theory on, **1:**99
    goal-directed firms and, **1:**96
    institutional theory on, **1:**99
    knowledge-based view on, **1:**98
    managerial theory of firm and, **1:**97–98
    noncooperative game theory and, **1:**96–97
    organization theory and, **1:**96
    resource-based view on, **1:**98
    simulation and, **1:**243
    strategic management theory and, **1:**95
    transaction-cost theory and, **1:**96, 109
Behaviorism, 1:99–102
    cognitive approach *vs.*, **1:**183
    criticism/future, **1:**101–102
    limitations of approach, **1:**101–102
    on international production, **2:**708
    on learning, **2:**802
    organizational behavior modification, **1:**100–101, 102
    Pavlov's classical conditioning experiment, **1:**100
    Skinner's operant conditioning, **1:**100
    Thorndike's law of effects, **1:**100
Behavior science, on punishment/violence
    in organizations, **4:**1335
Bell, D., **2:**568
Bell, G., **3:**939
Bem, D., **1:**187–188
Benchmarking prescriptions, **4:**1301
Benders, J., **3:**850
Bendix, R., **1:**88, **2:**636, **3:**863
Benedict, R., **4:**1371
Bennis, W., **3:**1073, **4:**1330
Bentham, J., **4:**1215–1216
Berg, P. O., **3:**1191
Berger, P., **1:**260, **2:**562, 684, 685, 721, **4:**1427
Beriain, J., **3:**915
Berle, A., **3:**872, 879, 937, 1211
Bern, S., **2:**544–545
Best alternative to this negotiated agreement (BATNA), **3:**951
Best practices, **4:**1296
Best Value, **3:**842
Beyer, J., **3:**1064, **4:**1256–1257
Bhaskar, R., **4:**1245
Bicycle business, **2:**734
Big five personality traits, **4:**1307
Binary logic, **3:**999
Biological view, on emotion, **2:**429

Biology, and cognitive approach, **1:**185
Biomimicry, **2:**456
Biosociation, **4:**1407
Black, D., **4:**1252
Black box, firm as, **3:**877, 879
Black box problem, **2:**617
Blue-collar activity, **3:**1209
Blumer, H., **2:**697, **4:**1500
   on fashion, **2:**503–504, **3:**851
Board of directors, **1:**299
Boas, F., **2:**472
Boje, D., **3:**944, 1052–1053
Boston Consulting Group (BCG), **3:**1182
Boulding, K. E., **3:**998, **3:**1000
Boundaries, formal organizations, **2:**518
Boundaryless career, 1:102–104
   criticism on, **1:**103
   descriptive research stream, **1:**103
   future, **1:**103–104
   instrumental research stream, **1:**103
   normative research stream, **1:**103
   organizational career *vs.*, **1:**102
Boundary objects, **3:**1091
Bounded awareness, and decision making and, **1:**227
Bounded decision making, **1:**226–227
Bounded emotionality, 1:104–106
   bounded rationality and, **1:**105
   criticism/future, **1:**105–106
   feminist organizational theory and, **1:**104, 105
   gender differences and, **1:**106
   organizational norms and, **1:**105
   outside pressures on, **1:**105–106
   rationality and, **1:**104–105
Bounded rationality (BR), 1:106–109, 363, **3:**860
   antirationalism and, **1:**61
   behavioral theory of firm on, **1:**108–109
   coordination and, **1:**282
   decision making and, **1:**226–227
   formal organizations and, **2:**515
   game theory and, **2:**533
   global rationality and, **1:**107
   in transaction cost theory, **3:**1060
   managerial rationality and, **3:**871
   normal accidents and, **3:**991
   of agent, **1:**43, 47
   satisficing concept in, **1:**106, 107
Bourdieu, P.
   habitus concept of, **1:**47, 162, 212, 344, **3:**865, 997
   on constructivism, **1:**261
   on cultural capital, **1:**344, **3:**864–865
   on fields, **3:**1074
Boyzatis, R. E., **4:**1608
Braceros, **1:**151
Brain drain, **1:**152
Braverman, H., **1:**162
Breaugh, J. A., **4:**1360–1361
Bremen Group, **3:**1040–1041
Bridge identity politics, **4:**1569
Brinkshaw, J., **4:**1566–1567

Broadcasting mode of imitation, **3:**853
Brown, A. D., **3:**943
Brundtland Report, **4:**1492
Buchanan, J., **4:**1252
Buckley, P. J., **2:**709, **3:**1065
Burawoy, M., **2:**636, **4:**1490
Bureaucracy, 1:109–113
   adhocracy *vs.*, **1:**33, 34
   characteristics of, **1:**110–111
   dehumanization by, **1:**112
   individual decision making in, **1:**112
   innovation stifled by, **1:**112
   large organization as, **1:**112–113
   moderately coupled, **1:**235
   rational, **1:**87
   rationalization of rationality and, **1:**113
   routinization by, **1:**112
   subsytems in, **1:**112
   See also **Bureaucratization; Machine bureaucracy**
Bureaucratic insurgency, **4:**1435
Bureaucratization, 1:113–118
   criticism on, **1:**117–118
   dehumanization, **1:**117
   future, **1:**118
   history of, **1:**114
Burke, E., **1:**256–257
Burke, K., **1:**406, **1:**408
Burnham, J., **3:**872–873
Burns, J. M., **2:**790, 791
Burns, T., **3:**891, 892, 1009–1010, 1045
Burrell, G., **4:**1217, 1219, 1221–1222, 1244–1245
Burton, R., **1:**244
Business ethics, 1:118–122
   approaches to, **1:**119
   capitalistic issues, **1:**120
   concerns of, **1:**120–121
   criticism on, **1:**121–122
   deontological ethics, **1:**119
   future, **1:**122
   organizational issues, **1:**120
   overview, **1:**118–119
   special issues, **1:**120–121
   teleological ethics, **1:**119
   virtue ethics, **1:**119
   work of business ethicists, **1:**121
Business history, 1:122–128
   case studies, **1:**126
   Chandler and, **1:**124–125
   foci of, **1:**123
   intellectual origins of, **1:**123
   organization studies and, **1:**126–127
   overview, **1:**123–124
   shift in, **1:**125–126
   sources for, **1:**123
Business journalism, 1:128–131
   criticism/future, **1:**129–131
   expansion of, **1:**129
   functions of, **1:**129
   influence of, **1:**130

management knowledge and, **1:**130
overview, **1:**128–129
public knowledge and, **1:**129–130
research needs, **1:**130–131
Business networks (BN), 1:131–135
cultural approach, **1:**132, 133
defining, **1:**131–132
economic theory on, **1:**134
exchanges in, **1:**132
network diamond, **1:**132
nodes in, **1:**133
overview, **1:**131–132
relational approach, **1:**132, 133
sociological approach, **1:**133
structural/positional approach, **1:**132, 133
Business process redesign. *See* **Reengineering**
Business process reengineering. *See* **Reengineering**
Business system approach, **2:**686
Business system concept, **4:**1599
Butler, J., **2:**543, 546, 633
Butterfly effect, **1:**156, 230
Buyer-supplier relationships, 1:135–137
criticism on, **1:**136
future, **1:**136
obligational contracting, **1:**135
overview, **1:**135–136
relational contracting, **1:**135–136

Calabresi, G., **2:**777, **2:**778
Call centers, 1:139–142
as mass customized bureaucracy, **1:**139
as new Taylorism, **3:**1101
feminized nature of, **1:**141
future, **1:**141–142
inbound, **1:**139
in-house, **1:**140
institutions, **1:**140
labor process theory, **1:**141
location of, **1:**140
markets, **1:**139–140
outbound, **1:**139
outsourced, **1:**140
products, **1:**140
regulatory issues, **1:**140
repetitive/uncomplexwork of, **1:**141
union recognition, **1:**141
Voice over Internet Protocol, **1:**140
work-life balance, **1:**141
Callon, M., **1:**27, 28, **4:**1580
Camus, A., **3:**1071
Canadian Accounting Standards Board, **1:**11
Capital asset pricing model, **1:**148
Capitalism, models of, 1:142–148
casino/turbo capitalism, **1:**146
concluding comments, **1:**147
contingent constraints, **1:**143
control imperative, **1:**143
criticism on, **1:**145–146
elite in, **1:**144

human capital and, **1:**146–147
informational capitalism, **1:**146
knowledge economy thesis on, **1:**146
logic of industrialization, **1:**144
paradigm break theories, **1:**145
postcapitalism, **1:**142
universal constraints, **1:**142–143
Capital markets, 1:148–150
capital assist pricing model, **1:**148
Chicago Board Options Exchange, **1:**149
criticism/future, **1:**149
efficiency of, **1:**148
financial assets, **1:**148
money market *vs.,* **1:**148
overview, **1:**148–149
portfolio theory, **1:**148
regulation of, **1:**148–149
risk-return relationships, **1:**148, 149
Capital movement, migration, and maquiladoras, 1:150–154
costs of, **1:**154
maquiladoras, **1:**153, **2:**763
migrant labor and labor market, **1:**150–152
U.S.-Mexico border, **1:**152–153
See also **Regionalization and capital movement**
Carnap, R., **2:**830, **4:**1602
Carroll, G. R., **3:**1043, **3:**1059
Case studies, organizational ethnography, **3:**1066
Case study approach, **4:**1340
Casino capitalism, **1:**146
Casson, M., **1:**96, **2:**709, **4:**1458
Castells, M., **3:**971–972, 973
Catastrophe theory, **1:**230
Causal mapping, **1:**189–190
Causal power, **3:**1164
Cellular automata, **1:**233, 243
Centralized network, **3:**972
Chaebol, **3:**1111
Chain mode of imitation, **3:**853
Chandler, A. D.
business history and, **1:**124–125, 126
on multidivisional form, **1:**235, 250
on organizational form, **3:**929, 1045
on strategic management, **3:**1181, **4:**1471, 1474
on visible hand, **1:**144
Change management *vs.* organizational development, **3:**1050–1051
Chanlat, J., **3:**1063
Chaos theory (CT), 1:154–157
butterfly effect, **1:**156
complexity theory and, **1:**230
criticism, **1:**156–157
definitional issues, **1:**154–155
disipative structures and, **1:**155
fractal organization, **1:**156
fuzzy set theory and, **1:**155–156
impossibility theorem, **1:**156
incompatibility principle, **1:**156
sytems tradition and, **1:**155

Taylorism and, **1**:155
three-body analysis, **1**:156
uncertainty principle, **1**:156
Charisma leadership. *See* **Leadership, charisma**
Charismatic authority, **1**:87
Cheater detection mechanism, **1**:199
Cheney, G., **3**:1083–1084
Chicago Board Options Exchange (CBOE), **1**:149
Chicago School
organizational ethnography and, **4**:1499, 1500
symbolic interactionism and, **4**:1499, 1500
Child, J., **3**:1063–1064, **4**:1462, 1463, 1464
Chodorow, N., **2**:538
Chomsky, N., **3**:998–999
Christensen, L., **3**:1083–1084
Chronotopic dialogism, **3**:999–1000, **4**:1456
Church, A. H., **3**:871
Circuit model of culture, **3**:851
Cisco model, **3**:971–972
Citizenship transformation, **3**:981
Civic virtue, **3**:1025
Civil society, 1:157–160
definition issues, **1**:157–158
democratization process and, **1**:158
global, **1**:159
human rights and, **1**:159–160
relevance to organizational studies, **1**:160
representative democracy and, **1**:158
Claiming value negotiation, **3**:950–951
Clans, **3**:907
Clark, K., **4**:1308
Clark, P., **4**:1553
Class, 1:160–163
class position of manager, **1**:160
deskilling thesis, **1**:162
labor process theory, **1**:162
life chances notion, **1**:161
on self-employment identities, **4**:1401
political economy of organization view, **1**:161–162
postmodernist approach to, **1**:162–163
relational approach to, **1**:161
skills and, **4**:1417
stratification approach to, **1**:161
"the multitude" notion, **1**:163
two camps approach to, **1**:161, 162
Classical conditioning experiment, of Pavlov, **1**:100
Classical liberalism, **2**:811
Classical management, 1:163–166
criticism/future, **1**:165–166
ethics and, **1**:166
general management principles, **1**:164
history of, **1**:163–165
management movements, **1**:164, 165
practitioner-scholar balance of, **1**:165
punctuated view of, **1**:165
return-on-investment measure, **1**:164
structural contingency theory and, **4**:1476
university curriculum, **1**:164
Classical theory of organizational decision, **3**:860

Clegg, S. R.
on concealed power, **3**:1045–1046
on consulting, **3**:848
on ideology and the organization, **2**:636, 637
on liberal technologies of regulation, **2**:816
on modernity, **3**:913–914
on organizational rules, **3**:1174
on power, **4**:1290
on power/domination, **3**:1007
on pressure group democracy, **2**:648
on social class, **1**:162
Client-centered counseling, **3**:1049
Climate of fear, **3**:1029
Climate of silence, **3**:1029
Clinical models, **4**:1340
Clinical perspective (clinical inquiry/research, C/R), 1:166–170
across cultural boundaries, **1**:168
basic characteristics of C/R, **1**:167
case example, **1**:168–169
C/R as client driven, **1**:167
C/R as oriented toward improvement, **1**:167
C/R as problem driven, **1**:167
criticism, **1**:169
future, **1**:169
intervention/data gathering as same process, **1**:167–168
overview, **1**:167
psychological contract is service for pay, **1**:168
reliability of, **1**:168
validity of, **1**:168
Clinton, W., **2**:782
Closed system approach (CSA), 1:170–171
criticism, **1**:171
future research directions, **1**:171
mechanistic view of organizations, **1**:170
open system approach and, **1**:170, 171
overview, **1**:170–171
Closed systems
general systems theory and, **2**:549
in formal organizations, **2**:515
social capital and, **4**:1424–1425
Social system, **4**:137, 1436
Taylorism as, **2**:549
Clusters, 1:171–173
as relational *vs.* geographical, **1**:172
cluster performance, **1**:173
criticism/future, **1**:172–173
global competitiveness and, **1**:173
mapping methods, **1**:172
overview, **1**:172
power issue in, **1**:173
Coaching, 1:173–178
as facilitation style, **1**:174
brief history of business coaching, **1**:176
business coaching, **1**:175
characteristics of efficient coach, **1**:174
cognitive behavioral theory and, **1**:174, 175
executive coaching, **1**:175, 176
future, **1**:177
life coaching, **1**:174–175

organizational coaching, **1**:175
overview, **1**:173–174
sports coaching, **1**:175
techniques used by coach, **1**:174
types, **1**:174–176
validity issues, **1**:176
Coalitions, 1:178–180
basic characteristics, **1**:179
context factors in, **1**:179
organizational politics and, **1**:178
Coase, R., **3**:877, 1060, **4**:1562
See also Coase theorem
Coase theorem, 1:180–181, 2:778
as invariance result, **1**:180–181
criticism/future, **1**:181
externalities and, **1**:180
Cocreation models, **1**:16
Codetermination, and industrial democracy, **2**:649
Coercion, 1:181–183
capacity of power and, **1**:182
means of, **1**:182
negotiation and, **1**:182
Nozick-style, **1**:182
overview, **1**:181–182
Coercive domination, **1**:401
Coevolution, **2**:482, 483, 484
Cognitive approach (CA), 1:183–186
affect *vs.* cognition, **1**:42
anthropology and, **1**:185
applied psychology and, **1**:184
artificial intelligence and, **1**:184
as abstract/mechanistic, **1**:185
behaviorism *vs.*, **1**:183
biology and, **1**:185
educational psychology and, **1**:184–185
fundamental assumptions of, **1**:183–184
linguistics and, **1**:185
neuropsychology and, **1**:184
on adult learning, **1**:36
on emotion, **2**:429
on learning, **2**:802–803
organizational psychology and, **1**:184–185
philosophy and, **1**:185
psychology and, **1**:184
social information processing and, **1**:185
universal laws and, **1**:184
Cognitive behavioral theory (CBT), **1**:174, 175
Cognitive cultural intelligence, **1**:345, 346, 348
Cognitive dissonance, 1:186–189
behavior justification component of, **1**:187
devaluing alternatives component of, **1**:187
external justification component of, **1**:186
free choice component of, **1**:186–187
implications for organizations, **1**:188
post-decision dissonance, **1**:187
self-concept violation component of, **1**:187
self-perception and, **1**:187–188
stay—leave decisions, **1**:187
Cognitive ergonomics, **2**:466

Cognitive mapping, 1:189–191
causal mapping, **1**:189–190
hybrid cognitive map, **1**:190
ideographic cognitive map, **1**:190
nomothetic cognitive map, **1**:190
repertory grid, **1**:189
revealed cognitive map, **1**:190
workplace cognition/behavior and, **3**:862
Cognitive resource view, on team diversity, **4**:1511–1512
Cognitive science
on information processing, **2**:667
on workplace cognition/behavior, **3**:860
Cohesion, 1:191–194
collaborative creativity, **1**:193
correlational research on, **1**:193
environment effect on, **1**:192
group goals and, **1**:192
groupthink, **1**:192, 194
interpersonal cohesion, **1**:191
levels of, **1**:191–192
need for new measures, **1**:193
networks, **1**:194
objective perspective on, **1**:193
organizational citizenship behavior and, **1**:191
perceived perspective on, **1**:193
task cohesion, **1**:191
virtual teams, **1**:193
Cohn, M. D., **3**:1095
Colby, K., **3**:1150
Coleman, J. S., **4**:1424
Collaboration and cooperation, 1:194–201
altruism, **1**:197
cheater detection mechanism, **1**:199
collaborative inertia, **1**:199
competition and, **1**:219–220
flexibility and, **1**:196
forms of, **1**:196–197
future of, **1**:199
illegitimate, **1**:197
joint ventures, **1**:196
negative outcomes of, **1**:197–198
networks, **1**:196
partnership, **1**:196
positive outcomes of, **1**:198
processes of, **1**:198–199
revealed *vs.* designed, **1**:195–196
stability and, **1**:196
strategic alliances, **1**:196
supplementary explanations of, **1**:197
Collaborative inertia, **1**:199
Collective action. *See* **Free-rider problem**
Collective bargaining, **2**:648
Collective democracy, **2**:649–650
Collective efficacy, **4**:1398–1399
Collective invocation, **3**:840
Collective-selection mechanism, fashion as, **2**:504
Collective social phenomena, 1:201–203
criticism, **1**:202

future, **1:**202–203
overview, **1:**201–202
Collectivism, 1:203–205
criticism, **1:**204–205
overview, **1:**204
Comanagement, **2:**648–649, **3:**1176
Command and control organizational design, **3:**1046
Commercial openness, **3:**961
Committee on Accounting Procedure, **1:**9–10
Communication, 1:205–208
critical perspective on, **1:**207–208
efficiency and, **1:**205–206
fidelity and, **1:**205–206
information-processing perspective on, **1:**205–206, 207
meaning-centered perspective on, **1:**205–206
media role in, **1:**208
Communicative action, 1:208–210
criticism, **1:**209
future, **1:**209–210
social nature of language and, **1:**208–209
Communicative action theory, **1:**208–209, 330–331
Communicative validity, **2:**722
Communitarian approach, **2:**463
Communities of practice, **3:**1091, 1093
Communities of practice (COP), 1:210–213
apprentices, **1:**210–211
criticism, **1:**210
future, **1:**212–213
knowledge-in-practice, **1:**212
knowledge management strategies, **1:**211–212
learning-in-working, **1:**211
legitimate peripheral participation and, **1:**210–211
networks of practice *vs.*, **2:**458
organizational learning and, **1:**211
situated learning theory and, **1:**210–211
storytelling and, **1:**211
Community and organizations, 1:213–217
criticism/future, **1:**216
employee community, **1:**214
fence line community, **1:**214
functional communities, **1:**213–125
globalization effects on decision making, **1:**214
impact community, **1:**214
Internet/cyber community, **1:**214
Internet effects on decision making, **1:**214
nongovernmental organizations, **1:**214–215
opinion/thought leaders, **1:**215
organizing skills, **1:**215–216
politics of community decision making, **1:**215–126
self-fulfillers, **1:**216
site/facility community, **1:**214
spatial communities, **1:**213, **1:**214
spontaneous groups, **1:**215
Comparative advantage, in international business, **2:**702
Comparative institutional theory, **4:**1566–1567
Competent domination, **1:**401
Competition, 1:217–220
analyzers, **1:**218
buyers, **1:**218
collaboration and, **1:**219–220
competitive advantage, **1:**218
corporate social responsiveness, **1:**219
cost leaders, **1:**218
defenders, **1:**218
differentiation strategy, **1:**218
direct competitor, **1:**217–218
effectiveness and, **1:**217
efficiency and, **1:**217
entrants, **1:**218
fashion and, **2:**503
focus strategy, **1:**218
imperfect, **3:**877
in two arenas, **1:**219
monopoly, **1:**217
moral limitations on, **1:**220
oligopoly and, **1:**217
perfect, **1:**217, **3:**877, **3:**879
product *vs.* factor markets, **1:**218–219
prospectors, **1:**218
reactors, **1:**218
substitute products/services, **1:**218
suppliers, **1:**218
traditional economic view, **1:**217
traditional strategic management view, **1:**217–218
See also **Competitive advantage**
Competitive advantage, 1:220–223
conditions for, **1:**218
core competencies and, **1:**221
distinctive capabilities and, **1:**221
entrepreneurs and, **1:**222
five forces approach to, **1:**221
imitation effects on, **1:**222
measurement issues, **1:**223
monopolies and, **1:**222
nonprice, **1:**222
primary activities and, **1:**221
sources of performance variations and, **1:**221–222
strategic intent and, **1:**221
strategic stretch and, **1:**221
support activities and, **1:**221
value chain concept, **1:**221
Competitive isomorphism *vs.* institutional isomorphism, **2:**680
Complex adaptive systems (CAS), 1:223–225
autopoietic systems, **1:**225
complex *vs.* complicated system, **1:**223–224
far-from equilibrium conditions, **1:**224
flocking behavior, **1:**224
overview, **1:**223–224
positive feedback effects, **1:**224
Complexity of decision making, 1:225–229
bounded awareness, **1:**227
bounded rationality, **1:**226–227
criticism, **1:**227–229
definition issues, **1:**226
stock options-based incentive programs and, **1:**228–229
technology effects on, **1:**227
See also **Decision-making theory**

Complexity theory, 1:229–234
   catastrophe theory, **1:**230
   cellular automata, **1:**233
   chaos theory, **1:**230
   characteristics of, **1:**230–231
   complexity system in, **1:**229
   emergence, **1:**231
   future, **1:**233–234
   general systems theory, **1:**229
   genetic algorithms, **1:**232–233
   implications for practice of management, **1:**233
   on hierarchy, **2:**588
   origins of, **1:**229
   research on, **1:**231–232
   self-organization, **1:**231
Complexity thinking, **3:**1047, **4:**1274
Complex organizations, 1:234–236
   complex organizational processes within, **1:**235
   future, **1:**235–236
   loosely coupled network, **1:**235
   moderately coupled bureaucracy, **1:**235
   overview, **1:**234–235
   sociological roots of, **1:**234–235
   tightly coupled firm, **1:**235
Complex system *vs.* complicated system, **1:**223–224
Compliance, 1:236–238
   expertise need for, **1:**237–238
   overview, **1:**236–237
   punishment/persuasion view, **1:**237
   regulator-regulee relation, **1:**237
   within organization, **1:**237
Complicated system *vs.* complex system, **1:**223–224
Compulsive procrastination, **4:**1306
Compulsory Competitive Tendering (CCT), **3:**842
Computer-based learning, 1:238–242
   advantages of, **1:**238–239
   criticism/future, **1:**240–242
   design issues, **1:**241–242
   enhanced interactivity and, **1:**241
   equivalency theory and, **1:**240–242
   learning objects in, **1:**239
   learning platform for, **1:**239–240
   outcomes *vs.* traditional course outcomes, **1:**240–242
   touch effect, **1:**241
Computer-based simulation research, 1:243–246
   agent-based model, **1:**244
   cellular automata method, **1:**243
   equation-based model, **1:**244
   ethics and, **1:**244–245
   generic algorithm method, **1:**243
   intelligent model, **1:**244
   NK fitness method, **1:**243
   procedural model, **1:**244
   rule-based model, **1:**244
   simplistic models, **1:**244
   stochastic method, **1:**243–244
   system dynamics method, **1:**243–244
   theory building need, **1:**244

   validation issues, **1:**244
   Virtual Design Team simulation, **1:**243
Computer-mediated communication (CMC), 1:246–248
   advantages of, **1:**247
   asynchronous, **1:**246
   coorientation, **1:**246
   effectiveness of, **1:**246
   efficiency of, **1:**246
   instant messaging as, **1:**246
   interpersonal skills need, **1:**246
   media for, **1:**247
   mobile, **1:**247–248
   participant location, **1:**247
   participants in, **1:**246
   relational development, **1:**246
   satisfaction in, **1:**246
   sources/destinations of, **1:**246–247
   technologies for, **1:**247–248
   timing issues, **1:**247
   Voice over Internet Protocol as, **1:**246
Computer-supported cooperative work (CSCW), **2:**467–468, 477
Comte, A., **2:**829, **4:**1439, 1601
Concentrated blockholder shareholding, **3:**1212
Concept theory, **1:**57
Concertive action, leadership as, **2:**784
Concrete experience (CE) learning mode, **2:**488, 490, 491
Condition-response, **1:**35–36
Conduct of conducts, **2:**563
Confessional ethnography, **2:**473
Confessional unionism, **4:**1589–1590
Configuration theory, 1:248–252
   criticism, **1:**251–252
   future, **1:**252
   internal organizational coherence and, **1:**250–251
   internal organization differentiation and, **1:**249–250
   multidivisional organization and, **1:**250
   overview, **1:**249–251
   structural-contingency theory and, **1:**249, 250–251
Confirmatory factor analysis (CFA), **4:**1348
Conflict, 1:252–256
   avoiding biases, **1:**255
   avoiding cognitive biases for integrative bargaining, **1:**254
   conflict types, **1:**254
   criticism/future, **1:**255
   definitional issues, **1:**253
   five strategy approaches, **1:**253
   goal interdependence, **1:**255
   integrative bargaining strategy, **1:**253–254
   motive-goal interdependence, **1:**254–255
   practical implications, **1:**255–256
   social theory on, **4:**1440
   strategies, **1:**255
Conflict of interest theory
   on corporate governance, **1:**298
   on marginalization, **3:**875
Confucianism, **3:**1108
Conglomerate discount, **3:**1182
Conglomerate form, unrelated, **3:**935

Conscientization, 3:858, 985
Consensus information, 1:80
Conservatism, 1:256–259
   criticism, 1:257–258
   liberalism *vs.*, 1:256–257, 258, 2:811–812
   overview, 1:256–257
Consistency information, 1:80
Conspicuous consumption, 2:503
Constructivism, 1:259–262
   agency *vs.* social structure, 1:260
   anchor-network theory and, 1:261
   deconstructivism and, 1:261–262
   Durkheimian sociology and, 1:261
   ethnomethodology and, 1:260
   formal *vs.* social organization, 1:260
   in organization theory, 1:259, 260
   in social theory, 1:259–260
   nominalists and, 1:259
   on adult learning, 1:36
   on ethnicity, 2:469
   on learning, 2:802
   phenomenological sociology and, 1:260
   Platonists and, 1:259
   positivism *vs.*, 2:459–2:460
   radical, 2:460
   realists and, 1:259–261
   reflexivity and, 4:1366
   symbolic interactionism and, 1:260
Construed external image (CEI), 3:1079
Consultants, 3:1048
Consumer culture, 1:262–265
   critiques of, 1:263
   culturalism and, 1:263
   cultural studies of, 1:263
   economics of happiness and, 1:264
   positive/negative externalities and, 1:264
   poststructuralism and, 1:263
   structuralism and, 1:263
   subjective well-being and, 1:264
Consumption models, 1:16
Contestable markets theory, 3:878
Contingency-based situational leadership theory, 2:797
Contingency theory
   on agency-structure debate, 1:47
   on behavioral theory of the firm, 1:99
   on formal organizations, 2:515
   on hierarchy, 2:586–587
   on organizational theory, 3:1197
   on truth, 4:1579
Contingent capital accumulation theory, 3:936
Contingent employment, 1:265–269
   consequences of, 1:266–267
   future, 1:267–269
   limited duration contract, 1:266
   temporary work agency, 1:266
   See also **Contingent workers**
Contingent values, 4:1606
Contingent workers, 1:269–271
   direct hire/in-house, 1:270
   diversity of, 1:270–271
   independent/freelance contractors, 1:270
   seasonal/part-time, 1:270
   temporary staffing agency, 1:269–270
   See also **Contingent employment**
Continuous reinforcement, 3:1002
Contract, relational, 1:97
Contracting. *See* **Outsourcing**
Contract theory, on behavioral theory of the firm, 1:97
Control, 1:271–275
   criticism, 1:274–275
   formal subordination of labor, 1:272
   future, 1:275
   labor process and, 1:273–274
   manufacturing consent to enable, 1:274
   procedural fairness and, 1:274
   real subordination of labor, 1:272
   rise of worker problem, 1:272–273
Convergence model, 1:275–277
   corporate governance and, 1:300–301
   directional convergence, 1:275
   divergence model *vs.*, 1:276–277
   final convergence, 1:276
   global convergence, 1:276
   globalization effect on, 1:277
   majority convergence, 1:276
   methodology needs, 1:277
   regional convergence, 1:276
Conversation, 1:275–281
   action/outcome orientation, 1:278
   criticism, 1:279–280
   organizational change role of, 1:279
   organizational learning role of, 1:279
   social construction of meaning, 1:278–279
Conversation analysis, 2:775–776
Conversion analysis, 2:476
Cooke, B., 4:1418, 1419
Cooperative, 4:1459
Coopetition, 1:199, 220, 4:1621
Coordinate and cultivate organizational design, 3:1046
Coordinated market economy (LME), 2:440
Coordination, 1:281–283
   bounded rationality and, 1:282
   information technology effects on, 1:282
   main mechanisms in, 1:281–282
   mutual adjustment, 1:282
   norm standardization, 1:281, 282
   of pooled dependencies, 1:281
   of reciprocal dependencies, 1:281
   of sequential dependencies, 1:281
   output standardization, 1:281
   relational, 1:282–283
   return to market concept, 1:282
   skill standardization, 1:281
   work standardization, 1:281
Copyright, 2:691–692
Corbett, M., 3:939–940
Corbin, J., 2:572
Core values, 4:1606

Corley, K., **3:**1083
Corporate branding, 1:283–286, **3:**1084
   perspective on, **1:**285–286
   self-identity and, **1:**284–285
   stakeholders and, **1:**285
   vision, culture, image and, **1:**285
Corporate citizenship, 1:286–289
   accountability and, **1:**288
   based on citizenship rights, **1:**288
   definition issues of, **1:**287–288
   descriptive view of, **1:**287
   future, **1:**288–289
   strategic aspect of, **1:**287
Corporate crime and corruption, 1:289–292
   alternative approach to explaining, **1:**290–291
   cost-benefit calculation of, **1:**290
   dominant approach to explaining, **1:**290
   limitations to research on, **1:**291
   normative assessment approach to, **1:**290
Corporate culture, 1:59, **1:292–297**
   beliefs/values in, **1:**295
   designing dispositions as goal of, **1:**293–294
   differentiated, **1:**296
   fragmented, **1:**296
   integrated, **1:**296
   leadership biography/history role in, **1:**294
   shared assumptions of, **1:**295
   superficial/visible, **1:**294–295
   total quality management as tool for, **1:**294
   value systems in, **1:**295–296
Corporate entrepreneurship, **2:**447
Corporate governance, 1:297–302
   agency theory on, **1:**297, 298, 300
   board of directors and, **1:**299
   conflict of interest and, **1:**298
   convergence of, **1:**300–301
   corporate social responsibility and, **1:**300, 301–302
   cross-national differences, **1:**299, 301
   globalization effect on, **1:**300–302
   worker/stakeholder focus of, **1:**299–300
Corporate identity, **3:**1079
Corporate image, **3:**1080, 1082
Corporate integrity, **2:**689–690
Corporate multiculturalism, **3:**927
Corporate reputation, **3:**1084
Corporate revolution, **3:**873
Corporate social responsibility (CSR), 1:5, **1:302–305**
   branding and, **1:**286
   civil society organizations and, **1:**303–304
   competition and, **1:**219
   creating impression of, **1:**303
   large corporations and, **1:**304
   shareholders and, **1:**302–303, **4:**1414
   small and medium-sized enterprises and, **1:**304
   See also **Corporate citizenship**
Corporate values, 1:305–308
   aligning core values, **1:**307
   culture of organization and, **1:**306
   espoused, **1:**306

   future, **1:**307–308
   individual values and, **1:**306–307
   lived, **1:**306
   outside stakeholder influence on, **1:**306
   overview, **1:**305–306
Corporation
   organizationally closed, **1:**91
   partnership *vs.*, **2:**741
   structurally open, **1:**91
Corporation/industry demography, **3:**1043
Coser, Lewis A., **2:**824
Costa, P., **4:**1237
Cost-benefit, of corporate crime/corruption, **1:**290
Cost leaders, and competition, **1:**218
Countertrade agreement, **4:**1459
Country similarity theory, **2:**702
Coup, as social movement, **4:**1435
Courtesy stigma, **3:**1180
Cox, J. W., **4:**1572–1573
Creativity, 1:308–313
   destructive influence of, **1:**312
   evolutionary view of, **1:**309–310
   novel/routine action trade-offs, **1:**311–312
   novelty/value as loosely coupled attributes, **1:**311
   selective retention process influence on, **1:**311
   variation process influence on, **1:**310
Credentialism, **4:**1416
Credit, **1:**8
Crime and corruption. *See* **Corporate crime and corruption**
Criminal law, **2:**779–780
Critical analysis, 1:313–316
   criticism, **1:**315–316
   deconstructionism and, **1:**315
   feminist critical organizational analysis, **1:**315
   of punishment/violence in organizations, **4:**1334
   on ideological managerialism, **1:**314
   postmodernism and, **1:**315
   poststructuralism and, **1:**315
   rationalism and, **1:**313–314
Critical discourse analysis (CDA), **1:**391
Critical feminist theory, **4:**1440, 1542
Critical linguists (CL), **1:**391
Critical management education (CME), 1:316–321
   emancipation issues in, **1:**319–320
   feminist perspective on, **1:**318
   future, **1:**320–321
   limitations of focus, **1:**318–319
   mainstream management education *vs.*, **1:**317, 318, 319
   nonreaction to, **1:**320
   process concerns of, **1:**318
   roots of, **1:**317–318
   See also **Critical management studies**
Critical management studies (CMS), 1:321–325, **2:**598
   antiperformativity theme in, **1:**322
   criticism, **1:**323–325
   denaturalization theme in, **1:**322
   future, **1:**325
   mainstream research *vs.*, **1:**321
   managerial rationality *vs.*, **3:**870

on oppression, **3:**1007
poststructuralism and, **1:**322–323
poststructuralism on, **1:**322–323
reflexivity theme in, **1:**322
See also **Critical management education**
Critical modernists, 1:325–327
criticism, **1:**327
future, **1:**327
overview, **1:**326–327
Critical multiculturalism, **3:**927
Critical organization theory, **4:**1221
Critical political economy, **2:**439–440
Critical realism, 1:66, 1:261, 1:327–329
on agency-structure debate, **1:**48
philosophy of science and, **4:**1245–1246
poststructuralism and, **1:**329
social world as layered in, **1:**328
social world as open system in, **1:**328
social world as transformational in, **1:**328
Critical social theory, **4:**1440–1441
Critical theory, 1:329–335
agency theory vs., **1:**50
communicative action theory and, **1:**330–331, 333–334
contributions of, **1:**332–334
critical metaphors for organizations, **1:**333
development within critical organization studies, **1:**332
ideology critique in, **1:**333
instrumental rationality in, **1:**333
key themes in, **1:**330–331
money code in organizations, **1:**333
on Enlightenment, **1:**330, 331
on managerial rationality, **3:**871
on organizational discourse, **3:**1053–1054
organizational research and, **1:**331–332
postmodernism and, **1:**331, 332
poststructuralism on, **1:**331, 332
weaknesses of, **1:**334
Critical Total Quality Management, **4:**1557
Crossan, M., **2:**202, 641, 642, **3:**1093, 1095, 1096
Cross-cultural management, 1:335–339
concept of culture, **1:**335–336
criticism, **1:**338
cultural difference, **1:**336–338
cultural diversity and, **1:**337
culture shock and, **1:**337–338
ethnocentrism and, **1:**337
future, **1:**338
individualism and, **1:**336, 337
long-term orientation and, **1:**336
masculinity and, **1:**336
passage of time and, **1:**337
power distance and, **1:**336
relationships with others and, **1:**338
relationship with environment and, **1:**337
Cross-cultural psychology, **2:**428
Cross-level analysis, 1:339–343
criticism, **1:**342–343
ecological fallacy and, **1:**340
future, **1:**343

hierarchical linear modeling in, **1:**341–342
levels of theory issues in, **1:**340–341
naïve pooling and, **1:**340
overview, **1:**339–342
statistics methods in, **1:**341–342
Cross-shareholding, **2:**749
Crozier, M., **1:**88, **3:**119, 1117
Cultural anthropology, **2:**427
Cultural approach, to consumer culture, **1:**263
Cultural approach, to networks, **3:**969–970
Cultural assimilation vs. multiculturalism, **3:**926–927
Cultural capital, 1:343–345
criticism, **1:**344–345
embodiment manifestation of, **3:**865
institutionalization manifestation of, **3:**865
objectification manifestation of, **3:**865
theoretical assumptions of, **1:**344
Cultural determinism, **3:**1111
Cultural diversity, **1:**337
Cultural hypersensitivity, **3:**928
Cultural intelligence (CQ), 1:345–350
artificial, **1:**184
behavioral, **1:**346, 347, 348
cognitive, **1:**345, 346, 348
criticism/future, **1:**348–350
emotional intelligence vs., **1:**346
general cognitive ability vs., **1:**346
metacognitive, **1:**345, 346, 347–348
motivational, **1:**345–347, 348
practical implications of, **1:**348
research results on, **1:**347–348
use in international management, **2:**713
Cultural pluralism, **3:**927
Cultural turn, **1:**59, **2:**580, **3:**1192
Culture. See **Organizational Culture**
Culture of dependency vs. enterprise culture, **2:**445
Culturepreneur, **2:**449
Culture shock, **1:**337–338
Customer capital, **2:**759
Customer surplus, **3:**877
Cybernetics, 1:350–354
complexity theory and, **1:**229
incentives/self-organizing systems, **1:**351–352
managing complex systems, **1:**352–353
process improvement/adaptive systems, **1:**351
reflexivity, **1:**353
See also **Viable system model**
Cyborg, **4:**1622
Cycle of learning, **2:**803
Cyert, R.
behavioral theory of the firm and, **1:**243
on coalitions, **1:**178
on organizational change, **3:**1021–1022
on profit maximization, **3:**879
Cynicism, 1:354–355
criticism, **1:**355
culture of, **3:**1144
future, **1:**355
overview, **1:**354

Cypert, D., **3:**939
Czarniawska, B., **2:**825, 826, **3:**1133
   on consulting, **3:**848
   on culture studies of employees, **3:**866
   on liminality, **2:**822–823
   on narratives, **3:**944
   on organization fields, **3:**1074
   on petrified narratives, **4:**1456
   on popular culture, **4:**1258–1259, 1260
   on translation, **3:**851
   on travels of ideas, **3:**852

Daft, R., **2:**723
Dahl, R. A., **4:**1252
Daosism, **3:**1108–1109
Darwin, C., **2:**429, **2:**477–480
Data, 1:357–359
analysis/interpretation, **3:**894–895
data coding, **3:**894
data collection, **3:**894
Davenport, T., **4:**1362
Davis, R., **1:**164
Deal, Terrence, **3:**1037, **4:**1378
Debit, **1:**8
Decentralization, 1:359–362
   centralization *vs.*, **1:**359
   distributed knowledge and, **1:**359–360
   incentives and the agency problem, **1:**360–361
   information overload and, **1:**361
   lateral communication and, **1:**361
   Management Information Systems, **1:**360
   organizational decision making and, **1:**360
   organizational design solution, **1:**360
Decentralized network, **3:**972, **3:**972
Decision-making theory, 1:362–366
   criticism, **1:**365–366
   decision making in organized anarchies, **1:**364–365
   edict tactic, **1:**365
   experience-based tactic, **1:**365
   formulating issues for decision, **1:**362
   future, **1:**366
   idea processes, **1:**362
   implementing decisions, **1:**365
   intervention tactic, **1:**365
   issue processes, **1:**362
   objective-directed processes, **1:**362
   on managerial rationality, **3:**871
   persuasion tactic, **1:**365
   power and decision making, **1:**363–364
   processes of deciding, **1:**362–363
   rational choice theory *vs.*, **1:**226
   rational economic model and, **1:**362–363
   readiness-based tactic, **1:**365
   reframing processes and, **1:**362
   See also **Complexity of decision making**
Decision making *vs.* sensemaking, **4:**1405
Decision theory. *See* **Behavioral theory of the firm**
Deconstruction, 1:366–370
   antirealism and, **1:**66
   constructivism and, **1:**261–262
   critical analysis and, **1:**315
   criticism, **1:**368–369
   discourse analysis and, **1:**391
   future, **1:**369
   literary theory and, **2:**825
   of CEO speech on taboos, **3:**1194–1195
   postmodernism and, **1:**368, **1:**369
   poststructuralism and, **1:**368
   preconceptions and, **1:**367–368
   reflexivity and, **4:**1366–1367
Decoupled system, **2:**833
Dedicated asset specificity, **1:**75
Deegan, J., **4:**1407
Deep-level demographics, **1:**378
Deficit approach, to ethnicity, **2:**469–470
Deftness, **1:**202
Dehumanization, 1:370–374
   criticism, **1:**373–374
   situational obligations, **1:**371–372
   total institutions and, **1:**371–374
Deinstitutionalization, 1:374–376
   criticism, **1:**375–376
   functional pressures on, **1:**375
   political pressures on, **1:**374–375
   social pressures on, **1:**375
Dejours, C., **3:**1120
Deleuze, G., **1:**54, **3:**973–974, 999, **4:**1282, 1283
Delphi technique, 1:376–378
   criticisms of, **1:**377–378
   ethics and, **1:**377
   overview, **1:**376–377
Deming, W. E., **4:**1549, 1550
Democracy. *See* **Organizational Democracy**
Democratic humanism, on empowerment, **2:**441
Democratic socialism, **2:**650
Demographic process, 1:378–380
   categorical approach, **1:**378
   compositional approach, **1:**378, 379
   contact hypothesis, **1:**379
   criticism, **1:**379
   deep-level demographics, **1:**378
   Euclidean distance score, **1:**379
   future, **1:**379
   relational approach, **1:**378
   self-categorization theory, **1:**379
   similarity-attraction paradigm, **1:**378–379
   social identity theory, **1:**378
   surface-level demographics, **1:**378
DeMott, B., **2:**824
Demsetz, H., **3:**879, 1060
Denaturalization, **1:**322
Density dependence theory, **3:**1057–1058
Dent, M., **3:**883
Denzin, N., **4:**1572
Deontological ethics, **1:**119
Depunctualization, **1:**29
Deregulation, **3:**961
Derivative work, **2:**691

Derived etic, **2**:478
Derrida, J.
   antirealism and, **1**:66
   on deconstruction, **1**:366–367, 391, **4**:1287
   on Lacan, **4**:1287
   on performance, **1**:408
   on postmodernism, **4**:1280, 1282–1283
Descartes, R., **1**:56, **2**:586, **3**:910, **4**:1371, 1484, 1608
Design science, **1**:14
Design space management, 1:380–381
   criticism/future, **1**:381
   overview, **1**:380–381
Deskilling thesis, **1**:162
Destructive price competition, **3**:972
Determinism
   multifactor, **3**:1111
   natural, **2**:452
   organizational, **3**:1011–1012
   positivist, **4**:1272
   rational, **2**:452
   social, **2**:452
   See also **Environmental determinism; Structural determinism; Technological determinism**
Deutero learning, **3**:1040
Dewey, J., **2**:696, **4**:1299, 1300, 1364, 1404
De Wit, B., **4**:1475
Dialectical materialism, **4**:1439
Dialogical scripting, **1**:382
Dialogic communication, **1**:382
Dialogism, **1**:382, **3**:999–1000
   architectonic, **4**:1456
   chronotopic, **3**:1000, **4**:1456
   stylistic, **4**:1456
Dialogue, 1:381–383
   appreciative inquiry, **1**:382
   core components of, **1**:382
   criticism, **1**:382–383
   definitional issues, **1**:381–382
   dialogical scripting, **1**:382
   dialogic communication, **1**:382
   future, **1**:383
   transformative, **1**:382
Diamond model, **2**:709
Diaries, **4**:1346
Diderot, D., **1**:408
Differentiated corporate culture, **1**:296
Differentiation of difference, as alterity, **1**:54
Differentiation rhetoric, **3**:1163
Differentiation studies, **4**:1256–1257
Diffusion, 1:383–385
   communication perspective, **1**:383–384
   criticism, **1**:384–385
   early sociological perspectives, **1**:383
   on management fashions/fads, **3**:849–850
   organizational perspective, **1**:384
Digital divide, 1:385–386, 2:559
Dilthey, W., **2**:583, 584, 721
DiMaggio, P., **3**:958, 976, 978, 1023, 1074, 1075, 1076, **4**:1316

Direct competitor, **1**:217–218
Direct hire/in-house contingent workers, **1**:270
Directional convergence, **1**:275
Discipline, 1:386–388
   downward hierarchical interactions, **1**:387
   horizontal/peer interactions, **1**:387
   normalization and, **1**:388
   self-discipline, **1**:387–388
   upward hierarchical interactions, **1**:387
Discourse
   organizational communication as, **3**:1034
   See also **Organizational Discourse; Strategic Discourse**
Discourse analysis (DA), 1:389–393, 2:774–775
   construction of reality and, **1**:391
   critical discourse analysis, **1**:391
   critical linguists, **1**:391
   critical linguists (CL), **1**:391
   criticism, **1**:391–392
   deconstruction and, **1**:391
   discourse formations, **1**:390
   future, **1**:392
   historical roots, **1**:389–390
   modern-day applications, **1**:390–391
   organizational, **1**:389
Discourse theory, **3**:1163–1164
Discriminating alignment hypothesis, **1**:75
Discrimination, 1:393–395
   disparate impact, **1**:393
   disparate treatment, **1**:393
   economic theory on, **1**:393
   globalization effects on, **1**:394
   group-based stereotyping and, **1**:394
   information-processing bias and, **1**:394
   intergroup dynamics and, **1**:394
   negative effects of, **1**:394
   workforce diversity and, **1**:393
Disidentity, **2**:634
Disipitative structures, **1**:155
Disorganization, 1:395–396
   confronting, **1**:395
   costs of, **1**:395
   practical approach, **1**:395–396
Dispersed leadership. *See* **Leadership, dispersed**
Dispersed ownership, **3**:1211–1212
Displayed emotional patterns, **2**:437
Dispositional approaches, to job satisfaction, **2**:738
Dispositional power, **3**:1164
Distance learning. *See* **Computer-based learning**
Distributed cognition, **3**:1089
Distributed network, **3**:972
Distributive bargaining, **3**:950–951
Distributive justice, **2**:463, **3**:1085, **4**:1305
Divergence model *vs.* convergence model, **1**:276–277
Diversity, 1:397–401
   anti-racism/sexism approach to managing, **1**:399
   in-group bias and, **1**:398
   labor force structure and, **1**:398
   minimal group studies on, **1**:398
   multiculturalist approach to managing, **1**:399

politics of diversity management, **1:**399
skills needed for managing, **1:**399–400
social categorization theory and, **1:**397–398
social identity and, **1:**397–398
types of, **1:**397
Division of labor, **1:**196, **2:**528, **3:**904, **4:**1553
Domination, 1:401–403
authoritarian, **1:**402
coercive, **1:**401
competent, **1:**401
criticism, **1:**402–403
future, **1:**403
hard coercive, **1:**402
ideological, **1:**402
impersonal, **1:**402
induced, **1:**401
instrumental, **1:**402
legitimate, **1:**401
manipulative, **1:**402
personal, **1:**401, 402
soft conducive, **1:**402
Domination critique, **3:**1158
Donaldson, L., **3:**1045
Double entry accounting system, **1:**8
Double-loop learning. *See* **Learning, double-loop**
Downs, A., **4:**1252
Downsizing, 1:403–406
as rhetoric, **1:**404
coping cycle and, **1:**405
criticism, **1:**405
fit and, **3:**956–957
survivor syndrome and, **1:**405
trends in, **1:**404–405
Downward influence, **2:**656, **2:**657
Dramaturgy, 1:406–409
act, **1:**406
actor, **1:**408
agency, **1:**406
agent, **1:**406
backstage behavior, **1:**406
dramatic persona and, **1:**407
faking it, **1:**407
front stage behavior, **1:**406
life as theater approach, **1:**406, 407
purpose, **1:**406
scene, **1:**406
social drama, **1:**406
theater as organization, **1:**407
theater in organization, **1:**407
theatrical technique/device approach, **1:**407
Drucker, P., **2:**713
Dualist school, on informal economy, **2:**659
Dual systems theory, on gender division, **2:**538–539
Du Gay, P., **4:**1323
Dukerich, J., **3:**1082–1083
Dunkerly, D., **2:**636
Dunlap, J., **3:**871
Dunning, J., **2:**709, **3:**933, **4:**1565
Duopoly, **3:**878

Du Pont, P., **1:**163–164
Durkheim, É.
on cohesion, **1:**191
on division of labor, **2:**528
on social facts, **4:**1602
on suicide, **4:**1335
social theory of, **3:**1166, **4:**1439
Durkheimian sociology, **1:**261
Dutton, J., **3:**1082–1083
Dynamic capabilities (DC), 1:409–411, 3:1022
as organizational routines, **3:**1171
criticism, **1:**410
evolution of, **1:**410
examples of, **1:**409
future, **1:**410–411
resource-based view of the firm on, **1:**409
Dynamic collectivism, **3:**1110–1111

Easterly-Smith, M., **3:**1096
Eclectic theory, **2:**703, **4:**1565–1566
Eco, U., **2:**722
Ecological change, 2:412–414
adaptation mechanisms for, **2:**413
adaptive outcomes of, **2:**413
criticism/future, **2:**414
organizational ecology *vs.*, **2:**412
retention effects, **2:**413
selection effects, **2:**413
stability effects, **2:**413–414
variation effects, **2:**413
Ecological rationality, **3:**862
Ecological validity, **3:**862
Ecology. *See* **Organizational Ecology**
Ecology theory, antirationalist stance in, **1:**62
E-Commerce, 2:415–416
assessment and, **2:**415
criticism, **2:**415–416
customer focus in, **2:**415
organizational learning and, **2:**415
Economic agency theory, **1:**43–44, **1:**45
Economic empowerment, **2:**441
Economic geography, **1:**172
Economic integration, in international business, **2:**703
Economic rationalism, 2:417–419
agency theory and, **2:**418
criticism, **2:**418
neoclassical economics on, **2:**417
overview, **2:**417–418
public choice theory and, **2:**418
transaction costs analysis and, **2:**418
Economic sociology, 2:419–422
criticism, **2:**421
mainstream economics *vs.*, **2:**419
on networks, **2:**420–421
overview, **2:**419–420
scope of, **2:**420–421
Economics of happiness, **1:**264
Economic theory
on behavioral theory of the firm, **1:**95

on business networks, **1:**134
on discrimination, **1:**393
on international production, **2:**708–709
Economic theory of social change, **4:**1439
Economy of social market, **3:**962
Educational psychology, **1:**184–185
Effectiveness, 2:422–425
   adaptation role in, **2:**424–425
   efficiency *vs.*, **2:**422–423
   levels of analysis, **2:**423–424
   measures of, **2:**423
   models of organizational effectiveness, **2:**423
   nature of change and effectiveness, **2:**424–425
Efficiency of McDonaldization, **3:**886
Egalitarian liberalism, **2:**811–812
Egocentric open systems theory, **3:**999
Ego ideal, **3:**941
Einstein, A., **2:**479
Eisenberger, R., **4:**1230, 1231
Elaboration likelihood model (ELM), **1:**78
Electronic battlefield, **3:**998
Elite theory, **3:**1024
E-mail, **1:**246, **2:**665
Emancipatory knowledge, **1:**35, **4:**1604
Embedded agency paradox, **2:**674–677
Emergent theory (ET), 2:425–426
   criticism, **2:**426
   grounded theory and, **2:**425–426
Emery, F., **2:**668, **4:**1449
Emic, 2:427–428
   cross-cultural psychology use of, **2:**428
   cultural anthropology use of, **2:**427
   insider/outsider and, **2:**427
   See also **Etic**
Emotion, 2:428–433
   aesthetic labor, **2:**433
   biological view on, **2:**429
   cognitive view on, **2:**429
   criticism, **2:**430–431
   emotional labor, **2:**430, 431–432
   emotion politics and power, **2:**431–433
   fun-at-work and, **2:**432
   positive organizational scholarship, **2:**432
   psychodynamic view on, **2:**429
   rationality and, **2:**431
   social constructionist view on, **2:**429–430
   toxic emotions, **2:**431
   toxic handler, **2:**431
Emotional dissonance, **1:**141
Emotional intelligence (EI), 2:433–436, 4:1428
   criticism/future, **2:**435
   cultural intelligence *vs.*, **1:**346
   emotional ability, **2:**434
   emotional competency, **2:**434–435
   emotional quotient, **2:**434
   multiple intelligences, **2:**434
   positive effects of, **2:**433–434
   practical intelligence, **2:**434
   social intelligence and, **2:**434

Emotional labor, **2:**430, 431–432, **3:**1101
Emotional patterns in organizations, 2:436–437
   displayed emotional patterns, **2:**437
   felt emotional patterns, **2:**436
   perceived threats and, **2:**436
   unconscious emotional contagion, **2:**436
Emotional quotient (EQ), **2:**434
Empathetic-logical approach, **1:**40
Empirical-analytical knowledge, **4:**1604
Employee community, **1:**214
Employee stock ownership, **4:**1226
Employment relations (ER), 2:437–441
   analytical framework for, **2:**438
   comparative studies on, **2:**440
   critical political economy and, **2:**439–440
   human resource management as, **2:**437–438
   industrial relations as, **2:**437
   institutional approach, **2:**440
   institutionalist, **2:**438
   overview, **2:**438
   tensions in trends in, **2:**439
   trends in, **2:**439
Empowerment, 2:441–442
   democratic humanism view, **2:**441
   economic, **2:**441
   effect on performance, **2:**442
   hierarchy and, **2:**587
   industrial democracy *vs.*, **2:**441
   psychological, **2:**441
   structural, **2:**441
Enabling infrastructure, **3:**1047, **4:**1274
Enacted environment, **3:**1064
Encapsulation, **4:**1274
Engels, F., **1:**161, 261
Engineering-managerial discourse, 2:442–445
   history of, **2:**443–444
   in country other than U.S., **2:**444
   mechanical engineers and, **2:**442–443
   systems ideology and, **2:**443
ENIAC (Electronic Numerical Integrator and Computer), **2:**664
Enlightenment, **3:**910, **4:**1438, 1439, 1601–1602
Énoncé, **4:**1286
Enriquez, E., **3:**1120
Enterprise culture, 2:445–446
   administrative reform and, **2:**445
   criticism/future, **2:**446
   culture of dependency *vs.*, **2:**445
   de-differentiation of, **2:**445
   entrepreneurship and, **2:**446, 449
   principles of, **2:**445
   privatization and, **2:**445
Entrant firm, **1:**218
Entrepreneurship, 2:447–451
   affect on everyday life and practices, **2:**450
   affect on organizational culture, **2:**448
   competition and, **1:**222
   corporate, **2:**447
   creative destruction and, **2:**447
   criticism, **2:**449–450

culturepreneur, **2:**449
economic sociology on, **2:**421
enterprise culture and, **2:**446, 449
entrepreneur mentality and, **2:**449
evolutionary approach to, **2:**448
future, **2:**450–451
interpretive approach, **2:**448
intrapreneurship, **2:**421, 447
narrative approach to, **2:**449
new venture creation and, **2:**447
opportunity/exploitation and, **2:**447–448
organizational politics and, **3:**1157–1158
social constructionist approach, **2:**448
stage models of, **2:**448
strategic choice and, **4:**1464
texture approach to, **2:**448–449
See also **Self-employment identities**
Environment. *See* **Organizational Environments**
Environmental determinism, 2:451–453
criticism/future, **2:**452–453
natural determinism and, **2:**452
on agency-structure debate, **1:**46
organizational adaptation and, **3:**1011
population ecology theory and, **2:**452
rational determinism and, **2:**452
social action view on, **2:**452
social determinism and, **2:**452
social systems view on, **2:**452
Environmentalism and organizations, 2:453–457
biomimicry, **2:**456
criticism, **2:**455
future, **2:**455–456
greenwashing, **2:**455
ISO 14001 certification, **2:**455
overview, **2:**454–455
sustainability, **2:**456
Environmental management systems (EMS), **2:**454–455
Epistemic communities (ECs), 2:457–459
criticism/future, **2:**458
overview, **2:**457–458
Epistemic culture, **2:**458
Epistemic relativism, **1:**30
Epistemological paradigm, **4:**1217
Epistemological positivism, **4:**1270
Epistemological relativism, **4:**1371
Epistemology, 2:459–462
constructivism, **2:**459, 460
organization science and, **2:**459–461
organization theory and, **2:**461, 462
positivism, **2:**459–460
representation, **2:**460–461
Equation-based model of simulation, **1:**244
Equifinality, **2:**506–507, 549, 550, **3:**999, 1011
Equilibrium theory, **1:**230
Equity alliance, **1:**51
Equity (E), **2:**462–463
See also Equity theory
Equity theory, 2:462–464
communitarian approach, **2:**463

distributive justice, **2:**463
liberal approach, **2:**463
libertarian approach, **2:**463
types of equity, **2:**463–464
Equivalency theory, on computer-based learning, **1:**240–242
Ergonomics, 2:464–468
cognitive, **2:**466
domain of, **2:**465–467
human computer interaction studies, **2:**467
organizational, **2:**467
overview, **2:**464–465
physical, **2:**465–466
safety-critical systems and, **2:**468
user as center of, **2:**465
virtual teamworking and, **2:**467–468
Ernst, B., **3:**850–851
Espoused corporate values, **1:**306
Essentialism
on ethnicity, **2:**469
on identity, **2:**630
strategic, **4:**1569
Ethical climate, **3:**1029
Ethics
accountability and, **1:**7
agency theory and, **1:**50
classical management and, **1:**166
computer-based simulation research and, **1:**244–245
exploitation, **2:**495
governmentality and, **2:**566
in negotiation, **3:**953
learning organization and, **2:**810
of managing identification, **2:**629
virtue, **4:**1624–1626
See also **Business ethics; Integrity**
Ethnicity, 2:468–471
being/becoming and, **2:**469
criticism, **2:**470–471
culturalist approach to, **2:**470
deficit approach to, **2:**469–470
essentialist view on, **2:**469, **2:**470
functionalist approach to, **2:**469
nonessentialist view on, **2:**469
social identity theory on, **2:**469
Ethnocentrism, **1:**337
Ethnographic realism, **2:**473
Ethnography, 2:471–475, **4:**1340
adjectival, **2:**473
audience for, **2:**473–474
confessional, **2:**473
ethnographic realism, **2:**473
fieldwork, **2:**471, **2:**472–473
national culture and, **3:**948–949
roots of, **2:**472
Ethnomethodological indifference, **2:**476
Ethnomethodology (EM), 2:475–478
accountability notion in, **2:**475–476
constructivism and, **1:**260
conversion analysis and, **2:**476, **2:**776
criticism, **2:**476–477

ethnomethodological indifference, **2**:476
future, **2**:477
qualitative interviewing, **4**:1343
reflexivity in, **2**:475–476
shop floor problem in, **2**:476
Etic, 2:478–479
derived, **2**:478
etic system, **2**:478
imposed, **2**:478
See also **Emic**
Etzioni, A., **1**:401, **4**:1230
Euclidean distance score, **1**:379
Événement, **2**:633–634
Evolutionary theory, 2:479–484
altruism and, **2**:482
applying to cognition, **2**:481–483
coevolution and, **2**:482, 483, 484
cognitive biases and, **2**:481–482
cross-cultural theorizing, **2**:483
descent with modification, **2**:479–480
dualism and, **2**:481
frequency-dependent selection, **2**:480
genotype, **2**:480
group selection and, **2**:482
handicap principle, **2**:482–482
interactionism and, **2**:483
kin selection, **2**:480
natural selection, **2**:480
neuroscience and, **2**:483
on behavioral theory of the firm, **1**:99
on innovation, **2**:671
on network coevolution, **3**:965–966
on organizational economics, **3**:1061–1062
on replication strategies, **4**:1374
phenotype, **2**:480
sexual selection, **2**:480
social contract algorithm and, **2**:481
standard social science model and, **2**:480–481
to entrepreneurship, **2**:448
See also **Organizational evolution**
Evolution by association, **3**:849
Ex ante opportunism, **3**:1004
Executive coordinator, **4**:1517
Executive coordinator, of team, **4**:1517
Existential movement, **3**:1070–1071
Exogenous motives, **4**:1332
Expatriation, **2**:705
Expectancy theory, 2:484–487
critical commentary, **2**:486–487
expectancy, **2**:485–486
future, **2**:487
instrumentality, **2**:485
valence, **2**:485
Experiential learning (EL), 1:38, 2:487–492, 803
abstract conceptualization learning mode, **2**:488, 490, 491
accommodating, **2**:489–490
active experimentation learning mode, **2**:489, 490, 491
affective complexity, **2**:490–491
assimilating, **2**:489

behavioral complexity, **2**:491
concrete experience learning mode, **2**:488, 490, 491
converging, **2**:489
diverging, **2**:489
experiential learning cycle, **2**:488–489
experiential learning theory of development, **2**:490–491
expert theory of development, **2**:490
foresight and, **2**:511–512
grasping knowledge, **2**:488
Kolb Team Learning Experience, **2**:492
learning style inventory, **2**:491–492
learning styles, **2**:489
perceptual complexity, **2**:491
reflexive observation learning mode, **2**:488, 490, 491
symbolic complexity, **2**:491
Team Learning and Development Inventory, **2**:492
transforming knowledge, **2**:488
Experimental design, **4**:1345–1346
Explicit contract, **1**:53
Explicit knowledge, 2:493–494
criticism/future, **2**:494
storytelling and, **4**:1457
tacit knowledge *vs.*, **2**:493–494, 754
Exploitation, 2:494–498
animal superexploitation, **2**:497
ethics, **2**:495
globalization and superexploitation, **2**:496
informatics of domination, **2**:498
micro *vs.* structural superexploitation, **2**:496–497
national resource superexploitation, **2**:497
performativity, **2**:495–496
sex labor superexploitation, **2**:497
story apologetics, **2**:497–498
superexploitation, **2**:495
Ex post opportunism, **3**:1004
Externalities. *See* **Coase theorem**
External team leader, **4**:1517
External trade theory, **2**:708

Facilitator power, **3**:1164
Failure-induced change theory, **3**:1022
Fairchild, Gregory, **3**:850
Fairness, **1**:274, **4**:1304, 1305
Family business, 2:499–502
concepts and constructs, **2**:501
fair process, **2**:502
family myths, **2**:501
family systems approach, **2**:500–501
genogram, **2**:501
parallel planning processes, **2**:501–502
psychodynamic perspective, **2**:500
three circles model, **2**:501
Fanon, F., **4**:1275
Far-from equilibrium conditions, **1**:224
Fashion, 2:502–505
as collective-selection mechanism, **2**:504
as conspicuous consumption, **2**:503
as reverential imitation, **2**:503
criticism/future, **2**:504–505

trickle-across effects and, **2:**503, 504
trickle-down effects and, **2:**503, 504
trickle-up effects and, **2:**503, 504
Fast and frugal heuristics, **3:**862
Fayol, H., **3:**1116–1117
   authority principle of, **1:**44
   on management, **1:**164, 165, 281
Federal Accounting Standards Advisory Board (FASB), **1:**10
Feldman, M., **3:**1090
Felt emotional patterns, **2:**436
Feminism. *See* **Radical feminism**
Feminismo popular, **4:**1569
Feminist critical organizational analysis, **1:**315
Feminist theory
   antirationalist stance in, **1:**61–62
   critical feminist theory, **4:**1440, 1542
   on gender division, **2:**538
   on management education, **1:**318
   on managerial rationality, **3:**871
   on qualitative interviewing, **4:**1343
   on value-free science, **4:**1604
Fence line community, **1:**214
Fidelity, **1:**205–206
Field theory, on organizational climate, **3:**1028–1029
Fieldwork, **3:**1066
Fifth generation innovation, **2:**672–673
Final convergence, **1:**276
Financial agency theory, **3:**935, 9:937
Financial participation, by employee, **4:**1226
Financial statements, **1:**8–9
Fincham, R., **3:**848
Fine, G., **4:**1407
Firms fundamental theorem of welfare economics, **3:**880
First order learning. *See* **Adaptive learning**
Fit, 2:505–507
   configurations and, **2:**506
   criticism, **2:**506–507
   external fit, **2:**506
   in neocontingency model, **3:**956
   interaction and, **2:**506
   internal fit, **2:**505–506
   research directions, **2:**507
Fitness landscape, **1:**232–233
Fitness of workable illegalities, **3:**1157
Five factor model. *See* **Personality, five-factor model**
Five forces, 2:507–509
   bargaining power of buyers, **2:**508
   bargaining power of suppliers, **2:**508
   competitive advantage and, **1:**221
   criticism/future, **2:**508–509
   existing competitors, **2:**508
   national diamond concept, **2:**508
   substitute products, **2:**508
   threat of entry, **2:**507–508
Flatter organizations, **2:**587
Flexible specialization, **2:**590, **4:**1278–1279
Flexible technology, **2:**656
Fligstein, N., **3:**935, 1074, 1076
Flocking behavior, **1:**224

Folkman, S., **4:**1307
Follett, M. P., **1:**164, 165, 199
Followership, 2:509–510
Foote-Whyte, W., **1:**22
Force-field analysis, on resistance, **4:**1377
Fordism, **1:**145, **4:**1548
Foreign direct investment (FDI), **2:**703, **3:**932–933, **4:**1368, 1610, 1634
Foresight, 2:510–514
   criticism, **2:**513
   experiential learning/scenario building, **2:**511–512
   foresight in practice, **2:**511
   process and scenario building, **2:**512–513
   QUEST mnemonic, **2:**512
   scenario planning, **2:**511–513
   strategic contexts, **2:**511
   strategic/critical conversation role in, **2:**513
Formal organizations, 2:514–521
   accountability of, **2:**516
   agency theory on, **2:**515
   bounded rationality and, **2:**515
   changes in levels of analysis, **2:**516
   changing conceptions, **2:**519–520
   changing features, **2:**518
   closed and open system models, **2:**515
   combined models, **2:**515
   common/divergent features, **2:**516–517
   common features, **2:**516–517
   contingency theory on, **2:**515
   divergent factors, **2:**517
   durability of, **2:**516
   enduring features, **2:**518
   form of, **2:**517
   institutional theory on, **2:**516
   knowledge-based theories on, **2:**515
   natural open system approaches, **2:**516
   organizational boundaries, **2:**518
   organizational components, **2:**519
   organizational ecology model, **2:**516
   organizational power, **2:**519
   organizational strategies, **2:**518–519
   rational and natural system models, **2:**514–515
   rational open system approaches, **2:**515
   reliability of, **2:**516–517
   resource dependence model of, **2:**516
   size of, **2:**517
   social organization *vs.*, **1:**260
   transaction cost analysis on, **2:**515
Formal rationality, **1:**114
Forty, A., **3:**852
Foucauldian turn, 2:521–523
Foucault, M.
   genealogical analysis and, **2:**547
   on discourse, **4:**1417
   on discourse formations, **1:**390
   on énoncé, **4:**1286
   on gaze, **4:**1286
   on governmentality, **2:**563–564, 565–566, 814
   on identity formation, **1:**54

on ideology, **2:**635
on knowledge, **4:**1429
on normalization, **1:**388
on panopticon, **1:**70, 390, **4:**1216
on politics, **1:**25, 26
on power, **1:**48, 212, **2:**449, 753, **3:**1007, 1008, **4:**1289–1291, 1335
on practices of self, **4:**1322
on social constructionism, **4:**1427
on subjectification, **4:**1486
on subjectivity, **2:**449
on truth, **4:**1580
See also **Foucauldian turn**
4I learning framework, **3:**1093, 1094
Fractal organization, **1:**156
Fragmentation studies, **4:**1257
Fragmented corporate culture, **1:**296
Frankfurt School, 2:523–525
consumer culture and, **1:**263
critical theory and, **1:**208–209, 322, 326, 331, **4:**1604
Freelance contractors, **1:**270
Freeman, C., **2:**764
Freeman, J., **3:**1043, 1056
Free market principal, **3:**960
Free-rider problem (FRP), 2:525–527
n-group and, **2:**526
order effect, **2:**526
selective incentives, **2:**526
surplus effect, **2:**526
tragedy of commons, **2:**527
Frege, G., **1:**56, **2:**830
Freire, P., **3:**858, 985
Frequency-dependent selection, **2:**480
Freud, S.
on human satisfaction, **2:**500
on narcissism, **3:**941
on sovereignty of subject, **1:**13
See also **Lacanian psychoanalysis**
Friedman, G., **3:**1117, 1118
Friedman, M., **2:**831, **3:**879, 959, **4:**1588
Friedman, T., **2:**764
Fromm, E., **3:**330, **4:**1351, 1488
See also Frankfurt School
Front stage behavior, **1:**406
Frost, P. J., **3:**1207–1208
Fukuyama, F., **2:**568, 811
Full Range Leadership (FRL) model, **2:**792
Functional community, **1:**213–125
Functionalism, 2:528–529
criticism, **2:**529
general systems theory and, **2:**528
on ethnicity, **2:**469
on humor, **2:**622–623
on learning, **2:**803
on organizational identity, **3:**1077
on punishment/violence in organizations, **4:**1334
overview, **2:**528–529
structural contingency theory and, **2:**528
Functionalist paradigm, **4:**1220

Functional magnetic resonance imaging (fMRI), **2:**483
Functional organizational structure, **3:**1186–1187
Fundamental attribution error, **3:**861
Future shock, **1:**34
Fuzzy set theory, **1:**57, 155–156

Gabriel, Y., **3:**945
Gadamer, H.-G., **2:**582, 583–584, **4:**1283
Gainsharing, **4:**1226
Galbraith, J. R., **1:**884
Game theory, 2:531–534
battle of the sexes, **2:**533
bounded rationality, **2:**533
coordination, **2:**532–533
fear *vs.* creed, **2:**533
future, **2:**533
hawk and dove, **2:**533
implications, **2:**533–534
intertemporal, repeated-trial games, **2:**531–532
market-based, **3:**877, 878
Nash equilibrium, **2:**532, 533
negative zero-sum games, **3:**1156–1157
noncooperative game theory, **1:**96–97
non-zero-sum games, **2:**532
on oligopoly, **3:**878
players, **2:**532
positive zero-sum games, **3:**1157
prisoner's dilemma, **2:**532, **4:**1303–1304
rational behavior, **2:**532
relational game, **2:**685
strategic games, **2:**531
utility, **2:**532
zero-sum games, **2:**532
Garbage can model, 1:364, 2:534–537
criticism, **2:**536–537
decision making by flight, **2:**535
decision making by oversight, **2:**535
decision making by resolution, **2:**535
organized anarchy, properties of, **2:**534–535
Gardener, H., **2:**434
Garfinkel, H., **1:**260, 391, **2:**475
Garratt, R., **2:**808–809
Gates, W., **1:**155
Gaze, **4:**1286
Geertz, C., **2:**472, **3:**1038
Gender
as seriality, **2:**546
in leadership theory, **2:**799
offshore labor and, **2:**765
sex *vs.*, **4:**1411
skills and, **4:**1417
Gender demographics, **3:**1101
Gender division, 2:537–540
criticism, **2:**539–540
macro-level theory on, **2:**538–539
meso-level theory on, **2:**538
micro-level theory on, **2:**538
poststructuralism on, **2:**540
Gendered assumptions, on scientific management, **3:**882

Gendered organization, 2:540–544
   criticism, 2:543–544
   gender, culture, and identity, 2:542–543
   gender in organizational theory, 2:541
   gender in organizations, 2:541–542
   organizational masculinity, types of, 2:541–542
   poststructuralism on, 2:543–544
Gender stereotypes, 2:544–547
   criticism, 2:545–546
   overview, 2:544–545
Genealogical analysis (GA), 2:547–548
   archaeology and, 2:548
   contingency concept in, 2:547
   criticism, 2:548
   descent concept in, 2:547–548
   emergence concept in, 2:548
   power concept in, 2:548
Generalized symmetry principle, 1:28
General knowledge, 1:360
Generally accepted accounting principles (GAAP), 1:8, 1:9
General systems theory (GST), 2:549–552
   closed systems in, 2:549
   complexity theory and, 1:229
   criticism, 2:550–551
   equifinality in, 2:549
   functionalism and, 2:528
   hard systems in, 2:550
   isomorphisms in, 2:549
   new sciences, 2:550–551
   open systems in, 2:549–550
   organismic metaphor in, 2:550
   reductive/analytic approaches, 2:551
   soft systems in, 2:550
Generative learning (GL), 1:32
Generative theory, on value-free conception of science, 4:1604–1605
Generic algorithms, 1:243
Genetic algorithms, 1:232–233
Genogram, 2:501
Genotype, 2:480
Genre analysis, 2:826
Gephart, R., 4:1340–1431
Gersick, Connie, 4:1508–1509
Gestalt approach, 2:804, 3:1028
G-8 group of nations, 2:703
Gherardi, S., 2:545, 3:857, 3:882
Ghoshal, S., 4:1566
Giddens, A.
   hermeneutics and, 2:584
   on interpretive theory, 2:720–721
   on modernity, 3:913, 914, 1090
   on power, 3:1007
   structuration theory of, 1:47–48, 3:1126, 1187, 4:1480–1481, 1483–1484, 1542
Gigerenzer, G., 3:862
Gilbreth, F., 1:164
Gilligan, C., 4:1608
Gioia, D. A., 3:1083
Glaister, K. W., 3:1065

Glaser, B., 2:572–573
Glass ceiling, 2:552–556
   affirmative action and, 2:554
   breaking through, 2:554–555
   deficit approach to, 2:470
   managing diversity, 2:554
   pay cap, 2:553
   persistence of existence of, 2:552–553
   reasons for existence of, 2:553–554
Global civil society, 1:159
Global convergence, 1:276
Globalization, 2:556–558
   activism and, 1:25–27
   criticism/future, 2:558
   effect on arts and organizations, 1:73
   effect on community decision making, 1:214
   effect on convergence, 1:277
   effect on corporate governance, 1:300–302
   effect on discrimination, 1:394
   effect on international business, 2:703–704
   hyperglobalizers, 2:557, 558
   interdependency and, 2:558
   neoliberal, 1:150, 4:1370
   redundant concepts of, 2:556
   risks associated with, 2:556
   skeptics, 2:557
   social theory on, 4:1441
   superexploitation and, 2:496
   transformationalists, 2:557
   trends in management learning, 3:855–856
   unevenness of processes of, 2:557–558
   variations in construction of, 2:557
   See also **International human resource management; International management; Multinational enterprises; Regionalization and capital movement**
Global rationality, 1:107
Global strategic rivalry theory, 2:702
Global supply chain, 2:702
Global village, 2:558–560
GLOBE project, 2:794, 3:1030
GNOSIS, 1:16
Goal-setting theory, 2:560–563
   challenging goals, 2:561
   clear communication and, 2:561
   criticism, 2:561–562
   future, 2:562
   participating and, 2:560–561
   rewarding and, 2:561
   role clarity and, 2:561
   stretch goals, 2:561
   supporting and, 2:561
Goffman, I., 1:354, 370–371
   on dramaturgy, 1:406–407, 4:1500, 1554
   on identity, 2:630, 631
   on ritual, 3:1168
   on stigma, 3:1178, 1180
Golden Shadow, 1:67
Goleman, D., 2:434–435
Gordon, A., 2:789–780

Gouldner, A., **4:**1230, **4:**1603
Governmental Accounting Standards Board (GASB), **1:**10
Governmentality, 2:563–568
   archaeological stage of, **2:**564
   biopolitics, **2:**565–566
   criticism/future, **2:**566–567
   disciplinary power, **2:**564–565
   ethical stage of, **2:**564
   ethics and, **2:**566
   genealogical stage of, **2:**564
Gramsci, A., **1:**391, **2:**580, 635
Grand narratives, 2:568–571
   criticism/future, **2:**570
   overview, **2:**568–570
   postmodernism critique of, **4:**1281
   postmodernism effect on, **2:**568–569
Grand theory, value-free conception of science, **4:**1603–1604
Granovetter, M., **2:**420, **3:**1005, **4:**1424, 1584
Grant, D., **3:**896, 898, 1052, 1055–1056
Greenfield investment, **4:**1610
Greenleaf, R. K., **2:**785–786
Greenwashing, **2:**455
Greenwood, R., **3:**958–959, **4:**1441–1442
Grewal, I., **4:**1568–1569
Greyser, S., **3:**1080, 1082
Grounded theory building (GTB), 2:571–574, 4:1340
   building, **2:**572
   coding in, **2:**572
   emergent theory and, **2:**425–426
   grounded, **2:**571
   theoretical sampling and, **2:**571–572
   theoretical saturation and, **2:**572
   theory, **2:**571–572
Ground projects, and identity, **2:**688
Group affective tone, **1:**202
Group-based stereotyping, **1:**394
Group cohesiveness *vs.* psychological safety, **4:**1329–1330
Group organizational therapy, **3:**1205
Group polarization, **4:**1524
Group selection, **2:**482
Groupthink, **4:**1329, 1524–1525, 1528–1529
Grüenberg, C., **2:**524
Guanxi, 2:574–575
Guattari, F., **3:**973–974, 999
Gulick, L., **1:**164
Gutenberg, E., **3:**1124–1125, 1127

Habermas, J.
   communicative action theory, **1:**208–209, 330–331
   hermeneutics and, **2:**584
   on discourse ethics, **1:**390
   on knowledge, **1:**35, **4:**1604
   on modernity, **3:**913, 914
   See also **Frankfurt School**
Habitus, **1:**47, 162, 212, 344, **3:**997
Hackman, J. R., **4:**1514–1515, 1523
Hall, S., **2:**469, **3:**946
Hammer, M., **3:**973, **4:**1362
Hampden-Turner, C., **1:**337

Handicap principle, **2:**482–482
Hannan, M. T., **3:**1043, 1056, 1059
Hard coercive domination, **1:**402
Hard system, **2:**550
Hardt, M., **3:**972, **3:**973
Hard Total Quality Management, **4:**1555, 1556
Hardware, computer, **2:**665
Hardy, C., **2:**676–677, **3:**1045–1046, **4:**1290
Hartmann, H., **2:**538–539
Harvard Business School, **1:**126, **3:**1203, **4:**1468–1469
Harvey, D., **3:**959
Hassard, J., **4:**1258, 1572–1573
Hatch, M. J., **3:**1083, **3:**1186–1187
Haute couture metaphor, **3:**851
Hawk and dove game, **2:**533
Hawthorne Studies, 2:577–580, 4:1554
   bank wiring observation room (1931–1932), **2:**578
   experiments in illumination (1924–1927), **2:**577
   Hawthorne effect, criticism, **2:**579
   ideological issues, **2:**579
   interviewing program (1928-1930), **2:**578
   methodological issues, **2:**579
   relay assembly test room (1927-1932), **2:**577–578
Hayek, F. A. von, **1:**360, **3:**959
Hedlund, G., **4:**1566
Hegel, G. W., **1:**109–110, 158, **2:**586
Hegemony, 2:580–582
   criticism, **2:**581–582
   in organization studies, **2:**581
   overview, **2:**580-581
Heidegger, M., **1:**65–66, **2:**582, 583
Heiden, E., **3:**1125
Heider, F., **1:**79–80
Heijunka, **2:**800
Heisenberg, W., **1:**156
Henderson, R. M., **4:**1308
Hennis, W., **4:**1321
Heraclitus, **3:**995, 1070
Herbst, D. P., **2:**808
Hermeneutics, 2:582–585
   contemporary, **2:**583–584
   criticism, **2:**584–585
   early, **2:**583
   future, **2:**585
   hermeneutic circle, **2:**585
   logical atomism and, **2:**582
   logical atomism tenets and, **2:**582–583
Heterarchy, **2:**587, 784, **3:**930–931,1046, **4:**1274
Heuristic-systematic model (HSM), **1:**78
Hidden transcripts, **1:**403
Hierarchical linear modeling (HLM), **1:**341–342
Hierarchy, 2:585–589
   alternatives to, **2:**587–588
   authority based on capability, **2:**587
   behavioral research on, **2:**588
   challenges to the hegemony of, **2:**586
   complexity theory on, **2:**588
   empowerment, **2:**587
   flatter organizations, **2:**587

future, **2:**588
heterarchy, **2:**587
learning organizations, **2:**587
neuroscience and, **2:**588
participative structures, **2:**587
peer-to-peer working and networking, **2:**587
self-organizing/self-managing team structures, **2:**587
systems theory, contingency theory, and hierarchy, **2:**586–587
triarchy theory, **2:**587
Hierarchical organizational design, **3:**1046
Hierarchy of needs, **2:**541
Higgins, M., **4:**1259
High-context communication, **2:**733
High involvement management, 2:589–593
criticism/future, **2:**591–592
developing knowledge dimension of, **2:**589
industrial relations and, **2:**590
information sharing dimension of, **2:**589
power dimension of, **2:**589
rewarding performance dimension of, **2:**589
High-performance workplace practices (HPWPs), **4:**1302
High reliability theory (HRT), **3:**990
High reliable organization (HRO), **3:**990, 991
High-risk technologies and organizations, 2:593–597
administrative risk, **2:**594–595
competitiveness risk, **2:**594
criticism/future, **2:**596–597
industry-level risk, **2:**594
inputs/outputs, **2:**593
product risk, **2:**595–596
risk and, **2:**593
societal risk and, **2:**593–594
strategy risk, **2:**594
Hinings, C. R., **3:**958–959, 1074, 1075, **4:**1441–1442
Hirsch, P. M., **3:**850
Historical analysis of organization theory, 2:598–600
criticism/future, **2:**599–600
overview, **2:**598–599
Historical-hermeneutic knowledge, **4:**1604
Hobbes, T., **2:**525, **2:**586
Hochschild, A., **2:**430, **4:**1635
Hofstede, G., **2:**598
on corporate culture, **1:**295
on cultural difference, **1:**336, 337, **2:**713
on national culture, **3:**946–947
on Nordic management, **3:**1134
on risk-taking, **2:**593
on Theory A/Theory J, **4:**1550
Holdup problem, **3:**1004
Holism, complexity theory on, **1:**229
Holland, J. L., **4:**1607–1608
Holliday, R., **4:**1258
Hollowing out, **3:**1210
Holocaust, **1:**372–373
Holographic identity, **3:**1078
Homo economicus, **3:**1013
Homo sacer, **3:**1195
Hood, C., **3:**979

Horizontal fit, **2:**614
Horizontal loose coupling, **2:**835
Horkheimer, M., **1:**263, 330
See also Frankfurt School
Hoskin, K., **2:**522, **3:**939–940
House, R. J., **2:**713, 780, 793, 794, **3:**1030
Huber, G. P., **3:**1094, 1095
Hudson Institute, **4:**1391–1392
Huizinga, J., **4:**1247
Human asset specificity, **1:**75, 76
Human capital, **2:**759, **4:**1415
Human-computer interaction, 2:600–605
criticism/future, **2:**603–604
overview, **2:**601–603
user acceptance, **2:**602–603
user-centered design, **2:**601–602
Human computer interaction (HCI) studies, **2:**467
Human conditioning experiments, **1:**100
Human engineering, 2:605–607
Humanism, 2:607–610
on adult learning, **1:**36
on organizational development, **3:**1049
overview, **2:**607–608
Human Relations School, 2:610–613, 3:1045
criticism/future, **2:**612
overview, **2:**610–612
Human relations theory, **3:**871, **4:**1476
Human resource management (HRM), 2:613–617
as distinctive approach to labor management, **2:**614–615
as function, **2:**613–614
as generic term, **2:**615–616
employment relations and, **2:**437–438, 440
origins of, **2:**653
See also **International human resource management; Recruiting**
Human rights, 2:617–620
civil society and, **1:**159–160
criticism/future, **2:**619–620
overview, **2:**618–619
Human system change, **3:**1049
Hume, D., **4:**1371, **4:**1602, 1624
Humor, 2:620–623
functionalism and, **2:**622–623
future, **2:**622–623
incongruity and, **2:**620–621
relief theory and, **2:**621
superiority theory and, **2:**621
Husserl, E., **2:**476, **4:**1240, 1242–1243
Huxley, J., **2:**609
Hybrid cognitive map, **1:**190
Hybrid identity, **4:**1569
Hybrid organizational structure, **3:**930, 1187
Hybrids methods, for job evaluation, **2:**736
Hymes, D., **1:**391
Hyperarchy, **3:**1184
Hyperglobalizers, **2:**557, **2:**558
Hyper-reality, **4:**1281
Hypertext, **3:**1188
Hypocrisy, 2:623–625

Icarus paradox, **1:**230
Idealism, **1:**65
Ideal type, **3:**1125
Identification, 2:627–630
　antecedents to, **2:**627, **2:**629
　collective-level identity *vs.,* **2:**628
　ethics and, **2:**629
　extracognitive aspects of, **2:**628
　identity *vs.,* **2:**628
　new contexts research on, **2:**629
　organizational management of, **2:**629
　organizational *vs.* affective commitment, **2:**628
　outcomes of, **2:**627–628
　process of, **2:**629
　social identity deidentification, **2:**632
　See also **Identity**
Identity, 2:630–634
　as mask, **2:**631, 633
　disidentity, **2:**634
　hybrid, **4:**1569
　identification *vs.,* **2:**628
　identity capital, **2:**631, 632
　identity formation, **2:**630–631
　identity performance and event, **2:**631, 633–634
　ideographic, **3:**1078
　project, **2:**634
　subjective identity formation, **2:**631
　workplace cognition/behavior and, **3:**861
　See also **Organizational identity; Social identity theory**
Identity-conferring commitments, **2:**688
Identity continuity, **3:**1078
Identity free alterity, **1:**55
Identity multiplicity, **3:**1078
Identity paradigm and alterity, **1:**54
Identity *vs.* alterity, **1:**54
Ideographic cognitive map, **1:**190
Ideographic identity, **3:**1078
Ideological domination, **1:**402
Ideological managerialism, **1:**314
Ideology, 2:634–637
　at organizational level, **2:**635–636
　at societal level, **2:**635
　criticism/future, **2:**637
　origins of *ideology,* **2:**635
Idiocentrism, **2:**645–646
Illegitimate collaboration, **1:**197
Image marketing, **3:**1080
Imitation modes, **3:**853
Impact community, **1:**214
Imperfect competition, **3:**877
Impersonal domination, **1:**402
Implicate order, **1:**224
Implicit contract, **1:**53
Imposed etic, **2:**478
Impossibility Theorem, **1:**156, **4:**1252
Impression management, 2:637–639
　characteristics of, **2:**638–639
　criticism/future, **2:**639
　exemplification tactic, **2:**638
　ingratiation tactic, **2:**638
　intimidation tactic, **2:**638
　realistic job preview and, **4:**1360
　self-promotion tactic, **2:**638
　supplication tactic, **2:**638
Improvisation, 2:639–643
　causal model of success, **2:**642
　future, **2:**641, **2:**642
　metaphor of, **2:**640–641
　performative aspects of, **2:**641
Incivility spiral, **4:**1638
Inclusive fitness, **2:**480
Income statements, **1:**8–9
Incommensurability, 2:643–645
　criticism/future, **2:**644
　de-facto, **2:**643
　desirability of, **2:**643–644
　noncommittal approach to, **2:**643
　weak, **2:**643
Incompatibility principle, **1:**156
Incongruity theory, **2:**620
Incorporated alterity, **1:**54
Incremental innovation, **2:**671, **4:**1308
Independent/freelance contractors, **1:**270
Indexicality, **3:**1164
Individualism, 2:645–647
　causes of, **2:**647
　cross-cultural management and, **1:**336, 337
　horizontal/vertical, **2:**646–647
　idiocentrics, **2:**645–646
　individuation *vs.,* **3:**1072
　institutional, **3:**1005
　methodological, **3:**995–996, **4:**1332, 1334
Individual leadership *vs.* team leadership, **4:**1514
Individuation *vs.* individualism, **3:**1072
Induced domination, **1:**401
Industrial democracy, 2:648–652
　codetermination, **2:**649
　collective democracy, **2:**649–650
　collective/representative combination, **2:**650
　comanagement, **2:**648–649
　empowerment *vs.,* **2:**441
　model overview, **2:**651
　pressure groups, **2:**648
　representative democracy, **2:**650
　self-management, **2:**650
Industrial economics, **4:**1465–1466
Industrial organization view
　on unemployment, **4:**1587
　on vertical integration, **4:**1610, **4:**1613–1614
Industrial relations (IR), 2:437, **2:**440, **2:652–654**
　criticism/future, **2:**653
　high involvement management and, **2:**590
　overview, **2:**652–653
　See also **Labor relations**
Industrial revolution (IR), 2:654–656
　causes of, **2:**654
　first, **2:**654, **2:**655–656
　overview of, **2:**655

second, **2:**654–655
third, **2:**655
Industry demography, **3:**1043
Industry-level risk, **2:**594
Industry organization (IO) economics, **3:**878
Inequity
material, **1:**61
symbolic, **1:**61
Influence, 2:656–659
antecedents effecting, **2:**657
assertiveness strategy, **2:**657
bargaining strategy, **2:**658
coalition strategy, **2:**658
criticism/future, **2:**658–659
downward, **2:**656, **2:**657
higher authority strategy, **2:**658
influence attempts, **2:**657–658
ingratiation strategy, **2:**657
outcomes of influence attempt, **2:**658
reason strategy, **2:**657
upward, **2:**656–657
Infocomm. *See* **Information and communication technology**
Informal economy, 2:659–660
dualist school on, **2:**659
employment regulation and, **2:**660
growth of, **2:**660
legalist school on, **2:**660
self-employment, **2:**659
structuralist school on, **2:**659–660
Informatics of domination, **2:**498
Informating, **2:**809
Information, 2:661–663
as way of knowing, **2:**752–753
criticism/future, **2:**663
data *vs.*, **2:**661
effects on coordination, **1:**282
overview, **2:**661–663
See also **Information and communication technology**; **Information processing**
Informational capitalism, **1:**146
Informational justice, **3:**1086
Information and communication technology (ICT), 2:664–667
conceptual overview, **2:**664–665
criticism, **2:**665–666
decentralization of decision making effects of, **2:**665
information processing and, **2:**668
innovation and, **2:**665
intellectual property, **2:**666
local government management and, **3:**844
outsourcing/offshoring and, **2:**665–666
reengineering and, **4:**1362
sexuality and, **4:**1411
societal applications of, **2:**664–665
support structures, **2:**666
virtual communities, **2:**665
See also Virtual organization
Information asymmetry, **1:**43
Information processing, 2:667–670
cognitive science on, **2:**667
criticism, **2:**669–670
data *vs.* information *vs.* knowledge, **2:**667
information systems and, **2:**668
information technology and, **2:**668
sociotechnical approach, **2:**669
systems theory on, **2:**668
technical-functional information, **2:**669
theory of information on, **2:**667
traditional approaches, questioning/expansion of, **2:**668–669
Information-processing bias, **1:**394
Information systems, **2:**667
Information technology (IT). *See* **Information and communication technology**
Information theory, **2:**667
In-group bias, **1:**398
Initial public offering (IPO), **3:**936
Innovation, 2:670–673
competitiveness and, **2:**671
criticism/future, **2:**673
evolutionary theory on, **2:**671
high- *vs.* low-tech, **2:**671
incremental, **2:**671
international level approach, **2:**671, **2:**672
national level approach, **2:**672
organizational level approach, **2:**672
process of, **2:**672–673
radical, **2:**671
research and development expenditure, **2:**670
technoeconomic paradigm shift, **2:**670
Innovation climate, **3:**1029, **3:**1030
Inpatriation, **2:**705
Instant messaging (IM), **1:**246
Institutional collectivism, **3:**1133
Institutional entrepreneurship, 2:674–678
criticism/future, **2:**677–678
embedded agency paradox, **2:**674–677
ideas for change, **2:**675–676
motivations for change, **2:**674–675
realizing institutional change, **2:**676–677
strategic choice and, **4:**1464
Institutional individualism, **3:**1005
Institutional isomorphism, 2:678–681
coercive mechanisms on, **2:**679
competitive isomorphism *vs.*, **2:**680
criticism/future, **2:**680–681
mimetic mechanisms on, **2:**679–680
normative mechanisms on, **2:**679
on organizational change, **3:**1023
population ecology and, **2:**678–679
Institutionalist employment relations, **2:**438
Institutional legitimacy, 2:682–683
criticism/future, **2:**682–683
social elements effect on, **2:**684
through assessment, **2:**682
through enactment, **2:**682
through imposition, **2:**682
Institutional logics, **3:**1023
Institutional theory, 2:683–688
criticism/future, **2:**687

on activities, **2:**686
on behavioral theory of the firm, **1:**99
on coercion, **2:**686
on externalization, **2:**684
on formal organizations, **2:**516
on imposition, **2:**686
on internalization, **2:**684
on legitimacy, **2:**684
on material resources, **2:**686
on normative institute, **2:**684
on objectification, **2:**684
on organizational change, **3:**1023
on organizational design, **3:**1046–1047
on organizational field, **3:**1076
on organizational rhetoric, **3:**1164
on procrastination, **4:**1307
on regulative institute, **2:**684–685
on social beliefs, norm, and rules, **2:**685
on social effect approach, **2:**687
on taken-for-granted reality, **2:**684
Instrumental domination, **1:**402
Instrumentality, in expectancy theory, **2:**485
Instrumental leadership, **2:**793
Instrumental rationality, **1:**197, 208, 333
Integrated corporate culture, **1:**296
Integrated model of job satisfaction, **2:**738
Integration rhetoric, **3:**1163
Integrative negotiation, **3:**951
Integrity, 2:688–690
  as social virtue, **2:**689
  corporate, **2:**689–690
  criticism/future, **2:**690
  ground projects, **2:**688
  identity-conferring commitments, **2:**688
  objectivism and, **2:**689
  overview, **2:**688
  pragmatism and, **2:**689
  See also **Ethics**
Intellectual capital, **2:**759
Intellectual property, 2:690–694
  copyright, **2:**691–692
  copyright infringement, **2:**691
  criticism/future, **2:**693
  derivative work, **2:**691
  ICT and, **2:**666
  license, **2:**692
  patents, **2:**692–693
  trademarks, **2:**693
  work made for hire, **2:**691
Intelligence. *See* **Cultural Intelligence**
Intelligent simulation model, **1:**244
Intended participation, by employee, **4:**1228
Interaction analysis, 2:694–696
  criticism/future, **2:**695
  overview, **2:**694–695
Interactionism, 2:696–698
  evolutionary theory and, **2:**483
  symbolic, **2:**697
Interaction justice, **3:**1085–1086, **4:**1305

Interaction ritual, **3:**1168
Interaction process analysis (IPA), **2:**694
Intercultural management, **3:**1013
Interest model, **2:**648
Intergroup conflict, 2:698–701
  avoiding, **2:**700
  competitive motivation, **2:**699
  compromising and, **2:**700
  conflict awareness, **2:**698
  conflict behavior, **2:**699–700
  conflict outcome, **2:**700
  contending, **2:**700
  individualistic motivation, **2:**699
  intentions (motivation), **2:**699
  organizational context and, **2:**700–701
  organizational effectiveness and, **2:**701
  over goals, **2:**698–699
  over issues, **2:**698
  over means, **2:**699
  prosocial motivation, **2:**699
  thoughts and emotions, **2:**699
Interlocking directorship, **2:**749
Intermittent reinforcement, **3:**1002
Internal/external goods of practice, **4:**1293
Internal-External Locus of Control Scale (I-E), **2:**827–828
Internalization. *See* **Vertical integration**
Internalization theory, **2:**709
Internal leader, **4:**1517
Internal organizational demography, **3:**1043
Internal team leader, **4:**1517
International Accounting Standards Board (IASB), **1:**10, 11
International business (IB), 2:701–704
  absolute advantage in, **2:**702
  balance of trade in, **2:**702
  comparative advantage in, **2:**702
  country similarity theory, **2:**702
  eclectic theory, **2:**703
  economic integration, **2:**703
  foreign direct investment, **2:**703
  globalization and, **2:**703–704
  global strategic rivalry theory, **2:**702
  global supply chain in, **2:**702
  international investment, **2:**703
  internationalization theory, **2:**703
  mercantilism, **2:**702
  multinational enterprises, **2:**702, **3:**931–934
  national competitive advantage theory, **2:**702–703
  ownership advantage theory, **2:**703
  portfolio investment, **2:**703
  product life cycle theory, **2:**702
  protectionism, **2:**702
  supranational agencies, **2:**703
International Financial Reporting Standards in EU, **1:**10
International human resource management (IHRM), 2:704–707
  criticism/future, **2:**706–707
  cultural factors in, **2:**705–706
  ethnocentric, **2:**705

expatriation, **2:**705
geocentric, **2:**705
inpatriation, **2:**705
polycentric, **2:**705
regiocentric, **2:**705
use of performance appraisals, **4:**1234
See also Human resource management
International investment, **2:**703
Internationalization school, 2:707–710
    behavioral theory on international production, **2:**708
    classical/neoclassical trade theory, **2:**708
    diamond model, **2:**709
    eclectic paradigm, **2:**709
    economic theory on international production, **2:**708–709
    external trade theories, **2:**708
    internalization theory, **2:**709
    international production theories, **2:**708
    product life cycle theory, **2:**709
Internationalization theory, **2:**703
International Labor Organization (ILO), **4:**1634, 1635
International management, 2:710–715
    controlling, **2:**713–714
    cultural context, **2:**712–713
    economic environment, **2:**711–712
    leading, **2:**713
    organizing, **2:**710–711
    PESTE analysis for, **2:**711, 714
    planning, **2:**711
    political environment, **2:**712
International Monetary Fund (IMF), **1:**26, 150, **2:**417, 703, 871, **3:**712, 980, 984, **4:**1368
International production theory, **2:**708
International team leadership, **4:**1517–1518
Internet, **2:**664
    effect on multinational enterprises, **3:**934
    effects on community decision making, **1:**214
    enacted liminality of, **2:**822
    local government management and, **3:**844
    operational effectiveness and, **3:**972
Internet/cyber community, **1:**214
Interorganizational relations and collaborations (IRC), 2:715–720
    alliances among competitors, **2:**716
    boundary issues, **2:**717
    competencies, **2:**716
    governance/governmentality/culture, **2:**719–720
    interorganizational advantage, **2:**718–719
    power/control issues, **2:**717
    relationship maintenance, **2:**718
    symbiotic cooperation between noncompetitor, **2:**717
    trust/trust-infusing mechanisms, **2:**718
    typology of, **2:**715–717
    vertical partnerships, **2:**716–717
Interpersonal accountability, **1:**6
Interpersonal justice, **3:**1086
Interpretive paradigm, **4:**1220
Interpretive theory, 2:720–724
    generalization/validity in, **2:**721–722

    language/social construction in, **2:**721
    on entrepreneurship, **2:**448
    on organizational identity, **3:**1077
    on organizational theory, **3:**1198–1199
Interpretive viability, **3:**850
Intertemporal, repeated-trial game, **2:**531–532
Intertextuality, **3:**1165
Interviews, **4:**1342–1344, **4:**1346
Interview society, **4:**1342
Intetextuality, **3:**1164
Intraorganizational communication, **2:**733
Intrapreneurship, **2:**421, **2:**447
Intuitive logics, **4:**1392
Invisible hand, **1:**180–181, **3:**872, **3:**959, **3:**1203
Iowa School, **4:**1499
Iron cage, **1:**113, **2:**504, **3:**870
Iron law of oligarchy, 2:724–727
    diverse types of political performance, **2:**725–726
Irony, **2:**774
Irrationality, 2:727–729
    antirationality *vs.,* **1:**63–64
    criticism/future, **2:**728–729
    overview, **2:**727–728
Irrationality of rationality, **3:**887
Irrealism, **1:**65
ISO 14001 certification, **2:**455
Isomorphism, **1:**116, **2:**549
    See also Institutional isomorphism
Issue management rhetoric, **3:**1162

James, W., **2:**696, **4:**1268, 1298, 1299, 1300, 1394
Japanese management, 2:731–735
    criticism/future, **2:**734–735
    embedded in Japanese context, **2:**733–734
    kaizen, **2:**731, 732, 733, 735, 801, **3:**801
    overview, **2:**732–733
    silver bullet, **2:**731
    See also **Just-in-time management; Karoshi; Keiretsu; Lean production**
Jazz metaphor, **3:**380, **3:**909
Jensen, M., **1:**43, 228, 360, 361, **3:**935, 1061
Jensen, P., **2:**492
Job characteristics model, **2:**738
Job evaluation, 2:736–737
    assessment, **2:**736
    classification, **2:**736
    criticism/future, **2:**736–737
    factor comparison, **2:**736
    hybrids methods, **2:**736
    job analysis, **2:**736
    job description, **2:**736
    point factor, **2:**736
    ranking, **2:**736
Jobs, S., **2:**781, **2:**782
Job satisfaction, 2:737–740
    affective events theory, **2:**738
    criticism/future, **2:**738–739
    dispositional approaches, **2:**738
    integrated model of, **2:**738

job characteristics model, **2:**738
person-environment (P-E) fit, **2:**738
social information processing approach, **2:**738
Joerges, B., **3:**852
Joint stock companies, 2:740–742
Joint ventures, **1:**75, 135, 517, **2:**715, 716, **4:**1459
    international, **1:**196, 335, **2:**701, 711, 932, **3:**856, **4:**1530
    managing diversity in, **1:**400
    organizational learning and, **3:**1093, 1096
    product innovation and, **4:**1310
    research and development, **1:**51
    resource dependent and, **4:**1383–1384
    risk management and, **4:**1388
Jung, C., **1:**67, **4:**1407
Justice. *See* **Organizational Justice**
Justice theory, **2:**813
Just-in-time management (JIT), 2:590, 742–745, 3:840
    criticism/future, **2:**744–745
    inventory cost reduction in, **2:**743
    kanban role in, **2:**743
    mass production systems *vs.*, **2:**742–743
    production cycle time reduction in, **2:**743
    push-pull systems and, **2:**743
    total production maintenance and, **2:**744
    workers and, **2:**743–744

Kahneman, D., **3:**871, 1022
Kairos, **3:**1165
Kaizen, **2:**731, 732, 733, 735, 801, **3:**801
Kant, I.
    on Enlightenment, **1:**326
    on hierarchy, **2:**586
    on humanism, **2:**608
    on nature as divine art, **1:**72
    on space/time, **4:**1551
Kanter, R. M., **2:**545, 586, 881–882, **3:**1043, 1631
Kaplan, C., **4:**1568–1569
Karoshi, 2:747–749
    criticism/future, **2:**748–749
    overview, **2:**747–748
Kauffman, S., **1:**232
Keenoy, T., **3:**899–900
Keiretsu, 2:749–750
    benefits, **2:**749–750
    costs, **2:**750
    criticism, **2:**750
Keller, K., **3:**1082
Kelley, R. E., **2:**509
Kelly, G. A., **1:**189
Keynesianism, on unemployment, **4:**1587, 1588
Kidder, T., **3:**1073
Kieser, A., **3:**848, 850–851
King, Jr., M. L., **2:**782
Kin selection, **2:**480
Klein, N., **2:**704
Kluckhohn, C., **4:**1607
Knight, F., **4:**1583, 1585
Knowing-doing gap, **1:**15

Knowledge, 2:750–753
    as power, **2:**753
    boundary objects, **2:**752
    dimensions of, **3:**1091
    emancipatory, **1:**35, **4:**1604
    embedded, **2:**759
    embodied, **2:**759
    embrained, **2:**759
    emcultured, **2:**759
    empirical-analytical, **4:**1604
    encoded, **2:**759
    epistemology of possession, **2:**751
    epistemology of practice, **2:**751–752
    explicit, **2:**493–494, 751, 754
    general, **1:**360
    historical-hermeneutic, **4:**1604
    information technology, **2:**752–753
    knowledge economy, **1:**146, 172, **2:**753
    know vs. knowledge, **3:**1091, **4:**1585–1586
    leaky, **3:**1091
    politics of, **4:**1428–1429
    practical, **1:**35
    specific, **1:**360
    sticky, **3:**1091
    tacit, **2:**751, 754, **4:**1503–1507
    technical, **1:**35
    ways of knowing, **2:**752–753
    See also **Actionable knowledge; Knowledge creation; Knowledge-intensive firms; Knowledge management; Organizational knowledge**
Knowledge-based theory, on formal organizations, **2:**515
Knowledge creation, 2:753–755
    combination mode of, **2:**754
    criticism/future, **2:**755
    externalization mode of, **2:**754
    full cycle assumption of, **2:**755
    internalization mode of, **2:**754
    new organizational knowledge, **2:**754
    socialization mode of, **2:**754
Knowledge creation cycle, **3:**1089
Knowledge economy, **1:**146, 172, **2:**753
Knowledge-in-practice, **1:**212
Knowledge-intensive firms, 2:755–758
    criticism/future, **2:**756–758
    embedded, **2:**756
    embrained, **2:**756
    organizational learning and, **2:**757
    overview, **2:**756
Knowledge management (KM), 2:758–762
    centralizing knowledge and, **2:**760
    combination stage of, **2:**759
    community approach to, **2:**760, **2:**761
    criticism/future, **2:**760–761
    embededness of knowledge and, **2:**759–760
    externalization stage of, **2:**759
    in professional service firms, **4:**1313
    intellectual capital and, **2:**759
    internalization stage of, **2:**759
    management fashion, **2:**761

socialization stage of, **2:**759
types of knowledge, **2:**759, **4:**1503
Knowledge management systems (KMS), **2:**663
Knowledge spillover, **3:**1018
Knowledge transfer, **1:**1–2, 172, 360, **2:**458, **3:**1018, 1020, **4:**1375, 1462
Knowledge transfer costs, **1:**1–2
Knowlegde work, **1:**274, **2:**457–458, 828, **3:**848, 1101, **4:**1548
See also **Knowledge-intensive firms**
Knowles, M., **2:**802, **4:**1364
Koestler, A., **4:**1407
Kohlberg, L., **3:**1072, **4:**1608
Kolb, D. A., **1:**38, **2:**487–489, 490, 492, 803, 804, 805, **4:**1364
Kolb Team Learning Experience (KTLE), **2:**492
Kondratieff, N., **2:**831–832
Kondratieff waves, **2:**831–832
Kornberger, M., **3:**848
Kotler, P., **3:**1080
Kristeva, J., **4:**1287
Krugman, P., **1:**172
Kuhn, T., **2:**467, 643, 830, **3:**1155, 1196, **4:**388, 1217, 1219, 1244, 1371, 1372
Kuznets, S., **2:**832
Kuznets swings, **2:**832

Labor and offshoring, 2:763–765
criticism/future, **2:**764–765
effect of ICT on offshoring, **2:**665–666
overview, **2:**763–764
Labor process theory (LPT), **1:**162, 274, **2:**767, **3:**1006–1007, **4:**1416–1417
Labor relations (LR), 2:765–769
collective actors in, **2:**766, **2:**767
criticism/future, **2:**768–769
new institutionalism and, **2:**767
outcomes of, **2:**766
pluralist view on, **2:**766
processes in, **2:**766
radical (Marxist) view on, **2:**766
rational choice institutionalism and, **2:**767–768
sociohistorical institutionalism and, **2:**767–768
unitary view on, **2:**766–767
See also **Industrial relations**
Labor reserve army, **4:**1588
Lacan, J., **4:**1286–1287, 1486
Lacanian psychoanalysis, 2:769–773
criticism/future, **2:**772
human change and learning, **2:**771
need, demand, and desire, **2:**771
post-Freudian Lacan, **2:**770
post-Lacanian Freud, **2:**770–771
postmodern Lacan, **2:**771–772
Lakoff, G., **2:**812
Language and organizations, 2:773–777
conversation analysis, **2:**775–776
criticism/future, **2:**776–777
discourse analysis, **2:**774–775
narrative analysis, **2:**775
overview, **2:**773–776
tropes, **2:**774
Language-in-use studies, **3:**1164
Lanier, J., **4:**1622
Lash, S., **3:**1090
Latent process perspective, **1:**77
Latham, G., **3:**922
Latour, B., **1:**27–28, **2:**816–817, **3:**851, **4:**1580
Law and economics, 2:777–780
Coase theorem, **2:**778, 779
criminal law, **2:**779–780
normative analysis of, **2:**778
positive analysis of, **2:**778
property/liability rules, **2:**778–779
Lawler, E., **2:**589–590
Law of effect, **1:**100, **3:**1001
Law of requisite variety, **3:**998
Lawrence, P., **3:**1064, **4:**1602
Lawrence, T. B., **2:**676
Lazarus, R., **4:**1307
Leader-member exchange theory, **2:**797
Leadership
individual *vs.* team, **4:**1514
neurotic, **2:**429
visionary, **4:**1362–1363
Leadership, charisma, 2:780–784
process, **2:**781–782
recent research, **2:**782–783
theory, **2:**781
transformational leadership *vs.*, **2:**782, 793
Leadership, dispersed, 2:784–785
as collective action, **2:**784
as collective flexibility, **2:**784
paradoxes of, **2:**785
Leadership, servant, 2:785–788
emancipation paradox, **2:**788
functional characteristics of, **2:**786–787
lack of empirical verification, **2:**787
necessary attributes for, **2:**786
Leadership, styles, 2:788–790
criticism/future, **2:**789–780
employee orientation, **2:**789
high relationship-low task, **2:**789
high task–high relationship, **2:**789
high task–low relationship, **2:**789
low task–high relationship, **2:**789
production orientation, **2:**789
relationships behaviors, **2:**789
situational approach, **2:**789
task behaviors, **2:**789
Leadership, transactional, 2:790–792
criticism/future, **2:**791
overview, **2:**790–791
transformational leadership *vs.*, **2:**792–793
Leadership, transformational, 2:792–795
charisma leadership *vs.*, **2:**782, 793
criticism/future, **2:**793–794
emotional intelligence and, **1:**85

Full Range Leadership model, **2:**792
instrumental leadership, **2:**793
research instrument, **2:**783
transactional leadership *vs.,* **2:**792–793
Leadership theory, 2:795–800
behaviorism on, **2:**796–797
contingency-based situational leadership, **2:**797
gender in, **2:**799
leader-member exchange, **2:**797
leadership as substitutable/dispersible, **2:**798
leadership *vs.* management, **2:**798
origins/key concepts, **2:**795–798
positive psychology, **2:**797–798
subordinate in, **2:**799
trait-based approach to, **2:**796
See also **Leadership, charisma; Leadership, dispersed; Leadership, servant; Leadership, transactional; Leadership, transformational**
Leaky knowledge, **3:**1091
Lean production, 2:800–801
design for manufacturing and assembly, **2:**801
heijunka, **2:**800
kaizen, **2:**801
total preventive maintenance, **2:**800
Toyota Production System, **2:**800
See also **Japanese management; Just-in-time management; Total Quality Management**
Learning, **2:**801–805
as group process, **2:**803
behavioral theory on, **2:**802
cognitive theory on, **2:**802–803
constructivist theory on, **2:**802
experiential, **1:**38, **2:**803
functionalism, **2:**803
history in organization studies, **2:**803–804
organizational-level, **2:**803
sociocultural theory on, **2:**802
team learning, **4:**1525
See also **Adaptive learning; Adult learning; Learning, double-loop; Learning organization; Team learning**
Learning, double-loop, **1:**15, 22, 32, 279, **2:**803, 2805–808, **3:**1088, 1093
criticism/future, **2:**806–807
overview, **2:**805–806
single-loop learning *vs.,* **2:**806–807
Learning, single-loop, **1:**32, 279, **2:**803, **3:**1088, 1093–1094
double-loop learning *vs.,* **2:**806–807
Learning anxiety, **4:**1330
Learning-by-doing, **4:**1395–1396
Learning-in-working, **1:**211
Learning organization (LO), 2:808–811
ethics and, **2:**810
hierarchy, **2:**587
ideals issues, **2:**810
informating concept, **2:**809
ontological issues, **2:**810
organizational learning *vs.,* **3:**1092
overview, **2:**808–810
personal mastery, **2:**809

shared vision, **2:**809–810
systems thinking, **2:**810
team learning, **2:**809
working with mental models, **2:**809
See also **Management learning**
Learning organization theory, **1:**32
Learning style inventory (LSI), **2:**491–492
Learning theory, **2:**709
Lebensführung, **4:**1321–1322
Legalist school, on informal economy, **2:**660
Legitimate domination, **1:**401
Legitimate peripheral participation (LPP), **1:**210–211
Lenin, V. I., **1:**161
Leopold, E., **3:**851
Lévi-Strauss, C., **3:**1122, **4:**1285, 1286, 1440, 1481
Lewin, K.
action research and, **1:**21
field theory of, **3:**1021, 1028–1029
on resistance to change, **4:**1377
on understanding systems, **1:**167
Liberalism, 2:811–814
classical, **2:**811
conservatism *vs.,* **1:**256–257, 258, **2:**811–812
criticism/future, **2:**812–813
equity theory, **2:**463
modern, **2:**812
New Deal/egalitarian, **2:**811–812
tender-minded, **2:**812
Liberal market economy (LME), **2:**440
Liberal multiculturalism, **3:**927
Liberal technologies of regulation, 2:814–817
alliance concept, **2:**815
criticism/future, **2:**816–817
degree of risk, **2:**815
knowledge producer significance, **2:**815
line of historical development, **2:**815
overview, **2:**814–816
regulation at distance, **2:**815
shared modes of perception/cognition, **2:**815
Libertarian approach, to equity theory, **2:**463
Licensing, **2:**692, **4:**1459
Life as theater concept, **1:**406, 407
Life chances concept, **1:**161
Life circle hypothesis, **4:**1611
Life cycle, 2:817–821
criticism/future, **2:**820–821
decline and death stage, **2:**819
family business, **2:**500
founding stage, **2:**818
growth stage, **2:**818
maturity stage, **2:**818
renewal stage, **2:**818–819
research on, **2:**819–820
stages, **2:**818–819
Life routine procrastination, **4:**1306
Lifetime employment, **2:**733
Life-world, **2:**583, 584, 585, 722, **4:**1240, 1241–1242, 1283
Lightfoot, G., **4:**1259
Likert, R., **3:**1029

Lim, J., **4:**1231
Liminality, 2:821–824
  communitas and, **2:**822
  health application, **2:**822
  place application, **2:**822
  professions application, **2:**822
  work organization application, **2:**822–823
Limited duration contract (LDC), **1:**266
Limited liability shareholders, **4:**1413
Linguistic turn, **1:**48, 74, **2:**367, 580, 773, 774, 776, **3:**851, 944, 947, 1052, 1056, **4:**1300, 1343
Linguistiscs, **1:**185
Linstead, S., **2:**631, 633, 634
Lippit, G., **3:**1048
Lippit, R., **3:**1048
Lippman, W., **2:**544
Literary theory, 2:824–827
  as analytical tool, **2:**825–826
  as guide to literature, **2:**824–825
  deconstruction and, **2:**825
  genre analysis, **2:**826–827
  narratology and, **2:**825–826
Lived corporate values, **1:**306
Living storytelling, **4:**1457
Local government. *See* **Management and organization of local governments**
Locke, E., **3:**920, 921, 922
Locke, J., **1:**55–56
Locus of causality, **1:**80
Locus of control, 2:827–829
  Internal-External Locus of Control Scale, **2:**827–828
Logical atomism, **2:**582, **2:**721, **2:**830
Logical positivism, 2:721, **829–831, 4:**1270–1271
  Vienna Circle and, **2:**829–830
Logic of industrialization model of capitalism, **1:**144
Long-wave theory, 2:831–833
  hegemonic cycles, **2:**832–833
  Kondratieff waves, **2:**831–832
  Kuznets swings, **2:**832
  long-term societal cycles, **2:**832
Loose coupling, 2:833–836
  causal indeterminacy/equivocality and, **2:**834
  coupling/decoupling dialectical interactions, **2:**834
  decoupled system, **2:**833
  horizontal, **2:**835
  loosely coupled networks, **1:**235
  noncoupled system, **2:**833
  normal accidents and, **3:**989
  procedural loose coupling, **2:**835
  tightly coupled system, **2:**833
  vertical, **2:**835
Lorenz, E., **1:**156, 230
Lorsch, J., **3:**1061, **4:**1602
Lubit, R., **3:**942
Luckmann, T., **2:**562, 684, 685, 721, **4:**1427
Luhmann, N.
  autopoietic systems, **1:**225, **3:**1126, **4:**1437
  criticism approach of, **2:**550
  on agency *vs.* social structure, **1:**260

Lukes, S., **1:**402, **4:**1289
Lyotard, J.-F., **2:**568, 569, **3:**911, **4:**1280–1281, 1284

Mach, E., **2:**830
Machine bureaucracy, 3:837–838
  central features, **3:**837–838
  criticism, **3:**838
Macoby, M., **3:**942
Macve, R., **2:**522
Magic in organizing, 3:838–842
  belief in magic *vs.* believing in magic, **3:**841
  historical overview, **3:**839
  magic as a cultural phenomenon, **3:**839
  magic as a particular experience, **3:**840
  magic as illusionism, **3:**839–840
  magic as label, **3:**841
  magic as organizing, **3:**840–841
  magic of organizing and, **3:**841–842
Maguire, S., **2:**676–677
Maitlis, S., **3:**1207, **3:**1208
Majority convergence, **1:**276
Majority shareholders, **4:**1413
Malinowski, B., **2:**472, **2:**610
Malpractice, **4:**1296
Management and organization of local governments, 3:842–845
  criticism/future, **3:**843–844
  overview, **3:**842–843
Management and public policy, 3:845–847
  criticism/future, **3:**846
  overview, **3:**845–846
Management by fear, **4:**1550
Management consultants, 3:847–849
  criticism/future, **3:**848
  overview, **3:**847–848
Management contracts, **4:**1459
Management fashions and fads, 3:849–855
  diffusion studies, **3:**849–850
  haute couture metaphor, **3:**851, **3:**853
  prêt-à-porter metaphor, **3:**851
  translation theory of managerial fashions, **3:**851–853, 868–869
Management Information Systems (MIS), **1:**360, **2:**668
Management knowledge, **1:**130
Management learning (ML), 3:855–860
  complexity of, **3:**859
  globalization trends in, **3:**855–856
  in formal/informal contexts, **3:**856–857
  pedagogical practice, **3:**856
  reflexive critique role in global, **3:**857–858
  rethinking pedagogical practice, **3:**858–859
Management movements, **1:**164, **1:**165
Managerial accounting, **1:**10
Managerial and organizational cognition (MOC), 3:860–863
  actor-observer effect and, **3:**861
  attribution theory and, **3:**861
  behavioral theory on, **3:**860–861
  classical theory of organizational decision, **3:**860

cognitive science on, **3:**860
criticism/future, **3:**861–862
identity theory and, **3:**861
perceived environment effect on, **3:**861
satisficing and, **3:**861
self-categorization theory and, **3:**861
Managerial capitalism, 3:863–864
criticism/future, **3:**864
overview, **3:**863–864
Managerial cultural capital, 3:864–867
criticism, **3:**866–867
overview, **3:**865–866
Managerialism, 3:867–870
as repackaging older ideas, **3:**868
evangelical tone of, **3:**869
ideologist view of, **3:**869–870
management fashion and, **3:**868–869
quantification facet of, **3:**869
Managerial rationality, 3:870–872
critical management studies *vs.,* **3:**870
critical theory on, **3:**871
decision-making theory on, **3:**871
feminist research on, **3:**871
human relations view, **3:**871
organizational theory on, **3:**872
postcolonial studies on, **3:**871
Managerial revolution, 3:871, **872–874**
corporate revolution and, **3:**873
criticism/future, **3:**874
economic ramifications, **3:**874
origins of, **3:**874
overview, **3:**872–873
professionalization of management and, **3:**873
Managerial sensemaking, **1:**37
Managerial theory of firm (MTF), **1:**97–98
Manipulative domination, **1:**402
Mannheim, K., **4:**1598
Maquiladoras. *See* Capital Movement, Migration, Maquiladoras
March, J.
behavioral theory of the firm and, **1:**243
deconstruction of work of, **2:**825
on choice/decision making, **3:**1095
on classical management, **1:**165
on coalitions, **1:**178
on cooperation, **1:**194
on corporate leadership, **3:**1073
on creativity, **1:**310
on decision making, **1:**225–226
on exploration/exploitation, **3:**1093
on imitation, **3:**853
on organizational change, **3:**1021–1022
on organizational knowledge, **3:**1088
on organizational-level learning, **2:**803
on profit maximization, **3:**879
Marcuse, H., **1:**263, **1:**330, **3:**871
See also Frankfurt School
Marginalization, 3:874–876
at individual level, **3:**875
at intergroup level, **3:**875

at organizational level, **3:**875
at societal level, **3:**875–876
criticism/future, **3:**876
Market-based theory (MBT), 3:876–881
criticism/future, **3:**880–881
customer surplus, **3:**877
duopoly, **3:**878
game theory, **3:**877, **3:**878
imperfect competition, **3:**877
industry organization (IO) economics and, **3:**878
knowledge/innovation issues, **3:**878–379
market system efficiency, **3:**879–880
microeconomics and, **3:**877
monopoly, **3:**877, 878
oligopoly, **3:**877–878
perfect competition, **3:**877, 879
price-output decisions, **3:**879
Marketing rhetoric, **3:**1162
Marshall, A., **1:**172
Martin, J., **3:**1194–1195
Marx, K.
economic sociology and, **2:**419
influence on social theory, **4:**1439
on capitalism, **1:**143, **1:**144
on competition, **4:**1309
on constructivism, **1:**261
on control, **1:**271–273
on division of labor, **3:**904
on ideology, **2:**635
on international labor market, **2:**496
on oppression, **3:**1006
on performativity, **2:**495
on production technology, **2:**635
on social class, **1:**160–161, 162, **4:**1401
on superexploitation, **2:**497
on surplus value, **2:**494
Marxism
Frankfurt School on, **2:**524
on labor relations, **2:**766
on oppression, **3:**1006
on radical humanism, **4:**1353
on unemployment, **4:**1587, **4:**1588
Marxist feminist theory, **2:**538
Masculinities and management, 3:881–884
cross-cultural management and, **1:**336
dominant masculine discourses, **3:**882
gendered assumptions on scientific management, **3:**882
gendered character of organizations/work, **3:**882–883
performativity and, **3:**883
women managers, **3:**882, **3:**883
Maslow, Abraham, **1:**216, **2:**541, **3:**920–921
Mass customized bureaucracy (MCB), **1:**139
Mass production systems, **2:**742–743
Mass social movements, **4:**1435
Master-servant relations, **2:**733
See also Leadership, servant
Material inequity, **1:**61
Materialist positivism, **4:**1270
Mathematical economics, **2:**831

Matrix organization, 3:884–886, 1045, 1187
Maximizing behavior, **1:**98
Maximum principle, **2:**463
Mayer, J. D., **2:**434, **3:**1046
Mayntz, R., **3:**1125–1126
Mayo, E., **2:**610–612
Mazza, C., **2:**822–823, **3:**851
McCallum, D., **1:**163
McCrae, R., **4:**1237
McDonaldization, 2:598, 704, **3:**838, **886–888**
  calculability of, **3:**886
  control through nonhuman technology of, **3:**886
  efficiency of, **3:**886
  irrationality of rationality and, **3:**887
  predictability of, **3:**886
McDonalds approach. See **Replication strategy**
McGregor, D., **2:**784, **4:**1545–1546, 1548, 1549–1550
McLaren, P., **3:**927
McLuhan, M., **2:**558, 559, 560, **3:**974
Mead, G. H., **1:**260, 285, **2:**630, 696–697, **4:**1499
Means, G., **3:**872, 879, 937, 1211
Measurement, 3:888–891
  cohesion studies issues, **1:**193
  competition studies issues, **1:**223
  error in, **3:**890, **3:**894
  measures of effectiveness, **2:**423
  reflective/formative, **3:**889–890
  See also **Meta-analysis**; **Qualitative approaches**;
    Quantitative models and methods
Mechanistic organizations, **3:891–893**, **3:**1045
  criticism/future, **3:**892–893
  overview, **3:**891–892
Meckling, W., **1:**43, 360, 361, **3:**1060
Media role, in communication, **1:**208
Meister approach, **2:**686
Melamed, A. D., **2:**778
Memes, **3:**965
Memory
  organizational, **3:**1088
  transactive, **4:**1526
Mercantilism, **2:**702
Meritocratic principle, **2:**469
Merleau-Ponty, M., **4:**1240, 1242–1243
Merrick, D., **4:**1395
Merton, R.
  on bureaucracies, **1:**33, **2:**528
  on identity, **2:**630
  on middle range theories, **3:**901
  on no new ideas, **3:**852
Meta-analysis, 3:893–896
  data analysis/interpretation, **3:**894–895
  data coding, **3:**894
  data collection, **3:**894
  error and, **3:**894
  problem formulation, **3:**894
  significance levels/null hypothesis, **3:**894
  stages in, **3:**894
  vote-counting, **3:**893–894
Metacognitive cultural intelligence, **1:**345, 346, 347–348

Metaphor and organization, 2:774, **3:896–900**
  goodness of fit and, **3:**898–899
  haute couture, **3:**851
  idealism and, **3:**899
  inequalities and, **3:**899
  irony and, **3:**899–900
  jazz metaphor, **3:**380, 909
  manifestations of, **3:**896–897
  metonymy and, **3:**899
  organizational routines and, **3:**1170
  organization as brains, **3:**897
  organization as culture, **3:**897
  organization as flux and transformation, **3:**898
  organization as machine, **3:**897
  organization as organism, **3:**897
  organization as political system, **3:**897–898
  organization as powerful instrument of domination, **3:**898
  organization as psychic prison, **3:**898
  permanent visibility metaphor, **4:**1491
  postmodernism on, **3:**899
  prêt-à-porter, **3:**851
  reification and, **3:**899
  schismatic, **3:**896–897
  synecdoche and, **3:**899
Metaphysics of presence, **1:**63
Metering problem, in team production theory, **3:**1060
Methodological individualism, **3:**995–996, **4:**1332, 1334
Methodological paradigm, **4:**1217
Metonymy, **2:**774, **3:**899
Meyer, J., **3:**872, **3:**975, 1023, 1074, 1075
Meyer, R., **4:**1475
M-form. See **Multidivisional form**
Michels, R., **2:**724
Microeconomics, **3:**877
Micro vs. structural superexploitation, **2:**496–497
Middle-range theory, 3:901–902
Migration. See **Capital Movement, Migration, and Maquiladoras**
Miles, R., **3:**1012
Milgram, N., **4:**1307
Milgram, S., **1:**371–372
Military organization (MO), 3:902–907
  centralization/decentralization, **3:**903–904
  conservation/innovation, **3:**905
  integration/differentiation, **3:**904
  formalization/informalization, **3:**905–906
Mill, J. S., **2:**607
Mindfulness, **1:**202, 286, **3:**1018, 1160, **4:**1241
Miner, J. B., **3:**920
Minimal group studies on diversity, **1:**398
Minimal network, 3:907–908
Minimal structure, 3:908–910
Mintzberg, H.
  on adhocracy, **1:**33–34
  on coordination, **1:**281, 282
  on entrepreneurship, **2:**448
  on machine bureaucracy, **3:**837, 838
  on organizational categories, **2:**461
  on strategic management, **4:**1472, 1473
Mitlin, D., **3:**986

Mobile computer-mediated communication, **1**:247–248
Model II theories-in-use, **1**:14–15
Model I theories-in-use, **1**:14–15
Moderately coupled bureaucracy, **1**:235
Modernism, 3:910–913
   criticism/future, **3**:912
   overview, **3**:910–912
   postmodernism *vs.*, **3**:911–912
   See also **Modernity**
Modernity, 3:913–916
   criticism/future, **3**:914–915
   multiple modernities, **3**:915
   myths of, **3**:915
   overview, **3**:913–914
   reflexivity and, **3**:915
Modern liberalism, **2**:812
Modular product innovation, **4**:1308
Mohanty, C. T., **4**:1568
Monopoly, **1**:217, 222, **3**:877, 878, **4**:1611
Mooney, J., **1**:164, 165
Moore, L. F., **3**:901–902
Morale, 3:916–917
Moral hazard, 3:917–919, 1061
   agency relationship and, **3**:918
   dealing with, **3**:918–919
   hidden action and, **3**:918
   hidden information and, **3**:919
   monitoring costs and, **3**:918
   opportunistic behavior and, **3**:1004
   origins in insurance industry, **3**:918
Moral reasoning, **4**:1608
Moral *vs.* epistemological relativism, **4**:1371
Morgan, G., **3**:837, 838, 896–898, **4**:1217, 1219,
   1221–1222, 1244–1245
Morin, E. M., **2**:550, 551, **3**:1072, 1073
Motivation, 3:919–926
   emotions, **3**:923–924
   goals, **3**:922–923
   incentives, **3**:924–925
   needs, **3**:920–921
   needs deprivation, **3**:921
   self-efficacy, **3**:924
   values, **3**:921–922
   See also **Theory X**; **Theory Y**; **Theory Z**
Motivational cultural intelligence, **1**:345–347, 348
Multiculturalism, 3:926–929
   as dangerous trend, **3**:928
   as fostering cultural hypersensitivity, **3**:928
   backlash and, **3**:928
   corporate, **3**:927
   critical, **3**:927
   cultural assimilation *vs.*, **3**:926–927
   cultural pluralism and, **3**:927
   liberal, **3**:927
   political correctness and, **3**:928
   roots of, **3**:926
Multidimensionality of performance, **3**:1152
Multidivisional form (M-form), 1:235, 250, 359,
   3:929–931, 1045
   heterarchy and, **3**:930–931

   hybrid organization *vs.*, **3**:930
   move from N-form to, **3**:1183–1184
   U-form *vs.*, **3**:929–930
   See also **Multisubsidiary form**
Multifactor determinism, **3**:1111
Multifactor Leadership Questionnaire (MLQ), **2**:793
Multinational corporations (MNCs). *See* **International human resource management; International management**
Multinational enterprises, 2:702, **3:931–934**
   international commerce drivers, **3**:931–932
   Internet effect on, **3**:934
   liability of foreignness and, **3**:932
   policy liberalization and, **3**:931–932
   reasons to engage in FDI, **3**:932–933
   technology change and, **3**:932
   See also **Transnational corporations**
Multiple intelligences, **2**:434
Multiple modernities, **3**:915
Multiple parallel subculture, **3**:927
Multisubsidiary form (MSF), 3:934–938
   advantage over MDF, **3**:937–398
   change from MDF to, **3**:936–937
   contingent capital accumulation theory on, **3**:936
   controlling interest and, **3**:934
   divisions and, **3**:934
   domestic *vs.* foreign competition and, **3**:936
   efficiency of, **3**:938
   financial agency theory on, **3**:935
   initial public offerings and, **3**:936
   LBO strategy, **3**:935–937
   multidivisional form *vs.*, **3**:937–938
   trusts and, **3**:934, **3**:935
   unrelated conglomerate form and, **3**:935
Multiteam system (MTS), **4**:1526–1527
Mumby, D., **2**:636
Murphy, A., **4**:1608
Music and work, 3:938–940
   future, **3**:940
   ocularcentrism and, **3**:938
   other setting, **3**:938–939
   work/consumer environments, **3**:938–939
Mutual adjustment, **1**:282
Mutualism, in network coevolution, **3**:964
Mystical spirituality, **3**:1176
Mythical fixed pie, **3**:952
Myths, **1**:67–68, **3**:980, **3**:1192

Narcissism, 3:941–944
   criticism/future, **3**:943–044
   ego ideal and, **3**:941
   organizational ideal and, **3**:942–943
   overview, **3**:941–943
Narratives, 2:449, 775, 825–826, **3:944–945,** 1033–1034
   See also **Storytelling**
Narrative therapy, **4**:1457
Nash equilibrium, **2**:532, 533
National competitive advantage theory, **2**:702–703
National culture, 3:945–950
   attitude scales and, **3**:947–949
   interpretive approach to, **3**:948–949

overview, **3**:945–947
social psychology view on, **3**:946–947
National diamond concept, **2**:508
Natural determinism, **2**:452
Natural open system approach, **2**:516
Natural/rational system models, **2**:514–515
Natural selection, **2**:480
Natural unemployment rate, **4**:1588
Need hierarchy theory, **3**:920–921
Needs deprivation, **3**:921
Negative reinforcement, **3**:1002
Negative trends, **3**:972
Negative zero-sum games, **3**:1156–1157
Negativity *vs.* true alterity, **1**:54
Negotiation, 3:950–953
anchoring/adjustment, **3**:952
best alternative to this negotiated agreement, **3**:951
cognitive biases, **3**:952
cultural differences, **3**:953
distributive bargaining, **3**:950–951
emotions, **3**:952–953
ethics, **3**:953
framing issues/people, **3**:952
integrative, **3**:951
irrational escalation of commitment, **3**:952
mythical fixed pie, **3**:952
Negri, Antonio, **1**:972, 973
Neoclassical economics, 3:953–955
criticism/future, **3**:953–954
on economic rationalism, **2**:417
overview, **3**:953–954
Neocontingency model, 3:955–957
ambiguity of fit construct in, **3**:956
overview, **3**:955–956
possible decrease of variables in, **3**:956–957
Neoinstitutional theory, 1:374, 3:957–959
criticism/future, **3**:958–959
on agency-structure debate, **1**:47
on environmental determinism, **2**:681
on organizational theory, **3**:1197–1198
on professions, **4**:1316–1317
on rationality, **3**:872
overview, **3**:957–958
Neoliberal globalization, **1**:150, **4**:1370
Neoliberalism and organization, 3:959–963
commercial openness strategy, **3**:961
criticism/future, **3**:962–963
deregulation strategy, **3**:961
economy of social market and, **3**:962
free market principal, **3**:960
individual freedom principal, **3**:960
limited state principal, **3**:960
main characteristics of neoliberalism, **3**:959
principals, **3**:960–961
privatization strategy, **3**:961
strategies, **3**:961
Neo-Marxism
on managerial revolution, **3**:874
on radical humanism, **4**:1353
on rationality, **3**:871

Neopragmatism, **4**:1395
Neostructuralism, **4**:1288
Nested stability, **2**:734
Network coevolution, 3:963–967
biological view on, **3**:964
comparison of alternatives and, **3**:965
competitive, **3**:964
components of actor in, **3**:965
detrimental, **3**:964
direct/indirect, **3**:964
industry level, **3**:965–966
learning and, **3**:965
main mechanisms in, **3**:965
memes, **3**:965
mutualism, **3**:964
neutral, **3**:964
parasitism, **3**:964
reciprocity and, **3**:964
selection and, **3**:965
symbiosis, **3**:964
Network of the multitude, **3**:973
Network organizational structure, **3**:1187
Networks, 1:196, 3:967–971
critical commentary/future, **3**:968–970
cultural approach to, **3**:969–970
economic sociology and, **2**:420–421
loosely coupled, **1**:235
overview, **3**:967–968
relational approach to, **3**:968–969
social network analysis on, **3**:968
structural/positional approach, **3**:968
structural theory of action on, **3**:968
See also **Actor-network theory**; **Network coevolution**; **Network society and organizations**
Network society and organizations, 3:971–975
aborescent networks, **3**:974
centralized network, **3**:972
decentralized network, **3**:972
distributed network, **3**:972
network of the multitude, **3**:973
rhizome networks, **3**:973–974
striated networks, **3**:974
Networks of practice *vs.* communities of practice, **2**:458
Neurath, O., **2**:830
Neuropsychology, **1**:184
Neuroscience
evolutionary theory and, **2**:483
on hierarchy, **2**:588
Neurotic leadership, **2**:429
New Class Theory, **3**:874
New Deal/egalitarian liberalism, **2**:811–812
New economic model, **1**:150
New geographical economics, **1**:172
New institutional economic theory, **3**:980
New institutionalism, 3:975–979
field level focus of, **3**:977–978
labor relations and, **2**:767
legitimacy of, **3**:977
limitations/extensions of, **3**:976–977
overview, **3**:975–976

stage in, **3:**976
transnational level of, **3:**978
New public management (NPM), 3:842, 843, 846, **3:979–984**
   antipolitical tendencies of, **3:**982–983
   as ideology, **3:**980
   as practical reform, **3:**980
   future, **3:**983
   government as service provider focus, **3:**982
   implementation variation, **3:**980–381
   management theory on, **3:**980
   myth theory on, **3:**980
   new institutional economic theory and, **3:**980
   quantification in, **3:**869
   reform effects, **3:**981–982
New Right ideology, **2:**418
New sciences, general systems theory on, **2:**550–551
New sociology of science (NSS), 30
New venture creation, **2:**447
N-group, and free-rider problem, **2:**526
Nicklisch, H., **3:**1124
Nicolini, D., **3:**1096
Nietzsche, F., **4:**1371
NK fitness method, **1:**243
No liability shareholders, **4:**1413
Nominalism, **1:**65, 259
Nomological analysis, **2:**720
Nomothetic cognitive map, **1:**190
Non Accelerating Inflation Rate of Unemployment (NAIRU), **4:**1588
Nonaka, I., **2:**754–755, 758, 759, **3:**1089, **4:**1503–1505
Noncooperative game theory, **1:**96–97
Noncoupled system, **2:**833
Nonequity alliance, **1:**51
Nongovernmental organizations, 3:984–987
   as change agent, **3:**985
   corporate social responsibility and, **1:**303
   criticism/future, **3:**986–987
   history of, **3:**984–985
Nongovernmental organizations (NGOs), **1:**214–215
Nonimee shareholders, **4:**1413
Nonprice competitive advantage, **1:**???
Nonprofit organizations, 3:987–989
   CEO-board relation, **3:**988–989
   overview, **3:**987–988
Non-zero-sum game, **2:**532
No-one-in-charge experiments, **2:**784
Normal accidents, 3:989–992
   as unavoidable, **3:**990–991
   bounded rationality and, **3:**991
   high reliable organization and, **3:**991
   high reliability theory on, **3:**990
   linear interactions and, **3:**990
   loosely coupled events and, **3:**989
   multiple failures, **3:**989
   nonlinear interactions and, **3:**990
   redundancy and, **3:**991
   risk reduction strategy, **3:**991–992
   system accidents, **3:**989
   tightly coupled events and, **3:**989

Normalization, Foucault on, **1:**388
Normann, R., **3:**1134
Normative assessment, of corporate crime and corruption, **1:**290
North American Free Trade Agreement (NAFTA), **1:**153, **2:**703, 712, **4:**1370
Not-for-profit. *See* **Nongovernmental organizations; Nonprofit organizations**
Nozick-style coercion, **1:**182
Numerical action, leadership as, **2:**784

Objectivism, integrity and, **2:**689
Objectivity, 3:993–994
   aperspectival, **3:**993
   ontological/absolute, **3:**993
Observations, quantitative, **4:**1346
Obsolescence, **3:**1145
Obsolescence, liability of, **3:**1145
Ocularcentrism, **3:**939
OECD (Organization for Economic Co-operation and Development), **1:**237, **2:**421, **3:**842, 980, 983, **4:**1420
Offshoring. *See* **Labor and offshoring**
Ohono, T., **2:**742
Old institutionalism, **3:**958
Oligopoly, **1:**217, **3:**877–878
Ontological/absolute objectivity, **3:**993
Ontological paradigm, **4:**1217
Ontology, 3:994–997
   atomistic conception of reality, **3:**995
   batteries of dispositions, **3:**996–997
   becoming, **3:**995, **3:**996–997
   being, **3:**995, 996
   methodological individualism, **3:**995–996
   reducibility thesis, **3:**996
   roots of, **3:**995
Open coding, **2:**572
Open systems, 3:997–1000
   binary logic and, **3:**999
   boundaries and, **1:**171
   closed systems *vs.*, **1:**170
   criticism, **3:**998–1000
   dialogism and, **3:**999–1000
   first-order cybernetics, **3:**998, 999
   general systems theory on, **2:**549–550
   in formal organizations, **2:**515
   natural, **2:**516
   rational, **2:**515
   second-order cybernetics, **3:**998
   social capital and, **4:**1425
   social system as, **4:**137, 1436
   third-order cybernetics, **3:**999
Operant conditioning, 1:100, **3:1000–1004**
   application, **3:**1003–1004
   extinction, **3:**1002–1003
   free-operant, **3:**1001
   instrumental conditioning *vs.*, **3:**1001
   punishment, **3:**1003
   reinforcement, **3:**1001–1002
Operating adhocracy, **1:**33–34

Operating philosophy, and values, **4:**1608–1609
Opinion/thought leader, **1:**215
Opportunistic behavior, 3:1004–1005
  asset specificity and, **3:**1004
  ex ante/ex post opportunism, **3:**1004
  holdup problem and, **3:**1004
  moral hazard, **3:**1004
  transaction cost theory and, **3:**1060
Oppression, 3:1005–1009
  as domination, **3:**1006
  as subjugation, **3:**1006–1007
  criticism/future, **3:**1007–1008
  labor process theory on, **3:**1006–1007
  racist, **3:**1007
  resistance to, **3:**1006
  sexist, **3:**1007
Order effect, **2:**526
Organ, D., **3:**1025
Organic organizations, 3:1009–1011, **3:**1045
  criticism/future, **3:**1009–1010
  link to environment type, **3:**1009
  organic-mechanistic type, **3:**1009
  rapid change environment of, **1:**170
Organisation for Economic Co-operation and Development (OECD), **1:**237, **2:**421, **3:**842, **3:**980, **3:**983, **4:**1420
Organizational accountability, **1:**5–6
Organizational adaptation, 3:1011–1012
  criticism/future direction, **3:**1011–1012
  enacted environment, **3:**1011
  equifinity and, **3:**1011
  organizational determinism *vs.*, **3:**1011–1012
  strategy type and, **3:**1012
  task environment, **3:**1011
Organizational anthropology, 3:1012–1014
Organizational art. *See* **Arts and Organizations**
Organizational behavior modification (OB Mod), **1:**100–101, 102
  See also Coercion; Organizational behavior
Organizational behavior (OB), 3:1014–1017
  criticism/future, **3:**1016–1017
  overview, **3:**1014–1016
Organizational capabilities, 3:1017–1020
  as competitive advantage, **3:**1018–1019
  criticism, **3:**1019
  dynamic, **3:**1018
  future, **3:**1019–1020
  knowledge transfer, **3:**1018
  organizational learning and, **3:**1017–1018
  routines relation to, **3:**1018
Organizational change, 3:1020–1025
  Carnegie School on, **3:**1021–1022
  cultural and cognitive perspectives on change, **3:**1023–1024
  ecological perspectives, **3:**1022–1023
  institutional perspectives, **3:**1022–1023
  Lewinian field theory, **3:**1021
Organizational citizenship behaviors, 3:1025–1028
  altruism, **3:**1025
  causes of, **3:**1026

  civic virtue, **3:**1025
  consequences of, **3:**1026–1027
  courtesy, **3:**1025
  criticism/future, **3:**1027–1028
  general compliance, **3:**1025
  sportsmanship, **3:**1025
  types of, **3:**1025–1026
Organizational climate, 3:1028–1031
  climate of fear, **3:**1029
  climate of silence, **3:**1029
  ethical climate, **3:**1029
  field theory on, **3:**1028–1029
  innovation climate, **3:**1029, 1030
  organizational culture *vs.*, **3:**1028–1029
  proximal climate, **3:**1029
  safety climate, **3:**1029
  service climate, **3:**1029
Organizational closure, **1:**90
Organizational commitment, **2:**628
Organizational communication, 3:1031–1035
  as contradiction, **3:**1035
  as discourse, **3:**1034
  as goal accomplishment tool, **3:**1032
  as narrative, **3:**1033–1034
  as networks, **3:**1032–1033
  as performance, **3:**1033
  as symbol, **3:**1033–1034
  as voice, **3:**1034
  conduit image of, **3:**1031–1032
  criticism/future, **3:**1034–1035
  overview, **3:**1031–1032
  tensions in, **3:**1035
Organizational culture, 3:1035–1039
  corporate values role in, **1:**306
  criticism/future, **3:**1038–1039
  culture and, **3:**1035–1036
  entrepreneurship affect on, **2:**448
  gender division and, **2:**538
  generated in/from organizations, **3:**1036–1037
  interpretive approach to, **3:**1038
  organizational change and, **3:**1023–1024
  organizational climate *vs.*, **3:**1028–1029
  organizational dynamics and, **3:**1037–1038
  organizational image and, **3:**1083
  various perspectives/approaches, **3:**1036–1038
Organizational culture *vs.*, **3:**1028–1029
Organizational democracy, 3:1039–1042
  actual benefits, **3:**1041–1042
  characteristics of, **3:**1040–1041
  decision-making in, **3:**1041
  possible benefits, **3:**1041
  shared residual claims in, **3:**1041
  supportive organizational structure in, **3:**1041–1042
Organizational demography, 3:1042–1044
  demography of corporations/industries, **3:**1043
  demography of workforce, **3:**1043
  formal demography *vs.*, **3:**1044
  internal organizational demography, **3:**1043
  minority tokens, **3:**1043

population studies *vs.*, **3:**1044
principles guiding analysis, **3:**1043
Organizational design, 3:1044–1047
  archetypes, **3:**1047
  command and control, **3:**1046
  coordinate and cultivate, **3:**1046
  enabling infrastructure, **3:**1047
  hetearchy, **2:**587, 784, **3:**930–931, 1046, **4:**1274
  hierarchy/alternatives to, **3:**1046
  institutional theory, **3:**1046–1047
  matrix, **3:**884–886, 1045, 1187
  mechanistic, **3:**891–893, **3:**1045
  necessity of, **3:**1047
  organic, **1:**170, **3:**1009–1011, 1045
  overview, **3:**1044–1046
  power and, **3:**1045–1046
  responsible autonomy and, **3:**1046
  U-form, **3:**929–930, 1045, 1181–1183
  See also **Design Space Management; Multidivisional form; Multisubsidiary form**
Organizational determinism vs. organizational adaptation, **3:**1011–1012
Organizational development (OD), 3:1047–1052
  assumptions about change efforts in, **3:**1050
  change management *vs.*, **3:**1050–1051
  client-centered counseling in, **3:**1049
  consultants for, **3:**1048
  criticism/future, **3:**1050–1051
  democratic principles in, **3:**1049
  humanistic orientation, **3:**1049
  human system change and, **3:**1049
  social-ecological systems orientation in, **3:**1049–1050
  social system knowledge in, **3:**1048–1049
  third-party change agent and, **3:**1049
  underlying values, **3:**1049–1050
  unfreeze-movement-refreeze formula in, **3:**1051
Organizational discourse, 3:1052–1056
  critical discourse analysis, **3:**1053
  critical view, **3:**1054
  criticism/future, **3:**1054–1056
  integrated approach, **3:**1053
  levels of discourse, **3:**1052–1053
  macro approach, **3:**1053
  meso approach, **3:**1053
  micro approach, **3:**1053
  modes of engagement, **3:**1053–1054
  positivist view, **3:**1053–1054
  postmodern view, **3:**1054
  See also See **Strategic Discourse**
Organizational discourse analysis (ODA), **1:**389
Organizational ecology, 3:1056–1059
  core concepts, **3:**1057
  core theories, **3:**1057–1058
  corporation demography and, **3:**1043
  criticism/future, **3:**1058–1059
  density dependence theory, **3:**1057–1058
  of formal organizations, **2:**516
  on organizational theory, **3:**1197–1198
  relative inertia theory of, **3:**1057
  resource partitioning theory of, **3:**1058
  See also **Ecological change**
Organizational economics, 3:1059–1062
  agency theory, **3:**1061
  business strategy, **3:**1062
  evolutionary theory, **3:**1061–1062
  on organizational theory, **3:**1198
  property rights and the theory of the firm, **3:**1061
  team production theory, **3:**1060–1061
  transaction cost economics, **3:**1060
Organizational environments, 3:1062–1066
  buffering and, **3:**1064
  coping with, **3:**1064–1065
  criticism/future, **3:**1065
  enacted environment, **3:**1064
  levels of reality in, **3:**1063
  resource dependency view on, **3:**1065
  subjective *vs.* objective, **3:**1063–1064
Organizational ergonomics, **2:**467
Organizational ethnography, 3:1066–1067
  anthropological view, **3:**1066–1067
  case studies, **3:**1066
  fieldwork, **3:**1066
  future, **3:**1067
  participant observation, **3:**1066
  pitfalls of, **3:**1067
Organizational evolution, 3:1068–1070
  criticism/future, **3:**1069
  overview, **3:**1068–1069
Organizational existentialism, 3:1070–1074
  collective *vs.* personal meanings, **3:**1072
  criticism/future, **3:**1072–1073
  example of existential authors, **3:**1071
  individuation *vs.* individualism, **3:**1072
  overview, **3:**1070–1072
Organizational field, 3:1074–1077
  criticism/future, **3:**1075–1076
  institutional theory on, **3:**1076
  overview, **3:**1074–1075
  population ecology on, **3:**1075–1076
  societal sector concept, **3:**1076
  structuration in, **3:**1075
Organizational identity, 3:1077–1081
  construed external image, **3:**1079
  corporate identity, **3:**1079
  criticism/future, **3:**1080
  culture and, **3:**1079
  desired image, **3:**1079
  future image, **3:**1079
  identity continuity, **3:**1078–1079
  identity in/identity of, **3:**1077–1078
  identity management, **3:**1079
  identity multiplicity, **3:**1078
  issues in, **3:**1078–1079
  levels of analysis, **3:**1079
  organizational change and, **3:**1024
  organizational reputation, **3:**1079

origins of, **3:**1077
projected image, **3:**1079
See also **Organizational image**
Organizational image, 3:1081–1084
   adaptive instability and, **3:**1083
   construed external image, **3:**1082
   corporate branding, **3:**1084
   corporate image, **3:**1082
   corporate reputation, **3:**1084
   criticism/future, **3:**1083–1084
   desired future image, **3:**1082
   organizational culture and, **3:**1083
   overview, **3:**1081–1082
   projected image, **3:**1082
   pseudoreality and, **3:**1083
   transparency and, **3:**1082
   See also **Organizational identity**
Organizational justice, 3:1084–1087
   distributive, **3:**1085
   group-level approaches, **3:**1087
   informational, **3:**1086
   interactional, **3:**1085–1086
   interactions among types of justice, **3:**1086–1087
   interpersonal, **3:**1086
   overview, **3:**1085–1086
   procedural, **3:**105
Organizational knowledge, 3:1087–1092
   knowledge in, of, by organization, **3:**1088
Organizational language. *See* **Language and organizations**
Organizational learning, 1:202, 3:1092–1097
   adaptive learning as, **1:**32
   applications of, **3:**1095–1096
   Carnegie School influence, **3:**1022
   cognition and behavior, **3:**1093
   communities of practice and, **1:**211
   congenital learning, **3:**1094
   deutero learning, **3:**1094
   e-commerce affect on, **2:**415
   effect on capabilities, **3:**1017–1018
   experiental learning, **3:**1094
   exploration/exploitation tension, **3:**1094
   grafting, **3:**1094
   4I framework, **3:**1093, **3:**1094
   incremental learning, **3:**1094
   knowledge-intensive firms and, **2:**757
   learning and performance, **3:**1095
   multilevel perspective, **3:**1092–1093
   process, **3:**1094
   searching/noticing, **3:**1094
   strategic choice and, **4:**1464
   transformational learning, **3:**1094
   types of learning, **3:**1093–1094
   vicarious learning, **3:**1094
Organizational literature, African, 3:1097–1100
   context/relevance, **3:**1098
   criticism/future, **3:**1098–1099
   external environment, **3:**1097–1098
   indigenous management theme in, **3:**1099

kinship solidarity theme in, **3:**1099
knowledge transfers and, **3:**1099–1100
resource dependency theme, **3:**1099–1100
ubuntu, **3:**1099
Organizational literature, Anglo-Saxon, 3:1100–1104
   overview of, **3:**1100–1101
   U.S.-British differences, **3:**1101–1104
Organizational literature, Arabic, 3:1104–1108
   Algerian context, **3:**1106–1107
   culture and organizational practice, **3:**1106–1107
   dissemination of theories/techniques, **3:**1105–1106
   diversity divide and, **3:**1104
   Egyptian context, **3:**1106
   family-owned companies/self-taught management, **3:**1107
   language divide and, **3:**1104–1105
   main areas of interest, **3:**1105
   Tunisian context, **3:**1106
Organizational literature, Asian, 3:1108–1112
   China, **3:**1109
   Confucianism and, **3:**1108
   Daosism, **3:**1108–1109
   India, **3:**1109
   Indonesia, **3:**1109–1110
   Japan, **3:**1110
   Malaysia, **3:**1110
   overview, **3:**1108–1111
   Singapore, **3:**1110
   South Korea, **3:**1110–1111
   Vietnam, **3:**1111
Organizational literature, Brazilian, 3:1112–1113
   future, **3:**1113
   overview, **3:**1112–1113
Organizational literature, Eastern European, 3:1113–1116
   after political changes, **3:**1115
   before 1990, **3:**1114–1115
   criticism, **3:**1115–1116
   Hungary, **3:**1114
   Poland, **3:**1114
   Soviet Union, **3:**1114
   Yugoslavia, former, **3:**1114–1115
Organizational literature, Francophone, 3:1106–1123
   actor/power relationship/social regulation, **3:**1118–1119
   as diversified field, **3:**1118
   as original field, **3:**1121–1122
   cultures/symbolism/identities, **3:**1119–1120
   industrial sociology/organizational analysis, **3:**1116–1118
   management/strategy, **3:**1121
   psychic life/work/organization, **3:**1120–1121
   Quebec and, **3:**1117–1118
Organizational literature, Germanic, 3:1123–1128
   business economics and, **3:**1123–1125
   from sociology, **3:**1125–1126
   in new century, **3:**1126–1127
Organizational literature, Latin American, 3:1128–1133
   criticism commentary, **3:**1130–1132
   overview, **3:**1128–1130

**Organizational literature, Scandinavian,
   3:1133–1137**
  criticism/future, 3:1136–1138
  overview, 3:1133–1136
Organizationally closed corporation, 1:91
Organizational man, 3:1137–1139
Organizational memory, 1:202, **3:**1088, **1139–1142**
  demand-side elements, 3:1139–1140
  distributed structure, 3:1140
  integrating supply/demand sides, 3:1140
  overlapping, 3:1140
  performance impact, 3:1141–1142
  risk-based storage, 3:1140
  social retrieval, 3:1141
  supply-side conceptualizations, 3:1139
Organizational misbehavior, 3:1142–1144
  misbehavior by organizations, 3:1142–1143
  misbehavior in organizations, 3:1143
Organizational mortality, 3:1144–1146
  adolescence, liability of, 3:1145
  founder characteristics, 3:1146
  newness/smallness liabilities, 3:1144–1145
  obsolescence, liability of, 3:1145
  organizational ecology, 3:1145–1146
  real options, 3:1146
Organizational paradox, 3:1146–1149
  change-stability pair, 3:1147
  dialectic *vs.*, 3:1147
  dualities *vs.*, 3:1147
  forced merger in, 3:1148
  integration-differentiation, 3:1147
  integration in, 3:1148
  managing, 3:1148
  neutralization in, 3:1148
  open-closed paradox, 3:1147
  selection in, 3:1148
  separation in, 3:1148
  transcendence in, 3:1149
Organizational paranoia, 3:1149–1151
Organizational performance, 3:1151–1153
  multiple stakeholder approach, 3:1151–1152
  rational goal approach, 3:1151
Organizational philosophy, 3:1151–1153
  cognitive approach and, 1:185
  criticism/future, 3:1155–1156
  overview, 3:1154–1155
  realism in, 4:1357
  relativism in, 4:1371–1372
Organizational politics, 3:1156–1160
  as essentially contested concept, 3:1156–1157
  coalitions and, 1:178
  criticism/future, 3:1158–1159
  traditions in, 3:1157–1158
Organizational psychology, 1:184–185
Organizational reputation (OR), 3:1079
Organizational resilience, 3:1160–1161
  behavioral characteristics, 3:1161
  cognitive elements, 3:1160–1161
  context and, 3:1161

  environmental conditions, 3:1161
  rebound-oriented, 3:1160
Organizational rhetoric, 3:1162–1166
  context affect on, 3:1164
  criticism/future, 3:1163–1164
  differentiation rhetoric, 3:1163
  discourse theory, 3:1163–1164
  indexicality and, 3:1164
  institutional theory, 3:1164
  integration rhetoric, 3:1163
  intertextuality, 3:1165
  issue management rhetoric, 3:1162
  kairos, 3:1165
  language-in-use studies, 3:1164
  marketing rhetoric, 3:1162
  overview, 3:1162–1163
  polyvocality, 3:1165
  presence, 3:1165
  rhetorical congruence, 3:1163
  speech act theory and, 3:1164
  strategy rhetoric, 3:1163
Organizational rituals, 3:1166–1169
  interaction ritual, 3:1168
  in total institution, 3:1167
  organizational rites, 3:1167–1168
  organizational rituals, 3:1166–1167
  rites of conflict, 3:1168
  rites of degradation, 3:1167, 3:1192
  rites of enhancement, 3:1167, 3:1192
  rites of integration, 3:1168, 3:1192
  rites of passage, 3:1167, 3:1192
  rites of renewal, 3:1167–1138, 3:1192
  ritual equilibrium, 3:1168
Organizational routines, 3:1169–1173
  as generative systems, 3:1170–1171
  as genes, 3:1170
  as habits, 3:1170
  as programs, 3:1170
  as skills, 3:1170
  dynamic capabilities as, 3:1171
  metaphors for, 3:1170
  metaroutines, 3:1171
  organizational capabilities relation to, 3:1018
  stability/change and, 3:1171–1172
Organizational rules, 3:1173–1175
  criticism/future, 3:1174–1175
  extraorganizational rules, 3:1174
  reproduction rules, 3:1174
  social rules, 3:1174
  state rules, 3:1174
  strategic rules, 3:1174
  technical rules, 3:1174
Organizational spirituality, 3:1175–1178
  criticism/future, 3:1176–1177
  mystical spirituality, 3:1176
  religious spirituality, 3:1176
  secular spirituality, 3:1176
Organizational stigma, 3:1178–1181
  courtesy stigma, 3:1180

enactment of, **3:**1179–1180
status and, **3:**1178–1179
Organizational strategy, 3:1181–1185
central functions/services, **3:**1183
competitive, **3:**1181
conglomerate discount, **3:**1182
corporate, **3:**1181
criticism/future, **3:**1184–1185
from M- to N-form, **3:**1183–1184
from U- to M-form, **3:**1181–1183
future, **3:**1184–1185
hyperarchy, **3:**1184
linkage influence, **3:**1183
matrix, **3:**1183
parenting advantage, **3:**1182–1183
portfolio, **3:**1181
stand-alone influence, **3:**1183
value chimera, **3:**1184
Organizational structure, 3:1185–1188
causal model of, **3:**1186
criticism/future, **3:**1187–1188
functional structure, **3:**1186–1187
hybrid structure, **3:**1187
hypertext, **3:**1188
ideal type, **3:**1186
matrix structure, **3:**1187
multidivisional structure, **3:**1187
network structure, **3:**1187
structure-in-process, **3:**1187
Organizational subcultures, 3:1188–1190
criticism/future, **3:**1189–1190
overview, **3:**1188–1189
Organizational support theory, **4:**1230
Organizational symbolism, 3:1191–1194
artifacts, **3:**1192
criticism/future, **3:**1192–1193
myths, **3:**1192
rites and ceremonies, **3:**1192
verbal symbols, **3:**1191–1192
Organizational taboos, 3:1194–1196
Organizational theory (OT), 3:1196–1200
contingency theory on, **3:**1197
epistemology and, **2:**461, **2:**462
interpretive theory on, **3:**1198–1199
neoinstitutional analysis on, **3:**1197–1198
on behavioral theory of the firm, **1:**96
on managerial rationality, **3:**872
on social constructionism, **4:**1429–1430
organizational ecology on, **3:**1197–1198
organizational economics on, **3:**1198
postmodernism and, **3:**1199
postpositivism on, **3:**1200
radical humanism and, **3:**1199
radical structuralism and, **3:**1199
resource dependence view on, **3:**1197
scientistic orientation of, **3:**1196
social constructivism and, **3:**1199–1200
sociological approach, **3:**1196–1197
subjectivist approach to, **3:**1196

subjectivist epistemology and, **3:**1199–1200
See also **Organization theory, historical analysis**
Organizational therapy, 3:1200–1203
areas of intervention, **3:**1201
client, **3:**1203
group organizational therapy, **3:**1202
steps in intervention process, **3:**1201
therapist training, **3:**1202–1203
transference reactions as change tool, **3:**1201–1202
triangle of relationships, **3:**1201
Organizational toxicity, 3:1203–1205
criticism/future, **3:**1205
sources of, **3:**1204
Organization science (OS). *See* **Epistemology**
Organization theory, historical analysis, 3:1205–1208
criticism/future, **3:**1205–1207
overview, **3:**1205–1206
Organized oblivion, **3:**852
Organizing reflection concept, **4:**1365
Orlikowski, W., **3:**1091, **4:**1482–1483
Orton, J. D., **2:**833, 834
Oswick, C., **3:**896, 898, 899–900, 1053
Otherness. *See* **Alterity (otherness)**
Ouchi, W. G., **3:**908, 930, **4:**1549–1550
Output standardization, **1:**281
Outsourcing, 3:1208–1211
arms length, **2:**1210, **3:**1209
criticism/future, **3:**1209
long-term, **3:**1209
Ownership, Location, Internationalization (OLI) paradigm, **3:**933
Ownership advantage theory, **2:**703
Ownership and control, 3:1211–1214
agency problem, **1:**360, **3:**1061, 1211
concentrated blockholder shareholding, **3:**1212
criticism/future, **3:**1213–1214
dispersed ownership, **3:**1211–1212
private benefits of control, **3:**1212
Ozcelik, H., **3:**1207, 1208

Panopticism, **1:**70–71, **1:**390, **4:**1215–1217
Paradigm incommensurability, 4:1217–1218
discursive view, **4:**1218
epistemological, **4:**1217
integrationist view, **4:**1217
pluralist view, **4:**1218
protectionist view, **4:**1217–1218
See also **Paradigms**
Paradigms, 4:1218–1222
Burrell-Morgan framework, **4:**1217, 1219, 1221–1222
epistemological, **4:**1217
functionalist paradigm, **4:**1220
interpretive paradigm, **4:**1220–1221
methodological, **4:**1217
methods/research interests, **4:**1219
ontological, **4:**1217
philosophy of science on, **4:**1244–1245
radical humanism paradigm, **4:**1221
radical structuralism paradigm, **4:**1221
See also **Paradigm incommensurability**

Paradigm wars, **3:**993, **4:**1217
Paradox, 4:1222–1225
   acceptance of, **4:**1222–1223
   confrontation of, **4:**1223
   relation of, **4:**1223–1224
Parasitism, in network coevolution, **3:**964
PARC (people, architecture, routines, and culture), **3:**1045
Pareto principle, **3:**880, **3:**954
Parington, A., **3:**851
Parker, M., **4:**1259
Parmenides, **3:**995
Parsons, T., **1:**89
   functionalist view of, **4:**1440, 1602
   on action frame of reference, **3:**995–996
   on coercion/inducement, **1:**402
   on identity, **2:**630
   on social behavior, **2:**528
   on social systems, **4:**1437
   reception of views of, **4:**1603
Parsons, W., **1:**128, 129
Partial reinforcement, **3:**1002
Partial reinforcement extinction effect (PRE), **3:**1003
Participant observation, **1:**58, **3:**1066
Participation, 4:1225–1229
   actual, **4:**1228
   conditions for success, **4:**1226–1227
   criticism/future, **4:**1227–1429
   defining, **4:**1225
   employee stock ownership, **4:**1226
   financial, **4:**1226
   forms of, **4:**1225–1226
   gainsharing, **4:**1226
   intended, **4:**1228
   motives for, **4:**1226
   outcomes of, **4:**1226
   participative management, **4:**1225
   profit sharing, **4:**1226
   quality circles, **4:**1225
   quality of life committees, **4:**1225
   representative, **4:**1225
   self-managed work teams, **4:**1225
Participative management, **4:**1225
Participative structures, on hierarchy, **2:**587
Participatory action research (PAR), **1:**22, **3:**985, **4:**1340
Partnership, **1:**196
   corporation *vs.*, **2:**741
Part-time contingent workers, **1:**270
Pascal, B., **4:**1371
Passeron, C., **1:**344
Patents, **2:**692–693
Patriarchy, **1:**87, **2:**538
Pavlov's classical conditioning experiment, **1:**100
Peer-to-peer working and networking, **2:**587
Peirce, C., **4:**1298, 1299, 1300
Penrose, E. T., **3:**879, **4:**1401, 1466–1467
Pentland, B., **3:**1090
Perceived organizational support (POS), 4:1229–1233
   additional support relationships, **4:**1231
   organizational support theory on, **4:**1230

   perceived supervisor support, **4:**1230–1231
   perceived team support, **4:**1231
   procedural justice and, **4:**1230
   psychological contract and, **4:**1232
   reciprocity norm and, **4:**1230
   social exchange theory on, **4:**1230
   work status and, **4:**1231–1232
Perceived supervisor support (PSS), **4:**1230–1231
Perfect competition, **1:**217, **3:**877, 879
Performance
   gender/sex as, **2:**543, 546
   organizational communication as, **3:**1033
Performance appraisal (PA), 4:1233–1235
   criticism/future, **4:**1233–1234
   effectiveness from employee perspective, **4:**1233–1234
   effectiveness from supervisory perspective, **4:**1233
   overview, **4:**1233
   See also **Performance-driven evaluation**
Performance-driven evaluation (PDE), 4:1235–1236
   See also Performance appraisal
Performativity
   exploitation and, **2:**495–496
   masculinities and, **3:**883
   of organizational improvisation, **2:**641
Permission marketing, **2:**415–416
Perrow, C., **1:**234–236, **2:**593–594
   on normal accidents, **3:**989–990, 991, 992
Personal construct theory, **1:**189
Personal domination, **1:**401, 402
Personality, five-factor model, 4:1236–1239
   agreeableness, **4:**1238
   conscientiousness, **4:**1238
   criticism/future, **4:**1238–1239
   extraversion, **4:**1237
   neuroticism, **4:**1237–1238
   openness to experience, **4:**1238
Personality types, **4:**1607–1608
Personal psychology, **3:**1101
Person-environment (P-E) fit, **2:**738
Persuasion research, **1:**79
PERT (program evaluation and review technique), **4:**1319
Peters, T., **1:**155, **3:**867–368, 869–870, **4:**1378
Pettigrew, A., **2:**448
Pfeffer, J., **1:**77–78, 79, 219, **2:**665–666, 738, **3:**909, 1043, 1063, 1064–1065, 1289
Phenomenology, 4:1239–1243, 1485
   epoché concept in, **4:**1242–1243
   life-world concept, **4:**1240, **4:**1421
   organization concept, **4:**1242
   relationality concept, **4:**1240–1441, 1242, 1243
   representation concept, **4:**1242
Phenotype, **2:**480
Phillips, N., **4:**1258
Philosophy. *See* **Organizational philosophy**
Philosophy of science, 4:1243–1246
   critical realism and, **4:**1245–1246
   ontology-epistemology debate, **4:**1243–1244
   paradigms and, **4:**1244–1245

postmodernism and, **4:**1245
reflexivity and, **4:**1245, 1246
Physical asset specificity, **1:**75
Physical ergonomics, **2:**465–466
Physical needs, **3:**920
Piaget, J., **1:**82, **2:**804, **3:**998, 1122, **4:**1364, 1440
Pike, K. L., **2:**427, 428, 478–479
Pindar, C. C., **3:**901–902
Plato, **2:**586, 795–796, **4:**1371, 1596–1597
Platonists, and constructivism, **1:**260
Play, 4:1247–1249
   criticism/future, **4:**1249
   overview, **4:**1247–1429
Pluralist view, on labor relations, **2:**766
PMBOK (project management body of
   knowledge), **4:**1319
Podcast, **1:**246
Poetic license, **3:**945
Poincaré, H., **1:**156, **1:**230, **2:**830, **3:**1122
Polanyi, K., **2:**419, **2:**420, **4:**1503–1506, **4:**1505
Polanyi, M., **2:**758–759
Political anatomy of human body, **2:**565
Political correctness and, **3:**928
Political economy of organizations,
   1:161–162, **4:1249–1251**
   criticism/future, **4:**1250–1251
   internal/external economy, **4:**1250
   internal/external polity, **4:**1250
Political science, on new public management, **3:**981
Politics, 4:1251–1255
   criticism/future, **4:**1253–1255
   overview, **4:**1251–1253
   See also **Politics of organizational culture**
Politics of organizational culture, 4:1255–1257
   differentiation studies, **4:**1256–1257
   fragmentation studies, **4:**1257
   integration studies, **4:**1256
Pólos, L., **3:**1059
Polyphonic dialogism, **3:**999
Polyvocality, **3:**1165
Pondy, L. R., **3:**998, 999, 1191
Poor, V., **1:**164
Poor Laws, 117
Popper, K., **2:**773, 830, **4:**1603–1604
Popular culture, 4:1257–1260
   criticism/future, **4:**1260
   emplotment device, **4:**1258–1459
   overview of, **4:**1258–1259
Population ecology, **2:**678–679
   on environmental determinism, **2:**452
   on organizational change, **3:**1023
   on organizational fields, **3:**1075–1076
Porter, M., **2:**709, **3:**972, **4:**1380, 1466, 1471–1472, 1599–1600
Portfolio investment, **2:**703, **4:**1368
Portfolio matrix, **3:**1181
Position Analysis Questionnaire (PAQ), **4:**1416
Positioning school, **4:**1380
Positive organizational behavior (POB), **4:**1267

Positive organizational scholarship (POS), 1:307,
   2:432, **4:1260–1266**, 1267
   as not value-neutral, **4:**1261–1262
   individual level of analysis, **4:**1263
   organizational in, **4:**1261
   organizational level of analysis, **4:**1263
   overview, **4:**1262–1265
   positive in, **4:**1261
   scholarship in, **4:**1261
Positive psychological capital, **2:**798
Positive psychology, 4:1266–1270
   on leadership, **2:**797–798
   organization studies and, **4:**1267–1268
   positive organizational behavior, **4:**1267
   positive organizational scholarship, **4:**1267
   scientific rigor, objective truth, and ream, **4:**1269
Positive reinforcement, **3:**1002
Positive zero-sum games, **3:**1157
Positivism, 4:1270–1273
   constructivism *vs.*, **2:**459–**2:**460
   criticism/future, **4:**1271–1272
   epistemological, **4:**1270
   materialist, **4:**1270
   on organizational discourse, **3:**1053–1054
   on truth, **4:**1579, **4:**1580
   overview, **4:**1270–1271
   positivist determinism, **4:**1272
   See also **Logical positivism**
Positivist determinism, **4:**1272
Post-bureaucratic organizations, 4:1273–1275
Postcapitalism, **1:**142
Postcolonial theory (PT), 4:1275–1278
   antirationalism and, **1:**62
   criticism/future, **4:**1277
   on gender research, **2:**546
   on managerial rationality, **3:**871
   on value-free conception of science, **4:**1604
   overview, **4:**1275–1277
Post-decision dissonance, **1:**187
Post-Fordist economy, 2:590, **4:1278–1280**
   criticism/future, **4:**1279–1280
   flexible specialization in, **4:**1278–1279
   overview, **4:**1278–1279
   See also **Liberal technologies of regulation**
Posthuman, **2:**609
Postmodernism, 4:1280–1283
   antirationalism and, **1:**63
   critical analysis and, **1:**315
   critical theory, **1:**331, 332
   criticism/future, **4:**1282–1283
   deconstruction and, **1:**368, 369
   effect on grand narratives, **2:**568–569
   influence on architecture and organizations, **1:**69–70
   modernism *vs.*, **3:**911–912
   on class, **1:**162–163
   on critical theory, **1:**331, 332
   on metaphor, **3:**899
   on organizational discourse, **3:**1053–1054
   on organizational identity, **3:**1077

on organizational theory, **3:**1199
on truth, **4:**1579–1580
overview, **4:**1280–1281
philosophy of science and, **4:**1245
Postmodernity, 4:1283–1285
criticism/future research, **4:**1285
life-world concept, **4:**1283
overview, **4:**1283–1285
Postmodern Lacan, **2:**771–772
Postpositivism, **2:**831, **3:**1200
Poststructuralism, 4:1285–1288
antirationalism and, **1:**62–63
consumer culture and, **1:**263
critical analysis and, **1:**315
critical management studies and, **1:**322–323
critical realism and, **1:**329
critical theory and, **1:**331, **1:**332
criticism/future, **4:**1287–1288
deconstruction and, **1:**368
on agency-structure debate, **1:**48
on gender division, **2:**540
on gendered organization, **2:**543–544
on punishment/violence in organizations, **4:**1335
on sustainable development, **4:**1494
overview, **4:**1286–1287
Powell, W., **3:**958, 976, 1023, 1074, 1075, **4:**1316
Power, 4:1288–1291
as tangible resource control, **4:**1288–1289
criticism/future, **4:**1290–1291
non-decision making as dimension of, **4:**1289
organizational design and, **3:**1045–1046
overview, **4:**1288–1290
professions and, **4:**1316
Power, M., **3:**869
Power distance, **1:**336
Power sharing, **3:**1176
Powers of association, **1:**16
Practical intelligence, **2:**434
Practical knowledge, **1:**35
Practice, 4:1291–1298
aesthetics of organization and, **1:**39
best practices, **4:**1296
criticism/future, **4:**1294
engaging with dynamic nature of, **4:**1294–1297
internal/external goods of practice, **4:**1293
interpractice dynamics, **4:**1295–1296
intrapractice dynamics, **4:**1295
malpractice, **4:**1296
practising, **4:**1294–1295
promising practices, **4:**1296
relation with intention/practical judgment, **4:**1293–1294
relation with rules/routines, **4:**1292–1293
Practice turn, **3:**996
Pragmatic validity, **2:**722
Pragmatism, 4:1298–1301
abductive inference and, **4:**1299
as radical theory of experience, **4:**1299
as theory of truth, **4:**1298–1299
criticism/future, **4:**1299–1301

fixing a belief, **4:**1299
integrity and, **2:**689
scientific management and, **4:**1394–1395
Praxeology, **3:**1114
Preference shareholders, **4:**1413
Premise reflection, **1:**36, 37
Prescriptive theory, 4:1301–1303
benchmarking prescriptions *vs.*, **4:**1301
criticism/future, **4:**1302–1303
high-performance workplace practices, **4:**1302
Presence, rhetorical, **3:**1165
Prêt-à-porter metaphor, **3:**851
Price-output decisions, **3:**879
Prigogine, I., **1:**155
Prisoner's dilemma, 2:532, **4:1303–1304**
Prisons, **4:**1215–1216
Privatization, **3:**961
Procedural justice (PJ), 3:105, **4:1304–1306**
criticism/future, **4:**1305–1306
distributive justice and, **4:**1305
fairness and, **1:**274, **4:**1304, **4:**1305
interactional justice and, **4:**1305
Procedural loose coupling, **2:**835
Procedural simulation model, **1:**244
Procrastination, 4:1306–1308
academic, **4:**1306
compulsive, **4:**1306
criticism/future, **4:**1307–1308
decisional, **4:**1306
individual, **4:**1307
intraindividual, **4:**1306–1307
life routine, **4:**1306
Product innovation, 4:1308–1311
criticism/future, **4:**1310–1311
incremental, **4:**1308
modular, **4:**1308
overview, **4:**1308–1310
process innovation *vs.*, **4:**1308–1409
radical, **4:**1309–1310
strategic learning role in, **4:**1310
Product life cycle theory, **2:**702, **2:**709
Profanity notion, **3:**1195
Professional service firms (PSFs), 4:1311–1315
criticism/future, **4:**1314
knowledge in, **4:**1313
managing professionals, **4:**1313–1314
scale/significance of, **4:**1312–1313
Professions, 4:1315–1318
criticism/future, **4:**1317–1418
neoinstitutionalist focus on, **4:**1316–1317
power perspective, **4:**1316
trait-based approach, **4:**1315–1316
Profit sharing, **4:**1226
Program for International Student Assessment (PISA), **4:**1416
Project identity, **2:**634
Project management (PM), 4:1318–1321
criticism/future, **4:**1319–1320
overview, **4:**1318–1319

PERT program for, **4:**1319
PMBOK program for, **4:**1319
Promotion escalator, **2:**734
Property rights, **3:**1061
Prospect theory, **3:**1022
Protectionism, **2:**702
Protestant ethic, 4:1321–1324
    Calvinism and, **4:**1321
    criticism/future, **4:**1322–1423
    Lebensfuhrung concept, **4:**1321–1322
    Weber on, **1:**293, **4:**1321–1322
Proximal climate, **3:**1029
Pseudoreality, **3:**1083
Psychoanalytic approach, 4:1324–1327
    criticism/future, **4:**1326–1327
    on gender division, **2:**538
    organizations and, **4:**1324–1326
    psychoanalyzing organizations, **4:**1326
    studying organizations psychoanalytically, **4:**1326
    toward management, **3:**1120–1121
Psychodynamics
    of work, **3:**1120
    on emotion, **2:**429
    on family business, **2:**500
    on organizational identity, **3:**1077
Psychological capital, **2:**798
Psychological contract, 4:1327–1329
    features, **4:**1327–1328
    mutuality and, **4:**1328
    types, **4:**1328
    violation of, **4:**1328–1329
Psychological empowerment, **2:**441
Psychological needs, **3:**920–921
Psychological safety, 4:1329–1332
    criticism/future, **4:**1331–1332
    group cohesiveness *vs.*, **4:**1329–1330
    team, **4:**1329, **4:**1330
    themes and findings, **4:**1330–1331
    trust role in, **4:**1330
Psychological tendency, **1:**76–77
Psychology
    cognitive approach and, **1:**184
    on leadership, **2:**797–798
Public choice theory, 4:1332–1334
    criticism/future, **4:**1333–1334
    economic rationalism and, **2:**418
    overview, **4:**1333
Public knowledge, and business journalism, **1:**129–130
Pugh, D., **3:**1197
Pullen, A., **2:**631, 632–633, 634
Punctuated equilibrium, **1:**29, **1:**30, **1:**165, **4:**1508–1509
Punishment and violence in organizations, 4:1334–1337
    behavior science on, **4:**1335
    functionalist approach, **4:**1334
    future, **4:**1336
    organization as entity approach, **4:**1334
    organization as process approach, **4:**1334
    poststructuralist approach, **4:**1335
    power-knowledge concept and, **4:**1335
    social science on, **4:**1335
Putnam, L., **3:**899–900
Putnam, R. D., **4:**1424

Qualitative approaches, **3:**888–889, **4:**1339–1342
    case study, **4:**1340
    cause and effect issues, **4:**1340
    clinical models, **4:**1340
    criticism, **4:**1340–1431
    ethnography, **4:**1340
    grounded theory, **4:**1340
    lack of generalization in, **4:**1340
    participatory action research, **4:**1340
    personal bias in, **4:**1340
    strategies in, **4:**1339–1340
    thick description and, **4:**1340
    variability, **4:**1340
    See also **Qualitative interview; Quantitative models and methods**
Qualitative interview, 4:1342–1344
    criticism/future, **4:**1343
    localist, **4:**1343
    neopositivist, **4:**1342
    romanticist, **4:**1342
Quality circles, **4:**1225
Quality culture, **4:**1550
Quality movement, **3:**1152
Quality of life committees, **4:**1225
Quality of Working Life (QWL), **2:**441
Quantitative models and methods, 3:889, 4:1344–1348
    advanced methods, **4:**1347–1348
    analysis at multiple levels, **4:**1348
    analytical methods, **4:**1347
    archival data, **4:**1346
    basic statistical methods, **4:**1347
    central terms, **4:**1344
    confirmatory factor analysis, **4:**1348
    data collection methods, **4:**1346
    diaries, **4:**1346
    experimental design, **4:**1345–1346
    interviews, **4:**1346
    observations, **4:**1346
    questionnaires, **4:**1346
    reliability, **4:**1346–1347
    research designs, **4:**1345–1346
    sampling methods, **4:**1345
    structural equation modeling, **4:**1347–1348
    survey design, **4:**1345
    triangulation, **4:**1348
    validity, **4:**1347
    See also **Qualitative approaches**
Quebec, **3:**1117–1118
Questionnaires, **4:**1346
QUEST mnemonic, **2:**512
Quetelet, Adolphe, **1:**56

Racist oppression, **3:**1007
Radical constructivism, **2:**460

Radical feminism, 4:1349–1351
  criticism/future, **4:**1349–1350
  overview, **4:**1349–1350
Radical humanism, 3:1199, **4:**1351–1355
  current "reformist" management debate on, **4:**1352–1353
  ruptures in alienated work, **4:**1353–1354
Radical humanism paradigm, **4:**1221
Radical innovation, **2:**671, **4:**1308, 1309–1310
Radical structuralism, **3:**1199
Radical structuralism paradigm, **4:**1221
Randall, D., **3:**1138
RAND Corporation, **2:**376, **3:**972, **4:**1391
Rational bureaucracy, **1:**87
Rational choice institutionalism, **2:**767–768
Rational choice theory (RCT), 4:1355–1356
  criticism/future, **4:**1355–1456
  decision-making theory vs., **1:**226
  on relational games, **2:**685
  overview, **4:**1355
  See also **Public choice theory**
Rational determinism, **2:**452
Rationality
  antirationalism vs., **1:**61, 62–63
  critical analysis and, **1:**313–314
  ecological, **3:**862
  emotion and, **2:**431
  formal, **1:**114, **3:**870
  instrumental, **1:**197, 208, 333
  irrationality of, **3:**887
  neoinstitutional theory on, **3:**872
  rationalization of, **1:**113
  substantive, **3:**870
  See also **Bounded rationality**
Rationalization of rationality, **1:**113
Rational/natural system models, **2:**514–515
Rational open system approaches, **2:**515
Rawls, J., **2:**463, **x**813, **4:**1253, 1492, 1595
Reagan, R., **2:**781–782, **3:**959
Realism, 4:1356–1359
  constructivism and, **1:**259–261
  critical, **1:**66, **1:**261
  criticism/future, **4:**1358–1359
  overview, **4:**1356–1358
  See also **Antirealism**
Realistic, Investigative, Artistic, Social, Engineering, and Conventional personality types, **4:**1607–1608
Realistic information hypothesis, **4:**1360
Realistic job preview, **4:**1360
Reality
  construction of, **1:**391
  hyper-reality, **4:**1281
  See also **Ontology**
Reay, T., **3:**1074, **3:**1075
Recognition heuristic, **2:**482
Recruiting, 4:1359–1362
  context of, **4:**1359
  criticism/future, **4:**1360–1361
  internal/external, **4:**1360
  standard practice, **4:**1359–1360

Redding, W. C., **3:**1031
Reducibility thesis, **3:**996
Redundancy, **2:**593, **x**694, **3:**989, 990, 991, 992, 1141–1142, **4:**1377
Reengineering, 3:852, **4:**1362–1364, **x**1393
  criticism/future, **4:**1363
  information technology role in, **4:**1362
  overview, **4:**1362–1363
  visionary leadership role in, **4:**1362–1363
Reflective action learning sets (RALS), **1:**19
Reflective practice, 4:1364–1366
  characteristics of critically informed, **4:**1365
  organizing reflection concept, **4:**1365
  reflection-in-action concept, **4:**1364
  roots of, **4:**1364
Reflective practitioner, **3:**856, **4:**1364
Reflexive modernization, **3:**1090, **3:**1091
Reflexivity, 4:1366–1368
  actionable knowledge and, **1:**15
  constructionist approach to, **4:**1366
  criticism/future, **4:**1367
  deconstructionist approach to, **4:**1366–1367
  in critical management studies, **1:**322
  modernity on, **3:**915
  philosophy of science on, **4:**1245, 1246
  role in global management learning, **3:**857–858
Reflexive observation (RO) learning mode, **2:**488, 490, 491
Regional convergence, **1:**276
Regionalization and capital movement, 4:1368–1371
  capital flow and, **4:**1368
  criticism/future, **4:**1370
  foreign direct investment, **4:**1368
  global south inflows, **4:**1369
  overview, **4:**1368–1370
  portfolio investment, **4:**1368
Relational aesthetics, **1:**74
Relational approach
  to class, **1:**161
  to networks, **3:**968
Relational contract, **1:**97
Relational coordination, **1:**282–283
Relational games, **2:**685
Relational serendipity, **4:**1407
Relational social capital, **4:**1424–1425
Relative inertia theory, **3:**1057
Relativism, 4:1371–1374
  criticism/future, **4:**1371–1372
  in philosophy, **4:**1371–1372
  moral vs. epistemological, **4:**1371
  stronger vs. weaker forms of, **4:**1371–1372
Reliability, **2:**722
  quantitative data, **4:**1346–1347
  validity vs., **3:**890
Reliability coefficient, **3:**890
Relief theory, **2:**621
Religious spirituality, **3:**1176
Remunerative power, **1:**401
Repertory grid, **1:**189

Replication strategy, 3:1068–1069, **4:**1374–1376
 accuracy issues, **4:**1375–1376
 Arrow core template, **4:**1374–1375
 process of replication, **4:**1375
 replicators/replica, **4:**1375
 research implications, **4:**1376
 source, **4:**1374
Representation, **2:**460–461
Representative democracy, **2:**650
Representative participation, by employee, **4:**1225
Requisite variety law, **1:**352
Research and development (R&D), **1:**1, 51, **4:**1459
Research-oriented action research (RO-AR), **1:**22, 23
Residual property rights, **3:**1061
Resistance to change, 4:1376–1379
 as reasonable response to traumatic event, **4:**1378
 classical foundational studies, **4:**1377
 criticism/future, **4:**1379
 deficiency concept of, **4:**1378
 management-oriented research bias, **4:**1377–1378
 modalities of resistance, **4:**1378
 poor management as cause, **4:**1378
 sluggish organizational structures as cause, **4:**1378
 target of, **4:**1378–1379
 though commission, **4:**1378
 though omission, **4:**1378
Resource allocation. *See* **Coase theorem**
**Resource-based view of the firm (RBV),
 1:**409, **4:**1379–1382
 criticism/future, **4:**1382
 definition of concepts, **4:**1380
 ex ante/ex poste limits to competition, **4:**1381–1382
 heterogeneity and, **4:**1381
 strategic discourse and, **4:**1466–1467
 strategic human resource management, **4:**1469
 superior resources, **4:**1381
 underlying assumptions and deductions, **4:**1380–1382
 uniqueness of resources, **4:**1381
 vertical integration and, **4:**1610, 1611, 1612,
  1613–1614
Resource dependence, 4:1383–1385
 adaptation/dominance and, **4:**1383–1384
 collective strategy, **4:**1383
 criticism/future, **4:**1384–1385
 focus on resources, **4:**1383
 in formal organizations, **2:**516
 on organizational environments, **3:**1065
 on organizational theory, **3:**1197
 proprietary strategy, **4:**1383
 resource environment, **4:**1383
 strategic choice and, **4:**1385
 strategic contingencies theory on, **4:**1384
Resource partitioning theory, **3:**1058
Responsible autonomy, **3:**1046, **4:**1274
Return-on-investment, **1:**164
Return to market, **1:**282
Revealed cognitive map, **1:**190
Revealed *vs.* designed collaboration, **1:**195–196
Reverential imitation, fashion as, **2:**503

Reverse culture shock (RCS), 4:1385–1387
 criticism/future, **4:**1386–1387
 overview, **4:**1386
Reynaud, J.-D., **3:**1119
Rhetorical congruence, **3:**1163
Rhizome networks, **3:**973–974
Rhoades, L., **4:**1231
Rhodes, C., **3:**848, **4:**1258–1259, 1260
Ricardo, D., **2:**708, **3:**954–955, **4:**1252
Richardson, G., **3:**879
Ricoeur, P., **2:**584
Riker, W., **4:**1252
Rio Earth Summit, **4:**1492
Risk
 in liberal technologies of regulation, **2:**815
 spare, **2:**468
Risk homeostasis, **2:**468
Risk management, 4:1387–1389
 criticism/future, **4:**1388–1389
 organizing activities for, **4:**1387–1388
Rites of conflict, **3:**1168
Rites of degradation, **3:**1167, 1192
Rites of enhancement, **3:**1167, 1192
Rites of integration, **3:**1168, 1192
Rites of passage, **3:**1167, 1192
Rites of renewal, **3:**1167–1138, 1192
Ritual equilibrium, **3:**1168
Rituals. *See* **Organizational Rituals**
Ritzer, G., **2:**598, 704, **3:**838
Roberts, J., **3:**1045
Robinson, S. L., **3:**1207–1208
Robinson, W. S., **1:**339–340
Rogers, E., **3:**849
Rokeach, M., **4:**1607
Role theory, on gender division, **2:**538
Roper, D., **3:**882
Rorty, R., **3:**993, 994, **4:**1298, 1300, 1371, 1395
Rothschild-Whitt, J., **2:**649
Rotter, J., **2:**827, 828
Rowan, B., **3:**975, 1023
Rowntree, B., **1:**165
Roy, D., **4:**1551, 1635–1636
Rule-based simulation model, **1:**244
Rule utilitarianism, **4:**1594, 1595
Russell, B., **1:**56, 57, **2:**721, 830
Russell, R. F., **2:**786–787
Ryder, R., **2:**609

Sacks, H., **1:**391, **2:**776
Safety climate, **3:**1029
Sagan, S., **2:**593–594, **3:**991
Said, E., **4:**1275
Sainssulieu, R., **3:**1119
Saint-Simon, H. de, **4:**1601
Salancik, G. R., **1:**77–78, 79, 219, **2:**665–666,
 738, 835, **3:**909, 1063, 1064–1065
Salovey, P., **2:**434
Sampling methods, **4:**1345
Samuelson, P., **2:**831

Sandberg, J., **2:**722
Sapir, E., **2:**503, 505, **3:**949
Sarbanes-Oxley Act, **1:**7
Sartre, J.-P., **2:**608
Satisficing, **1:**106, 363, **3:**861, 879
   antirationalism and, **1:**61
Saussure, F. de, **1:**391, **4:**1286, 1440
Scenario planning (SP), 4:1391–1393
   criticism/future, **4:**1391–1392
   foresight in, **4:**1391
   intuitive logic approach to, **4:**1392
   overview, **4:**1391–1392
Schein, E.
   on corporate culture, **1:**293–294, 295
   on corporate values, **1:**306
   on entrepreneurship, **2:**448
   on psychological safety, **4:**1330
Schiller, F., **1:**74, **2:**608
Schismatic metaphor, **3:**896–897
Schizogenic, **3:**882
Schleiermacher, F., **2:**583, 584, 721
Schlick, M., **2:**830, **4:**1602
Schmalenbach, E., **3:**1124
Schön, D., **2:**802–803, 805, 806–807, 809,
   810, **3:**856, 1096, **4:**1364
Schultz, A., **1:**12, 259
Schultz, M., **3:**1083
Schumpeter, J.
   on competition, **1:**222, **3:**879
   on creative destruction, **3:**966
   on entrepreneurship, **2:**447, **4:**1400–1401
   on product innovation, **4:**1308, 1309
Schwartz, H. S., **3:**942–943
Schwartz, S. H., **4:**1607
Schwartz Value Survey, **4:**1607
Science and technology studies (STS), **4:**1541
Science of the state, **2:**565
Scientific administration, **2:**654
Scientific inscriptions, 28
Scientific management, **1:**44, 155, 274
   as closed system, **2:**549
   Theory X and, **4:**1547–1548
   worldwide, **2:**444
Scientific management, 4:1393–1397, 4:1551–1553
   criticism/future, **4:**1396
   dehumanization effects of, **1:**111
   division of labor in, **4:**1553
   empirical examination in, **4:**1553
   individual competition in, **4:**1553
   learning-by-doing, **4:**1395–1396
   methodology of, **4:**1394–1395
   pragmatic approach of, **4:**1394
   Taylor on, **1:**155, 272, 293, **4:**1393–1396
Scott, R., **3:**975, 1046, 1074, 1075, **4:**1316
Seasonal/part-time contingent workers, **1:**270
Second Wave feminism, **4:**1408
Secular spirituality, **3:**1176
Securities and Exchange Commission (SEC),
   1:9, 148–149

Selection bias, **3:**1056
Selective coding, **2:**572
Selective incentives, and free-rider problem, **2:**526
Self-categorization theory, **3:**861
Self-discipline, **1:**387–388
Self-efficacy, 4:1397–1400
   collective efficacy, **4:**1398–1399
   diverse effects of, **4:**1397–1398
   diverse organizational impact of perceived, **4:**1399–1400
   motivation and, **3:**924
   sources of, **4:**1397
Self-employment identities, 4:1400–1403
   classical accounts of self-employment, **4:**1400–1401
   criticism/future, **4:**1402
   personal traits/motivation of self-employed, **4:**1401
   social class view on, **4:**1401
   social constructionism on, **4:**1401–1402
   social identity formation, **4:**1400
   See also **Entrepreneurship**
Self-managed work teams, **4:**1225
Self-marginalization, **3:**875
Self-organization, **1:**231
Self-referential, autopoietic social system, **4:**1437
Self-serving bias, **1:**81
Seligman, M., **4:**1266–1267
Selznick, P., **3:**957–958, 1074, **4:**1300
Semiology, **1:**391, **4:**1286
Semiotics theory, **4:**1440
Semler, R., **2:**784
Sen, A., **4:**1252
Sender-message-receiver-feedback information
   processing model, **3:**999
Senge, P., **2:**809–810
Sensemaking, 1:13, 37, 206, 2:834, 4:1403–1406
   action learning and, **1:**38
   criticism/future, **4:**1404–1405
   in handoff activities, **4:**1405
   properties of, **4:**1403–1404
   vs. decision making, **4:**1405
   what sensemaking is not, **4:**1404
Sensitivity to initial conditions, **1:**156
Sensory feedback, **3:**920
Serendipity, 4:1406–1408
   biosociation and, **4:**1407
   criticism/future, **4:**1407–1408
   overview, **4:**1406–1407
   relational, **4:**1407
   time factor in, **4:**1407
Servant leadership. *See* **Leadership, servant**
Service and relationship management, **3:**1134
Service climate, **3:**1029
Service mark, **2:**693
Sevón, G., **3:**1133
Sexist oppression, **3:**1007
Sex labor superexploitation, **2:**497
Sexuality, 4:1408–1412
   case studies on, **4:**1410
   heterosexual relationships/liaisons, **4:**1409–1410
   lesbians/gay men experiences, **4:**1410

sexualed organizations, **4:**1410–1412
sexual harassment, **4:**1408–1409
Sexual selection, **2:**480
Shadow, **1:**67
Shareholders, 4:1413–1414
   concentrated blockholder, **3:**1212
   corporate social responsibility and, **1:**302–303, **4:**1414
   criticism/future, **4:**1413–1414
   limited liability, **4:**1413
   majority, **4:**1413
   no liability, **4:**1413
   nominee, **4:**1413
   preference, **4:**1413
Sheldon, Oliver, **1:**164, 165
Shop floor problem, **2:**476
Shotter, J., **4:**1583
Silver bullet, **2:**731
Silverman, D., **1:**260, **4:**1500
Similarity-attraction paradigm, on team diversity, **4:**1511
Simmel, G., **1:**401
   on fashion, **2:**503–505, **3:**851
   on networks, **3:**967
   on organizational change, **3:**1021–1022
   on social organization as human works of art, **1:**72
   symbolic interactionism of, **4:**1439
   tertius gaudens notion of, **2:**421
Simon, H.
   deconstruction of work of, **2:**825
   on bounded rationality, **1:**106–107, 363, **3:**860, 1125
   on classicists, **1:**165, 166
   on cognitivism, **1:**183
   on cooperation, **1:**194
   on managerial decision making, **1:**225
   on organizational knowledge, **3:**1088
   on organizational-level learning, **2:**803
   on organization as thing/arena, **2:**834
   satisficing heuristic of, **3:**861
Simulacra, **4:**1281
Single-loop learning. *See* Learning, single-loop
Single-person organization, **3:**981
Site/facility community, **1:**214
Site specificity, **1:**75
Situated learning theory, **1:**210–211
Skill, 4:1414–1418
   as individual attribute, **4:**1415
   as job attribute, **4:**1415
   measuring, **4:**1415–1416
   social construction of, **4:**1416–1417
   standardizing, **1:**281
Skinner, B. F., **1:**35–36, **3:**1001
Slavery, 4:1418–1419
   criticism/future, **4:**1419–1420
   new, **4:**1418–1419
   numbers of enslaved persons, **4:**1418
   old, **4:**1418, x1419
   organizational complexity of, **4:**1419
   organizational hierarchy of, **4:**1419
Small and medium-sized enterprises (SMEs), 4:1420–1423
   corporate social responsibility and, **1:**304
   criticism/future, **4:**1422–1423
   overview, **4:**1420–1421
   success strategies, **4:**1421–1422
Smith, A., **1:**180–181, **2:**654, 702, 708, **4:**1252, 1395
Smith, W., **4:**1259
Snow, C., **3:**1012
Social action, **2:**452
Social anthropology, **3:**1195
Social capital, 4:1423–1426
   appropriability of, **4:**1424
   criticism/future, **4:**1425–1426
   effects of, **4:**1424
   embededness of, **4:**1424
   learning and, **2:**803
   reciprocity of, **4:**1424
   relational, **4:**1424–1425
   sources of, **4:**1425
   trust and, **4:**1577
Social categorization theory, on diversity, **1:**397–398
Social class. *See* **Class**
Social cognitive theory, **2:**802
Social constructionism, 4:1426–1430
   centrality of language in, **4:**1428
   on emotion, **2:**429–430
   on entrepreneurship, **2:**448
   on gender division, **2:**539–540
   on identity, **2:**630
   on marginalization, **3:**875–876
   on truth, **4:**1579
   organizational theory and, **3:**1199–1200
   politics of knowledge and, **4:**1428–1429
   practices of inquiry, **4:**1430
   scholarship of critique and, **4:**1429
   social origins of knowledge, **4:**1427–1428
   theory of the organization and, **4:**1429–1430
Social construction of technology (SCOT), **4:**1541
Social contract, **1:**5
Social determinism, **2:**452
Social development theory, on ICT, **2:**665
Social-ecological systems, **3:**1049–1050
Social exchange theory, **4:**1230
Social facts, **1:**261, **4:**1602
Social identity deidentification (SIDE), **2:**627
Social identity theory (SIT), 4:1430–1432
   continuity concept in, **4:**1431
   criticism/future, **4:**1432
   demographic process, **1:**378
   ethnicity and, **2:**469
   ground boundaries, **4:**1431–1432
   on diversity, **1:**397–398
   on group-based stereotyping, **1:**394
   on marginalization, **3:**875–876
   on team diversity, **4:**1511
   status enhancement concept in, **4:**1431
Social information processing, **1:**185, **2:**738
Social intelligence, **2:**434
Socialism, democratic, **2:**650
Socialization, 4:1432–1434
   criticism/future, **4:**1433

gender division effects on, **2:**538
overview, **4:**1433
Social learning theory
   adult learning and, **1:**36
   on adult learning, **1:**36
Social loafing, **4:**1524, **4:**1528
Social movements, 4:1434–1436
   bureaucratic insurgency, **4:**1435
   coup, **4:**1435
   mass movements, **4:**1435
   organizational activism, **4:**1435–1436
   organizational change and, **3:**1024
   relevance to organizations, **4:**1434–1435
Social network analysis (SNA), **3:**968
Social networks, and team diversity, **4:**1512
Social (nonorganizational) demography, **3:**1044
Social organization *vs.* formal organization, **1:**260
Social-psychology, **1:**394, **3:**946–947
Social regulation theory, **3:**1119
Social science, on punishment/violence in organizations, **4:**1335
Social sciences realism, **4:**1356, **4:**1357–1358
Social structure *vs.* agency, **1:**260
Social system, 4:1436–1438
   AGIL functions of, **4:**1437
   closed, **4:**137, **4:**1436
   criticism/future, **4:**1437–1438
   environmental determinism and, **2:**452
   face-to-face interaction as, **4:**1437
   open, **4:**137, 1436
   self-referential, autopoietic, **4:**1437
   social component of, **4:**1436
   systemic component of, **4:**1436–1437
Social system knowledge, **3:**1048–1049
Social theory, 4:1438–1441
   classic tradition, **4:**1438–1439
   conflict theory, **4:**1440
   critical, **4:**1440–1441
   critical feminist theory, **4:**1440
   dialectical materialism, **4:**1439
   economic theory of social change, **4:**1439
   Frankfurt School influence on, **4:**1439, 1440–1441, 1604
   globalization effect on, **4:**1441
   integrated/balanced, **4:**1441
   semiotics theory, **4:**1440
   sociological theory *vs.*, **4:**1438
   structural-functionalism, **4:**1440
   structuralism, **4:**1440
Social view of learning, **3:**857
Societal accountability, **1:**4–5
Societal effects, **4:**1279
Societal risk, **2:**593–594
Societal sector *vs.* organizational field, **3:**1074
Sociocultural theory, on learning, **2:**802
Sociohistorical institutionalism, **2:**767–768
Sociological approach, 4:1441–1445
   approach to power, **4:**1443–1444
   business networks and, **1:**133
   criticism/future, **4:**1442–1444

   overview, **4:**1441–1442
   power/efficiency separation in, **4:**1442
   to organizational theory, **3:**1196–1197
Sociological theory, *vs.* social theory, **4:**1438
Sociology of business firms, **3:**1119
Sociology of work and employment, 4:1445–1448
   criticism/future, **4:**1446–1448
   overview, **4:**1445–1446
Sociology of scientific knowledge (SSK), **4:**1366
Sociology of translation. *See* **Actor-network theory**
Sociotechnical systems (STS), 2:668, **4:1448–1451,** 1540
   core characteristics of, **4:**1449
   criticism/future, **4:**1450–1451
   psychological requirements, **4:**1449–1450
   regional varieties of, **4:**1449
Socrates, **2:**795–796
Soft conducive domination, **1:**402
Soft system, **2:**550
Soft Total Quality Management, **4:**1556–1557
Software, computer, **2:**665
Sourcing agreements, **4:**1459
Sowell, T., **2:**812
Spare risk, **2:**468
Spatial community, **1:**213, **1:**214
Spatial organization, 4:1451–1452
Specific knowledge, **1:**360
Specific property rights, **3:**1061
Speech act theory, **3:**1164
Spencer, H., **2:**503
Spontaneous groups, **1:**215
Sportsmanship, **3:**1025
Sproull, L. S., **3:**1095
Sputnik, **2:**664
Stage model
   of entrepreneurship, **2:**448
   on team development, **4:**1507–1508
Stakeholders, 3:1133, **3:**1152, **4:1452–1454**
   corporate branding and, **1:**285
   corporate governance focus on, **1:**299–300
   criticism/future, **4:**1453–1454
   influence on corporate values, **1:**306
   involuntary, **4:**1453
   overview, **4:**1453
   types of, **1:**213
   voluntary, **4:**1453
Stalker, G. M., **3:**891, 892, 1009–1010, 1045
Standard social science model, **2:**480–481
Starbuck, W. H., **3:**1065, **4:**1543, 1545
Stark, M., **4:**1360–1361
Statement of cash flows, **1:**9
Statement of stockholder's equity, **1:**9
Statistical generalization, **2:**722
Statistical methods, basic, **4:**1347
Status, and organizational stigma, **3:**1178–1179
Stein, M., **3:**943
Stereotyping, group-based, **1:**394
Stevens, S., **3:**889
Sticky knowledge, **3:**1091
Stigler, G. J., **4:**1611

Stochastic method, of simulation, **1:**243–244
Stock options-based incentive programs, **1:**228–229
Stone, A. G., **2:**786–787
Storper, M., **1:**172
Story apologetics, **2:**497–498
Storytelling, 4:1454–1458
    antenarrative, **4:**1458
    architectonic dialogism, **4:**1456
    as dialectic, **4:**1455–1456
    as heteroglossic, **4:**1456
    chronotopic dialogism, **4:**1456
    collective, **4:**1455
    communities of practice and, **1:**211
    criticism/future, **4:**1455–1458
    distributed, **4:**1455
    fragmented, **4:**1454–1455
    living, **4:**1457
    managerial approach, **4:**1455
    nonlinear, **4:**1454
    organizational complexity and, **4:**1457
    petrified narratives, **4:**1456
    polpi, **4:**1457
    polyphonic approach, **4:**1455
    stylistic dialogism, **4:**1456
    tacit/explicit knowledge, **4:**1457
    teller/listener, **4:**1457
    See also **Metaphor and organization**; Tropes
Stouffer, Samuel, **3:**904
Strategic alliances (SAs), 1:196, 4:1458–1462
    commentary/future, **4:**1461–1462
    needs of firms seeking, **4:**1459–1460
    process of, **4:**1460–1461
    types of, **4:**1459
    See also Joint ventures
Strategic choice, 4:1462–1465
    coevolution of, **4:**1464
    institutional entrepreneurship, **4:**1464
    organizational evolution, **4:**1463–1464
    organizational learning, **4:**1464
Strategic contingencies theory, **4:**1384
Strategic discourse, 4:1465–1468
    criticism/future, **4:**1467
    industrial economics on, **4:**1465–1466
    resource-based theory on, **4:**1466–1467
    See also **Organizational discourse**
Strategic essentialism, **4:**1569
Strategic human resource management, 4:1468–1471
    criticism/future, **4:**1469–1470
    overview, **4:**1468–1469
Strategic industrial cooperation agreement, **4:**1459
Strategic knowledge arbitrage, **1:**1
Strategic knowledge serendipity, **1:**1
Strategic learning, and product innovation, **4:**1310
Strategic management, 3:1133–1134, 4:1471–1475
    challengers, **4:**1472–1473
    conventional view, **4:**1471–1472
    criticism/future, **4:**1474
    disputes/accord, **4:**1473–1474
    on behavioral theory of the firm, **1:**95

Strategic momentum, **1:**201
Strategy rhetoric, **3:**1163
Stratification approach, to class, **1:**161
Strauss, A., **2:**572
Stretch goals, **2:**561
Striated networks, **3:**974
Strodtbeck, F., **4:**1607
Strong reciprocity, **2:**482
Structural capital, **2:**759
Structural contingency theory, 4:1475–1477, 4:1602
    classical management theory and, **4:**1476
    configuration theory and, **1:**249, 250–251
    criticism/future, **4:**1476–1477
    diversification and, **4:**1476
    functionalism and, **2:**528
    human relations theory and, **4:**1476
    organizational size and, **4:**1476
    overview, **4:**1475–1476
    task uncertainty and, **4:**1476
Structural determinism, 4:1477–1479
    criticism/future, **4:**1478
    overview, **4:**1477–1478
Structural empowerment, **2:**441
Structural equation modeling (SEM), **4:**1347–1348
Structural functionalism, 4:1479–1480
    on general systems theory and, **2:**549
    on social theory, **4:**1440
    symbolic interactionism *vs.*, **4:**1499
Structuralism
    consumer culture and, **1:**263
    on gender division, **2:**538
    on informal economy, **2:**659–660
    on social theory, **4:**1440
    Structurally open corporation, **1:**91
Structural/positional approach, to networks, **3:**968
Structural theory of configuration, **2:**448
Structural unemployment, **4:**1588
Structural *vs.* micro superexploitation, **2:**496–497
Structuration, 4:1480–1484
    adaptive structuration theory, **4:**1483
    as grand theory, **4:**1482
    criticism/future, **4:**1483–1484
    duality of technology in, **4:**1482
    key theses in, **4:**1481–1482
    on agency-structure debate, **1:**47–48
    on technology, **4:**1542
Structure. *See* **Organizational Structure**
Sturdy, Andrew, **3:**848, 850
Stylistic dialogism, **3:**999, **4:**1456
Subcontracting. *See* **Outsourcing**
Subjective identity formation, **2:**631, 632–633
Subjective well-being, **1:**264
Subjectivity, 4:1484–1487
    criticism/future, **4:**1486–1487
    organizational theory and, **3:**1199–1200
    overview, **4:**1484–1486
Subordination, 4:1487–1490
    criticism/future, **4:**1489
    overview, **4:**1488–1489

Suchman, L., **3**:1089
Suicide, **4**:1335
Superexploitation. *See* **Exploitation**
Superiority theory, **2**:621
Superstructuralism, **4**:1288
Supply chain, **4**:1459
Supranational agencies, **2**:703
Surface-level demographics, **1**:378
Surplus effect, and free-rider problem, **2**:526
Surplus value, **2**:494
Surveillance, 4:1490–1491
Survey design, quantitative, **4**:1345
Survivor syndrome, **1**:405
Sustainable development (SD), 4:1491–1495
    criticism/future, **4**:1493–1494
    overview, **4**:1492–1493
    poststructuralism on, **4**:1494
Sutton-Smith, Brian, **4**:1247
Sveiby, K.-E., **2**:759
Sweatshops, 4:1495–1498
    antisweatshop campaign, **4**:1495–1496
    clothing/apparel production, **4**:1496–1497
    criticism/future, **4**:1496–1498
    globalization and, **4**:1496, 1497–1498
    overview, **4**:1495–1496
    regulation and, **4**:1497
Swift trust, **1**:400
Symbiosis, in network coevolution, **3**:964
Symbolic inequity, **1**:61
Symbolic interactionism, 2:697, **4**:1439, **1498–1501**
    constructivism and, **1**:260, **4**:1499
    criticism/future, **4**:1500–1501
    overview, **4**:1498–1499
Symbolic management, **3**:1024
Symbolism. *See* **Organizational Symbolism**
Synecdoche, **2**:774, **3**:899
System accidents, **3**:989
System dynamics method, of simulation, **1**:243–244
System 4 model, **3**:1029
Systems ideology, **2**:443
Systems theory, **1**:155
    on information processing, **2**:668
    on learning organization, **2**:810–811
    on sociotechnical systems, **2**:668
    See also **General systems theory**

Taber, T., **2**:789–780
Taboos. *See* **Organizational Taboos**
Tacit knowledge, 4:1503–1507
    communication in Japanese organizations and, **4**:1504–1505
    criticism/future, **4**:1505–1506
    explicit knowledge *vs.*, **2**:493–494, 754, 758–759
    in scientific management, **4**:1395
    original idea of Polanyi, **4**:1505–1506
    popular writing and, **4**:1506–1507
    seeds of misunderstanding about, **4**:1503–1504
    storytelling and, **4**:1457
Tajfel, H., **4**:1400
Takeuchi, H., **4**:1504–1505

Talk-in-interaction, **2**:775
Tarde, G., **3**:849, 852
Task aversiveness, **4**:1307
Task environment, **3**:1011
Tastes and preferences approach, **1**:393
Tavistock Institute, **1**:21–22, **2**:808, **3**:1203–1204, **4**:1449
Taylor, C., **3**:926
Taylor, F., **1**:69, 155, 163, 164, 272, 293, 370, 380, **2**:443, 541, **3**:871, **4**:1393–1396
Taylor, M., **2**:551
Taylorism. *See* **Scientific management**
Team, self-managed work teams, **4**:1225
Team development, 4:1507–1510
    adjourning, **4**:1508
    criticism/future, **4**:1509
    forming, **4**:1508
    norming, **4**:1508
    performing, **4**:1508
    punctuated equilibrium model, **4**:1508–1509
    stage model of, **4**:1507–1508
    storming, **4**:1508
Team diversity, 4:1510–1514
    cognitive resource view on, **4**:1511–1512
    criticism/future, **4**:1512–1513
    impact on workgroup outcomes, **4**:1512
    similarity-attraction paradigm on, **4**:1511
    social identity theory on, **4**:1511
    social networks and, **4**:1512
    taxonomies of, **4**:1510–1511
    theory on work group diversity, **4**:1511–1512
Team leadership, 4:1514–1519
    affective processes, **4**:1515–1516
    cognitive processes, **4**:1515
    coordination processes, **4**:1516
    criticism/future, **4**:1518
    executive coordinator, **4**:1517
    external leader, **4**:1517
    individual leadership *vs.*, **4**:1514
    internal leader, **4**:1517
    international, **4**:1517–1518
    motivational processes, **4**:1515
    stages of team development, **4**:1516
    team leadership functions, **4**:1514–1515
    types of team leaders, **4**:1517
    vertical *vs.* shared leadership, **4**:1516–1517
Team learning, 4:1519–1522
    criticism/future, **4**:1521
    degree of change, **4**:1520
    nature of knowledge, **4**:1521
    permeability, **4**:1520
    process *vs.* outcome, **4**:1521
    source of variance in, **4**:1520–1521
Team Learning and Development Inventory (TLI), **2**:492
Team performance, 4:1522–1526
    between-group conflict, **4**:1524
    dyads/sets of teams, **4**:1525–1526
    group polarization, **4**:1524
    group synergy, **4**:1524
    groupthink, **4**:1524–1525

input-process-output models, **4:**1522–1523
inputs, **4:**1523
managing teams, **4:**1526
processes, **4:**1523
process losses, **4:**1524–1525
situational constraints, **4:**1523
social affiliation, **4:**1525
social facilitation, **4:**1525
social loafing, **4:**1524
synergistic gains, **4:**1525
team learning, **4:**1525
team task, **4:**1524
within-group conflict, **4:**1524
workteam, **4:**1522
Team process, 4:1527–1530
   balance of member contributions, **4:**1527
   cohesion, **4:**1528
   communication, **4:**1527
   coordination, **4:**1527
   dysfunctional tendencies, **4:**1528–1529
   effort, **4:**1528
   groupthink, **4:**1528–1529, 1529
   mutual support, **4:**1528
   quality of teamwork, **4:**1527–1528
   social loafing, **4:**1528
Team production theory, **3:**1060–1061
Team psychological safety, **4:**1329
Teams, cross-cultural (CCTs), 4:1530–1533
   criticism/future, **4:**1532–1533
   detriments to, **4:**1530–1531
   heterogeneity relation to effectiveness, **4:**1531–1532
   leader role in, **4:**1531
   nature of task for, **4:**1531
   overview, **4:**1530–1532
   reasons to develop, **4:**1530
   well-functioning, **4:**1531
Teams, virtual, 2:467–468, **4:1533–1536**
   criticism/future, **4:**1535–1536
   overview, **4:**1533–1535
Technical-functional information, **2:**669
Technical knowledge, **1:**35
Technological determinism (TD), 4:1536–1539
   determinism concept, **4:**1537
   ideology and, **4:**1539
   social effects of, **4:**1538–1539
   technological determinism, **4:**1537–1538
   technology concept, **4:**1537
Technological unemployment, **4:**1587
Technology, 4:1539–1543
   actor-network theory on, **4:**1541
   critical feminism on, **4:**1542
   criticism/future, **4:**1542
   decision making via, **1:**227
   effect on workplace incivility, **4:**1637–1638
   flexible, **2:**656
   Fordist system, **4:**1540
   science and technology studies, **4:**1541
   social construction of technology on, **4:**1541
   sociotechnological studies, **4:**1540–1541

   structuration theory on, **4:**1542
   workplace studies, **4:**1541–1542
   See also **Information and communication technology**; Internet; **Technological determinism**
Teleological ethics, **1:**119
Temporary staffing agency, **1:**269–270
Temporary work agency (TWA), **1:**266
Tender-minded liberalism, **2:**812
Tenne, Rachael, **4:**1307
Tertius gaudens, **2:**421
Testimonios, **4:**1569
Texture approach, to entrepreneurship, **2:**448–449
Thatcher, M., **3:**959
Thatcherism, **2:**445
Theater as organization, **1:**407
Theater in organization, **1:**407
"The multitude" notion, **1:**163
Theory A, **4:**1550
Theory Building, 4:1543–1545
   criticism/future, **4:**1544–1545
   overview, **4:**1543–1544
Theory in the flesh, **4:**1569
Theory J, **4:**1550
Theory of the firm, **3:**1061, **3:**1125
   See also Behavioral theory of the firm
Theory X, 2:784, **4:1545–1547**
   Theory Y *vs.,* **4:**1547–1549
Theory Y, 2:784, **4:1547–1549**
   as way of seeing/not being, **4:**1548
   Theory X *vs.,* **4:**1547–1549
Theory Z, 4:1549–1551
Thick description, **4:**1340
Third Italy, **4:**1279
Third-party change agent, **3:**1049
Third sector organization. *See* **Nongovernmental organizations**
Third way, **1:**199
Thompson, E. P., **4:**1635
Thorndike, E. L., **2:**434, **3:**1001
Thought experiments, **2:**773
Thought worlds, **2:**662
Threat-rigidity hypothesis, **3:**1022
Three-body analysis, **1:**156
Three circles model, **2:**501
360-degree appraisal, **1:**387
Three Mile Island nuclear incident, **1:**235–236
Tightly coupled events, **3:**989
Tightly coupled system, **1:**235, **2:**833
Time-collective of management, **3:**853
Time famine, **4:**1636
Time-space relations, 3:1101, **4:1551–1555**
   banana time, **4:**1551
   clock and calendar time, **4:**1551
   criticism/future, **4:**1554–1555
   scientific management and, **4:**1551–1553
   time as social construction, **4:**1553–1554
TINA (There Is No Alternative), **3:**980
Tocqueville, A. de, **2:**724–725
Todorova, G., **3:**1017–1018

Toffler, Alan, **1:**155
Tokenism, **2:**421, 542–543
Token minority theory, **3:**1043
Total generalization, **2:**722
Total institution, **1:**370–372, **2:**518
Total normativization, **3:**905
Total preventive maintenance (TPM), **2:**800
Total production maintenance (TPM), **2:**744
**Total Quality Management (TQM), 2:808, 3:869,
    4:1555–1558**
  as corporate culture tool, **1:**294
  critical, **4:**1557
  hard, **4:**1555, 1556
  high quality management and, **2:**590
  local government and, **3:**842
  soft, **4:**1556–1557
Toyota Production System, **2:**800
TQM. *See* Total Quality Management
Trademarks, **2:**693
Trade unions, **2:**727
Traditional authority, **1:**87
Tragedy of commons, **2:**527
Trained incapacity, **1:**196
Training, 4:1558–1562
  costs, **4:**1558–1559
  criticism/future, **4:**1560–1561
  earnings, **4:**1558
  macro level, **4:**1559
  micro level, **4:**1559–1560
  time, **4:**1559
Trait-based approach
  to leadership, **2:**796
  to professions, **4:**1315–1316
Transactional leadership. *See* **Leadership, transactional**
Transaction-costs economics (TCE) theory.
    See **Transaction cost theory**
Transaction cost theory, 1:74–75, 76, 4:1562–1564
  criticism/future, **4:**1563–1564
  on behavioral theory of the firm, **1:**96, 109
  on economic rationalism, **2:**418
  on formal organizations, **2:**515
  on organizational economics, **3:**1060
  on outsourcing, **3:**1209
  on vertical integration, **4:**1610–1611, 1613–1614
  overview, **4:**1562–1563
Transactive memory, **4:**1526
Transformational leadership. *See* **Leadership,
    transformational**
Transformational perspective, **3:**1160
Transformative dialogue, **1:**382
Transgressive validity, **2:**722
Transhuman, **2:**609
Translation theory, **1:**16, 29
  of managerial fashions, **3:**851–853, 868–869
**Transnational corporations (TNCs),
    4:1564–1567**
  comparative institutional theory on, **4:**1566–1567
  criticism/future, **4:**1567
  global firms, **4:**1566

international firm, **4:**1566
management of, **4:**1566
multinational company, **4:**1566
reasons to locate overseas, **4:**1565–1566
transnationality index, **4:**1565
See also **Multinational enterprises**
Transnationality index, **4:**1565
**Transnational/postcolonial feminist theorizing,
    4:1568–1571**
  criticism/future, **4:**1566–1570
  overview, **4:**1568–1569
Transscientific fields, **2:**458
Triadic elicitation procedure, **1:**189
Triangulation, 4:1348, 4:1571–1573
  overview, **4:**1572
  researcher stance and, **4:**1572–1573
Triarchy theory, **2:**587
Trice, H., **4:**1256–1257
Trickle-across effects, fashion and, **2:**503, 504
Trickle-down effects, fashion and, **2:**503, 504
Trickle-down process, **3:**853
Trickle-up effects, fashion and, **2:**503, 504
Trist, E., **2:**668, **4:**1449
Trompenaars, F., **1:**337
Tropes, **2:**774
Trust, 4:1573–1579
  benevolence dimension of, **4:**1574
  competence dimension of, **4:**1574, 1576–1577
  context and, **4:**1576
  criticism/future, **4:**1576–1578
  dimension overlap, **4:**1577
  integrity and, **4:**1574, 1577
  perceived trustworthiness, **4:**1573–1574
  relationship and, **4:**1575–1576
  social capital *vs.*, **4:**1577
  sources of trust judgments, **4:**1574–1576
  trustee, **4:**1574–1575
  trustor, **4:**1575
Truth, 4:1579–1581
  criticism/future, **4:**1580–1581
  overview, **4:**1579–1580
Tryce, H. M., **3:**1064
Tuckman, B., **4:**1507–1508
Turbo capitalism, **1:**146
Turing, A., **3:**998
Turner, J., **4:**1400
Turner, V., **2:**821–822
Turnkey contract, **4:**1459
Tversky, Amos, **3:**871, 1022
Two camps approach, to class, **1:**161, 162
Tyranny of identity, **1:**54

Ubuntu, **3:**1099
U-form. *See* Unitary (U-form) organization
Uncertainty, 1:156, 4:1583–1587
  asset specificity and, **1:**76
  overview, **4:**1583–1585
Unconscious attitudes, **1:**77
Unconscious emotional contagion, **2:**436

Unemployment, 4:1587–1588
  cyclical underemployment, **4:**1587
  labor reserve army, **4:**1588
  natural unemployment rate, **4:**1588
  structural, **4:**1588
  technological, **4:**1587
  underemployment, **4:**1587
Unfreeze-movement-refreeze formula, **3:**1051, **4:**1377
Unionism, 4:1588–1593
  confessional, **4:**1589–1590
  crises on global scale, **4:**1590–1591
  criticism/future, **4:**1591–1592
  golden age of, **4:**1590
  origins of unions, **4:**1589
  services of unions, **4:**1589
  transmission belts for, **4:**1590
Unitary (U-form) organization, **3:**929–930, 1045, 1181–1183
Unitary view, on labor relations, **2:**766
United Nations, **1:**288, **2:**456, **4:**1369, 1492, 1493, 1565
United Nations Development Program (UNDP), **1:**152
United Nations Universal Declaration on Human Rights, **2:**618
Universal laws, **1:**184, **2:**567, **4:**1394
Unrelated conglomerate form, **3:**935
Upward influence, **2:**656–657
Urwick, L., **1:**164–165
Utilitarianism, 4:1593–1596
  act/rule, **4:**1594–1595
  aggregation and, **4:**1594
  criticism/future, **4:**1595–1596
  hedonism and, **4:**1593
  preferences and, **4:**1593–1594
  respect for persons and, **4:**1595
Utopia, 4:1596–1598
  criticism/future, **4:**1597–1598
  overview, **4:**1596–1597

Valence, in expectancy theory, **2:**485, **3:**921
Validity
  communicative, **2:**722
  ecological, **3:**862
  in computer-based simulation research, **1:**244
  of action research, **1:**22–23
  pragmatic, **2:**722
  quantitative data, **4:**1347
  reliability *vs.*, **3:**890
  transgressive, **2:**722
Valuative wage discrimination, **4:**1627, 1628
Value chains, 1:221, **4:1599–1601**
  criticism/future, **4:**1600–1601
  overview, **4:**1599–1600
  primary activities, **4:**1599, 1600
  support activities, **4:**1599–1600
  value systems and, **4:**1600
Value chimera, **3:**1184
Value-free conception of science, 4:1601–1606
  criticism/future, **4:**1603–1605
  domain assumptions and, **4:**1603
  "facts" and, **4:**1603
  feminist theory on, **4:**1604
  generative theory on, **4:**1604–1605
  grand theory and, **4:**1603–1604
  knowledge production and, **4:**1604
  language affect on, **4:**1605
  methodology issues, **4:**1604
  overview, **4:**1601–1603
  postcolonial theory on, **4:**1604
Values, 4:1606–1610
  contingent values, **4:**1606
  core values, **4:**1606
  humanistic operating system on, **4:**1609
  intellectual operating system on, **4:**1608–1609
  motivation and, **3:**921–922
  pragmatic operating system on, **4:**1608
Van Gennep, A., **2:**821, **3:**1166
Variability, **4:**1340
Veblen, T., **1:**196, **2:**503, 504, **3:**850, **4:**1439
Veil of ignorance, **2:**463
Verbal symbols, **3:**1191–1192
Vernon, R., **2:**702, 709
Verstehen, **1:**56, **2:**721, 723, **4:**1439, 1602
Vertical integration (VI), 4:1610–1616
  critical commentary/future, **4:**1611–1614
  foreign direct investment, **4:**1610
  greenfield investment, **4:**1610
  industrial organization view on, **4:**1610, 1613–1614
  life circle hypothesis of, **4:**1611
  monopolistic advantage of, **4:**1611
  resource-based view on, **4:**1610, 1611, 1612, 1613–1614
  transaction costs economics on, **4:**1610–1611, 1613–1614
Vertical loose coupling, **2:**835
Vertical *vs.* shared leadership, **4:**1516–1517
Viable system model (VSM), 4:1616–1618
  criticism/future, **4:**1617
  overview, **4:**1616–1617
Vienna Circle, **2:**773, 829–830, **4:**1602
Violence, 4:1618–1620
Virilio, P., **3:**974–975
Virtual communities, **2:**665
Virtual Design Team (VDT) simulation, **1:**243
Virtual organization, 1:171, **2:**518, **4:1620–1622**
  interorganizational, **4:**1621
  intraorganizational, **4:**1621
Virtual reality, 4:1622–1624
Virtual teams. *See* **Teams, virtual**
Virtue ethics, 4:1624–1626
  as explanation of behavior, **4:**1626
  future, **4:**1626
  human nature and, **4:**1625
  in business life, **4:**1625–1526
  inclinations and emotions, **4:**1624–1625
  principles and, **4:**1624
Visible hand, **3:**872, 959
Vision, culture, image (VCI) and, **1:**285
Visionary leadership, **4:**1362–1363
Voice
  organizational communication as, **3:**1034
  organizational justice and, **3:**1085

Voice over Internet Protocol (VoIP), **1:**140, 246
Volition concept, in aesthetics of organization, **1:**39
Voluntaristic agency, **1:**46, 47
von Bertalanffy, Ludwig, **2:**549, **3:**998
VRIN (valuable, rare, inimitable, and nonsubstituable), **1:**219
Vroom, V., **3:**921
Vygotsky, L., **2:**665

Wage inequities, **4:**1627–1628
    allocative wage discrimination, **4:**1627–1628
    valuative wage discrimination, **4:**1627, 1628
    within-job wage discrimination, **4:**1627
Waldo, D., **2:**824
Wallemacq, A., **3:**971
Walton, R., **2:**589–590
Waterman, R., **3:**867–368, 869–870
Watts, D., **3:**971
Webb, B., **2:**650, **4:**1588–1589
Webb, S., **2:**650, **4:**1588–1589
Weber, M.
    influence on social theory, **4:**1439
    iron cage concept, **1:**113, **4:**1439
    on authoritarian systems, **1:**110
    on authority, **1:**87, **3:**1196–1197
    on bureaucracy, **1:**33, 109, 110, 111, **1**113–115, 118, **3:**1057, 1157, 1186
    on capitalism, **1:**144
    on capitalism and culture, **1:**293
    on charisma, **1:**72, 84–85, **2:**780, 796
    on charismatic authority, **1:**87
    on control, **1:**271–272, 273
    on convergence, **1:**276
    on domination, **3:**1125
    on economic sociology, **2:**419
    on generalizations, **2:**722
    on ideal case, **2:**784
    on ideal-typical bureaucracy, **3:**1197
    on influence and power, **2:**657
    on leadership, **2:**796
    on legitimacy, **2:**682
    on methodological individualism, **3:**995
    on modernity, **3:**913
    on organizational design, **3:**1045
    on organizational power, **2:**814
    on Protestant ethic, **4:**1321–1322
    on rationality, **3:**870–871
    on rational-legal authority, **1:**88
    on relativism, **4:**1371
    on social action, **1:**11, 12
    on social class, **1:**161
    on social domination, **1:**84–85
    on social reality, **1:**259
    on social *vs.* natural sciences, **4:**1602
    on sovereignty of subject, **1:**13
    on traditional authority, **1:**87
    on violence in organizations, **4:**1335–1336
Webster, E. J., **4:**1543, 1545
Weick, K. E.
    on conversation, **1:**279
    on enacted environment, **3:**1064
    on goals, **2:**562
    on improvisation, **2:**640
    on loose coupling, **2:**833, 834, 835
    on minimal structure, **3:**909
    on organizational design, **1:**380, 381
    on organizing process as self-fulfilling prophecy, **3:**840
    on perceived environment, **3:**861
    on sensemaking, **1:**37, 206, **2:**834, **3:**1089, 1160
    on variation in organizing, **2:**448
Weiner, B., **1:**81, 82
Welch, J., **2:**781, 782
Wheeler, J., **4:**1608
Whetten, D., **2:**628, **3:**1077–1079
Whistle-blowing, **1:**79, 82, 116, 120, **3:**1143, **4:**1145, 1189, 1624
Whitehead, S., **3:**883
Whyte, W., **3:**863–864, 1137–1138, **4:**1258
Wiener, N., **3:**974, 998
Williams, M., **2:**722
Williamson, O., **3:**1004, 1060, 1209, **4:**1583
Wittgenstein, L., **1:**56, **2:**582–583, 721, 773, 830, **4:**1585–1586
Wolff, R., **3:**1074
Woodward, J., **3:**1186, **4:**1540, 1602
Work enrichment theory, **2:**590
Worker problem, and control, **1:**272–273
Worker rights, 4:1628–1630
    criticism/future, **4:**1630
    overview, **4:**1628–1629
Work-family balance, 4:1630–1635
    behavior-based conflict, **4:**1632
    energy-based conflict, **4:**1632
    levels of analysis, **4:**1633
    research direction, **4:**1633
    research foci, **4:**1633
    time-based conflict, **4:**1632
    work and life integration, **4:**1633
    work-family conflict, **4:**1631–1632
    work-family enrichment, **4:**1631, 1632–1633
    work-family role conflict, **4:**1631
Workforce demography, **3:**1043
Working time, 4:1635–1636
Work made for hire, **2:**691
Work motivation theory, **3:**921
Workplace design *vs.* agency, **1:**44–45
Workplace incivility, 4:1636–1639
    incivility spiral, **4:**1638
    intent issues, **4:**1638
    low intensity antisocial behavior effect on, **4:**1637
    outcomes of, **4:**1638–1639
    reasons for, **4:**1637–1638
    technology effect on, **4:**1637–1638
Workplace spirituality, **3:**1176–1177
Workplace studies, **1:**391, **4:**1541–1542
Workplace violence. *See* **Violence**
Work standardization, **1:**281
Work teams, self-managed, **4:**1225

World Bank, **1:**1, 26, 150, **2:**417, 703, 871, **3:**712, 980, 983, 984, 985, **4:**1368, 1369, 1421, 1493
World Trade Organization (WTO), **1:**26, 150, **2:**703, **3:**712, **4:**1370, 1567
World Wide Web, **2:**665

Yoon, J., **4:**1231
Yukl, G., **2:**789–780, 794

Zaccaro, S. J., **4:**1515, 1517
Zadeh, L., **1:**155–156
Zarathustra, **3:**1070
Zero-sum game, **2:**532, **3:**1157
Zero transaction costs, **1:**181
Zey, M., **3:**936–937
Zucker, S., **3:**975